CLASSICAL PHILOLOGY

STEWART IRVIN OOST, *Editor*

DAVID M. NOVAK, *Editorial Assistant*

VOLUME 74

JANUARY–OCTOBER 1979

THE UNIVERSITY OF CHICAGO PRESS

CHICAGO, ILLINOIS

CONTENTS FOR VOLUME 74

AVERY, HARRY C., The Three Hundred at Thasos, 411 B.C. 234
BAILEY, D. R. SHACKLETON, The Loeb Manilius 158
BALDI, PHILIP, A Structural Ambiguity in Latin 49
BALDWIN, BARRY, Zosimus and Asinius Quadratus 57
BAYLESS, WILLIAM N., The Chronology of Priscus Fragment 6 154
BOEGEHOLD, ALAN L., Thucydides' Representation of Brasidas before Amphipolis 148
BURNETT, ANNE, Desire and Memory (Sappho Frag. 94) 16
CAMERON, ALAN, Propertius 1. 1 and Constantine the Sicilian 58
CAMERON, AVERIL, A Nativity Poem of the Sixth Century A.D. 222
DREWS, ROBERT, Argos and Argives in the *Iliad* 111
HANSEN, MOGENS HERMAN, The Duration of a Meeting of the Athenian *Ecclesia* 43
HUNT, J. M., Latin Textual Criticism 340
KEANEY, JOHN J., Moschopoulos and the Scholia to the *Batrachomyomachia* 60
———, A New MS of the *Vaticanus Paradoxographus* 156
KONSTAN, DAVID, A Note on Theocritus *Idyll* 18 233
MALTBY, ROBERT, Linguistic Characterization of Old Men in Terence 136
MORITZ, HELEN E., Refrain in Aeschylus: Literary Adaptation of Traditional Form 187
MOULTON, CARROLL, Homeric Metaphor 279
MURGIA, CHARLES E., Notes on the *Dialogus* of Tacitus 245
O'MARA, MECHTILDE, *Curuca* and Juvenal *Satire* 6 242
REDFIELD, JAMES, The Proem of the *Iliad:* Homer's Art 95
REEVE, MICHAEL, The Textual Tradition of Donatus' Commentary on Terence 310
RENEHAN, ROBERT, Poet or Plato in Plutarch? 244
ROSS, DAVID O., JR., Two Rustic Notes 52
RUBINCAM, CATHERINE REID, Thucydides 1. 74. 1 and the Use of ἐς with Numerals 327
SCHAPS, DAVID, The Found and Lost Manuscripts of Tacitus' *Agricola* 28
———, An Unnoticed Rule of Plautine Meter 152
SYME, RONALD, The *Patria* of Juvenal 1
THOMAS, RICHARD F., Theocritus, Calvus, and *Eclogue* 6 337
WALSH, GEORGE B., Public and Private in Three Plays of Euripides 294
WEISS, ROSLYN, Aristotle's Criticism of Eudoxan Hedonism 214

BOOK REVIEWS

Allen and Furley (eds.): *Studies in Presocratic Philosophy*, vol. 2: *The Eleatics and Pluralists* (Sprague) 176
Baldwin: *Studies in Aulus Gellius* (Marshall) 173
Binns (ed.): *The Latin Poetry of English Poets* (Russo) 261
Boardman: *Athenian Black Figure Vases* (Price) 82
Castrén: *Ordo populusque Pompeianus: Polity and Society in Roman Pompeii* (Morgan) 257
Dietrich: *The Origins of Greek Religion* (Jameson) 250
Duncan-Jones: *The Economy of the Roman Empire: Quantitative Studies* (Oost) 86
Edmunds: *Chance and Intelligence in Thucydides* (Adshead) 354
Erbse (ed.): *Scholia Graeca in Homeri "Iliadem"* (*Scholia Vetera*) (Combellack) 179
Goold (ed.): *Manilius: "Astronomica"* (Bailey) 158
Greenhalgh: *The Year of the Four Emperors* (Bradley) 258
Guthrie: *A History of Greek Philosophy*, vol. 4: *Plato: The Man and His Dialogues: Earlier Period* (Sprague) 174

Haehling: *Die Religionszugehörigkeit der hohen Amtsträger des Römischen Reiches seit Constantins I. Alleinherrschaft bis zum Ende der Theodosianischen Dynastie (324–450 bzw. 455 n. Chr.)* (Novak) **362**
Higgins: *Xenophon the Athenian: The Problem of the Individual and the Society of the "Polis"* (Redfield) **352**
Kassel (ed.): *Aristotelis "Ars rhetorica"* (Solmsen) **68**
Marshall: *Crassus: A Political Biography* (Twyman) **356**
Mehl: *Tacitus über Kaiser Claudius: Die Ereignisse am Hof* (Shotter) **259**
Pollitt: *The Ancient View of Greek Art: Criticism, History, and Terminology* (Price) **253**
Preus: *Science and Philosophy in Aristotle's Biological Works* (Sprague) **84**
Reynolds (ed.): *L. Annaei Senecae "Dialogorum" libri duodecim* (Bailey) **76**
Saïd: *La faute tragique* (Redfield) **351**
Schellhase: *Tacitus in Renaissance Political Thought* (Momigliano) **72**
Sommerstein: *The Sound Pattern of Ancient Greek* (Nagy) **266**
Starr: *Political Intelligence in Classical Greece* (Oost) **88**
Stillwell, MacDonald, and McAllister (eds.): *The Princeton Encyclopedia of Classical Sites* (MacKendrick) **78**
Talbert: *Timoleon and the Revival of Greek Sicily 344–317 B.C.* (Oost) **85**
Teodorsson: *The Phonemic System of the Attic Dialect 400–340 B.C.* (Wyatt) **264**
Tränkle: *Livius und Polybios* (Gruen) **170**
Usener: *Glossarium Epicureum* (Furley) **178**
Vermeule: *Götterkult* (Jameson) **250**
Ward: *Marcus Crassus and the Late Roman Republic* (Twyman) **356**
White: *Farm Equipment of the Roman World* (Rodgers) **74**
Willis: *Latin Textual Criticism* (Hunt) **340**
Woodman: *Velleius Paterculus: The Tiberian Narrative (2. 94–131)* (Sumner) **64**

BOOKS RECEIVED

89–94, 181–86, 268–77, 366–73

CLASSICAL PHILOLOGY

VOLUME 74, NUMBER 4

October 1979

HOMERIC METAPHOR, *Carroll Moulton* 279

PUBLIC AND PRIVATE IN THREE PLAYS OF EURIPIDES, *George B. Walsh* 294

THE TEXTUAL TRADITION OF DONATUS' COMMENTARY ON TERENCE *Michael Reeve* 310

THUCYDIDES 1. 74. 1 AND THE USE OF ἐς WITH NUMERALS, *Catherine Reid Rubincam* 327

THEOCRITUS, CALVUS, AND *Eclogue* 6, *Richard F. Thomas* 337

REVIEW ARTICLE: LATIN TEXTUAL CRITICISM, *J. M. Hunt* 340

REVIEWS IN THIS ISSUE 351

S. SAÏD: *La faute tragique* (Redfield).—W. E. HIGGINS: *Xenophon the Athenian: The Problem of the Individual and the Society of the "Polis"* (Redfield).—L. EDMUNDS: *Chance and Intelligence in Thucydides* (Adshead).—B. A. MARSHALL: *Crassus: A Political Biography*, and A. M. WARD: *Marcus Crassus and the Late Roman Republic* (Twyman).—R. VON HAEHLING: *Die Religionszugehörigkeit der hohen Amtsträger des Römischen Reiches seit Constantins I. Alleinherrschaft bis zum Ende der Theodosianischen Dynastie* (*324–450 bzw. 455 n. Chr.*) (Novak).

CLASSICAL PHILOLOGY

A Quarterly Journal devoted to research in the Languages, Literatures, History, and Life of Classical Antiquity

VOLUME 74 NUMBER 1

January 1979

THE UNIVERSITY OF CHICAGO PRESS

Editorial correspondence: The Editor, *Classical Philology*, Box I, Faculty Exchange, The University of Chicago, Chicago, Illinois 60637. N.B. To be considered for publication, all material submitted must be typewritten, with both texts and footnotes double-spaced, and on stout paper with ample margins.

Published January, April, July, and October. Subscription rates, U.S.A.: institutions, 1 year $24.00, 2 years $43.20, 3 years $61.20; individuals, 1 year $18.00, 2 years $32.40, 3 years $45.90; students, $14.40 (with signature of faculty member). Other countries add $1.50 for each year's subscription to cover postage. Single copy rates: institutions $6.50; individuals, $5.00. Back volumes available from 1965 (vol. 60). Single issues and reprinted volumes through 1961 (vols. 1–56) available from Walter J. Johnson, Inc., 355 Chestnut Street, Norwood, New Jersey 07648. Volumes available in microfilm from University Microfilms, 300 North Zeeb Road, Ann Arbor, Michigan 48106; in microfiche from J. S. Canner & Co., 49–65 Lansdowne Street, Boston, Massachusetts 02215. Checks should be made payable to CLASSICAL PHILOLOGY, The University of Chicago Press, 5801 Ellis Avenue, Chicago, Illinois 60637.

Claims for missing numbers should be made within the month following the regular month of publication. The publishers expect to supply missing numbers free only when losses have been sustained in transit and when the reserve stock will permit.

Subscribers are requested to notify the Press and their local postmaster immediately of change of address. All changes of address should provide *both* the old and the new address. *Please allow four weeks for the change.*

The articles in this journal are indexed in the *Humanities Index*.

Second-class postage paid at Chicago, Illinois.

ISSN 0009-837X

CLASSICAL PHILOLOGY

VOLUME 74, NUMBER 1

January 1979

THE *Patria* OF JUVENAL, *Ronald Syme* 1

DESIRE AND MEMORY (SAPPHO FRAG. 94), *Anne Burnett* 16

THE FOUND AND LOST MANUSCRIPTS OF TACITUS' *Agricola, David Schaps* 28

THE DURATION OF A MEETING OF THE ATHENIAN *Ecclesia, Mogens Herman Hansen* 43

A STRUCTURAL AMBIGUITY IN LATIN, *Philip Baldi* 49

TWO RUSTIC NOTES, *David O. Ross, Jr.* 52

ZOSIMUS AND ASINIUS QUADRATUS, *Barry Baldwin* 57

PROPERTIUS 1. 1 AND CONSTANTINE THE SICILIAN, *Alan Cameron* 58

MOSCHOPOULOS AND THE SCHOLIA TO THE *Batrachomyomachia, John J. Keaney* 60

REVIEWS IN THIS ISSUE 64

A. J. WOODMAN: *Velleius Paterculus: The Tiberian Narrative (2. 94–131)* (Sumner).—R. KASSEL (ed.): *Aristotelis "Ars rhetorica"* (Solmsen).—K. C. SCHELLHASE: *Tacitus in Renaissance Political Thought* (Momigliano).—K. D. WHITE: *Farm Equipment of the Roman World* (Rodgers).—L. D. REYNOLDS (ed.): *L. Annaei Senecae "Dialogorum" libri duodecim* (Shackleton Bailey).—R. STILLWELL, W. MACDONALD, and M. H. MCALLISTER (eds.): *The Princeton Encyclopedia of Classical Sites* (MacKendrick).—J. BOARDMAN: *Athenian Black Figure Vases* (Price).—A. PREUS: *Science and Philosophy in Aristotle's Biological Works* (Sprague).—R. J. A. TALBERT: *Timoleon and the Revival of Greek Sicily 344–317 B.C.* (Oost).—R. DUNCAN-JONES: *The Economy of the Roman Empire: Quantitative Studies* (Oost).—C. G. STARR: *Political Intelligence in Classical Greece* (Oost).

MANUSCRIPT ACCEPTANCE POLICY

While it is our policy to require the assignment of copyright on most journal articles, we do not usually request assignment of copyright for other contributions. Although the copyright to such a contribution may remain with the author, it is understood that, in return for publication, the journal has the non-exclusive right to publish the contribution and the continuing right, without limit, to include the contribution as part of any reprinting of the issue and/or volume of the journal in which the contribution first appeared by any means and in any format, including computer assisted storage and readout, in which the issue and/or volume may be reproduced.

COPYING BEYOND FAIR USE

The code on the first page of an article in this journal indicates the copyright owner's consent that copies of the article may be made beyond those permitted by Sections 107 or 108 of the U.S. Copyright Law provided that copies are made only for personal or internal use, or for the personal or internal use of specific clients and provided that the copier pay the stated per-copy fee through the Copyright Clearance Center Inc.

To request permission for other kinds of copying, such as copying for general distribution, for advertising or promotional purposes, for creating new collective works, or for resale, kindly write to the publisher.

If no code appears on the first page of the article, permission to reprint may be obtained only from the author.

THE *PATRIA* OF JUVENAL

RONALD SYME

I

Simple truth can take a long time to percolate. The personal detail concerning Juvenal that the *vitae* and the scholiasts serve up with complacency is only a farrago, concocted from the poems. That was declared by Johannes Vahlen, long ago.[1] Nothing emerges to contradict or refute. As the orator Domitius Afer once observed, *hoc artificium periit.* Or, on a lower-key and Juvenalian note, stale cabbage, *crambe repetita.*

Nonetheless, the biography of the poet has proved an alluring theme in recent time, issuing an abundant discourse, and not without confident asseverations.[2] Brief affirmations of skepticism or denial intervene.[3] They are not always given heed. And the traffic keeps on.[4]

That being so, while faith and credulity persist, it is something of a paradox that doubts should be voiced in passing about Juvenal's Italian home, *tuo . . . Aquino* (3. 319).[5] The phrase might indicate, it is true, not the *patria*, but merely a sojourn of predilection. Thus, in a poem of Martial, his eloquent friend Licinianus will repair for the winter to the sunny shores of Tarraconensis: "aprica repetes Tarraconis litora / tuamque Laietaniam" (1. 49. 21–22). Now Licinianus, as is patent, belongs to Bilbilis, in the interior (1. 49. 1 ff., 4. 55).

On that line of argument, the inscription found in the vicinity of Aquinum has to be explained or disallowed. The standard text runs as follows:

> C[ere]ri sacrum / [D. Iu]nius Iuvenalis / [trib.] coh. [I] Delmatarum / II[vir] quinq., flamen / divi Vespasiani / vovit dedicav[itq]ue / sua pec.
>
> [*CIL*, 10. 5382 = *ILS* 2926]

That text calls for various comment, some of it disturbing. The document is not extant; it has not been seen for nearly two centuries. Shortly before 1772 it was transmitted by "magistrates of Aquino" to a certain Orlandi, who made the first publication. A better version was provided by P. Cayro of that city, in 1808.[6]

1. "Juvenal und Paris," *Gesammelte philologische Schriften*, vol. 2 (Leipzig and Berlin, 1923), pp. 181 ff. The article originally appeared in *SBBerl*, 1883, pp. 1175 ff.
2. Notably in G. Highet, *Juvenal the Satirist* (Oxford, 1954), pp. 4–41, 233–45.
3. Thus U. Knoche, *Die römische Satire* (Berlin, 1949; 3d ed. Göttingen, 1971), pp. 88 ff.; idem, *Gnomon* 29 (1957): 52 f. (reviewing Highet); R. Syme, *Tacitus* (Oxford, 1958), p. 499; M. Coffey, *Roman Satire* (London, 1976), pp. 121 f.
4. J. Gérard, *Juvénal et la réalité contemporaine* (Paris, 1976), pp. 5 ff.; E. Cizek, "Juvénal et certains problèmes de son temps: Les deux exils du poète et leurs conséquences," *Hermes* 105 (1977): 80 ff. And it may be noted that Highet "nous paraît un peu trop critique," according to A. Michel, "La Date des *Satires:* Juvénal, Héliodore et le tribun d' Arménie," *REL* 41 (1963): 316, n. 1.
5. Knoche, *Satire*, p. 89.
6. See the annotation at *CIL*, 10. 5382.

0009-837X/79/7401-0001$01.30

First of all, the command of a Dalmatian cohort. The manuscript texts showed no space for a numeral, which was inserted by Mommsen. Again, the supplement *trib.* Cayro's text apparently had *trib.* That would permit *praef.* That title is desiderated for the commander of an ordinary cohort (i.e., *quingenaria*).[7] A tribune commands a *cohors milliaria.* But that kind of regiment would not be the first post to be held by an equestrian officer (and perhaps his sole post). Finally, the two *cohortes milliariae Delmatarum* were created in the time of Marcus Aurelius.[8]

For attribution to the satirist Juvenal a cohort of Dalmatians carried an attraction not easy to withstand. Other regiments (*quingenariae*) are attested in Britain, a region in which the poems appeared to disclose a marked and even personal interest.[9]

Yet the man may not be the satirist, so some have opined. No matter, and nothing need be lost save the anxious or optimistic search for provinces in which Dalmatian cohorts had their stations (they are numerous). The officer and magistrate who set up the dedication to Ceres might be another member of the family, perhaps the father. No reason need therefore debar Aquinum as the residence of these Junii.

Their *ultima origo* is another matter. Domicile or birthplace is not the same as a *patria.* A modest observation now becomes pertinent, albeit not conclusive. When a local worthy makes or receives a dedication in his home town, a common and intelligible habit attaches to his *nomen* the tribe as well as the filiation. This time both are absent.

Aquinum supplies three inscriptions of Roman knights, each of whom held the posts of *tribunus militum* and *praefectus fabrum.* Two register the tribe, the Oufentina.[10] The third omits it. This man, after (or during) a varied and a successful career in the days of Tiberius Caesar, became *patronus* of the town. Since he had been a *quattuorvir* at Verona, he looks like an immigrant from Transpadane Italy.[11]

II

A brief excursus is in place. Though the document cannot be verified, nobody seems to doubt that it is genuine. A gentle suspicion insinuates. As with literary products, a clear motive is often enough to arouse dubitation.

At Ameria local zeal duly reveled in a plethora of bogus Roscii, now segregated.[12] And further, one gained admittance to *CIL* 11 but can hardly pass muster.[13] To come closer to home (if that is the word), Rocca d'Arce,

7. As assumed without argument by E. Birley, *Roman Britain and the Roman Army* (Kendal, 1953), p. 20. Similarly, *PIR*² J 765.

8. Dessau's note gave a reference to *ILS* 2616 (Salonae): one of the pair.

9. Namely coh. I in 122, coh. II in 105 (*CIL*, 16. 69, 51). C. Cichorius had uttered a salubrious admonition (s.v. "Cohors," *RE* 4 [1900]: 283 f.).

10. *CIL*, 10. 5399, 5401 (= *ILS* 6291).

11. *CIL*, 10. 5393 = *ILS* 6286 (Q. Decius Saturninus).

12. *CIL*, 11. *548–68.

13. *CIL*, 11. 4349.

lying half way between Aquinum and Arpinum, has its inscriptions of the Cicero family. Why not? The place is near the site of Q. Cicero's property, called Arcanum. All condemned, however: fabrications of Grossi early in the nineteenth century.[14]

One piece in the collection deserves scrutiny. It honors the orator's son (*suff.* 30 B.C.), describing him as "cos., pro cos. prov. Asiae, leg. imp. / Caes. Aug. in Syria" (*CIL*, 10. *704). The extant sources that reveal these two provincial governorships are far from obvious: the elder Seneca and Appian.[15] Observe, moreover, the formulation of the second post. It is the correct style at that time for a legate in the *provincia* of Caesar Augustus—which not all scholars have discerned.[16]

It might not have exceeded the talent or the scruples of an erudite antiquary to furnish from Aquino desirable confirmation of the Third Satire—though the disappearance of the stone is no credit to the local magistrates. A dedication to Ceres was suitable, since the poet himself names *Ceres Helvina* (3. 320).[17]

Preoccupation with Juvenal neglects the inscription reported on the other face of the stone. It presents peculiar features.[18] That is not enough in itself to cast discredit on the Juvenal inscription.

To conclude. It cannot be proved that the document from Rocca d'Arce is genuine, that from Aquino a forgery. Such is not the point and purpose of these remarks. Advantage will accrue if speculation about the poet's life and career eschews the inscription. For the scholar (as previously for scholiasts) the only source resides in the poems—and their author is artful, perverse, and secretive.

III

It suits the satirist to parade from time to time in the garb of a poor client.[19] To infer impoverishment or a disaster that deprived him of rank and estates, that is a sad misconception.[20] It overlooks both what can be established (the demands of the genre and the persona of a satirist) and what cannot, namely the temperament of an author, perhaps predisposed to ferocity and discovering in invective a congenial outlet and liberation.

14. *CIL*, 10. *700–706.

15. Sen. *Suas*. 7. 13; App. *BC* 4. 51. 221.

16. See further the review of A. E. Gordon's *Potitus Valerius Messala Consul Suffect 29 B.C.* in *JRS* 45 (1955): 160 = *Roman Papers* (Oxford, 1978), p. 270.

17. Juvenal elsewhere mentions the goddess six times.

18. *CIL*, 10. 5426: ". . . iuvaberit / huic universus populus / Aquinatium tabulam / aeneam patronatus tra / ditam sed et statuam / perpetuabilem cum pic / turam similitudinis / eius hoc in loco ad peren / nem testimonium censuer[e] / constituendam." The word *perpetuabilis* is not found anywhere else. However, that reason, or others, cannot exclude or disprove a document of late antiquity.

19. Such is a common theme in Martial, who, addressing his friend, has "dum per limina te potentiorum / sudatrix toga ventilat" (12. 18. 4–5). For Juvenal's dependence on Martial, and for his essential frivolity, see G. B. Townend, "The Literary Substrata to Juvenal's Satires," *JRS* 63 (1973): 148 f.

20. Eloquently expressed by Highet in the summary of his reconstruction (*Juvenal the Satirist*, p. 41).

It will be useful to adduce opportunities in the wider world that beckoned to alert young men from the *municipia* with moderate aspirations and some proficiency in polite letters. That is, military posts—and also paramilitary, for the *praefectus fabrum* should not be neglected.

In contrast to *laticlavii*, there was no uniform age of entrance, no regularity in service or prospects.[21] A pair of examples from Pliny's circle is instructive. First, in the year 101 Pliny requested the governor of Britain to accord a military tribunate to Suetonius Tranquillus (*Epist.* 3. 8. 1). Tranquillus, the son of Laetus, who had fought as tribune in a legion at Bedriacum, was born (so it may be conjectured) in the year of peace, hence aged about thirty at the time.[22] Second, Pliny's friend from the studious years, Voconius Romanus of Saguntum. Pliny's natal year was 61 or 62 (probably the latter). In 100 Pliny wrote to an army commander called Priscus, soliciting some post or other for Romanus, who had recently been provincial high-priest of Tarraconensis (2. 13. 4).[23]

Tenure of a single post in what is called the *militia equestris* is by no means infrequent. Thus the two knights from Aquinum already noted, or two writers from Spain, Cornelius Bocchus and the agronome Junius Columella.[24] Further, a number of the local dignitaries who end as high-priests at Tarraco.[25]

That is to say, persons with no clear vocation for the military life, no hope or ambition to rise higher in an equestrian career. Their motives do not evade conjecture: travel and recreation, attachment to a friend or a patron, local prestige when they came back after a brief sojourn with the armies.[26]

Like others of the educated class, Juvenal may have chosen to embark on this avenue. With success or with failure, who can tell? The poems breathe no hint of any patron. By an innovation in the author's technique, the last five are dedicated to friends, so it appears. None can be identified.[27]

Aquinum is styled a *frequens municipium* by Cicero, a great city by Strabo.[28] Yet it cannot show a Roman senator, Republican or imperial.[29]

21. Birley, *Roman Britain*, p. 135.

22. For the conjecture that Tranquillus was born in 70, see "The Enigmatic Sospes," *JRS* 67 (1977): 44 (discussing "Sospes" and "Innocens").

23. Priscus is to be identified as Javolenus Priscus, legate of Syria: cf. "Pliny's Less Successful Friends," *Historia* 9 (1960): 365 f. = *Roman Papers*, pp. 480 f.

24. *ILS* 2920–21 (Bocchus), 2923 (Columella).

25. See the lists in G. Alföldy, *Flamines provinciae Hispaniae Citerioris* (Madrid, 1973), pp. 33 ff.

26. "Pliny the Procurator," *HSCP* 73 (1969): 208 = *Roman Papers*, p. 748.

27. Viz., Corvinus, Calvinus, Fuscinus, Volusius Bithynicus, Gallius. The persons addressed have all been proved fictitious ("erwiesen") according to Knoche, *Satire*, p. 89. The claim is excessive.

Further, it might do no harm to concede Umbricius (3. 21) as the authentic name of a friend. But Persicus, addressed in 11. 57, is presumably debarred because of his wife's adultery (187 ff.).

28. Cic. *Phil.* 2. 106; Strabo 5, p. 237.

29. Unless it be P. Barronius Barba, curule aedile in the late Republic (*ILS* 5562). Because of the extremely rare *nomen* (three instances at Aquinum), cf. T. P. Wiseman, *New Men in the Roman Senate* (Oxford, 1971), p. 217.

According to the *Historia Augusta*, Aquinum was the home of Pescennius Niger. The engaging piece of fiction endows him with "Annius Fuscus" for father, "Lampridia" for mother; and the grandfather was *curator Aquini*. The biographer goes on to deprecate the invention, as is his fashion, with a note of scholarly caution: "quod quidem dubium etiam nunc habetur" (*Pesc.* 1. 3). Aquinum, it is surmised, owes its evocation to his scholiastic milieu and acquaintance with the poems of Juvenal.[30] Nor are any of the higher knights there discoverable. That deficiency, however, is not enough to consign Aquinum to the downward path of Ulubrae. The region was rich and prosperous. Nor, again, is it legitimate to suppose that Aquinum was harmed by close proximity to three other towns in the valley of the Liris, each at an equal distance of less than a dozen kilometers: Casinum, Interamna Lirenas, Fabrateria Nova.[31]

The great family in the neighborhood was established at Casinum: the Ummidii, of ancient opulence. They had recently come into possession of the Roman palace inhabited by the jurist Cassius Longinus—by what means, it evades ascertainment.[32] When describing Neronian confiscations, Juvenal alludes to the mansion. A regiment of soldiers, he says, "Longinum et magnos Senecae praedivitis hortos / clausit" (10. 16–17). *Longinus* indicates the mansion—not the person, as commentators and translators assume. There is a faint chance that the choice of this particular derives from personal knowledge.[33]

Subjoined to the notorious inscription, these observations are independent of that document. The design is to illustrate the milieu, to indicate occupations accessible to the better sort from *municipia* in Italy or in provinces of the Roman West.

Juvenal's knowledge of foreign parts has not failed to arouse curiosity and some inordinate expectations. Its nature and origin demands discrimination. In the first instance literature, given the author's manner and habits, elsewhere beyond dispute. Juvenal does not attack the living (1. 170 f.). His Rome is mainly the *imperium vetus* of Claudius and Nero, as well as the recent age of Domitian.[34] But personal experience comes in—at least for one country.

30. For an engaging parallel in Renaissance fiction, observe the *vita* published by J. Dürr (*Das Leben Juvenals*, Wissenschaftliche Beilage zum Programm des Kgl. Gymnasiums in Ulm, Prog. 561 [Ulm, 1888]). It assigns the poet "Septumuleia" for mother—and also for his sister, who married "Fuscinus." The author took "Fuscinus" from 14. 1. The other *nomen* is rare, municipal, and plausible—cf. *Septumuleius ille Anagninus* who got hold of the head of C. Gracchus and claimed a reward (Cic. *De or.* 2. 269).

31. The latter two towns do not offer senators either. Juvenal happens to mention Fabrateria, along with Frusino (3. 224).

32. Pliny *Epist.* 7. 24. 8.

33. C. Ummidius Quadratus was consul suffect in 118. He and his aged grandmother are the subject of Pliny's letter, a showpiece. For the family, see "The Ummidii," *Historia* 17 (1968): 72 ff. = *Roman Papers*, pp. 659 ff.

34. His "Domitianic experience" tends to be overvalued, largely because of *Satire* 4. Thus Knoche: "obwohl Juvenals Satiren sich ganz vorwiegend mit der Schreckenszeit beschäftigen" (*Satire*, p. 90).

IV

In *Satire* 15 Juvenal recounts a murderous feud between two villages. Terminating the long *exordium*, he claims to know Egypt:

> horrida sane
> Aegyptos, sed luxuria, quantum ipse notavi,
> barbara famoso non cedit turba Canopo.
>
> [15. 44–46]

Juvenal does not assert that he was in Egypt at the time, but he assigns the incident to a precise date, *nuper consule Iunco* (15. 27). Now L. Aemilius Juncus was consul suffect with Sex. Julius Severus in 127, entering office on the first day of October. Dating by *suffecti*, that is precise—but anomalous in a literary text. Who knew, who cared? That year had six *suffecti*. The significance of the item has seldom been perceived.

The only other consular date in the poems registers a year by the *ordinarius*. Addressing Calvinus, Juvenal exclaims, "stupet haec qui iam post terga reliquit / sexaginta annos Fonteio consule natus?" (13. 16–17). The sixtieth year stamped a man as *senex* indubitably, and in a senator it excused attendance at the high assembly. The poet himself avows an affection for birthdays, as in the previous poem, "Natali, Corvine, die mihi dulcior haec lux" (12. 1). Now the consulship of Fonteius Capito (in 67) was not a year of notoriety like 68, introduced by Silius Italicus: Nero's end, and Silius, orator and poet, living on as the last survivor of the Neronian consuls. The conjunction of the two consular dates permits a hypothesis. Each meant something to Juvenal. He may have seen the light of day in the autumn of the year 67.[35] Other estimates have shown a wide fluctuation.[36] The matter thus acquires some importance. Less, however, than the time of writing.[37]

When or why Juvenal visited the land of Nile, there is no clear indication. Perhaps on military service (either as tribune in a legion at Alexandria, or as commander of a regiment elsewhere), perhaps in the retinue of a prefect of Egypt. The next governor after Cornelius Gallus, namely Aelius Gallus, had Strabo with him, not yet known as "Strabo the geographer," who shared an excursion as far as Syene.

Attention has also been drawn to Meroe, mentioned twice in the poems. First, the votary of Isis will journey under divine injunction to the southern frontier of Egypt and get water from torrid Meroe (6. 527–28). Second, among examples of deformity, the large breasts normal among Negresses at Meroe (13. 163). That item, so commentators with gravity aver, stands unique in writings of the ancients.[38] Why, Meroe is only about nine hundred

35. As suggested in *Tacitus*, pp. 774 f.

36. As at different times by Highet. Thus "probably c. 50," *OCD*[1], p. 475; "about 55," "The Life of Juvenal," *TAPA* 68 (1937): 505; "about 60," *Juvenal the Satirist*, p. 5 (cf. p. 50); "between 50 and 65," *OCD*[2], p. 571.

37. There are no valid reasons for supposing that Juvenal had published anything before 117.

38. J. E. B. Mayor in his commentary ad loc. (2d ed., London, 1878); Highet, *Juvenal the Satirist*, p. 31.

miles distant from the end of Egypt: from the *porta Syenes*, as it is designated (11. 124).[39]

This item need not detain, save for a fleeting glance at the exotic seduction of far Meroe, euphonic name. It is commemorated in the famous Greek quatrain on the subject of death.[40] Strange therefore that Meroe had no appeal for any of the Augustan poets, keen as they are on remote geography, save only Propertius: "Cepheam hic Meroen fuscaque regna canat."[41]

V

Four passages which mention Britain are noteworthy on various counts:

(*a*) The reference to Roman conquests in the far North:

> arma quidem ultra
> litora Iuvernae promovimus et modo captas
> Orcadas ac minima contentos nocte Britannos.
>
> [2. 159–61]

(*b*) Fabricius Veiento in Domitian's council of state is moved to foretell splendid news from the island:

> regem aliquem capies aut de temone Britanno
> excidet Arviragus.
>
> [4. 126–27]

(*c*) An aspirant to the centurionate is given advice ironically:

> dirue Maurorum attegias, castella Brigantum.
>
> [14. 196]

(*d*) The spread of rhetorical education to the world's end is illustrated thus:

> Gallia causidicos docuit facunda Britannos,
> de conducendo loquitur iam rhetore Thyle.
>
> [15. 111–12]

The rubric is respectable, an attraction to insular conceit and an incentive to the quest for Juvenal's area of service as an equestrian officer. The question stands thus: do any of those passages entail and demand his presence in Britain?

The third is a general reference to disturbed regions in the frontier zone, valid at any time in the reign of Hadrian subsequent to initial trouble on the borders of Dacia. For the rest, literature appears to be the answer, notably the *Agricola* and the *Historiae* of Cornelius Tacitus. The chieftain Arviragus may have been named in the latter work.

Another foreign name is stylish indeed, Iuverna instead of Hibernia. It is found in Pomponius Mela (3. 53), not to recur until the late days, in the

39. Cf. Tac. *Ann*. 2. 61. 2: "Elephantinen ac Syenen, claustra olim Romani imperii."
40. *Anth. Pal*. 10. 3.
41. Prop. 4. 6. 78.

Historia Augusta. Glory is predicted for a descendant of the emperor Tacitus, who will impose a Roman governor in Ceylon and send a proconsul to Ireland (*Tac.* 15. 2). Parading Taprobane and Iuverna, the ingenious author did not require Thyle, which Juvenal adopts for adornment (15. 112).[42]

The preceding verse has eloquent Gaul instructing Britain in the forensic art. That might be taken as an allusion to civilizing operations conducted by a Roman governor. Agricola shaped his policy *ut . . . eloquentiam concupiscerent*. But Agricola, it may be noted in passing, came out with a preference for the untutored talents of the natives: "ingenia Britannorum studiis Gallorum anteferre" (*Agr*. 21. 2). However, there is no call to insist on what may be only a stylized commonplace.

Nor will the great whale in British seas impress, "quanto delphinis ballaena Britannica maior" (10. 14). A final item will serve as a test case. Montanus, the gourmet present at Domitian's council, had an exquisite taste in oysters:

Circeis nata forent an
Lucrinum ad saxum Rutupinove edita fundo
ostrea callebat primo deprendere morsu.
[4. 140–42].

Oysters from Rutupiae, at first sight that is vivid and precise. The British bivalve came in fact to high esteem shortly after the invasion. Awarding the palm among eight varieties of oyster to the product of Cyzicus, the eminent authority of Licinius Mucianus declared them *dulciora Britannicis*.[43]

Yet *Rutupino* should not deceive. It simply means "British."[44] In this device the satirist had been anticipated by a stylish performer in another genre. Lucan introduced *Rutupinus* along with *Caledonius* into Latin poetry:

aut vaga cum Tethys Rutupinaque litora fervent,
unda Caledonios fallit turbata Britannos.
[*Phars*. 6. 67–68]

VI

Africa might be another matter. Juvenal employs *Maurus* no fewer than eight times (it is absent from Martial), and also *Maura* as the name of an unchaste woman (6. 307–8, 10. 224). Likewise *Gaetulus*, six times (against once in Martial): the massive epithet appealed, as notably in *Gaetulum Ganymedem* (5. 59).

It is hazardous to claim significance for any such phenomenon: Horace also liked *Gaetulus* (three times in the *Odes*). But the passage describing cheap oil imported in Numidian boats made of reeds might invite attention:

illud enim vestris datur alveolis quod
canna Micipsarum prora subvexit acuta,
propter quod Romae cum Boccare nemo lavatur.
[5. 88–90]

42. Iuverna can thus be added to the Juvenalian echoes registered by A. D. E. Cameron, "Literary Allusions in the Historia Augusta," *Hermes* 92 (1964): 363 ff.

43. Pliny *NH* 32. 62.

44. F. Haverfield, "Three Notes," *CR* 21 (1907): 105; idem, s.v. "Rutupiae," *RE*, 2. Reihe 1 (1914): 1284. As that scholar pointed out, Rutupiae (Richborough) does not grow oysters.

The name Boccar is not elsewhere on attestation, not even in Martial, who produces some peculiar and enigmatic specimens.[45] It is patently Punic. Indeed, "Boccar" instead of "Bucar" should probably be read in Livy (three times: an officer of Syphax).[46]

Again, the huts of the Moors, *Maurorum attegiae* (14. 196). The word occurs elsewhere only on an inscription in Germania Superior.[47] The origin is not clear. Some invoke Celtic. The standard term for huts in Africa is *mapalia*, brought into Latin poetry by Virgil (*Georg.* 3. 340); and Martial has *Gaetula mapalia* (10. 13. 7).

What then emerges? Only the notorious word-fancier, it might appear. His tastes come out clearly in the naming of fictitious characters. Thus "Laronia" and "Tongilius" (2. 36, 7. 130), taken, along with less obtrusive specimens, from his friend Martial.[48]

Those *gentilicia* are extremely rare. Similarly, the exploitation of technical or alien terms not normally admitted to the high style. They can be used for effects of comedy or bathos. For example, Juvenal in a solemn passage calls the spear of a Roman god *Martis frameam* (10. 79). The word is German, so Tacitus states in the *Germania* (9. 1). He avoids it in the historical writings.

Next, a transaction of recent history that stands prominent in the early poems, and in its way unique:

> exul ab octava Marius bibit et fruitur dis
> iratis, at tu, victrix, provincia ploras.
>
> [1. 49–50]

Juvenal reverts to it later on;

> cum tenuis nuper Marius discinxerit Afros.
>
> [8. 120]

He refers to the prosecution of Marius Priscus, terminated in January of the year 100. The vivid repercussion of a recent event has generally been assumed, hence valid for dating: the First Satire was composed in the near sequel.

Not at all. The indictment of a proconsul of consular rank was something memorable, and probably without parallel during the whole reign of Trajan. Moreover, it passed into the realm of literature. As Pliny states, *ego et Cornelius Tacitus* conducted the case (*Epist.* 2. 11. 2).

Juvenal therefore alludes to the account in a modern classic, the correspondence of Pliny, rather than to a prosecution that occurred in the year 100. Whether or no with veiled malice toward the eminent advocates who achieved so little, that is a question irrelevant to the present context.

45. Thus Baccara (6. 59. 2, 7. 92. 2, 11. 74. 1); Lattara (11. 47. 2); Ligurra (12. 51. 2).

46. Cf. the apparatus to Livy 29. 32 in the edition of R. S. Conway and S. K. Johnson (Oxford, 1935).

47. *CIL*, 13. 6054 = *ILS* 3204 (Niederbronn): "deo Mercurio attegi / am teguliciam comp / ositam Severinius / Satullinus c(ivis) T(ribocus) ex vo / to posuit l. l. m."

48. Mart. 2. 32. 5, 2. 40. 1. Martial also produced "Tongilianus" (2. 52. 1, 12. 88. 1).

Finally, no marked or especial concern for Africa need be deduced, despite the double mention of the proconsul's misdeeds.

And now for something quite different. Describing old age and its bodily degradation, the poet calls up for comparison the wrinkled cheeks of elderly apes in the woods near Thabraca,

> tales aspice rugas
> quales, umbriferos ubi pandit Thabraca saltus,
> in vetula scalpit iam mater simia bucca.
>
> [10. 193–95]

The first emergence in poetry of towns or tribes with novel names is a topic of some mild interest. The source and the reason can often be divined. Names of specific tribes in Cantabria and Asturia are not easy to come by. But Horace supplies the Concani, who drink the blood of horses.[49] The poet reflects contemporary warfare.

No known transactions of history brought in Thabraca, or any exotic product. It is not mentioned by any other poet except Claudian. With Claudian the word is not decorative but precise. The insurgent Gildo was captured and killed there, early in the year 398.[50]

Thabraca was an ancient harbor on the coast of Numidia, close to its eastern boundary. The *umbriferi saltus* of Juvenal are discovered westward from Tabarka along the shore or inland to the southeast, in the Oued Zeen. As concerns apes, one may rest content with *quaerere distuli* or invoke testimony from Posidonius. On a journey from Gades to Italy Posidonius was moved to laughter when observing the appearance and comportment of those creatures (male and female) in a wooded grove along the shore of Africa.[51]

The cool glades near Thabraca and their denizens may have been familiar as a piece of common knowledge. Perhaps not. The sentence explains itself—that does not always happen with Juvenalian allusions. Another explanation avails: Juvenal had been in Africa, and the family may come from Africa.

VII

For long ages the persuasion prevailed that Juvenal was Italian, he must be Italian. His love of old Italy and his hatred of foreigners were duly enlisted.[52] And amusing consequences ensue. Cornelius Tacitus has been hailed an "Italico giovenaliano."[53]

The frequentation of Roman social history imports a severe doubt. One looks toward the provinces of the West—and a quieter tone now becomes perceptible.[54]

49. Hor. *Odes* 3. 4. 34, whence Silius 3. 311.
50. Claud. *Cons. Stil.* 1. 359.
51. Strabo 18, p. 827.
52. Highet, *Juvenal the Satirist*, pp. 233, 255.
53. P. Treves, *Il mito di Alessandro e la Roma d'Augusto* (Milan, 1953), p. 159.
54. Thus "Juvenal perhaps was not of Italian origin" (Coffey, *Roman Satire*, p. 120).

Nomenclature affords guidance in the investigation of local origins. The procedure can only be experimental; the prospects are limited when a *gentilicium* is common, indistinctive, and widespread; and statistics are often delusive.

What then can be done with D. Junius Juvenalis?[55] Junii are very numerous both in Spain and in Africa. Given the comparative totals of inscriptions in the two regions, Spain carries a heavy advantage.[56] Junius is one of the *nomina* spread through grants of the citizenship by proconsuls—but that is not the only explanation.

In favor of Spain, some might be moved to invoke Martial's warm affection for young Juvenal, first conveyed in two poems of the year 92.[57] Not valid. Immigrants from all the lands came together at the capital, and some families formed potent and enduring alliances. Nor can Juvenal's estate at Tibur acquire significance (11. 65), albeit a resort where many Spaniards congregated.[58]

Martial avowed his yearning for Bilbilis (rivers, mountains, and the names of obscure villages); and he was generous in proclaiming a Spanish origin for friends of any rank or condition. But not for Juvenal, despite three poems. There is a clear parallel. Pliny is sparing with local topography (only Lacus Larius) but exuberant in praise and promotion of a larger *patria;* that is, the Transpadana. Pliny does not annex Tacitus to *illa nostra Italia.*

Now Juvenal nowhere discloses an interest in anything Spanish. Reticences can be detected in some of the extraneous. Quintilian betrayed no sign of his own origin. In a cursory reference to dialect words he says, "licet omnia Italica pro Romanis habeam" (1. 5. 56). He goes on to make a distant and ostensibly nescient reference to a word current in Spain.[59] Yet the immigrant professor was in a position to offer much more: archaisms in Spanish Latinity or words brought to the peninsula from towns of Italy.

VIII

Taken alone, the *nomen* Junius tells nothing. Recourse can be had to *praenomina,* generally negligible and neglected. Some of them adhere to *gentilicia* by tradition or from a kind of elective affinity, while others appear repugnant. For example, one seldom comes upon A. Claudius, P. Caecilius, T. Cornelius.

Decimus attached to Junii is familiar from history and literature, as witness D. Junius Brutus (*cos.* 137 B.C.), who campaigned in Spain; D. Junius Silanus (*cos.* 62), who opened a momentous debate in the senate;

55. The full name stands at the beginning of the biography attached to the Codex Montepessulanus: the earliest, and the original, of the scholiastic *vitae.* The scholium elucidates the *praenomen* Decimus. The item has never been impugned.

56. Nearly two columns in *CIL* 2 against about two and a half columns in *CIL* 8.

57. Mart. 7. 24, 7. 91. Also in 100 or 101 (12. 18).

58. *Tacitus,* p. 602.

59. Quint. 1. 5. 57: "et *gurdos,* quos pro stolidis accepit vulgus, ex Hispania duxisse originem audivi."

D. Junius Brutus Albinus, serving for long years under the proconsul of Gaul, then governor there and in the Cisalpina, consul designate for 42.

One might expect to discover repercussions in nomenclature among clients in the western provinces. The results are a surprise and a shock. In such Junii as carry a *praenomen* on the inscriptions, the percentage is minimal.[60]

Spain abounds in Junii (the ninth name in order of frequency), but Spain yields a solitary specimen of the desired collocation: a wealthy lady, Junia D. f. Rustica, honored for her buildings and benefactions at a small *municipium* near Malaca.[61] Africa in *CIL* 8 registers four Decimi Junii out of eighty-four; but three examples in eight have recently accrued at one town, Lepcis Magna.[62]

Narbonensis registers a blank; and, for that matter, Transpadana (the "provincial" zone of the Cisalpina) shows only one example.[63] Nonetheless, for Juvenal's origin a thought might go to Tres Galliae, in view of the early renown engrossed by the Gallic orators. All Julii—except Marcus Aper, one of the interlocutors in the *Dialogus* of Tacitus. Aper was often and easily taken to be a Julius. Better, the parent of Flavius Aper, consul suffect shortly before 105, grandfather of M. Flavius Aper (*cos*. 130).[64] Therefore D. Junius Juvenalis might be enlisted in the ranks of those *causidici* who gave instruction to natives of Britain.

However, no sign in the poems points to Tres Galliae, to Narbonensis, or to Transpadane Italy. The *cognomen* now comes in. It indicates either low-class Italian or a provincial origin.[65] Observe, for example, "Iuvenalis e primoribus Tungrorum" (Tac. *Hist*. 4. 66. 3), and C. Julius Juvenalis (*suff*. 81), one of the rare Gallic senators on record in the period.[66] *CIL* 13 furnishes six specimens of the *cognomen*, *CIL* 8 a dozen.[67]

IX

The data about nomenclature are registered as relevant, but not decisive; and it is expedient here as elsewhere to declare limitations in the method. For Juvenal's *ultima origo* nothing debars Africa, even Thabraca, slipped in at a late stage in the poems, like the two consular dates which permit an inference about the age of this elusive fellow.

Thabraca is sparse on record. Yet it happens to stand on conspicuous show in an early writer, Pomponius Mela, as he follows the coast eastward: "Hippo Regius et Rusicade et Thabraca" (1. 33). Thabraca acquired the status of a *colonia* or a *municipium* from either Caesar or the Triumvirs. A

60. Viz., *CIL* 2 (1/63), 8 (4/84), 12 (0/21), 13 (2/13).
61. *CIL*, 2. 1956 (Cartima).
62. *Inscriptions of Roman Tripolitania*, nos. 517 (two men), 645.
63. *CIL*, 5. 3396 (Verona, a magistrate).
64. As argued in "People in Pliny," *JRS* 58 (1968): 139 f. = *Roman Papers*, p. 701 f.
65. *Tacitus*, pp. 799 f.
66. "Helvetian Aristocrats," *Mus. Helv*. 34 (1977): 138 f.
67. Also one in *CIL* 2, four in *CIL* 12.

dedication to Lepidus, set up *d(ecreto) d(ecurionum)*, has recently brought the town into due notoriety.[68]

The site had strategic value: a harbor (there are very few along that coast) with a road running south through the mountains to open country at Bulla Regia. The inscriptions of Thabraca are not numerous or remunerative; but Thuburnica, about thirty kilometers to the west of Bulla, discloses early settlement with a plethora of rare Italian *gentilicia* and an abnormal variety of tribes.[69]

Juvenal himself designates Africa next to Gaul as a nurse of forensic oratory, *nutricula causidicorum* (8. 148). In the days of his early manhood an African town far less promising than Thabraca delivered the first of them, namely Septimius Severus from Lepcis. In an ode of the year 95 Statius extols his amiable talent, "est et frementi vox hilaris foro; / venale sed non eloquium tibi" (*Silv.* 4. 5. 49–50). The young man was well to do—the father had an estate at Veii (5. 54–55).[70] Furthermore, the prose preface to Book 4 brings up a welcome fact. Severus was a *condiscipulus* of Vitorius Marcellus. This is the excellent young man (*suff.* 105) to whom Quintilian dedicated his great work. Sober scholars have not been reluctant to reckon Juvenal among the pupils.[71]

Lepcis did not acquire the full status of a Roman colony until the year 110; and the first magistrate under the new ordinances was L. Septimius Severus, precisely.[72] Immigrant or native, the extraction of these Septimii has been a question for debate.[73] Statius comes out with a firm pronouncement, "non sermo Poenus, non habitus tibi, / externa non mens: Italus, Italus" (4. 5. 45–46). The fervor of that asseveration is perhaps superfluous if the ancestry of Severus was in fact Italian.

The rise of the new Romans from the western lands is the triumph of the educated class, parallel (but generally antecedent) to their emergence in the service of the Caesars, with senatorial rank soon to ensue. Spain and Narbonensis lead the way and go on to produce a dynasty of emperors.

Africa puts up its first consul in 80, a Pactumeius from Cirta, the family Campanian by origin. Writers and scholars from Africa became prominent

68. *AE*, 1959, no. 77 = *ILLRP* 1276. See further J. Guey and A. Pernette, "Lépide à Thabraca," *Karthago* 9 (1958): 81 ff. An inscription of the second century presents the title, "colonia V. P. Thabracenorum" (*Inscriptions latines de l'Algérie*, 1. 109).

69. L. Teutsch, *Das Städtewesen in Nordafrika in der Zeit von C. Gracchus bis zum Tode des Kaisers Augustus* (Berlin, 1962), pp. 14 ff. The Furfanii are a family of local notables, one of them honoring C. Marius as *conditor coloniae* (*AE*, 1951, no. 81), with some exaggeration. Observe also four Velonii, an Etruscan name absent from *CIL* 11. One of them, with the tribe Lemonia, has for *patria*]*onia* (*CIL*, 8. 787). Borne also by the Furfanii, Lemonia is the tribe of Bononia.

70. Cf. *HASev.* 4. 5, with the emendation of M. Hammond, "Septimius Severus, Roman Bureaucrat," *HSCP* 51 (1940): 144.

71. F. Vollmer, s.v. "Iunius (Iuvenalis)," *RE* 10 (1917): 1042; Vollmer adduces 6. 75, 6. 280, 7. 186 ff.

72. *Inscriptions of Roman Tripolitania*, nos. 353, 412.

73. For Italian origin, T. D. Barnes, "The Family and Career of Septimius Severus," *Historia* 16 (1967): 87 ff.; for native, A. R. Birley, *Septimius Severus, the African Emperor* (Garden City, N.Y., 1971), p. 36.

toward the middle years of the Antonine century. Rational curiosity will look about for predecessors.

Hippo Regius yields a dedication to Suetonius Tranquillus, set up early in the reign of Hadrian, after he had become the secretary *ab epistulis*.[74] At first sight, his *patria*—though Pisaurum is not excluded for the *ultima origo* of the family (because of the occurrence of their rare nomen).[75] Attempts were made to appropriate Suetonius for Ostia. They have recently been canceled.[76] As for Junius Juvenalis, the argument leads toward Africa—but Thabraca does not have to be the *patria*.

X

The present disquisition puts emphasis on facts and the scarcity of facts, on plain nescience in a field that has been infested with credulity and romance. In consonance, the "exile of Juvenal" is eschewed.[77]

However, if license be conceded at the end to mitigate aridity, the notion of a festival to celebrate the sixtieth birthday of a professor in the last years of Domitian (a somber season) might amuse a philosophical mind. Quintilian himself was emboldened to proclaim an efflorescence of Roman oratory in this epoch, exhibiting already some *consummati patroni*, worthy rivals to classic performers in the old time; and younger men are coming on.[78]

A fine company of disciples might convene for a discreet symposium, men whose births fall between 57 and 70. In the forefront perhaps Cornelius Tacitus, and perhaps also his friend Fabius Justus (*suff.* 102). Resplendent success had endowed Tacitus with a priesthood by the time of his praetorship (in 88), but Justus soon gave up eloquence for the career of provinces and armies, taking him to consular commands in Moesia Inferior and in Syria. Next, and beyond a doubt, the loyal and alert Pliny (*pr.* 93), and Pliny's close coeval Vitorius Marcellus.[79]

At the tail end might be surmised without discomfort some persons of lower rank, such as Severus, the young man from Punic Lepcis—or Juvenal. Perhaps likewise Suetonius Tranquillus, whose career as an advocate was to be cut short through diffidence and superstition.[80]

74. *AE*, 1953, no. 73.

75. *Tacitus*, pp. 780 f.

76. F. Zevi, "Nuovi documenti epigrafici sugli Egrili ostiensi," *MEFR* 82 (1970): 302 f.; R. Meiggs, *Roman Ostia*² (Oxford, 1973), pp. 515 f.

77. For Knoche it was only "vielleicht . . . eine Legende" (*Satire*, p. 91). Coffey goes some way further: "probably invented in the fourth century" (*Roman Satire*, p. 122). *PIR*² J 765 is firm and negatory. The poet is now hounded into exile not once but twice by Cizek: "Juvénal et certains problèmes de son temps," pp. 80 ff.

78. Quint. 10. 1. 122: "namque et consummati iam patroni veteribus aemulantur et eos iuvenum ad optima tendentium imitatur ac sequitur industria."

79. For Pliny as a disciple, *Epist.* 2. 14. 9, 6. 6. 3.

80. Terrified by a dream, Suetonius asked Pliny to have the case postponed (*Epist.* 1. 18. 1). He is next found soliciting (and rejecting) a military tribunate in Britain (3. 8. 1).

To posterity the satirist Juvenal remains an isolated and enigmatic figure (he willed it thus). No friend is both verifiable and tangible, except for Martial.[81]

Wolfson College, Oxford

81. Young Juvenal lurks somewhere on the fringe of Pliny and Tacitus, of Statius perhaps, and of Suetonius. That he should fail to gain entry to Pliny's letters has evoked surprise and illicit inferences about both persons (e.g., Highet, *Juvenal the Satirist*, p. 19). Many other people of various categories, far superior in birth, rank, and attainments, are also absent. There is no sign that Juvenal had written anything before the last installment of the correspondence was given to the world (109?).

DESIRE AND MEMORY (SAPPHO FRAG. 94)

ANNE BURNETT

THE fragment that is numbered 94 in Voigt and in Lobel–Page has been a favorite since its discovery,[1] for it seems to preserve what many think of as the quintessentially Sapphic qualities. It has scenes of Lesbian life as soft as Swinburne's dreams, and it crosses these (or so we are told) with the sharp sense of anguish that today's scholar always seeks in Sappho's work. A favorite girl has gone and the poet, after a brave farewell, takes her lyre and confesses to us the depth of her despair, beginning τεθνάκην δ' ἀδόλως θέλω. The wish for death, according to the unanimous contemporary reading, strikes a deep chord that is held throughout the poem, adding shadows to the brighter melodies that are touched and put aside. This description is itself so seductive, with its tension between past pleasure and present despair, that few critics have attempted a closer interpretation of the piece; but there is one full and subtle reading, made along these lines, which I should like first to applaud and then to differ with.

Wolfgang Schadewaldt[2] discovers a song that is a triple portrait of the singer, placed against a background of triply layered time. He finds a frenzied grieving Sappho in a time of loss (the poetic present), a calm and gnomic Sappho in a time of parting (the recent past), and a tender, solicitous Sappho in a time of love (the deeper past). All melt together in a complex picture of longing and pain that is yet touched with irony, as the poet views both the old happiness and the old wisdom with the eye of her present pain. "Hier wurzelt auch jene sapphische 'Ironie,' die schon das Altertum gespürt und mit der sokratischen verglichen hat und die unser Gedicht fein schattiert."[3] The irony is really a form of *aidōs*, Schadewaldt explains, a modest and civil corrective that works upon a poem of passion to make it the reproduction "eines Gefühls, in dem Schmerz, Liebe und Gefasstheit der Seele unscheidbar in eins gehn."[4]

The magic of the critic's own passion, as he writes, is so great that for the moment it obscures all difficulties. When the air has cleared, however, and one turns back to the fragment, it is to discover that under Schadewaldt's reading the poem does not resolve itself into oneness, whatever may have happened to its "Gefühl." For Schadewaldt, the emotion that the poem reproduces first and last, the "Grundegefühl," is the anguish of loss; but

1. W. Schubart, "Neue Bruchstücke der Sappho u. des Alkaios," *SBBerl.*, phil.-hist. Kl., 1902, pp. 195 ff., esp. p. 202.
2. "Zu Sappho," *Hermes* 71 (1936): 363–73; cf. idem, *Sappho* (Potsdam, 1950), pp. 114–19.
3. "Zu Sappho," p. 373.
4. Ibid., p. 371.

0009-837X/79/7401-0002$01.09

if this is so then one of its parts negates two others, for he would have this emotion repudiate the explicit lesson of the Sapphic lines and also undo their sensual influence. Sappho will be saying one thing to her listener's mind (and powerfully involving his senses in the reception of her words), while she denies her own statement with a counter-message sent to his heart. There is refreshment, even joy, in memory, says the rational, consoling Sappho of the parting scene. Separate, finite pleasures that have come to an end can be fused into an infinite pleasure ever available, says the description of the common life. But then, if we read with Schadewaldt, an assertion of present despair tramples both of these statements to the ground and labels them as error. The poem's own counsels are useless by its own demonstration—"es hilft nichts"[5]—and instead of receiving the revived delights of the past, the present invades that lovely past with its own misery. The piece is tragic, its conclusion finally that both the beauty and the wisdom of the past contained the seeds of this present agony—there is "ja eine Art Tod im Dasein in der Liebe."[6]

Has Sappho really spread the matchless *mille fleurs* tapestry of stanzas five through ten in order to stain it with her wish for death? I am unable to believe that she has, and this, along with a conviction that the tragic is not her mode,[7] is the true cause of my resistance to Schadewaldt's compelling reading. There are, however, several concrete points that have confirmed me in this stand. Consider the two stanzas that occupy lines 6 through 11 and contain the formal exhortation to memory and continuing joy—stanzas which Schadewaldt's poem will go on to discredit. These are, for him, on the fictional level commonplace farewells infused with a lover's particular meaning: an anxious and pressing "Do not forget me!" On another level they represent for him an attempt at self-mastery that fails, a mask of composure that is let slip as soon as the girl is gone.[8] This section of the poem, then, portrays the gnomic Sappho, an impotent creature upon whom the anguished Sappho of the present smiles with irony. When one listens without prejudice, however, these stanzas give no hint of being

5. Ibid., p. 370.

6. Ibid., p. 367. A second line of interpretation should be noted, though it is not so convincing as Schadewaldt's. According to it this is a song that holds a reproach in ambush among its remembered wreaths because the girl has defected to another school. "On sent, l'on devine," wrote T. Reinach, "que la poétesse a dû éprouver une déception et que, sous cette tendre évocation, se cache un reproche: après tant de souvenirs et sans doute de promesses, l'amie, l'élève, a dû trahir sa foi". ("Nouveaux fragments de Sappho," *REG* 15 [1902]: 60 ff., esp. 65). Since it is really impossible to hear any accusation or suggestion of betrayal in the words given to the Sappho of the song, Wilamowitz offered an altered scheme (*Sappho und Simonides* [Berlin, 1913], p. 50). Sappho would like to die because all she has tried to teach the girl has been forgotten (Wilamowitz took line 9 literally), but the song is meant to be sung, not to the departed girl, but to Sappho's still present circle. It is an admonition to those who have remained loyal: they should not repeat the girl's careless forgetfulness or they too will cause their mistress pain and agony.

7. Though Plutarch reports that the Mixolydian was her invention (*De mus.* 16 = *Mor.* 1136D), I do not believe that Sappho made of Eros an Erinys; that in the ancient world was a figure for impossibility (Demetr. *Eloc.* 132).

8. Note G. Perotta, *Saffo e Pindaro* (Florence, n. d.), p. 150, who describes a Sappho who suffers much more than the girl does, as she speaks her words of comfort, one who disguises the "ardent pain" of her heart as a melancholy memory of past joy.

other than what they seem: the formal presentation of that part of the poem's thought that is paraphrasable.

Nothing betrays weakness or pretense in the Sapphic lover who speaks here, and nothing suggests that she is alienated from the poetic persona who controls the final song. On the contrary, the lines themselves are firm and strong; they are fixed into the poem in such a way as to suggest that what they say is of significance; and they control the subsequent shape of the piece. The opening ἔγω (6) proudly identifies the voice as that of the poet-lover, and the near rhyme of the two clausulae, πεδήπομεν and ἐπάσχομεν (8 and 11), sets the stanzas apart as a pair with special affinities one with the other. They offer in effect a small closed system where the theme is plainly marked by the crowded repetition of μέμναισ' (8) and ὄμναισαι (10). The idea of intellectual control over experience is extended by the coordination of οἶσθα and αἰ δὲ μή that clasps the two units together, and it is associated with the emotions in the pairing of the participles, "rejoicing"[9] and "remembering," in lines 7 and 8. A claim is being made for the power of the mind; and, as if in demonstration, this pair of stanzas is sharply marked by wit. The second speaker, Sappho, takes up a phrase from the first, the girl, and caps it triumphantly as if they were engaged in formal stichomythy; and as a result the girl's trite δεῖνα πεπόνθαμεν (4) stands corrected and transformed. With her κάλ' ἐπάσχομεν (11), Sappho emends "the dreadful" to make it beautiful, while she reads "experience" not as suffering but as pleasure; and in this way she works the poem's transition into the stanzas of recollection. It is her exercise of mind that allows all the beauties of the past life to pour out now like fruits from a cornucopia, but her mind has also marked these beauties for her persuasive purposes. The sweet moments of the past are here in the Sappho-lover's speech in order that they may replace δεῖνα with κάλα. Revived in memory they will justify the exhortation χαίροισ' ἔρχεο (7), for Sappho has not in fact pled anxiously that *she* should be recalled. Rather, "Remember me!" has expanded, in the lines that follow, to become "Remember beauty and pleasure!"—and this larger remembrance is offered as a happy talisman that can be taken anywhere.

Such is the exhortation to remember. It is followed by a demonstration of memory in action, offered fictionally to the senses of the girl, and by the poem as a whole to ours. Sappho has suggested that remembering can bring joy, and she now makes her statement fact in a passage that provides all of the poem's immediate sensory pleasures, and that also leaves a permanent mark upon the listener's memory. Her song does not produce images of a grieving woman or a departing girl; instead it leaves behind the rich residue of impressions made by the perfumes and wreaths, the flowers and cushions

9. D. Page, *Sappho and Alcaeus* (Oxford, 1955), p. 77, reports that χαίροισ' cannot mean what it seems to mean, because rejoicing "would be out of place here." He gives the word its neutral, Attic, fifth-century usage, as a phrase of dismissal. Nevertheless, in every other Sapphic occurrence, the word has what Page himself calls its "old meaning." The wedding wishes are particularly telling here (frags. 116 and 117V); at 22. 14V and 96. 5V there is clearly a happy pleasure in the word, and at 155V the expression can only be ironic, as Maximus of Tyre tells us it is, if its overt meaning is strongly joyful.

and music of the stanzas of remembrance. We, in other words, have been turned into vivid proofs of the truth of her "gnomic" thesis, so how can the poem be treating that thesis as useless or invalid? On the other hand, if it is valid and proved to be so, why has the counsel of memory not had its effect upon both of the lovers equally? Why can the girl remember and rejoice, while the woman can only weep?[10]

The fact is that there is a radical disharmony between every preserved part of this song and its singer's wish to die. Gordon Kirkwood,[11] recognizing this, supposed that the closing stanzas contained a reversal wherein Sappho gathered herself together with new strength, after giving ear to her own advice. He believed that such a poem would be a testimonial to the power of its own teaching, but one wonders if it could be taken seriously. A sense of unsteady fluctuation would be created, as the lesson was shown to be ineffective in one moment, effective in the next; and meanwhile the opening wish would suffer such devaluation that it would seem a piece of silly affectation, easily relinquished. Denys Page also saw the problem of the ineffective counsel, but he attacked the question of how this pleasure-filled poem could contain a wish for death in another way.[12] The true purpose of the piece, he said, is the description of the Sapphic life, the parting is merely a fictional occasion, and the longing to die a commonplace expression. He has been resisted with amusing fervor[13] by certain critics who (exactly like himself) believe that a poet's "sincerity" is impugned if conscious artistry is attributed to him. For them Sappho either sings with a noose around her neck or else she is "insincere"; and, though Page is willing to find "nothing profound" in her work, they are not—they loyally demand "genuine suffering" from her.

On the point of convention, however, Page is certainly right. The literary wish to die is a useful turn of speech that allows one to mark the thing that makes life desirable. So Achilles says *αὐτίκα τεθναίην* (*Il.* 18. 98) when he can no longer be of service to Patroclus; and Mimnermus echoes *τεθναίην* (frag. 1. 2 Diehl) when the Aphrodite-days are past. Anacreon, probably for amorous reasons, prays for death's release (*ἀπό μοι θανεῖν γενοῖτο* 411*a* Page), and the Sapphic corpus too contains another example of this topos (95V), so there can be no real question about the traditional nature of the wish in fragment 94. Page is nevertheless wrong in thinking that a mere recognition of this fact will solve the problem of our poem's inner consistency. The question of whether or not the woman Sappho sought death has never been a proper one, nor could it be resolved by proving that she spoke of the matter in trite phrases. The legitimate question is whether or

10. If I understand C. del Grande correctly, he proposes that the memories should make the girl sad, if she retained them, but that they are soon to be effaced by "more violent joys and pains" (of which the poem says nothing), so that Sappho alone will remember and regret: ΦΟΡΜΙΓΞ (Naples, 1959), p. 123.

11. *Early Greek Monody* (Ithaca, N.Y., 1974), pp. 135–36.

12. *Sappho and Alcaeus*, p. 83.

13. H. Saake, *Zur Kunst Sapphos* (Munich, 1971), pp. 190 ff.; idem, *Sappho Studien* (Munich, 1972), p. 90. C. M. Bowra believed that this was the first, literal use of an expression that then became conventional (*Greek Lyric Poetry*² [Oxford, 1961], p. 192).

not Sappho's song presents its lover-poet as seriously wishing for death, and this question cannot be resolved by simply putting the test of conventionality.[14] A thought, a sentiment, or an emotion may find literary expression either in a new-coined or in a conventional way; in either of these cases, it may be given its whole self-claimed value or only a part of that value, but this evaluation is established by and important to the work (not the artist's life) and can be discovered only in that work.[15] In the present instance, our song may offer its familiar wish at full or partial value, and as long as it remains in the poet-lover's mouth we are faced with the same two possibilities. Either the message of memory is countermanded by a fully evaluated topos (as Schadewaldt and most others suppose), or else the wish to die is reduced to a mere fit of vapors by memory's medicine (as Kirkwood has suggested). Page and his "commonplace" have thus not resolved the problems of interpretation; and I think it is time to ask whether Sappho in fact does really say, in her poetic persona, that she longs to die.[16]

The words τεθνάκην δ' ἀδόλως θέλω are by a freak of chance the first to be readable in this Sapphic fragment. They are in actuality the second line of a stanza that may or may not have begun the poem, but they have assumed the dominance that belongs naturally to an opening line. They are generally taken as the de facto beginning of the poem, simply because critics like to think of them that way: "schwerlich wird dieser Anfang sich weit zurückerstreckt haben," says Schadewaldt,[17] confident that what he has called the beginning must be so. After the same fashion and with no better reason, these first surviving words are forced into the mouth of the poem's singer. The stanza in which they appear depicts a dramatic situation, and the line that follows the wish places us in the middle of a fully realized scene in which two speakers engage in direct discourse; but the wish to die is nevertheless plucked from this context and set out in naked prominence by every recent editor.[18] The words are to be sung in a voice different from that used

14. Note, e.g., G. Lanata, "Sul linguaggio amoroso di Saffo," *QU* 2 (1966): 72, who finds the wish-to-die topos to be expressive of "un momento tipico dell'esperienza saffica dell'eros"—at once serious and conventional.

15. See the vigorous and sensible remarks of S. Radt, "Sapphica," *Mnemosyne*, ser. 4, 23 (1970): 347: "Im Gedicht haben wir es also nur mit dieser 'imaginative experience' zu tun—ihr Verhältnis zur erlebten Wirklichkeit spielt für die Beurteilung des Gedichts überhaupt keine Rolle." He quotes R. Wellek and A. Warren, *Theory of Literature* (New York, 1949), p. 74: "The frequently adduced criterion of 'sincerity' is thoroughly false, if it judges literature in terms of biographical truthfulness, correspondence to the author's experience or feelings as they are attested by outside evidence."

16. One further attempt to coordinate the present wish to die with the past counsel of memory should be noted. It is that of G. Caduff, "Zu Sapphos Fr. 94 LP. (= 96 D.)," in R. Muth (ed.), *Serta Philologica Aenipontana*, vol. 2 (Innsbruck, 1972), pp. 9–12. Caduff argues that Sappho's desire for death is an outburst of jealous pain caused by an act of erotic treason newly discovered. Some fresh event has occurred, he says, between the time of the consolation speech and the present moment of despair; Sappho has learned that the girl, since her departure, has proved her forgetfulness by a new liaison.

17. Schadewaldt, "Zu Sappho," p. 370; see also H. Jurenka, "Die neuen Bruchstücke der Sappho und des Alkaios," *Zeitschr. Österr. Gymn.* 53 (1902): 291.

18. It seems to have been Reinach, acting on a suggestion from Henri Weil, who inaugurated the present way of reading the first surviving line: "avec H. Weil j'attribue ces paroles à Sappho, non à son interlocutrice; il est facile, malgré cette parenthèse, de rattacher le vers 2 à celui où l'amie devait être désignée" ("Nouveaux fragments," p. 65). Wilamowitz followed, and Schadewaldt, giving the line to Sappho, adds, "wie heute nicht mehr bezweifelt wird" ("Zu Sappho," p. 364).

for the rest of the song, we are told, for this is an aside, a kind of moan that rises from the very heart of the woman who performs for us.

The resulting effect has been so popular that the fragment is coming to be known as "The Confession Song," quite as if this were as objective a description of it as "The Ostrakon" is of fragment 2.[19] Nevertheless, neither text nor sense necessarily assigns the death wish to the singer, and the privilege of hearing Sappho admit to her terrible agony is bought at a certain price. When the first surviving line is in this way ascribed to the poet's own voice, there is an awkward jerk in the developing exposition of the scene, as the connection between line and line is broken. Schadewaldt asserts that this asyndeton is "ganz selbstverständlich" because of the poet's strong emotion,[20] but his argument has a certain circularity; and in fact the break is especially noticeable in this Lesbian form, where each new statement as a rule flows directly from the one before. When the wish to die is given to the extra-dramatic Sappho there is in addition an anomalous time shift between the two lines—a leap from a generalized present into an actualized past—and a further wrench as well, as the form of the discourse alters. An immediate, personal exclamation is replaced by a distanced and objective narrative, and a nameless "she" bounds onto the stage without any introduction or linguistic signal to ease our comprehension. These difficulties are real, and they are created by the accepted reading of the wish to die; they have, however, been glossed over by a host of scholars who were eager to hear Sappho confess to her total despair.

Or is there perhaps something about the wish itself that is necessarily appropriate only to the singer of the song? The fact that there is a second Sapphic wish to die might seem to establish a precedent in the poet's favor; but in truth the other passage is wholly unlike the present one, and a close examination of it leaves one less, rather than more, convinced of the accepted attribution in fragment 94. The second wish occurs in a poem that refers to Gongyla and is probably in some sense erotic in subject; the wish is not an aside, however, not an anguished moan from singer to audience, nor does it even belong to the surface-present of the poem. It is instead submerged in an elaborately artful scene between Hermes and the poet, a scene from the past in which she had asked him to take her down to Acheron: "I said to him, 'Master, . . . and a longing for death has taken hold of me . . .' " (95. 8–11V). The wish is, in other words, distanced and dramatic and wholly unlike the wish generally attributed to Sappho the singer of fragment 94. Indeed, if the Acheron wish suggests anything for the interpretation of our poem, it is that our wish too may belong to the dramatic scene, and this idea is strengthened by a verbal point as well. When speaking to Hermes, Sappho says very simply *κατθάνην δ' ἴμερός τις ἔχει με* (95. 11V). She does not have to assure him that she means all she says, and her plainness makes one wonder why, in an aside to her audience, she should protest her earnestness with the urgent adverb, *ἀδόλως*. The word is usually translated "honest-

19. Saake regularly refers to it as "das confessio-Gedicht."
20. "Zu Sappho," p. 364.

ly" or "truly", but it is uncommon enough to keep its explicitly privative sense.[21] It lays claim to an absence of guile, a refusal to use trickery, and, as it does so, it brings those very notions into play. To protest that one is straight is to depict a listener who suspects one of crookedness—surely a curious portrait of Sappho's audience of admiring girls, and yet it is to them that her assurance is offered, if the wish to die is hers.

Why ἀδόλως? The speaker with this word assures someone that her wish for death is neither trick nor trap, and it is not hard to catch the tone of her avowal, for the striking word betrays it. The notion of the δόλος has its Sapphic context in the Hymn to Aphrodite, where the goddess is given the epithet δολόπλοκος because she plays ensnaring tricks upon mankind. She may pretend to help or she may pretend not to hear, just as individual lovers may feign concern or jealousy or indifference in imitation of her tricks. The normal speech of love is full of the snares of exaggeration and placation—it is that πάρφασις ἥ τ' ἔκλεψε νόον that Aphrodite kept in her elaborate kirtle (*Il.* 14. 217)—and just because it is tricky, love's speech is likewise full of protestations of sincerity ("honestly" and "I really mean it"), though these too may be only a part of the game. Fragment 94 concerns the parting of two lovers, and so it is natural to suppose that its insistent reassurance belongs to this same amorous mode. The poem does not need to claim innocent guilelessness as it addresses posterity, nor does Sappho as she sings to a small group of friends;[22] but the girl who would persuade her mistress that she is loath to leave may feel called upon to "cross her heart and hope to die" as she speaks of her unhappiness. She alone can easily say τεθνάκην δ' ἀδόλως θέλω.

Since only opinion forbids it and so much in the poem recommends it, I propose to read the initial line of fragment 94 in the simplest way (the way of the first editor), as belonging to the girl:[23]

. . . .

"I don't deceive you, I want to die!"
Weeping she tried to leave me
and more than once she said,
"How frightfully we suffer, Sappho!
I go against my will!"

21. Generations of American students have recognized this quality with the inelegant but accurate translation, "no kidding." H. Fränkel reports that "protestations like 'in good faith' and 'truly' are frequent in Sappho" (*Early Greek Poetry and Philosophy*, trans. M. Hadas and J. Willis [New York, 1975], p. 179), but he does not supply citations. Presumably he refers to such turns of speech as ἦ μήν, but these are in no sense parallels for ἀδόλως.

22. Unless one assumes that Sappho is saying to her audience: "I tricked the girl with my counsel of memory, but I do not now trick you."

23. Arnold Gomme attempted to revive Schubart's way of reporting the wish for death, but the suggestion was made in the course of an article that contained a few rather imprudent remarks on other matters, and it was not taken seriously: see "Interpretations of Some Poems of Alkaios and Sappho," *JHS* 77 (1957): 255–66. I know of only two other scholars who give the words to the girl: Del Grande, ΦΟΡΜΙΓΞ, p. 24; and J. Danielewicz, "Sappho's Subjective Lyrics," *Eos* 58 (1969–70): 168: "She cites the girl's own words full of despair and sorrow τεθνάκην δ' ἀδόλως θέλω, as well as her own consoling answer. . . ." (Sappho's remarks about the common life are, according to this critic, "full of motherly cordiality"!) D. Gerber, *Euterpe* (Amsterdam, 1970), p. 175, says

The reassignment doesn't affect the girl at all. In her mouth the line is affectionately melodramatic and she remains the same effusive creature that she was. Her ἀδόλως is in the style of her ἦ μάν, both of them examples of the exaggeration and emphasis that might be thought of as typical of the very young. The poem, on the other hand, undergoes a considerable change when its persona is relieved of the solemn wish to die. As soon as the girl absorbs the line, her wise companion joins the Sappho who sings the song and we no longer have to apprehend a frenzied present singer divided against two peaceful selves from the past. The words that she addressed to the girl in the scene of farewell are now the real burden of the song, and they do not have to be heard accompanied by the performer's inharmonious lament. The garlands of the remembered life no longer wither under ironies, and the extreme artistry of the stanzas of recollection applies itself directly to a meaning that is luminous and clear. The poem, insofar as we have it, becomes a whole, and in it Sappho delivers one of her plainest lectures on love's philosophy.

The disconsolate girl thinks that parting is the end of life and love, but her wiser mistress commands her to go her way rejoicing. Memory can turn momentary pain into an enduring joy, and her continuing speech gives precise instructions in the discipline that is to shape this transforming meditation. "I should like to remind you," Sappho says, "of the facets of love which, when correctly recalled, can outlive our separation." She proceeds point by point, and just beneath her explicit program two rather surprising implicit conditions appear. The girl is to remember, not her lover but herself, and of herself, not her own person, not even vivid moments of her own history, but a schema of experience. She is to think of a series of three habitually repeated gestures, and these will lead her to an equally prismatic memory of satisfied desire.

Crowning oneself with flowers, at the side of the beloved (πάρ' ἔμοι, 14), is the first gesture that thought should revive, for Sapphic flower crowns marked a girl as ready for love. Such wreaths were worn to seek favor from the Charites, dispensers of attractiveness (81. 6–7V),[24] and they were themselves redolent of desire (ἐράτοι, 81. 4V), like the crown that Alcman mentions, where a wanton Eros sports among the blossoms (58P). A flower crown was reminiscent of Aphrodite's own (of roses at Eur. *Med.* 840), and this is why the Horae put a wreath of spring blooms in Pandora's hair when she was sent out on her mission of seduction (Hes. *Erga* 73–75). The

"we should not completely discount the possibility . . . ," but he does not entertain it; Kirkwood, *Monody*, p. 263, takes the matter more seriously, admitting that the line could be given to the girl and that such an arrangement would ease the asyndeton. Finally, however, he dismisses the idea as "impossible" on the grounds that the "style of the beginning is so unlike the style of what follows," without explaining what he means. In *Frühgriechische Lyriker*, vol. 3: *Sappho, Alkaios, Anakreon*, trans. Z. Franyó, ed. B. Snell (Berlin, 1976), the Greek text as usual leaves the line outside the quotation, but the translation marks it as part of the girl's speech. (The referee of this article has kindly drawn my attention to Francis Cairns, *Generic Composition in Greek and Roman Poetry* [Edinburgh, 1972], pp. 50 ff.)

24. On the notion that the Charites bestow a *charis* that marks readiness for love, see Lanata's discussion of frag. 49V, "Linguaggio amoroso," pp. 63 ff.

second gesture to be remembered is the placing of the garland that will draw attention to a tender, vulnerable throat (*ἀμφ' ἀπάλαι δέραι*, 16),[25] again a re-enactment of one of Aphrodite's coquetries, though her decorations were of gold (*Hymn. Hom. Ven.* 88).[26] Such a garland took its name, *hypathymis,* from the fact that it hung down over the breasts, and the breasts and the body are the focus of the third gesture to be recalled, the application of perfumes. Both Alcaeus and Anacreon speak of myrrh poured upon the breast,[27] but here there seems to be a second and richer unguent as well, and one is reminded of Archilochus' ambiguous salute to the girl whose perfumed hair and breasts could rouse a greybeard's lust (48 West). Scented unguents and salves were the major ingredients in any recipe for provocation, which is why Hera begged perfumes from Aphrodite's *kistē* when she meant to numb Zeus's wits with sex (*Il.* 14. 171–72), and why Aphrodite herself applied scent before she journeyed to Anchises' hut (*Hymn. Hom. Ven.* 61–62). She took a pot of myrrh with her to the Judgment (Soph. *Krisis,* frag. 361 Pearson and note) and she gave a phial of the same sweet salve to Phaon who, using it, became the darling of the ladies of Mytilene (Ael. *VH* 12. 18). In *Lysistrata* oil of myrrh is a telling weapon in the women's arsenal, along with diaphanous frocks and foolish little shoes (946), and there is a girl in middle comedy who has a different scent for each one of her body's parts (Antiphanes *Thorikioi, CAF,* 2:53).

With her three remembered gestures the girl of Sappho's lesson marks herself as courting love, and in stanza eight she is taught to remember its achievement.[28] It is silly to quibble over the precise nature of the moments that the poem here recalls; all we need to know is that the Homeric phrase *ἐξίης πόθον* (23) conveys the idea of release by way of satisfaction, and that Sappho's own usage fixes *pothos* as erotic.[29] The Sappho of the dramatic scene thus tells the girl to think of the familiar triple preparation of crowning, garlanding, and perfuming, and in this way to reach the heartening

25. With this *ἀπαλὴ δειρή* compare the *ἁβρὸς αὐχήν* of the shorn boy of Anacreon 347P. On *ἀπαλός*, see M. Treu, *Von Homer zur Lyrik*² (Munich, 1968), pp. 178–83, who notes a change from the subjective Homeric meaning to the affective, erotic, Sapphic use.

26. At *Hymn. Hom.* 6. 10–11, Aphrodite makes all the immortals want her for their wife by thus bedecking herself: *δειρῇ δ' ἀμφ' ἁπαλῇ καὶ στήθεσιν ἀργυφέοισιν / ὅρμοισι χρυσέοισιν ἐκόσμεον.*

27. Alcaeus 362. 3V; Anacreon 363P. Note G. Zuntz, "De Sapphus Carminibus ε̄ 3, ε̄ 4, ε̄ 5," *Mnemosyne*, ser. 3, 7 (1939): 87: "Ego pectoris quoque mentionem in v. 18 vel v. 19 fuisse coll. Athen. 674c et 678d sqq. divinaverim." At a symposium perfumes were applied chiefly to the head; but, where drinking was not the chief occupation, they were rubbed into the flesh (see Athen. 691F–692, citing Philonides' *On Perfumes and Wreaths*).

28. This is something like what Christopher Dawson perceived in Mimnermus 2: "the briefest of short stories: *κρυπταδιὴ φιλότης*, a quiet, stolen kiss or embrace; then *μείλιχα δῶρα*, further concrete inducements; and finally *εὐνή*, the consummation" ("Random Thoughts on Occasional Poems," *YClS* 19 [1966l: 49).

29. Attempts have been made to treat this Sapphic *pothos* as non-erotic: see, e.g., J. M. Edmonds, *Lyra Graeca*², vol. 1 (Cambridge, Mass., 1928), p. 243, who thought the condition was hunger; Bowra, *Greek Lyric Poetry*², p. 191, who proposed a wish for absent friends; or C. Theander, "Studia Sapphica," *Eranos* 34 (1936): 59 ff., who suggested homesickness. These were presumably assuaged by eating, the exhaustion of the festival, and sleep, respectively. Nevertheless, it is generally recognized that lines like *καὶ ποθήω καὶ μάομαι* (36V) and *ἦλθες, †καὶ† ἐπόησας, ἔγω δέ σ' ἐμαιόμαν / ὂν δ' ἔψυξας ἐμὰν φρένα καιομέναν πόθωι* (48V) establish the erotic meaning beyond doubt: see, e.g., Zuntz, "De Sapphus Carminibus," pp. 89–90; Lanata, "Linguaggio amoroso," p. 70; Page, *Sappho and Alcaeus*, pp. 79–80.

memory of fulfilled desire. In the meantime the poem has moved through three stanzas that evoked but never directly described first the hair on which a crown would rest, then the throat that garlands might touch, and finally the sheen of anointed flesh. As a result, the couch of the eighth stanza receives the sinking weightlessness of an image at once powerfully sensual and perfectly insubstantial and, strangest of all, the figure seems to be alone. This soft cot is a place for lovemaking,[30] but as a partner for the girl's remembered self the poem proposes only the transparent companion of the initial garlanding (the ἔμοι of line 14).[31] All the ink spent in trying to remove the sexuality from this moment has indeed been wasted, for nothing can change the fact that sex both is and is not here.[32] The event is one that occurred, or rather is to be thought of as having occurred, repeatedly, but it has been removed from history, from narrative, and from any contact with the mundane world. The couch is neither indoors nor out; it rests upon nothing, neither carpet nor grass, because it does not contain lovers at all, but only the girl's seductiveness and its success. Sappho's art has already done for it what the trained memory will do, for it has taken from blunt objects and fleeting sensations their enduring essence.

This is not the end of the Sapphic lesson, however, for there is another and actual sense in which the past will endure. The passage that revives the frequent pilgrimages to the couch does not come to an end with that private culmination but moves forward instead to what is evidently its real goal in a burst of festal activity. The ninth and tenth stanzas are badly damaged, but the words "sacred" and "grove" are there, terms for musical sound and a dancing chorus can perhaps be recognized, and the rhetorical shape is clear: no sacred feast or celebration was held from which the lovers stayed away (26). These two public and festive stanzas thus cap the lines about escape from desire, outweighing them and drawing the remembered private acts of love into public and sacred scenes that the poem now imagines. It is as if the pair rose from the couch of their satisfaction and danced away into a populous complex of song and procession, or indeed as if their lovemaking

30. On the erotic associations of *μαλθακός*, see J. M. Bremer, "Meadow of Love," *Mnemosyne*, ser. 4, 28 (1975): 268 f.

31. This is denied by many, even F. Lasserre, who admits the erotic quality of *ἐξίης πόθον*, but insists, "Il ne s'agit pas d'un amour de Sappho." He is arguing for the conventional quality of the poem, but is unable to admit any middle ground between poems that were fully public, as choral poetry was, and poems that were the private record of actual and immediate emotion: see "Ornaments Erotiques," *Serta Turyniana* (Urbana, 1974), p. 24, n. 35.

32. See, e.g., Martin West, "Burning Sappho," *Maia* 22 (1970): 322, where the author attempts to answer questions that need never have been asked. He tries to follow Bowra in the notion that *pothos* means "a longing for one who is absent" and may therefore be satisfied by a reunion. Faced with the couch, he proposes that "in settling down to sleep in companionable proximity . . . they finally found contentment." Then he cites the undeniably amorous *δαύοισ' ἀπάλας ἐταίρας ἐν στήθεσιν* (126V). Finally he abandons the idea of a Girl Scout overnight by announcing: "It may be that still more intimate things sometimes occurred in the dark hours. The point . . . is that Sappho is not telling us so in fr. 94." (Night and sleep have entered his picture out of modesty and because he believes that the poem is a record of specific experience; there is nothing about either in Sappho's lines, so far as we can read them.) All of this speculation is as unnecessary as it is embarrassing because Sappho *does* tell us that erotic satisfaction is found, over and over again, on the couch; but she also makes it perfectly clear that we are not to take any interest in the precise nature of that satisfaction. See the splendid outburst of Zuntz, "De Sapphus Carminibus," p. 89.

had itself been a gesture, a part of some larger pageant of prescribed observances. The idea that individual lovers belong to a community of celebrants is thus enforced by the progress of the song, as private cult and public celebration are made one by poetic fiat.[33]

It is part of Sappho's instruction, then, that the girl should view herself and be viewed by others as a creature engaged in a repeated rite of embellishment, devotion, and celebration. The thrice reiterated "many . . . many . . . many . . ." (πόλλοις . . . πόλλαις . . . πόλλωι, 12, 15, and 18)[34] keeps the three actions balanced and equal each to the others, while it also creates the sense of habitual and ceaseless renewal. Love is not a discrete experience: it is a part of the common life of the *thiasos*, and of its common observance as well; and this last notion provides a final reason why the departing girl should rejoice, while suggesting as well an explanation for the last problem of the poem. "Go rejoicing and holding me in memory," Sappho says, "for you know how we followed after you!" (οἶσθα γὰρ ὤς σε πεδήπομεν, 8). The whole counsel of memory seems, in these lines, to hang upon the γὰρ clause, but the expression is a baffling one. It is often rendered, "You know how we have cherished you," just to get past the difficulty, though no parallel for any such meaning can be found.[35] A second interpretation proposes this as an erotic compliment meant to suggest that the entire company has been in love with the girl,[36] though this too depends upon a figurative use of the verb that is unexampled. If, however, μεθέπεσθαι is allowed to keep its literal sense, it will convey the idea that the girl has led them all much as a chorus leader might a dancing band. Perhaps Sappho means to remind her that she has been, for a time, the manifestation of *charis* among them, the one who danced first in the cult of love, who carried the sacred objects, performed the sacred acts, and set the pace for them all—the best, in other words, as Helen was among the Spartan girls (Theoc. 18. 24 ff.). When she is gone someone else will take her place in the *thiasos*, and presumably in Sappho's preference as well, but her own experience is indestructible. Within the large conceit of love as ritual, the individual episode is given permanence, for no single act can be rendered futile by completion since the cult will continue forever.

Neither grief nor regret is compatible with such a view of love, and so Sappho evokes the undeniable pang of parting, only to erase it with her song. The "sheer and absolute sorrow" and "abandoned hysteria"[37] that have been attached to its singer have no place at all in her poem, and even

33. Something of this sort is perceived by T. McEvilley, "Sapphic Imagery and Frag. 96," *Hermes* 101 (1973): 268, who writes, "Fragment 94 does not present exactly a rite nor exactly a party, but a private occasion which involved the symbolic objects common to both." Cf. Saake, *Kunst*, p. 200, who supposes that the gestures are part of an actual cult of the Muses.

34. It should be noted that the πόλλωι of line 18 is the conjecture of Achille Vogliano; Bowra prints πάνται.

35. See Page, *Sappho and Alcaeus*, p. 77.

36. Lanata, "Linguaggio amoroso," p. 65.

37. Bowra, *Greek Lyric Poetry*², p. 197, and R. Bagg, "Love, Ceremony and Daydream," *Arion* 3 (1964): 47. It is hard to avoid the conclusion that the scholarly determination to discover a miserable woman behind Sappho's poems is connected with the scholarly recognition of the nature of the love she refers to. The unexpressed reasoning seems to be: unnatural, therefore unhappy.

the figure of Sappho as lover dims, since it plays but an exemplary role in the exemplary fiction of parting. The poem is not *reportage* but thought cast into a poetic mode, its imagined "event" just firm enough to launch the poet's reflections, for the essential quality here is not raw emotion but perfected meditation. The same quality distinguishes all of the longer Sapphic pieces, and surely it was this presence of thought—this absence of immediate frenzy—that made Plato call the poet wise (Ael. *VH* 12. 19) and caused Horace to speak of her approvingly as *mascula*[38] (*Epist.* 1. 19. 28).

University of Chicago

38. E. Fraenkel, *Horace* (Oxford, 1957), p. 346, n. 3, quotes the deathbed recantation of Philipp Buttman, who had suggested that the word was meant to describe Sappho's sexual preference: "Meine wirkliche Schuld gegen beiden [Sappho and Horace] gut zu machen, halte ich für eine meiner heiligsten Pflichten, ehe ich aus diesem Kreise der redenden Menschengeschlechter scheide; welche ich hiermit erfülle."

THE FOUND AND LOST MANUSCRIPTS OF TACITUS' *AGRICOLA*

DAVID SCHAPS

OF THE two manuscripts with which this paper will deal, neither is currently available to scholars. The Hersfeldensis, discovered in the middle of the fifteenth century, seems to have vanished from sight shortly thereafter; the Aesinas, discovered in Iesi at the beginning of the current century by Cesare Annibaldi, was apparently taken from its owners during World War II, and I have been unable to locate any scholar who knows its present whereabouts. It was Annibaldi's belief[1]—and that of most scholars after him[2]—that he had rediscovered, in the Aesinas, a fragment of the lost Hersfeldensis. I think that the weight of evidence now available is heavily against this conclusion; but, as received opinion lies ponderous on the other side, I shall be required to reproduce much of the evidence, almost all of which is available elsewhere, in order to demonstrate what is known and what is not.

Reconstruction of the Hersfeldensis, with which we shall deal first, is a problem more properly historical than paleographical. The first clear mention of it is in a letter of Poggio Bracciolini dated November 3 (1425), in which he informs Niccolò Niccoli that "quidam monachus amicus meus ex quodam monasterio Germaniae"[3] has some books that he is willing to trade; "inter ea volumina est Iulius Frontinus et aliqua opera Cornelii Taciti nobis ignota."[4] The news caused some excitement in humanist circles[5] and a certain amount of competition to get hold of the manuscript. A letter of

My thanks to Professors J. P. Elder, Herbert Bloch, and Mason Hammond of Harvard University for their guidance, encouragement, and helpful suggestions. They are not responsible for my mistakes. Thanks also to a journal referee, whose suggestions I have adopted at a few points.

1. *L' "Agricola" e la "Germania" di Cornelio Tacito nel MS. latino N. 8 della biblioteca del Conte G— Balleani in Iesi* (Città di Castello, 1907), pp. 75–78.

2. G. Wissowa, introduction to *Taciti "Dialogus,"* etc. (Leyden, 1907), *non vidi*; R. P. Robinson, *The "Germania" of Tacitus: A Critical Edition* (Middletown, Conn., 1935), pp. 12–13; P. Lehmann, "Paläographische Beurteilung des Codex Hersfeldensis," in R. Till, *Handschriftliche Untersuchungen zu Tacitus "Agricola" und "Germania"* (Berlin–Dahlem, 1943), p. 11. All editors of Tacitus' minor works have repeated this judgment, but not, so far as can be told, after any particular consideration of the matter. The lone, but firm, dissenter is C. W. Mendell, "Manuscripts of Tacitus' Minor Works," *MAAR* 19 (1949): 133–45; his views are repeated in his *Tacitus: The Man and His Work* (New Haven, 1957), pp. 241–54.

3. That the monastery was Hersfeld is stated in other letters, reproduced in R. Sabbadini, *Storia e critica di testi latini* (Catania, 1914), pp. 272, 275, n. 2; a more readily available summary of the documents bearing on the Hersfeld manuscript will be found in G. Brugnoli (ed.), *Suetoni "De grammaticis et rhetoribus"*[2] (Leipzig, 1963), pp. viii–xiv. For a bibliography of modern discussions of the Hersfeldensis, see Brugnoli, p. xxviii, and E. Koestermann, *Taciti "Germania," "Agricola," "Dialogus de oratoribus"* (Leipzig, 1964), pp. xxxi–xxxiii.

4. Sabbadini, *Storia e critica*, p. 263.

5. Ibid., pp. 264–73.

0009-837X/79/7401-0001$01.30

il Panormita (Antonio Beccadelli) of the following April[6] describes the discovery in more detail:

> Compertus est Cor. Tacitus de origine et situ Germanorum. Item eiusdem liber de vita Iulii Agricolae isque incipit: "Clarorum virorum facta" caeterave. Quinetiam Sex. Iulii Frontonis liber de aquaeductibus. . . . Item eiusdem Frontonis liber alter. . . . Et inventus est quidam dyalogus de oratore et est, ut coniectamus, Cor. Taciti, atque is ita incipit: "Saepe ex me requirunt" et caetera. Inter quos et liber Suetonii Tranquilli repertus de grammaticis et rhetoribus: huic inicium est: "Grammatica Romae."[7]

It is clear that Panormita is describing the same find that Poggio had mentioned; but he was to be disappointed in his expectation of seeing the manuscript *proxime et de repente.* When, in fact, Poggio's connection returned, he brought with him an "inventarium plenum verbis, re vacuum";[8] this was in 1427. In 1429, again, he arrived in Rome *absque libro;*[9] and in 1431, when the cardinals Cesarini and Albergati were about to travel to Germany and France on ecclesiastical business, Niccoli prepared for them a list of valuable books to be sought out. The second item in his *Commentarium* reads:

> In Monasterio hispildensi haud procul ab alpibus continentur haec opuscula. videlicet.
>
> Iulii Frontini De aquae ductis quae in vrbem inducunt liber .j. Incipit sic. "PERSECVTVS ea. . . ." &c. Continet hic liber xiij.
>
> Item eiusdem frontini liber incipit sic. "Cum omnis res. . . ." &c. Continet .xi. folia.
>
> Cornelii taciti de origine & situ germanorum liber incipit sic. "Germania omnis a galiis rhetiisque & pannoniis rheno & danubio fluminibus a sarmatis datisque & mutuo metu a montibus separatur" etc. Continet autem xij folia:—Item in eodem codice:—
>
> Cornelii taciti De uita Iulii agricole Incipit sic. "Clarorum uirorum facta moresque posteris tradere antiquitus usitatum, ne nostris quidem temporibus, quamquam uniuersa suorum etas obmisit." Qui liber continet .xiiij. folia. Item in eodem codice:—
>
> Dialogus De oratoribus qui incipit sic. "Sepe ex me requiris iuste fabi, cur cum priora secula tot eminentium oratorum ingeniis, gloria, floruerint: nostra potissimum etas deserta & laude eloquentiae orbata:" qui liber continet xviij. folia. Item in eodem codice continetur liber—
>
> Suetonii Tranquilli De grammaticis & rhetoribus, qui incipit sic. "Grammatica romae ne in usu quidem olim nedum in honore ullo" &c. Continet hic liber folia vij.
>
> Ammiani Marcellini rerum gestarum libri xviij. Qui peruenerunt usque ad obitum Valentis imperatoris: qui est finis hystoriae.[10]

6. Ibid., p. 270, n. 6. Panormita was, in this matter, Poggio's competitor rather than his associate, and it is probable that his information came from the monk himself, not from Poggio (C. W. Mendell, "Discovery of the Minor Works of Tacitus," *AJP* 56 [1935]: 114–16).
7. Sabbadini, *Storia e critica*, p. 270.
8. Ibid., p. 272.
9. Ibid., p. 275, n. 2.
10. Ibid., pp. 4–7; more accurately in R. P. Robinson, "The Inventory of Niccolò Niccoli," *CP* 16 (1921): 251–55, from whom my text is taken.

Four of the items, as Niccoli indicates, all belong to one codex; so it is apparent that the Frontinus and the Ammianus Marcellinus[11] were separate. There can be no doubt that Niccoli is describing the same "Iulius Frontinus et aliqua opera Cornelii Taciti" that Poggio and Panormita had mentioned; the detail in which he is able to describe the works shows that he had before him, either in the original or in a copy, the inventory—*plenum verbis* indeed—that his friend Poggio had gotten from the Hersfeld monk. This being the case, we may be confident that his description is reasonably accurate, being derived from a firsthand apograph; since, however, the monk himself was apparently a man of small talent and little scholarship,[12] there are numerous mistakes in detail, not all of which were necessarily in the manuscript itself.

Nothing came of Niccoli's list; although Cesarini did indeed reach Nuremberg, he did not, apparently, search out the codices. But the manuscript did reach Rome, for the papal secretary Pier Candido Decembrio saw it there in 1455, and described it in detail in his notebook.

> Cornelii taciti liber reperitur Rome visus 1455 de Origine et situ Germanie. Incipit: "Germania omnis a Gallis retiisque et panoniis Rheno et danubio fluminibus a Sarmatis dacisque mutuo metu aut montibus seperatur. cetera occeanus ambit." Opus est foliorum XII in columnellis. Finit: "Cetera iam fabulosa helusios et oxionas ora hominum vultusque corpora atque artus ferarum gerere. quod ego ut incompertum in medium relinquam." Utitur autem cornelius hoc vocabulo "inscientia" non "Inscitia."
>
> Est alius liber eiusdem de Vita Iulii agricole soceri sui. in quo continetur descriptio Britanie Insule nec non populorum mores et ritus. Incipit: "Clarorum virorum facta moresque posteris tradere antiquitus usitatum. ne nostris quidem temporibus quamquam incuriosa suorum etas ommisit." Opus foliorum decem et quattuor in columnellis. Finit: "Nam multos veluti inglorios et ignobiles oblivio obruet. Agricola posteritati narratus et traditus superstes erit."
>
> Cornelii taciti dialogus de oratoribus. Incipit: "Sepe ex me requiris iuste fabi cur cum priora secula tot eminentium oratorum ingeniis gloriaque floruerint, nostra potissimum etas deserta et laude eloquentie orbata vix nomen ipsum oratoris retineat." Opus foliorum XIIII in columnellis. Post hec deficiunt sex folia. nam finit: "quam ingentibus verbis prosequuntur. Cum ad veros iudices ventum." Deinde sequitur: "rem cogitare nihil abiectum nihil humile." Post hec sequuntur folia duo cum dimidio. et finit: "Cum adrisissent discessimus."
>
> Suetonii tranquilli de grammaticis et rhetoribus liber. Incipit: "Grammatica rome nec in usu quidem olim nedum in honore ullo erat. rudi scilicet ac bellicosa etiam tum civitate necdum magnopere liberalibus disciplinis vacante." Opus foliorum septem in columnellis. Finit perprius: "Et rursus in cognitione cedis mediolani apud lucium pisonem proconsulem defendens reum. cum cohiberent lictores nimias laudantium voces ita excanduisset. ut deplorato Italie statu quasi iterum in formam provincie redigeretur. M. insuper brutum cuius statua in conspectu erat invocaret legum

11. Of which a fragment, rediscovered in 1876, is preserved in the Marburger Staatsarchiv. According to Lehmann, "Beurteilung," p. 12, it has no "graphic relation" to the Aesinas.

12. A number of his letters, "in naiver Form und wirrer Gedankenfolge, sprachlich eine Mischung von Rhöndeutsch und Latein," have been published in L. Pralle, *Die Wiederentdeckung des Tacitus* (Fulda, 1952), a book whose extremely tendentious theses have somewhat obscured the interest of the documents reproduced in it. The monk's name was Heinrich von Grebenstein (ibid., p. 24).

ac libertatis auctorem ac vindicem." Ultimo imperfecto columnello finit: "diu ac more concionantis redditis abstinuit cibo." Videtur in illo opere Suetonius innuere omnes fere rhetores et Grammatice professores desperatis fortunis finivisse vitam.[13]

The description matches Niccoli's,[14] but where Niccoli had ascribed eighteen pages to the *Dialogus*, Decembrio mentions fourteen, then six folia missing, then two and a half folia at the end. The difference may be ascribed simply to the carelessness of the monk who was Niccoli's ultimate source;[15] or, more elegantly, we may suppose that the six missing folia were represented in the manuscript itself by six blank columns—that is, one and a half folia—to bring the total to eighteen.[16] No one, at any rate, will suppose (at least, no one has supposed) that Decembrio saw some other codex, identical with the Hersfeldensis in all but the number of blank pages in the *Dialogus*.

I am sure that at this point the reader will grant me that the existence and content of this manuscript have now been established beyond a doubt: it contained the *Germania*, the *Agricola*, the *Dialogus*, and Suetonius, in that order. The number of folia, for all but the third item, is also established, nor is there any reason to doubt Decembrio's comment that all the works were written in columns. One of our descriptions, that of Niccoli, derived from an eyewitness account, while Decembrio was himself an eyewitness. The accounts of Niccoli and Panormita, while independent of each other, presumably have a common source in the monk who provided the information; Decembrio's is independent even of the monk.

If I seem to be belaboring the obvious, it is because the subsequent history and contents of this manuscript are by no means so clear. In a manuscript containing the *Germania*, the *De grammaticis*, and the *Dialogus* (in that order, which is not the order attested for the Hersfeldensis), we find a note saying, "Hos libellos Iovianus Pontanus excripsit nuper adinventos et in lucem relatos ab Enoc Asculano quamquam satis mendosos. MCCCCLX Martio mense."[17] Enoch of Ascoli, who is here credited with the discovery of these works, had been commissioned in 1451 by Pope Nicholas V to search for manuscripts in northern Europe; he had traveled as far as Denmark, and perhaps farther, returned through Germany, and arrived in Rome in the spring of 1455 with a number of codices.[18] Whether the Hersfeldensis was among them is a question which has generated no

13. Sabbadini, *Storia e critica*, pp. 279–80, reproduced with insignificant variations in Robinson, "*Germania*," pp. 8–9.

14. Except for a number of variants of transcription, for which see Robinson, "*Germania*," pp. 9–13.

15. Sabbadini, *Storia e critica*, p. 282.

16. Robinson, "*Germania*," pp. 12–13, modifying K. Barwick, "Umfang der Lücke in Tacitus *Dialogus de oratoribus*," *RhM* 68 (1913): 279–85 (cf. ibid., pp. 638–39), who thought Decembrio had simply been mistaken (cf. Robinson, "*Germania*," p. 14, n. 5). For another suggestion, see Koestermann's edition, p. viii, n. 2.

17. Leidensis XVIII Perizonianus Q. 2, f. 1, reproduced photographically in Wissowa's edition of the *Dialogus* and (Pontano's notes only) in B. L. Ullman, "Pontano's Handwriting and the Leiden Manuscript of Tacitus and Suetonius," *IMU* 2 (1959): 309–335.

18. Sabbadini, *Storia e critica*, pp. 276–78.

small debate among scholars;[19] it need not concern us here. What is worth noting is that the manuscript took more than four years to reach Pontano, who was no backwoods scribe but an important humanist; and that, when it did, he failed to copy—or to mention the existence of—the *Agricola*.

More striking, however, is a letter of Poggio's son Jacopo, not published until 1958.[20] The letter is a description of manuscripts already found and manuscripts still to be sought, and most of it is a recapitulation, practically verbatim, of Niccoli's commentary.[21] The section dealing with the Hersfeldensis reads:

> Cornelii taciti de origine: et situ germanorum: item in eodem codice
> Cornelii taciti de Vita Iulii agricole. Incipit sic. "Clarorum virorum facta moresque posteris tradere antiquitus usitatum: ne nostris quidem temporibus: quanquam Universa suorum aetas omisit." Continet xiiij. folia. Item in eodem codice Suetonii tranquilli de grammaticis: et rhetoribus: verum nostris temporibus Pii Pontificis opera in Italiam venit. Suetonius hic: et Cornelius de situ et origine germanorum: et de oratoribus. Sed corruptus: et laceratus.[22]

In the first section of this note (up to the words *et rhetoribus*), Jacopo gives us the information from Niccoli's list, omitting three items: he does not mention the *Dialogus de oratoribus*, nor does he give the *incipit* or the number of folia for any work except the *Agricola*. The first omission is apparently a scribal slip;[23] the reason for the other two omissions (the *incipit*s and the number of folia) is made clear by the words added by Jacopo himself (*verum nostris temporibus*, etc.), listing all the works except the *Agricola* and saying that they have "come to Italy." If we take Jacopo's words at their face value, he seems to have known of a Hersfeld codex (or group of codices, if *corruptus et laceratus* refers to the *De oratoribus* alone)[24] which contained all the material except the *Agricola*. Indeed, from his care in transcribing the entire description of the *Agricola*, one might reasonably suppose that he thought himself to be describing a still unknown work—that he was, in 1475,[25] entirely unaware that the *Agricola* was in Italy. The whole note is very carelessly written and is far from certain evidence,[26] but it does provide further grounds for believing that the manu-

19. Robinson, "*Germania*," pp. 351–56, denied it; and Mendell, "Manuscripts," thought Enoch had brought to Rome a different manuscript of the *Germania*, the Suetonius, and the *Dialogus*—a view which has not found supporters, particularly since it is now clear that the Hersfeld *Agricola* disappeared early. Most scholars accept Pontano's account, though Koestermann, in his edition, pp. vii–viii, hesitates.

20. N. Rubinstein, "An Unknown Letter by Jacopo di Poggio Bracciolini on Discoveries of Classical Texts," *IMU* 1 (1958): 383–400.

21. He seems, however, not to be copying Niccoli's commentary, but Poggio's own notes (or the monk's inventory itself); for he shares many readings with Panormita (ibid., pp. 389–90).

22. Ibid., pp. 398–99.

23. Perhaps not by Jacopo, but by a copier: our text is not Jacopo's original.

24. The *item in eodem codice*, like the present tense of *continentur*, is mere mechanical copying of his source, not independent testimony.

25. Rubinstein, "Letter," p. 386, n. 2. The Toletanus had in fact already been copied by this time (see n. 41).

26. At the end he writes: "Nam post patris mortem omnia hec reperta sunt: Donatus super eneidis Frontinus de aqueductibus: et aliud opus suum. . . . Cornelius tacitus. Suetonius. . . . ," from which we might as easily draw the opposite inference, that both Tacitean works had been

script, once it became available, no longer contained the *Agricola*; it may, in fact, have been dismembered completely.[27] There is no extant manuscript in which the *Agricola* is joined to any of the Hersfeldensis material except for Vat. Lat. 4498; but this is a miscellaneous collection including many different works, among which are these four, in a different order and not consecutive. It is surely not a copy of the entire Hersfeldensis, nor have we any such copy.

Now Decembrio had surely seen the entire manuscript in 1455—but other humanists do not seem to have had access to it immediately. Pontano, in a note to the manuscript mentioned above,[28] says that Bartolomeo Fazio's *mors immatura* prevented him from seeing the Suetonius: Fazio died in November 1457. When Aeneas Sylvius Piccolomini published his own *Germania* in 1458, he seems to have had some idea of the contents of Tacitus' work, but no firsthand knowledge.[29] If it was indeed Aeneas Sylvius (who became Pope Pius II that August) who made the Hersfeld works available,[30] he will hardly have done so until he saw them himself. But for this period, at least, there is nothing to suggest that he, or anyone else, managed to get his hand on the Hersfeld *Agricola*.

When the *editio princeps* of Tacitus appeared in 1472, it did not include the *Agricola*. But a copy did reach Italy; it was copied by 1474 at the latest, and before the end of the century it had been printed. If the preceding discussion were all we knew of *Agricola* manuscripts, we should surely presume that the Hersfeld *Agricola* had turned up at last, to form the basis for the printed text. To indicate why that cannot be so, we must consider another found and lost manuscript, the Aesinas.

The Aesinas is a parchment manuscript of seventy-six folia containing "Dictys' " *Bellum Troianum* (fifty-one folia, of which the first one and a half are blank), the *Agricola* (fourteen folia), and the *Germania* (ten folia). Most of the *Bellum Troianum*, and one gathering (eight folia) of the *Agricola*, are in a Carolingian minuscule of the ninth or tenth century;[31] a few folia at the beginning and end of the first two works are in a fifteenth-century hand, as is all of the *Germania*. Annibaldi attributed this hand to Stefano Guarnieri, the founder of the library which later passed by marriage to the counts Balleani, in whose possession it was when it was discovered. A few leaves which are now blank or written over in Guarnieri's hand had on them Carolingian writing which has been erased: among these, the outer folia of the last quaternion were originally a *unio* constituting the last two

found. Jacopo is at any rate wrong about Frontinus, which had been found by his own father in 1429, not to mention the Hersfeldensis, which Decembrio had seen before Poggio's death.

27. As argued by G. Brugnoli, "La vicenda del codice hersfeldense," *RCCM* 3 (1961): 68–90.

28. Leidensis XVIII Perizonianus Q. 2, f. 47v. Cf. p. 31.

29. See J. Perret, *Recherches sur le texte de la "Germanie"* (Paris, 1950), pp. 146–51.

30. See R. Wuensch, "Zur Textgeschichte der Germania," *Hermes* 32 (1897): 56; Ullman, "Pontano's Handwriting," p. 323; Brugnoli, "Vicenda," p. 87. As the *CP* referee points out, Jacopo's words ("Pii Pontificis opera in Italiam venit. Suetonius hic . . .") may as easily mean that Aeneas Sylvius had a hand in arranging Enoch's trip.

31. This was Annibaldi's judgment. Wissowa in his edition considered it to be "certainly" tenth-century; while Lehmann, "Beurteilung," p. 12, says that this date "für den Kenner kann . . . gar nicht zur Debatte gestellt werden, sondern nur die Zeit von etwa 830–850."

folia of the *Agricola*. One of these two folia—the last, which has not been written over—was read entirely by Annibaldi.

Since the codex as we have it is a mixture of medieval and Renaissance hands, it obviously was not bound in its current binding until Guarnieri's time; presumably he bound it himself, having first recopied missing or illegible parts. Since the repaired parts include the juncture of the *Bellum Troianum* and the *Agricola*, it is not immediately clear whether these two works had been bound together when Guarnieri obtained them. The fact that the *Agricola* ended with a *unio* suggests strongly that it was written to be the last item in the codex; but it surely does not prove that more items had not been added before Guarnieri's time, as he himself added the *Germania*.[32] It cannot, therefore, be used as evidence for the state of the manuscript before Guarnieri bound it.

The *Agricola* quaternion, considered by itself, fits Decembrio's description almost perfectly. It is *in columnellis*; and, if continued in the same format (as it was by Guarnieri), it would make an *opus foliorum decem et quattuor*.[33] This, really, is all the information Decembrio gives us, except for the *incipit* and *explicit*. The *incipit* of the ninth-century manuscript is lost. As for the *explicit*, it is indeed visible, though erased, on folio 76v of the Aesinas; and though it differs in two words from Decembrio's copy (Decembrio wrote *multos veluti ingloriosos* where the Aesinas reads *multos veterum velud ingloriosos*), these are easy copyists' inaccuracies which hardly indicate that Decembrio had a different manuscript in front of him.[34] Decembrio, not being a modern paleographer, did not leave an account that would tell us in what sort of script his manuscript was written; but the Aesinas, which appears to have been written in the vicinity of Fulda,[35] would be a likely enough candidate for a manuscript found at nearby Hersfeld six hundred years later.

The sum of these facts, as Annibaldi recognized but his successors did not, is no more than a presumptive indication that the Aesinas is Decembrio's manuscript. The number of pages in so short a treatise would probably be nearly the same in any manuscript of roughly the same style; and the disposition into columns, while never the rule, was common throughout the Middle Ages. The approximate agreement of the *explicit*s, in the absence of any other known manuscript tradition, proves nothing positive; that the

32. On the question of whether Guarnieri had before him a medieval *Germania*, see Koestermann's edition, pp. xxi–xxii, and more recently M. Winterbottom, "The Manuscript Tradition of Tacitus' *Germania*," *CP* 70 (1975): 4.

33. Robinson, "*Germania*," p. 17, also observed that the Hersfeldensis, if it began on page 1 and was bound in quaternions, will have begun a new gathering, as the Aesinas does, on the fifth folium of the *Agricola*.

34. Mendell, "Manuscripts," p. 138 and *Tacitus*, p. 285, argued that Decembrio's reading was the better one and therefore, perhaps, independent; but the omission of *veterum* before *veluti*, even if it should be correct, hardly demonstrates an independent source.

35. Robinson, "*Germania*," pp. 26–30, and Lehmann, "Beurteilung," pp. 12–13. It should be noted that both consider the script more French than German, and they choose Fulda chiefly because of the influence of Lupus of Ferrières there, and because of the assumption that the Aesinas is the manuscript that was in Hersfeld in the fifteenth century.

script may come from Fulda[36] is also only suggestive, since we do not know, after all, in what script the Hersfeldensis was written.

Nevertheless, if nothing stood in the way, we should surely accept these correlations as an adequate proof—the more so as we know of no manuscript of the *Agricola* except the Hersfeldensis that survived the Middle Ages. It has become clear in recent decades that the *Agricola* was not, as had been believed, completely unknown from Cassiodorus to Poggio; it was imitated by Adam of Bremen in the eleventh century[37] and by Peter the Deacon at Monte Cassino in the twelfth.[38] But there is nothing to indicate that either of their manuscripts, or any manuscript except the Hersfeldensis, reached the humanists of the fifteenth century.

We should like, then, to identify the Aesinas with the Hersfeldensis, if nothing stood in the way. There is, in fact, only one matter that stands in the way, but it is rather a bulky one: the fifty-one folia of Dictys' *Bellum Troianum* which make up two-thirds of the Aesinas manuscript and which cannot have been in the Hersfeldensis. For, if there is one thing that the numerous testimonia about the latter establish with certainty, it is the contents and disposition of the codex. Had we only one such testimony, we might suggest that the Italians were not interested in the Dictys, which was well known; but the Frontinus had been found by 1431, and Niccoli cited it anyway. The Suetonius, too, had turned up by Decembrio's time, but he did not for that reason neglect to note that it existed in his manuscript. It is in the highest degree unlikely that both the uncultured monk—from whose catalog Panormita, Niccoli, and Jacopo derived their information—and Decembrio, who recorded even the number of blank pages in the *Dialogus*, independently reached the same decision to omit all mention of a work that, if it were there, would comprise fully half the codex. If we can believe anything at all about the codex Hersfeldensis, we must believe that it did not contain Dictys' *Bellum Troianum;* and scholars have, sometimes grudgingly, recognized this.[39]

It follows that the Aesinas *Agricola*, if it is in truth a relic of the Hersfeld *Agricola*, cannot have been bound with the Dictys at the beginning of the fifteenth century. But the contrapositive is: if it was bound with the Dictys at the beginning of the fifteenth century, it was *not* part of the Hersfeld manuscript, whatever its other points of similarity with Decembrio's account.

The matter cannot be judged from the present binding (see p. 34). As for the whereabouts of the Aesinas before the fifteenth century, we have no testimonia—unless, of course, it is the Hersfeldensis. We have no account of

36. "Typisch fuldisch," however, "ist der Aesinas nicht" (Lehmann, "Beurteilung," p. 13).

37. Mendell, *Tacitus*, pp. 284–85. Adam may be imitating Einhard, in which case Einhard knew the *Agricola*.

38. Herbert Bloch, "A Manuscript of Tacitus' *Agricola* in Monte Cassino about A.D. 1135," *CP* 36 (1941): 185–87.

39. Thus Robinson, "*Germania*," p. 20, with some hesitation; Mendell, *Tacitus*, pp. 280–83, with some vehemence.

how the ninth-century manuscript got into Guarnieri's hand,[40] nor of what manuscript he did get. Of our Renaissance manuscripts of the *Agricola*, all, apparently, derive from the Aesinas in either its present state or its pre-Guarnieri form, but none indicates any connection with either the Dictys or the Hersfeldensis.[41]

We must, then, judge the Aesinas entirely by its internal evidence. If this evidence indicates that the Dictys and the *Agricola* were originally two independent manuscripts, we shall surely presume that they remained independent until they reached Guarnieri, who consolidated them; the *Agricola* will have been part of the Hersfeld manuscript, separated (as we saw) before it was published, and eventually rebound into the Aesinas. If, on the other hand, the evidence requires us to believe that they originally formed part of a single codex, we shall have no choice but to conclude that they continued to do so until they reached Guarnieri, and that he merely repaired the codex. It is surely too much to presume that two parts of a single codex, separated before it ever reached Italy and rebound in different bindings, happened independently to fall into the hands of the same provincial humanist six hundred years after they were written, and that he chanced to bind them again into the same book!

Most of the paleographical evidence has already been published,[42] and it suggests strongly that the two parts belonged originally together. The size of the page (220 × 273 mm.), the style of writing, the disposition into columns, the size of the columns (60 × 203 mm.), the number of lines per page, the space between the columns (17 mm.), the method of ruling (hard point, with prickings at the outer margin) are all identical.[43] The two parts were not, apparently, written by the same hand; but, since there are a number of different hands within the Dictys itself,[44] the appearance of yet another hand (perhaps even two additional hands[45]) is not particularly notable. R. P. Robinson, indeed, believed that the marginal notes in the *Agricola* were written by the same scribe who wrote folia 27v, 28, and 29r of the Dictys,[46] though P. Lehmann disagreed;[47] Robinson also "suspected" that the hand that wrote the text of the *Agricola* appears on folium 29v of the Dictys,[48] a matter on which Lehmann did not express an opinion.

On the face of it, the identity between the two parts of the Aesinas is much stronger than the identity between the Aesinas *Agricola* and the Hersfeld *Agricola*. About the latter we can say only three things: that it was divided into columns (the Dictys is as well); that it ran fourteen folia (which

40. We first hear of Guarnieri as being interested in manuscripts in 1462 (Annibaldi, *L' "Agricola,"* p. 10, n. 1) and the repair was probably done sometime between this date and 1474 (1471?), when the Toletanus (see n. 41) was copied from Guarnieri's codex.

41. Vat. Lat. 3429 and 4498, and Cod. Toletanus 49, 2 in the capitular library of Toledo. For a description, see E. de Saint Denis (ed.), *Tacite: "Vie d'Agricola"* (Paris, 1967), pp. xxiii–xxvi. On Vat. Lat. 4498, see p. 33.

42. By Annibaldi, Robinson, and Lehmann, qq. v.

43. Lehmann, "Beurteilung," p. 11, who saw the manuscript, adds that both use the same type of parchment.

44. Robinson, *"Germania,"* pp. 20–22.

45. Ibid., pp. 23–24.

46. Ibid., p. 21.

47. Lehmann, "Beurteilung," p. 11.

48. Robinson, *"Germania,"* pp. 22–24.

is equivalent to saying that the number of words per page is approximately the same in the Hersfeld *Agricola*, the Aesinas *Agricola*—and the Dictys); and that it was, at the beginning of the Renaissance, in the general area of Germany in which the Aesinas seems to have been written. Of the Dictys and the Aesinas *Agricola* we can with certainty say that they were, at the least, produced in the same scriptorium at the same time.[49] Since, as we argued earlier (p. 35), the two possibilities are mutually exclusive—the Aesinas *Agricola* cannot be identical with the Hersfeld *Agricola* and *also* have been originally bound together with the Dictys—the weight of probability would seem to be in favor of the Dictys as an original part of the Aesinas, and therefore against the likelihood that the Aesinas *Agricola* is a remnant of the Hersfeldensis. C. W. Mendell[50] had already come to that conclusion; and B. L. Ullman, though he expressed himself more cautiously, did consider the possibility.[51]

In point of fact, though, the connection between the Aesinas *Agricola* and the Dictys is closer than has been noticed hitherto. The manuscript, as was mentioned, appears to be lost; and a complete facsimile edition (that is, one including the Dictys) has never been published. But a set of photographs was made in Rome in the early years of World War II by the Istituto di Patologia del Libro. At least two complete sets of these copies are still in existence: one was used, and partially published, by Rudolf Till;[52] and later Werner Eisenhut used it in preparing his Teubner edition of Dictys.[53] The other was obtained by Harvard University from the American Embassy in Rome, through the agency of Professor (now emeritus) Mason Hammond, in 1947. I was privileged some years ago to examine the Harvard photographs, and I observed, in addition to the information already published elsewhere and summarized here, a pattern which could hardly be coincidental.

The manuscript, as has been noted, was pricked in the margin at regular intervals and ruled from margin to margin[54] with a hard point—a normal practice designed to keep the lines straight. The prickings are reasonably plain in at least one folium of each quaternion; and, as the reader can see for himself by comparing the figures on pages 38–40,[55] the prickings all

49. On this everyone is agreed: cf. Annibaldi, *L' "Agricola,"* p. 74; Robinson, *"Germania,"* p. 19; and Lehmann, "Beurteilung," p. 11. In fact Lehmann ("auf einem mehr als 35 jährigen paläographischen Studium von vielen Codices der verschiedensten Länder, Stätten und Zeiten in Original und in Reproduktionen fussend," as he boasted) could apparently find no other manuscript so close to the Aesinas *Agricola* as the Aesinas Dictys.

50. Mendell, "Manuscripts," pp. 133–45, and *Tacitus*, pp. 282–85.

51. "Robinson believed that one of the Dictys scribes entered marginal notes in the *Agricola*. Lehmann in denying this made it possible to assume that the Dictys was combined with the *Agricola* after the latter was torn away from its fellows in the Hersfeld book. But if the two were together from the beginning the Iesi manuscript is hardly likely to have been the Hersfeldensis" (Ullman, "Pontano's Handwriting," p. 324).

52. In his 1943 edition (cf. n. 2). A later edition omitted the photographs—and the dedication to Heinrich Himmler.

53. *Dictyis Cretensis "Ephemeridos belli Troiani libri,"* ed. W. Eisenhut (Leipzig, 1958), p. ix.

54. That is, in our case, from outer margin to outer margin of each *bifolium*. On the practice in general, see L. W. Jones, "Pricking Manuscripts," *Speculum* 21 (1946): 389–403.

55. The folia whose margins are shown are 22 and 41 (both from the Dictys), 62 (*Agricola*), 69 (*Agricola* palimpsest), and 76 (*Agricola* erased). The prickings are clearer on some folia than on

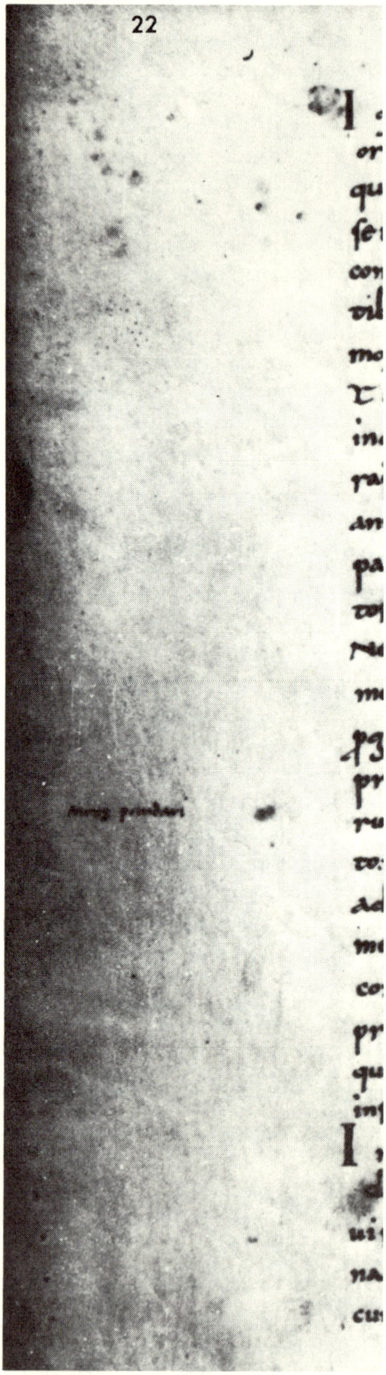

41

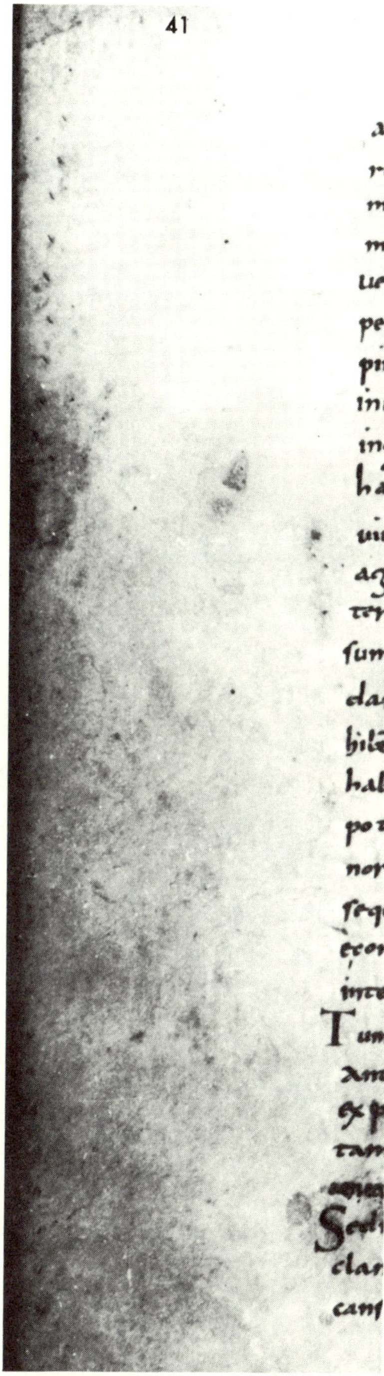

62

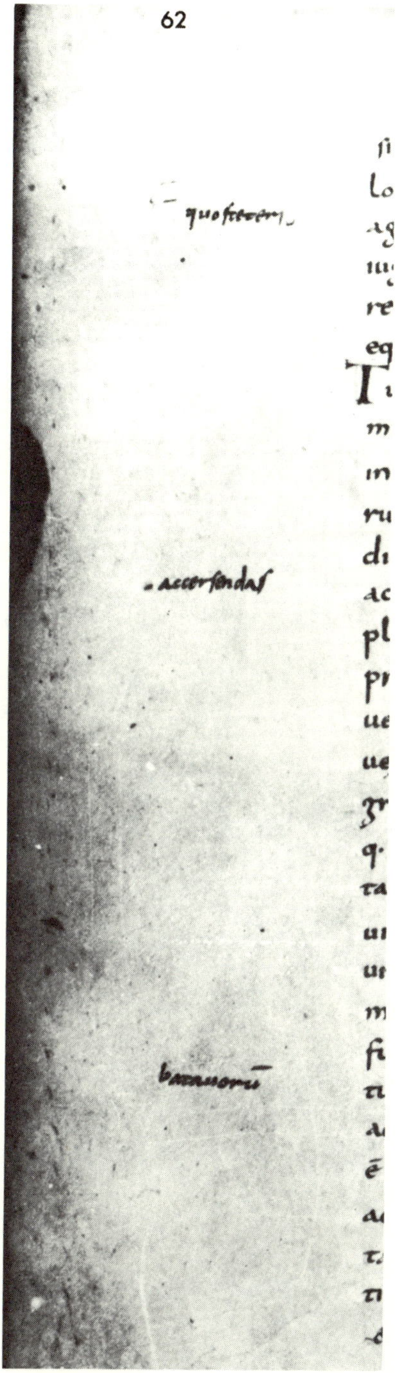

67

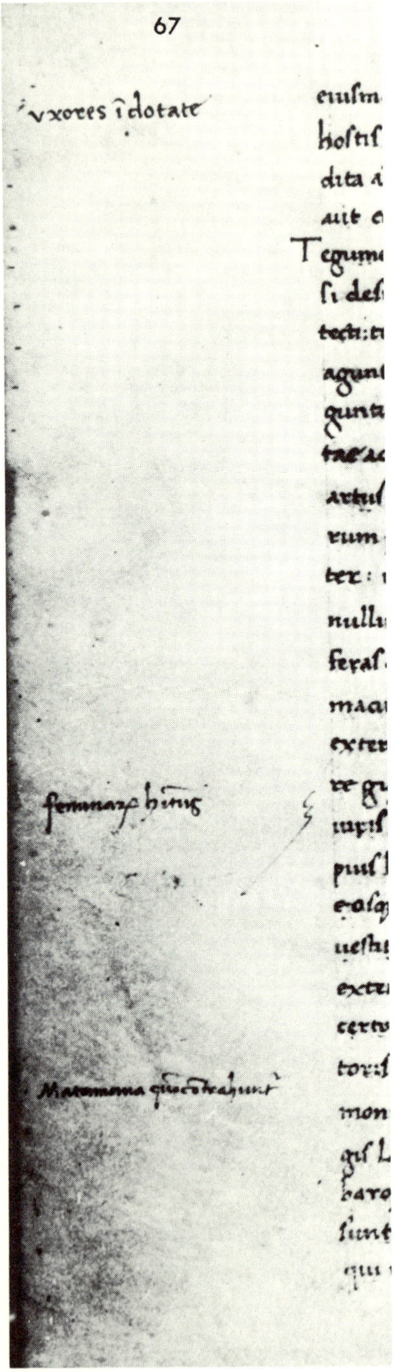
vxores i dotate

eiusm
hostis
dita
ait
Tegume
si des
tecti:
agunt
gunta
tae ac
artus
rum
tex:
nullu
feras
maca
exter
re gr
iupis
pius
eosq
uesti
exter
certo
tor:
mon
gis L
baro
sunt
qui

feminaz hinc

Matrimonia que contrahunt

76

show the same irregular pattern. Starting from the top, they approach the edge of the page, coming closest somewhat more than halfway down; then they turn markedly inward toward the bottom. Details, too, correspond: for example, if we draw a line through the top pricking and the one immediately below it, we will find, continuing our line downward, that it will always fall to the right of the third pricking. Examples can be multiplied according to the reader's ingenuity.

Normally, books were pricked one gathering at a time; a few cases are known of the same pattern being repeated throughout an entire book.[56] No case, as far as I have heard or read, is known of the same pattern being repeated in two different books. In view of the other paleographical evidence, all of which shows the closest connection between the Dictys and the Aesinas *Agricola*, there is surely no temptation to believe that we have before us the first such case. The book, apparently, was pricked and ruled in one sitting: one gathering at a time, to be sure, and with at least two different awls—but with the same jagged measuring rod[57] from start to finish.

It is a coincidence that the Aesinas *Agricola* has fourteen folia and is divided into columns, as was the Hersfeld *Agricola*; and, as Ullman observed, "Scholars do not like to resort to coincidence as an explanation. Usually there is a relationship between coincident facts."[58] But this coincidence is naturalness itself compared to the chance that would be required for a single book, which had been written six hundred years earlier and five hundred miles away, and which had been torn apart and rebound with other material, to arrive in two halves in Italy at the same time, for the two halves to find their way into the hands of the same collector, and for them to be bound together, purely by accident, into the same codex once again. If our numerous testimonies about the contents of the Hersfeldensis mean anything at all, there is no third possibility, and between the two theories there is little room for doubt.

This conclusion means that we are ignorant of three things we thought we knew: the original composition of the Aesinas, its medieval home, and the fate of the Hersfeldensis. For the first, it is worth pointing out that, although we have been forced to the conclusion that the Aesinas Dictys and *Agricola* were originally bound together, it does not necessarily follow that there was nothing else in the book. In fact, the opposite seems nearly certain; for both the Dictys and the *Agricola* were bound (as far as we can tell) in quaternions, but there is not sufficient material between the last

---

others, but for each gathering there is at least one folium that allows us to ascertain the pattern, which is the same wherever the prickings are visible. Space prevents me from offering more examples than the five here given.

My thanks to Ms. Donna Moseman of Widener Library's Photographic Service for her help in obtaining the photographs, and to the Classics Department of Harvard University for permission to publish them.

56. Jones, "Pricking Manuscripts," pp. 395–96. Jones's explanation for the repetition of the irregularity—a spiked double frame—is not the only one that can be given, nor is it possible for the Aesinas, where two different points have been used, one flat (as at 41 and 62) and one round (as at 22); see the figures.

57. Or, perhaps, the jagged edge of an old ruled parchment.

58. Ullman, "Pontano's Handwriting," p. 318.

Carolingian page of the Dictys and the first such page of the *Agricola* to fill a quaternion (Guarnieri's binding has only five folia between these two places). At least one other work probably stood between the Dictys and the *Agricola*; if it was one that interested its readers more than the other two items, it may well have fallen out in part or entirely, leaving the other two works mutilated as Annibaldi found them. This work, if it was there, might conceivably have been the *Germania*, if it was written slightly broader than Guarnieri's; for eleven folia, with the other five, would give us an even two quaternions. But it might just as well have been any other work, and speculation on the matter is probably vain.

Nor is there much basis on which to decide where the Aesinas was until it reached Guarnieri's hands. Perhaps in the place where it had been written, which may have been Fulda; but perhaps not. Mendell thought the Aesinas was the manuscript that Peter the Deacon saw at Monte Cassino; this hypothesis is as possible as anything else, but Mendell's attempt to prove the point was a failure.[59] We should do better, in the current state of our knowledge, to admit that we do not know.

As for the Hersfeld *Agricola*, so long sought after, brought to Italy after three decades only to be removed from the codex and lost—we have no evidence at all that it was ever found. All our manuscripts of the *Agricola* descend from the Aesinas, not the Hersfeldensis; except for the lucky Decembrio, and perhaps Enoch of Ascoli, we know of no Italian who ever saw it. It may have been destroyed in the years that have passed since that time; or it may be sitting unnoticed on the shelf of an Italian library, waiting for its Annibaldi.

Bar-Ilan University

59. He claimed ("Manuscripts," pp. 139–40, and *Tacitus*, pp. 283–85) that the words *Historiam Cornelii cum Omero* in a Cassinese booklist referred to the Aesinas, but (*a*) the order of the items in the entry is the reverse of their order in the Aesinas; (*b*) the *Agricola* is not a *historia*, but a *vita*, and calls itself such; (*c*) this is a list of books copied at Monte Cassino under the abbot Desiderius (1058–67), which the Aesinas certainly was not. E. A. Lowe, "The Unique Manuscript of Tacitus' *Histories*," *Casinensia* (Monte Cassino, 1929), pp. 260–61 = *Palaeographical Papers*, ed. Ludwig Bieler (Oxford, 1972), 1:291–92, was presumably right in understanding that the reference was to Cornelius Nepos' translation of Dares.

NOTES AND DISCUSSIONS

THE DURATION OF A MEETING OF THE ATHENIAN *ECCLESIA*

Modern historians sometimes imply, without further discussion, that a meeting of the Athenian *ecclesia* usually lasted one whole day. What evidence can be produced in support of this assumption? According to one source, the amount of business dealt with by the assembly was so enormous that an applicant to the people sometimes had to wait more than a year before his case came up for decision (ps.-Xen. *Ath. Pol.* 3. 1). In connection with important issues we are informed that many speakers addressed the people during the debate (Thuc. 1. 139. 4, 3. 36. 6, 6. 15. 1; Xen. *Hell.* 1. 7. 12). From other sources we can infer that a politician was allowed to speak twice on the same subject,[1] and we do not know of any restriction on the speaking time. The waterclock seems to be a device designed for use in the courts in the Agora, not for assembly meetings on the Pnyx. Since Athenian loquacity is a commonplace (e.g., Thuc. 3. 38. 2–7, 3. 40. 2–3; Dem. 3. 14–15, etc.), it is tempting to think that a meeting which started early in the morning must usually have lasted all day and not have been closed until evening.

But do we possess any direct evidence that bears on the duration of a meeting of the Athenian assembly? Numerous passages in Aristophanes, most of them from the *Ecclesiazusae*, constitute sufficient proof that a meeting was opened early in the morning. At *Ecclesiazusae* 740–41 early meetings are described as a statutory requirement, and it is often mentioned that citizens have to set out before dawn to arrive in due time (*Eccl.* 283–84, 291, 390–91; cf. 20–21, 84–85). Other sources can also be cited (Ar. *Thesm.* 376; Plut. *Phocion* 15). The only evidence to the contrary is the introductory scene of the *Acharnians*, where Dicaeopolis sits in splendid isolation on the Pnyx, waiting for the opening of the session and looking down over the Agora, which is already packed with people (*Ach.* 19–22). But in this passage Aristophanes is making much of the Athenian citizens' apathy toward their political institutions: the comic effect is achieved by putting Dicaeopolis alone on the Pnyx although a κυρία ἐκκλησία ἑωθινή has been summoned.

It is much more difficult to find evidence for the assumption that a meeting was not closed until the day was over. To the best of my knowledge, only two sources can be cited.

(1) Xenophon *Hellenica* 1. 7. 7: ἔδοξε δὲ ἀναβαλέσθαι εἰς ἑτέραν ἐκκλησίαν· τότε γὰρ ὀψὲ ἦν καὶ τὰς χεῖρας οὐκ ἂν καθεώρων . . . This meeting took place shortly before the *Apaturia* (*Hell.* 1. 7. 8), which were celebrated some time in the second half of Pyanopsion (J. D. Mikalson, *The Sacred and Civil Calendar of the Athenian Year* [Princeton,

1. Euryptolemus addressed the people twice during the second *ecclesia* held after the battle at Arginusae (Xen. *Hell.* 1. 7. 12 and 16 ff.). Euktemon spoke twice during the *ecclesia* held in Skirophorion 354/353 (Dem. 24. 12 and 13).

A law quoted by Aeschines (1. 35) contains the provision that a *rhetor* is liable to a maximum fine of fifty drachmas ἐάν τις λέγῃ . . . δὶς περὶ τοῦ αὐτοῦ ὁ αὐτὸς τῆς αὐτῆς . . . But the document inserted in Aeschines' speech is probably spurious (cf. E. Drerup, "Über die bei den attischen Rednern eingelegten Urkunden," *Jahrb f. class. Phil.*, suppl. 24 [1898]: 307–8).

1975], p. 79), i.e., in the beginning of November. A continuous meeting from dawn to dusk at this time of the year must have lasted about eleven hours (W. Kubitschek, *Grundriss der antiken Zeitrechnung* [Munich, 1928], p. 182). It would, however, be rash to base a generalization on this piece of evidence, since it concerns a very special meeting of the assembly: the first hearing of the six generals put on trial after their victory at Arginusae.

(2) Demosthenes 24. 9–15, on a meeting of the assembly held in Skirophorion 354/353 (Dem. 24. 15) or shortly before. Euktemon had moved a proposal concerning the collection of a debt to the state; a *graphe paranomon* was brought against the proposal, but it was upheld by the court (Dem. 24. 14). Euktemon describes the successive stages through which the proposal passed in the following words: ἀλλὰ πρῶτον μὲν τῆς βουλῆς κατεγνωκυίας, εἶτα τοῦ δήμου μίαν ἡμέραν ὅλην ἐπὶ τούτοις αὐτοῖς ἀναλώσαντος, πρὸς δὲ τούτοις δικαστηρίοιν δυοῖν εἰς ἕνα καὶ χιλίους ἐψηφισμένων . . . (Dem. 24. 9). This passage is difficult to interpret. First, μίαν ἡμέραν ὅλην need not mean more than that the *ecclesia* spent one whole meeting on this item on the agenda. Second, Euktemon is undoubtedly exaggerating, for he is eager to convey the impression that everybody approved of his proposal. We know from Aristotle (*Ath. Pol.* 43. 6) that the people usually had to deal with a minimum of nine items; it looks suspicious that in this case they discussed one single item for more than twelve hours. Moreover, Euktemon does not explicitly state that the assembly passed his proposal, probably because it was indicted as unconstitutional before it was put to the vote. So he emphasizes instead how thoroughly the matter was discussed. I admit, however, that the passage is open to a literal interpretation, and that, so interpreted, it gives us a second example of a special meeting of the assembly where one item was discussed from dawn to dusk.

On the other hand, numerous sources indicate that the meetings of the assembly were often considerably shorter.

(3) When the first Athenian embassy to Philip, sent in the spring of 346, returned to Athens, Demosthenes proposed and carried a decree prescribing a meeting of the assembly on Elaphebolion 8. Aeschines criticizes Demosthenes' proposal: Δημοσθένης . . . γράφει ψήφισμα . . . ἐκκλησίαν ποιεῖν τοὺς πρυτάνεις τῇ ὀγδόῃ ἱσταμένου τοῦ Ἐλαφηβολιῶνος μηνός, ὅτ' ἦν τῷ Ἀσκληπιῷ ἡ θυσία καὶ ὁ προαγών, ἐν τῇ ἱερᾷ ἡμέρᾳ . . . (Aeschin. 3. 67). Nothing in Aeschines' text indicates that the *proagon* and the sacrifice to Asclepius were postponed because of the *ecclesia*. Indeed, since the *ecclesia* held on Elaphebolion 18 was the second meeting of the assembly after the Dionysia and the Pandia, it is most unlikely that the festival had been adjourned and held one day later than usual (cf. M. H. Hansen, "How Often Did the *Ecclesia* Meet?" *GRBS* 18 [1977]: 57–58). We must accordingly assume that one day was sufficient time for a meeting of the assembly, the sacrifice to Asclepius, and the *proagon* of the Greater Dionysia. The *ecclesia* cannot have filled more than a part of the day.

(4) After the conclusion of the peace with Philip on Elaphebolion 19, a meeting of the assembly was held on Elaphebolion 25 to discuss the oaths on the peace. Demosthenes was one of the *proedroi*, and Aeschines relates that Demosthenes put to the vote a proposal made by Philocrates that the oath on the peace be taken on the same day by the allies' representatives in Athens, the *synedroi:* ἀποδοῦναι δὲ τοὺς ὅρκους τοῖς πρέσβεσι τοῖς παρὰ Φιλίππου ἐν τῇδε τῇ ἡμέρᾳ τοὺς συνέδρους τῶν συμμάχων (Aeschin. 3. 74). We know from Aeschines' speech *On the Embassy* that the proposal was passed and put into effect: ὡς δ' ἡ παροῦσα ἐκκλησία διελύθη, ἐξώρκιζον τοὺς συμμάχους οἱ τοῦ Φιλίππου πρέσβεις ἐν τῷ στρατηγίῳ τῷ ὑμετέρῳ (Aeschin. 2. 85). Once more, the conclusion is that the meeting of the assembly was over before the end of the day.

(5) In 343 the Megarians applied secretly to Athens for military assistance. As a *strategos*,

Phocion arranged a meeting of the assembly and persuaded the Athenians to vote for his proposal to relieve the Megarians. Immediately after the *ecclesia*, the signal was given for calling up the army, and the Athenian forces set out the same day: τῶν δὲ Μεγαρέων ἐπικαλουμένων κρύφα, φοβούμενος ὁ Φωκίων τοὺς Βοιωτοὺς μὴ προαισθόμενοι φθάσωσι τὴν βοήθειαν, ἐκκλησίαν συνήγαγεν ἕωθεν, καὶ προσαγγείλας τὰ παρὰ τῶν Μεγαρέων τοῖς Ἀθηναίοις, ὡς ἐψηφίσαντο, τῇ σάλπιγγι σημήνας εὐθὺς ἀπὸ τῆς ἐκκλησίας ἦγεν αὐτοὺς τὰ ὅπλα λαβόντας (Plut. *Phocion* 15. 1). This piece of evidence points to one more occasion when the *ecclesia* must have concluded its business within a few hours.

(6) In 339 Philip's capture of Elatea took the Athenians by surprise. The event was reported to Athens in the evening; the next day the citizens assembled on the Pnyx, without any summons, while the council in the *bouleuterion* discussed the situation and prepared the agenda. The meeting of the assembly was not opened until the council had finished its session in the *bouleuterion:* τῇ δ' ὑστεραίᾳ ἅμα τῇ ἡμέρᾳ οἱ μὲν πρυτάνεις τὴν βουλὴν ἐκάλουν εἰς τὸ βουλευτήριον, ὑμεῖς δ' εἰς τὴν ἐκκλησίαν ἐπορεύεσθε, καὶ πρὶν ἐκείνην χρηματίσαι καὶ προβουλεῦσαι πᾶς ὁ δῆμος ἄνω καθῆτο (Dem. 18. 169).

(7) In addition to these four examples ([3]–[6]) of *ecclesiai* held in the period 346–339, we have two descriptions in Aristophanes' comedies of meetings of the assembly. The *Acharnians* opens with an ἐκκλησία κυρία held on the Pnyx. Dicaeopolis hopes for a discussion of peace, but the debate instead is on the continuation of the war. In despair and disgust, Dicaeopolis avails himself of a simple device to stop the meeting: he interrupts, saying that he has felt a drop of rain. This is a sign from heaven that the *ecclesia* is inauspicious, and the *prytaneis* are bound to adjourn the meeting (*Ach.* 167–73). In the *Ecclesiazusae*, the decision to hand over the city to the women is made in an *ecclesia* packed with women who have stolen their husbands' clothes and disguised themselves as men. After the vote whereby the political power is transferred to the females, the assembly is closed. On his way home Chremes, one of the few male participants, meets Blepyrus, who is necessarily dressed in his wife's robe. Chremes describes how the meeting went, and Blepyrus is surprised to hear that the *ecclesia* is already over; but the dialogue between the two men does not convey the impression that the meeting normally would have lasted all day:

> Βλ. ἀτὰρ πόθεν ἥκεις ἐτεόν; Χρ. ἐξ ἐκκλησίας.
> Βλ. ἤδη λέλυται γάρ; Χρ. νὴ Δί' ὄρθριον μὲν οὖν.
>
> [*Eccl.* 376–77]

To summarize, we have four examples and two descriptions in comedy of *ecclesiai* that fill only a fraction of a day. Against the evidence presented, it may be objected that at least two of the examples, (5) and (6), and perhaps (3) and (4) as well, describe emergency meetings, where the session was curtailed because a prompt decision was required. Similarly, the *ecclesia* in the *Acharnians* is closed prematurely. And the assembly described in the *Ecclesiazusae* is unique. No generalizations can be based on emergency meetings and comic scenes.

However, it is possible to adduce other sources to show that even regular meetings must have been shorter than a whole day. We know from the *Constitution of Athens* that the *prytaneis* summoned the council each and every day, with the exception of ἡμέραι ἀφέσιμοι: οἱ . . . πρυτανεύοντες . . . συνάγουσιν καὶ τὴν βουλὴν καὶ τὸν δῆμον, τὴν μὲν οὖν βουλὴν ὅσαι ἡμέραι, πλὴν ἐάν τις ἀφέσιμος ᾖ, τὸν δὲ δῆμον τετράκις τῆς πρυτανείας ἑκάστης (*Ath. Pol.* 43. 3). The word ἀφέσιμος is almost a *hapax* in Greek literature. It does not occur again until Aelius Aristides (*Orat.* 50[26]. 98), in a passage which does not provide any clue to the exact meaning of the word. Nor is it explained by any of the lexicographers. Since it is derived from ἀφιέναι, it certainly denotes a day on which the council was not summoned, but which days were ἀφέσιμοι? The translation offered by LSJ is "holiday," which may be on the right lines but is no more than a guess. Neither the assembly (Aeschin. 3. 67) nor the court (schol. Ar. *Vesp.* 663) was summoned on festival days, and we may assume that the council's ἡμέραι ἀφέσιμοι included festival days. Mikalson's careful investigation of attested meeting days of the council (*Athenian Year*, pp. 193–97) points to the conclusion that the *boule* (like the *ecclesia*) did not meet on annual festival days but (unlike the *ecclesia*) was regularly summoned on monthly festival days. In one respect, then, the interpretation "festival days" is too comprehensive; in another, it is too narrow, since not only (annual) festival days, but also ἡμέραι ἀποφράδες were presumably ἀφέσιμοι.[2] On the other hand, there is nothing in Aristotle's text to indicate that the ἡμέραι ἀφέσιμοι included the assembly's meeting days—quite the contrary. Two passages in the orators do in fact substantiate the assumption that the forty days reserved for meetings of the assembly were meeting days of the council as well.

(8) In the speech *Against Timarchus* Aeschines relates an event which took place in the archonship of Nicophemus (361/360). Timarchus was a member of the council that year; and, during a meeting of the assembly, he was charged with embezzlement and prostitution by Pamphilus of Acherdus, who proposed and carried a decree that the people at the end of the year bestow the usual honors on the council only if the councillors forthwith excluded and punished Timarchus. After the *ecclesia*, when the councillors returned to the *bouleuterion*, Timarchus was first excluded by the ἐκφυλλοφορία, but this preliminary condemnation was reversed in the subsequent vote taken by ballot. The change of scene from the *ecclesia* to the *bouleuterion* is described by Aeschines as follows: μετὰ ταῦτα, ὡς ἐπανῆλθεν ἡ βουλὴ εἰς τὸ βουλευτήριον . . . (Aeschin. 1. 112). The phrase implies that the councillors went from the Pnyx to the *bouleuterion*, and that the meeting of the council was held on the same day as the *ecclesia*.

(9) In 19. 70 Demosthenes refers to the curse proclaimed in the assembly against corrupt and treacherous politicians. He has the text read out to the jurors, whereupon he makes the following comment: ταῦθ' ὑπὲρ ὑμῶν, ὦ ἄνδρες Ἀθηναῖοι, καθ' ἑκάστην τὴν ἐκκλησίαν ὁ κῆρυξ εὔχεται νόμῳ προστεταγμένα, καὶ ὅταν ἡ βουλὴ καθῆται, παρ' ἐκείνῃ πάλιν. The crucial word is πάλιν, by which Demosthenes stresses that the curse was, in some way or another, proclaimed twice. We miss the point if we take the passage to mean no more than that the curse was read out both to the people and to the councillors. What Demosthenes says rather is that, on a meeting day of the *ecclesia*, the curse was proclaimed first in the assembly and then, again, in the council.

Comparing passages (8) and (9) with Aristotle's statement (*Ath. Pol.* 43. 3), I conclude that the councillors were regularly summoned on the meeting days of the *ecclesia* and that the hours left after the *ecclesia* was concluded were sufficient for a session of the council.

The council probably met not only after, but also before, a meeting of the assembly. It is a well-known fact that the nine *proedroi* were picked by lot from among the 450 *bouleutai* who did not serve as *prytaneis*, one from each of the remaining *phylai*. The *proedroi* must have been chosen before the opening of the *ecclesia*, and the sortition must have been conducted in the presence of the councillors. So the *proedroi* were appointed during a meeting of the council held either

2. Cf. J. D. Mikalson, " Ἡμέρα ἀποφράς," *AJP* 96 (1975): 26–27.

early in the morning immediately before the *ecclesia* or late in the afternoon of the preceding day. No direct information allows us to make a choice between these two possibilities, but some circumstantial evidence can be produced. A study of the Athenian calendar seems to lend support to the view that the *proedroi* were appointed late in the afternoon of the preceding day. The Athenians reckoned the ἡμέρα (in the sense of a twenty-four-hour period) from sunset to sunset—not from sunrise to sunrise, as the Egyptians did, or from midnight to midnight, as we do (E. Bickerman, *Chronology of the Ancient World* [London, 1968], pp. 13–14; O. Neugebauer, *A History of Ancient Mathematical Astronomy* [Berlin, 1975], 3:1067 ff.). So the ἐπιστάτης τῶν πρυτάνεων, who was in office for a twenty-four-hour period, was probably appointed at the beginning of the day, i.e., at sunset (G. Busolt and H. Swoboda, *Griechische Staatskunde* [Munich, 1920–26], p. 1029). Analogy would suggest that the *proedroi* were appointed during the meeting of the council held in the afternoon. The *proedroi*, however, did not serve continuously for twenty-four hours like the ἐπιστάτης τῶν πρυτάνεων. Their only task was to preside over the meetings of the council and of the assembly held within the period. Moreover, several sources show that the Athenians reckoned the day from sunset to sunset only for calendar purposes. For all other purposes, their day began at sunrise (G. Bilfinger, *Der bürgerliche Tag* [Stuttgart, 1888], pp. 102–154). Meetings prolonged through the evening and the night were not rated as meetings over two days, and in such cases the word ὑστεραία is unambiguously applied to the period starting the next morning (e.g., Dem. 57. 9–15). Similarly, the elaborate sortition of the jurors took place in the morning immediately before the hearing of the cases (Arist. *Ath. Pol.* 63–65). The analogy of the *proedroi* to the jurors is stronger than the analogy of the *proedroi* to the ἐπιστάτης τῶν πρυτάνεων. The principal reason for using the lot was to prevent corruption (cf. Aeschin. 3. 3). Sortition would not have produced the desired effect if the *proedroi* had been appointed twelve to sixteen hours before the opening of the meeting over which they were to preside. I therefore prefer the view that the *proedroi* were appointed during a short session of the council held at sunrise, immediately before the meeting of the assembly.

It may be useful to give a summary account of one of the forty meeting days of the assembly. At sunrise the *prytaneis* summoned the councillors to a short meeting, for the sole purpose of appointing the nine *proedroi* of the day and, among them, the ἐπιστάτης τῶν προέδρων. While this session was being held, the citizens ascended the Pnyx and entered the auditorium controlled by the six ληξίαρχοι (Poll. 8. 104) and the thirty συλλογεῖς τοῦ δήμου (ibid.; *IG*, 2–3². 1749B). Not long after sunrise the councillors went from the *bouleuterion* to the Pnyx for the opening of the *ecclesia*. We do not know how long a meeting lasted. It is apparent from Aristophanes that the citizens carried food and wine with them to the Pnyx (*Eccl.* 306–8), but even a meeting of five or six hours would have been long enough for a snack to be welcome. Admittedly, a public action heard by the jurors filled a whole day (Xen. *Hell.* 1. 7. 28; Arist. *Ath. Pol.* 67; Aeschin. 3. 197; cf. Busolt–Swoboda, *Staatskunde*, p. 1161), but it is significant that the courtrooms in the Agora were roofed (Antiphon 5. 11). The *ecclesiai* were open-air meetings where the citizens were exposed to the rain and the sun. We know from Aristophanes that a session was adjourned if it began to rain (*Ach.* 171), and I doubt that the Athenians, during the summer, extended their meetings over the afternoon. Only on special occasions, during a political crisis, did a meeting continue until it was too dark to survey the hands raised when the vote was taken (Xen. *Hell.* 1. 7. 7 and [perhaps] Dem. 24. 9).[3] In the winter, when days were shorter, the meetings obviously began later, and a session of the same duration would have filled a greater part of the day. The principal business of the *ecclesia*, however, was foreign policy, as is evident from a survey of all decrees preserved on stone or referred to in the literary sources. It is a well-known fact that interstate relations were cut down to a minimum during the period from October to March. So the meetings of the assembly were probably considerably shorter between Boedromion and Anthesterion and may have been closed at noon or shortly afterward—just as, for other reasons, the summer meetings probably were.[4] After the *ecclesia*, the councillors were summoned to their daily meeting in the *bouleuterion*. The other citizens who had attended the *ecclesia* in the morning had time left for half a day's work, at least, if they resided near the Pnyx, either in Athens or in the Piraeus.

This description of a typical meeting day must lead to a modification of two important statements usually made about Athenian democracy. If an *ecclesia* normally filled no more than part of the day, the number of man-days lost because of the democratic institutions was considerably smaller than is often assumed, and the subvention paid out for attendance was a full compensation for the lost working hours. A working day in Athens probably extended from sunrise to sunset.[5] So it must have varied according to the season, from about nine hours in the winter to about fourteen hours in the summer (cf. Kubitschek, *Grundriss*, p. 182). But the duration of an *ecclesia* probably varied, too, in accordance with the business at hand, which was no doubt greatly reduced from late autumn to early spring. An *ecclesia* lasting, e.g., six to seven hours in the summer and four to five hours in the winter filled the same fraction of a working day, and most of the participants, who must have been town dwellers, would have had sufficient time left to supplement the dole paid out for attendance with half a day's wages. On

3. Νύξ ἐν μέσῳ at Aeschin. 3. 71 does not imply (*pace* R. A. De Laix, *Probouleusis at Athens* [Berkeley, 1973], p. 185, n. 68) that the meeting held on Elaphebolion 18 filled the whole day until sunset.

4. This assumption is supported by the epigraphical evidence. Mikalson (*Athenian Year*, p. 182) has counted all the exactly dated decrees. Dividing the year into two halves (Boedromion–Anthesterion and Elaphebolion–Metageitnion), we obtain the following figures: Boedromion–Anthesterion 52 decrees, Elaphebolion–Metageitnion 93 decrees. Mikalson, however, deals exclusively with the civil calendar, and accordingly he has no reference to decrees which record the number of the prytany but give no information about the day of the month. I have counted 79 fourth-century decrees (403–322) preserved on stone which record the number of the prytany. Following Mikalson, I have excluded all examples based on debatable restorations. Of these 79 decrees, 29 are passed within the period Pryt. 3–7, whereas no fewer than 50 can be assigned to the period Pryt. 8–2. Both these investigations indicate that the *ecclesia* passed many more decrees during the summer than during the winter. I admit, however, that the distribution within the two periods is remarkably uneven. Pryt. 8 (roughly equal to Elaphebolion) and Pryt. 10 (roughly equal to Skirophorion) are the two busiest periods; I have found very few examples from Pryt. 1 (roughly equal to Hekatombaion).

5. Bickerman, *Chronology*, p. 13, without reference to any source. I am not able to produce evidence concerning the classical period, but I do not doubt that some important sources for Italy, Palestine, and Egypt in the Roman period can be applied to fourth-century Athens. (*a*) In Egyptian apprenticeship contracts, it is regularly stated that the working day extends from sunrise to sunset: ἀπὸ ἀνατολῆς ἡλίου μέχρι δύσεως *BGU*, 4. 1021. 13; *POxy*. 725. 12, 1647. 20. (*b*) In the parable of the laborers in the vineyard (Matt. 20), the last group is hired during the eleventh hour and works for one hour only. The hour of the ancients was one-twelfth of the day from sunrise to sunset (Kubitschek, *Grundriss*, p. 182), and so the working day must have been coextensive with the daylight hours. (*c*) Columella *Rust*. 11. 1. 17–18.

this theory there is no longer any foundation for the assumption made by several historians that the μισθὸς ἐκκλησιαστικός only compensated the Athenian citizens in some measure for loss of working time,[6] and we can reject the view that the poorer citizens even in the fourth century may have been debarred from attending the *ecclesia*. On the other hand, assuming that an *ecclesia* usually did not fill more than part of the day enables us to give a simple explanation of the higher rate for an ἐκκλησία κυρία. It is apparent from the *Constitution of Athens* (43. 3–6) that there were more items on the agenda for an ἐκκλησία κυρία than for other meetings of the assembly. Such a meeting was probably more time-consuming, and consequently the subvention paid for attendance had to be raised in order to provide full compensation for the working hours lost.

The thesis suggested in this article is based on a study of the scanty sources. I conclude my argument by anticipating an a priori objection which will doubtless be raised against my reconstruction: that it is impossible for six thousand participants, all of whom have the right to speak, to discuss and vote on a dozen decrees within a few hours. My answer is that it *is* possible: it happens in Switzerland today. In a few of the smaller cantons, magistrates are still elected and laws are still passed by the *Landsgemeinde*, which in Glarus, for example, is attended by about five thousand citizens who vote on all proposals by a show of hands. Every citizen is entitled to address the assembly, and the number of items on the agenda is comparable to the description found in the *Constitution of Athens* (43. 3–6). Nevertheless, such meetings last for no more than two to four hours.[7]

MOGENS HERMAN HANSEN
University of Copenhagen

6. G. Glotz and R. Cohen, *Histoire grecque*, vol. 3 (Paris, 1936), p. 16; P. Cloché, *La démocratie athénienne* (Paris, 1951), p. 210; V. Ehrenberg, *The Greek State* (Oxford, 1960), p. 55; C. Mossé, *Les institutions politiques grecques* (Paris, 1967), p. 46; De Laix, *Probouleusis*, p. 176. Cautiously stated by A. H. M. Jones, *Athenian Democracy* (Oxford, 1957), p. 18.

7. W. Stauffacher, *Die Versammlungsdemokratie in Kanton Glarus* (Zurich, 1962), pp. 284–85; H. Ryffel, *Die Schweizerischen Landsgemeinden* (Zurich, 1903), pp. 80–109, 270–324.

For valuable discussions of various problems I should like to thank Dr. A. Bülow-Jacobsen, Prof. J. Christensen, Mr. J. A. Crook, Mr. G. T. Griffith, Dr. C. M. Taisbak, and the anonymous referees of *Classical Philology*.

A STRUCTURAL AMBIGUITY IN LATIN

In a revealing passage of the *Institutiones grammaticae* (ed. H. Keil, *Grammatici Latini*, vol. 3, pp. 177–78, §§139–41), Priscian offers observations on the nature of reciprocal conjunction which point up some interesting usages in Latin syntax. He remarks that there are several means of expressing the reciprocal notion ("each other, one another"), giving the following examples:

(1) Terence *Adelphoe* 827–28: "video amare inter se."
"I see them loving each other."

(2) Terence *Adelphoe* 271: "age, inepte, quasi nunc non norimus nos inter nos, Ctesipho."
"Carry on foolishly, Ctesiphon, as if we don't now know each other."

(3) Vergil *Aeneid* 11. 121: "conversique oculos inter se atque ora tenebant."
"They hold their eyes and faces turned on each other."

In each of these examples, the reciprocal notion is conveyed by the preposition *inter* plus the reflexive pronoun (*se*, etc.).

According to Priscian, another technique of expressing reciprocity is the use of *inter se* together with the adverb *invicem:*

(4) ego et tu nosmet ipsos invicem amamus inter nos.
"You and I, we love each other indeed, each the other between ourselves."

(5) tu et ille invicem amatis inter vos.
"You and he love each the other between you."

Compare also:

(6) Livy 33. 6. 12: "cum inter se innexi rami vinculum invicem praebeant"
"Since the interwoven branches bind each other together"

(7) Livy 9. 43. 17: "invicem inter se gratantes"
"Congratulating each other"

Finally, Priscian gives examples of the following type, in which *invicem* plus the reflexive pronoun is used alone, without *inter:*

(8) ego et tu nostri invicem miseremur.
"You and I, we have compassion for each other."

(9) tu et ille invicem vobis indulgetis.
"You and he, you gratify each other."

(10) iste et ille invicem se potiuntur.
"This one and that one, they are masters of each other."

Compare also:

(11) Manilius 2. 275: "linea . . . inque vicem extremis iungit se finibus ipsa."
"Indeed the line joins up with itself at the very ends."

(12) Tac. *Agr.* 6 *init.*: "vixerunt mira concordia, per mutuam caritatem et invicem se anteponendo."
"They lived in extraordinary harmony, through mutual affection, with each holding [the interests of] the other more important."

Priscian notes that, without *invicem*, sentences like (8)–(12) would be ambiguous with respect to the reflexive or reciprocal interpretations (for example, sentence [8] could mean "You and I have compassion for ourselves" or "You and I have compassion for each other"). Thus, in addition to his fundamental purpose of describing the Latin usage in relation to the Greek reciprocal pronoun ἀλλήλο-, Priscian is pointing out and attempting to account for the potential ambiguity in sentences such as (8)–(12). To illustrate this ambiguity, he gives the following sentence, where *se* is used alone:

(13) iste et ille se amant.
"This one and that one love each other."
"This one and that one love themselves."

Compare also:[1]

(14) Livy 6. 28. 1: "nam cum esset Praenestinis nuntiatum . . . patres ac plebem in semet ipsos versos . . ."

1. Examples with *se* alone are infrequent, since the *se* is usually modified by *ipsi* or some other intensifier.

"For when it was announced to the Praenestini . . . that patricians and plebeians had turned against each other . . ."

(15) Caesar *BG* 2. 19. 6: "ipsi sese confirmaverant."
"They had encouraged each other."

Using Priscian's example (13) as an illustration, we see that two rules of Latin syntax, that of conjunction reduction (which takes the sentence "iste amat illum et ille amat istum" and reduces it to "iste et ille amant illum et istum"), and that of reflexivization (which replaces the object pronouns *illum et istum* by *se*), have intersected to produce a structurally ambiguous sentence type. This ambiguity, like most ambiguities, was usually resolved in the various instances in which it occurred by the surrounding context. But when it was not obvious that context would make explicit whether the intended meaning was reflexive or reciprocal, Latin, lacking a reciprocal pronoun like the Greek ἀλλήλο- made use of several syntactic devices.[2] The first, and probably the oldest, was the use of the prepositional phrase *inter se*, as illustrated in examples (1)–(3). This construction is found most frequently among the earlier writers, and it appears to be the fundamental means of expressing reciprocity in Latin. In addition, we find a multiple, hypercharacterized construction which utilizes both *inter se* and *invicem*, as in examples (4)–(7). Here the adverb *invicem*, which in its original sense meant "in place of" (cf. *vice versa, mutua vice, in vicem*, all of which deal with changing place), shows a semantic evolution whereby the original meaning "in place of" develops the meaning "by turns, alternately"—compare A. Ernout–A. Meillet, *Dictionnaire étymologique de la langue latine*[4] (Paris, 1959), pp. 1059–60, s. v.[3] It is this meaning which we find when *invicem* is used alongside *inter se* in redundant constructions such as (4)–(7).

From the meaning "by turns, alternately," *invicem* undergoes still another semantic shift, in this case to the meaning of reciprocity itself, which is typically carried by *inter*. This development is illustrated by examples (8)–(12), where *invicem* occurs with the reflexive pronoun alone. This stage is most likely a co-existing alternative with the next stage, where *invicem* takes on the meaning "each other, one another" (cf. *TLL*, 7.2:176 [II]). *Invicem* adopts this meaning from the reflexive pronouns, especially *se*, with which it was so frequently associated and with which it frequently occurred. Thus, from its repeated collocation with *se*, *invicem* actually takes on the meaning of *se* itself.[4] Once *invicem* has arrived at this stage of expanding its meaning, even the reflexive pronoun can be eliminated as unnecessary and redundant, as for example:

(17) Lucan 7. 177: "inque vicem voltus mirantur."
"And they wonder at each other's faces."

2. I will not deal in this paper with the familiar Latin *alter alterum* construction, since it has no bearing on what follows. Cf. R. Kühner–C. Stegmann, *Ausführliche Grammatik der lateinischen Sprache*, vol. 2.1[2] (Hannover, 1912), p. 616.

3. This meaning of alternation is clearly illustrated by Quint. 1. 3. 11: "[pueri] positis invicem . . . quaestiunculis aemulantur" ("boys compete by posing trifling questions to each other"); and by Tac. *Ann.* 13. 38. 1: "commeantibus invicem nuntiis" ("with messengers alternately coming and going").

4. This is a fairly productive process of semantic change in language. A similar example from English would be the *auto* of *automobile*, "self-moving," which has now taken on the meaning of car itself.

(18) Pliny *Epist.* 7. 20. 7: "ut invicem ardentius diligamus"
"That we should love each other still more warmly"
(19) Quintilian 9. 4. 129: "homines, manibus invicem apprehensis, gradum firmant."
"Men, having linked hands with each other, steady their steps."

In (17)–(19), the reciprocal interpretation of *invicem* ("each other") and not the sequential one ("by turns, alternately") is fully apparent, since it is clear that the action in each sentence is simultaneous for every agent involved.

Schematically, then, I would represent the derivation of this reciprocal complex as follows:

Stage I	*se*
Stage II	*inter se*
Stage III	*inter se invicem*
Stage IV	*invicem se*
Stage V	*invicem*

It is important to note that this schematization does not assume a chronological progression and should not be considered a reconstruction. These stages may be best viewed as representing stylistic options rather than a diachronic chain. In other words, there was probably no time at which any of these options would have been ungrammatical once *invicem* came to be used to disambiguate reciprocals and reflexives. This semantic and syntactic development is motivated entirely by the need to distinguish more easily the reciprocal from the reflexive interpretation of sentences like Priscian's "iste et ille se amant," and as such is a dynamic example of Latin's well-known intolerance for ambiguity and lack of clarity. That Priscian recognized this ambiguity as a linguistic problem and attempted to deal with it at all is a credit to his independence and creativity. Those who would berate him as a mere translator of Apollonius would do well to look at the entire *Institutiones*. There is a wealth of valuable insight in it.

PHILIP BALDI
The Pennsylvania State University

TWO RUSTIC NOTES

1. VARRO *Rust.* 1. 5. 4 AND THE STRUCTURE OF SCROFA'S DISCOURSE

Scrofa, the principal speaker of the first half of Book 1 of Varro's *De re rustica*, is a lecturer of method: he first outlines his subject and then, at the beginning and conclusion of each part and section, reminds his audience of his progress and of what is to come. His outline (1. 5. 3–4) is as follows (there are four "parts," each of which has two "sections"):[1]

I. cognitio fundi (discussed in chaps. 6–16)
  A. quae ad solum pertinent terrae (6–10, 14–15)
  B. quae ad villas et stabula (11–13)

1. "Parts" and "sections" (and later "subsections") are my terms of convenience. In such outlines (*divisio, dividere*), Varro uses *pars, genus*, and *species* loosely, often interchangeably: see M. Fuhrmann, *Das systematische Lehrbuch* (Göttingen, 1960), pp. 72–74. Cf. the first sentence of 1. 5. 4, with Heinrich Keil's convincing emendation, "de his quattuor generalibus partibus singulae minimum in binas dividuntur species" (for "de his quattuor generibus singulae . . ."). References

II. quae in eo fundo opus sint ac debeant esse culturae causa (17–22)
  A. de hominibus per quos colendum (17–18)
  B. de reliquo instrumento (19–22)
III. quae in eo praedio colendi causa sint facienda (23–26)
  A. quae ad quamque rem sint praeparanda
  B. ubi quaeque facienda
IV. quo quicque tempore in eo fundo fieri conveniat (27–37. 3)
  A. quae ad solis circumitum annuum sint referenda (27–36)
  B. quae ad lunae menstruum cursum (37. 1–3)

The neatness of this division obviously appealed to Varro, for some of the material turns out not to fit quite so easily. For instance, II is actually handled in a triadic arrangement, *instrumenti genus vocale* (men, 17–18), . . . *semivocale* (beasts, 19–21), . . . *mutum* (equipment, 22); and III is actually dealt with as a whole and in somewhat different terms (23. 1 ". . . duo consideranda, quae et quo quidque loco maxime expediat serere," what to plant where). Such discrepancies, noted by some scholars, need cause no alarm and should only emphasize for us the importance Varro attached to his four-part, eight-section *divisio*.[2] What is alarming, however, is a complete lapse in the handling of I, where outline and discussion are totally and irreconcilably at odds. Though some scholars have noted this as another minor slip on Varro's part, no one has regarded it as serious or offered a solution.

At the beginning (6. 1), I A is divided further into four "subsections": "igitur primum de solo fundi [i.e., I A , 'quae ad solum pertinent terrae'] videndum haec quattuor, qua sit forma, quo in genere terrae, quantus, quam per se tutus." Sure enough, each subsection is dealt with in turn—the situation of the land (6. 2–7. 4), types of soil (7. 5–9. 7), measurements of land (10), and types of enclosures (14–15) —all purposefully concluded by the methodical lecturer (at the end of 15): "igitur primum haec, quae dixi, quattuor videnda agricolae, de fundi forma, de terrae natura, de modo agri, de finibus tuendis." But what, then, is all this we have just heard at length (11–13), in the subsection on measurements, about the villa (its location in relation to winds, sun, and water) and the other farm buildings? Consulting our notes of Scrofa's initial outline, we see that he appears to have included, under the subsection *de modo agri*, the whole of I B ("quae ad villas et stabula"). Is this unexpected inclusion (or intrusion) a nicety of arrangement, however uncharacteristic of Varro's procedure elsewhere? Or is it a structural blunder? In any case, since we have had both sections in I as given in the outline, II should follow, and with this expectation we turn again to the text, picking up, after

to Keil are to his edition of Cato and Varro: vol. 1.1: Cato *De agri cultura* (Leipzig, 1882); vol. 1.2: Varro *Res rusticae* (Leipzig, 1884); vol. 2.1: commentary on Cato (Leipzig, 1894); vol. 2.2: commentary on Varro (Leipzig, 1891); vol. 3.1: index to Cato, compiled by R. Krumbiegel (Leipzig, 1897): vol. 3.2: index to Varro, also by Krumbiegel (Leipzig, 1902).

2. So Fuhrmann, *Lehrbuch*, p. 70, on Varro's general disposition of his subject: "Schon diese Stellen zeigen, dass Varro einer konsequenten systematischen Trennung der Materien grossen Wert beimisst und dass er die erstmal von ihm durchgeführte Dreiteilung der gesamten Landwirtschaft als erheblichen wissenschaftlichen Fortschritt ansieht." Cf. the elaborate triadic *divisio* of Book 2 (outlined at 2. 1. 12 "ita fiunt omnium partes minimum octaginta et una . . ."). Varro's use of *minimum* in the first sentence of 1. 5. 4 indicates his awareness that outline and discussion will not agree in every detail.

This note is as much concerned with Varro's structure (now misunderstood) of Book 1 (Scrofa's discourse) as with the text of 1. 5. 4 (the source of the misunderstanding); hence its length and detail.

Scrofa's summary (at the end of 15), with chapter 16: "relinquitur altera pars, quae est extra fundum . . ." But as we read, we find nothing of the subject matter of II, nor can we relate what we are being told to the initial outline.[3]

As we reread 16, however, it becomes obvious what we have. This *altera pars* has four subsections (*species*), listed at the outset (16. 1), just as in 6. 1 the four subsections of I A were listed: the safety of the region, accessibility of markets, availability of transportation, influences of neighboring farms. Following the discussion of each of these subsections, Scrofa sums up (17. 1): "de fundi quattuor partibus, quae cum solo haerent, et alteris quattuor, quae extra fundum sunt et ad culturam pertinent, dixi. nunc dicam, agri quibus rebus colantur." Clearly enough, *here* is the conclusion of I and the beginning of II. Here, too, we have a clear statement of I, its two sections, each in turn with its four subsections, from which we may abstract the outline:

I. cognitio fundi
  A. quae cum solo haerent (in four subsections)
  B. quae extra fundum sunt et ad culturam pertinent (in four subsections)

Comparing this with Scrofa's first outline (5. 4), we recognize again that I B is the villain of the piece. Not only did the *villae et stabula* (the I B of the initial outline) cause confusion when we heard about them in the third subsection (11–13) of I A, but here (17.1), when Scrofa sums up the division of I, they have disappeared. And it should be perfectly clear that the subject matter of I B, as given in the revised outline, has valid credentials—first, because the otherwise inexplicable "relinquitur altera pars, quae est extra fundum" (16.1) can only introduce I B; second, because the summary of 17. 1 is guaranteed by the discussion of 16 (whereas the "quae ad villas et stabula" of 5. 4 is not guaranteed by, or embedded in, its context); and third, because we can now see an obvious division of I (A internal considerations || B external considerations).

The only recourse now is emendation, and there is only one form it can take: "quae ad villas et stabula" must be ejected from Scrofa's initial outline at 5. 4, and its place given to some form of the words we have at both 16. 1 and 17. 1:

> de his quattuor generalibus partibus singulae minimum in binas dividuntur species, quod habet prima ea quae ad solum pertinent terrae et altera quae extra fundum sunt.[4]

3. This unusual and serious incongruity between outline and discussion has been either ignored, regarded as careless, or explained away. Keil, *Commentarius*, p. 28, simply presents Varro's disposition of material; H. Dahlmann, s.v. "M. Terentius Varro," *RE*, suppl. 6 (1935): 1188, finds perfect order ("Den Dispositionspunkten, die er 5,3 aufführt, folgt die Darstellung ganz glatt und klar"); nor is Fuhrmann, *Lehrbuch*, pp. 72–74, in spite of the fact that arrangement is his primary concern, aware of any difficulty. F. Zahlfeldt, *Quaestiones criticae in Varronis "Rerum rusticarum" libros tres* (Berlin, 1881)—unavailable to me—"attributes the discrepancy to Varro's careless form" (so, citing Zahlfeldt, J. Skydsgaard, *Varro the Scholar*, Analecta Rom. Inst. Danici, suppl. 4 [Copenhagen, 1968], p. 12, n. 7). Skydsgaard notes that "the discrepancy between the introductory systematization and the actual description has been only superficially discussed in the previous literature" (p. 12, n. 7); on pp. 12–15, he recognizes the difficulty, seems to find such discrepancies characteristic, and concludes only that "Scrofa has decisively broken the general outline given by himself, the breach apparently motivated by the word 'modus,' which gives rise to the train of thought: unit of area→the ideal size of the farmstead→its location generally" (p. 13).

4. The paradosis is ". . . quod habet prima ea quae ad solum pertinent terrae et alterum quae ad villas et stabula." Keil first deleted *alterum*, noting (*Commentarius*, p. 27), "*alterum* inde ab Aldina

"Et quae ad villas et stabula" may have been added, perhaps as a marginal note, by a reader (at any time) to account for what is after all a large and important block of material (11–13, in itself twice as long as the real I B); and this addition may then have been taken as the second *species* (section) and so replaced *quae extra fundum sunt.*[5]

2. CATO *Agr.* 1. 7

I give Keil's text, my own apparatus criticus (after Keil), and the Loeb translation of W. D. Hooper and H. B. Ash (Cambridge, Mass., 1934):

> praedium quod primum siet, si me rogabis, sic dicam: de omnibus agris optimoque loco iugera agri centum: vinea est prima, *si vino bono* vel si vino multo est, secundo loco hortus inriguus, tertio salictum . . .

post agris, *non post* dicam, *interpunxit Merula et* -que *del.* *post* loco *addidit* emito *Merula,* si emeris *Iucundus* (*Keil in Commentario suo*) si vino bono *addidit Ursinus, alia alii ex Varrone De re rustica* 1. 7. 9 vel *a Florentino Politianus*

> If you ask me what is the best kind of farm, I should say: a hundred iugera of land, comprising all sorts of soils, and in a good situation; a vineyard comes first if it produces bountifully wine of a good quality; second, a watered garden; third, an osier-bed . . .

So has this sentence, almost without exception, been printed, punctuated, translated, and understood since the Renaissance; but there are real difficulties of both sense and syntax.

(1) *De omnibus agris* cannot mean "comprising all sorts of soils,"[6] nor, even if it could, does Cato want to say that here. Cato, as Varro read him,[7] is ranking cash crops: the prospective buyer (to whom this chapter is addressed) will consider whether what the land is suited for will be profitable or not (the well-known "scito idem agrum quod hominem. . ." immediately precedes this sentence). What Cato is *not* saying (as should be evident from the simple fact of the list) is that one's sixty-six acres should be producing all sorts of crops (though this is what our texts lead readers and translators to suppose).

editione omissum erat," but then had second thoughts: "scribendum erat potius . . . *et altera quae ad villas et stabula.*" In his *editio minor* (Leipzig, 1891), he printed ". . . [et] altera quae ad villas et stabula." G. Goetz, in his edition (Leipzig, 1922), emended to *iterum. Altera* should be read (the Parisinus gives *alteram,* with *eam* for *ea*): *prima* and *altera* then stand for *species* (not *pars*), which is why Varro continues *secunda pars* . . . (cf. n. 1).

5. It is, of course, possible to read ". . . quod habet prima ea quae ad solum pertinent terrae et ad villas et stabula, et altera quae extra fundum sunt." (The omission of *quae extra fundum sunt*—and the consequent confusion which finally produced *alterum*—would then be due to a copyist's taking *ad villas et stabula* as the second *species.*) I do not, however, regard this as a likely possibility, because Varro intentionally simplifies and (cf. n. 2 and *minimum in binas species* at 5. 4) even distorts for the sake of clarity, simplicity, and balance of *divisio;* he would thus not have thought it necessary in the initial outline to mention buildings (a mention which would, in fact, distract from the neatness of the internal/external opposition).

6. This is not the *templum de marmore* usage (material). "Comprising all sorts of fields" requires *ex,* as Varro *Rust.* 1. 6. 2 "et ex iis tribus quartum," describing a "composite" farm comprising two or three of the basic types of land (*campestre, collinum, montanum*).

7. *Rust.* 1. 7. 9 "Cato quidem . . . gradatim praeponens alium alio agrum meliorem dicit esse in novem discriminibus, quod sit primus ubi vineae possint esse bono vino et multo, secundus ubi hortus irriguus," etc.

The idea of a farm "comprising all sorts of soils" is therefore foreign to this sentence (whether or not such a farm is desirable or possible is not at issue here).

(2) For the same reason, *optimoque loco* is at least suspect: frequently *locus* does mean "situation" or "site," but is this meaning relevant here?

(3) There is an awkwardness in the structure of the sentence evident even in translation (e.g., the Loeb translators' semicolon serves only to make an impossible sequence tolerable): what is the relation of *iugera agri centum* to *vinea est prima?* Merula and Iucundus saw the difficulty, but their solutions are noted by only one modern editor, and by him only in his commentary, without comment of any sort.

I suggest: "praedium quod primum siet, si me rogabis, sic dicam de omnibus agris: optimo loco iugera centum vineae, *si vino bono* vel si vino multo est, secundo loco hortus inriguus, tertio salictum . . ." Four points may be made in explanation.

(1) Merula's punctuation seems necessary and apt:[8] *dicam de omnibus agris* makes sense of *de* and is precisely what Cato must want to say.

(2) If we place a full stop after *agris*, the *-que* (*optimoque*) is no longer required, and was in fact omitted by Merula. Further considerations guarantee the deletion. P. Theilscher saw that *loco* means not "the situation of the farm," but "place in a ranked list."[9] This should have been an obvious enough possibility: Cato's enumeration continues *secundo loco . . . tertio . . .* etc. And, as noted earlier, reference to the farm's situation is not germane to this sentence.

(3) Cato's norm for a profitable olive grove is 240 *iugera* (10. 1 "quo modo oletum agri iugera CCXL instruere oporteat"), for a vineyard 100 *iugera* (11. 1 "quo modo vineae iugera C instruere oporteat"): these headings suggest, then, a solution to the awkwardness of expression mentioned earlier.

(4) *Vinea est prima* has the ring of a (Carolingian?) marginal gloss. It contributes to the awkwardness (rendering *iugera* superfluous) and violates the system of enumeration.

It is not difficult to understand the course of the corruption. As soon as *optimo loco* was understood to refer to the situation of the farm (a common meaning, after all, and one that occurs twice just before: 1. 3 *loco salubri* and 1. 5 *loco bono siet*), and as soon as *de omnibus agris* was taken with what follows (again an easy misunderstanding), then *-que* became a necessary addition. A further inevitable consequence of the misunderstanding of *optimo loco* is that the first-place prize would appear unawarded, and a conscientious reader would then have noted in his margin *vinea est prima*, which became established in the text.

DAVID O. ROSS, JR.
University of Michigan

8. Given by Keil, *Commentarius*, p. 9; R. F. Thomas has kindly checked for me Merula's text in the *editio princeps* (Venice, 1472) at Harvard University.

9. *Des Marcus Cato Belehrung über die Landwirtschaft* (Berlin, 1963), p. 180. His text and translation (". . . will ich es so sagen: von allen Böden, und an bester Stelle, ist, 100 Morgen [gross], Weinland das erste . . .") seem to ignore this insight.

Optimo (*loco*) is odd and, as far as I know, unparalleled in this meaning, but W. V. Clausen has pointed out to me that "presumably Cato used it (instead of *primo*) in order to avoid confusion, having just written *praedium quod primum siet*."

ZOSIMUS AND ASINIUS QUADRATUS

At 5. 27. 1 of his *New History*, Zosimus affects to weigh up the discrepant views of Olympiodorus of Thebes and Asinius Quadratus on the origins of Ravenna, pronouncing for the latter's opinion. Those few scholars who have studied the matter assert, without demonstration, that this is largely a charade: Zosimus only knew of Quadratus because Olympiodorus himself had adduced him.[1]

To the extent that Zosimus does not actually claim to have looked up Quadratus in so many words, the implication is unfair. Given that Olympiodorus set out the views of Quadratus with his customary precision and detail, there need be no issue. Zosimus read both versions in his prime post-Eunapian source, and awarded the palm to Quadratus. He may have honestly preferred the latter. Or to be cynical (which is usually pardonable in the case of Zosimus), the author of the *New History* wished to obnubilate his dependence upon Olympiodorus by seeming to desert him on a point of objective scholarship.

However, the point deserves investigation for a number of reasons. Analysis of the sources and methods of Zosimus is far from exhausted; Asinius Quadratus is a figure of wider importance vis-à-vis later writers; and there is an outside chance that Zosimus did look him up. Finally, if the traditional view is to be maintained (as I think it should), it requires a firmer foundation than mere assertion.

Asinius Quadratus was a natural source of information for an Olympiodorus. The latter is markedly interested in geographical matters.[2] It is for such items that Quadratus is almost invariably cited.[3] The signal exception is the *Historia Augusta*, where the egregious biographer twice[4] adduces him as a source for the Parthian campaigns of Verus and Avidius Cassius. This is the earliest extant reference to Quadratus.[5] It is just possible that it reflects a vogue for his work. Since the *HA* does not so much create fashions as follow them, and since the geographical expertise of Quadratus is not invoked until the fifth and sixth centuries, this may constitute a small argument in favor of the dating of the *HA* to the last decade of the fourth century or later.

The historical span of Quadratus' writings is mentioned by Evagrius (*HE* 5. 24). More pertinent to Zosimus is the case of Agathias of Myrina, who cites Quadratus once (1. 6. 3) on the name of the Alamanni. Agathias' claim to scholarly research, too, is open to doubt.[6] It serves, however, to reinforce the reputation of Quadratus as a name worth dropping.

Agathias was no polymath. But he could have looked up the odd authority on a matter of particular interest to himself,[7] if only to lend his work an occasional patina of erudition. Honest work is not automatically precluded by suspect motives.

1. See L. Mendelssohn's Teubner (Leipzig, 1887), ad loc.; F. Jacoby, *FGrHist*, 2C, p. 303; E. A. Thompson, "Olympiodorus of Thebes," *CQ* 38 (1944): 45; J. F. Matthews, "Olympiodorus of Thebes and the History of the West," *JRS* 60 (1970): 88.
2. The point is fully illustrated by Thompson, "Olympiodorus," p. 45.
3. See Jacoby's collection, *FGrHist* 97: the fragments are mostly from Stephanus.
4. *Verus* 8. 1; *Avid. Cass.* 1. 1.
5. Cf. R. Syme, *Emperors and Biography* (Oxford, 1971), p. 59.
6. The limitations of Agathias are exposed by Averil Cameron, *Agathias* (Oxford, 1970), p. 112.
7. That is the view of Cameron, loc. cit.

Quadratus was to hand, with the added attraction of fashion. All of these points obtain in the case of Zosimus: he too *could* have consulted a source outside Olympiodorus.

But the traditional suspicions are probably well founded. A little after the Ravenna sequence, Zosimus offers (5. 29. 3) one of the very few testimonies to the third-century poet Pisander. In point of fact, it is one of the earliest.[8] The same material is exploited by Sozomen (*HE* 1. 6. 4), who drew on Olympiodorus for his ninth book in particular.

Olympiodorus would appear to be the common source here. The quick appearance of the Quadratus and Pisander references, one shortly after the other, in that part of Zosimus which is flagrantly derived from Olympiodorus, is suggestive, especially when we consider the rarity of named authorities in the *New History*. Apart from the ones under review, they boil down to: Homer, Herodotus, Polybius, the emperor Julian, and Syrianos the philosopher.[9] These are more widely dispersed: there is no agglomeration comparable to the one in question. The allusions to Quadratus and Pisander come in the first paragraphs after that point in Book 5 where Zosimus switches from Eunapius to Olympiodorus. The conclusion is obvious and tempting.

And there is one further reinforcement. At 1. 47, Zosimus commences his notorious dependence upon Eunapius. In this very paragraph, he vaguely adduces "certain historians" on the matter of Claudius' brother, Quintillus. In the opening sentence of the *New History*, where one or more elusive[10] sources are being exploited, there is a sloppy evocation of Polybius. A pattern is discernible. Wherever Zosimus begins to use a particular source, there is prompt adducing of authorities followed by long stretches without any such allusions. As a historiographical technique, it is a non-starter. But the assumption that Zosimus begins each major segment with a short-lived reproduction of his sources' sources, with equally swift abandonment thereof, is all too plausible, since it requires nothing more subtle than the plain evidence of his narrative as a whole. The odds against the outside chance lengthen: Olympiodorus remains a firm favorite as the source of Zosimus' knowledge of Asinius Quadratus.

BARRY BALDWIN
University of Calgary

8. See the *testimonia* assembled (with bibliography) in E. Heitsch, *Die griechischen Dichterfragmente der römischen Kaiserzeit* (Göttingen, 1964), 2:44–46.
9. Consult the register in the introduction to F. Paschoud's Budé (Paris, 1971), p. xxxvi.
10. Ibid., pp. xxxiv–lxiii; Dexippus will surely have been a major (if not the sole) source, given his popularity in later times and the fact that Eunapius both admired and continued him.

PROPERTIUS 1. 1 AND CONSTANTINE THE SICILIAN

In the concluding section of an article that has cast much new light on Propertius 1. 1 (*CQ*, n.s. 24 [1974]: 94–110), Francis Cairns has recently compared that poem with a long anacreontic poem by a writer of the early tenth (rather than late ninth) century, Constantine the Sicilian. The first sixty lines describe how the poet caught sight of and attempted to catch Eros, who finally turned and shot him; lines 77 ff. run as follows:

> συνομηλίκων χορεία,
> συναρήξατε προθύμως . . .
> τί δὲ φάρμακόν ποθ' εὕρω,
> κραδίην ἐμὴν δροσίζον.
> φάρμακον ἐξ 'Ελένης εἴ τις ἐφεύροι
> ἡμετέραις φιάλαις ἐγκαταμῖξαι.

"Here," writes Cairns (p. 109), "we have first an appeal to the speaker's contemporaries for help and advice. Then the speaker wishes for a φάρμακον. This word in itself can refer equally to magic or to orthodox medicine. But the phrase ἐξ 'Ελένης which qualifies φάρμακον favours a religious/magical interpretation." Cairns acknowledges a suggestion of A. J. Beattie "that Constantine's poem seems to refer to worship of Helen as a love-goddess," which he takes as a "further hint at the learned Hellenistic source from which this lyric may ultimately derive." On this assumption he infers that "in these lines we have appeals resembling those of Propertius to the witches and to his friends (1. 1. 19–30)," concluding (p. 110) that "it is impossible to dismiss the thematic correspondences between them as coincidence."

Alas, Constantine's source can be identified with certainty: none other than Homer. He is alluding to the opiate that Helen, no love goddess but the reinstated wife of Menelaus, mixed with Telemachus' wine to dissipate his grief at Sparta:

> αὐτίκ' ἄρ' εἰς οἶνον βάλε φάρμακον, ἔνθεν ἔπινον
> νηπενθές τ' ἄχολόν τε, κακῶν ἐπίληθον ἁπάντων . . .

[*Od.* 4. 220–21]

There is also another text to be taken into account. Constantine's poem is transmitted in two MSS: in one (now apparently defective) together with some other early Byzantine anacreontics (see Bergk, *PLG*, 3[4]:339 f., 370), and in another (Paris. suppl. gr. 352) embedded in an anthology of classical epigrams, most but not all of which reappear in Palatinus gr. 23, the *Palatine Anthology* (Cramer, *Anecd. Par.*, 4:380–83). Despite the unfounded recent denial of R. Aubreton ("La Tradition des épigrammes de l'*Anthologie palatine*," *REA* 70 [1968]: 67), both anthologies may be presumed to derive from the now lost collection put together by Constantine Cephalas, a contemporary of Constantine the Sicilian, circa 900. One of the epigrams that does not feature in the *Palatine Anthology* is:

> Τυνδαρέη κρητῆρα κερασσομένη παρὰ δεῖπνον
> δάκρυα Τηλεμάχοιο κατέσβεσεν ἐς μίαν ὥρην.
> εἰ δὲ ῥόδα προσέμιξε παρηγορέοντι κυπέλλῳ,
> εἶχε μένειν ἄκλαυστος, ἕως νόστησεν 'Οδυσσεύς

[E. Cougny, *Appendix nova epigrammatum* (Paris, 1890), chap. 5, no. 52]

Here the poet is suggesting an improvement on Helen's drug (for the mixing of roses with wine, cf. *Anacreontea* 5. 2 f.). I shall elsewhere be presenting reasons for supposing that Constantine himself is the compiler of this little anthology (*Studies in the Greek Anthology*, forthcoming). Whether it was this epigram (presumably late imperial) or its Homeric model that suggested the Helen motif to Constantine, the reference in his own poem to the mixing of the φάρμακον in a cup of wine puts it beyond doubt that it was a drug like Helen's he had in mind, something to make him forget his pain. No reference then to love potions or witches—and no lost Hellenistic poem.

The other parallels between Propertius and Constantine adduced by Cairns add up to no more than commonplaces: a warning for others to beware of love, and the benefits of travel as a cure for it. Cairns himself draws attention to "marked differences between the treatment of some of the themes in the two texts" (p. 110). With the disappearance of the most striking of the supposed coincidences, the idea of a common "learned tradition of erotic poetry" behind both Propertius and Constantine is probably best abandoned.

ALAN CAMERON
Columbia University

MOSCHOPOULOS AND THE SCHOLIA TO THE *BATRACHOMYOMACHIA*

There is contained in two manuscripts[1] of the *Batrachomyomachia*, U = Ambrosianus H 22 (saec. xv) and P° = Ottobonianus Gr. 150 (saec. xv/xvi), a set of scholia (to verses 1–208) which is attributed in P° (fol. 110r) to Moschopoulos: Ὁμήρου Βατραχομυομαχία μετ' ἐξηγήσεως ὠφελιμωτάτης τοῦ Μοσχοπούλου.[2] The attribution has not, to my knowledge, been questioned; but, in their text tradition and contents, these scholia present so many anomalies when compared with the texts and practices of Moschopoulos that their cumulative effect makes it almost certain that they were not composed by him.

THE TEXT

It is certain that the *Batrachomyomachia* was never part of the poetic *sylloge* of Moschopoulos (*Iliad* 1–2. 493, Hesiod *Opera et dies*, Pindar *Olympians* 1–8, the Byzantine triads of Sophocles [*Aj.*, *El.*, *OT*] and Euripides [*Hec.*, *Or.*, *Phoen.*], and Theocritus *Idylls* 1–8).[3] The text of the *Batrachomyomachia* is not found in any MS containing the whole, or the majority of the components, of the *sylloge*, although it is occasionally found in a MS which contains part of the *sylloge* (e.g., Baroccianus 46: Hesiod with scholia of Tzetzes and Moschopoulos; Ambrosianus L 73: Moschopoulos' commentary on the *Iliad;* Casanatensis G IV 16: Hesiod, Moschopoulos' commentary on Theocritus). No component of the *sylloge* and no other work of Moschopoulos is in U or P°.

1. The first three scholia are found without attribution in Uª (Ambr. H 22, foll. 184 ff.). I use the sigla and edition (pp. 198–308) of A. Ludwich, *Die Homerische Batrachomachia des Karers Pigres* (Leipzig, 1896), cited hereafter as Ludwich.

2. E. Miller, *Catalogue des manuscrits grecs de la bibliothèque de l'Escurial* (Paris, 1848), p. 330, no. 41, listed a MS containing *Batr.* with the scholia of Moschopoulos, scholia of Tzetzes to Hesiod, and Apollodorus' *Bibliotheca.* The MS came into the possession of Cardinal Ottoboni in Rome and was later incorporated in the Vatican's holdings by Benedict XIV (Miller, p. 305). It is tempting to identify the Escorial MS with P°; but, if Miller's description is correct, the identification is not possible (Ludwich, p. 119).

3. For bibliography see "Moschopoulos and Harpocration," *TAPA* 100 (1969): 204, n. 13, and "Moschopulea," *ByzZ* 64 (1971): 303, n. 1.

Second, it is normal for MSS containing Moschopoulos' scholia to carry the same text[4] of the work on which the scholia comment. The texts of the *Batrachomyomachia* in P°, U, and Uª belong to different recensions: P° to A. Ludwich's[5] class III³, U to I², and Uª to I³. Further, the scholia in U comment upon a recension different from the one in U.[6]

THE CONTENTS

The contents[7] of the scholia in U and P° show even more anomalies by the standards of Moschopoulos' usual practice. Each of these anomalies is, perhaps, not of much weight by itself, but again I stress their cumulative effect. The criteria I use are (*a*) manner of citation, (*b*) authors cited, (*c*) works used, (*d*) faulty quotations, and (*e*) comparison of the content of the scholia with analogous passages in Moschopoulos' Περὶ σχεδῶν.[8]

(*a*) *Manner of citation*. The scholiast frequently refers to Homer as οὗτος ὁ ποιητής (28; cf. 2 ὁ ποιητὴς οὗτος, 4 παρὰ τῷ ποιητῷ τούτῳ). The standard mode of reference in Moschopoulos is παρ' Ὁμήρῳ; and he would not have used the scholiast's expression, for the demonstrative pronoun so used is superfluous.[9] When Moschopoulos quotes Scripture, the quotation is anonymous.[10] The scholiast, on the other hand, cites Δαβίδ (2: Ps. 5:3) and ὁ Ψαλμῳδός (165: *immo* 1 Kings 2:10).

(*b*) *Authors cited*. The scholiast uses Eustathius and frequently (7, 8, 30, et alibi) refers to him as ὁ Θεσσαλονίκης. Moschopoulos also uses Eustathius,[11] but never cites him by name—he also never cites Tzetzes and the scholiast does (1). In his scholia to Homer and Hesiod,[12] Moschopoulos cites Porphyry and Proclus but, with a single exception,[13] never elsewhere cites an ancient scholarly source. In contrast, the scholiast refers (usually, if not always, from an intermediate source like Eustathius or the *Etymologicum magnum*) to Theodosius and Herodianus (124: from Eustathius), Choiroboscus (13, 24), Aristophanes ὁ γραμματικός (98: from Eustathius), and to Aristocles' Περὶ διαλέκτων (69: from Eustathius). Finally, citations of Cornutus are unexampled in Moschopoulos, but he is quoted by the scholiast (171: Κορνοῦτος ὁ ἱστορικός): the quotation is fictitious and seems to be a garbled reminiscence of a passage in Tzetzes.[14]

4. I avoid the phrase "Moschopoulean recension" because of the doubts recently expressed by R. D. Dawe, *Studies on the Text of Sophocles* (Leyden, 1973), pp. 55–57.

5. Ludwich, p. 56.

6. Cf. Ludwich, *Index lectionum in Regia Academia Albertina* (Königsberg, 1891–92), p. 25, where O is Ludwich's earlier *siglum* for U.

7. In what follows, numbers, unless otherwise specified, refer to lines of *Batr.*

8. Περὶ σχεδῶν = *Manuelis Moschopuli "De ratione examinandae orationis libellus"* (Paris, 1545). On this work, see "Moschopulea," pp. 303 ff.

9. Π. σχ. 17. 29: ὡς ὅταν εἴπω "ὁ ποιητής" εὐθὺς γὰρ τὸν Ὅμηρον ἐξόχως νοεῖν δίδωμι.

10. Π. σχ. 5. 26: ὡς τὸ "ἃ ὁ θεὸς ἐκάθηρε, σὺ μὴ κοινοῦ" (Acts 10:15 = 11:9); 7. 27: ὡς τὸ "δανείζεται ὁ ἁμαρτωλὸς καὶ οὐκ ἀποτίσει" (Ps. 36:21). Sometimes Moschopoulos makes general reference to Scriptural usage (Π. σχ. 25. 23: παρὰ τῇ συνηθείᾳ τῆς θείας γραφῆς; ad Pind. *Ol.* 1. 1 [52. 13 Abel]: παρὰ τῇ θείᾳ γραφῇ).

11. Compare especially the discussion of Σμινθεῦ (*Il.* 1. 39) in Moschopoulos (L. Bachmann [ed.], *Manuelis Moschopuli Scholiorum Homericorum, particula prima* [Prog. Rostock, 1835], p. 10) with Eustathius ad loc. (1:56 Van der Valk).

12. In the scholia to Hesiod, he is especially reliant on Proclus: cf. M. R. Dimitrijevič, *Studia Hesiodea* (Leipzig, 1899), pp. 46–48.

13. The exception is the citation of Gorgon of Rhodes (*FGrHist* 515 F 18) ad Pind. *Ol.* 7. 1 (214. 7 Abel), which he got from the *scholia vetera*.

14. Cf. Ludwich, p. 275: "Freilich steht in der Ἐπιδρομὴ τῶν κατὰ τὴν Ἑλληνικὴν θεολογίαν παραδεδομένων des Kornutos nichts davon, dass er die Kentauren für Thessalien erklärte."

(*c*) *Works used.* Moschopoulos never refers to or quotes the Hesiodic *Scutum*, as the scholiast does (141), nor the *Batrachomyomachia* itself. A large number of the scholia contain the kind of etymologizing familiar in (and in many cases drawn from[15]) the *Etymologicum magnum.* I would not affirm that Moschopoulos never dipped into that farrago, but he does not make the kind of systematic use of it evident in the scholia.

(*d*) *Faulty quotations.* When Moschopoulos quotes from memory, as I assume he does at least occasionally for Homer and Scripture, the quotations are either accurate or slightly (but not misleadingly) inaccurate.[16] Quotations of more difficult authors—Sophocles, Euripides, Aristophanes—are precise. No one will claim precision for the scholiast. Doubtless some of the faulty quotations are the result of the oral nature of the scholia,[17] and it is probably the fault of a "wenig achtsam Zuhörer"[18] that we find errors like σαυτῆς for σ' αὐτῆς (4, quoting *Il.* 6. 490). For the majority of errors, however, blame must be assigned to the scholiast himself. Examples need not be multiplied. I point to 2, where εὔχετο δ' Ἀπόλλωνι ἄνακτι is a conflation of *Iliad* 4. 119 and 1. 35–36; to 94, where Euripides *Orestes* 5–7 (Τάνταλος / κορυφῆς ὑπερτέλλοντα δειμαίνων πέτρον / ἀέρι ποτᾶται) is rendered ὃς προσδειμαίνων πέτρον ἀέρι ποτᾶται; and to 152, where τόθ' εἶναι καὶ δείσαντες is apparently a corruption of Aristophanes *Ranae* 133 τόθ' εἶναι καὶ σὺ σαυτόν.

(*e*) *Moschopoulos'* Περὶ σχεδῶν. For the sake of convenience, Moschopoulos uses the same explanatory material in different contexts; and it is worth noting that the kind of correspondence which can be observed between his scholia and the Περὶ σχεδῶν cannot be paralleled in the *Batrachomyomachia* scholia. I begin with the latter.

Scholia 1: χόρος σημαίνει δύο· χόρος ὁ τοῦ κύκλου· καὶ ἐτυμολογεῖται ἀπὸ τοῦ τὴν χεῖρα ὀρέγειν καὶ παρέχειν. ἢ παρὰ τὸ χάρα. ἤ, ὃ καὶ κρεῖττον, παρὰ τὸ κόρος ἢ χόρτασις. γίνεται κόρος κατὰ τροπὴν τοῦ κ̄ εἰς χ̄, μεταπεσόντος καὶ τοῦ τόνου· κορεσθέντες γὰρ οἱ ἄνθρωποι ἀνίστανται εἰς τὸ παίζειν καὶ χορεύειν. καὶ χόρος τὸ πλῆθος.

Π. σχ. 76. 17–18: χόρος, πλήθους κατὰ κύκλον στροφὴ ἐναρμόνιος.

Scholia 10: γένειον ἐνταῦθα τὸν πώγωνά φησι. διὰ διφθόγγου δὲ γράφεται, ὡς περιεκτικὸν ὂν τῶν τριχῶν, ὡς τὸ βαλανεῖον, νοσοκομεῖον, ἰατρεῖον, ξενοδοχεῖον καὶ ἄλλα.

Π. σχ. 67. 16–17: γένειον, αἱ κατὰ τὰς σιάγονας τρίχες.

For contrast, we may adduce:

Mosch. ad[19] *Il.* 1. 151: ἢ ὁδὸν ἐλθέμεναι] ἤγουν εἰς λόχον· καὶ παρὰ τοῖς ῥήτορσίν ἐστι τοῦτο ἐν χρήσει. Δημοσθένης "ἢ ἐν ὁδῷ καθελών"[20] ἤγουν ἐνέδρᾳ. εἰ δὲ ψιλωθείη, φασιν, ἡ προτέρα, τὸν βάθμον σημαίνει.

Π. σχ. 132. 7–10: ὁδὸς, ἡ πορεία καὶ ὁ λόχος, ὡς παρὰ Δημοσθένει "ἢ ἐν ὁδῷ καθελών." τοιοῦτον εἶναι, φασί, καὶ τὸ Ὁμηρικόν "ἢ ὁδὸν ἐλθέμεναι."

15. Cf., e.g., Ludwich's comments at 11 and 69. The phrase ἐτυμολογεῖται ἀπό is a favorite of the scholiast, but I have noted only one instance of it in Moschopoulos (Π. σχ. 109. 20).

16. For example, the proper reading in Acts 10 and 11 (cf. n. 10) is ἐκαθάρισεν; at Π. σχ. 29. 15, μετὰ τοῖσιν ἔβη is a mistake for μετὰ δέ σφιν ἔβη.

17. Cf. 8: ἐν θνητοῖσι] τοῦτο τὸ πάθος προσχρηματισμὸς λέγεται, ὡς πρώην εἰρήκαμεν ἐν τῷ "δέλτοισι" (3).

18. Ludwich, p. 121.

19. Bachmann, *Moschopuli Scholia Homerica*, p. 19.

20. From Harpocration, s.v.

Mosch. ad[21] *Il.* 1. 179 : καὶ σοῖς ἑταροῖσιν] ἑταῖροι, οἱ προσοικειωθέντες κατὰ φιλίαν· φίλοι, οἱ οἰκεῖοι καὶ κατὰ γένος προσηκόντες· ἔται, οἱ συνέστιοι φίλοι· γείτονες, οἱ πλησίον μένοντες.

Π. σχ. 121. 1–9 : φίλος, ὁ οἰκεῖος καὶ κατὰ γένος προσήκων, ὡς παρ' Ὁμήρῳ . . . διαφέρει δὲ τοῦ ἑταίρου ὅπερ (ὥσπερ?) ὁ ἔτης τοῦ γείτονος. φίλος μὲν γὰρ αὐτό, ὅπερ εἴρηται, ἑταῖρος δ' ὁ προσοικειωθεὶς κατὰ φιλίαν, ἅπερ Ὅμηρος διακρίνων λέγει . . . ἔτης δὲ συνέστιος φίλος, γείτονες δὲ οἱ πλησίον μένοντες.

I subjoin two smaller pieces of evidence to add to the cumulative effect. The *Lexicon* of Harpocration is used occasionally in the Moschopoulos scholia to the *Iliad*[22] but is not one of the sources of this scholiast. The Συλλογὴ Ἀττικῶν ὀνομάτων, usually[23] but wrongly[24] attributed to Moschopoulos, does contain material drawn from his commentaries: it does not, I think, contain material from these scholia.

I conclude, then, that the attribution of these scholia to Moschopoulos in P° is wrong. Presumably the conjectural attribution was based on the analogy of Moschopoulos' scholia to Homer and Hesiod.

JOHN J. KEANEY
Princeton University

21. Bachmann, *Moschopuli Scholia Homerica*, p. 20.
22. Cf. "Moschopulea," p. 318, n. 45.
23. Still so by Dawe, *Sophocles*, p. 58.
24. Cf. "Moschopulea," pp. 314–15.

BOOK REVIEWS

Velleius Paterculus: The Tiberian Narrative (2. 94–131). Edited with an Introduction and Commentary by A. J. WOODMAN. Cambridge Classical Texts and Commentaries, No. 19. New York and London: Cambridge University Press, 1977. Pp. xix + 292. $26.50.

"This preposterous volume is the first instalment of a commentary on Velleius Paterculus," so Woodman announces in his preface, pointing out that no commentary of comparable scale or scope has been published since the beginning of the nineteenth century. "The neglect of Velleius by commentators has extended to scholars in most other branches of classical learning and is due almost entirely to his treatment of the man who occupies what is marginally the largest single portion of his work—Tiberius. A historian who describes Tiberius in such enthusiastic terms, it is argued, cannot be trusted on any other matter and his work may be safely dismissed. The Tiberian narrative, which forms the last thirty-eight chapters of Velleius' work and covers the years 23 B.C.–A.D. 29, is thus of primary importance for any consideration of his history as a whole." Hence the appearance of the present volume at this time.

What is the proper approach to a writer who like so many in the imperial age resorted to panegyric? Pliny on Trajan, Ammianus on Julian come to mind. Caution obviously is necessary. Velleius, a scion of the Italian gentry, was imbued with unreserved admiration for his *imperator* and *princeps*, Tiberius Caesar, and expressed it overflowingly in the closing chapters and epilogue of his miniature universal history. Even if one does not endorse a wholly black-painted presentation of Tiberius, Velleius' enthusiastic adulation can be hard to take. It has earned him the contempt of many modern scholars, notably of Sir Ronald Syme, a critic more disposed to savor the delicious innuendo of the "subversive" Tacitus than to stomach the outpourings of the loyal Velleius, which he has recently characterized as mendacious ("Mendacity in Velleius," *AJP* 99 [1978]: 45–63). To the list of stereotypes mustered in my "The Truth about Velleius Paterculus: Prolegomena," *HSCP* 74 (1970): 257—"the bluff old soldier, the nonentity, the ham-fisted amateur, the sleazy toady"—must, it seems, be added "the crafty liar."

Syme's indictment of Velleius was drawn up before the appearance of W.'s commentary, though subsequent to the publication of a significant article by that scholar: "Questions of Date, Genre and Style in Velleius: Some Literary Answers," *CQ* 25 (1975): 272–306.[1] W. and Syme represent completely opposite attitudes to Velleius. W. is very conscious of Syme as the standard-bearer of the denigrators of Velleius, and is constantly to be found defending the historian against his attacks. Indeed, if Syme's position were accepted, a good deal of W.'s work would have to be discarded as misconceived. It therefore is incumbent on the reviewer of this book to confront the issue squarely, and it will be useful to compare and

1. Syme makes no reference to Woodman's chapter on Velleius published in *Empire and Aftermath*, ed. T. A. Dorey (London, 1975), pp. 1–25.

assess the rival treatments at points where Syme claims to have unmasked Velleius' mendacity.

Syme attaches great significance ("Mendacity," pp. 45-48, 63) to a statement which comes at the end of a rapid summary of Tiberius' achievements in foreign affairs: "magni etiam terroris bellum Africum et cotidiano auctu maius auspiciis consiliisque eius brevi sepultum est" (Vell. 2. 129. 4). He urges that this war cannot have appeared very alarming *at Rome*, and that it was by no means quickly buried. W. simply notes that "the war in fact lasted 8 years (A.D. 17-24)," and implies that Velleius' *brevi* is indefensible (p. 270, ad loc.). He shows no concern about "magni terroris bellum," and it would be unreasonable to blame him. This routine phrase does not seem to call for much comment. Syme himself, when faced with the task of epitome, once wrote of Tacfarinas stirring up "a serious insurrection" (*OCD*², p. 1033). The whole thing is no more than a typically inexact cliché—the serious war terminated with exemplary dispatch. Velleius is, as usual, lauding Tiberius rather than someone else (*auspiciis consiliisque eius*).

Syme has his guard up against the imaginary threat that one might try to defend Velleius' inexactitude by the plea that he did not know the details of the African War because he was absent from Rome at the time ("Mendacity," pp. 50 f.). Hence an urgent need to denounce my suggestion ("Truth," p. 277—though it is as old as Beatus Rhenanus) that the general mentioned in Tacitus *Annals* 3. 39 (*P. Vellaeus* M) might actually be Velleius. The idea may have been particularly offensive because, if it were accepted, one would have to give Velleius credit for being an efficient soldier. Unless and until the "real" P. Vellaeus turns up in a document, there is no reason to rule out the identification peremptorily.

The role of Tiberius in the East in 20 B.C. is exaggerated by Velleius ("Mendacity," pp. 54 f.). Who can deny it? However, an aspect of Syme's argument was sabotaged by W. in advance (pp. 124 f.). The text of Velleius 2. 101. 1 on which Syme relies is not secure, depending on an emendation by Lipsius: "ante aliis provinciis ad visendum obitis in Syriam missus." The paradosis is †*adsidendum* (*ad sedandum* P), and even if *ad visendum* were right (cf. 94. 4, *ad visendas*), "the allusion is presumably to Gaius' preliminary trip to the Balkans in 1 B.C.," not, as Syme appears to assume, to a tour of the East. Syme assigns to C. Caesar the phrase "omnibus ad Orientem visis provinciis" (101. 3), which actually belongs to Velleius himself.

In the Alpine War of 15 B.C. Velleius represents Nero Claudius Drusus as *adiutor* to his brother Tiberius (2. 95. 1). W. compares Cn. Piso's position as legate of Syria, *adiutor* to Germanicus (Tac. *Ann.* 3. 12. 1). Syme, on the other hand, is convinced that Velleius is prevaricating. "False. Drusus was not a subordinate or auxiliary of his elder brother" ("Mendacity," p. 55). Yet Tiberius was an ex-praetor, Drusus merely an ex-quaestor (cf. "Germanicus and Drusus Caesar," *Latomus* 26 [1967]: 435). Velleius' word *adiutor* (not exactly official, as W. thinks) does not misrepresent the situation at the level of rank and seniority.

Syme's objection ("Mendacity," p. 56) to Velleius' account of the first Julia scandal is based on a wrong interpretation of an unfashionable (but not necessarily incorrect) reading in 100. 5. He prints "quasi [quas in *Woodman*] cuiuslibet uxore violata poenas pependere [pependissent, pependere *Woodman*], cum Caesaris filiam et Neronis violassent coniugem," and interprets "they suffered only the normal and legal penalty for adultery." This statement he contrasts with Tacitus' observation (*Ann.* 3. 24. 2) that Augustus punished the lovers of his daughter and granddaughter with death or exile, "nam culpam inter viros ac feminas vulgatam gravi nomine laesarum religionum ac violatae maiestatis appellando, clementiam maiorum suasque ipse leges egrediebatur." "Not therefore 'mere adultery,'" Syme comments. But Velleius' meaning is that they, i.e., Quinctius Crispinus, Ap. Claudius, Sempronius Gracchus, and Scipio, with some less notable senators and knights, paid the same penalty for their *treasonable* adultery as they would have paid for ordinary adultery, namely, exile. Syme is unable to refute Velleius' statement with any contradictory details from Tacitus. His use of "Dio" 55. 10. 15 (epitome!)—Iullus Antonius ἀπέθανε μετ' ἄλλων τινῶν ἐπιφανῶν ἀνδρῶν οἱ δὲ λοιποὶ ἐς νήσους ὑπερωρίσθησαν—cannot be described as exemplary. Syme knows better than anyone that in the Empire, when one source says that a prominent person was killed, another that he was punished with death, and a third that he killed himself ("ipse sceleris a se commissi ultor fuit," Velleius), the solution of the equation is compulsory suicide. It is unsatisfactory to intimate that "it may not be quite certain whether [Antonius] was executed or persuaded to take his own life."

At 101. 1 a slight textual change, which W. revives from Lipsius—"convento prius Ti. Nerone qui [cui *codd.*] omnem honorem ut superiori habuit"—would dispose of Syme's objection ("Mendacity," p. 57) that "the deference exhibited by the prince [C. Caesar] 'ut superiori' is a fiction." It would now be Tiberius' deference to the prince, who was, as W. points out, *superior* by virtue of the *maius imperium*. On the other hand, Tiberius was *superior* by virtue of age, and the subject under discussion is Gaius Caesar's behavior, not Tiberius'. Retaining the paradosis, it is not hard to envisage that Gaius treated Tiberius with cold politeness, which Velleius, probably an eyewitness, proceeds to dress up in his usual style. Syme is very likely right to regard *convento . . . Ti. Nerone* as a misleading expression suggesting that Gaius went to visit Tiberius: Suetonius and Dio indicate that the opposite happened. W. misses this subtlety.

But he almost gains Syme's grudging admission ("Mendacity," p. 61) that he has solved the problem of 2. 106. 2 f. ("Questions of Date," pp. 304 f.). That which "numquam antea spe conceptum, nedum opere temptatum est" was not (of course) the march to the Elbe but the combined operation of army and fleet in that campaign. "A new and novel interpretation" according to Syme, its seed had been lurking in an obscure note in the commentary of F. Kritz (Leipzig, 1840), p. 447, ad 2. 106. 3, now restored to the light by W. (p. 144).

Velleius 2. 112. 7 on the *exitus* of Agrippa Postumus is analyzed by Syme ("Mendacity," pp. 61 f.) into three statements, corresponding to (*a*) *abdicatio* and removal to Surrentum (A.D. 6); (*b*) banishment to Planasia (A.D. 7); (*c*) *exitus* = death (A.D. 14). W. (p. 171; cf. "Questions of Date," p. 305) argues that *exitus* may mean "final state of a person," and "since Postumus' 'final state' was banishment to Planasia, and since this took place in A.D. 7, the precise year which V. is here discussing, it is surely his banishment, not his death, to which reference is being made. V. is thus not guilty [of placing the death here in order to dissociate Tiberius from it] but he is guilty of later passing over Postumus' death in silence." Syme dismisses this interpretation "without further ado" on the strength of his own analysis of the passage, as if that were unquestionable. In fact, the stages indicated by Velleius are slightly at odds with Syme's: (*a*) "qualis esset apparere coeperat" refers to something in A.D. 5 (*iam ante biennium*); (*b*) the alienation of Augustus and Tiberius should then refer to what happened in A.D. 6 (the date from the *Fasti Ostienses*); (*c*) "moxque crescentibus in dies vitiis dignum furore suo habuit exitum" refers to the banishment in A.D. 7. Yet the debate is somewhat unreal. In truth, the third stage was exile and oblivion A.D. 7–14; I would not quarrel with Syme's formulation, that Velleius seeks "to veil the fate of Agrippa Postumus."

Finally, 2. 120. 1–2. Syme ("Mendacity," p. 58 f.) doubts Velleius' description of "a vigorous resumption of active warfare in A.D. 10," but is apparently prepared to accept it for A.D. 11. The basis for this "strong doubt" is that Zonaras (10. 37) describes a time in A.D. 10 when Tiberius "did not see fit to cross the Rhine, but kept quiet, watching to see that the barbarians did not cross." Does this testimony carry enough weight to erase Velleius' detailed description of how Tiberius crossed the Rhine and invaded the German interior that year? W. (p. 207) agrees with R. Seager (*Tiberius* [London, 1972], p. 45) "that Tiberius did cross the Rhine in A.D. 10" and discounts the testimony of "Dio 56. 24. 6" (i.e., Zonaras). Since, however, the testimony of Dio-Zonaras is isolated from context, one ought to suspect that the Greek historian was writing about the earlier phase of the campaign of A.D. 10, which was defensive and is in fact described by Velleius (120. 1) before the invasion of Germany: "mittitur ad Germaniam, Gallias confirmat, disponit exercitus, praesidia munit . . . ultro Rhenum cum exercitu transgreditur," etc.

Enough probably has been set forth to show that W. is a knowledgeable, resourceful, and resolute champion of his author. He is not a scholar inclined to flee from controversy. His judgments are firmly expressed, their reasons sharply and fully articulated. He deserves to be given a hearing.

The book includes a substantial introduction, which is in two parts. The first (pp. 3–28) deals extensively with the history of the text, which is a particularly interesting one. The main critical problem concerns the status of Amerbach's apograph (A). W. takes the view that this MS was not copied directly from the Murbach codex but from the same copy of the codex as was used for the printing of the *editio princeps*. He does not, accordingly, put a high value on A. "It is because the Oxford text of Ellis and the Teubner texts of Halm and Stegmann have unanimously and heavily sided with A that the apograph's importance is still overestimated today" (p. 24, n. 3).

The second part of the introduction (pp. 28–56) discusses Velleius' standing as a historian under the title "History, Biography or Panegyric?" This essay involves a useful survey of "personalities and patriotism in Latin historiography," to illustrate the fact that Velleius' concentration on those themes is not abnormal but belongs well within the historiographic tradition. Very much to the point is the consideration of the last twenty-two books of Livy (pp. 34–40). "Historians of Augustus were presented with splendid material and themes which they could elaborate with all the patriotic fervour traditional, as we have seen, to Roman historiography. If these foreign campaigns were contemporary, as they were for

Livy, there was an additional benefit: by concentrating in this direction the historian need not compromise himself by dwelling upon events of a delicate political nature" (p. 30). W. reasonably concludes that Velleius' history is a characteristic product of its time. He adds the suggestion that Syme's apologia for Ammianus' treatment of Julian "could with equal justice be applied to the Tiberian portion of V.'s narrative" (p. 56, referring to Syme, *Ammianus and the Historia Augusta* [Oxford, 1968], p. 94).

There follows W.'s text of Velleius 2. 94–131 with very full critical apparatus (pp. 57–92). W.'s own conjectures on this portion of the text add up to twelve, all printed in his text; the more significant or interesting are at 94. 4, "⟨Tigrani, filio⟩ Artauasdi⟨s⟩"; 96. 2, "consul" (vocative); 110. 1, "rumpit interdum, ⟨modo⟩ moratur"; 111. 4, "euasimus, ⟨exhausimus⟩"; 114. 2, "iam ⟨tamquam⟩ in hoc solum portatum instrumentum balinei"; 125. 2, "paene in ultimam ⟨cladem⟩."

The commentary occupies pages 95–282 and, as can be seen from this statistic, is extremely detailed. W. gives an admirably complete account of the work of earlier commentators. The notes are a treasury of information about Velleian usage, enhanced by a thorough collation of parallels. Even those who would deny Velleius' usefulness as a Tiberian historian would be well advised not to neglect what W. has to offer here. The volume is rounded off by three substantial indexes ("General," "Latin words," "Persons"). In the excellent general index, profit will accrue from following up the entries under such headings as "consolatory literature," "panegyric," "topoi."

All in all, it is to be hoped that Woodman's herculean efforts will be rewarded by a quickening of interest in Velleius, the only Latin historian of Roman affairs to have survived from the period between Livy and Tacitus.

G. V. Sumner
University of Toronto

Aristotelis "Ars rhetorica." Edidit RUDOLFUS KASSEL. Berlin and New York: Walter de Gruyter & Co., 1976. Pp. xix + 259. Mk. 198.

Professor Kassel has established his text on exceptionally solid foundations. In a book published five years prior to this edition, *Der Text der Aristotelischen Rhetorik* (Berlin–New York, 1971), he furnished information about every extant MS, examined the relation between individual MSS as well as between groups and families, and defined precisely the place in the stemma and the value of all *subsidia editionis* except the Arabic translation (which cannot yet be used), but including the Latin translations. A (= Parisinus 1741, tenth cent.), which was for some time the *codex unicus*, is still the *codex optimus*. It has remarkably few descendants. The head of the other class, β, is not extant but its readings may, as Kassel showed us, be recovered through a methodical use of available MSS and reconstructed hyparchetypes. The *recensio* in this preliminary study is a model performance from which any future editor of a Greek text may learn. Since I am to review the new text, I must not linger over the prolegomena; suffice it to add that the archetype (ω) of the entire transmission remains a somewhat elusive entity. I admit that we cannot do without it—though I wonder why the transposition in all witnesses of 1. 9. 1367b26–1368a10 into a lacuna of Book 3 is not used by Kassel as the strongest proof of a common ancestor. For practical purposes the archetype equals the readings common to the two classes, plus some *variae lectiones*. Kassel wisely refrains from suggesting a date for ω. Realistically speaking, there is little hope of getting to the other side of the dark centuries of Byzantine culture. For the *Rhetoric* we have no Alexander of Aphrodisias and no Simplicius.

Turning now to the edition, we may say at once that we are on much firmer ground than were earlier students of the work. And what is true of the text holds good also of the apparatus. We know not only the importance of A, but also whence the corrections in A^2 and A^{rec} are derived, and we similarly know in the case of every siglum what weight we are to assign to the MS or family that it represents. But great as is the progress gained from the superb *recensio*, K. has achieved no less by his careful and astute interpretation of Aristotle's argument. He avoids unnecessary alterations, and in a considerable number of instances where good readings had been questioned (e.g., 1360b36, 1370a19, b28, 1378a32, 1401b14, probably also 1402b6) he shows that what has caused offense is actually good Aristotelian usage. The points at issue may be small, but K. would probably (like myself) subscribe to Eduard Norden's opinion that classical scholars must not keep company with the praetor who *minima non curat*. Most of K.'s own emendations strike me as felicitous. Some are decidedly elegant.

1375b35 ff.: for events of the future, writes Aristotle, χρησμολόγοι may serve as "witnesses," οἷον Θεμιστοκλῆς ὅτι ναυμαχητέον τὸ ξύλινον λέγειν (λέγων A: λέγει β) τεῖχος. Themistocles does not need a predicate in this sentence, but the "wooden wall" needs an indication that it has a meaning.

1395b31: discussing the kinds of materials from which the speaker should draw his proofs, Aristotle says he may draw them from opinions (δοκοῦντα), but not from everybody's opinions. οὐκ ἐξ ἁπάντων τῶν δοκούντων ἀλλ' ἐκ τῶν ὡρισμένοις (ὡρισμένων ω) λεκτέον, οἷον ἢ τοῖς κρίνουσιν ἢ οὓς ἀποδέχονται. Surely K.'s change here is necessary.

1403b36 ff.: Aristotle has said that diction and delivery add nothing of real value to a speech, and that concern about these matters is rightly considered boorish. But rhetoric is altogether oriented toward δόξα rather than toward truth, and therefore some study of delivery is necessary, ἐπεὶ τό γε δίκαιον μηδὲν πλείω ζητεῖν περὶ τὸν λόγον ἢ ὡς μήτε λυπεῖν μήτ' εὐφραίνειν. As it stands (and has often been printed), the sentence can hardly pass for Greek. It becomes Greek only through K.'s change of ζητεῖν to ζητεῖ.

The temptation to quote and discuss some more emendations (as at 1366a35, 1379a11, 1383b5, 1385a5, 1391b17, 1417b25) is strong, but considerations of space forbid it. Inevitably there are occasions—though rather few—where K. has put into the text a conjecture which must not remain there.[1]

A procedure which K. is not the first to use, but which he pursues more systematically and with far better understanding than his precursors, is the identification of material added "later," that is, after the drafting of the original text. These additions may consist of a single word, a clause, a sentence, or even a whole section. There is a great deal of such material in our text of the *Rhetoric*, and not

1. I understand why at 1396a3, where Aristotle expounds what kind of knowledge a speaker has to have at his fingertips for the subject περὶ οὗ δεῖ λέγειν καὶ συλλογίζεσθαι εἴτε πολιτικῷ συλλογισμῷ εἴθ' ὁποιῳοῦν, K. prefers to read εἴτ' ⟨ἐν⟩ πολιτικῷ συλλόγῳ. But since Aristotle insists on the need to have τὰ ὑπάρχοντα (the material or rather the premises) specifically in order to συνάγειν (= συλλογίζεσθαι, a6 f.), the text must remain unchanged.

all of it can be laid at the door of interpolators. On the contrary, as soon as we get away from the most trivial insertions and find ourselves dealing with more complex and interesting accretions, they usually turn out to be the result of Aristotle's own second (or even third) thoughts, or they represent alternative versions put down by him. To be sure, there is no limit to the degree of complexity: second thoughts, interpolations, and awkward attempts to smooth out rough edges may all come together to make life hard for the editor (1367b26–1368a10 is a case in point). K. remains undaunted; more often than not he unravels the tangled condition of the text.[2] As I have said, earlier critics, too, discovered alternative versions—they could scarcely help it—but the passages seem to have embarrassed them and brought them to their wits' end. When K. separates secondary material from the main body of the text (using a special kind of double bracket to mark Aristotle's own additions), he knows what he is doing and why it is legitimate (*Der Text*, p. 114). An Aristotelian *pragmateia* was not published, like tragedies, epinikia, and other literary compositions; as a technical treatise, it remained at the disposal of its author, who could at any time change, shorten, augment, or rewrite the first draft. In other works of Aristotle—most notably the *Metaphysics* and the *Physics*, yet also the *De generatione animalium*—editors and textual critics have borne this special condition in mind. But in the *Rhetoric* the notion that unity is desirable and that every effort should be made to vindicate it has maintained itself with astonishing tenacity. Actually, K.'s procedure shows that the recognition of second thoughts does not necessarily conjure up the dreaded specter of "development." Although not opposed to development, K. prefers to settle his textual problems without reference to the possibilities and perspectives opened by this approach. In his view, as soon as scholars have surer ground to walk on, they may attack broader questions with increased confidence (*Der Text*, p. 115). This is an outlook and a policy with which one may certainly come to terms; I for one would even admit that few or none of the alternative versions in K.'s text reflect a serious change of orientation in Aristotle's thought. On the other hand, sections that in this edition rest peacefully side by side are bound to appear incompatible as soon as their content, especially the underlying logical doctrine, is analyzed.

Between his text and his apparatus K. has reserved some space for what he calls "Zitate und Anspielungen," though his formulation "alles . . . was der Leser bei der kritischen Lektüre des Textes unmittelbar zur Verfügung haben sollte" (*Der Text*, p. 114) fits the collection better. For here are assembled items as diverse as late echoes—clear or faint—of Aristotle's thoughts, parallels in Aristotle himself and in other writers, and passages quoted or alluded to. The reader will not always find it easy to decide what function a reference or quotation is meant to have. He may also wonder why, when Byzantine rhetoricians figure so often, Aristotle's

2. At times K.'s decisions, while convincing, give rise to new problems. This is not the place to discuss them, nor can we here consider whether there are not other passages in the *Rhetoric* which call for a similar critical approach. However, I wish to offer a suggestion for 1363b35 ff., where K. diagnoses trouble. The text reads *καὶ τὰ μείζονος ἀγαθοῦ ποιητικὰ μείζω* [i.e., "are themselves greater goods"]. *τοῦτο γὰρ ἦν τὸ μείζονος ποιητικῷ εἶναι. καὶ οὗ τὸ ποιητικὸν μεῖζον ὡσαύτως* [*ὡσαύτως* = "is itself a greater good"]. The sequence of thought here is disturbed, but everything will be in order if the clause *καὶ οὗ . . . ὡσαύτως* is placed before *τοῦτο γὰρ ἦν*. Perhaps the mistake arose when a note jotted down by Aristotle was incorporated in the text.

own ethical treatises and his *Topics* are not cited where they offer significant parallels. *Topics* 3 is so close to the discussion of the choice between two ἀγαθά in *Rhetoric* 1. 7 that a blanket reference might have sufficed. Of the rhetorical *topoi* set forth in *Rhetoric* 2. 23, the τόπος τοῦ μᾶλλον καὶ ἧττον (1397b12 ff.) and the τόπος ἐκ τῶν ἐναντίων ("is the opposite present in the opposite?" 1397a7 ff.) are likely to have most parallels in the *Topics*. For the doctrine that *hedone* is a good or the greatest good (1362b5 ff., 1364b23 ff.), the impressive passage about Eudoxus' sponsorship of this thesis (*EN* 10. 2) ought to have been mentioned; it is also the thesis of Philebus in Plato's dialogue. The blueprint of a scientific *psychagogia* in the *Phaedrus* (270B ff.; 271B10 ff.) is the historical background for the analysis of the emotions in *Rhetoric* 2. Why are we never referred to it? On the *techne* of Theodectes we need more information than Valerius Maximus 8. 10, the only passage quoted at 1410b2, furnishes; even if scholars are not agreed about Aristotle's use of his friend's *techne*, they are agreed on not trusting Valerius (see especially W. Kroll, s.v. "Rhetorik," *RE*, suppl. 7 [1940]: 1052, 1061 ff.; G. Kennedy, *The Art of Persuasion in Greece* [Princeton, 1963], pp. 80 f. and n. 65). At 1406b8 f. Aristotle quotes Gorgias' stylistic adventure χλωρὰ καὶ ἔναιμα τὰ πράγματα as an example of tasteless metaphor. The passage which in Demetrius *Eloc.* 116 illustrates the same kind of aberration, τρέμοντα καὶ ὠχρὰ τὰ γράμματα, cannot be used as *testimonium* for Aristotle's quotation. The right way of dealing with the two passages is to combine them into an antithesis which does Gorgias honor: τρέμοντα ⟨μὲν⟩ καὶ ὠχρὰ τὰ γράμματα, χλωρὰ ⟨δὲ⟩ καὶ ἔναιμα τὰ πράγματα (see LSJ, s.v. χλωρός III).

I admit that, since the *testimonia* have to be a mixed bag, it is not possible to satisfy everybody everywhere. What distresses me more (on the assumption that K. meant to provide not only a well-constructed but also a readable text) is the failure to break up long chapters into smaller units. As presented by K., the second chapter of Book 1 is a swamp. I could not imagine how anyone not thoroughly familiar with the intricacies of Aristotle's logic could wade through it from one end to the other without sinking, and even an expert may turn with relief to an earlier edition. In A. Roemer's Teubner text of 1914, the chapter has been divided into eight paragraphs, each of them embodying a self-contained argument. L. Spengel in his famous edition of 1867 had done essentially the same, while W. D. Ross in his OCT of 1959 resorts to additional devices that may help the readers.[3] 1. 6 and 2. 5 are other chapters where earlier editors made a break—and not only in the interest of the readers—for at 1362b29 and at 1383a15 Aristotle changes the subject. In 3. 14, a chapter of more than eighty lines, the subject changes sufficiently at 1415a5 and b33 to warrant a new paragraph, and at a21 a new point of view is introduced rather suddenly, a fact indicated by Roemer and Ross, but not by K.

3. K. himself seems to have lost the thread at the end of 1. 2. As we learn from 1358a2 ff., oratorical arguments need not be strictly rhetorical or dialectical, but may be based on the premises of a specific subject (such as ethics or physics, a18 ff.). As the speaker takes a firmer hold on these materials, he quite properly moves out of rhetoric or dialectic (αὐτῶν, a9), although the audience does not realize that he is shifting his ground: λανθάνουσί τε τοὺς ἀκροατὰς καὶ μᾶλλον ἁπτόμενοι κατὰ τρόπον μεταβαίνουσιν ἐξ αὐτῶν. K.'s lacuna after ἀκροατάς is a mistake, and the insertion of ἢ after ἁπτόμενοι makes the sentence, for me at least, unintelligible. Further on, at a23, τὰς προτάσεις is very probably an interpolation meant to explain ταῦτα.

In a second edition—provided it deserves the name and is not a mechanical reprint—it should be easy to remove these few shadows from an otherwise splendid performance. To the numerous merits that have been pointed out one more should be added, the indexes. Both of them are reliable and very useful, and it was a wise decision to keep the *index auctorum* apart from the *index graecus*, which includes all proper names other than authors.

Friedrich Solmsen
University of North Carolina

Tacitus in Renaissance Political Thought. By KENNETH C. SCHELLHASE. Chicago and London: The University of Chicago Press, 1976. Pp. xiii + 270. $16.00

All the great Greek and Latin historians of antiquity were models for historians of later generations, but only Tacitus came to have wider significance for politicians, moralists, and religious leaders for about three centuries from the Reformation to the French Revolution. First, he gave the Germans that picture of German virtues and German leaders (Arminius) which decisively contributed to their self-confidence in their struggles with the Roman Church and with the *Welsch* nations. Secondly, he transmitted an ambiguous image of monarchy which (as Guicciardini observed) could both teach tyrants to secure their tyranny and teach those who live under tyrants to behave prudently. On the other hand he could easily be turned into a guide for active opponents of absolutism whenever and wherever (England, Holland, and later France) conditions became propitious for political reform. These developments of Tacitus' teaching are of course entirely modern, but they have their roots in his ambiguities and also in his almost prophetic foresight, because he was afraid of the Germans and looked anxiously out of the corner of his eye at Jews and Christians.

The story of the modern fortunes of Tacitus has been told several times since Giuseppe Toffanin—not without predecessors—wrote his classic book *Machiavelli e il "Tacitismo"* (Padua, 1921). In recent years research on "Tacitism" has multiplied and has been especially fruitful in the Spanish area. The Spanish studies by E. Tierno Galván ("El tacitismo en las doctrinas políticas del siglo de oro español," *Anales de la Universidad de Murcia*, 1948, pp. 895–988; reprinted in *Escritos (1950–1960)* [Madrid, 1971]), F. Sanmartí Boncompte (*Tácito en España* [Barcelona, 1951]), and J. A. Maravall (*La Philosophie politique espagnole au XVIIe siècle* [Paris, 1955]) have been accompanied by those of J. von Stackelberg on Tacitus in Italy and France (*Tacitus in der Romania* [Tübingen, 1960]) and of Else-Lilly Etter, more generally, on *Tacitus in der Geistesgeschichte des 16. und 17. Jahrhunderts* (Basel, 1966). In a chapter of twenty pages on "Tacitism" in the collective volume *Tacitus* edited by T. A. Dorey (London, 1969), P. Burke brilliantly characterized the main features of this phenomenon. In the same year André Stegmann produced an interesting programme for new research and evaluation, the developments of which, if they were published, are not known to me ("Le Tacitisme: Programme pour un nouvel essai de définition," *PPol* 2 [1969]: 445–58).

Professor K. C. Schellhase in his book goes over all the evidence again and attempts a synthesis. He does not aim at new discoveries, but shows on every page a remarkable command, if not of the original texts, at least of the modern literature: only the Spanish section is patently defective. The book is useful.

As the limits of the research are so clearly and honestly marked, critical observations must correspondingly be confined to the relation between the new book and previous research. It seems to me that S. is inclined to attribute too much importance to the early Florentine references to Tacitus. He consequently believes that Tacitus lost political importance when he was no longer interpreted in republican terms, as Leonardo Bruni had done in his *Laudatio florentinae reipublicae* about 1401–4. No doubt H. Baron discovered a very significant reference to Tacitus *Histories* 1. 1 in the text of the *Laudatio* of which he later became the first editor (*From Petrarch to Leonardo Bruni* [Chicago, 1969]; the reference is on p. 247). But such a prominent use of a passage of Tacitus to describe the effects of the transition from a republican to a monarchic regime is somehow untypical of the fifteenth-century humanist: Bruni himself owed much more to Polybius than to Tacitus. The fact remains that Tacitus' reputation soared in the sixteenth century. As has long been recognized, it was not so much founded on a specific doctrine as on a mental attitude. During the Counter-Reformation, Tacitus was taken to express a pessimistic vision of political life, an ambiguous nostalgia for freedom which was at the same time an implicit (or explicit) recognition that true liberty, if it had ever existed, was out of reach. What is more, this attitude was not read into Tacitus by his sixteenth- and seventeenth-century readers. It was there, only waiting to be developed in various directions by the commentators. It explained politics and guided politics. I am therefore at a loss to understand why S. denies genuine political interests to Justus Lipsius (p. 134), and declares: "The tradition of the application of Tacitus to political reality, which had begun with Bruni in 1403, did not survive the death of Boccalini in 1613" (p. 150). In 1640 Nicolas Perrot d'Ablancourt declared in the dedication to Richelieu of his translation of Tacitus' books on Tiberius: "C'est luy [Tacite] qui a engendré toute la politique d'Espagne et d'Italie . . . c'est luy que les Princes de la Maison d'Autriche consultent encore tous les jours dans la nécessité de leurs affaires."

K. A. Blüher in his fine book *Seneca in Spanien* (Munich, 1969), which does not seem to have been used by S., has some very illuminating pages on the questions about Seneca which Tacitus suggested to his Spanish readers. Did Seneca behave with the prudence one is entitled to expect from the minister and confidant of a monarch? Did the Roman state derive advantage from Seneca's dissimulation? Such were the questions that the biographers of Seneca, Juan Francisco Fernandez de Heredia (1642) and Juan Baños de Velasco y Acebedo (1674), tried to answer—and very real (and political) questions they were, in an age in which a satisfactory relation between a monarch and his minister(s) was the first requirement of politics.

For England S. himself has to admit different chronological limits to political Tacitism (p. 157). But there is very little Tacitism in the controversy between the great scholar whom he calls "a certain Salmasius" (p. 164; the index takes the name for a pseudonym!) and Milton. As Salmasius and Milton were quarreling about the divine rights of kings, the Old Testament and St. Paul were more to the point than Tacitus. "Si fuit, cur Paulus de eo non intellexit? Cur praetermisit?" This is a fair example of Salmasius' way of arguing (*Ad Johannem Miltonum responsio, opus posthumum* [London, 1660], p. 303). It is interesting that Salmasius quotes Tacitus to lessen the ancient liberties of the Germans (*Defensio regia* [Leyden, 1649], p. 239). Milton used Tacitus with greater emphasis, and rather cheaply accused Salmasius of getting his Tacitus secondhand, but he too relied mainly on the Bible. It comes as another surprise to hear from S. that Jeremy Taylor in *The Rule of Conscience* (or *Ductor dubitantium*) "showed even greater skill in ransacking Tacitus to support the rightful rule of the King" (p. 165). If a book was ever ransacked by Jeremy Taylor, it was of course the Bible.

A careful reading of Milton, Salmasius, and Jeremy Taylor at least teaches us what Tacitus was not: a text to be used to settle questions about the divine rights of kings.

Arnaldo Momigliano
University of Chicago

Farm Equipment of the Roman World. By K. D. WHITE. Cambridge–London–New York–Melbourne: Cambridge University Press, 1975. Pp. xvii + 258 + 16 pls.; 66 figs. in text. $35.00.

This is a companion volume to the author's *Agricultural Implements of the Roman World* (Cambridge, 1967); with the earlier volume it shares its raison d'être, its methodology, and its presentation of data. White aims at the same wide audience: readers of Latin literature, scholars of ancient agriculture, lexicographers, and historians. The value of this work, as of the former, lies not so much in its peculiar usefulness for a certain category of student as in its pioneering attempt to set archaeological evidence alongside literary evidence. Since they are so much better acquainted with literature than most (I do not say all) literary specialists are with archaeology, I cannot say how useful these books will be to archaeologists. The information White has collected will surely interest large numbers of classicists and medievalists, not just the historians of technology. Shortcomings are inevitable, perhaps, in a pioneering study such as this; if I seem negative, it is in the hope that the book will be used to its best advantage, and I do not mean to underrate a very laudable achievement.

W. comes equipped as a historian, and in particular as the English-speaking world's specialist in Roman agriculture (see his *Roman Farming* [London, 1970]). He is not a philologist, nor does he pretend to be; he wants to help us all out of a muddled confusion to which editors and translators have generously contributed (p. xi). A hard-core philologist will find much to grumble about in W.'s superficial treatment of etymologies, spelling, and closely related words: e.g., *festuca*, *fistuca* (pp. 5 ff.)—what does Festus' *ferula* have to do with this implement, and do we not want Palladius' *fisticula* (5. 7. 2)? At best, superficial philological comments are irrelevant; at worst, they are misleading or erroneous (cf. my remark in "Notes on Palladius 1. 42," *BICS* 18 [1971]: 50, n. 6). W. is generally unhelpful on textual variants. Some which he gives do not require even passing attention in a work of this sort (e.g., Pliny *HN* 31. 27, discussed p. 184, n.—for the *pelvis* it would have been more to the point to compare *Geopon*. 2. 4. 2; or *Moretum* 62, discussed p. 25, n.). At other times we may wonder about the authenticity or the accuracy of an important word (e.g., *festucisque* in Caesar *BG* 4. 17. 4, mentioned p. 6, n., or *serias* in Varro *Rust*. 1. 55. 5, mentioned p. 185, n.). It is nice to have Mynors' emendation *quae* for *quos* in Isidore *Etym.* 20. 14. 13 (p. 56, n., and again p. 99, n.; in the latter case the text gives the reference as 14. 13!), but I am less sure of W.'s defence of *de eo* in Cato *Agr.* 154 (pp. 141, n., 155, n.; Mazzarino's Teubner [1962] has *deco*). I note with pleasure that W. cites (p. 37, n.) S. Hedberg's edition of Columella (Uppsala, 1968); with dismay that he seems to have used older editions (p. 120, citing Columella 4. 4. 2, he has *recumbens* for *recubans*).

W.'s interpretative comments sometimes depart too far from his texts. Columella's *cophini* (11. 3. 51), used for forcing cucumbers, are not necessarily "of a quite different shape and larger dimensions" (p. 74) than those used for carrying dirt or manure, for they are to be filled with earth and carried indoors or outdoors until weather permits the cucumbers to be set in the ground (baskets and all). "The usual conical shape, with flat bases" (p. 73) would suit this purpose well, since cucumbers have a deep root-system. Juvenal's *cophinus* (3. 14) seems out of place here: Forcellini's "dogmatic" definition (which includes the scholiast's comment on this line) does not adequately explain the poet's choice of this word, used only rarely in classical Latin for something other than a container with dirt (W. does not notice the connection with the New Testament κόφινος, but cf. p. 75). A commoner Latin word for "bread basket" (if that is what Juvenal's Jews used their *cophinus* for) is *canistrum*. On this object (p. 63) W. is right about *canistros* = *fiscos* at Palladius 12. 17. 1, but he ought to have made clear that Palladius' source was Greek (cf. *Geopon.* 9. 19. 7, with κύρτους) since this "seems to be the sole instance of the term [*canistrum*] in the agronomists" (it is not: Pallad. 11. 10. 1 *canistris*, based on Columella 12. 52. 10 *fiscis*). For another scholar's warning on W.'s interpretations, see H. W. Pleket, "Technology in the Greco-Roman World: A General Report," ΤΑΛΑΝΤΑ 5 (1973): 45, n. 143.

Many such difficulties may have arisen as this book grew from "an assortment of notes" (p. xi). For *corbis* (pp. 56 ff.) W. cites Palladius 3. 10. 6, but he says that Palladius' *corbicula* "will probably have been only a few inches in diameter." W. did not apparently copy enough onto his notecard, for Palladius goes on to say "quae mensuram pedis vel aliquanto minus circini spatio possit implecti."

I miss some items which might usefully have been included in a book of this sort: e.g., *sabanum* (Pallad. 7. 7. 3), or *vectis* (Cato 28. 2, where it appears side by side with *festuca*, discussed by W. on p. 6). I also miss references to agricultural writers from which we might glean further information: e.g., on *cistella* (pp. 63 ff.) Palladius 4. 10. 35; on *saccus* (pp. 91 ff.) Palladius 3. 25. 11; on *cribrum* (pp. 102 f.) Palladius 3. 25. 6 and 11. 14. 13; on *cribellum* (W. does not mention the diminutive here, although he does so normally) Palladius 3. 24. 6 and 7. 11; on *trulla* (pp. 192 f.) Faventinus 21 and Palladius 1. 13. 2. The last example is, I grant, the plasterer's trowel, but this raises a more general question: how do we distinguish between "farm equipment" and the more general "household equipment" (city dwellers use pots and pans); or should we reject as "agricultural implements" items which are, strictly speaking, the working tools of tradesmen (I try never to be too far from a screwdriver)? Farmers are versatile, as they have to be, and all of our ancient agricultural writers stress the need for equipment on the premises. The specific recommendation to have a *serrula* on hand for pruning does not imply that you won't need a *serra* (and a good deal more often, I should think), but *Agricultural Implements* (pp. 116 ff.) dismisses *serra* very briefly. So here with *trulla*. I do not really blame W. for putting some limits to his task, especially since he could legitimately ask, "Don't you know about saws?" (I would answer, "Enough, I suppose, for my purposes, and I am learning to use a trowel.") I raise the point only to suggest that much further work will be needed for a comprehensive study of ancient tools and technology.

A second general question: are we justified in dealing with "the Roman world" through Latin eyeglasses? It is true that four Latin agricultural treatises have survived more or less intact, whereas the Byzantine *Geoponica* contain no more than the *disiecta membra* of a host of writers who flourished from the second to the sixth centuries after Christ. W. acknowledges (p. 131) that this text has value, but would it not have been desirable to include it among the literary sources?

But now to details. Author and publisher must share the blame where it is impossible to determine whose fault lies behind errors of inaccurate or inconsistent references, or blank spaces in the printed text. I give only examples (and not necessarily the most important or annoying ones).

P. xv: (André title) "*termes de botanique*" (not "*t. botaniques*"). *P. 6:* (Columella reference) 8. 15. 7 (not 8. 5. 7). *P. 14:* cross-reference (to pp. 11–12) missing. *P. 16:* (Bloch in translation): J. E. Anderson, 1967 (see pp. 18, 241). *P. 16: OGV* (not in list of abbreviations) = *The Oxford Book of Greek Verse in Translation*, ed. T. F. Higham and C. M. Bowra (Oxford, 1938). *P. 54:* cross-reference (to p. 88) missing. *P. 38:* (reference to Appendix A) Fig. 60, p. 230 (not Fig. 43). *P. 86:* Pritchett (not Pritchard). *P. 131:* Palladius 1. 18. 2 (not 1. 1. 2).

To summarize: the weaknesses of this work, by and large, are weaknesses of detail. I urge users to be cautious, as scholars must always be with any work of reference. My objections are essentially minor (and pedantic, as often as not); they must not obscure my true evaluation of an important contribution to scholarship, one which I have read with keen interest and no small profit.

R. H. Rodgers
University of California, Berkeley

L. Annaei Senecae "Dialogorum" libri duodecim. Recognovit brevique adnotatione critica instruxit L. D. REYNOLDS. Oxford: Clarendon Press; New York: Oxford University Press, 1977. Pp. xx + 327.

In technical expertise, sound scholarship, and independent judgment this edition lives up to the standard set by Reynolds' *Epistulae Morales* (OCT, 1965). Its virtues far outweigh occasional shortcomings.

"Omnibus apparet codicem Ambrosianum textus Dialogorum fundamentum esse semperque futurum" (p. xviii). The preface of nineteen pages includes a detailed description of this MS. The problem of the *recentiores*, in this case also *deteriores*, has been much debated; R. provides a formidable bibliography extending from Gertz (1874) to Grimal (1969). His own researches lead him to conclude that most of them descend from a copy of the Ambrosianus itself. A much smaller group, from which he selects two witnesses, represents a different tradition, much corrupted and interpolated, but containing some independent truth. These results can the more readily be taken on trust because they appear to have little or no effect upon the text.

This text is not merely superior to any previously available, it is "good enough to live with": i.e., with our present resources it seems unlikely that it can ever be greatly bettered. A comparison of the first fifty pages with the Teubner text by E. Hermes (1905) gives an average of rather less than one divergence per page. Sometimes there is little to choose, but the general superiority of the Oxford text is obvious. In all, this text admits over fifty conjectures made subsequent to 1905, of which the great majority deserve their place. R. himself contributes twenty-three, including a number of combinations or slight improvements (but still improvements) of earlier attempts. In the apparatus, which is of course technically flawless, the *deteriores* are seldom cited except where the Ambrosianus is in trouble. It is hospitable to deserving conjectures and includes at least thirteen more by R.

I have the impression that this critic is happiest with conjectures "of the type commonly called brilliant—neat and pretty changes of a letter or two." Now and again he offers an unacceptable text with nothing in the apparatus to show that it has ever been challenged: so in 4. 15. 1, 6. 26. 4 (where Hermes acknowledged the need for emendation), 7. 16. 2. At 10. 11. 1 the text reads "iam uero cum illos aliqua imbecillitas mortalitatis admonuit, quemadmodum pauentes moriuntur, non tamquam exeant de uita, sed tamquam extrahantur!" People do not ordinarily die (in terror or otherwise) when admonished of mortality by some physical infirmity. A verb is needed after *admonuit.* R. once suggested that it might be *adfligit* or *adfliguntur* (see my "Emendations of Seneca," *CQ* 20 [1970]: 359). Now he seems to think that the problem is solved beyond need for comment by an exclamation point. Perhaps there *is* an exclamation: *quemadmodum pauent!*

I append a few more cavils.

2. 12. 2: "illis talorum nucumue et aeris minuti auaritia est, his auri argentique et *orbium.*" *Orbium* for *urbium* (Ageno) is supported by 12. 11. 6 "aurum argentum et magni leuatique mensarum orbes." But can *orbes* = *mensae* without more aid from the context? Must we not add *mensarum?*

2. 14. 1: tanta quosdam dementia tenet ut sibi contumeliam fieri putent posse a muliere. quid refert quam ⟨beatam⟩ habeant, quot lecticarios habentem, quam oneratas aures, quam laxam sellam?" The supplement *beatam* (*diuitem* vel *nobilem* vel *famosam* Karsten) may have been suggested by my proposal "quam beata, quot lecticarios habente" mentioned in the apparatus. No text which fails to dispose of the insufferable *habeant* ("suspectum," says the apparatus) deserves to be printed. If R. was not inclined to adopt the only conjecture which effectively does that, he would have done better to obelize. An obelus would also have been desirable in 13. 2 on the previous page, where Viansino should not have been followed even "dubitanter."

5. 10. 4: "ille rogari *iniuriam* iudicat, hic non rogari contumeliam." Axelson's *iniuriam* is sense, but the paradosis *inuidiam* is Seneca. Some people feel that to be asked a favor puts them in an invidious position (a refusal may look ungracious or stingy). For *inuidia* thus, compare Martial 3. 21, "Proscriptum famulus seruauit fronte notatus. / non fuit haec domini vita, sed inuidia."

6. 1. 2: "fudistique lacrimas palam et gemitus deuorasti quidem, non tamen hilari fronte texisti." "Locus obscurior," says the apparatus. One hardly sees why. Marcia wept openly for her father (a victim of Tiberius), and though she did not audibly *groan,* she made no effort to look cheerful.

6. 3. 2: "nec plus doluit [*sc.* Livia] quam aut honestum erat Caesare aut aequum saluo." *Aequum saluo* (Abel) for *aequo maluo* is fine as far as it goes, but what is the meaning of the clause? "Quam aut honestum aut aequum erat Caesare saluo"? Surely not. Sense calls for something like "quam aut honestum erat Caesare ⟨uidente⟩ aut aequum saluo." The adjectives mean "seemly" and "fair"; *Caesare* = *Augusto.*

6. 14. 2: "Bibulus . . . qui toto honoris sui anno ⟨in⟩ inuidiam collegae domi latuerat." *In* (Thörnell) gives the right sense, but classical stylists tended to avoid such assonance. They did not write *in initio*, *in iniuriam* (the conjectural reading in Trajan's letter to Pliny [10. 109] is not affected), or *in inuidiam*. They did write *ad invidiam*, as the *Thesaurus* testifies.

10. 4. 6: "nondum horum effugerat insidias: filia et tot nobiles iuuenes adulterio velut sacramento adacti iam infractam aetatem territabant *Iullusque* et iterum timenda cum Antonio mulier." *Iullus* (Waltz) for *plus* (championed by Grimal) is far from an improvement on *Paul(l)us* (Rubenius). Why mention Jullus Antonius twice? The conspiracy of L. Aemilius Paullus is noticed by Suetonius (*Aug.* 19). Either way Seneca has made one of his historical gaffes. He took Jullus, who in fact was adulterously involved with the elder Julia, for the husband of the younger, who was in fact married to Paullus.

11. 9. 9: "omnibus illo nobis commune est iter: quid fata deflemus? non reliquit ille nos sed antecessit. est, mihi crede, magna felicitas in ipsa *necessitate* moriendi. nihil ne in totum quidem diem certi est: quis in tam obscura et inuoluta ueritate diuinat utrumne fratri tuo mors inuiderit an consuluerit?" R., like some of his predecessors, reads *necessitate* (Heylbut) for *felicitate*. It is not clear why there is great happiness in the necessity of dying. Reasons can be imagined, but they have nothing to do with this context (it would be different if Seneca had written *magna consolatio*). I suspect that the paradosis is right after all. Polybius' brother was fortunate in his dying because, as Seneca has just said, "antequam quicquam ex suo fauore fortuna mutaret, stantem adhuc illam et munera plena manu congerentem reliquit." Seneca means that a man is lucky indeed if he dies lucky.

9. 17. 8 and 10. 8. 2: I doubt the need for R.'s exclusions; indeed, in the latter place *aegros* is helpful as showing that *mortis periculum* refers to sickness.

In attractiveness of format and meticulous printing this volume conforms to the currently high standard of its series. A chapter number has fallen out on page 172, and there is a small lacuna in the last line of page 44 (apparatus). The name of E. A. Lowe, honorably mentioned on page vi, is misspelled in a footnote. For *in Beneuento* on the same page the printer can hardly be held responsible.

D. R. Shackleton Bailey
Harvard University

The Princeton Encyclopedia of Classical Sites. Edited by RICHARD STILLWELL, WILLIAM L. MACDONALD, and MARIAN HOLLAND MCALLISTER. Princeton, N.J.: Princeton University Press, 1976. Pp. xxii + 1019 + 24 pp. of maps. $125.00.

This book brings to fruition a project vast in concept, international in scope. It covers, and pinpoints on twenty maps, nearly 3,000 sites, dating from 750 B.C. to A.D. 365, described by 398 contributors from 17 countries. Nearly all the important sites are described by their excavators, or by persons of recognized expertise: Baatz does the Saalburg; Bass, shipwrecks; Bean, Turkish sites; Broneer, Isthmia; Lady Brogan, the Libyan hinterland; F. E. Brown, Cosa; Caskey, Ceos; Castagnoli, Lavinium; Cunliffe, Fishbourne; Doppelfeld, Cologne; C. W. J. Eliot, Attic sites; Erim, Aphrodisias; Euzennat, Moroccan sites; Février, Le Glay, Souville, and Charles Picard, sites in Algeria and Tunisia; Frere, British sites; Gentili, Piazza Armerina; the late Michael Gough, Cilician sites; Nicholas Hammond, Albanian sites; Hanfmann, Sardis; Hull, Colchester; Joffroy, Chatillon; the late Dame Kathleen Kenyon, Jerusalem; Phyllis Lehmann, Samothrace; Meiggs, Ostia and Portus; Mylonas, Eleusis; the late Ernest Nash, Rome; Petsas, Pella; Pippidi, Histria; the Richardsons, Etruscan and Italian sites; L. Robert, Claros; Henry Robinson, Corinth; Salmon, Samnite sites; Schönberger and Von Petrikovits, the German *limes;* Scranton, Kenchreai; Stillwell, Morgantina; Travlos, Athens; Ward Perkins, Libyan sites; Donald White, Cyrene; Wilkes, Dalmatian sites; Yalouris, Olympia; and the late Rodney Young, Gordion.

Twenty-five long and informative articles account for sixteen percent of the space: Akragas (by Orlandini), Antioch (by Lassus), Aphrodisias, Athens, Byzantium (a palmary article by W. L. MacDonald), Corinth, Cyrene, Delos (by Bruneau), Delphi (by Roux), Eleusis, Ephesus (by Mitsopoulou-Leon), Epidauros (by Yalouris), Kos (by Picozzi), the various *limites*, Lugdunum (by Le Glay), Miletus (by Kleiner), Olympia, Ostia, Palmyra (by Rey-Coquais), Pergamon (by Schäfer), Pompeii (a splendid article by L. Richardson), Rhodes (by Wycherley), Rome (in sixteen columns, a miracle of compression), Timgad (by Lassus), and Vienne (by Le Glay).

The general reader will often find his knowledge of these sites brought up to date with the most recent scholarly discussion. The bibliography of the Delos article contains a useful table of contents to the multivolume *Explorations de Délos*. Under Hildesheim, we learn that the silver treasure is firmly dated too late to have belonged to the ill-starred Quinctilius Varus. Iris Love writes on Knidos without claiming to have found the head of Aphrodite. Nash on Rome reminds us that the columns in the Via delle Botteghe Oscure belong not to Bellona but to the Lares Permarini, and updates his bibliography beyond *Pictorial Dictionary of Ancient Rome*[2] (New York, 1968). Tusa on Selinus assigns Temple C to Apollo, A to Leto, O to Artemis, G to Zeus, F to Athena, E to Hera, and D to Aphrodite. On the other hand, some general books (all with plans or illustrations) escaped the bibliographic net or appeared too late to be noticed: V. Karageorgis, *The Ancient Civilization of Cyprus* (Geneva and New York, 1969); R. F. Hoddinott, *Bulgaria in Antiquity* (London, 1975); J. von Elbe, *Roman Germany* (Mainz, 1975); R. J. A. Wilson, *Roman Remains in Britain* (London, 1975).

Although the allotment of space seems on the whole just, minor sites in France are in my judgment overrepresented. Space saved here might have made more room for some or all of the following omissions: Arae Philaenorum, Bu Ngem, Cartennae, Cydamus, Deva (Romania), El Khroub, Fontaines Salées, Gemellae, Hippo Diarrhytus, Kbor Klib, Kerkouane, the *limes* in the Maghreb and Tripolitania, Milev, Munda, Sarmazigethusa Dacica, Thabraca, Thapsus, Thubursicum Bure, Uchi Maius, Ucubi (Tunisia).

On occasion contributors fail to reveal the subjects of works of art or the contents of documents—e.g., the archaic metopes from the Foce del Sele, the Idalion and Valentia "tablets," the Sarsina "deposit," the Urba mosaic, the reliefs on the Porte Noire at Besançon. Key figures or facts are omitted from accounts of sites —e.g., Protagoras from Abdera; the Pharos, one of the wonders of the world, from Alexandria; St. Paul from Damascus; the swine from Gadara; Vergil's education from Mantua, Cremona, and Milan; the cause of Scipio's exile from Liternum; Nero's doctor's wall from Massilia; Prosper Mérimée from Saintes; Thales and

Hippodamus from Miletus; Sappho's brother from Naucratis; the soldier who took Decebalus' head to Rome from Cavala; Cicero's slave Tiro from Patras; the battle from Pharsalus; the symbolic significance of its name from Philippi; the importance of its aqueduct from Segovia; Rupert Brooke from Skyros; the uniqueness of its three Capitolia from Sbeitla; the magnificent silver tetradrachms from Syracuse; the Warrior of Capestrano from Chieti; the colonization of Cyrene from Thera; and Horace from Venusia. There is a regrettable tendency to play down picturesqueness: the fact that Labraunda's tame fish wore gold necklaces and earrings (!), and came when called; the British vertebra in the Dorchester museum, with a Roman soldier's spear point stuck in it; the graffito of Phidias from Olympia; the production of the *Bacchae* at Pella, and the death there of Euripides, torn apart by dogs; and the vignette of Petra, "rose-red city half as old as time."

It is sad to have to report that this whole splendid concept has been ill served by its translators, especially from French and Italian. Minor typographical errors have been reported to the editors privately; some that might mislead the unwary are here recorded. References are by lemma, then (where necessary) by page, column, and line number (the last always counted from the top of the column).

Acholla 6 b 48: for "Revel" read "Thiasos." *Ad Confluentes 8 b 41:* for "Franconian" read "Frankish." *Althiburos 45 a 6:* not "Berger" but "Berber." *Ammaedara 50 a 31:* not "Medjerba" but "Medjerda." *50 a 32:* the page number of the *CRAI* paper should be 221. *Antioch:* add to the bibliography at 63 b 37 Irving Lavin's magnificently illustrated account of the mosaics, with parallels, *DOP* 17 (1963): 181–286. *Ardea 85 b 17:* and B. Tilly, *Vergil's Latium* (Oxford, 1947); in general, foreign contributors neglect bibliography in English. *Arelate 87 a 46:* add mention of a replica of the shield inscribed with Augustus' virtues, from the cryptoportico. *Asculum Picenum 99 b 71:* by "reticulate road" is meant "grid of streets." *Athens 107 a 39:* mention of Aristeides is omitted in the historical account; *109 a 44:* for "the Andronikos of Kyrrhos" read "the Tower of the Winds, by A. of K." *Augusta Emerita 114 b 66:* for "Otto" read "Otho." *Aventicum 131 b 35:* add the gold bust of M. Aurelius. *Banasa 141 a 39:* for "right of the city" read "citizenship." *Barcino 143 a 18:* for "had been surrounded" read "was then surrounded." *Bulla Regia 171 b 40:* for "Amphitrite or Neptune" read "A. and N." *Buthrotum 175 a 52:* for "Pompeius Atticus" read "Pomponius A." *Caesena 183 b 50:* for "epithet of a curve" read "the epithet 'curva.' " *Calama 185 a 29:* for "statute" read "status." (The translators are particularly ignorant about Roman constitutional terms.) *Cannae 192 a 60:* add vol. and p. of De Sanctis: vol. 3.2, pp. 60–64, 131–66. *Carnuntum 199 b 8:* "Heidentor" does not mean "giant gate." *Carthage 202 a 46:* add the mosaic of Dominus Julius in Bardo, and the horse-mosaic at the Antiquarium. *Centum Cellae 212 b 58–59:* for "Constance" read "Constantius." *Cerro de los Santos 214 a 39:* of the 300 sculptures, many were fakes. *Cirta 225 a 444:* for "embossments" read "rustication" or "drafting"; correct also at Plataia 717 b 10. The translators have constant trouble with this term, and, like at least 75 other technical words, it does not occur in the glossary. *225 a 31:* Sidi M'Cid, it should be noted, is the name of a bridge. *Claros 226 b 34:* the bibliography should cite G. E. Bean, *Aegean Turkey* (London, 1967), pp. 190–96. *Conimbriga 237 a 30:* the Cantabri are not a family but a tribe. *Cyrene 255 b:* to the bibliography add S. Stucchi, *Architettura Cirenaica* (Rome, 1975). *Daulis 259 b 12:* for "Placeière" read "Flacelière." *Delos 263 b 9:* Stesileos is not a private organization but the head of one; *51:* for "Den of Cythnos" read "Cave of K." *Dodona 280 b 7:* for "Tauzenorakel" read "Tauben-." *Ebora 290 b 44:* for "García y

Bellido" read "García y. B." *Entremont 306 a 3:* for "crouching" read "in tailor or Buddha pose" (correct also under Glanon, 356 b 37). *Ephesos 308 b 34:* there is also a scene from an *Iphigeneia; 309 a 7:* for "isolating" read "insulating." *Eporedia 315 b 42:* add U. Ewins, "The Early Colonisation of Cisalpine Gaul," *PBSR* 20 (1952): 70 ff. *Forum Julii 336 b 19:* for "Giapidi" read "Iapyges"; so also under Iulium Carnicum 422 b 31, and Tergeste 894 a 56. *Gadir 341 b 24:* for "Galbus" read "Balbus." *Grand 365 a 36:* note that this Roman mosaic is the largest in Europe. *Gyphtokastro 369 a 21:* a second edition of Martin appeared in Paris, 1974. *Hadria 370 a 47:* for "Malcia" read "Maecia"; *48:* for "another colony, but of 'Roman right' " read "another Roman colony." *Hadrian's Wall 371 b 4:* no hint of the importance of Housesteads. *Heloros 382 a 48:* the Supplement to *EAA* appeared in 1970. *Herculaneum 388 a 26:* the bibliography should mention J. J. Deiss, *Herculaneum: Italy's Buried Treasure* (New York, 1966). *Hippo Regius 394 b 57:* for "Zarytos" read "Diarrhytos." *Incoronata 410 a 33:* for "pyre-shaped" read "pear-shaped." *Industria 410 b 43:* for "Erwin" read "Ewins" (correct also under Vardagate 954 b 55). *Iomnium 414 a 50:* correct references to *MélRom* are to 65 (1953): 127–28; 67 (1955): 127–48. *Ithaca 421 a 42:* for "Proci" read "suitors." *Iulia Traducta 422 a 27:* Zelis is not the modern Algiers, but lay near Tingis. *Jebel Oust 425 b 55: IMT* (*Inventaire des mosaïques de Tunisie*) is not in the list of abbreviations. *Kerkyra 450 a 17:* for "Kapo" read "Kato"; *451 a 36:* before "94" insert "*BCH.*" *Koroni 463 b 40:* "E.M." is Ernst Meyer. *Limes of Djerdap 511 a 49:* for "Anasthasia" read "Anastasius." *Lucus Augusti 528 a 60:* for "Celeste" read "Caelestis." *Lugdunum 529 a 42:* the year is not 117 but 177. *Lykosoura 537 b 18:* for Δεσταιvας read Δεσποίνας. *Macomades 540 a 18:* for "recovered" read "taken away." *Matauros 559 a 8:* for "N. W. van Buren, 'New Letters' " read "A. W. van Buren, 'Newsletter' "; *564 a 63:* for "Massilian" read "Massylian." *Melita 569 a 4:* for "bishop's see from the suffragio" read "seat of a suffragan bishop." *Mogontiacum 587 a 44:* the Eichelstein is a large mausoleum, not a tombstone. *Mont-Lassois 593 a 33:* for "vial" read "*phiale*"; for "navel" read "boss." *Mt. Oeta 598 a 36:* the *Kl. Pauly* entry is to be found under "Oite." *Naxos 612 a 31:* for "Horn. *Hymni* I" read "*Hom. Hymn.* III." *Nemausus 617 a 14:* for "Plotinus" read "Plotina." *Novar 630 b 32:* by "colonial village" is meant "seaside resort"; so also under Tipasa 925 a 43. *Olbia 642 b 1:* for "Mysia" read "Moesia." *Olbia (Sardinia) 643 b 35:* for "Foci" read "Phocaeans"; *40:* Nero's mistress was Acte, not Atte. *Oplontis:* most scholars do not agree with De Franciscis' identification of the site. *Oxyrhynchus 663 b 21:* the series reached vol. 39 in 1972. *Parndorf 677 b 34:* for "public" read "imperial." *Paros 678 b 59:* for "Dris" read "Dryos." *Passau 679 a 42:* for "Boiodunum" read "Boiodurum." *Peiraeus 684 a 43:* for "GommeI" read "Gomme I"; there are no illustrations. *Pella 685 a 31:* by "exaggeration" is meant "minimizing." *Pergamon 691 b 16:* "two-part latrine" means for ladies and gentlemen. *Philae 704 a 70:* "Philometer" refers to Ptolemy Ph., and the preferred spelling is Philometor. *Piazza Armerina 711 b 43:* no mention of Carandini's different dating of the mosaics (after 320). *Pollentia* (Italy) *722 b 1:* for "Hygenus" read "Hyginus." *Pontchevron 727 b 19:* Genabum is not Gien but Orléans. *Portus 731 b 17:* the bibliography should mention H. Thylander, *Inscriptions du Port d'Ostie*, 2 vols. (Rome, 1952). *Potentia 734 a 39:* for "derived from" read "planted in." *Rome 765 b 67:* Augustus was not born on the Palatine; *769 b 6:* mention of the subterranean basilica at Porta Maggiore is omitted. *Romula-Malva:* the identification of the site is not generally recognized. *Rotomagus 773 a 24:* for "Suindinum" read "Subdinum." *Samos 802 b 50:* altars "exceptional with respect to the axis" are off-center. *Sanxay 807 a 58:* it is worth noting that the ancient theater had parking space. *Segesta 817 a 64:* for "W" Mediterranean read "E." *Sinope 842 a 61:* for "red earth" read "ruddle." *Sphakteria 857 a 4:* the bibliography should mention A. W. Gomme, *Historical Commentary on Thucydides*, vol. 3 (Oxford, 1956) pp. 482–89. *Stabiae 858 b 56:* for "Sannio" read "Sarno." *Sumelocenna 868 a 34: ORL* (*Der obergermanisch-rätische Limes des Römerreiches*) is not in the list of abbreviations. *Surrentum:* the bibliography has been left untranslated.

Syracuse 873 b 54: the bibliography should mention M. I. Finley, *Ancient Sicily* (New York, 1968). *Tarraco 883 a 52:* for "Palatine" read "Palacio." *Tegea 890 a 1:* for "peristalsis" read "peristasis." *Tergeste 894 b 37:* by "Knidia" is meant the Aphrodite of Knidos. *Thamugadi 899 b 30:* for 200 colonists read 12,000; *901 b 60:* this new inventory of mosaics is buried in the bibliography, see under S. Germain. *Thugga 919 a 13:* for "Immurita" read "Immunitas." *Tibiscum 921 a 31:* the correct page reference to *Oraşe* is 37–42. *Tipasa 925 a 62 and b 57:* to "Tomb of the Christian" add "Woman"; correct also at Hippo Regius 395 a 21. *Tomis 928 b 18:* for "Ovid came . . . to die" read "Ovid came . . . and died there seven years later." *Troizen 936 a 69:* the Themistokles decree is not universally considered a fourth-century forgery. *Tropaeum Traiani 937 b 45:* for "3800 names . . . are inscribed" read "3800 names . . . were inscribed." *Tuscana 941 b 46:* for "dado" read "cube." *Uthina 949 a 51:* for "Mornay" read "Mornag." *Utica 950 a 55:* by "historiated" capitals are meant capitals with human heads. *Vasio 956 b 42:* for "Diadoumena" read "Diadoumenos." *Velvina 962 a 61:* by "Fraser and Lorat" is meant Fraser's review of Lorat. *Verona 969 a 65:* for "Gabii" read "Gavii." *Volaterrae 987 b 62:* for "Cic. *Att.* 16. 4" read "16. 8. 3"; for "owners" read "owner."

Paul MacKendrick
University of Wisconsin

Athenian Black Figure Vases. By JOHN BOARDMAN. New York: Oxford University Press, 1974. Pp. 252; 383 ills. in text. $10.00.

Boardman is already a veteran at handbook writing (*Greek Art* [New York, 1964]; *Greek Art and Architecture* [New York, 1967]; *Pre-Classical: From Crete to Archaic Greece* [London, 1967]; *Greek Burial Customs* [Ithaca, 1971]). Here he has managed to put quite a lot of information into 120 pages of text; the rest of the book consists of photographs, charts, and indexes.

The word "Athenian" in his title, rather than the usual "Attic," implies no restriction on the contents of his survey. He prefers the term "Athenian" because, as he observes, the distribution of pottery finds within Attica cannot serve as a criterion for locating workshops outside Athens—although he himself admits that certain early black-figure painters are represented only at Vari, and that there is evidence for local workshops in other townships such as Eleusis and Brauron: see page 182 and figure 317.

In the preface B. says that he has made parts of his book more archaeological than art historical in the interest of providing general information for his readers. Yet "it has seemed best [but why?] to omit . . . any detailed consideration of the techniques of potting and painting" (p. 7). In fact he gives no description at all of the artists' technique in applying the unique clay color or of the subtleties of firing. Consequently the beginner who has not read J. V. Noble's *Techniques of Painted Attic Pottery* (New York, 1965; it is mentioned in B.'s bibliography) would get the impression that the Athenians splashed black paint on the figures. All B. says about technique is that "it involves *painting figures in black silhouette*, incising all linear detail so that the pale clay shows through the black, and adding, if required, touches of red and white paint, all applied before the vase was fired" (p. 9; my emphasis). The words italicized are misleading, since the figures were not painted in black, but in a concentrated clay color that looked only a little darker than the terracotta background, which was painted with a diluted slip. Only after controlled firing did the figures turn black; there are several examples in which, because the firing was unsuccessful, they did not turn black. This information is important for both archaeological and art historical purposes. The black-figure technique of the ancient vase painters was a difficult achievement, which has been investigated and understood in detail only recently. It is responsible for the everlasting, "built-in," black color of the vases.

B.'s short but lively introduction (pp. 9–13) summarizes the state which modern study of these vases and of their potters and pot-painters has reached. In the next six chapters he examines the development of black-figure styles from the seventh century B.C. to the latest examples in the middle of the fifth century; a special chapter is devoted to the Panathenaic amphoras. A chapter on miscellaneous small groups of vases follows, then others on "Shapes, Names and Functions," "Relative and Absolute Chronology," and "General Decoration." The last two chapters deal briefly with iconography—mythic, religious, and other.

The text, though concise, is very informative. Thanks in part to B.'s habit of continual reference to illustrations, it gives the impression of being a series of well-planned lectures with slides; the book is probably the outcome of the course on Attic black figure which B. has been giving at Oxford for many years. There is little space for discussion of controversies or for presentation of new views, but the information is reliable and up to date, and it includes useful historical notes here and there.

B. naturally has to avoid the use of Greek in a handbook, and so he does not reproduce the inscriptions found on vases. He does, however, note that many vases were signed. Unfortunately, he does not always say which ones, and when he does discuss a particular work of a particular painter (e.g., Sophilos on pp. 18–19), he does not say whether the vase is actually signed—and whether as "painted by" (*egrapse*) or "made by" (*epoese*)—or whether it is merely attributed. In the captions of the photographs also, though he sometimes speaks of a vase as being signed, he does not distinguish how. Occasionally the inscription may be legible in the photograph (as in figure 25), but these days not every student can read Greek, and certainly not archaic *boustrophedon*. It would have been useful to have consistently singled out the signed vases, especially those signed "painted by," because one must form an idea of a painter's style first of all from the vases which were certainly painted by him. Attributions of unsigned vases may be disputed and are often changed.

B. gives a good account of influences between one workshop and another, and of influences on exported wares. He offers some good short characterizations of individual artists like this on Amasis: "through temperament or training he was able to add something of delicacy and wit to a style which seemed always to work against these qualities" (p. 56). The sections on the "Age of Red Figure," on the "bilinguists" who used both black-figure and red-figure techniques, and on the different classes of cups are lucidly written and informed. Yet of necessity they are concise, where the material to be covered is vast, with the result that some artists are mentioned only with a reference to an illustration, or with no reference at all (e.g., Skythes, p. 106). The compressed presentation is likely to be confusing for a beginner, although it makes a useful précis for more knowledgeable students. B.'s chapters on iconography are not as comprehensive as his discussion of styles, as one may see from his section on satyrs and comic choruses (he might have added to the bibliography here G. M. Sifakis' *Parabasis and Animal Choruses* [London, 1971]). For representations of runners and other athletes, I would like to call attention to two studies written at the University of Chicago by Brian Legakis, his 1970 M.A. thesis "The Foot Race in Greek Painting," and his 1977 doctoral dissertation "Athletic Contests in Archaic Greek Art." But on the whole, B.'s bibliography is very up to date.

The book is well produced. There are only a few inconsistencies in the Greek terminology (e.g., on p. 113 "hydriae" but "pelikai"; p. 186 "hydriai"); the Latinized form "amphorae" is used throughout. The illustrations provided are numerous and interesting, though not always good. They give an adequate idea of shapes, styles, and iconography; but one could wish for a few enlargements and figures which would show the fineness of line in details.

In sum, Boardman has written a useful short manual for classical students and teachers. But if the purpose of the book is, as the publisher's advertisement on the flap of the dust jacket declares, to enable readers to study the many aspects of vase painting without having to resort to other books, then it has not entirely succeeded. Its compression and scholarly detail make it difficult to read for a beginner or amateur, and the photographs do not provide an adequate basis for the study of artists' hands. But after all, no chapter of art history can be presented, even in elementary form, through only a single book. Boardman has contributed something better than the equivalent chapters in R. M. Cook's more general manual *Greek Painted Pottery* (London, 1961). The book digests a lot of recent research, brings everything together from the viewpoint of an expert, and is a real bargain for the price.

Theodora Hadzisteliou Price
Naperville, Illinois

Science and Philosophy in Aristotle's Biological Works. By ANTHONY PREUS. Studien und Materialien zur Geschichte der Philosophie, kleine Reihe, vol. 1. Hildesheim and New York: Georg Olms, 1975. Pp. ix + 404. Mk. 88.

Although it has long been the fashion to refer to Aristotle as a biologist, it has been less fashionable actually to read his more strictly biological works. This situation is gradually being rectified (to the great benefit of Aristotelian studies), and Preus's volume is a case in point.

The book centers primarily upon the *Parts of Animals* and the *Generation of Animals*, works in which, P. rightly observes, "the philosophical concepts and the observational data meet" (p. 1). It is somewhat surprising, however, to find no mention of the important methodological passage at *De generatione animalium* 760b28 ff. (on the generation of bees): "the facts, however, have not been sufficiently grasped; if ever they are, then credit must be given rather to observation than to theories, and to theories only if what they affirm agrees with the observed facts" (trans. A. Platt [Oxford, 1912]). It is certainly true that Aristotle's discussion of animal generation, for instance, is conducted within the context of matter and form and that his association of female with matter and male with form has metaphysical (and probably ethical) roots. P., however, tends to imply that

Aristotle arrived at an account of animal generation with which he was satisfied. In my view, the fact that he employs more than one explanatory model in, say, his attempt to account for the transfer of soul (the contribution of the male being compared first to the fig juice which causes milk to set, and then to the act of the carpenter who shapes a bed from the wood) indicates that he is not entirely satisfied with either. P. thinks that the explanatory models are a *cause* of some of Aristotle's difficulties, rather than aids to explanation. But surely no particular model was *forced* upon Aristotle; he chose them himself for what each could contribute to the reconcilement of philosophy and observation.

The real virtue of P.'s book consists in his having made a serious study, on the whole very well documented, of a number of crucial topics in Aristotle's biology, and in having demonstrated that these topics are important for the general study of Aristotle. He has, for instance, made a detailed examination of the complex topic of necessity (deciding that conditional necessity is the kind most relevant to biological explanation) and of the nature of Aristotelian teleology. With respect to the latter, he sensibly concludes that "entities are to be comprehended in terms of themselves and not in terms of something else" (p. 249). Furthermore, expressions such as "Nature does nothing in vain" (P. makes a special study of these) are to be understood as references to purposive process on the part of biological individuals and not in any theological or transcendental sense.

It interested me that P. referred, in the final sentence of his book, to the *charm* of Aristotle's biology. Charm it certainly has, and it is to P.'s great credit that he has conveyed this quality with considerable success.

The index of passages, partly, I should judge, because of publisher's restrictions, is so constructed as to be almost useless.

Rosamond Kent Sprague
University of South Carolina

Timoleon and the Revival of Greek Sicily 344–317 B.C. By R. J. A. TALBERT. Cambridge Classical Studies. Cambridge and New York: Cambridge University Press, 1974. Pp. xii + 235. $15.00 (in U.S.A.).

This is an excellent book, although not for beginners. Its readers would do well to come equipped with a good knowledge of both Plutarch's and Diodorus' accounts of the career of Timoleon; acquaintance with a modern synthesis on the same subject will not be amiss either. There are some petty annoyances which will confront the reader, but they do not detract from the book's solid merit. The book is a revised dissertation for the University of Cambridge, and was originally conceived as a commentary on Plutarch's *Life of Timoleon.* Talbert judged that a true biography was impossible to write in view of the dearth of evidence, and ended up with a series of interconnected studies of the main problems relating to Timoleon's career. Such an organization inevitably entails repetition, but it seems that the author has repeated himself more frequently than necessary. The chapter dealing with "Military Studies" (pp. 52–77) is particularly flagrant in this respect. Repetition is more the fault of the writer than of the copy editor, but the latter is mainly to be credited for the fact that it is always "the R. Crimisus" (and similarly for other rivers), the site of Timoleon's most important battle, never "the River

Crimisus," or the most natural and simple form, "the Crimisus." And does the English language now boast a verb "to tirade" (p. 22)? The date 317 B.C. in the title marks, of course, the beginning of Agathocles' regime and of the overthrow of Timoleon's settlement.

But putting aside minor vexations, one can surely admit that T.'s book is an important advance in the study of Timoleon. Naturally T. disagrees not infrequently with his immediate predecessor in English, H. D. Westlake, and he regularly rejects the extravagances of interpretation found in M. Sordi's work on Timoleon. T.'s own judgment is cool and balanced: he eschews farfetched theories; and, if this conservatism frequently produces a note of uncertainty about the solutions of various problems, he regularly contributes something, even if it is less than a final solution. He begins with a discussion of the extant ancient accounts. Not unexpectedly, he fails to find the ultimate sources of Plutarch and Diodorus, but he does offer valuable criticism of existing theories. Plutarch's account is more hagiography even than moral biography; it is not T.'s fault therefore that we are left wondering how it was that late in life a relatively undistinguished (as far as we can tell) Corinthian was able to show himself a first-rate statesman and general, and to become the greatest benefactor that Greek Sicily was ever to know in antiquity. Since this is the sort of question that Plutarch ordinarily tries to answer when he can, we may assume that the information was not available to him either. After all, it explains nothing to say that Timoleon (or any one else) was a "late bloomer."

Historians of antiquity (especially since Rostovtzeff) are always lauding the use of archaeology in combination with literary sources, but in actual fact, apart from details, we do not very often practice what we preach. Hence it is a welcome contribution when T. is able to show how archaeology and the literary texts confirm each other on the subject of Timoleon's benefits to Sicily, increased prosperity and trade during the period, the importation of colonists from the mother country, and the rebuilding of cities and towns, many of which had lain more or less desolate since the terrible destruction wrought by the Carthaginians in 406 and 405 B.C. (pp. 146–60). One wishes for some illustrations of these matters, but, in view of the high cost of books nowadays, it is better not to press the point.

Stewart Irvin Oost
University of Chicago

The Economy of the Roman Empire: Quantitative Studies. By RICHARD DUNCAN-JONES. Cambridge and New York: Cambridge University Press, 1974. Pp. xvi + 396; 17 tables in text. $22.50.

At present a fashionable subject for historical research is "quantitative history"; it is to be expected that the study of ancient history will by no means be exempt from this trend. Not that such an approach to the study of ancient Greece and Rome is new: one has only to remember such works as Beloch's *Bevölkerung* and Frank's *Economic Survey* in past generations. But the fact remains that ancient statistics are relatively scarce and frequently untrustworthy (especially as transmitted in literary works). Duncan-Jones is usually aware of this problem, as the numerous qualifications he introduces into his reports and analyses of figures regularly show. In general, one can only laud the caution with which he proceeds.

The book deals almost exclusively with the western half of the empire (especially Italy and Africa) during the Principate. It begins with an interesting analysis, correcting past discussions, of the finances of the younger Pliny, and goes on to discuss the economics of agriculture, especially as deducible from Columella. It is worth noting here that the analysis of Columella (pp. 43–44, 45) bears out M. I. Finley's recent strictures (in his Sather Lectures, *The Ancient Economy* [Berkeley, 1973]) on the rudimentary and quite inadequate notions the ancients had of cost accounting. Next come discussions of prices and price levels in Africa and Italy. Much of this section is not readable in the usual sense, but the annotated collections of prices will be very useful for reference. Since not only here but throughout the book much of the evidence comes from inscriptions, the lack of an epigraphical index is most unfortunate. Note, however, the interesting discussion of prices in the novel (pp. 238–56, *Historia Apollonii Tyriensis*, as well as Petronius and Apuleius). Contrary to previous writers, D.-J. demonstrates that little reliance can be placed on these figures; they are as fictional as their contexts. Then there are some remarks on demography and the size of cities, followed by an important and careful study of the *alimenta*. Slips seem uncommon. The reviewer would be more cautious in accepting ancient estimates of the fortunes of very wealthy Romans (pp. 343–44). Fortunes estimated at three or four hundred million sesterces are particularly suspect; these numbers probably mean no more than we do when we say that so-and-so is a multimillionaire (cf. "The Career of M. Antonius Pallas," *AJP* 79 [1958]: 128, n. 57).

Even today some scholars think that the way to compare prices between one age and another is to translate the money terms into gold. D.-J.'s procedure of translating such terms into the amount of wheat a given sum would buy (pp. 4–5) is far more significant (in fact, one may say that using gold equivalents is both meaningless and misleading—though even wheat may mislead, for the value of cereals to the ancient Mediterranean diet was far greater than it has been in other times and places; the cost of living for a family of, say, four during a given time interval is a better standard, if the information exists).

At least once D.-J. lapses into anachronism: "To some extent the proliferation of town monuments was the result of Roman liking for the grandiose, rather than the fulfilment of genuine social needs" (p. 260). But there is no reason to understand what our age calls "social needs" as being the same throughout all history. Most medievalists, for example, would concede that the great cathedrals of the High Middle Ages, built from relatively small resources, were nonetheless constructed to fill a keenly felt social need of the time and place. And so the possibility should at least be envisaged that, mutatis mutandis, Roman grandiosity also filled a social need of its time and place. It should be otiose to remark that a fundamental point concerning the historian's understanding of any past society is involved.

Nevertheless, this is a good, careful book from which any student of the Principate will profit.

Stewart Irvin Oost
University of Chicago

Political Intelligence in Classical Greece. By CHESTER G. STARR. Mnemosyne, suppl. 31. Leyden: E. J. Brill, 1974. Pp. vii + 48. Fl. 18.

Probably almost every instructor of graduate students in almost every subject from time to time reminds them that the most important single aspect of successful research is learning to ask oneself the right questions. Certainly C. G. Starr has shown over and over again in his published works that he knows how to ask the right questions. It would seem that no one before Starr has thought to ask himself the questions: how did the Greeks collect political intelligence, and what did they do with it once they had it?

S. assembles and interprets the evidence that intelligence was gathered from spies, deserters, traitors, cavalry patrols, ambassadors, merchants, and aristocrats (with their connections across city-state boundaries). Councils, assemblies, executives, and politicians evaluated the data thus obtained. A minor regret: S. does not define "intelligence," but he means information about diplomatic, military, and political (in the narrow sense) matters. Technology changed so slowly in antiquity that collecting information on that subject was seldom important. A major regret: S., as his title declares, did not go on to study the Hellenistic Age or Rome, although occasionally comparative examples are taken from those very similar times and places.

Stewart Irvin Oost
University of Chicago

BOOKS RECEIVED

[Not all works submitted can be reviewed, but those relating to the subject matter of this journal are regularly listed under "Books Received." Offprints from periodicals and parts of books will not be listed unless they are published (sold) separately. Books submitted are not returnable.]

Argos: Revista de la Asociación Argentina de Estudios Clásicos (AADEC), año 1, no. 1. Buenos Aires: Asociación Argentina de Estudios Clásicos, 1977. Pp. 95 + 1.

AUSTIN, M. M., and VIDAL-NAQUET, P. *Economic and Social History of Ancient Greece: An Introduction.* Translated and revised by M. M. AUSTIN. Berkeley and Los Angeles: University of California Press, 1977. Pp. xv + 397; 4 maps in text. First English language edition 1977; originally published in France as *Économies et sociétés en Grèce ancienne* by Librairie Armand Colin, Paris (first edition 1972, second edition 1973).

BARNES, JONATHAN; SCHOFIELD, MALCOLM; SORABJI, RICHARD (eds.). *Articles on Aristotle, 2: Ethics and Politics.* Edited by JONATHAN BARNES, MALCOLM SCHOFIELD, RICHARD SORABJI. New York: St. Martin's Press, 1978. Pp. xiv + 254 + frontispiece. $19.95.

BENGTSON, HERMANN. *Griechische Geschichte von den Anfängen bis in die römische Kaiserzeit.* Handbuch der Altertumswissenschaft, sec. 3, part 4. 5., durchgesehene und ergänzte Auflage. Munich: Verlag C. H. Beck, 1977. Pp. xix + 633 + 2 + 11 folding maps; 1 map in text. Mk. 84.

BERTELLI, LUCIO. *Historia e Methodos: Analisi critica e topica politica nel secondo libro della "Politica" di Aristotele.* Historia, Politica, Philosophica; Il Pensiero Antico–Studi e Testi, 3. Turin, etc.: G. B. Paravia & Co., 1977. Pp. iv + 91.

BERTIER, JANINE; BRISSON, LUC; COMBÈS, JOSEPH; TROUILLARD, JEAN. *Recherches sur la tradition platonicienne (Platon, Aristote, Proclus, Damascius).* Histoire des Doctrines de l'Antiquité Classique. Paris: Librairie Philosophique J. Vrin, 1977. Pp. 143.

BOLCHAZY, LADISLAUS J. *Hospitality in Early Rome: Livy's Concept of Its Humanizing Force.* Chicago: Ares Publishers, Inc., 1977. Pp. iv + 135. $10.00.

BRAZDA geb. BRÉE, MONIKA KAROLA. *Zur Bedeutung des Apfels in der antiken Kultur.* Diss., Bonn. Bonn, 1977. Pp. 141.

BRENK, FREDERICK E., S.J. *In Mist Apparelled: Religious Themes in Plutarch's "Moralia" and "Lives."* Mnemosyne, suppl. 48. Leyden: E. J. Brill, 1977. Pp. xiii + 306.

BRUCKNER, FRIEDRICH. *Interpretationen zur Pseudo-Seneca-Tragödie "Octavia."* Diss., Erlangen-Nuremberg. Nuremberg: Offsetdruckerei Hogl, 1976. Pp. viii + 258.

BRUNO, VINCENT J. *Form and Color in Greek Painting.* New York: W. W. Norton & Company, Inc., 1977. Pp. 123 + 16 pls. $15.00.

BURKERT, WALTER. *Griechische Religion der archaischen und klassischen Epoche.* Die Religionen der Menschheit, vol. 15. Stuttgart-Berlin-Cologne-Mainz: Verlag W. Kohlhammer, 1977. Pp. 508 + 2; 2 maps on endpapers. Mk. 98.

California Studies in Classical Antiquity, vol. 9. Berkeley–Los Angeles–London: University of California Press, 1977. Pp. viii + 202 + 9 pls.; 13 figs. in text. $12.50.

CELLUPRICA, VINCENZA. *Il capitolo 9 del "De interpretatione" di Aristotele: Rassegna di studi: 1930–1973.* Pubblicazioni del Centro di Studio per la Storia della Storiografia Filosofica, 1. Bologna: Società Editrice Il Mulino, 1977. Pp. 188. L. 8,000 (paper).

CHERNISS, HAROLD (trans.). *Plutarch's "Moralia" in Seventeen Volumes,* vol. 13, part 2 (1033A–1086B). Loeb Classical Library, no. 470. With an English Translation by HAROLD CHERNISS. Index Compiled by EDWARD N. O'NEIL. Cambridge, Mass.: Harvard University Press; London: William Heinemann, Ltd., 1976. Pp. xxvi + 369–885 + 8. $7.00.

COHEN, GETZEL M. *The Seleucid Colonies: Studies in Founding, Administration and Organization.* Historia, Einzelschriften, vol. 30. Wiesbaden: Franz Steiner Verlag GmbH, 1978. Pp. xiv + 95 + 2 + 1 folding map. Mk. 28 (paper).

COPLEY, FRANK O. (trans.). *Lucretius: "The Nature of Things."* Translated by FRANK O. COPLEY. New York: W. W. Norton & Company, Inc., 1977. Pp. xxi + 177. $10.95.

DEDOUS, CHRISTINA. *Ho rolos tou chorou stis Bakches.* Panepistēmion Iōanninōn, Philosophikē Scholē, D' Hedra Klassikēs Philologias. Iōannina, 1975. Pp. 26.

DELATTE, L.; GOVAERTS, S.; DENOOZ, J. *Index du Corpus Hermeticum.* Centro di Studio del C. N. R.; Lessico Intellettuale Europeo, 13. Rome: Edizioni dell' Ateneo & Bizzarri, 1977. Pp. xxiv + 359. L. 15,000 (paper).

EBEL, CHARLES. *Transalpine Gaul: The Emergence of a Roman Province.* Studies of the Dutch Archaeological and Historical Society, vol. 4. Leyden: E. J. Brill, 1976. Pp. x + 113.

EBENER, DIETRICH (trans.). *Euripides: Tragödien,* parts 2 (*"Alkestis," "Hippolytos," "Hekabe," "Andromache"*), 3 (*"Herakles," "Die Kinder des Herakles," "Die Hilfeflehenden"*), and 4 (*"Elektra," "Helena," "Iphigenie im Lande der Taurer," "Ion"*). 3 vols. Schriften und Quellen der alten Welt, 30: 2, 3, 4. Griechisch und Deutsch von DIETRICH EBENER. Berlin: Akademie-Verlag, 1975, 1976, 1977. Pp. 380 + 8 pls.; 271 + 8 pls., 467 + 7 pls. Mk. 38; 32; 58.

EVANS, J. D. G. *Aristotle's Concept of Dialectic.* Cambridge–London–New York–Melbourne: Cambridge University Press, 1977. Pp. x + 150. $12.95.

FRAENKEL, EDUARD. *Due seminari romani di Eduard Fraenkel: "Aiace" e "Filottete" di Sofocle.* Sussidi Eruditi, 28. A cura di alcuni partecipanti. Premessa di L. E. ROSSI. Rome: Edizioni di Storia e Letteratura., 1977. Pp. xxxiv + 83 + 2. L. 5,000 (paper).

GIANNANTONI, GABRIELE (ed.). *Scuole socratiche minori e filosofia ellenistica.* Pubblicazioni del Centro di Studio per la Storia della Storiografia Filosofica, 4. A cura di GABRIELE GIANNANTONI. Bologna: Società Editrice Il Mulino, 1977. Pp. 255. L. 8,000 (paper).

GIRARD, RENÉ. *Violence and the Sacred.* Translated by PATRICK GREGORY. Baltimore and London: The Johns Hopkins University Press, 1977. Pp. vii + 333. $17.50. Originally published in Paris in 1972 as *La Violence et le sacré.*

GRANT, MICHAEL (ed.). *Greek Literature: An Anthology.* Translations from Greek Prose and Poetry Chosen by MICHAEL GRANT. Harmondsworth: Penguin Books, Ltd.; New York: Penguin Books, Inc., 1976. Pp. 491 + 3; 1 map in text. £1.00 (U.K.), $2.50 (U.S.A.) (paper).

GRUBE, G. M. A. (trans.). *Plato's "Meno."* Translated by G. M. A. GRUBE. Indianapolis: Hackett Publishing Company, Inc., 1976. Pp. iv + 33.

Harvard Studies in Classical Philology, vol. 81. Cambridge, Mass., and London: Harvard University Press, 1977. Pp. viii + 306 + 5 pls.

HATHORN, RICHMOND Y. *Greek Mythology.* Beirut: American University of Beirut, 1977. Pp. x + 422. $14.00. Distributed in the U.S.A. by Syracuse University Press.

HAWKES, C. F. C. *Pytheas: Europe and the Greek Explorers.* The Eighth J. L. Myres Memorial Lecture. A Lecture delivered at New College, Oxford on 20th May, 1975. Revised and amplified, with ten maps. Oxford: B. H. Blackwell, Ltd., 1977. Pp. ii + 46; 10 maps in text. £2.00 (paper).

HECK, ADRIANUS VAN. *Breviarium urbis Romae antiquae.* Viatorum in usum composuit ADRIANUS VAN HECK. Leyden: E. J. Brill; Rome: G. Bretschneider, 1977. Pp. xxvi + 599; 18 plans in text.

Historiographia antiqua: Commentationes Lovanienses in honorem W. Peremans septuagenarii editae. Symbolae Facultatis Litterarum et Philosophiae Lovaniensis, ser. A, vol. 6. Leuven: Leuven University Press, 1977. Pp. v + 350 + 1 loose sheet (Tabulae Gratulatoriae addenda). Fr. 1,200.

HOHTI, PAAVO. *The Interrelation of Speech and Action in the "Histories" of Herodotus.* Commentationes Humanarum Litterarum, 57 (1976). Helsinki: Societas Scientiarum Fennica, 1976. Pp. 151.

Illinois Classical Studies, vol. 2 (1977). Urbana-Chicago-London: University of Illinois Press, 1977. Pp. viii + 332.

IRWIN, TERENCE. *Plato's Moral Theory: The Early and Middle Dialogues.* Oxford: Clarendon Press; New York: Oxford University Press, 1977. Pp. xvii + 376. $21.00.

JOLY, ROBERT (ed.). *Corpus Hippocraticum: Actes du Colloque hippocratique de Mons (22–26 septembre 1975).* Editions Universitaires de Mons, Série Sciences Humaines, 4. Édités par ROBERT JOLY. Mons: Université de Mons, 1977. Pp. 374 + 1 map + 1 folding chart.

JONES, JULIAN WARD, and JONES, ELIZABETH FRANCES (eds.). *The Commentary on the First Six Books of the "Aeneid" Commonly Attributed to Bernardus Silvestris; Commentum Quod Dicitur Bernardi Silvestris Super Sex Libros "Eneidos" Virgilii.* A New Critical Edition by JULIAN WARD JONES and ELIZABETH FRANCES JONES; Nunc Denuo Ediderunt JULIANUS JONES et ELIZABETHA JONES. Lincoln and London: University of Nebraska Press, 1977. Pp. xxxiv + 163.

KASTEN, HELMUT (trans.). *Cicero: Staatsreden*, part 2: "*Dankrede vor dem Senat,*" "*Dankrede vor dem Volke,*" "*Rede für sein Haus.*" "*Über die konsularischen Provinzen,*" "*Über die Gutachten der Haruspices,*" "*Gegen Piso.*" Schriften und Quellen der alten Welt, vol. 27. Lateinisch und Deutsch von HELMUT KASTEN. 3., unveränderte Auflage. Berlin: Akademie-Verlag, 1977. Pp. 303. Mk. 28.

KING, CHARLES. *Hieroglyphs to Alphabets.* New York: Crane Russak, 1977. Pp. 133; 10 ills. in text. $9.50.

KIRKWOOD, G. M. (ed.). *Poetry and Poetics from Ancient Greece to the Renaissance: Studies in Honor of James Hutton.* Cornell Studies in Classical Philology, vol. 38. Ithaca and London: Cornell University Press, 1975. Pp. 236.

KLEIN, JACOB. *Plato's Trilogy: "Theaetetus," the "Sophist," and the "Statesman."* Chicago and London: The University of Chicago Press, 1977. Pp. vii + 200. $16.00.

KLEINER, FRED S., and NOE, SYDNEY P. *The Early Cistophoric Coinage.* Numismatic Studies, no. 14. New York: The American Numismatic Society, 1977. Pp. vii + 129 + 38 pls. $22.00 plus 35 cents postage.

LEFKOWITZ, MARY R. *The Victory Ode: An Introduction.* Noyes Classical Studies. Park Ridge, N.J.: Noyes Press, 1976. Pp. vi + 186. $18.00.

LILJA, SAARA. *Dogs in Ancient Greek Poetry.* Commentationes Humanarum Litterarum, 56 (1976). Helsinki: Societas Scientiarum Fennica, 1976. Pp. 156.

MERKELBACH, REINHOLD. *Die Quellen des grieschischen Alexanderromans.* Zetemata, vol. 9. Zweite, neubearbeitete Auflage unter Mitwirkung von JÜRGEN TRUMPF. Munich: Verlag C. H. Beck, 1977. Pp. 285 + 2. Mk. 208 (paper).

MORELAND, FLOYD L., and FLEISCHER, RITA M. *Latin: An Intensive Course.* Berkeley–Los Angeles–London: University of California Press, 1977. Pp. xvi + 459. $10.95 (paper).

MORFORD, MARK P. O., and LENARDON, ROBERT J. *Classical Mythology.* 2d ed. New York: Longman, 1977. Pp. xvi + 524; 22 figs. + 26 ills. in text. $14.95 (cloth), 7.95 (paper).

MORGAN, KATHLEEN. *Ovid's Art of Imitation: Propertius in the "Amores."* Mnemosyne, suppl. 47. Leyden: E. J. Brill, 1977. Pp. v + 116. Fl. 32 (paper).

O'BRIEN, JOAN V. *Guide to Sophocles' "Antigone": A Student Edition with Commentary, Grammatical Notes, & Vocabulary.* Carbondale and Edwardsville: Southern Illinois University Press; London and Amsterdam: Feffer & Simons, Inc., 1978. Pp. xiv + 208. $10.00 (cloth), 5.95 (paper).

PAGE, DENYS (ed.). *The Epigrams of Rufinus.* Cambridge Classical Texts and Commentaries, vol. 21. Edited with an Introduction and Commentary by DENYS PAGE. Cambridge–London–New York–Melbourne: Cambridge University Press, 1978. Pp. xii + 115. $19.95.

PETRONE, GIANNA. *Morale e antimorale nelle commedie di Plauto: Ricerche sullo "Stichus."* Palermo: Palumbo Editore, 1977. Pp. 85. L. 2,800 (paper).

PISI, GIORDANA. *Fedro traduttore di Esopo.* Università degli Studi di Parma, Pubblicazioni della Facoltà di Magistero, 4. Florence: La Nuova Italia Editrice, 1977. Pp. 93. L. 3,000 (paper).

PLEPELITS, KARL (trans.). *Chariton von Aphrodisias: "Kallirhoe."* Bibliothek der griechischen Literatur, vol. 6. Eingeleitet, übersetzt und erläutert von KARL PLEPELITS. Stuttgart: Anton Hiersemann, 1976. Pp. viii + 200. Mk. 94.

Proceedings of the 1st International Humanistic Symposium at Delphi September 25–October 4, 1969; Praktika tou A' Diethnous Anthrōpistikou Symposiou en Delphois 25 Septembriou–4 Oktobriou 1969. Hellenic Society for Humanistic Studies, International Centre for Classical Research, 2nd series: Studies and Researches, 20, 21; Hellēnikē Anthrōpistike Hetaireia, Diethnes Kentron Klassikōn Ereunōn, seira deutera: Meletai kai Ereunai, 20, 21. 2 vols. Athens, 1970, 1971. Pp. xii + 415 + 6; viii + 295 + 6 + 2 pls.

PUCCI, PIETRO. *Hesiod and the Language of Poetry.* Baltimore and London: The Johns Hopkins University Press, 1977. Pp. vii + 152. $9.50.

REES, ENNIS (trans.). *The "Iliad" of Homer.* The Library of Liberal Arts. Translated by ENNIS REES. Indianapolis: Bobbs-Merrill Educational Publishing, 1977. Pp. xiv + 530. $5.95 (paper). Copyright 1963 by Ennis Rees; copyright 1977 by The Bobbs-Merrill Company, Inc.

REPICI, LUCIANA. *La logica di Teofrasto: Studio critico e raccolta dei frammenti e delle testimonianze.* Pubblicazioni del Centro di Studio per la Storia della Storiografia Filosofica, 2. Bologna: Società Editrice Il Mulino, 1977. Pp. 247. L. 12,000 (paper).

ROWE, CHRISTOPHER. *An Introduction to Greek Ethics.* New York: Barnes & Noble Books (a division of Harper & Row Publishers, Inc.), 1977. Pp. 143. $10.00. First published 1976 by Hutchinson & Co. (Publishers), Ltd., London; published in the U.S.A. 1977 by Harper & Row Publishers, Inc., Barnes & Noble Import Division.

SAÏD, SUZANNE. *La faute tragique.* Textes à l'appui: histoire classique. Paris: François Maspero, 1978. Pp. 536.

SALE, WILLIAM. *Existentialism and Euripides: Sickness, Tragedy and Divinity in the "Medea," the "Hippolytus" and the "Bacchae."* Ramus Monographs. Berwick, Victoria, Australia: Aureal Publications, 1977. Pp. iii + 142. Recommended price: $A 8.50 (plus postage and packing where applicable) (paper). Business Address: Department of Classical Studies, Monash University, Clayton, Victoria 3168.

SETÄLÄ, PÄIVI. *Private Domini in Roman Brick Stamps of the Empire: A Historical and Prosopographical Study of Landowners in the District of Rome.* Annales Academiae Scientiarum Fennicae, Dissertationes Humanarum Litterarum, 10. Helsinki: Suomalainen Tiedeakatemia, 1977. Pp. 316. Mk. 55 (paper). Distributor: Akateeminen Kirjakauppa (The Academic Bookstore), Helsinki.

STAMATIS, E. S. (ed.). *Euclidis "Elementa,"* vol. 5, pars 1: *Prolegomena critica, Libros XIV–XV, Scholia in Libros I–V continens.* Bibliotheca Scriptorum Graecorum et Romanorum Teubneriana. Post I. L. HEIBERG edidit E. S. STAMATIS. Leipzig: BSB B. G. Teubner Verlagsgesellschaft, 1977. Pp. lxxxix + 234 + 3. Mk. 54.

STRAUME-ZIMMERMANN, LAILA. *Ciceros "Hortensius."* Europäische Hochschulschriften, ser. 15: Klassische Philologie und Literatur, vol. 9. Bern: Herbert Lang; Frankfurt/M: Peter Lang, 1976. Pp. 283.

STRONG, DONALD, and BROWN, DAVID (eds.). *Roman Crafts.* New York: New York University Press, 1976. Pp. 256 + 12 pls.; 390 ills. in text. $35.00. First published in 1976 by Gerald Duckworth & Co., Ltd., The Old Piano Factory, 43 Gloucester Crescent, London NW 1.

TEBBEN, JOSEPH R. *Homer-Konkordanz; A Computer Concordance to the "Homeric Hymns."* Alpha–Omega, Reihe A: Lexika–Indizes–Konkordanzen zur klassischen Philologie, 35. Hildesheim and New York: Georg Olms Verlag, 1977. Pp. viii + 226.

THORNTON, AGATHE. *The Living Universe: Gods and Men in Virgil's "Aeneid."* Mnemosyne, suppl. 46. Leyden: E. J. Brill, 1976. Pp. xiii +223. Published in New Zealand by the University of Otago Press, Dunedin.

TSAGARAKIS, ODYSSEUS. *Nature and Background of Major Concepts of Divine Power in Homer.* Amsterdam: B. R. Grüner Publishing Co., 1977. Pp. xviii + 160. Fl. 60 (paper).

VERMASEREN, MAARTEN J. *Cybele and Attis: The Myth and the Cult.* Aspects of Greek and Roman Life. Translated from the Dutch by A. M. H. LEMMERS. London and New York: Thames and Hudson, 1977. Pp. 224; 112 ills. in text. $27.50.

VERMEULE, CORNELIUS C., III. *Greek Sculpture and Roman Taste: The Purpose and Setting of Graeco-Roman Art in Italy and the Greek Imperial East.* Jerome Lectures, 12th series. Ann Arbor: The University of Michigan Press, 1977. Pp. xii + 137 + 100 figs. on plates. $18.50.

WADDELL, HELEN (trans.). *More Latin Lyrics, from Virgil to Milton.* Translated by HELEN WADDELL. Edited and with an Introduction by DAME FELICITAS CORRIGAN. New York: W. W. Norton & Company, Inc., 1977. Pp. 392. $12.95.

WELLIVER, WARMAN. *Character, Plot and Thought in Plato's "Timaeus"-"Critias."* Philosophia Antiqua, vol. 32. Leyden: E. J. Brill, 1977. Pp. vi + 65 + frontispiece. Fl. 20 (paper).

WENDER, DOROTHEA (trans.). *Hesiod: "Theogony," "Works and Days"; Theognis: "Elegies."* The Penguin Classics. Translated with an Introduction by DOROTHEA WENDER. Harmondsworth: Penguin Books, Ltd.; Baltimore: Penguin Books, Inc., 1976. Pp. 170 + 6. 60p (U.K.), $1.95 (U.S.A.) (paper). This translation first published 1973, reprinted 1976.

WEST, M. L. (ed.). *Hesiod: "Works & Days."* Edited with Prolegomena and Commentary by M. L. WEST. Oxford: Clarendon Press; New York: Oxford University Press, 1978. Pp. xiii + 399. £15.00 (in U.K.), $37.50.

WHITEHEAD, DAVID. *The Ideology of the Athenian Metic.* Cambridge Philological Society, suppl. vol. no. 4. Cambridge: The Cambridge Philological Society, 1977. Pp. vi + 200.

WILKINSON, L. P. *The "Georgics" of Virgil: A Critical Survey.* Cambridge–London–New York–Melbourne: Cambridge University Press, 1978. Pp. xii + 364. $9.95 (paper). First published 1969; first paperback edition 1978.

WISTRAND, ERIK. *Miscellanea Propertiana.* Studia Graeca et Latina Gothoburgensia, 38. Göteborg: Acta Universitatis Gothoburgensis, 1977. Pp. 84 + 2. Kr. 50 (paper). Distributors: Acta Universitatis Gothoburgensis, Box 5096, S-402 22 Göteborg, Sweden.

WRIGHT, JOHN (ed.). *Essays on the "Iliad": Selected Modern Criticism.* Bloomington and London: Indiana University Press, 1978. Pp. ix + 150. $10.95.

STATEMENT OF OWNERSHIP,
MANAGEMENT AND CIRCULATION
(Required by 39 U.S.C. 3685)

1. Title of publication: CLASSICAL PHILOLOGY

a. Publication number: 116240

2. Date of filing: October 1, 1978.

3. Frequency of issue: Quarterly

a. No. of issues published annually: 4

b. Annual subscription price: $24.00

4. Location of known office of publication: 5801 S. Ellis Avenue, Chicago, Illinois 60637.

5. Location of the headquarters or general business offices of the publishers: 5801 S. Ellis Avenue, Chicago, Illinois 60637.

6. Names and addresses of publisher, editor, and managing editor:
Publisher: The University of Chicago Press, 5801 S. Ellis Avenue, Chicago, Illinois 60637
Editor: Stewart I. Oost, 5801 S. Ellis Avenue, Chicago Illinois 60637
Managing Editor: None

7. Owner: The University of Chicago Press, 5801 S. Ellis Avenue, Chicago, Illinois 60637

8. Known bondholders, mortgagees, and other security holders owning or holding 1 percent or more of total amount of bonds, mortgages or other securities: None.

9. The purpose, function, and nonprofit status of this organization and the exempt status for Federal income tax purposes have not changed during preceding 12 months.

10. Extent and nature of circulation:

	Average Number Copies Each Issue During Preceding 12 Months	Single Issue Nearest To Filing Date
A. Total number copies printed	1,700	1,700
B. Paid circulation:		
1. Sales through dealers and carriers, street vendors and counter sales		
2. Mail subscriptions	1,327	1,395
C. Total paid circulation	1,327	1,395
D. Free distribution: samples, complimentary, and other free copies	38	38
E. Total distribution (sum of C and D)	1,365	1,433
F. Copies not distributed:		
1. Office use, leftover, unaccounted, spoiled after printing	335	267
2. Returns from news agents		
G. Total (sum of E and F)	1,700	1,700

11. I certify that the statements made by me above are correct and complete.

JEAN W. SACKS, Assistant Director

ILLINOIS CLASSICAL STUDIES

VOLUME III 1978

Miroslav Marcovich, *Editor*

Contents

1. Xenophanes on Drinking-Parties and Olympic Games
MIROSLAV MARCOVICH
2. *Philoctetes* and Modern Criticism
P. E. EASTERLING
3. The *Bacchae* as Satyr-Play?
DAVID SANSONE
4. Apollonius Rhodius and the Papyri
MICHAEL W. HASLAM
5. The Third-Century B.C. Land-Leases from Tholthis
JEAN BINGEN
6. More of Nemesion's Notes: P. Corn. inv. 18
JOHN F. OATES
7. Grenfell's Gift to Lumbroso
HERBERT C. YOUTIE
8. Two Greek Documents from Provincia Arabia
NAPHTALI LEWIS
9. Some Roman Elements in Roman Egypt
J. F. GILLIAM
10. Rules for Musical Contests
ORSAMUS PEARL
11. Two Literary Papyri in an Archive from Panopolis
WILLIAM H. WILLIS
12. Augustine and Manichaeism in Light of the Cologne Mani Codex
LUDWIG KOENEN
13. The Sahidic Version of Kingdoms IV
GERALD M. BROWNE
14. The Role of the Papyri in Etymological Reconstruction
HENRY AND RENÉE KAHANE
15. Juvenal, Satire 12: On Friendship True and False
EDWIN S. RAMAGE
16. Tacitean *Nobilitas*
REVILO P. OLIVER
17. Three Textual Notes
CHAUNCEY E. FINCH

Mark Naoumides (1931–1977): List of Publications

CLASSICAL PHILOLOGY

A Quarterly Journal devoted to research in the Languages, Literatures, History, and Life of Classical Antiquity

VOLUME 74 NUMBER 2

April 1979

THE UNIVERSITY OF CHICAGO PRESS

Editorial correspondence: The Editor, *Classical Philology*, Box I, Faculty Exchange, The University of Chicago, Chicago, Illinois 60637. N.B. To be considered for publication, all material submitted must be typewritten, with both texts and footnotes double-spaced, and on stout paper with ample margins.

Published January, April, July, and October. Subscription rates, U.S.A.: institutions, 1 year $24.00, 2 years $43.20, 3 years $61.20; individuals, 1 year $18.00, 2 years $32.40, 3 years $45.90; students, $14.40 (with signature of faculty member). Other countries add $1.50 for each year's subscription to cover postage. Single copy rates: institutions $6.50; individuals, $5.00. Back volumes available from 1965 (vol. 60). Single issues and reprinted volumes through 1961 (vols. 1–56) available from Walter J. Johnson, Inc., 355 Chestnut Street, Norwood, New Jersey 07648. Volumes available in microfilm from University Microfilms, 300 North Zeeb Road, Ann Arbor, Michigan 48106; in microfiche from J. S. Canner & Co., 49–65 Lansdowne Street, Boston, Massachusetts 02215. Checks should be made payable to CLASSICAL PHILOLOGY, The University of Chicago Press, 5801 Ellis Avenue, Chicago, Illinois 60637.

Claims for missing numbers should be made within the month following the regular month of publication. The publishers expect to supply missing numbers free only when losses have been sustained in transit and when the reserve stock will permit.

Subscribers are requested to notify the Press and their local postmaster immediately of change of address. All changes of address should provide *both* the old and the new address. *Please allow four weeks for the change.*

The articles in this journal are indexed in the *Humanities Index.*

Second-class postage paid at Chicago, Illinois.

ISSN 0009-837X

CLASSICAL PHILOLOGY

VOLUME 74, NUMBER 2

April 1979

THE PROEM OF THE *Iliad:* HOMER'S ART, *James Redfield* 95

ARGOS AND ARGIVES IN THE *Iliad*, *Robert Drews* 111

LINGUISTIC CHARACTERIZATION OF OLD MEN IN TERENCE, *Robert Maltby* 136

THUCYDIDES' REPRESENTATION OF BRASIDAS BEFORE AMPHIPOLIS, *Alan L. Boegehold* 148

AN UNNOTICED RULE OF PLAUTINE METER, *David Schaps* 152

THE CHRONOLOGY OF PRISCUS FRAGMENT 6, *William N. Bayless* 154

A NEW MS OF THE *Vaticanus Paradoxographus*, *John J. Keaney* 156

REVIEW ARTICLE: THE LOEB MANILIUS, *D. R. Shackleton Bailey* 158

REVIEWS IN THIS ISSUE 170

H. TRÄNKLE: *Livius und Polybios* (Gruen).—B. BALDWIN: *Studies in Aulus Gellius* (Marshall).—W. K. C. GUTHRIE: *A History of Greek Philosophy*, vol. 4: *Plato: The Man and His Dialogues: Earlier Period* (Sprague).—R. E. ALLEN and D. J. FURLEY (eds.): *Studies in Presocratic Philosophy*, vol. 2: *The Eleatics and Pluralists* (Sprague).—H. USENER: *Glossarium Epicureum* (Furley).—H. ERBSE (ed.): *Scholia Graeca in Homeri "Iliadem"* (*Scholia Vetera*) (Combellack).

MANUSCRIPT ACCEPTANCE POLICY

While it is our policy to require the assignment of copyright on most journal articles, we do not usually request assignment of copyright for other contributions. Although the copyright to such a contribution may remain with the author, it is understood that, in return for publication, the journal has the non-exclusive right to publish the contribution and the continuing right, without limit, to include the contribution as part of any reprinting of the issue and/or volume of the journal in which the contribution first appeared by any means and in any format, including computer assisted storage and readout, in which the issue and/or volume may be reproduced.

COPYING BEYOND FAIR USE

The code on the first page of an article in this journal indicates the copyright owner's consent that copies of the article may be made beyond those permitted by Sections 107 or 108 of the U.S. Copyright Law provided that copies are made only for personal or internal use, or for the personal or internal use of specific clients and provided that the copier pay the stated per-copy fee through the Copyright Clearance Center Inc.

To request permission for other kinds of copying, such as copying for general distribution, for advertising or promotional purposes, for creating new collective works, or for resale, kindly write to the publisher.

If no code appears on the first page of the article, permission to reprint may be obtained only from the author.

THE PROEM OF THE *ILIAD:* HOMER'S ART

JAMES REDFIELD

In his proem (*Il.* 1. 1–7) the poet of the *Iliad* asks his Muse for the *Iliad*, and in asking for it has to say what it is. The proem thus states in brief compass the whole of which it is the introductory part. It is a kind of lyric at the head of the epic, a masterpiece of compression; here, even more than elsewhere, every word is made to tell.

The proem has been the object of special attention by the philologists.[1] What follows incorporates much from those predecessors. I shall be concerned, briefly, with establishing and construing the text, and also, at greater length, with interpreting it. These problems require us to set the text within a context, to display its language as a use of epic diction, its emphases as a choice of epic themes, its devices as an exploitation of an epic genre. We thus examine, in this one instance, the interplay between the "tradition" of the poet and his "individual talent."

T. S. Eliot reminds us, in the essay from which I draw these terms, that all poets are traditional. Nevertheless, Homer is a traditional poet in a special sense. The *Iliad* is, or at the very least is like, oral poetry, poetry created in performance by the rapid and relatively unreflective mobilization of traditional means. As we come to understand such poetry better, we begin to invent the philologies appropriate to it. Philology then reveals that the oral poet also is a creator. He handles his materials freely, and therefore meaningfully. I shall often draw attention to expressions atypical of epic usage; such expressions do not separate Homer from his tradition but rather display him as its master. The oral poet, like others, stretches his tradition as he puts it to use. I do not intend, therefore, a contrast between "formulaic" and "invented" language, but between more and less familiar or expected uses of the formulaic language, between (to borrow a contrast from the linguists) more marked and less marked expressions. Both have their place in epic art; both, indeed, appear in the proem.

I begin by setting out a text and offering an (unpoetic) translation:

Μῆνιν ἄειδε, θεά, Πηληϊάδεω Ἀχιλῆος
οὐλομένην, ἣ μυρί' Ἀχαιοῖς ἄλγε' ἔθηκε,

Thanks are due to Paul Friedrich, to Gregory Nagy, and to the *CP* referee for many helpful suggestions; they are not responsible for this final version, which they have not seen.

1. See S. E. Bassett, "The Proems of the *Iliad* and the *Odyssey*," *AJP* 44 (1923): 339–48; B. A. van Groningen, "The Proems of the *Iliad* and the *Odyssey*," *Meded. Ned. Akad. van Wetensch.*, Afd. Letterkunde, n.s. 9, no. 8 (1946): 279–94; W. W. Minton, "Homer's Invocations of the Muses: Traditional Patterns," *TAPA* 91 (1960): 292–309; A. Pagliaro, "Il proemio dell'*Iliade*," *Nuovi Saggi di critica semantica*² (Messina–Florence, 1963), pp. 3–46; K. Rüter, *Odysseeinterpretationen* (Göttingen, 1969), esp. pp. 28–34: "Die traditionellen Elemente des Epenproömiums." I have been particularly careful to acknowledge in detail my debt to Pagliaro; his brilliant commentary stimulated me to write the present essay.

0009-837X/79/7402-0001$01.44

πολλὰς δ' ἰφθίμους ψυχὰς Ἄϊδι προΐαψεν
ἡρώων, αὐτοὺς δὲ ἑλώρια τεῦχε κύνεσσιν
οἰωνοῖσί τε δαῖτα, Διὸς δ' ἐτελείετο βουλή
ἐξ οὗ δὴ τὰ πρῶτα διαστήτην ἐρίσαντε
'Ατρεΐδης τε ἄναξ ἀνδρῶν καὶ δῖος 'Αχιλλεύς

The wrath sing, goddess, of Peleus' son Achilles,
That cursed wrath, which inflicted countless pangs on the Achaeans;
Many potent shades she sent to Hades
Of heroes, and them she was preparing as prey to dogs,
And for birds a feast, and the word of Zeus was coming to completion
From that time when first those divided after quarreling,
The son of Atreus, king of men, and bright Achilles.

Certain features of this translation will be explained in the course of the paper, but there are two points which must be explained at the outset; on both points I follow Pagliaro. First, at the famous crux in line 5 I have adopted δαῖτα (the reading of Zenodotus, Athen. 12F), rather than πᾶσι, the reading of the manuscript tradition. Δαῖτα is confirmed by passages in tragedy which seem to paraphrase the proem, especially Aeschylus *Suppliants* 800–801: κυσὶν δ' ἔπειθ' ἕλωρα κἀπιχωρίοις / ὄρνισι δεῖπνον οὐκ ἀναίνομαι πέλειν. (Cf. also Eur. *Hec.* 1078, *Ion* 504–5.) Athenaeus reports ancient objections to οἰωνοῖσί τε δαῖτα on the ground that δαίς could be used only of human meals. Such objections could well have motivated the weak emendation πᾶσι, while it is hard to see why πᾶσι would have been replaced by δαῖτα. Furthermore, τεῦχε fits well with δαῖτα but would be odd with no object but ἑλώρια, since one is said, in the Homeric idiom, to "make" a meal but not to "make" prey.[2]

The second point has to do with the referent of ἐξ οὗ in line 6. If we take it with ἐτελείετο in line 5 (as did Aristarchus: schol. ad loc.), then the plan or word of Zeus is represented as being in the process of fulfillment from the moment of the quarrel. If we take it with ἄειδε in line 1 (the choice of most moderns), the Muse is being asked to begin the story from the point of the quarrel. But elsewhere, when it is a question of beginning a story at a certain point, the adverb used is spatial: τῶν ἀμόθεν γε . . . εἰπέ (*Od.* 1. 10), ἔνθεν . . . ὡς (*Od.* 8. 500); cf. οἴμης τῆς (*Od.* 8. 74) and the spatial metaphor in μετάβηθι (*Od.* 8. 492). 'Εξ οὗ, by contrast, is a temporal expression, and is employed when a process has been going on, or a condition has obtained, since a certain moment.[3] An audience familiar with the Homeric idiom would thus take ἐξ οὗ with ἐτελείετο rather than with ἄειδε.

This interpretation of ἐξ οὗ gives us a proem which unfolds smoothly as a consecutive sentence, moving from the wrath, to its consequences, to its

2. These points are derived from Pagliaro's defense of δαῖτα in an essay first published in 1948, "Un riflesso Pitagorico nella tradizione del testo Omerico," *Saggi di critica semantica*[2] (Messina–Florence, 1961), pp. 127–31, and from his restatement of his arguments in "Proemio," pp. 35–37. The "correct" emendation would be κύρμα; cf. the phrase ἕλωρ καὶ κύρμα: *Il.* 5. 488, 17. 151; *Od.* 3. 271, 5. 473 (Pagliaro, "Proemio," p. 35, n. 21).

3. Pagliaro, "Proemio," pp. 11–12, reviews epic usage of ἐξ οὗ and quotes, as the closest parallel to the proem, *Od.* 11. 167–68: ἀλλ' αἰὲν . . . ἀλάλημαι . . . ἐξ οὗ τὰ πρώτισθ' ἑπόμην 'Αγαμέμνονι δίῳ; he also compares *Od.* 14. 379.

connection with Zeus, and then to the crucial moment when divine purpose and human action intersected. I now proceed to a detailed study of that sentence.

The first word, *μῆνιν*, states the topic of the poem. Three points about this much-studied word are fundamental to the proem.[4] First, *μῆνις* and its derived verb *μηνίω* are used throughout the *Iliad* by both characters and narrator for Achilles' anger against Agamemnon (the noun occurs at *Il.* 9. 517, 19. 35, 19. 75—and a peculiar derived form, *μηνιθμός*, at *Il.* 16. 62, 16. 202, 16. 282; the verb at *Il.* 1. 422, 1. 488, 2. 769, 2. 772 = 7. 230, 9. 426, 12. 10, 18. 257, 19. 62); *μῆνις*, among the various Homeric words for anger, is the specific name of Achilles' wrath.[5] Second, the noun is in epic diction restricted, except for Achilles, to gods (the verb is used of other humans);[6] Achilles' anger is godlike, and others fear him as they would an angry god. Third, *μῆνις* includes an element of moral outrage; it is provoked by a bond broken, a hierarchy disrupted.[7] *Μῆνις* taps a cosmic power released by the disorder of a basic order. Achilles' anger thus has the demonic destructive power of a justified curse.

Achilles' anger is, of course, literally a kind of divine anger; with the

4. E. Schwyzer, "Drei griechische Wörter," *RhM* 80 (1931): 209–17; H. Frisk, "ΜΗΝΙΣ. Zur Geschichte eines Begriffes," *Eranos* 44 (1946): 28–40; J. Irmscher, *Götterzorn bei Homer* (Leipzig, 1950), pp. 5–8; P. Considine, "Some Homeric Terms for Anger," *Acta Classica* 9 (1966): 15–25; C. Watkins, "A propos de ΜΗΝΙΣ," *Bull. Soc. Ling. de Paris* 72 (1977): 187–209.

5. Achilles does not normally speak of his own rage as *μῆνις* but rather as *χόλος*—see esp. *Il.* 18. 107–10, where he speaks of the *χόλος* that drips down sweeter than honey and rises like smoke. Other speakers and the narrator also use *χόλος* and other words for anger far more frequently than *μῆνις*. Watkins, "A propos de ΜΗΝΙΣ," p. 194, notes that Homeric speakers never use *μῆνις* for their own state of mind, and concludes that such usage is definitely taboo (although the taboo does not extend to the verb [*Il.* 9. 426, 19. 62] or to the derived form *μηνιθμός* [*Il.* 16. 62, 16. 202]). It seems easier, however, to conclude that *μῆνις* means an objective relation, an anger dangerous to someone (and therefore usually so classified from the outside), while *χόλος* and *κότος*, "bile" and "rancor," are subjective conditions, experienced by the angry person.

Achilles applies words derived from *μῆνις* to his own frame of mind only when he is speaking of it as a definite position to which he is committed. Probably his rage does not become a *μῆνις* until after Athena's intervention and his oath by the scepter; at this point a flash of rage is transformed into a settled determination. The first use of the term after the proem applies it only indirectly to Achilles; after the oath *Ἀτρεΐδης δ' ἑτέρωθεν ἐμήνιε* (*Il.* 1. 247). Agamemnon responds to *μῆνις* with *μῆνις*. The first application to Achilles is Thetis' imperative: *μήνι'* (*Il.* 1. 422); later the narrator, describing the new state of affairs, says of Achilles: *ὁ μήνιε* (*Il.* 1. 488). Evidently there is something settled and lasting about *μῆνις*; it is "colère durable" (P. Chantraine, *Dictionnaire étymologique de la langue grecque*, vol. 3 [Paris, 1968], s.v.).

6. We must be alert to differences in the semantic range of nouns and their denominative verbs; in other cases also the range of the verb is the wider. For instance, *νέμεσις* is a human emotion, "not used of the gods in Homer" (LSJ, s.v.), but the derived verbs *νεμεσάω* and *νεμεσίζομαι* are frequently used of the gods—of their outrage with one another and with men. *Αἰδώς* is a feeling evoked in men by their relations with other men or (twice) in a god by another god, but the verb *αἰδέομαι* is used also of human respect for the gods (cf. H. Ebeling, *Lexicon Homericum* [Leipzig, 1885], s.vv.).

7. Zeus may feel *μῆνις* against a god who disregards his authority (*Il.* 5. 31–34; *Od.* 5. 146–47) or who defies his thunderbolt (*Il.* 15. 122; cf. 15. 115–18). Men rouse the *μῆνις* of Apollo if they dishonor his priest (*Il.* 1. 75; cf. 1. 94–95), think themselves equal to the gods (*Il.* 5. 444; cf. 5. 440–42), or defy fate (*Il.* 16. 711 = 5. 444; cf. 16. 707–8). The *μῆνις* of an unnamed god may follow failure of sacrifice (*Il.* 5. 177–78), defilement of an enemy (*Il.* 22. 358; cf. 22. 338–43), or failure to bury a friend (*Od.* 11. 72–73). Zeus (*Il.* 13. 623–25; *Od.* 14. 283–84) or unnamed gods (*Od.* 2. 66–67) may be roused to *μῆνις* against those who break the bond of hospitality. Similarly, human *μῆνις* is provoked by offenses against authority (*Il.* 1. 247) or merit (*Il.* 13. 460), against host (*Od.* 16. 376–82) or guest (*Od.* 17. 10–15).

help of his goddess mother he can bring the gods into action to avenge his wrongs. In so doing he lets loose in the world a power which is greater than himself and ultimately beyond his control. The proverb says: χαλεπὴ δὲ θεοῦ ἔπι μῆνις, "the wrath of a god is harsh, when it comes" (*Il.* 5. 178). Divine μῆνις can bring the plague (*Il.* 1. 75) or civil strife (*Od.* 3. 134–36); it can set a city in flames (*Il.* 21. 522–24). Achilles' wrath is on such a scale; aimed at Agamemnon, it reaches out to bring destruction on his whole community.

Furthermore, Achilles, although he is half a god, is still a man; we are reminded in the second half of this line that he is son of Peleus. His wrath thus falls on his own people and ultimately, through Patroclus, on himself. The first line of the *Iliad* qualifies the hero in terms of his divine wrath and his human father, and thus places him between god and man. This ambiguous status is the source of his tragedy. The chosen starting point of the epic thus has implications which are unfolded in the poem's overall plot.

The words ἄειδε, θεά place the proem within a generic type, the invocation to the Muse.[8] At the same time the words chosen are atypical of the genre. Normally the Muse is asked, not to "sing," but to "say."[9] The Muses are themselves singers, and sing among the gods as the bards sing among men (*Il.* 1. 603–4; *Od.* 24. 60–61; *Theog.* 36–52), but the bard who invokes the Muse does not expect to bring their song into the world of men; rather the Muse, who gives song to men (*Od.* 8. 64, 8. 498; *Theog.* 104; Hes. frag. 310 M.–W.; Archil. frag. 1 West), will "impel the bard to sing" (*Od.* 8. 73). The Muses "teach" the bard (*Od.* 8. 488) and "make to grow" in him the οἶμαι, the paths of song—that is, themes and stories. They are the daughters of Memory (*Theog.* 54; Solon 1. 1 West) and remind the bard of what he might otherwise forget (*Il.* 2. 492). They are a source of information, and their inspiration guarantees the truth of the song. But the voice which is heard is not that of the Muse, but of the bard. When, therefore, the bard asks the Muse not to "speak" to him but to "sing," a complex relation is somewhat simplified. The bard in effect claims that his song is the authentic voice of the goddess.

As the poet brings the Muse directly on the stage, so he addresses her, relatively informally, as θεά. This vocative is proper, not to a prayer such as this invocation, but to face-to-face conversation with a goddess; in such a context the word has a tone of formal propriety.[10] Similarly, in a prayer

8. There are five invocations internal to the *Iliad:* 2. 484–93, 2. 761–62, 11. 218–20, 14. 508–10 16. 112–13. There are also the initial invocations of the *Odyssey* (1. 1–10), and *Erga* (1–10), and the *Eoiai* (Hes. frag. 1 Merkelbach and West). The *Theogony* begins with a complex hymn to the Muses, which closes with an invocation of them (104–15). The invocatory first lines of the *Thebais* and *Epigonoi* are preserved: T. W. Allen (ed.), *Homeri Opera,* 5:112.

9. In Homer the verb is ἔννεπε if the Muse is singular (*Il.* 2. 761; *Od.* 1. 1), ἔσπετε if the Muses are plural (*Il.* 2. 484, 11. 218, 14. 508, 16. 112).

10. Vocative θεά is twice used by superior to inferior deities (*Il.* 15. 93, 24. 104)—perhaps to reassure them that their status will be respected, as Hermes says he will tell the truth "as one god to another," θεὰ θεόν (*Od.* 5. 97). Humans use it most often to signal their recognition of a goddess (*Il.* 1. 216, 5. 815, 18. 182; *Od.* 13. 312, 20. 37; cf. *Hymn. Hom. Ven.* 185), or to signal the relevance of divine status as when Achilles calls Thetis' attention to her power (*Il.* 1. 401) or Odysseus tells Calypso why he cannot trust her (*Od.* 5. 173, 5. 178).

a speaker who has already called a goddess by name may also call her θεά (*Il.* 10. 290; *Od.* 20. 61); we find this usage in the proem to the *Odyssey*, where θεά (*Od.* 1. 10) is anaphoric to Μοῦσα (*Od.* 1. 1). To pray to a goddess simply as θεά, however, assumes that the correct goddess will know she is being addressed, and this in turn assumes a preexisting relation between speaker and goddess. There are only two other instances of this form of address in Homer (*Il.* 10. 462, 23. 770—the narrator tells us that both prayers are to Athena): both are by Odysseus to the goddess who is always close to him (cf. *Il.* 10. 278–79; *Od.* 3. 221–22, 13. 314–15).

The first three words of the *Iliad* thus introduce us into a numinous world; a godlike wrath will be sung by a bard who is himself close to the divine source of song.

These first three words, with their consecutive trochaic word breaks, are metrically anomalous, and it has been held that they are "nonformulaic."[11] One can as easily think, however, that ἄειδε, θεά (metrical anomaly and all) was the regular expression in a proem after a trochaic topic word ending in a consonant, and this notion is confirmed by the only parallel case in early epic, the first line of the *Thebais:* Ἄργος ἄειδε, θεά, πολυδίψιον ἔνθεν ἄνακτες (Allen, *Homeri Opera*, 5:112). Since, moreover, μῆνις was the traditional name for Achilles' wrath, since a proem usually began with a topic word,[12] and since Πηληϊάδεω Ἀχιλῆος is the usual name-formula for Achilles in the genitive case after the masculine caesura, we can hold that the entire first line was "dictated" to the poet from the moment he chose his topic. And this conclusion would seem to invalidate the analysis offered above, since the poet could not mean anything special by words he had no choice about.

This view vastly overrates the rigidity of formulaic composition; we should be cautious about deriving strict rules from evidence which is after all fragmentary. Πηληϊάδεω Ἀχιλῆος (in violation of the principle of economy) has, in fact, an alternative in this position: μεγαθύμου Πηλεΐωνος (*Il.* 18. 226, 19. 75—in the second instance modifying μῆνις). Invocations of the Muse, at least in the *Hymns*, do not always begin with a topic word (*Hymn. Hom. Ven.* 1; *Hymn.* 19. 1). Another, less gifted, bard might have begun, Μοῦσα μοι ἔννεπε μῆνιν Ἀχιλλῆος θείοιο. . . . And in any case formulae are meaningful. I concede that, as an adjective becomes fixed in combination with a noun, and as the combination becomes a normal unit in a specific metrical context, the two parts lose independent meaning. The whole combination becomes "lexicalized"; ποδάρκης δῖος Ἀχιλλεύς hardly means anything different from Ἀχιλλεύς (although even here the greater length of the combined form adds an emphasis). But it is also true that the latent implications in the most familiar combinations can be contextually evoked; if the context made us think of Achilles' feet, we would notice ποδάρκης in a different way.[13] The first line of the *Iliad* is rich in such implications.

11. By J. A. Russo, "A Closer Look at Homeric Formulas," *TAPA* 94 (1963): 235–47, esp. p. 240.

12. See Van Groningen, "Proems," p. 284.

13. We can observe the poet avoiding unwanted implications (and violating the principle of economy) at *Il.* 23. 168, where the next line begins with a reference to the feet of Patroclus, and Achilles is called (uniquely) μεγάθυμος instead of πόδας ὠκύς. See W. Whallon, *Formula, Character and Context* (Washington, D.C., 1969), p. 59.

Whether we ascribe the richness to the poet or to his tradition, it remains a poetic success.[14]

There is, however, a different, stylistic, point about formulaic composition, which is exemplified by this first line. The first three words are highly "marked"; even if they are normal in a proem, a proem itself is a highly marked environment, in contrast to the run of the narrative. The second hemistich, which consists of the expression most usual in this syntactic and metrical context, is less marked. The first line thus exemplifies the familiar rule that hexameters become more formulaic toward the end. We hear the line as composed from left to right. The poet, having set himself a metrical problem in the first part of his line, solves it with an item from his formulaic repertoire. This involves a shift from relatively free, and therefore relatively meaningful, syntagmata, to relatively lexicalized units. The first hemistich consists of three lexemes; the second, in effect, of only one. Information is thus transmitted at an uneven rate. The run of the meter, with its alternation of asymmetrical hemistichs, is complemented by a variation of semantic density, and this contributes to that correlation of semantics with phonology characteristic of poetic utterance.

Similarly, phonology correlates with syntax. The first word of line 2, οὐλομένην, an adjective in concord with the first word of line 1, exemplifies another general stylistic feature: the tendency toward ambiguous syntactic end-stopping of the line. What has appeared to be a closed syntactic unit is, in effect, reopened by the first item of the following line. Ἡρώων in line 4 works much the same way. Milman Parry has called this feature "unperiodic enjambement."[15] It helps the singer to dramatize the process of his thought; he seems to think one line at a time (as he no doubt often did in the process of oral composition). Having established the μῆνις as his theme, he now finds something more to say about it.

From one point of view οὐλομένην adds little, since it is a notably unspecific negative adjective, covering a range from inadequate to unfortunate to harmful to outrageous. It is a term of general rejection. It is, however, also an adjective applied, exclusively in the *Iliad* and predominantly in the *Odyssey*, to persons (*Il.* 5. 876, 14. 84, 19. 92; *Od.* 4. 92, 11. 410, 17. 484, 18. 273, 24. 97). Four times in the *Odyssey* it is applied to objects, always with a touch of personification; the things mentioned (Circe's drugs, *Od.* 10. 394; Achilles' armor, *Od.* 11. 555; the belly, *Od.* 15. 344, *Od.* 17. 287) are more than mere instruments, and have a kind of life of their own. So we can say that οὐλομένην personifies the μῆνις.[16]

We should also note that this adjective is used elsewhere in the epics exclusively in speeches; it has a tone of subjectivity, and expresses a personal rejection of another person or personified thing. The bard thus brings before us his own reaction to, almost his distaste for, his theme.

14. As Michael Nagler, *Spontaneity and Tradition* (Berkeley and Los Angeles, 1974), p. 61, says, "It is necessary to recall . . . from time to time . . . that the art language cannot compose for a poet or even, in the last analysis, restrict what he means to say."

15. "The Distinctive Character of Enjambement in Homeric Verse," *TAPA* 60 (1929): 200–220, esp. pp. 205–7.

16. This personification is noted by Pagliaro, "Proemio," p. 5, n. 6.

The personification is developed in the relative clause which follows: ἣ μυρί' Ἀχαιοῖς ἄλγε' ἔθηκε. Elsewhere the giver or sender of ἄλγεα is a god or a curse.[17] It is once said that gods and men can inflict ἄλγεα on each other (*Il.* 5. 384), but the only particular human actor who inflicts ἄλγεα is Achilles (*Il.* 22. 422). Ἄλγε' ἔθηκε thus has the same semantic range as μῆνις; the relative clause reinforces our sense of the μῆνις as a numinous agent.

In the next three lines the poet specifies the ἄλγεα. The problem here is not what the poet means to say, but why he says it. We might expect at this point some foretaste of the plot; instead the fate of the heroes is stated in the most general terms. Their shades were sent to Hades, while they were left to the birds and dogs. This last statement, further, is puzzling because in the *Iliad* no bodies are ever left to the birds and dogs; such treatment of the dead, while often threatened, and even attempted, is never enacted.[18] The proem thus presents a scene which will not occur in the poem.

Let us begin by examining one puzzling phrase: ἰφθίμους ψυχάς. Ἴφθιμος is an obscure adjective; it may well be that by Homer's time it was an archaic word, used only in the epic language, and of uncertain meaning to the poet himself. But it does seem to have implications of potency—of physical strength, or fertility, or both.[19] The ψυχή, on the other hand, is the typically impotent thing; it has no function for the living man except to leave him at death, and its later fate is a mere existence, twittering and flittering in the dark underworld.[20]

Line 3 is similar to *Iliad* 11. 55, where, as Zeus sends down a rain of blood, we are told that he intended πολλὰς ἰφθίμους κεφαλὰς Ἄϊδι προϊάψειν. Similarly, in Hesiod fragment 204. 118–19 M.–W., we are told of Zeus's intentions for the Trojan War:

> . . . π]ολ̣λ̣ὰς Ἀΐδηι κεφαλὰς ἀπὸ χαλκὸν ἰάψ[ει]ν
> ἀν]δ̣ρ̣ῶν ἡ̣ρ̣ώων.

In the proem the subject is not Zeus but the μῆνις; nevertheless, we are about to be told that all this was somehow a fulfillment of Διὸς . . . βουλή. The poet seems in the proem to be drawing upon familiar language for Zeus's intention to produce destruction at Troy.

Ἰφθίμους κεφαλάς in *Iliad* 11. 55 is closer to normal Homeric usage than is ἰφθίμους ψυχάς in line 3 for two reasons: κεφαλή is a word elsewhere accompanied by adjectives (although nowhere else by the adjective ἴφθιμος), and ἴφθιμος is used with another word for "head" in a fixed line employed four times in descriptions of arming: κρατὶ δ' ἐπ' ἰφθίμῳ κυνέην εὔτυκτον ἔθηκεν.

17. Zeus: *Il.* 2. 39, 2. 375, 18. 431, 24. 241; *Od.* 4. 722. Zeus and Poseidon: *Il.* 13. 346. Apollo: *Il.* 1. 96, 1. 110. The South Wind: *Od.* 12. 427. Unnamed gods: *Il.* 19. 264; *Od.* 14. 39. Curses: *Od.* 11. 279, 19. 330. It will be noted that the distribution of ἄλγεα is close to that of μῆνις; both are particularly associated with Zeus and Apollo.

18. Cf. Pagliaro, "Proemio," pp. 29–33. For a sensitive review of all relevant passages, see C. Segal, *The Theme of the Mutilation of the Corpse in the "Iliad,"* Mnemosyne, suppl. 17 (Leyden, 1971).

19. See J. Warden, "ΙΦΘΙΜΟΣ: A Semantic Analysis," *Phoenix* 23 (1969): 143–58; and Pagliaro, "Proemio," pp. 21–23.

20. Cf. Pagliaro, "Proemio," p. 22.

On the other hand, line 3 of the proem "is the only instance in the *Iliad* or the *Odyssey* where ψυχή is qualified by a descriptive epithet. This would suggest that of the two lines 11. 55 is the prototype."[21] The poet, in other words, has in the proem varied his familiar language in order to replace κεφαλάς by ψυχάς.

The substitution was made easy for him by the close association of the ψυχή with the head,[22] and by the fact that the ψυχή of the dead man is regularly said to be sent to Hades, as in the formulaic phrase ψυχὴν δ' Ἄϊδι κλυτοπώλῳ (three times). The poet is working with the resources of the formulaic language. Nevertheless, line 3 is odd. The oddity is not entirely semantic, for "potent shades" is not much odder than "potent heads"—the head is not a potent part of Homeric man, whose power lies in his limbs and midriff. The real oddity is syntactic; the poet has produced a unique syntagm: ψυχή + adjective. We must seek his motivation for including ψυχή in the line at the expense of the normal syntactic privileges of that word. The explanation is to be found in the use of αὐτούς in line 4.

Αὐτός is a pronoun which "topicalizes" its antecedent. A person or object is marked as the focus of interest, in contrast to other items which, although they may be syntactically parallel, are of less interest to the speaker. Very often αὐτός focuses attention on a person in contrast to his parts or possessions.[23] Thus in lines 3 and 4 the ψυχή, a part or possession, departs, while the dead hero remains on the field.

In the normal expression, κεφαλὰς Ἄϊδι προϊάψειν, the κεφαλή is in fact metaphorical for the ψυχή.[24] The poet could not, however, use the normal expression followed by αὐτούς; the literal sense would have asserted itself. He would have seemed to say that a part of the body was sent away while the body remained on the field. The poet therefore inserted ψυχάς, not because he particularly wanted ψυχάς, but because he wanted an acceptable substitute for κεφαλάς.

Αὐτούς, then, motivates ψυχάς.[25] The dead bodies are spoken of as the heroes themselves, the ψυχαί as mere accessories. We should note that this notion is peculiar to the proem.[26] Usually the dead person goes to Hades

21. Warden, "ΙΦΘΙΜΟΣ," p. 154. Pagliaro (not cited by Warden) reviews much the same material and comes to similar conclusions: "Proemio," pp. 23–29.

22. R. B. Onians, *The Origins of European Thought* (Cambridge, 1951), pp. 95 ff.; Warden, "ΙΦΘΙΜΟΣ," pp. 153–57.

23. Cf. P. Chantraine, *Grammaire homérique*, vol. 2 (Paris, 1963), p. 156; and Pagliaro, "Proemio," p. 10, n. 7.

24. Pagliaro, "Proemio," pp. 24–25, says (and I agree) that, even if the phrase reflects some earlier custom of decapitating the enemy, in the Homeric idiom "to send the head to Hades" simply means "to kill."

25. That αὐτούς in line 4 requires ψυχάς in line 3 has been seen since ancient times: cf. schol. ad 7. 330, 11. 55; it has been held (cf. G. M. Bolling, *The Athetized Lines in the "Iliad"* [Baltimore, 1944], pp. 43–44) that ψυχάς was substituted for κεφαλάς when lines 4 and 5 were interpolated in the proem. My own interpretation is close to that of Pagliaro, "Proemio," p. 23.

26. *Contra* E. Rohde, *Psyche*[4] (Tübingen, 1907), p. 5. The closest parallels are *Il.* 16. 856–58 = 22. 362–64 (with a difference of proper name in the last line). Here the ψυχή goes off to Hades, while the victor continues to harangue the corpse: τὸν καὶ τεθνηῶτα προσηύδα. Τόν here is unemphatic; the victor speaks to the corpse as if it were not dead, treats it, irrationally, as a person. Rohde also cites *Il.* 23. 103–7, but this passage makes no reference to the dead body, only to the fact that Patroclus' ψυχή looks just as he did in life.

and leaves his body behind.[27] With some perturbation of normal usage the poet here focuses our attention on the fate of the dead bodies. This focus, I would suggest, looks forward to the last third of the epic. Achilles' μῆνις, announced in the proem as the theme, is (in a narrow sense at least) concluded by the beginning of Book 16, when Achilles declares that his rage has passed (*Il.* 16. 60–61). Thereafter Achilles' story centers on the deaths of two heroes and the fates of their bodies. Patroclus dies, his body is recovered from the enemy, and Achilles gives him an elaborate funeral. Achilles takes his revenge, kills Hector, and attempts to feed his body to the dogs. Finally Hector also is recovered by his city and properly buried. In its overall structure the *Iliad* moves from themes involving the social relations of the heroes—themes of honor and of the destruction which springs from dishonor—to themes involving the defilement and purification of the dead. The proem, formally, refers only to the first part of this story, to the destruction brought by the μῆνις on the Achaeans. Yet in its structure the proem shows a parallel development, as it traces the consequences of the μῆνις from suffering (ἄλγεα) to death to defilement.

The notion of defilement is made concrete in the words that follow: ἑλώρια τεῦχε κύνεσσιν / οἰωνοῖσί τε δαῖτα. The use of τεύχω here, as a causative over an embedded nominal-predicate sentence (i.e., to mean "made *x* into *y*"), is highly marked and unique in the *Iliad;* the normal Homeric causative is τίθημι.[28] Τίθημι is the verb in line 2, where, oddly enough, τεῦχε would have fitted comfortably (cf. ἄλγεα τεύχει at *Il.* 1. 100 and related phrases at *Il.* 13. 346 and *Il.* 21. 585), just as θῆκε would have fitted in line 4.[29] If we seek a poetic motivation for τεῦχε, we find it, I think, in a further oddity: τεύχω is not a normal verb with ἑλώρια, since one is not said to "make" prey but to "leave" it (ἐᾶν, λείπειν). Τεύχω, on the other hand, is one of the normal verbs for preparing a meal.[30] As we go through the chiastic series, prey–dogs, birds–feast, the choice of verb is justified only by the last item. Τεῦχε (in contrast to the more neutral θῆκε) thus serves to knit the whole expression together, and puts a special stress on δαῖτα.

27. In similar phrases with προϊάψειν the object is a simple personal pronoun (*Il.* 5. 190, 6. 487; cf. 8. 367, 21. 47–48); the vanquished is sent to Hades. The ψυχή continues the adventures of the bodily person, as in Polydamas' rough joke: some Argive has been pierced with a spear "and now I suppose he can use it as a staff while walking down to the house of Hades" (*Il.* 14. 456–57). The dead hero—that is, the dead body—must be protected, but at the same time he has gone away in the form of his ψυχή. Thus Patroclus says: "Bury me as quick as you can, that I may pass within the gates of Hades, for the ψυχαί keep me away" (*Il.* 23. 71–72). He is both there and here.

28. Cf. Ebeling, *Lexicon Homericum*, s.v. τίθημι 5. There are two causative uses of τεύχω in the *Odyssey* (13. 190–91, 13. 397), but there also the normal causative verb is τίθημι. Perfect middle forms of τεύχω are used in Homer as agentless passives, and thus as simple copulas; contrast *Il.* 6. 300 τὴν γὰρ Τρῶες ἔθηκαν Ἀθηναίης ἱέρειαν, where we have a stated agent with τίθημι, with the agentless use of τεύχω at *Il.* 16. 604–5 ὅς Διὸς ἱρεὺς . . . ἐτέτυκτο.

29. Ἄλγε' ἔθηκε is a normal expression; cf. *Il.* 22. 422. The problem is not that ἔθηκε is out of place in line 2, but that τεῦχε is out of place in line 4. The whole sentence would be more normal if the two verbs were reversed.

30. Pagliaro, "Riflesso," p. 130, assembles the evidence for τεύχω used with δαίς, δόρπον, and δεῖπνον, and for the verbs used with ἕλωρ, as part of his argument for reading δαῖτα as against πᾶσι. In none of the passages involving meals is the use of τεύχω causative; in *Od.* 9. 291 and 9. 344, where we might have expected some such phrase as τοὺς . . . τεῦχε . . . δόρπον, we find instead that the material of the meal is made the object of a subordinate participial clause.

Δαῖτα has been the problem word in the proem since ancient times.[31] The association of dogs with birds is familiar in threats of defilement (*Il.* 2. 393, 8. 379, 13. 831, 17. 241, 18. 271, 22. 42, 22. 335, 22. 354, 24. 411; *Od.* 3. 259), but the association of prey with feasting is not.

Elsewhere in the *Iliad* ἕλωρ (the developed form ἑλώρια is unique to the proem) is used of the dead body left to despoilment by the enemy (*Il.* 5. 488, 5. 684, 17. 151, 17. 667, 18. 93), in the *Odyssey*, of bodies left as carrion for animals (*Od.* 3. 271, 5. 473, 24. 292).[32] The notion of ἕλωρ thus marks an intersection of the human and animal spheres. The warrior's "catch" is sometimes mutilated with bestial playfulness (*Il.* 11. 146–47, 13. 202–5, 14. 498–500, 20. 481–83). At war, as the *Iliad* similes often remind us, man becomes to man as man to beast or beast to beast; war negates society.

The δαίς, by contrast, is in Homer the institution wherein society preeminently becomes peaceful (cf. *Il.* 1. 573–83, 9. 68–78). A δαίς is literally a "sharing"; through the sharing of meat at the δαίς status is respected (*Il.* 12. 310–21) and merit is recognized (*Od.* 8. 474–83). Here man is joined with man and with god through council, hospitality, song, sacrifice, and prayer.

The use of δαῖτα for the carrion meal of the beasts is thus a strong and (as the ancient critics complained) rather repulsive metaphor. While ἑλώρια points to an intersection between categories, δαῖτα suggests the deletion of the categorical contrast between men and beasts. The complex phrase suggests the analogies: warriors:victims::dogs:prey and birds:carrion:: men:meat.

More than once in the *Iliad* it is suggested that these two analogies could be collapsed into warrior:victim::man:meat, that the perfection of victory would be actually to consume the vanquished (*Il.* 3. 23–28, 13. 198–202, 18. 161–64, 22. 261–65, 24. 212–13). The most explicit statement is by Achilles just before he kills Hector (*Il.* 22. 346–54): "If only I could cut you into raw meat and eat you myself," he says, but as it is: κύνες τε καὶ οἰωνοὶ κατὰ πάντα δάσονται. (In this context we may hear in δάσονται an echo of the cognate noun δαίς: "the birds and dogs will share you out [as at a feast].")

At only one other place in Homer is δαίς used as in the proem for the meal of an animal: Apollo says (*Il.* 24. 33–54) that Achilles in defiling Hector's body ἄγρια οἶδεν; he is like a lion who comes down on the flock ἵνα δαῖτα λάβῃσιν. The lion feasts [like a man]; if we fill out the symmetrical ellipses of what I take to be a complex comparison, we shall say that Achilles is like a beast [who feeds on his prey].[33]

Achilles of course is no cannibal; rather the theme of cannibalism represents, as a logical extreme case, the dehumanization of the enemy, his

31. The vulgate tradition, as we saw, emended it away; Zenodotus, who read δαῖτα, athetized lines 4 and 5; cf. Pagliaro, "Proemio," p. 5.

32. And once (*Od.* 13. 208) of property left abandoned.

33. A pictorial reflection of this theme of latent cannibalism can be seen in Attic vase paintings, by Oltos and the Brygos painter, of Achilles feasting over Hector's body; the blood from the meat of the feast (picked out in red paint by Oltos) runs down onto the corpse beneath the table. These items are nos. 20*g* and 20*i* in K. Friis Johansen, *The "Iliad" in Greek Art* (Copenhagen, 1967), p. 267.

reduction to a mere thing to be mastered. I have argued elsewhere that such dehumanization is central to the terror of the *Iliad*.[34] Here I add that δαῖτα in the proem (as in Apollo's simile) suggests the same theme, as it were, inside out. In the poem men become bestial; in the proem the carrion-eating beasts do a man-like thing. What is presented in the proem as an objective fact about beasts appears in the poem (where no bodies are ever eaten by the beasts) as a subjective tendency of men, who in battle become somewhat like predators or scavengers.[35]

The proem adds that all this was somehow according to the will of Zeus: Διὸς δ' ἐτελείετο βουλή. At least five interpretations of this much-discussed phrase[36] can be defended; while there are objections to them all, I shall be arguing my way through four in favor of the fifth.

First, the poet may have in mind no specific plan or intention of Zeus; he may mean simply that these events, like all events, were somehow "god's will."[37] Agamemnon and Achilles themselves speak of their quarrel this way: since it happened, Zeus must have willed it (*Il.* 19. 86–90, 19. 270–74). But this way of talking is characteristic only of the characters in epic, not of the epic narrator, who, when he speaks of the βουλή of Zeus (e.g., *Od.* 1. 86; *Theog.* 465, 730; *Erga* 71, 79, 99; *Hymn. Hom. Cer.* 9; *Hymn. Hom. Ven.* 23) means some definite plan or contrivance of the god.[38] Similarly, Zeus himself, when he speaks of the fall of Troy Ἀθηναίης διὰ βουλάς (*Il.* 15. 71), means the contrivance of the Trojan Horse.

A second interpretation would hold that the quarrel between Achilles and Agamemnon was itself contrived by Zeus for some purpose of his own. The evidence for this interpretation is Proclus' reference, at the end of his account of the *Cypria*, to a Διὸς βουλὴ ὅπως ἐπικουφίσῃ τοὺς Τρῶας Ἀχιλλέα τῆς συμμαχίας τῆς Ἑλληνικῆς ἀποστήσας (Allen, *Homeri Opera*, 5:105).[39] This interpretation receives, however, no support from the text of the *Iliad;* there the quarrel is the result, not of divine contrivance, but of human error. Agamemnon refuses to return the priest's daughter and thus brings down the plague; the assembly called by Achilles (instigated by Hera, not Zeus—*Il.* 1. 55) to correct this error is badly handled and brings about further error.[40]

34. J. M. Redfield, *Nature and Culture in the "Iliad": The Tragedy of Hector* (Chicago, 1975), pp. 183–203.

35. Pagliaro, "Proemio," pp. 29–34, gives a somewhat different account of the transformation: defilement, which appears in the poem as a threat (that is, as a rhetorical element), appears in the proem as a fact of experience. The poet, he says, thus displays his detachment from the literary tradition; he is able to revive a somewhat faded rhetorical terror to vivid actuality.

36. W. Kullmann, "Ein vorhomerisches Motiv im Iliasproömium," *Philologus* 99 (1955): 167–92, includes extensive bibliographical notes referring to earlier discussions of the phrase.

37. This position has been held: cf. Kullmann, "Motiv," p. 167, n. 2. S. E. Bassett, "The Three Threads of Plot of the *Iliad*," *TAPA* 53 (1922): 53, refers to it as "today the most commonly accepted interpretation."

38. Cf. Kullmann, "Motiv," p. 168, n. 1.

39. Cf. ibid., pp. 177–78, and Kullmann's *Die Quellen der "Ilias,"* Hermes Einzelschriften, 14 (Wiesbaden, 1960), pp. 210–11.

40. Cf. A. Lesky, "Göttliche und menschliche Motivation im homerischen Epos," *SBHeidelberg*, phil.-hist. Kl., 1961, pt. 4, pp. 16–17; and Redfield, *Nature and Culture*, pp. 91–98.

A third interpretation (probably now the most popular)[41] refers Διὸς . . . βουλή in the proem to the events which follow the quarrel in the poem, to the intervention by which Zeus, in order to make the Greeks feel the consequences of Achilles' μῆνις, contrives a temporary success for the Trojans. Within the *Iliad* itself Διὸς βουλή and related phrases usually refer to this intervention by Zeus (cf. *Il.* 11. 79, 12. 235–42, 13. 347–50, 13. 523–25, 15. 592–602, 16. 121, 17. 331–32). I see, however, two objections to finding this meaning in the proem. First, if we take ἐξ οὗ with ἐτελείετο, the statement will, by this interpretation, be untrue; the intervention of Zeus does not immediately follow the quarrel but occurs only after a lapse of many days (cf. *Il.* 1. 423–27). Zeus does not finally take charge of the battle until the beginning of Book 8. (Perhaps this difficulty, as much as anything else, has caused critics to take ἐξ οὗ with ἄειδε, a syntactic interpretation which, as we saw, is unsatisfactory on other grounds.) Second, the contrivance of Hector's brief success originates, not with Zeus, but with Thetis, who demands it of Zeus as an ἐέλδωρ (*Il.* 1. 504). The poet reminds us of this fact in the course of his narrative (*Il.* 13. 347–50, 15. 69–77, 15. 592–602), and Athena says of Zeus: Θέτιδος δ' ἐξήνυσε βουλάς (*Il.* 8. 370). But the language of the proem seems to imply the initiative of Zeus himself; the Διὸς . . . βουλή is mentioned as a primary fact about the poem to follow, whereas within the poem it is a secondary result of other events. Such misrepresentation of the poem by the proem is (as we have seen) far from impossible, but it should be motivated, and I see no clear motive for it here.

A fourth interpretation refers to the proem of the *Cypria*, where it is said that Zeus determined to lighten the earth of her burden of men; he therefore stirred up war against Troy where ἥρωες κτείνοντο. Διὸς δ' ἐτελείετο βουλή (Allen, *Homeri Opera*, 5:118). The view that Διὸς . . . βουλή has the same referent in the identical phrases of the proems of the *Cypria* and the *Iliad* has been impressively championed by Wolfgang Kullmann, who has collected from the *Iliad* more than a dozen passages where some general intention of Zeus to massacre the heroes may be implied.[42] This evidence is not quite persuasive; not one of these passages brings the implication to the surface. We can find Kullmann's meaning in them only if we read them with the *Cypria* (and other non-Iliadic passages—especially *Erga* 156–73 and Hes. frag. 204. 96–119 M.–W.) in our minds.[43] The plan of Zeus to exterminate the heroes may be a latent theme in the *Iliad*, but it remains latent; the Homeric story is focused on the responsibility of the human actors for their own destruction. Even the intervention of Zeus on behalf of the Trojans (the Διὸς βουλή within the poem) is the result of Achilles' initiative to Thetis; the god, as it were, becomes an instrument of the man.

41. Kullmann, "Motiv," p. 169, n. 1; this interpretation goes back to Aristarchus and was championed by Bassett, "Three Threads," p. 54.

42. Kullmann, "Motiv," pp. 170–75 (citing *Il.* 2. 3–4, 2. 37–40, 11. 52–55, 12. 13–18, 12. 20–23, 13. 222–27, 19. 86–88, 19. 270–74, 20. 21); pp. 190–92 (citing *Il.* 2. 110–15, 9. 17–25, 12. 231–50, 14. 69–70, 22. 208–12). The latter group are held to refer "indirectly" to the plan of Zeus. Cf. also Kullmann's "Zur Διὸς βουλή des Iliasproömiums," *Philologus* 100 (1956): 132–33, citing *Il.* 14. 83–87 and 17. 647.

43. Cf. Kullmann, *Quellen*, p. 47, n. 2.

We may move toward a fifth interpretation by observing that our phrase occurs in one other place in early hexameter: *Odyssey* 11. 281–97 tells of a seer whose θεοῦ . . . μοῖρα cast him in prison until the fated time was fulfilled; then Iphicles his captor released him, Διὸς δ' ἐτελείετο βουλή. The scholiast (ad loc.) explains the phrase: "because Zeus had told the seer that he would be overcome by Iphicles." In other words, the seer recognized the will of Zeus in the correspondence of the event to his foreknowledge of it.

This association of Διὸς βουλή with foreknowledge and prophecy is strengthened by passages in which that phrase means the content of an oracle (*Od.* 14. 328 = 19. 296; *Hymn. Hom. Ap.* 132; *Hymn. Hom. Merc.* 538). *Odyssey* 8. 73–82 suggests that Διὸς . . . βουλή may have this meaning in the *Iliad* proem also. Here Demodocus sings of the quarrel between Achilles and Odysseus which arose at a feast, and how Agamemnon rejoiced in his heart that the best of the Achaeans were quarreling, since Apollo had spoken to him when he came to Delphi:

τότε γάρ ῥα κυλίνδετο πήματος ἀρχὴ
Τρωσί τε καὶ Δαναοῖσι Διὸς μεγάλου διὰ βουλάς.

[*Od.* 8. 81–82]

This story should belong to the first arrival of the Greeks at Tenedos,[44] and is most economically explained by assuming that Agamemnon had received an oracle that Troy would fall after the best of the Achaeans quarreled. The oracle had a false and premature fulfillment in a quarrel between Achilles and Odysseus; the true fulfillment was the quarrel between Achilles and Agamemnon (the real "best of the Achaeans") which opens the *Iliad*.[45] By this interpretation the words in lines 5 and 6 of the proem mean: "the will of Zeus [as foretold] was [finally] coming to pass from the time those two divided . . ." (hence my translation: "the word of Zeus"). The promise given long ago at Delphi when "the beginning of trouble was in motion" (*Od.* 8. 81) was at last to be kept.[46]

In fact the train of events which originates with the quarrel in Book 1 of the *Iliad* leads to the death of Hector, which assures the fall of Troy (*Il.* 24. 380–85); thus it is true that the μῆνις, while it brings great suffering on the Greeks, also makes certain their promised victory.

This interpretation is subject to one mighty objection: no one in the *Iliad* ever speaks of the μῆνις as the fulfillment of a prophecy. But we can say that this interpretation is not inconsistent with the poem, and is consistent with epic linguistic usage.

44. In other words, this was the quarrel portrayed by Sophocles in the *Syndeipnoi* (frags. 139–53 Nauck).

45. This is the interpretation of Pagliaro, except that he places the quarrel at Aulis ("Proemio," pp. 17–20); I also derive from him the interpretation of the proem in the light of Demodocus' story.

46. Agamemnon may actually be referring to this oracle and its deceptive fulfillment when he complains that the promises of Zeus have not been kept (*Il.* 2. 110–18 = 9. 17–25). He cannot be referring to the omen described by Odysseus (*Il.* 2. 299–332), since this predicted success in the tenth year, and it is exactly the nine-year delay of which Agamemnon complains (*Il.* 2. 134–35).

Within the proem Διὸς δ' ἐτελείετο βουλή draws attention to the paradoxical relation between Zeus and the Achaeans. Zeus wills the victory of the Achaeans, but their victory comes about only because they endure a crushing disaster. The proem develops from wrath to suffering to death to defilement before it comes to Zeus. The frame continually widens; it begins with the single hero, then includes his living community, then the human dead, then the animals—birds and dogs. Finally it includes also the god; we move abruptly from the lowest to the highest. The association of Zeus with the carrion scavengers is reinforced by the aspect of the verbs. Ἔθηκε and προΐαψεν are aorists, while τεῦχε and ἐτελείετο are imperfects; we are thus led to associate the verbs in pairs, and to see, not the death of the heroes, but their defilement, as the special accomplishment of Zeus.

Yet here also the proem is at odds with the poem. Zeus does not will the defilement of the dead; on the contrary, he arranges the funerals of Sarpedon (*Il.* 16. 666–83) and Hector (*Il.* 24. 110–19). If we take Zeus as the high god, representative of the gods in general, the contrast is even sharper; for, while the gods may require the destruction of mortals, they do not, as Hera explicitly says (*Il.* 16. 450–57), require their defilement (although they may predict it: *Il.* 8. 379–80). If we ask why the defilement of the dead does not occur in the *Iliad*, the simple answer is that the gods prevent it. Hera sees to it that the Trojans do not capture the body of Patroclus (*Il.* 18. 165–86), and Thetis keeps the maggots from him (*Il.* 19. 30–33). Aphrodite keeps the dogs from Hector (*Il.* 23. 184–87) and Apollo protects his body (*Il.* 23. 188–91, 24. 18–21).

But the implication of the proem is partly right: the gods desire and contrive the reciprocal violence which leads the heroes to fear and to intend the defilement of the dead. God sends war, and as war feeds on itself the heroes become more vindictive than even the gods. At one point, when Zeus says that Hera might wish to eat Priam and his children raw (*Il.* 4. 31–36), the poet suggests that even the gods might be drawn into bestial impurity. At the end, with the gods' help, there is purity and healing, as there was for Niobe (*Il.* 24. 613–14). But in the proem, by his association of Zeus with the vultures, the poet suggests the demonic power of the forces which Zeus lets slip.

From this point the proem winds down to its conclusion; lines 6 and 7 give the sense of an ending. We return to the human world, to a particular action and particular actors. Ἐξ οὗ δή focuses on a particular moment, which is then specified by the remainder of line 6. Διαστήτην, while returning us to the theme (Achilles' withdrawal from battle) with which the proem began, introduces a development from the singular to the dual; what had appeared in line 1 as Achilles' solitary wrath now is shown to have its source in a quarrel between two parties. There is thus a shift from theme to plot, from the μῆνις to its causes. In the process the wrath is somewhat "demystified"; we shift from the numinous μῆνις to the more mundane ἔρις which underlies ἐρίσαντε. Διίστημι, similarly, is a rather colorless verb, meaning "divide" or "go in opposite directions": its five other uses in

Homer (*Il.* 12. 86, 13. 29, 16. 470, 17. 391, 21. 436) have no connotation of hostility.

Ἐρίσαντε, an aorist participle, states an event prior in time to the finite verb it modifies;[47] we might translate the phrase, "parted, having quarreled." Line 7 names the subjects of the verb. The poet is telling his story backward; the proem is not in narrative but in logical order. It responds to the questions: What story is it? Why is it worth telling? How does it begin and with whom?[48]

Line 6 is hardly familiar; there are no complex units in it which recur, and the words of which it is made have no fixed places in the line[49]—with the exception of τὰ πρῶτα, which appears here in its normal place just before the caesura.[50] Line 7, on the other hand, is entirely composed of familiar phrases, mostly in their familiar positions. Ἀτρεΐδης occurs more than half the time at the beginning of the line, and δῖος Ἀχιλλεύς is invariably at the end of the line. The motion from free composition to fixed language, and from compact to diffuse transmittal of information (line 7 consists, in effect, of two proper names), which, as we saw, is characteristic of the structure of the line, is here expanded in scale, so that the motion is from a free line to a formulaic line. Just as the familiar line-ending formulae give a sense of closure to a particular line, so here the familiar phrases of line 7 give a sense of closure to the proem as a whole.

Yet, just as there is a touch of the familiar in line 6, so there is an unfamiliar touch in line 7. Ἄναξ ἀνδρῶν, most frequently used (as here) as an epithet of Agamemnon, occurs in Homer some fifty times. Everywhere else, however, it occurs just after the caesura. Here and only here the phrase has been shifted to the first half of the line.[51] Our attention is drawn to the phrase, so that its latent semantics are brought to the surface. While Agamemnon is always ἄναξ ἀνδρῶν, the epithet has a special relevance here; the quarrel between Agamemnon and Achilles was so dangerous and insoluble precisely because Agamemnon was "king of men."

Since the verbal phrase in line 6 is in the dual, it requires two names to supply its subject; line 6 looks forward to line 7, and the syntax is not complete until the last word in that line: Ἀχιλλεύς. This completion of the syntax, when it arrives, also contributes to a sense of having reached a full stop. The proem as a whole moves from the accusative μῆνιν to the nominative Ἀχιλλεύς, from the hero's act as the object of song, to the hero as

47. Cf. R. Kühner, *Ausführliche Grammatik der griechischen Sprache*, vol. 1^2 (Hannover, 1869), p. 199.

48. In actually beginning his story, the poet goes back one further step and asks: who provoked them to quarrel? He then goes back one step further still, and tells how Agamemnon angered Apollo, how Apollo's anger led to the plague, and how the plague led to the quarrel.

49. Of the sixteen instances of ἐξ οὗ cited by Pagliaro ("Proemio," pp. 11–12), about half occur at the beginning of the line. I suggest, however, that it is misleading to take this as a formulaic feature; more properly it is an outcome of the tendency in the Homeric style for metrical and syntactic segments to correspond, so that items which open a clause tend also to open the line. On the originality of διαστήτην ἐρίσαντε, see Russo, "Closer Look," p. 246.

50. Πρῶτον and πρῶτα which, taken together, appear more than 140 times in Homer, appear more than twice as often just before the caesura as in all other positions put together.

51. As noted by Pagliaro, "Proemio," p. 38.

actor. The link between the first word and the last frames the whole as a unity;[52] the proem is over, and the poem is ready to begin.

In conclusion a few general remarks may be in order. The proem has long been admired for its clarity and compactness;[53] here we have also examined the poetic devices which make it expressive: personification—in the development of μῆνιν through οὐλομένην and ἄλγε' ἔθηκε; metaphor—especially in δαῖτα; variation of tone—in the contrast between μῆνιν and ἐρίσαντε. We have found the proem to be a formed unity with a beginning, middle, and end, beginning and ending with Achilles, and centering on the dogs and birds, and on Zeus.

The proem does not tell us what the story will be, but suggests, by the elements chosen for inclusion, what the story will be about. The *Iliad*, it tells us, will explore the relations between man, beast, and god; it will be a story of suffering and death, and will go beyond this to tell of the ultimate fate of the dead. The fundamental device of the proem, as in all of Homer, is parataxis; the relevance of elements to one another is implied by their mere conjunction. This is an art of resonance and implication; precisely because the elements are familiar they come before us charged with meaning.

Where so much is familiar, further, every unfamiliar touch is meaningful—a fresh phrase like ἰφθίμους ψυχάς; a familiar word used in an unfamiliar way, like τεῦχε; even a familiar phrase in an unfamiliar position, like ἄναξ ἀνδρῶν. The familiar itself, balancing the unfamiliar, could be used to give the style shape, and vary its pace. The epic tradition may be thought of as the ground against which Homer displayed the figure of his art.

University of Chicago

52. Cf. Bassett, "Proems," p. 340; and Rüter, *Odysseeinterpretationen*, p. 30, n. 6.
53. Cf. Rüter, *Odysseeinterpretationen*, p. 33.

ARGOS AND ARGIVES IN THE *ILIAD*

ROBERT DREWS

For almost a century, from Heinrich Schliemann's discovery to Michael Ventris', it was the preponderant opinion that the heroes of the Homeric poems were at home in Mycenaean Greece, the palaces of the LH III period. The Linear B tablets, however, have revealed a society fundamentally different from the society the *Iliad* describes, and scholars who disagree on much else are agreed that Mycenaean Greece no longer seems to furnish a credible model for the heroic society. There has been, as a result, a tendency to accept M. I. Finley's thesis that "the world of Odysseus" existed during the Dark Age of Greece—especially the tenth and ninth centuries—and apparently on both sides of the Aegean.[1] That thesis, too, has been undermined, mostly by excavations at Lefkandi, Smyrna, Argos, Fortetsa, and other Dark Age sites. What archaeologists have found there does not square with the "Homeric" picture of the Dark Age which Finley has drawn. The difficulty has been stated forcefully and concisely by A. M. Snodgrass, who finds the world which Homer describes "unimaginable in dark age Greece."[2] Nor, finally, can Homer's own eighth century have supplied much to his picture of heroic society. The world of the Euboean and Corinthian traders which has come to light at Al Mina, Pithecusae, and Eretria may be reflected here and there in the *Odyssey*, but it seems far removed from the world recalled in the *Iliad*.

Since the heroic society has not been found where many had expected to find it, it may be worthwhile to revive an old hypothesis. A century ago William D. Geddes published an argument that the Homeric epics originated in the area which in classical times corresponded to Malis, Achaea Phthiotis, and Thessaly,[3] and which for the sake of convenience I shall call "Thessaly." Geddes' suggestion received vigorous though dubious support in Germany during the 1880s, when August Fick, convinced that the epics had indeed originated in Thessaly, "translated" the *Iliad* and the *Odyssey* back into

This article grew out of an underclass seminar at Vanderbilt University in the spring of 1976. Participants in the seminar were Wayne Childers, Yunghi Choe, Mary Quint, Celia Rawlings, and Thomas Surface. For the *Iliad*, I have used the translation of Lang, Leaf, and Myers (London, 1897); for the *Odyssey*, Butcher and Lang (New York, 1906); for Strabo and Pausanias, the Loeb editions of H. L. Jones (London, 1927) and W. H. S. Jones (London and New York, 1918), respectively. Translations from other Greek authors are my own.

1. *The World of Odysseus* (New York, 1954; rev. ed., 1965), pp. 40–43; cf. G. S. Kirk, *The Songs of Homer* (Cambridge, 1962), pp. 126–38. The convenient anthology edited by C. G. Thomas, *Homer's History: Mycenaean or Dark Age?* (New York, 1970), expresses in its title the present range of choices.

2. *The Dark Age of Greece* (Edinburgh, 1971), p. 392; cf. the same scholar's "An Historical Homeric Society?" *JHS* 94 (1974): 114–25.

3. *The Problem of the Homeric Poems* (London, 1878). The theory, in rudimentary form, was first put forward by Giambattista Vico.

0009-837X/79/7402-0002$02.00

the Aeolic dialect of that region.[4] Because of, or despite, such efforts, the Thessalian hypothesis seemed about to prevail. R. C. Jebb stated matter-of-factly his belief that the *Iliad* was descended from a poem written in Thessaly in or after the eleventh century.[5] The fullest exposition of the thesis appeared in Paul Cauer's *Grundfragen der Homerkritik*, published initially in 1895 and in a second edition in 1909.

Even before Geddes' book had been published, however, Schliemann's finds at Mycenae had begun to make headlines in Europe and America. With his subsequent discoveries at Tiryns, and then Sir Arthur Evans' on Crete, there stood revealed "the whole pre-Hellenic Aegean civilization. . . . Herewith was swept away at once the whole fabric of assumptions on which the theories of the first three-quarters of the nineteenth century were based." Those were the words of Walter Leaf,[6] in 1915. Needless to say, Leaf was fascinated with Mycenaean and Minoan Greece and had nothing but scorn for the Thessalian hypothesis. By Martin Nilsson's time there was no longer much doubt that the Peloponnese was the heart of the heroes' world. As for the Thessalian hypothesis, Nilsson noted with satisfaction that "the popularity of this view has vanished to a certain extent."[7] It is time, I think, to revive it.

The advantages of such a hypothesis are considerable. If Thessaly was the home of the heroes, it would be less mysterious that Mt. Olympus was the home of the gods or that Thessaly was, as H. J. Rose pointed out, such "a very ancient and fruitful source of mythology."[8] If southern Greece borrowed its heroic notions from the north, it would be easier to understand why it took its Hellenic name from an otherwise undistinguished people on the Malian gulf. Agamemnon's ad hoc suzerainty over the other Achaean kings could be explained as analogous to the practice of the Thessalian *koinon*, whose otherwise independent barons recognized the hegemony of a *tagos* in wartime.[9] And a Thessalian origin of the Greeks' tradition about the Trojan War would account for the Aeolisms in Homer's Greek.

These and other considerations were as apparent in the nineteenth century as they are today. To the arguments marshalled by Geddes and Cauer, however, must now be added the discovery that, in what might be called "mainstream" Greece (Attica, Boeotia and Euboea; the Isthmus and Peloponnese; and, eventually, Ionia), there is little room for a heroic society during either the LH III or the Submycenaean and Protogeometric periods. This area was characterized during the Mycenaean period by a "rationing" economy and society which were centered in the palaces,[10] with Thebes

4. *"Odyssee"* (Göttingen, 1883); *"Ilias"* (Göttingen, 1886).

5. *Homer: An Introduction to the "Iliad" and the "Odyssey"*[5] (Boston, 1894), p. 168.

6. *Homer and History* (London, 1915), p. 2.

7. *The Mycenaean Origin of Greek Mythology* (Berkeley, 1932), p. 232.

8. *A Handbook of Greek Mythology* (New York, 1928), p. 256.

9. H. D. Westlake, *Thessaly in the Fourth Century B.C.* (London, 1935), pp. 25–26, described the *koinon* of the Thessalian baronies during the Archaic and Classical periods: "Its main function was in the event of war to elect a national commander and to mobilize a national army. This commander, who was known as a ταγός, was in theory appointed only for the duration of the current crisis."

10. M. I. Finley, *The Ancient Economy* (Berkeley, 1973), p. 28, suggested the adjective.

the northernmost site at which the symbols of that society, Linear B tablets, have been found.

North and west of Boeotia lay the hinterland. The tumulus burials which have recently been excavated in the Haliacmon valley, north of Mt. Olympus, suggest ties to the central Balkans rather than to the more civilized Mediterranean world.[11] For the area south of Olympus, unfortunately, archaeology does not provide much more than an argumentum ex silentio. Vincent Desborough noted that the Spercheus valley "has been singularly unproductive of Mycenaean remains of any sort. . . . If any conclusion on this meagre evidence is legitimate, it is that the region was rather marginal so far as the Mycenaeans were concerned."[12] Archaeologists have had slightly more success in Thessaly proper. Early in this century A. J. B. Wace and M. S. Thompson reported that "Mycenean wares . . . are found in certain quantities in Thessaly, but before North Greece could become civilised, all civilisation for a time was swept away."[13] Although some *tholos* tombs were visible near Dhimini, Sesklo, and Marmariani, and although Mycenaean pottery was found at some sites near the coast, Wace and Thompson concluded that "Mycenean influence never succeeded in permeating Thessaly, which always continued in a backward and barbarous state of civilisation."[14] Since Wace and Thompson wrote, more Mycenaean pottery has been found in Thessaly, and at Iolkos there has been unearthed a building which its excavator, D. R. Theochares, designated as a "palace."[15] Overall, however, the material record of Late Bronze Age Thessaly is not very impressive. To be sure, in contrast with Macedonia to the north, the physical remains in Thessaly are to some extent "Mycenaean." But when one compares Thessaly proper (to say nothing of the Spercheus valley) with southern Greece, the difference is striking. From Gla and Orchomenus southward there are imposing Mycenaean remains, and in Boeotia as well as in the Peloponnese there manifestly were palaces. In all of Thessaly one palace has been reported. Most important, no Linear B tablets have yet been found at Iolkos, and thus there is no evidence that in Thessaly during the LH III period life and society were organized in the Mycenaean fashion. The region as a whole was apparently innocent of literacy, bureaucracy, massive fortifications, and the other blessings of civilization which stamp Mycenaean Greece as an advanced society.

There is also linguistic evidence that Thessaly was not a part of Mycenaean civilization. Abandoning the view that successive "waves" of Greeks hurled themselves into Greece during the second millennium, linguists are now concluding that all the Greeks arrived at once, bringing with them a

11. For a summary of the finds at Vergina, see N. G. L. Hammond, *A History of Macedonia*, vol. 1 (Oxford, 1972), pp. 271, 328–36.

12. *The Last Mycenaeans and Their Successors* (Oxford, 1964), pp. 126–27.

13. *Prehistoric Thessaly* (Cambridge, 1912), p. 249.

14. Ibid., p. 255. Although some of the tombs are from the Bronze Age, more seem to date from the beginning of the Iron Age; cf. M. S. F. Hood, "*Tholos* Tombs of the Aegean," *Antiquity* 34 (1960): 166–76.

15. "Iolkos," *Archaeology* 11 (1958): 18. For the pottery, see Desborough, *Last Mycenaeans*, pp. 131–35.

single, uniform "proto-Greek" language; and that, as the Greeks spread out in their new homeland, their language became differentiated into various dialects.[16] In the south, innovations were frequent and led to the formation of "Mycenaean Greek." This dialect, which by historical times had again bifurcated into Arcado-Cypriote and Attic-Ionic, seems to have extended throughout mainstream Greece—from Cnossus and the Peloponnese through Euboea and Attica into Boeotia. The language of the recently published tablets from Thebes, at any rate, is not detectably different from that attested at Pylos, Cnossus, and Mycenae.[17] Those Greeks who were linguistically most conservative—the ancestors of the Dorians and West Greeks—perhaps lived in and beyond the Pindus range. The Aeolic dialect seems to have emerged in the buffer zone between the innovating southerners and the isolated northwesterners.[18] If, by the end of the Bronze Age, the form of Greek spoken in the south had diverged from the form of Greek spoken west and north of Boeotia, then it is logical to assume that there had also been some cultural divergence. More than that, if proto-Aeolic was more conservative than Mycenaean Greek, then one may assume that in proto-Aeolic Greece social change (specifically, Minoanizing and Orientalizing tendencies) had been less in evidence than in mainstream Greece, although neither area could have been so isolated as the land occupied by the ancestors of the Dorians.

It is ironic that our thesis requires a demonstration that Thessaly was less civilized than southern Greece. It was precisely because Thessaly seemed so backward that Leaf and others assumed that heroic society must have been centered in the Peloponnese. Nilsson, for example, believed that Greek mythology and the Homeric epics sprang from the splendid Mycenaean capitals. A place so primitive as Thessaly, "which never . . . was penetrated by either the Mycenaean or the historical Greek culture," could have played no part.[19] I doubt that anyone would use such an argument today. To the contrary, the fact that Thessaly was generally more backward than Mycenaean Greece now speaks in favor of a Thessalian origin for the Greeks' heroic traditions. It is precisely because mainstream Greece, in both the Late Helladic period and the Dark Age, appears too domesticated, too settled, too orderly, that we are obliged to look elsewhere for the heroic society.

It is reasonable, then, to suggest that Troy VII*a* was sacked by warriors from Thessaly. Traces of the fact may adhere to the tradition. Achilles came from the Spercheus valley; and two other Thessalian heroes—Protesilaus and Philoctetes—were also crucial to the story,[20] although

16. For the current consensus on this matter, see R. A. Crossland, "Retrospect and Prospects," in *Bronze Age Migrations in the Aegean: Archaeological and Linguistic Problems in Greek Prehistory*, ed. R. A. Crossland and A. Birchall (Park Ridge, N.J., 1974), p. 343.

17. T. G. Spyropoulos and J. Chadwick, *The Thebes Tablets*, vol. 2 (Salamanca, 1975), p. 85.

18. See J. Chadwick, "The Greek Dialects and Greek Prehistory," *G&R*, n.s. 3 (1956): 48. The conclusions reached by W. Wyatt, Jr., "The Prehistory of the Greek Dialects," *TAPA* 101 (1970): 627–28, seem compatible with this, although Wyatt does away with the conventional nomenclature.

19. *Mycenaean Origin*, p. 237.

20. Cf. Kirk, *Songs of Homer*, p. 155.

neither figures in the action of the *Iliad*. We need not imagine that so modest a place as Troy VII*a* succumbed to a fleet of more than forty or fifty ships. The expedition against Troy was probably not an international venture joined by kings from as far away as Crete and Pylos, but rather a raid, led by three or four of the coastal barons of Thessaly. That the peoples of this region conducted such raids is certain, since by the dawn of the first millennium the Troad and much else in the northeast Aegean had been taken over by speakers of the Aeolic dialect.[21] A legend embedded in the Catalog of Ships credits Achilles with the sacking of two other cities in the Troad, Thebe and Lyrnessus; and for Oileus (father of another Thessalian baron) the cataloger uses the epithet, "sacker of cities."[22] Although we need not list them among the Sea Peoples, it is at least probable that toward the end of the Bronze Age the less civilized Greeks of Thessaly participated in various and sundry raids upon the cities within their horizon.

In attempting to prove the Thessalian hypothesis, Cauer used a variety of arguments,[23] some of which seem still convincing, others farfetched. An argument which is potentially conclusive was stated by Cauer in his chapter, "Achäer, Danäer, Argeer." Briefly stated, the argument is that each of the three names which Homer uses for the heroes who went to Troy—Achaeans, Danaans, Argives—originally applied to peoples in Thessaly.

To Cauer's brief treatment of the Danaans[24] I can add nothing. As for the Achaeans, since 1924 many scholars have identified them with the Ahhiyawa mentioned in Hittite texts.[25] This identification seems capable of neither proof nor disproof, and there is still a lively debate about where the Ahhiyawa lived. The most recent study of the Achaean name concluded, as did Cauer, "che nell'epos in origine il nome di Achei indicasse solo un popolo della Tessaglia, la patria di Achille, e che quindi non sia originario per l'Acaia peloponnesiaca il nome di Acaia, ma solo per l'Acaia Ftiotide."[26] (It is therefore distressing to observe that there is a growing tendency among linguists to refer to the dialect of the LH Peloponnese as "Achaean" rather than "Mycenaean." The admonitions of R. A. Crossland on this point should be heeded.[27])

Cauer's presentation of the names "Argos" and "Argives"[28] needs reinforcement. A fresh look at the old evidence in the light of the new should

21. Like the "Dorian Invasion," the migration of Aeolic Greeks into the northeast Aegean left little or no archaeological imprint; cf. Desborough, *Last Mycenaeans*, p. 255.

22. *Il*. 2. 691, 2. 728.

23. *Grundfragen der Homerkritik*^{2} (Leipzig, 1909), pp. 191–237.

24. Ibid., pp. 220–22.

25. For an up-to-date discussion of the problem, see J. D. Muhly, "Hittites and Achaeans: Ahhijawā *redomitus*," *Historia* 23 (1974): 129–39.

26. A. Sacconi, "Gli Achei in età micenea ed in Omero," *Živa Ant*. 19 (1969): 15.

27. "Retrospect and Prospects," p. 341.

28. *Grundfragen*, pp. 223–35. Cauer, in turn, was indebted to the "glänzende Vermutung" arrived at almost simultaneously by G. Busolt, *Griechische Geschichte*, vol. 1^2 (Gotha, 1893), p. 223, and K. J. Beloch, *Griechische Geschichte*, vol. 1 (Strassburg, 1893), p. 157, "dass die homerischen Dichter ursprünglich unter Argos nur das thessalische verstanden haben."

leave little doubt that in the heroic tradition those terms originally had Thessalian rather than Peloponnesian connotations.

In a note on the meaning of "Argos" in Homer, D. L. Page[29] states that "Ἄργος may denote (*a*) the town Argos, (*b*) the district Argos, especially as the home of Agamemnon (the epithets πολυδίψιον, ἱππόβατον presumably refer specially to the Argive plain); (*c*) Greece in general, sometimes with special reference to southern Greece (the Peloponnese as a whole), sometimes comprising the country entire, the place from which all the Achaeans came to Troy,—this I take to be a usage derived from the paramount importance of the district governed by the great overlord." Page's set of definitions, and the explanation thereof, was in more rudimentary form first hammered out by Strabo, and has been repeated ever since.[30] A complete listing, as found in G. Autenrieth's dictionary,[31] would include yet another meaning. I suppose that this other meaning was ignored by Page (as it certainly was by Leaf[32]) because it occurs in the Catalog of Ships. But it is for that reason the most important of all for our purposes. Leaf regarded the Catalog as a late and supposititious document. But if, as Page has so forcefully argued and as most other scholars today agree, the Catalog of Ships is a very old poem (composed in either the LH IIIC or, more likely, the Submycenaean period),[33] then the meaning of "Argos" in the Catalog is our best clue to the evolution of the name.

There is, in the Catalog of Ships, a reference to the city of Argos in the Peloponnese, and we shall examine that reference in due course. On the other hand, the cataloger does not seem to have used the names "Argives" and "Argos" in the sense in which they are so familiar in the *Iliad* proper, as equivalents for all the Greek heroes and their homeland. The Argives in this broader sense do appear, it is true, at *Iliad* 2. 725, in the entry on Philoctetes. That hero had been left with his wound on the island of Lemnos; "yet were the Argives soon to bethink them beside their ships of king Philoctetes." But the entry on Philoctetes, like that on Protesilaus, was not composed by the cataloger. Our Catalog of Ships, it is generally agreed, was at one time a survey of the contingents assembled at Aulis; with a few

29. *History and the Homeric "Iliad"* (Berkeley, 1959), p. 164, n. 33.

30. Strabo 8. 6. 5. The set of meanings offered by Cauer, *Grundfragen*, pp. 226–28, is less vulnerable than Leaf's (*Homer and History*, pp. 193–95), but is still very much influenced by Strabo's analysis and presuppositions.

31. *A Homeric Dictionary*[4], trans. R. Keep (New York, 1888), s.v.

32. In his discussion of the meanings of "Argos" in Homer, Leaf (*Homer and History*, p. 193) declared that "the problem of its use is, for our purpose, somewhat simplified when we notice that the much discussed Pelasgian Argos of *Il*. ii. 681 is not a Homeric term, but occurs only in the Catalogue."

33. In the most recent full-length study, R. Hope Simpson and J. F. Lazenby, *The Catalogue of the Ships in Homer's "Iliad"* (Oxford, 1970), pp. 156–67, conclude that the Catalog was composed during the LH IIIC period. Because I believe that the cataloger was profoundly mistaken about both the nature of the Trojan War and the character of Mycenaean society, I prefer to place him in the Submycenaean rather than the LH IIIC period. Unlike the Catalog of Ships, the Catalog of Trojan Allies (*Il*. 2. 816–77) was perhaps a creation of Homer's own time; cf. J. M. Cook, "Two Notes on the Homeric Catalogue," *Studi micenei ed egeoanatolici*, 1967, pp. 103–9. I have presented a supporting argument in "The Earliest Greek Settlements on the Black Sea," *JHS* 96 (1976): 20–22; cf. S. Burstein, "Fragment 53 of Callisthenes and the Text of *Iliad* 2. 850–55," *CP* 71 (1976): 339–41.

minor alterations, this ancient poem was fitted to its present function—a review of all the host besieging Troy in the tenth year of the war. Now, although Philoctetes and Protesilaus were both alive and well at Aulis, by the tenth year of the war the one was dead and the other languishing on Lemnos. Their two entries in the Catalog, therefore, had to be revised in order to fit the new context. All of this has been noted frequently;[34] what is important for our purposes is the corollary that the "Argives" of 2. 725 were not put there by the original cataloger. There is thus no evidence that in the days of the cataloger "Argos" and "Argives" had yet acquired their Panhellenic connotations (nor were the Achaeans at this time anything other than the subjects of Achilles).[35]

We come, then, to the meaning disregarded by Leaf and Page. After listing the contingents from all the rest of the Greek world—from Boeotia through the Dodecanese—the cataloger continues:

> Now all moreover that dwelt in the Pelasgian Argos and inhabited Alos and Alope and Trachis and possessed Phthia and Hellas the home of fair women, and were called Myrmidons and Hellenes and Achaians; of all these, even fifty ships, Achilles was captain.
>
> [*Il.* 2. 681–85]

Such a translation of 681 implies that the Pelasgic Argos was part of Achilles' kingdom, perhaps a town like Alos or Alope, or a district like Hellas or Phthia. Both the translation and the implication are wrong. The Greek text for these lines is as follows:

> *νῦν αὖ τοὺς ὅσσοι τὸ Πελασγικὸν Ἄργος ἔναιον*
> *οἵ τ' Ἄλον οἵ τ' Ἀλόπην οἵ τε Τρηχῖνα νέμοντο*
> *οἵ τ' εἶχον Φθίην ἠδ' Ἑλλάδα καλλιγύναικα*
> *Μυρμιδόνες δὲ καλεῦντο καὶ Ἕλληνες καὶ Ἀχαιοί*
> *τῶν αὖ πεντήκοντα νεῶν ἦν ἀρχὸς Ἀχιλλεύς.*

The translation of Lang, Leaf, and Myers, it will be noted, does nothing at all with the *τοὺς* of 681 and incorrectly renders the *νῦν* of the same line, not as a temporal adverb, but as a colorless conjunction. These are small but deadly errors. Every serious philological analysis of 681 has concluded that the line is not part of the entry on Achilles' kingdom (682–85), but rather a proem which introduces the entire Thessalian section (682–759) with which the Catalog closes. And so the Pelasgic Argos, far from being merely a part of Achilles' kingdom (as it appears, for example, in the maps provided by R. Hope Simpson and J. F. Lazenby[36] or by F. Stubbings[37]), was the cataloger's term for all nine Thessalian baronies which this section contains.

34. See, e.g., V. Burr, ΝΕΩΝ ΚΑΤΑΛΟΓΟΣ: *Untersuchungen zum homerischen Schiffskatalog*, Klio Beiheft 49 (Berlin, 1944), pp. 129–30, 136; Page, *History and the Homeric "Iliad,"* p. 149; Kirk, *Songs of Homer*, p. 155; Hope Simpson and Lazenby, *Catalogue*, pp. 159–60.
35. See p. 130.
36. *Catalogue*, map 7 (p. 127).
37. *CAH*, vol. 2^2, pt. 2 (Cambridge, 1975), map 9 (p. 344).

On a grammatical problem such as this, our best authorities are the ancient scholars. In explanation of 681, one scholiast remarks that for *τοὺς* the reader must supply a "tell me" or an "I shall sing" from the first proem (*μακρόθεν ὑπακούεται τὸ "ἔσπετε" ἢ τὸ "ἐρέω"*). Another scholiast observes that at this line the poet "makes a second beginning of the Catalog; for Thessaly is a large and low plain." A third scholiast found in 681 the artistry *τοῦ Ὁμήρου φιλοτέχνως ὥσπερ προοιμιαζουμένου.*[38]

Modern editors agree with the scholiasts. D. B. Monro explained the line as marking "a transition to a different part of the map. *τούς* is used as if *ἐρέω* or some equivalent word were to follow."[39] Leaf himself admitted as much, but found the line just one more proof that the Catalog was the work of a botcher.[40] For Viktor Burr, the line was the most obvious indication that the Thessalian section of the Catalog (681–759) was originally an independent, self-contained entity: "Dies tritt schon rein äusserlich dadurch in die Augen, dass B 681 mit *νῦν αὖ τούς* an den Beginn des Prooimion (B 484) erinnert und direkt an *ἐρέω* (B 493) oder an *ἔσπετε* (B 484) anknupft."[41] Günther Jachmann saw in 681 the solemnity "eines emphatischen Introitus."[42] Alexander Pope's translation, "Now, Muse, recount Pelasgic Argos' powers," preserves both the solemnity and the meaning of the line.

For a definition of the Pelasgic Argos, the best evidence is the Catalog itself. Ancient commentators on the Catalog gave their opinions, and most of them suggested Thessaly *tout court*. That is certainly possible, since historical Thessaly might have been perceived as a unit (and so might have had a name) before the arrival of the Dorian Thessali. The Pelasgic Argos is mentioned in a very early oracle, but we cannot be sure what Apollo meant by it, or even that he knew what it was:[43]

> Best of all is the land of the Pelasgic Argos,
> The horses of Thessaly, the women of Lacedaemon,
> And the men who drink the waters of fair Arethusa.
> But better still than these, are they who dwell
> 'twixt Tiryns and Arcadia, rich in flocks,
> Argives in linen corslets, goads of war.
> But you, Aegians, are neither third nor fourth
> Nor twelfth, nor in the count nor of account.

Strabo has a great deal to say about the Pelasgic Argos, as about other places mentioned in the Catalog. At 5. 2. 4, in his explanation of "Pelasgic,"

38. This scholiast reports Zenodotus' observation that without the proem of 681 the Thessalian section of the Catalog would be "ill-joined" with what precedes it. For all scholia, see the edition of H. Erbse, *Scholia Graeca in Homeri "Iliadem,"* 4 vols. (Berlin, 1969).

39. *Homer: "Iliad" Books I–XII*³ (Oxford, 1890), ad loc.

40. *The "Iliad,"* vol. 1² (London, 1900), ad loc.

41. *Schiffskatalog*, p. 87.

42. *Der homerische Schiffskatalog und die "Ilias"* (Köln-Opladen, 1958), p. 184.

43. H. W. Parke and D. E. Wormell, *The Delphic Oracle*, 2 vols. (Oxford, 1956), 2:1 (no. 1). Parke and Wormell (1:82–83) date the oracle to the early seventh century.

he is precise about the geographical limits:

> Thessaly is called "the Pelasgian Argos" (I mean that part of it which lies between the outlets of the Peneius River and Thermopylae as far as the mountainous country of Pindus) on account of the fact that the Pelasgi extended their rule over these regions.

He discusses the term again at 9. 5. 5:

> Some take the Pelasgian Argos as a Thessalian city once situated in the neighborhood of Larisa but now no longer existent; but others take it, not as a city, but as the plain of the Thessalians, which is referred to by this name because Abas, who brought a colony there from Argos, so named it.

Both the detail of 5. 2. 4 and the lame speculation of 9. 5. 5 show that Strabo and his contemporaries knew nothing about the name other than what could be deduced from the Catalog itself. A careful reading of 681, as we have seen, excludes the possibility that the Pelasgic Argos was a Thessalian city and shows that it must have the definition which Strabo gives it at 5. 2. 4. Originally it may not even have been a proper noun. The article (or demonstrative), τό, suggests a common noun.[44] Strabo states that in Thessaly and Macedonia *argos* was the word for "plain," and he is supported by a number of ancient texts. The argument has been fully stated by T. W. Allen, and I shall add only (*contra* Allen) that the plain in question must certainly have been the great Thessalian plain, far and away the largest in Greece.[45] However that may be, by the cataloger's time "the Pelasgic Argos" was no longer a common noun, since for him the term embraced not only the plain, but also the Pelion-Ossa range and the mountainous country of Phthiotic Achaea and Malis.

We may conclude that, when the Catalog of Ships was composed, "the Pelasgic Argos" was a term used for the entire area from the Spercheus river north to the Peneus, and from the sea west to the Pindus range. We may infer, furthermore, that before the composition of the Catalog of Ships there was already in circulation a poem celebrating the contingents which had sailed against Troy from the Pelasgic Argos. This inference is based on the proemic nature of 681 and also on the otherwise inexplicable position of the Thessalian section at the end of the present Catalog.[46] In

44. T. W. Allen, *The Homeric Catalogue of Ships* (Oxford, 1921), p. 108: "The word . . . is a common noun (for we must not invent a city bound only to disappear)."

45. Strabo 8. 6. 9. Allen, *Catalogue*, pp. 108–9, identified the Pelasgic Argos with the Spercheus valley. Allen's discussion of the line entirely omits the grammatical difficulties, and is devoted to a defense (*contra* Leaf) of its antiquity. Hope Simpson and Lazenby, who retain Allen's identification, hardly deal with 681 at all; their comments (*Catalogue*, p. 175, n. 106) ignore both the νῦν and the τούς.

46. As Hope Simpson and Lazenby, *Catalogue*, p. 175, n. 6, note, "the isolated position of the Thessalian contingents at the end is, in any case, a problem. Allen, *Catalogue*, p. 39, maintained that it reflects the fact that Thessaly was the last area of the Greek world conquered by the Mycenaeans. Jachmann, *Schiffskatalog*, pp. 184 ff., suggested that the cataloger chose to end with the

this early form of the tradition, at least nine chieftains—among them, Achilles, Protesilaus, and Philoctetes—were said to have supplied three hundred ships for the venture. This figure in the present Catalog has puzzled many scholars. Hope Simpson and Lazenby observe that "the numbers from Thessaly seem out of all proportion to the rest," and Page warns that "the figures for Thessalian districts . . . are much too high."[47] The puzzle disappears if one accepts the Thessalian hypothesis: in the earliest stage of the heroic tradition about the sack of Troy, the "Argives" were all Thessalian.

During the period in which the Catalog of Ships was composed (perhaps the Submycenaean period), what had until then been sung by Aeolic bards as an exploit of the Pelasgic Argives became a far grander event. At a time when the geography of Mycenaean Greece was still remembered, but the character of its civilization had been forgotten, the descendants of the southern, Mycenaean Greeks enlisted their own ancestors in the Trojan War. (The borrowing may have taken place in Boeotia, where at the end of the LH III period speakers of the old Mycenaean dialect seem to have been joined by newly arrived immigrants from the Aeolic north.) But the collective name which bards had been using for the warriors and their homeland did not change. Instead, "Argos" became synonymous with the homelands of the Mycenaean as well as of the Aeolic forebears. For the bards of the Dark Age, "Argos" was heroic Greece, and heroic Greece included all those regions from which warriors were now claimed to have gone to Troy.

So it happens that, in the *Iliad* proper, "Argos" and "Argives" no longer have Thessalian connotations. Even the formula, "horse-pasturing Argos," though probably coined for the Thessalian plain,[48] has a new meaning. According to Autenrieth, Ἀργεῖος in Homer means "an inhabitant of Ἄργος; frequently in plural as collective designation of Greeks." The noun, Ἄργος, is defined by the same authority as "in widest sense, the whole of Greece."[49] These definitions are convenient, but they are not entirely accurate. "Argives" was not an eighth-century word for "Greeks"; it did not apply to Homer's contemporaries nor even to all the Greeks of Agamemnon's day (the Dorians, for example). Instead, Homer's Argives were quite simply "the heroes who fought against the Trojans." The Argives (or the Achaeans,

Thessalians because their heroes were much more renowned than those of the Dodecanese. I agree with Burr's description of *Il.* 681–759 (*Schiffskatalog*, pp. 86–87): "Diese Verse bilden einen selbständigen, in sich abgeschlossenen zweiten Hauptteil des Katalogs." Burr (pp. 106–7) also suggested that the lines originally described a mustering of ships at Thessalian Halos.

47. *Catalogue*, p. 161; *History and the Homeric "Iliad,"* p. 152.

48. "Best of all," said the oracle, were "the horses of Thessaly," and that was probably as true for the LH period as it was for the early seventh century. Leaf's identification (*Homer and History*, p. 194) of Peloponnesian Argos as the original "pasture-land of horses" was an *ex cathedra* verdict: "in the pools which fringe the marshy land along the southern shore brood mares can still [!] be seen from the train plashing with their colts through the rank grass; and with this fact falls to pieces a whole tissue of theory which assumes that a 'horse-breeding Argos' must be in Thessaly."

49. *Dictionary*, s.vv.

or the Danaans) and the Trojans are the two parties in the conflict. The dichotomy is clearest where both opponents are mentioned: "Why must the Argives make war on the Trojans?" Or, as Achilles says to Patroclus, "Would that not one of all the Trojans might escape death, nor one of the Argives."[50] Similarly, Argos in the *Iliad* is the land across the Aegean whence these heroes have come, with primarily narrative rather than geographical connotations. If one must supply an equivalent, "the home of the Argives" will be safe, though circular; "heroic Greece" will do (Homer's own Ionia, for example, was obviously not included), although "the heroic Greek mainland" (as opposed to the surrounding islands) may occasionally be required. All the heroes besieging Troy had come from Argos, and all hoped to return to it. At *Iliad* 15. 372 Nestor prays Zeus not to let the Trojans triumph, "if ever one of us in wheat-bearing Argos did burn to thee fat thighs of bull or sheep." And Odysseus promises Achilles at *Iliad* 9. 283 that, "if we win to the richest of lands, even Achaian Argos," Agamemnon will treat Achilles as a favorite son.

Aside from the reference, in the Catalog of Ships, to the Pelasgic Argos, there are 217 instances of the noun, "Argos," and the adjective, "Argive," in the *Iliad*.[51] Of these, 209 (ninety-six percent) carry the common meaning set forth above. As for the eight other passages, the reference in six of them is to the city on the Inachus river, in the northeast Peloponnese; in the other two passages the reference may be either to the city of Argos or to the "home of the Argives." Those are the only meanings which "Argos" and "Argive" have in the *Iliad*.

Other definitions are not only superfluous but wrong. Here belong Autenrieth's (or Leaf's, or Page's) second and third definitions: the kingdom of Agamemnon, and the Peloponnese. The lists presented by Autenrieth and other modern scholars are more elaborate, and therefore more mischievous, than the list in Strabo (8. 6. 5) on which they depend. Although I cannot quote in full Strabo's long discussion, it may be useful to quote from it, so that the quality of Strabo's analysis can be assessed. For it is on that analysis that the conventional views are founded:

> Let me mention in how many ways the term "Argos" is used by the poet. . . . In the first place, the city is called Argos: "Argos and Sparta," "And those who held Argos and Tiryns." And, secondly, the Peloponnesus: "In our home in Argos," for the city of Argos was not his [i.e., Agamemnon's] home. And, thirdly, Greece as a whole; at any rate, he calls all Greeks Argives, just as he calls them Danaans and Achaeans.

The perceptive reader may be unconvinced of the necessity of Strabo's second definition, for, although it is true that Agamemnon did not live in the city of Argos, nothing prevents us from giving to "Argos" in this

50. *Il.* 9. 337–38, 16. 98–99.

51. To the passages listed in the index of the OCT "*Iliad*," s.v. Ἀργεῖος, should be added 12. 37.

passage (*Il.* 1. 30) its usual meaning—"the home of the Argives."[52] Nor are Strabo's supplementary proofs any more convincing:

> To prove that by Argos the poet means the Peloponnesus, we can add the following examples: "Argive Helen," and "There is a city Ephyra in the inmost part of Argos," and "mid-Argos," and "and that over many islands and all Argos he should be lord."

Not many readers, I think, will be persuaded that by "Argive Helen" the poet must have meant "Peloponnesian Helen." As for Strabo's second example, even if Ephyra should be identified with Corinth (as Strabo thought), it could hardly be described as lying μυχῷ Ἄργεος ἱπποβότοιο (*Il.* 6. 152).[53] Whatever "mid-Argos" means, the phrase appears only in the *Odyssey*. Strabo's final proof is no more acceptable than the rest, but in the interest of economy I shall use its demolition to bring down another section of the Argological labyrinth.

Autenrieth, Leaf, and others declare that in the *Iliad* "Argos" may also stand for Agamemnon's own kingdom in the northeast Peloponnese. This misconception, though not fostered by Strabo, was common in antiquity in a slightly different form. The Attic tragedians refer to Agamemnon's capital as either Mycenae or Argos, and in one and the same play Euripides vacillates so often between the two names that he appears to be using them as synonyms. Strabo noted this equivocation and explained it as an understandable result of the fact that the two cities were only fifty stades from each other.[54]

In the *Iliad*, however, Homer did not confuse the two. Agamemnon's city is always Mycenae; and in those few passages where the city of Argos appears, it is sometimes Diomedes' capital, never Agamemnon's. Homer's clarity on this matter is what we would expect from a good storyteller. We would not expect of Homer what Autenrieth, Leaf, and others seem to believe: that Homer occasionally used the name of Diomedes' capital as a metaphorical equivalent for "Agamemnon's kingdom" (as, I suppose, a modern poet might refer to France as "London").

On what texts is such a bizarre thesis based? Here let us return to *Iliad* 2. 108; for, although Strabo opined that in this line "Argos" stands for the Peloponnese, Autenrieth presented it as the definitive example of "Argos" in the sense of "Agamemnon's realm." The context of this passage is the assembly of all the Achaeans, called and addressed by Agamemnon. The assembly was restive and would not cease from noise until Agamemnon

52. *Contra* Strabo, Autenrieth, *Dictionary*, s.v., believed that at *Il.* 1. 30 "Argos" was intended not as the Peloponnese but as the realm of Agamemnon. Autenrieth therefore offers only one passage from the *Iliad* (6. 152; see n. 53) in which "Argos" supposedly means "the Peloponnese." Leaf, *Homer and History*, pp. 194–95, lists seven such passages, but all are from the *Odyssey*.

53. There were four or five Ephyres in Greece (for the evidence, see Leaf, *Homer and History*, pp. 177–79), all of them unfortunately suspect: they tend to be either the "ancient" names of real places or the real names of places whose existence cannot be verified. I believe that the Ephyre of the Bellerophon story was originally either Aetolian or Thessalian Ephyre. Eumelus, who seems to have written his Corinthian epic ca. 700, claimed that Ephyre was the "ancient" name of Corinth (*Corinthiaca* frag. 1 Kinkel). But "Corinth" seems to be one of the oldest place-names in Greece.

54. Strabo 8. 6. 19; cf. Eur. *Or.* 98, 101, *IT* 508, 510.

stood up, bearing the scepter which was wrought by Hephaestus, conferred by Zeus, and held successively by Pelops, Atreus, and Thyestes.

> . . . and Thyestes in his turn left it to Agamemnon to bear, that over many islands and all Argos he should be lord. Thereon he leaned and spoke his saying to the Argives.
>
> [*Il.* 2. 107–9]

I shall not belabor the obvious point that the "Argos" of 108 and the "Argives" of 109 should not be completely unrelated. The whole story of the scepter's descent is told in order to explain why Agamemnon is lord—not over his own realm back at Mycenae, but over all these Argives assembled before Troy. It was the scepter which marked his authority to preside over the assembly (so far as I can find, no other Argive king at Troy had a scepter; when Odysseus wished to admonish the assembly, he had to borrow Agamemnon's).[55] A third piece of evidence that "Argos" in 108 stands for all of heroic Greece is the close parallel with passages in which that meaning is clear. At *Iliad* 1. 79 Calchas fears lest by his speech he might anger Agamemnon, who "ruleth all the Argives with might and whom the Achaians obey." Similarly, at *Iliad* 10. 32–33 a troubled Menelaus goes to wake his brother, who "mightily ruled over all the Argives."

So much for Autenrieth's major example. His second instance of Argos as Agamemnon's own kingdom comes a few lines further on (*Il.* 2. 115), when Agamemnon complains that, although Zeus had promised him that he would not return until he had wasted Troy, "now I see that he planned a cruel wile and biddeth me return to Argos dishonoured, with the loss of many of my folk." The line is repeated at *Iliad* 9. 22, Autenrieth's third instance. Although nothing prevents one from equating "Argos" in these lines with Agamemnon's kingdom (or, for that matter, with Mycenae or even with Clytemnestra's bed), one would not make such an equation except to support a preconception. There is no need to interpret "Argos" here in anything other than its normal sense—"the home of the Argives"—especially since in both instances the poet expressly presents Agamemnon as speaking his doleful words to "the Argives." And where there is no need, *entia non sunt multiplicanda.* The same must be said for *Iliad* 1. 30 (Agamemnon vows that he will not release Chryses' daughter: "Nay, ere that shall old age come on her in our house, in Argos, far from her native land"); for *Iliad* 13. 379 (Idomeneus, having slain Othryoneus, rails at the corpse: "We would give thee the fairest daughter of the son of Atreus, and bring her from Argos, and wed her to thee, if only thou wilt aid us to take the fair-set citadel of Ilios"); and for *Iliad* 4. 171 (after Menelaus is wounded,

55. In the *Iliad* kings have scepters when they are acting as kings (9. 156: Agamemnon will give to Achilles seven cities which he will rule with a scepter; cf. the sceptered king depicted on the shield of Achilles at 18. 557). Among the Argives assembled at Troy there was one scepter—Agamemnon's; see esp. 1. 279, 9. 38, 9. 99. For Odysseus' borrowing of the scepter, see 2. 46 and 2. 186. At 6. 159 we hear that Bellerophon had been driven by Proetus out of "the land of the Argives, whom Zeus had made subject to his sceptre." In other words, in an earlier day Proetus held the same overlordship among the Argive heroes which Agamemnon enjoys in the *Iliad*. For the *tagos* of the Thessalian *koinon*, see n. 9.

Agamemnon reckons with the possibility that his brother will die: "Yea in utter shame should I return to thirsty Argos"). Finally, in Autenrieth's seventh passage (*Il.* 15. 30) Zeus reminds Hera how, after she had driven Heracles off to Cos, "him did I rescue thence, and lead again to Argos, the pasture-land of horses." The "Argos" of this passage may have been intended either as the city of Argos or, since Cos was across the Aegean from heroic Greece, as "the home of the Argives."[56]

In summary, there is no support for the assertions of Strabo and Autenrieth that the poet of the *Iliad* sometimes used "Argos" as an equivalent for the Peloponnese or for Agamemnon's own kingdom. These "intermediate definitions" arose, as mentioned earlier, from the erroneous assumption that the name "Argos" as a synonym for Greece was borrowed from the city on the Inachus River.

That assumption was as widely held in antiquity as it is today. In his description of the city of Argos, Strabo states it as his personal opinion (8. 6. 9): "I think the fame of this city brought it about that the other Greeks were named after it." But it was the common opinion of all Greeks, promoted and exploited, to be sure, by the citizens of Argos. According to the *Certamen Homeri et Hesiodi*, the people of the city of Argos set up a statue of Homer in gratitude for the great honor he had brought to the city. The statue was set up, we are told, following Homer's recital in Argos, whither he had come after similar recitals in Delphi, Athens, and Corinth. For his performance at Argos the poet had sung, from the Catalog of Ships, the entry on Diomedes' kingdom.[57] Although we will dismiss the biographical items as amusing fantasy, we may be sure that long after the time of Homer the city of Argos did show its gratitude to the poet by a permanent memorial. In late antiquity, as the description left by Pausanias shows, the city of Argos was festooned with a bewildering number and variety of mythical memorabilia and relics, and about each monument the guides could tell interesting stories (Pausanias observed that, although the guides themselves did not always believe the stories, they continued to recite them because the citizenry insisted that the stories were true).[58]

Not only in the city in question, but throughout Greece, it was believed that Homer had called the Greeks "Argives" because of the towering prominence of the city of Argos in the Heroic Age. The Attic tragedians seem to have moved Agamemnon from Mycenae to Argos because they thought that in his day Argos was the greater of the two cities. Herodotus, in his playful description of the abduction of Io (2. 2. 2), casually notes that the Phoenician merchants came to Argos, since "in those days Argos stood out over everything in what is now called Greece." Pindar, celebrating the city in his Tenth Nemean, admits that the past glories of Argos are too

56. In the Catalog of Ships two heroes (Antiphus and Pheidippus) are listed as coming from Cos (2. 678), but they do not appear in the rest of the *Iliad*.

57. *Cert. Hom. et Hes.* 325.

58. Paus. 2. 23. 6. Pausanias (2. 16–24) itemizes the forest of monuments which the city of Argos had erected to the many "Argive" heroes. In one extraordinary precinct there were displayed Palamedes' dice (in the Temple of Tyche), the statues of the Seven and of the Epigoni, Danaus' tomb, and the cenotaph of the Argives killed at Troy (2. 20. 4–6).

many and too large for him to rehearse, although he does allude to Perseus and Danaë, Io, Danaus and the Danaids, Adrastus and the Seven against Thebes, Heracles, and Diomedes.

Bronze Age Argos retained its prestige until very recently. Allen spoke admiringly of "the powerful Argive monarchy (its power is shown apparently by the submission of the Theban Heracles to Eurystheus of Mycenae, certainly by the two wars which Argos waged against Thebes, which extirpated the house of Cadmus and left such a lasting impression on the Greek recollection)."[59] N. G. L. Hammond reckons the city as a leading power in the LH period: the Danaan name in the *Iliad*, he suggests, "may derive from the eponymous Danaus, whose dynasty at Argos was founded in the fifteenth century. The term Argeioi may derive from the same dynasty, or from the leadership imposed by Adrastus of Argos in the recent war of the Epigoni against Thebes."[60] Even R. A. Tomlinson, who admits that Bronze Age Argos was overshadowed by its neighbors, nonetheless assumes that "its name is used by Homer as a synonym for Greece" (as evidence, Tomlinson cites *Il.* 2. 108 and Strabo 8. 5. 5).[61]

All of this, I suggest, is fundamentally wrong. Our review will show that Homer's Argives are named for the Pelasgic Argos, not for the city of Argos; and I shall suggest the same for the "Argives" who assaulted Thebes. The limits of this study do not permit a detailed examination of the rest of the image, but I believe that the "Argives" in most of the "Argive" myths probably had Aeolic origins.

Although such depreciation of the city of Argos may appear radical, it is not entirely new. Nilsson did not attach these myths to the Pelasgic Argos, it is true, but he was convinced that they were not the patrimony of the city of Argos: "When Argos became the capital of the province, it tried of course to build up a mythology of its own; we have noticed these efforts, but they cannot deceive anybody."[62]

Nilsson's skepticism about the importance of Bronze Age Argos was awakened by the lack of any material evidence for it.[63] I have argued that the lack of palaces and Cyclopean walls, far from ruling out Thessaly as the home of the heroes, actually commends it to our attention; for we now know that the society characterized by these artifacts was quite unlike Homer's heroic society. Concerning the city of Argos, we have a very different question: was it one of the leading powers of the time? Was it powerful enough, for instance, to have rivaled Mycenae and Tiryns, and to have launched an expedition which destroyed distant Thebes? The Greeks of historical times recalled that Cnossus, Mycenae, Tiryns, Pylos, Thebes, and even Iolkos had once been preeminent, and the traditions have been confirmed by the archaeological record. The traditions about the city of Argos, on the other hand, are not supported by the material remains. This

59. *Catalogue*, pp. 61–62.
60. *A History of Greece to 322 B.C.* (Oxford, 1959), p. 66.
61. *Argos and the Argolid* (Ithaca, N.Y., 1972), p. 1.
62. *Mycenaean Origin*, pp. 67–68.
63. Ibid. p. 38 (survey of the Mycenaean remains at Argos).

was true when Nilsson wrote, and it is still true today, despite two decades of careful work at Argos by French archaeologists.[64] We are, in fact, only now able to state with some precision when Argos did become a significant center: in the late eighth century.

At the beginning of the Archaic period, Argos was one of the major powers in Greece. King Pheidon, whose floruit has been placed anywhere from ca. 725 to ca. 625 B.C., is said to have taken over Olympia, to have "restored the lot of Temenus," and to have imposed a system of weights and measures on the Peloponnese.[65] These traditions, however faulty, do find some support in the archaeological record: by ca. 725 Argos had become a fair-sized town, at any rate, and at least one remarkably wealthy tomb from the Late Geometric period has been found.[66] Argive Geometric pottery reached its acme in the period 725–700, and during that time exerted influence on the potters of Lacedaemon.[67]

Until the late eighth century, however, Argos was neither large nor prosperous. In his recently published history of Argos, Thomas Kelly has shown conclusively that modern reconstructions of an "Argive empire" during the Dark Age are without foundation.[68] A survey of the archaeological and literary evidence brought R. A. Tomlinson to the conclusion that Dark Age Argos was "a village, its population a few hundred at most, its ruler a village chief."[69] Kelly's verdict is even more emphatic: "its inhabitants were simple farmers, and there is nothing to suggest that they enjoyed any influence beyond the fields immediately surrounding their own settlement at the foot of the Larissa."[70] The historical (as opposed to the mythical) traditions about pre-Pheidonian Argos are remarkably unimpressive. Like all primitive societies, the early Argives recalled the beginnings of their community, and so we have a number of stories about the foundation of Dorian Argos (apparently no earlier than the eleventh century).[71] The subsequent period, through the Dark Age and most of the eighth century, left no traditions other than a defective kinglist. This list, Pheidon's pedigree, supplies the names of only five kings between the reigns of the founder (Temenus) and Pheidon.[72] There is, in short, no reason to think that between its foundation and ca. 725 Dorian Argos attracted any atten-

64. The French excavations are chronicled in *BCH*, beginning in 1953 and continuing to the present. For summaries in English, see J. M. Cook and J. Boardman, "Archaeology in Greece 1953," *JHS* 74 (1954): 152–53; M. S. F. Hood, "Archaeology in Greece," *Arch. Reports*, 1955, pp. 9–10; and Desborough, *Last Mycenaeans*, pp. 80–82. Two chamber tombs, dating from the LH I and LH III periods, were discovered near the Larissa in 1970. See the summary by J.-P. Michaud, "Chronique des fouilles en 1970," *BCH* 95 (1971): 867.

65. On Pheidon, see T. Kelly, *A History of Argos to 500 B.C.* (Minneapolis, 1976), pp. 94–129.

66. P. Courbin, "Une tombe géométrique d'Argos," *BCH* 81 (1957): 322–86.

67. See J. Coldstream, rev. of *La céramique géométrique de l'Argolide* by P. Courbin, *JHS* 88 (1968): 235–37.

68. *History of Argos*, pp. 38–46; cf. H. Bengtson, *Griechische Geschichte* (Munich, 1969), p. 84: "nur ein Phantasiegebilde."

69. *Argos and the Argolid*, p. 68.

70. *History of Argos*, p. 36.

71. These traditions are assembled and analyzed by Tomlinson, *Argos and the Argolid*, pp. 58–63, who also discusses the date of the foundation of Dorian Argos (pp. 64–66).

72. Diod. 7. 17 (citing Theopompus). There are nine names from Heracles to Pheidon.

tion even in its own bailiwick in the northeastern Peloponnese, to say nothing of the Greek world as a whole.

No more imposing was pre-Dorian, Bronze Age Argos. On the hill later known as the Aspis there was an LH III settlement with a cemetery on its southern slope, the Deiras ridge; on the more rugged acropolis to the north, in later times called the Larissa, traces of a fortress have been found. This inventory, which is comparable to the LH III remains at nearby Nauplion, Asine, and Berbati, is somewhat inferior to the material at Dendra (ancient Midea) and is dwarfed by the spectacular ruins of Tiryns and Mycenae. The settlement at Argos was in all likelihood nothing more than a satellite of one or both of the two great citadels. Perhaps the most telling measure of the impression made by Mycenaean Argos is the belief that it has not yet been found.[73]

If the *Iliad* was composed ca. 750, and if its contents are for the most part traditional, it is surprising that the village of Argos receives any mention at all. Yet it is mentioned, perhaps as many as eight times. A skeptic will be forgiven for suspecting that none of the passages is traditional, and that some of them are post-Homeric.

It is quite unlikely, for example, that Dark Age bards sang of "Hera of Argos and Alalcomenean Athene" (*Il.* 4. 8, 5. 908). The adjective Ἀργείη here undoubtedly refers to the city of Argos, just as "Alalcomenean" refers to a town in Boeotia. Pausanias tells us that the shrine at Alalcomenae was famous for an "ancient ivory statue" of Athena. If the statue (statuette?) made the cult famous, it must have been one of the earliest ivory sculptures known in Greece, which suggests an eighth century date for the work.[74] We can with some confidence fix the *terminus post quem* for Alalcomenae's prestige: the town does not appear in the Catalog of Ships, despite the fact that the cataloger treated Boeotia in exquisite detail. That is fairly conclusive evidence that in the Submycenaean period the place had no reputation. So far as the Argive Heraeum is concerned, available evidence suggests that Argos took over the site soon after 750; an elaborate terrace was built (dated by the pottery in its fill to ca. 725), and by the end of the eighth century a primitive temple may have been erected.[75] "Argive" Hera and "Alalcomenean" Athena might therefore have been appropriate epithets at the end of the eighth century. They could hardly have been current in Ionian Greece during the Dark Age.

Equally suspect is the reference to the city of Argos at *Iliad* 4. 52. After Zeus has lamented the eventual fate of his beloved Troy, Hera announces,

> Of a surety three cities are there that be dearest to me, Argos and Sparta and wide-wayed Mykene; these lay thou waste whene'er they are found hateful to thy heart.

73. Cf. J.-P. Michaud, "Chronique des fouilles en 1973," *BCH* 98 (1974): 604. For the LH material, see Kelly, *History of Argos*, pp. 10–12.

74. Archaeological evidence suggests that ivory was not imported to Greece between the thirteenth and the ninth centuries; cf. R. D. Barnett, "Early Greek and Oriental Ivories," *JHS* 68 (1948): 1–25.

75. See Tomlinson, *Argos and the Argolid*, pp. 232–35. The great temple of the Archaic period, which burned in 424, seems to have been erected early in the seventh century.

That Dark Age bards could have put the village of Argos in the storied company of Troy and Mycenae is surprising. The inclusion of Sparta in the same company dissolves belief and has made the line "a well-known anachronism":[76] before ca. 750 it is doubtful that an Ionian audience would have known where or what Sparta was. This is the sole mention of Sparta in the *Iliad*, apart from the Catalog of Ships (which may have circulated in Old Greece rather than in Ionia), where Sparta is listed as one of the nine towns of Lacedaemon which supplied ships for Menelaus. Sparta appears frequently in the *Odyssey*, as the home of Menelaus and Helen; but apparently it had not yet been so identified when the *Iliad* was composed (in the earlier epic Menelaus and Helen are tied only to the district of Lacedaemon). *Iliad* 4. 52 may reflect (as does the *Odyssey*) the prestige which Sparta acquired by her remarkable conquests in the middle and late decades of the eighth century.

There are doubtful references to the city of Argos at *Iliad* 15. 30 and 19. 115, both in connection with Heracles. In the Archaic period the city of Argos claimed Heracles, and Homer may also have associated him with that city. Since, however, Heracles is explicitly tied to Thebes at 19. 99, it is also possible that his association with the city of Argos stemmed from a misunderstanding of 15. 30 or 19. 115. At 15. 30 Zeus recalls how he had once fetched the exiled Heracles from Cos "to horse-pasturing Argos." In two passages in the *Odyssey* and in a fragment from the Hesiodic corpus, "horse-pasturing Argos" stands for the city of Argos,[77] but nowhere else in the *Iliad* does it have that meaning. Perhaps, therefore, the Argos of 15. 30 should have its normal equivalent, "the home of the Argives": Cos lay across the water from heroic Greece, and in restoring Heracles "to horse-pasturing Argos" Zeus brought him from the wrong side to the proper side of the Aegean. In the second doubtful reference (19. 115), Agamemnon tells the story of the births of Eurystheus and Heracles. In order to speed the former, Hera left the peak of Mt. Olympus,

> *καρπαλίμως δ' ἵκετ' Ἄργος Ἀχαιικόν, ἔνθ' ἄρα ᾔδη*
> *ἰφθίμην ἄλοχον Σθενέλου Περσηιάδαο.*

The purpose of Hera's journey was to ensure that Eurystheus rather than Heracles would "be lord among Argives." Since Heracles has already been identified in the story as a Theban, the Argos of which the one or the other would one day be lord cannot be the city of Argos, but must be all of heroic Greece (just as Agamemnon himself, at a later time, would be "lord of all Argos"). The Achaean Argos of 19. 115, like the Achaean Argos of *Iliad* 9. 283, might therefore be "the home of the Argives." But it is also possible,

76. G. P. Shipp, *Studies in the Language of Homer*² (Cambridge, 1972), p. 242; Shipp believes that the general context of 4. 52 is linguistically "late."

77. *Od.* 15. 224, 15. 274: Melampus had once fled from Pylos to Argos *hippoboton*, and now his descendant, Theoclymenus, returns from Argos *hippoboton* to Pylos. In the Catalog of Women (Hes. frag. 25. 36 Merkelbach and West) we are told that Hypermestre, after entering the rich bed of Oecles Ἄ[ρ]γει ἐν ἱπποβότῳ, gave birth to Amphiaraus. Since Argos as "the home of the Argives" would be pointless here, it must refer to the city of Argos.

as Page has eloquently argued,[78] that Agamemnon's entire speech of reconciliation is a late creation; if it is, "Achaean Argos" at 9. 283 and at 19. 115 may have different meanings. In any case, one would be ill-advised to argue from 19. 115 that the city of Argos was celebrated during the Dark Age.

Finally, three certain references to the city of Argos identify it as the home of Diomedes. At *Iliad* 14. 119–20 Diomedes explains to Agamemnon that his ancestors' home had been at Aetolian Pleuron, "but my father dwelt at Argos, whither he had wandered, for so Zeus and the other gods willed that it should be." Diomedes is again tied to the city of Argos at *Iliad* 23. 471. With the chariot race in full swing at the funeral games for Patroclus, the spectators ask Idomeneus (who had the best vantage point) to tell them who is in the lead. Idomeneus answers that the front runner is Αἰτωλὸς γενεήν, μετὰ δ' Ἀργείοισιν ἀνάσσει. A number of ancient and modern critics have athetized these passages for various improprieties. Their substantial arguments, available in commentaries, need not be repeated here. It may be pointed out, however, that the transfer of Tydeus to the city of Argos at 14. 119–20 is difficult to square not only with the first two words of 23. 471 (which suggest that Tydeus begat Diomedes in Aetolia) but also with *Iliad* 4. 99, where Agamemnon refers to "Aetolian Tydeus" and does so in a story which makes sense only if it is understood that Tydeus lived all his life in Aetolia:

> Never did I meet him nor behold him, but men say that he was pre-eminent amid all. Of a truth he came to Mykenai, not in enmity, but as a guest with godlike Polyneikes, to raise him an army for the war that they were levying against the holy walls of Thebes.

If Tydeus is understood as living in the city of Argos, a few miles down the plain from Mycenae, it is incomprehensible that Agamemnon should never have seen him, and that apparently only once (and then as a *xeinos*) did Tydeus ever visit Mycenae (it was because Mycenae and the city of Argos were so close together, Strabo said, that they were confused by the tragedians!).

The *locus classicus* for Diomedes' identification with the city of Argos is *Iliad* 2. 559–68, from the Catalog of Ships:

> And they that possessed Argos and Tiryns of the great walls, Hermione and Asine that enfold the deep gulf, Troizen and Eionae and Epidauros full of vines, and the youths of the Achaians that possessed Aigina and Mases, these were led of Diomedes of the loud war-cry and Sthenelos, dear son of famous Kapaneus. And the third with them came Euryalos, a godlike warrior, the son of king Mekisteus son of Talaos. But Diomedes of the loud war-cry was lord over all. And with them eighty black ships followed.

Let us investigate the possibility that, unlike the rest of the Catalog of Ships, this entry was composed long after the Submycenaean period.

78. *History and the Homeric "Iliad,"* pp. 313–15.

In other entries in the Catalog a high proportion of places were important in the Mycenaean period, but insignificant or even forgotten in historical times.[79] In contrast, eight of the nine towns which are listed in our entry were known in Strabo's time; most of these were more significant in the first millennium than in the second. On the other hand, one very important LH site—Midea—does not appear in our entry, nor do more modest places such as Prosymna and Berbati. Instead, we find Aegina, Troezen, and Epidaurus.[80] Equally remarkable is the magnitude of the kingdom delineated by these towns. What was later called the Argolid—the plain and the headland—is almost entirely contained within the kingdom: this restricts Agamemnon of Mycenae to a curiously gerrymandered state which controlled some undesirable land but none of the rich plain ostensibly guarded by the citadel of Mycenae. The anomaly was seized upon by scholars who denied the cataloger's familiarity with the political geography of the Bronze Age. Leaf, for example, delivered a magnificent tirade on the matter and concluded (unnecessarily) that the entire Catalog was a "curious product of a post-Achaian time."[81] The political argument, however, cannot by itself show 2. 559–68 to be a late concoction. For one can insist, as Page has done,[82] that the mere presence of two citadels—Mycenae and Tiryns—proves that the Argive plain was split into two kingdoms at the end of the Bronze Age. I do not find Page's argument convincing. (Midea was also heavily fortified, and traces of Mycenaean walls have been found, as noted earlier, on the "Larissa" at the city of Argos. Page's argument ought therefore to posit at least four kingdoms for the plain. The various citadels were more likely complementary, guarding the plain against marauders from land or sea.[83]) But the matter will probably remain undecided unless a new cache of Linear B tablets provides an answer.

A more incriminating clue was dropped in line 562, where we read of "the youths of the Achaians that possessed Aigina and Mases." By the eighth century all of the heroes who went to Troy were called "Achaeans," but when the Catalog of Ships was composed the Achaeans were still a specific people in Achilles' realm. In the narrative section of Book 2 (1–494) there are forty-seven references to "Achaeans" in the usual sense of "the heroes opposing Troy." The entire Catalog of Ships has only five references to Achaeans, and all five can be accounted for. The Achaeans of 684 are Achilles' followers. Those of 702 and 722 are, it is true, "Achaeans" in the wide sense, but they appear in the passages which explain the absence of Protesilaus and Philoctetes, passages which by common consent were

79. Page, ibid., pp. 120–22, notes that, of the 164 places named in the Catalog of Ships, "some forty names were known from only one source, the Catalogue."

80. Hope Simpson and Lazenby, *Catalogue*, p. 171, n. 8, regard the omission of Dendra/Midea as the most puzzling omission in the Catalog, There is at present no evidence for LH III occupation of Troezen and Epidaurus (ibid., pp. 62–63).

81. *Homer and History*, pp. 241–42.

82. *History and the Homeric "Iliad,"* pp. 129–31.

83. Leaf, *Homer and History*, pp. 208–9. Hope Simpson and Lazenby, *Catalogue*, p. 71, find it "hardly conceivable" that LH IIIB Mycenae could have been cut off from the Argive plain by independent fortresses at Tiryns and Argos, but think that this might have happened in the LH IIIC period. They assume, in any case, that the fortresses were built by the kings of Mycenae.

composed when the original Catalog of Ships assembled at Aulis was converted to its present function as a "march-past of the host" in the tenth year of the war.[84] In 530, which states that Locrian Ajax excels "all the Hellenes and Achaians," the Achaeans may or may not be the Locrians' western neighbors. Since they are paired with the "Panhellenes," however, they can be explained in only two ways: either both terms are Submycenaean and have a specific rather than a general meaning, or the terms refer to all the Greek heroes and date from the late Geometric period, when the people of Old Greece began to refer to themselves as "Hellenes."[85] Thus, the Submycenaean cataloger does not seem to have used "Achaeans" as an equivalent for "the heroes who fought against Troy." Such a use of the term in 562 seriously compromises the Argolid entry.

A fourth piece of evidence for the entry's late date does not appear in our texts at all. In some ancient texts of the *Iliad*, however, the entry closed with the lines (2. 568*a–b*),

> And in them men skilled in war were ranged in rows,
> Argives in linen corslets, goads of war.[86]

This last line is identical to a line in the oracle which the Aegians received at Delphi during the Archaic period.[87] Since ancient scholars knew that Apollo did not quote Homer, they presumably concluded that 568*a–b* could not possibly be so early as Homer, and accordingly excised them from the Catalog. By so doing, of course, they enhanced the respectability of what remained.

One additional consideration supports the view that the Catalog of Ships did not contain 2. 559–68 during the Dark Age, and this argument will serve as a bridge to another topic. The contingent was led, we are told, by Diomedes, Sthenelus, and Euryalus. Of these, Diomedes is said to have been lord over all; but Euryalus, the son of *anax* Mecisteus, was also of royal stock. The implication is that all three were kings at the city of Argos.[88] The mind boggles at the thought of three monarchical lines coexisting in the city of Argos. Even Pausanias found the situation remarkable: "The Argives are the only Greeks I know who were divided into three kingdoms."[89] On the other hand, we know very well that a number of kings ruled their independent kingdoms concurrently in the vast expanse of that other Argos, the Pelasgic Argos of the Aeolic north.

Throughout the *Iliad*, Diomedes, Sthenelus, and Euryalus are found together. Sthenelus is Diomedes' charioteer and close companion; Euryalus, too, always fights alongside Diomedes; and in the boxing match in Book 23

84. See n. 34.
85. In both the Catalog of Ships and the rest of the *Iliad*, Hellas is a small district on the Malian Gulf. In addition to 2. 683, see 9. 395, 9. 447, 9. 478, 16. 595; cf. Thuc. 1. 3. 2. For the later meaning, see Hes. *Erga* 653, and Hes. frag. 9 M.–W.
86. This is the text as given in *Cert. Hom. et Hes.* 325.
87. See n. 43.
88. For Sthenelus' kingship in Argos, see Paus. 2. 18. 5.
89. Paus. 2. 18. 4.

Diomedes acts as Euryalus' second.[90] The three are associated with each other in the *Iliad* because they were already familiar as comrades from another story. They were among the Epigoni against Thebes, and their fathers had been among the Seven.[91] At *Iliad* 4. 403–10 Sthenelus insists that Diomedes and he were superior to their fathers, Tydeus and glorious Capaneus, since the fathers had failed to take Thebes, whereas the sons had succeeded. At *Iliad* 23. 678 we are told that Mecisteus had vanquished all the sons of Oedipus. Thus, both the fathers and the sons were prominent among the champions of the Argives against the city of Thebes.

Which Argives? Can anyone who has considered the evidence believe that in the Late Bronze Age Thebes was destroyed (and it *was* destroyed) by an army dispatched from the city of Argos?[92] For that matter, can anyone explain why the village on the Aspis would have launched an expedition against faraway Thebes? Even under Pheidon, when it was at its height, the city of Argos is not known to have meddled in central Greece. To save the classical story, scholars have substituted Mycenae for the city of Argos;[93] but that will not do, for it contradicts the very best evidence we have: Agamemnon says very clearly (*Il.* 4. 381) that, when Aetolian Tydeus came to ask Mycenae's help against Thebes, Mycenae gave none. I do not wish to embark on a full-scale analysis of the legend of the Seven against Thebes; I will merely suggest that the legend could have a historical basis only if the "Argives" who assaulted Thebes (and whose sons took it) are identified as a coalition of Aeolic outlanders, rather than as an expedition from the city of Argos. Such an identification not only makes historical sense—marauders from Aetolia and Thessaly attempting, eventually with success, to sack a rich and attractive outpost of the civilized world—but also fits the oldest evidence that we have: *Iliad* 4. 370–99 and 6. 223, where Diomedes recalls Tydeus' departure "what time the Achaian host perished at Thebes." This phrase seems to reflect a tradition in which the "Achaeans" were still a specific people within Greece. Finally, Hesiod (*Erga* 161–63) says that the Race of Heroes perished at Troy and Thebes, the latter of which they had attacked "for the flocks of Oedipus." The words describe a marauders' raid, not a mission to restore Polynices.

90. Sthenelus and Diomedes: *Il.* 4. 364–67, 4. 403, 5. 107 ff., 5. 241, 5. 318, 5. 835, 9. 48, 23. 411; Euryalus and Diomedes: *Il.* 6. 20, 23. 677.

91. The evidence is presented under the individual entries in W. H. Roscher (ed.), *Ausführliches Lexikon der griechischen und römischen Mythologie*, 6 vols. (Leipzig, 1884–1937).

92. That is what we hear from the author of the *Thebais* in the Archaic period and from all subsequent writers. (Aeschylus' *Septem* may preserve an echo of an older tradition. Although Aeschylus thought that the Argives came from the city of Argos, his "Argives" are synonymous with his "Achaeans.") On the destruction of Thebes, see Stubbings, *CAH*, vol. 2², pt. 2 (Cambridge, 1975), pp. 166–69, who dates the destruction to the LH IIIB period and attributes it to the rulers of Mycenae (an attribution contradicted by our best evidence and supported by none). Recent discoveries suggest a late date: "the destruction of the 'first palace' has now been dated to c. 1300 B.C. by the burnt floors with early LH IIIB pottery. In the 'second palace' (on a different alignment), the burnt layer where the cylinders and jewellery were found contained *developed* LH IIIB pottery" (Hope Simpson and Lazenby, *Catalogue*, p. 36, n. 47). Thebes and Troy may have fallen in the same generation.

93. M. S. F. Hood, *The Home of the Heroes* (London, 1967), p. 115, thinks that the legends of the Seven and the Epigoni "retain a memory of the overthrow of a rival power at Thebes by the rulers of Mycenae." See n. 92 for Stubbings' view.

Omitting the rest of the legend, we note only the Aeolic heritage of the three "Argives" who are presented at 2. 559–68*b* as hailing from the city of Argos. That Diomedes was of Aetolian birth we have already seen (in the LH III period Aetolia was apparently part of proto-Aeolic Greece).[94] According to a fragment in the Hesiodic corpus, Euryalus was one of the suitors of Hippodamia,[95] and in Apollodorus' *Bibliotheca* he is one of the Argonauts as well as one of the Epigoni.[96] Sthenelus' father, Capaneus (whose glorious exploits ended only when he was slain by a thunderbolt at the gates of Thebes), bears a name which seems to be derived from *καπάνα*, the Thessalian word for "chariot."[97]

Just as Aeolic bards sang of the destruction of Troy by nine barons of the Pelasgic Argos, so, I would suggest, did they sing of an earlier siege and eventual sacking of Thebes by seven "Argive" barons and their sons. When the Pelasgic Argos had been forgotten, it was inevitable that the city of Argos should be credited with the expeditions against Thebes. When Greeks of the eighth century heard the dichotomy "Argives and Trojans," they understood that the "Argives" were heroic Greeks and that the Trojans were barbarians. The dichotomy "Argives and Thebans" required a different interpretation: since both parties were obviously Greek, the "Argives" here had to be more narrowly defined. In this way, I believe, the "Argive" kings—among them, Diomedes, Sthenelus, and Euryalus—came to be associated with the city of Argos.

The indulgent reader has, I hope, found some plausibility in this analysis of "Argos" and "Argives" in the *Iliad*, and may even agree that my reconstruction makes the best sense out of our varied and puzzling evidence. Assent, however, will probably be withheld unless another question can be answered: how did the city of Argos manage to perpetrate such a monumental fraud, such an outrageous distortion of Greek prehistory?

For an explanation, conspiracy need not be invoked when ignorance will suffice. The career of "Argos" and "Argives" in post-Homeric poetry is entirely reasonable, almost predictable. By the end of the eighth century, the city of Argos had become a city in fact, and was one of a handful of contemporary states in Old Greece which had attained some visibility in Ionia. In the world known to the poet of the *Odyssey*, there was one place in Old Greece named Argos, and that was the aggressive city not far from the ruins of Mycenae. The poet of the *Odyssey* seems to have drawn a conclusion which has been accepted ever since—Homer's "Argives" were named for the city of Argos. At any rate, we find in the *Odyssey* some of the same confusion about the name which we find in ancient and modern commentators. By "Argos" the poet of the *Odyssey* can mean either the

94. V. I. Georgiev, "The Arrival of the Greeks in Greece: The Linguistic Evidence," in *Bronze Age Migrations*, p. 252.

95. Hes. frag. 259*a* M.–W.

96. *Bibliotheca* 1. 9. 16, 3. 7. 2.

97. On *καπάνα*, see Athen. 10. 418D (quoting Aristophanes); cf. the entry "Kapaneus" by H. W. Stoll in Roscher, *Lexikon*, 2:951.

city of Argos or all of Old Greece, or some intermediate entity such as the Peloponnese.[98]

Although Argos and Argives do not appear in either the *Theogony* or the *Works and Days*, they can be found in the fragments of the catalog poetry, apparently composed in the seventh or sixth century, which went under Hesiod's name. In these fragments we see the city of Argos becoming the home of many heroes. Acrisius, grandfather of Perseus, "reigned in well-built Argos." The sons of Amphiaraus, one of the Seven, came "from nearby Argos" to enlist themselves as Helen's suitors. And a Danaus has been created: "Danaus made un-watered Argos well-watered."[99]

This fragment invites a closing argument. At *Iliad* 4. 171 Agamemnon says that, if Menelaus should die, "in utter shame should I return to thirsty (πολυδίψιον) Argos." The adjective was apt enough for the "home of the Argives," since Old Greece as a whole was "thirsty" in comparison with the wide and green river valleys of Ionia. Problems arose, however, when the "Argos" of 4. 171 began to be equated with the city of Argos: the latter community did not regard itself as deficient in water. Strabo found the epithet incomprehensible, "since the country lies in a hollow, and is traversed by rivers, and contains marshes and lakes, and since the city is well supplied with waters of many wells whose water-level reaches the surface."[100] The epithet had, however, been boldly appropriated. In the opening line of a *Thebais* an Archaic poet prayed unimaginatively, Ἄργος ἄειδε, θεά, πολυδίψιον ἔνθεν ἄνακτες.[101] The Argos about to be celebrated was surely the city of Argos.

Strabo noted that there were various expedients for reconciling Argos' epithet with her water. Several he dismissed as too labored, but one was convincing:[102]

> Now writers agree that the country has plenty of water, and that although the city itself lies in a waterless district, it has an abundance of wells. These wells they ascribe to the daughters of Danaüs, believing that they discovered them; and hence the utterance of this verse, "The daughters of Danaüs rendered Argos, which was waterless, Argos the well watered"; but they add that four of the wells not only were designated as sacred but are especially revered, thus introducing the false notion that there is a lack of water where there is an abundance of it.

To which one can only reply, with the Duke of Wellington, "If you can believe that, sir, you can believe anything."

Thus was Peloponnesian Argos, not always without difficulty, attached to many of the legends which had arisen in Pelasgic Argos. Some stories—

98. City of Argos: *Od.* 3. 180, 15. 224–74, 21. 108. Peloponnese (?): *Od.* 4. 174 and possibly the phrase, "from Hellas to mid-Argos" (*Od.* 1. 344, 4. 726, 4. 816, 15. 80; for the poet of the *Odyssey*, Argos and Hellas together seem to have included all of Old Greece). Realm of Agamemnon (?): *Od.* 3. 309.

99. Hes. frags. 129. 10, 197. 7, 128 M.–W.

100. Strabo 8. 6. 7.

101. *Thebais* frag. 1 Kinkel.

102. Strabo 8. 6. 8.

such as the Argonauts' voyage from Iolkos—retained a northern setting, perhaps because they were tied to Thessaly by an unambiguous place name. Other "Argive" legends, however, must have slipped their moorings and have been floating free by the end of the Dark Age. The city of Argos emerged in the eighth century to provide the reef on which they lodged.

Vanderbilt University

LINGUISTIC CHARACTERIZATION OF OLD MEN IN TERENCE

ROBERT MALTBY

FROM the time of Cicero the plays of Terence have been renowned for their purity of diction.[1] But emphasis on the refinement of Terence's writing, as contrasted with the more exuberant style of Plautus, has perhaps led critics to underestimate an important aspect of his work. It has generally been assumed, for example, that the same refined Latin is spoken by all Terence's characters in all situations. The traditional view is well represented by J. Marouzeau: "Son ton est celui de la bonne compagnie. . . . Le langage de ses personnages ne varie guère: hommes ou femmes, vieillards ou jeunes gens, maîtres ou esclaves, matrones ou courtisanes s'expriment dans la langue de l'auteur."[2] Similarly, G. P. Shipp states: ". . . all his characters, old and young, bond and free, speak a uniform Latin."[3]

More recently, it has been recognized that within the bounds of his refined style Terence is in fact capable of varying his language according to context and meter.[4] The aim of the present paper is to set out evidence which suggests that Terence may also have aimed at some kind of linguistic characterization of individuals. In particular, the language of his old men contains a number of pet expressions and long-winded turns of phrase, not normally used by other characters, as well as certain distinctive archaic and elevated lexical features. The term "archaic" in this context denotes words and phrases which were no longer in current use, whereas "elevated" refers more generally to any features, including archaisms, which were regularly restricted to formal language.

To begin, I offer for consideration two passages from the *Eunuch:*

(*a*) 971–75 (*senex*)
ex meo propinquo rure hoc capio commodi:
neque agri neque urbis *odium* me umquam *percipit.*
ubi *satias* coepit fieri commuto locum.
sed estne ille noster Parmeno? et certe ipsus est.
quem *praestolare,* Parmeno, hic ante ostium?

(*b*) 403–5 (Thraso)
. . . tum sicubi eum *satietas*[5]
hominum aut negoti siquando *odium ceperat*
requiescere ubi volebat, quasi . . . nostin? . . .

1. At Suet. *Vit. Ter.* 7, Cicero speaks of his *lectus sermo* and Caesar refers to him as *puri sermonis amator.*

2. *Térence, Comédies,* vol. 1 (Paris, 1942), p. 47.

3. *Terence's "Andria"* (Oxford, 1960), p. 55.

4. On differentiation of character through use of figurative language and imagery, see W. G. Arnott, "*Phormio Parasitus,*" *G&R,* n.s. 17 (1970): 32–33. On variation of language with meter, see H. Haffter, *Untersuchungen zur altlateinischen Dichtersprache* (Berlin, 1934), pp. 10–125.

5. Corrected to unmetrical *satias* in the second hand of some later MSS.

0009-837X/79/7402-0003$01.09

Both passages are written in iambic senarii and both contain similar ideas, but the words used to express them are slightly different. The first point of interest is the variation between the forms *satias* in (*a*) and *satietas* in (*b*). In Classical Latin the normal form was *satietas*, while *satias*, which was restricted mainly to the nominative singular, was probably archaic.[6] This distinction also holds good for Plautus, who normally uses *satietas*.[7] The only certain occurrence of *satias* is found in the context of formal religious language spoken by the young man Calidorus at *Pseudolus* 334: "ut hodie ad litationem huic suppetat satias Iovi." This is probably an intentional archaism.[8] Given that such a distinction in tone between *satias* and *satietas* existed both for Plautus and for classical writers, it seems unlikely that Terence alternated between the two simply for metrical convenience. But, before drawing any conclusion about the precise effect of *satias* in (*a*), let us first turn to a number of other peculiarities in the old man's speech.

The verb *percipit* (972) in its original sense (= *occupat*) is here a Terentian hapax. Elsewhere the use of the word in this sense is restricted to Plautus[9] and Lucretius[10] and was probably archaic in the classical period. Plautus *Truculentus* 467 and Lucretius 3. 80 provide parallels for the present phrase with *odium* as subject, but elsewhere, as in our "control" passage (*b*), Terence prefers to use *odium capit*.[11]

Another word which occurs in Terence only in this old man's speech is *praestolare* (975, 977). *Praestolor* meaning "wait for" (syn. *opperior*, *exspecto*) occurs six times in Plautus,[12] but the archives of the *Thesaurus Linguae Latinae* show that it is rare in the classical period (when it is constructed + dative)[13] and becomes common again only in Apuleius,[14] a writer well known for his archaizing tendencies.

The context of (*a*) is not one which in itself calls for high style or archaic diction. It is tempting to conclude that the effect of such forms as *percipit*, *satias*, and *praestolare* is to characterize the old man's speech in some way, perhaps as pompous or old-fashioned. One further piece of evidence seems to back up this conclusion. Whereas the classical *satietas* is used by a soldier (*b*) and a young man (*Phorm.* 834), the only other occurrence of *satias* is in the speech of the old *matrona* Sostrata (*Hec.* 594). It is perhaps no coincidence that the archaic form is restricted to the speech of old persons. Terence's choice of *satias* in both passages could have been motivated by the desire to give a realistic portrayal of their archaizing speech patterns.[15]

6. Restricted in prose to occasional occurrences in historical writing (Sallust [*Hist.*], Livy, and, later, Tacitus) and in verse mainly to Lucretius; cf. B. F. B. Axelson, *Unpoetische Wörter* (Lund, 1945), p. 27.
7. *Amph.* 472 (acc.), *Cist.* 70 (acc.), *Most.* 196 (abl.), *Poen.* 215 (nom.).
8. As possibly in a legal context at *Cist.* 502, where the text is unsound.
9. *Amph.* 1118, *Men.* 921, *Stich.* 341, *Truc.* 467.
10. Lucr. 3. 29, 3. 80, 5. 605.
11. So at *Hec.* 219, 580.
12. *Cas.* 578, *Epid.* 217, 221, *Most.* 1066, *Poen.* 1173, *Truc.* 336.
13. E.g., Cic. *Cat.* 1. 24, *Att.* 2. 15. 3; Caes. *BC* 2. 23. 3.
14. Apul. *Met.* 3. 3. 8, 4. 10. 1, 5. 4. 4, 5. 20. 6, 10. 20. 1.
15. In the case of Sostrata this effect is reinforced by the frequent use of abstract verb subjects, e.g., *mea praesentia* (587) and *mea longinquitas aetatis* (597), giving the impression of long-winded, rather elevated style. But this greater elaboration may be determined by the different verse medium (iamb. oct.); see Haffter, *Untersuchungen*, pp. 86–100.

Cicero's remarks about Crassus' mother-in-law in the *De oratore*[16] suggest that in real life the speech of old women, in particular, was characterized by archaism, and it is not difficult to imagine that this could also have been a feature of the language of more conservative old men.

We now turn from the two *Eunuch* passages to consider in more detail exactly what linguistic features are restricted mainly to old men. These may conveniently be discussed under four headings: archaisms, long-winded expressions, words linked semantically with the role of old men in the plot, and pet expressions of individual old men.

I. ARCHAISMS

In addition to the *satias/satietas* pair, a second example in Terence of an Early Latin (EL) form alongside its Classical Latin (CL) alternative is provided by the perfects *tetuli* and *tuli*. In this case the EL reduplicated form is the norm in Plautus,[17] and the simple form—which was to become regular in CL—occurs only rarely in his work.[18] Neither form appears to be restricted to particular characters or to particular contexts in Plautus, nor docs the CL form occur only in what are generally considered to be the later plays.[19] In Terence it is the CL *tuli* which is regular;[20] the EL *tetuli* occurs only twice. Once again, as with *satias*, both examples of the earlier form occur in the speech of old men: *Andria* 807–8 (Crito) ". . . haud auspicato huc me appuli; / nam pol, si id scissem, numquam huc tetulissem pedem" (iam. sen.); and *Andria* 832 (Chremes) "impetrasti: incepi, dum res tetulit. nunc non fert: feras" (troch. sept.). Donatus comments to the effect that the reduplicated form in each line is too elevated for the comic style: 808 "sed critici adnotant altius esse charactere comico 'tetulissem pedem' " (perhaps the reference here is to the whole phrase); 832 "compositum pro simplici est 'tetulit.' et altius quam decet comicum characterem dictum videtur." This clearly would not apply to Plautine comedy, where, as we have seen, *tetuli* is regular,[21] but by Terence's time this form could indeed have sounded archaic and have acquired an elevated tone.[22] The presence of other elevated features in the speech of Crito and Chremes suggests that Terence could be using the reduplicated forms here as a further means of characterizing their language as pompous. Crito's phrase "haud auspicato huc me appuli" is a clear example. The ablative participle *auspicato* used adverbially (= "auspiciously," lit. "the omens having been

16. *De or.* 3. 45: "equidem cum audio socrum meam Laeliam—facilius enim mulieres incorruptam antiquitatem conservant . . . eam sic audio, ut Plautum mihi aut Naevium videar audire."

17. *Amph.* 716, 800, *Bacch.* 482, 811, *Cist.* 650, *Men.* 381, 591, 630, *Most.* 471, *Rud.* 68, 893, 1040; also in Caecil. frag. 75 Ribbeck.

18. *Aul.* 433 (?), *Curc.* 644, *Poen.* 1076.

19. For an approximate chronological order of Plautus' plays, see K. H. E. Schutter, *Quibus annis comoediae Plautinae primum actae sint quaeritur* (Groningen, 1952); cf. W. B. Sedgwick, "The Dating of Plautus' Plays," *CQ* 24 (1930): 102–6.

20. *An.* 142, 178, 188, 443, 496, *Phorm.* 520, 579, *Hec.* 87, 128, 333, 568, 594, 685, 709, *Eun.* 82.

21. For the phrase *tetuli pedem*, cf. *Men.* 381 and 630, where no attempt at high style seems to be intended.

22. After Terence the reduplicated form occurs only as an intentional archaism at Lucr. 6. 672 and Catull. 63. 47, 63. 52, 66. 35.

taken") is a feature of formal religious language.[23] This one word ablative absolute construction, which except for a few common types[24] is rare in CL outside Livy, appears to be another characteristic of old men's language in Terence. Five out of six Terentian examples occur in the speech of old persons,[25] whereas the proportion of normal ablative absolutes used by this group is only 13/31.[26] The phrase *huc me appuli* probably means nothing more than "brought myself here"[27] and, like *tetulissem pedem* in the next line, is simply an elevated way of saying "I came." A similar fullness of expression is to be detected in Crito's words "dictast . . . atque habitast soror" in 809. Chremes' speech at 829–33 also contains elevated features. Shipp[28] points to the EL poetic device in 832 of repeating the same verb *fero* in two different senses: "allow" and "put up with." Similarly, the balanced phrases in 829 "in alio occupato amore, abhorrenti ab re uxoria," 830 "in seditionem atque in incertas nuptias," and in the medical metaphor at 831 (where the effect is reinforced by assonance) "eius labore atque eius dolore" are reminiscent of Crito's rather elevated and long-winded manner of speech at 807–9. Of course, other characters, slaves for example,[29] may, in certain circumstances, speak in an elevated tone, but the adoption of this tone outside contexts which would normally call for it as well as specifically archaic features of the type *satias* and *tetuli*[30] seem particularly characteristic of Terence's old men.

In view of such cases in which an EL form is given to old men, and its CL equivalent to other characters, one is less likely to look upon the restriction to old persons of other EL features, for which there is no exact CL equivalent in Terence's work, as purely fortuitous. That such restrictions are not

23. Cf. Plaut. *Persa* 607 in a mock military context of going into battle and Cic. *Rep.* 2. 5 of founding a city (= "under good omen").

24. E.g., *auspicato*, *optato*.

25. *An.* 533 (Chremes) *optato*, *An.* 807 (Crito) *auspicato*, *Phorm.* 756 (Sostrata) *composito*, *Hec.* 737 (Laches) *peccato*. The only exception is *Hec.* 94 (Philotis—*meretrix*) *praefinito*.

26. Examples from C. E. Bennett, *Syntax of Early Latin*, vol. 2 (Boston, 1914), pp. 367–68.

27. It is true that in CL *appello* has the meaning "bring (a ship) to shore," "put in at (a port)" and that this sense would fit the context here, where Crito has just arrived by sea from Andros; see E. Fantham, *Comparative Studies in Republican Latin Imagery* (Toronto, 1972), pp. 42–43. But: (1) in all its Plautine occurrences the word has its original meaning of "drive" with personal objects: *Asin.* 633 *me ad mortem*, *Bacch.* 378 *amicos ad probrum*, *Rud.* 1043 (*me*) *ad ignotum arbitrum*. There seems to be little reason, then, for rejecting this original meaning—"drive," "direct"—in Terence, even in the metaphorical examples with *animum* at *An.* 1 and 446, in favor of a specialized nautical sense, which is not attested until Afranius (137 Ribbeck). (2) The reflexive *me* argues against this specialized sense, where *navem* (even when not expressed as, e.g., in Caes. *BC* 2. 3. 21) must always be understood as the object of *appello* (unless one were to understand an ablative *nave*, as in the passive construction *propulsi navigiis* at Cic. 2 *Verr.* 5. 145; but there is no other example of the reflexive used with this construction). On the other hand, I see no reason to reject the majority reading in favor of *me attuli*, attested in Priscian 2. 68.

28. *Terence's "Andria,"* p. 187.

29. E.g., Syrus in his parody of Demea at *Ad.* 364–430.

30. It could be objected that the presence of the *tetuli* forms in the *Andria* simply reflects the early date of the play. Other EL forms found in the *Andria* are rejected by Terence in later plays, e.g., *medicor* at 831 and 944 (contrast *medeor* at *Phorm.* 822), *qui* for *ut* with verbs of striving at 6, 307, and 334, and *qui ne* for *ne* at 335. But, whereas these forms are not restricted to particular characters, the *tetuli* forms are used only by the old men Crito and Chremes, while all the other characters in the play use the normal CL *tuli:* 142 (Sosia), 178 (Davos), 188 (Simo), 443 (Davos), 496 (Simo).

merely statistical freaks is suggested, furthermore, by the fact that EL forms are not concentrated in the same way in the speech of other characters (except for rare examples of colloquial EL features being restricted mainly to slaves[31]). In general, EL features in Terence are either restricted to old persons or spread evenly throughout the characters. Evenly spread EL features (except for the examples from the *Andria* mentioned in n. 30) were probably not yet felt to be archaic in Terence's time. Examples of this second category include the verb *proviso* and the use of *postulo* + infinitive in the sense "intend doing."[32] Among the EL features restricted mainly to old persons, the following are worthy of note:

(1) *aio imperfect* (ten examples, eight by old persons). The verb *aio* (= "say") was already obsolescent in Terence, where it occurs, as in CL, mainly in the forms *ais* (*ain*), *ait*, *aiunt*. Table 1 shows that these forms are more frequent in Terence than they were in Plautus, whereas all other forms of the verb, except *ai(e)bant*, are less frequent than they had been in the earlier author. The imperfect tense is clearly one of the uses which is dying out by Terence's time, and eight of its ten occurrences in this author are to be found in the speech of old persons: *aibas*, *Adelphoi* 561 (Demea); *aiebas*, *Hautontimorumenos* 924 (Menedemus); *aibat*, *Andria* 932 (Chremes), *Adelphoi* 717 (Demea); *aiebat*, *Andria* 930 (Crito); *aibant*, *Andria* 534, 572 (Chremes), *Hecyra* 238 (Sostrata). (Note that *ai-* and *aie-* forms are used indiscriminately by both authors.) No such restriction is found in Plautus, where this tense is more common. There are two exceptions to this restriction in Terence. The first is the use of *aibas* at *Hautontimorumenos* 960 by the young man Clitipho. Here it may be significant that Clitipho is in conversation with the old man Menedemus. The second is the use of *aibat* at *Phormio* 480 by Geta. Here the slave may be adopting the tone of the old man Demipho, to whom he is referring, for humorous purposes: "ut aibat / de

TABLE 1

	Frequency[a]	
	Plautus	Terence
ais	108	43
ain	33	14
ait	45	25
aiunt	22	23
aio	23	1
ai(e)bas	13	3
ai(e)bat	32	4
ai(e)bant	9	3
aiam	1	0
aias	2	0
aiant	1	0
aibatis	1	0

[a] Terentian figures must be multiplied by 3.5 to compensate for the greater bulk of the Plautine corpus (20,959 lines to 6,074).

31. E.g.: *edormisco*, *Ad.* 786 (Syrus); *beo*, *An.* 106 (Sosia), *Eun.* 279 (Gnatho—parasite); *volup est*, *Hec.* 857 (Bacchis), *Phorm.* 610 (Geta).

32. See H. Bléry, *Syntaxe de la subordination dans Térence* (Paris, 1909), p. 23.

eius consilio sese velle facere." It may also be relevant that Geta himself, like the slave Syrus in the *Adelphoi*,[33] is portrayed as an old man.

(2) *propediem* (three examples, all by old men). *Propediem* (= "in a short time," lit. "at an early day") does occur in CL, but in contexts which suggest it is being used as an intentional archaism (e.g., Sall. *Cat.* 56. 4; Livy 1. 48. 7; Cic. *Div.* 1. 47; but also once in a letter at *Att.* 2. 1. 11). All three Terentian occurrences are restricted to the line-end, which suggests it was felt as archaic.[34] In all cases the speaker is an old man: *Hautontimorumenos* 160, 868 (Chremes) and *Adelphoi* 888 (Demea). The word occurs only three times in Plautus (again twice at the line-end), but there is no restriction on the characters using it: *Asinaria* 817 (*adulescens*), *Persa* 295 (*puer*), *Persa* 837 (*servus*).

(3) *uspiam* (two examples, both by old persons). The word occurs seven times in Plautus and probably already had an archaic or elevated ring about it as it is used mainly in mock epic passages, e.g., *Miles* 597 (*servus*). Its occurrence in Terence is restricted to the old man Micio, who uses it twice in the opening speech of the *Adelphoi* (28, 37).

(4) *faxim* (two examples, both by old men). Similarly, the EL subjunctive form *faxim* is restricted in Terence to the old man Demea, who twice uses the formula *lubens bene faxim* in his determined effort to be gracious (*Ad.* 887, 896).

II. LONG-WINDED EXPRESSIONS

Other linguistic phenomena restricted to old men in Terence are not specifically archaic in coloring. One group of such phenomena consists of particularly imposing or long-winded forms of expression, which would be well suited for characterizing the language of old persons as slow or ponderous.

This characteristic of old men's speech in Terence was clearly recognized by Donatus. For example, on *Adelphoi* 68 (Micio) "mea sic est ratio et sic animum induco meum," Donatus notes, (3) "senilis μακρολογία"—the reference is to the virtual tautology of the phrases *mea . . . ratio* and *sic . . . meum*. On *Adelphoi* 646 (Micio) ". . . ego dicam tibi," Donatus' comment is (2) "seniliter: nam iam dicendum fuit." Similarly, on the old man's speech quoted at *Eunuchus* 338–41:

> "scin quid ego te volebam?" "dic." "cras est mihi
> iudicium." "quid tum?" "ut diligenter nunties
> patri, advocatus mane mi esse ut meminerit."
> dum haec dicit abiit hora.

Donatus notes: 338 (1) "hic ostenditur odiosa tarditas senis apud festinantem Chaeream"; 340 "non 'ut sit' sed 'ut esse meminerit': o prolixitas."[35] A clear indication that this was in fact Terence's intention here is given in the text by the words "dum haec dicit abiit hora" (341).

33. *Ad.* 563. Syrus, too, can use old men's language when it suits him; cf. n. 29.

34. The greater metrical restriction at this position in the line led to the retention of old-fashioned formulae; see P. W. Harsh, "The Position of Archaic Forms in the Verse of Plautus," *CP* 35 (1940): 126–42.

35. Cf. Demipho's pleonasm *quem ais fuisse* for *quis fuerit* at *Phorm.* 380.

As was the case with the archaic features, there are at least two examples where synonyms are distributed significantly between old persons and other characters. These are:

(1) *prohibeo/veto*. Both words are used regularly in CL; neither is particularly archaic or colloquial. In Terence, however, the longer, more imposing *prohibeo* is used mainly by old men (nine of twelve examples), whereas the shorter *veto* is restricted to low characters. Old persons use *prohibeo* (*a*) in the formula *di . . . prohibeant: Andria* 568 (Simo), *Hautontimorumenos* 1038 (Sostrata), *Hecyra* 207 (Laches); and (*b*) in other contexts: *Andria* 54 (Simo), *Andria* 140 (Simo—quoting the hypothetical words of his son), *Phormio* 425 (Demipho), *Hautontimorumenos* 573 (Chremes), *Hecyra* 266 (Laches). For Terence, *prohibeo* definitely seems to have had an elevated ring. When not being used by old persons, it occurs in an extended version of the usual *di . . . prohibeant* formula at *Adelphoi* 275 (*Aeschinus—adulescens*) ". . . deos quaeso ut istaec prohibeant," and in the intentionally imposing language of the *miles gloriosus* figure, Thraso, at *Eunuchus* 808 ". . . tum me prohibeas / meam ne tangam?" picked up by the *adulescens* Chaerea at 809 "prohibeo inquam . . ." *Veto* is used by slaves (*Haut.* 378 [Syrus], *Phorm.* 709, 864 [Geta], *Hec.* 317 [Parmeno]) and by a parasite (*Phorm.* 417 [Phormio]).

(2) *sceleratus/scelestus*. In Plautus and Terence the most common form is *scelestus*. In CL and later Latin *sceleratus* becomes more frequent, and in Cicero it is always used, in place of *scelestus*, of persons. The longer form occurs only twice in Plautus, on both occasions in passages of abuse by slaves (*Epid.* 369 and *Persa* 275). In Terence the longer CL form *sceleratus* is restricted to old men (*An.* 159 [Simo], *Ad.* 553 [Demea]). All other characters in Terence use *scelestus*, which is never used by old men (*An.* 790 [Mysis], *Haut.* 312 [Clitipho], *Haut.* 790 [Syrus], *Eun.* 71, 668 [Phaedria], *Eun.* 817, 832 [Thais], *Ad.* 159 [Aeschinus]).[36]

A number of other expressions restricted to old persons, for which there are no exact synonyms in Terence, may also characterize their speech as ponderous or long-winded:

(1) *non clam me* (*te*) *est*. This phrase is found mainly in Plautus and Terence,[37] where it is used as the equivalent of *non ignoro*, or simply *scio*, introducing an indirect question or statement. Its restriction to old persons in Terence may be due to the fact that it was an elevated expression (which may have sounded archaic by his time) or simply that it was a long-winded circumlocution. Three of the four examples occur in the *Hecyra* and are spoken by old persons: 261 (Laches), 568 (Myrrina—*matrona*), 577 (Sostrata—*matrona*). The exception to this restriction occurs at *Andria* 287. Here the speaker is the young man Pamphilus, who is quoting the deathbed appeal made to him by Chrysis. The tone of the language in this section with its balanced phrases (288 ". . . ad pudicitiam et ad rem tutandam . . . ," 289–90 ". . . per hanc te dexteram et genium tuom / per . . . fidem per-

36. The EL and post-CL form *scelerosus* (not found in Plautus) occurs in Terence only at *Eun.* 643 (Pythias).

37. *TLL*, 3:1247.

que . . . solitudinem . . .") and the repeated "si . . . sive . . . seu" clauses at 292–94 is clearly elevated, and the use of the *non clam te est* construction at 287 probably adds to this formal effect.

(2) (*in*) *animum inducere*. Attention has been drawn to Donatus' remark about the "senilis μακρολογία" of Micio's phrase "mea sic est ratio et sic animum induco meum" (*Ad.* 68). There the tautology obviously contributes to the effect; but, when ten out of twelve further occurrences of *animum induco* or *in animum induco* are also spoken by old persons, it seems possible that Terence could have used the phrase as a typically senile circumlocution. Alternatively, the sententious nature of the phrase could have led to its association with old men (cf. features discussed in III). The phrase is used by old persons at *Andria* 572, 834, 883, *Hautontimorumenos* 1028, *Hecyra* 264, 277, *Adelphoi* 68, 597, and occurs in prologues spoken by old men at *Hautontimorumenos* 41, 49 and *Hecyra* 50. The two exceptions occur in the *Hecyra:* 99 (Philotis—*meretrix*), 292 (Parmeno—*servus*).

(3) *comperio*. This common CL word[38] is not found in Plautus. It is used in Terence mainly in the perfect as a synonym for *scio*. As with *non clam me est*, a phrase of similar meaning, it is restricted mainly to old men. In all but one (*Haut.* 121) of its occurrences in old men's speech, it introduces a complement clause in accusative + infinitive, whereas this construction is not found in the two exceptional uses by other characters. It is used by old men at *Andria* 90, 145 (Simo), *Phormio* 801 (Chremes), *Hecyra* 763, 779 (Laches), and *Hautontimorumenos* 121 (Menedemus), and by other characters at *Andria* 211 (Davos) ". . . primum iam de amore hoc comperit" (where the reference is to the old man Simo) and *Eunuchus* 825 (Pythias). The deponent form *comperior* (also found in the archaizing writers Sallust, Tacitus, and Apuleius) occurs only at *Andria* 902 in the speech of the old man Simo (on the significance of this, see n. 30).

III. WORDS LINKED SEMANTICALLY WITH THE ROLE OF OLD MEN IN THE PLOT

In all the restrictions discussed so far, the *form* of the word or phrase (e.g., archaic, long-winded) made it appropriate for the speech of old persons. There are cases, however, where the *meaning* of a word explains its restriction to one sort of character, since it fits in with some specific aspect of the character's behavior (e.g., culinary terms to parasites, military terms to soldiers). In fact, as was pointed out in the case of *in animum induco*, there may be some overlap between these categories; *non clam me est* and *comperire*, for example, also belong to the semantic field of "finding out," which is the traditional business of old men in plots of concealment. In this section, however, I list cases where the semantic value of the words alone leads them to be associated with old men. This is linguistic characterization in a wider sense than has been discussed so far.

38. Cicero was criticized for using this word too frequently in connection with the Catilinarian conspiracy (cf. *Att.* 1. 14. 5, *Fam.* 5. 5. 2), and he subsequently dropped it from his letters—but here the sinister implications of the word's meaning ("to have discovered by devious means and without making one's evidence plain"), not the tone of the word, was at issue.

(1) *paucis*. In view of the evidence for "senilis μακρολογία" discussed earlier, there is probably some intentional irony in Terence's distribution of the phrase *paucis* (abl. sc. *verbis* = "in a few words") in five of its six occurrences to old men. In the opening scene of the *Andria*, for example, after the promising "ades dum: paucis te volo . . ." at 29, Simo manages to exasperate Sosia (not to say the audience) by his long-winded exposition of the situation. Similarly, Simo's request to Chremes at *Andria* 538–43, with its lengthy introduction "per te deos oro . . . perque unicam gnatam . . . ," is introduced by the phrase "ausculta paucis . . ." (536). Here the OCT editors read *pauca* on the evidence of one MS (codex Parisinus) and Donatus; but, in view of other examples with verbs of listening, especially *Adelphoi* 806, it seems best to keep the majority reading here (omitting *et* before *quid*). At *Adelphoi* 806, Micio introduces his long central argument to Demea with the words "ausculta paucis . . ." The other examples of this phrase in the speech of old men occur at *Hecyra* 510 (Laches) "ades: audi paucis" and *Hautontimorumenos* 10 (prologue spoken by the old man Ambivius) "quam ob rem has partis didicerim paucis dabo." When not being used by old men, the only occurrence of *paucis* is in the exaggeratedly elevated pronouncement by the parasite Gnatho at the end of the *Eunuch:* "prius audite paucis: quod quom dixero si placuerit / facitote" (1067), where the use of parallel subordinate clauses introduced by *quom* and *si*, together with the EL imperative form, is reminiscent of ancient legal language.[39]

(2) *ades* (*imperative*). Except for the phrase *adeste aequo animo*, which occurs in Terence only in the prologues as part of the traditional *captatio benevolentiae* (*An.* 24, *Haut.* 35, *Phorm.* 30), the use of the imperatives *ades* and *adeste* (= "come [stay] here") is restricted in all but one case to old men. It occurs twice in combination with *paucis*. Again, the reason for the restriction is likely to be a "behavioral" one, namely, that old men are more likely to be ordering other people around. Examples are found at *Andria* 29 (Simo; with *paucis*), *Hecyra* 495 (textually doubtful), *Hecyra* 510 (Laches; with *paucis*), and *Phormio* 350 (Demipho). The only exception occurs at *Andria* 344, where the young man Pamphilus is addressing the slave Davos.

(3) *diminutives referring to persons*. The use of diminutives generally is not a feature of old men's speech. In fact, most diminutives in Terence's plays are restricted to low characters. Terence may have considered such colloquial features more appropriate to their speech.[40] The only diminutive forms used by old characters are those which refer to people: a diminutive was perhaps an appropriate word for an old man to use when referring to a younger person, particularly a social inferior. The following forms are used mainly by old persons:

(*a*) *adulescentulus*. Only in the more colloquial *Eunuch* is this word used by all characters with little difference in sense from the simple *adulescens*.[41]

39. Cf. *Lex XII Tab*. 8. 12: "si nox furtum faxit, si im occisit, iure caesus esto."

40. E.g., *Phorm*. 663, *Eun*. 284, 753, 531, *Phorm*. 36, 37, *Ad*. 585, 786, *An*. 369.

41. So in the *Eunuch* by a young man (539), a slave (931, 940), a soldier (423), and a maid (686, 943, 949, 1021).

Elsewhere the diminutive is restricted mainly to old men, usually with reference to their sons: *Hautontimorumenos* 51 (old man), *Hautontimorumenos* 93, 100, 113, 1045 (Menedemus; the first three expressing sympathy with the son he has wronged), *Hautontimorumenos* 477, 546 (Chremes), *Andria* 55, 910 (Simo), *Andria* 828 (Chremes), *Hecyra* 619 (Laches), *Adelphoi* 101 (Micio), 112 (Demea). Two exceptions occur in the *Phormio*, but in both cases the diminutive form is required by the sense. The first is in a slighting reference to a rival's play in the prologue: "quia nusquam insanum scripsit adulescentulum / cervam videre fugere et sectari canes" (6–7). In the second, the young man Phaedria, speaking to his father, is emphasizing the innocence of his young son Antipho: ". . . functus adulescentulist / officium liberalis . . ." (281–82).

(*b*) *adulescentula*. This term is applied by old persons to their sons' mistresses (*virgines* as opposed to *meretrices*). It is used in this way by Simo of Glycerium at *Andria* 118 and by Sostrata of Antiphila at *Hautontimorumenos* 654. Syrus the slave also refers to Antiphila in this way at *Hautontimorumenos* 602.

(*c*) *muliercula*. This is used by old men to refer to younger women, perhaps with a stronger subsidiary idea of their social inferiority than with *adulescentula*. It is so used at *Hautontimorumenos* 444 by Chremes of Antiphila and at *Phormio* 1017 by Demipho of Chremes' mistress, though here the intention may be to stress the insignificance of the affair.[42]

(*d*) *servolus*. This is used once by a slave to express self-pity at *Adelphoi* 566 (Syrus). Elsewhere it is used as a pejorative word for slaves, once by a young man at *Hautontimorumenos* 191 (Clitipho), but mostly by old persons: *Andria* 83 (Simo), *Hautontimorumenos* 471, 530 (Chremes), *Adelphoi* 27 (Micio), 480 (Hegio).

IV. PET EXPRESSIONS OF INDIVIDUAL OLD MEN

An individual old man in Terence may occasionally be given a pet expression as an idiosyncratic peculiarity of his speech. Such expressions need not belong to one of the categories already mentioned (though they often do), nor are old men the only characters to be given pet phrases.[43] This use by individual characters of a favorite phrase, which need not be lexically unusual, has already been detected in the plays of Menander,[44] so one should not perhaps be too surprised to find a similar device in his closest Roman imitator. The following examples are found in the speech of old men:

(1) *propterea quod*. This expression, which is not uncommon in CL, occurs in Terence only in the speech of the old man Simo at *Andria* 38 and 584. In both cases the simple *quod* (or *quia*) could be used, and the extended

42. See R. H. Martin, *Terence's "Phormio"* (London, 1959), ad loc.

43. Cf. Geta's preference for the adverb *modo* in the *Phormio* (59, 68, 93, 95, 109, 142, 149, 198, 221, 566, 624, 773, 859, 865 [2]) and, more understandably, Thais's use of *mi* + vocative in the *Eunuch* (86, 95, 144, 190, 455, 743); cf. Donatus on 95: (2) "vult enim Terentius velut peculiare verbum hoc esse Thaidis."

44. F. H. Sandbach, "Menander's Manipulation of Language for Dramatic Purposes," *Entretiens sur l'antiquité classique* 16 (1969): 113–43, esp. 122–24.

expression is probably intended to characterize Simo's language as long-winded.

(2) *ut tempus est diei*. This phrase, again perhaps a feature of long-winded speech, is used twice by Chremes at *Hautontimorumenos* 168 and 212 and occurs nowhere else in Terence.

(3) *inpuratus*. This EL and post-CL term of abuse is used only by the old man Demipho in the *Phormio* at 669 and 962 (in both cases as a substantive).

(4) *vostro* (*meo*) *impulsu*. The phrase occurs twice in Terence and is used only in the speech of the old man Laches in the *Hecyra*. The imposing "at my (your) instigation" fits in well with Laches' rhetorical style of speech. It is found in chiastic arrangement at 242 "ubi duxere impulsu vostro, vostro impulsu easdem exigunt." The other example occurs at 687 "impulsu duxisti meo."

(5) *adeo*. A penchant for this adverb in all its uses is an idiosyncratic feature of Laches' language in the *Hecyra*. He uses it seven times in sixty lines between 201 and 261, and nine of the twenty occurrences of the adverb in this play are to be put down to him (cf. n. 44 for Geta's use of *modo* in the *Phormio*).

Before leaving the subject of linguistic peculiarities of particular old men, it is worth noting that within individual plays the language of two old men may be contrasted. In the *Adelphoi*, for example, twice as many of the old-fashioned or long-winded expressions discussed earlier are given to the rustic Demea (six) as to the urban Micio (three). E. Fantham suggests that Demea's coarse metaphorical use of *olfacere* (*Ad*. 397) may be intended to characterize his ἀγροικία.[45] Other Terentian hapaxes in his speech may have a similar effect: for example, the EL local use of *prae* at 980 in the phrase *prae manu* of cash "ready to hand," the Plautine verb *perrepto* at 715, and two EL (and post-CL) forms based on Greek at 564 *patrisso* (πατρίζω) and 78 *mastigia* (μαστιγίας). No such hapaxes are found in Micio's language. Similarly, the language of Chremes in the *Hautontimorumenos* contains more non-CL forms than that of Menedemus: for example, *gratulor* in its EL sense of *gratias agere* at 879, *resto* in its EL military sense of "make a stand" or "resist" at 1007, and Plautine features such as the comic formation *advorsatrix* at 1007 and the string of abuse at 1033–34 ". . . gerro iners fraus helluo / ganeo's damnosus . . ." Again, what is significant is not so much the individual features in themselves as their accumulation in the language of Chremes and their relative absence from the speech of Menedemus.

The evidence suggests that, at least in the case of his old men, Terence did concern himself with finding an appropriate manner of speech to suit particular characters. This is perhaps only to be expected in a playwright who was more interested in psychological realism than in the comic possibilities of caricature and farce. The extent of Terence's debt to Menander

45. *Studies*, p. 62.

in this area has yet to be fully assessed,[46] but the presence of such characterization in Terence can no longer be denied. The question of how far such characterization applies to types other than old men in Terence has been left open for the moment. There is some evidence that slaves and "low" characters generally may use more colloquial language than do "high" characters, but the question is complicated by variations in language brought about by the demands of context. Syrus in the *Adelphoi*, for example, adopts an elevated style of language when duping Demea (364–430), which contrasts with the highly colloquial language of his drunken scene (763 ff.). Furthermore, there is some variation in language between the different plays of Terence which may be related to the dates of their composition (see n. 30) or to their stylistic coloring (the *Eunuch*, for example, tends to be more "Plautine" than the rest of the Terentian corpus). The interrelation of these various elements is complex and deserves further investigation. In the meanwhile it is hoped that the evidence concerning the language of Terence's old men has at least put an end to the myth that all his characters in all situations speak the same uniform Latin.

University of Sheffield

46. See Sandbach, "Manipulation," pp. 113–43; cf. J. Strauss, *Terenz und Menander: Beiträge zu einer Stilvergleichung* (Zurich, 1955); S. Zini, *Il linguaggio dei personaggi di Menandro* (Florence, 1938).

NOTES AND DISCUSSIONS

THUCYDIDES' REPRESENTATION OF BRASIDAS BEFORE AMPHIPOLIS

εἰ γὰρ δείξειε τοῖς ἐναντίοις τό τε πλῆθος καὶ τὴν ὅπλισιν ἀναγκαίαν οὖσαν τῶν μεθ' ἑαυτοῦ, οὐκ ἂν ἡγεῖτο μᾶλλον περιγενέσθαι ἢ ἄνευ προόψεώς τε αὐτῶν καὶ μὴ ἀπὸ τοῦ ὄντος καταφρονήσεως.

[Thuc. 5. 8. 3]

A. W. Gomme described 5. 8. 3 as "one of the most difficult of Thucydides' sentences"; and many other editors, translators, and readers have agreed, even when they have not said so in so many words.[1] There is a way, however, to read the sentence so that it yields good sense and fits its context. In the present paper, it is suggested first that Thucydides in other sentences used a mode of coordination very much like that of 5. 8. 3. Once that mode is identified and observed in these other contexts, it can be used to explain 5. 8. 3. Then, when 5. 8. 3 becomes comprehensible, Brasidas' soliloquy, as he assesses his chances at Amphipolis, shows a propriety and a consistency that readers in the past have wished for but not found. Finally, a welcome corollary of this new aspect of Brasidas is that it illustrates Thucydides' painstaking care when representing principal figures in his history.

1. A. W. Gomme, *A Historical Commentary on Thucydides*, vol. 3 (Oxford, 1956), pp. 642–43. The following, selective list with its summaries and examples of varying approaches documents a persistent intransigence. Σ sc_2 (C. Hude) *ἤγουν οὕτως ἐνόμισε περιγενέσθαι* Κλέωνος *καὶ τῶν περὶ αὐτὸν ἐπιτιθησόμενος κρύφα, ὅπερ ἐστὶ τὸ ἄνευ προόψεως, καὶ μὴ ἀπὸ τοῦ φανεροῦ ὅπερ ἐστὶ τὸ καταφρονήσεως τοῦ ὄντος*. L. Valla in H. Stephanus' second edition of Thucydides (Paris, 1588) translates, ". . . haud arbitrabatur magis proficere quam si improvisus esset ac vere contemptus." Thomas Hobbes in 1629 (ed. Richard Schlatter [New Brunswick, N.J., 1975]) translates: "For if he should have showed to the enemy both his number and their armour, such as for the present they were forced to use, he thought that thereby he should not so soon get the victory, as by keeping them out of sight and out of their contempt until the very point." Thomas Arnold in his commentary (Oxford, 1832) says Thucydides has tried ". . . to make the same words express two different things." E. F. Poppo begins a survey of explanations in his edition and commentary (Leipzig, 1835) with the words, "Haec verba magna laborant difficultate," and ends, "ut vides igitur, nobis magis, quid falsum, quam quid verum hic sit, videntibus nulla horum verborum enucleandorum ratio omnino satisfacit; meliorem tamen quum proponere nequeamus, vos, qui haec legitis, homines eruditissimi, ut difficultatem quam negatio parat . . . felicius expediatis, impense opto" (3.3:448). L. Herbst, *Zu Thukydides Erklärungen und Wiederherstellungen*, vol. 2 (Leipzig, 1893), pp. 135–39, says early in his discussion, "Man sieht nicht wie der Schriftsteller sich verständlicher hätte ausdrücken können . . ."; but then he offers no translation or paraphrase, fails to reconcile his explanation with the larger context of the immediate narrative, invokes a disputed phrase in Soph. *Ant*. 4 to justify his version, and finally confesses that he has not perhaps written the last word on the subject. J. Classen and J. Steup in the third edition of their commentary (Berlin, 1912) translate, "wenn er den Feinden seine Schwäche zeigte, glaubte er weniger auf den Sieg rechnen zu können als wenn diese sein Heer nicht vorher erblickten, und er nicht mit Nichtachtung der tatsächlichen Beschaffenheit der beiderseitigen Streitkräfte vorginge." D. Mervyn Jones, "The Scholiast on Aristophanes *Knights* 438 and Three Passages of Thucydides," *Proceedings of the Cambridge Philological Society* 177 (1951): 23–24, proposes either to regard *μὴ* as redundant or to supply *οὔσης* with *καταφρονήσεως* (Göller's solution, which Jones favors slightly). J. de Romilly in her edition and translation (Paris, 1967) describes her own paraphrase correctly as "assurément difficile" (p. 186). The standard English translations of today—R. Crawley's in the Modern Library (New York, 1934), Rex Warner's in the Penguin series (Bungay, 1954), and B. Jowett's (ed. P. A. Brunt [New York, 1963])—follow Hobbes for the sense of the passage.

The key to understanding 5. 8. 3 lies in a way of speaking that can be illustrated as well in English as in Greek. Sometimes in English a speaker will reinforce his message by adding a negatived, opposite conception. For example: "Come on time and don't be late." At other times—more often than not, in fact—the same speaker, in the interest of variety, takes one further step in his mind and leaves the mere opposite conception unspoken. Instead, he illustrates it with some attendant circumstance or result or specific instance. Thus, in the sentence, "Come on time and don't disappoint us," the prohibition, "Don't disappoint us," is not the opposite of "Come on time." It is a possible result of the implied opposite conception, "Don't be late." That is, before disappointment can become an issue, lateness must be present either in the words or the mind of the speaker.

Demosthenes' address to his troops at Pylos (4. 10. 2) contains a good example of Thucydides' use of this sort of antithesis:

> ἐγὼ δὲ καὶ τὰ πλείω ὁρῶ πρὸς ἡμῶν ὄντα, ἢν ἐθέλωμέν τε μεῖναι καὶ μὴ τῷ πλήθει αὐτῶν καταπλαγέντες τὰ ὑπάρχοντα ἡμῖν κρείσσω καταπροδοῦναι.

Demosthenes says, "I even see that most of the circumstances are on our side, if we are willing to stand fast and not betray our existing superiorities by being dismayed at the number of the enemy." In this sentence, as in the English example in the foregoing paragraph, two notions are presented in a way that might at a glance suggest a polarity. Under the strictest interpretation, however, the polarity does not exist. "Stand fast" and "not betray" are connected, to be sure, by *τε . . . καὶ μή*, which is a form of coordination often used to bind opposites together, but "not betray" is a specification or result of some conception like "flee," which is the exact opposite of "stand fast." We infer this opposite from the phrase, "not betray"; but, as in the English example the notion of lateness must precede disappointment, so here betraying cannot become an issue unless the notion of flight is in the mind or words of the speaker. The sequence can be illustrated in the following manner, where angle brackets enclose the unuttered, implicit opposite: ". . . if we are willing to stand fast and not ⟨flee and thereby⟩ betray," etc.

A few more examples (these, however, without *τε*) will help to establish this sort of elliptical antithesis as a characteristic Thucydidean formulation. *2. 39. 1:* "We present a city that is open to the world, and we do not ⟨keep it to ourselves and, for example⟩ prevent people from seeing and learning," etc.[2] *3. 39. 6:* "Let them now be properly punished for this crime and not ⟨escape proper punishment, as they will, for example, if you⟩ blame the few and let the demos go." *3. 40. 3:* "For it is right to feel pity for people like yourselves and not ⟨for people unlike yourselves, namely⟩ for people who will not feel pity in return and who are fated to be our enemies forever." *3. 40. 3:* "The orators who give you pleasure by their speeches will hold their contest in other, lesser circumstances and not ⟨in these important circumstances⟩ where the state will pay a lot for a little pleasure." *6. 10. 5:* "One must consider and not ⟨fail to consider, and thereby⟩ require the city to risk danger while on the high seas and to reach for another empire before securing the one we have."

2. Classen–Steup, ad loc.: "*καὶ οὐκ ἔστιν ὅτε . . . εὐψύχῳ* ist die Ausführung des *κοινὴν τὴν πόλιν παρέχομεν*." Essentially the same thing could be said, mutatis mutandis, concerning all the examples listed in this paper.

To return to 5. 8. 3, the relationship between the two elements associated by *τε . . . καὶ μὴ* can be expressed in exactly the same way: Brasidas thought he would not more likely prevail than he would without their seeing his troops beforehand and not with ⟨their having seen his troops beforehand, which would result in⟩ their becoming contemptuous as a result of their awareness of his true situation.[3]

Brasidas, in other words, is relinquishing one possible advantage, a feeling of contempt on the enemy's part, in favor of another, the element of surprise. Cleon might well feel contemptuous on making out the high number of peltasts in the total troop strength of the Peloponnesians, and Brasidas as a good general is weighing all possible advantages against each other. Thucydides does not say whether Brasidas regrets having to relinquish that possible advantage; he just shows Brasidas reckoning what he can and what he cannot have.

The reckoning that Thucydides abstracts and compresses may have been somewhat as follows: "I cannot count on the strength of my troops if we oppose the enemy face to face. We are about equal in number, but the Athenians and their allies have too many hoplites, and we on the other hand have too high a proportion of peltasts. Peltasts, no matter how brave, cannot stand against well-trained hoplites here. Now, if the Athenians see my men beforehand, they may fall into being contemptuous, since they are as aware as I am of the fundamental difference between light-armed and heavy-armed troops, and that treacherous feeling could lead them into some error that would be to my advantage. But I had better keep my troops hidden until the last minute. That way I may lose a tactical advantage, namely, the enemy's contempt—granted it would arise from seeing my actual numbers and armor—but surprise is best."

Thucydides 5. 8. 1–3 can then be translated: "Immediately as Brasidas caught sight of the Athenians in motion, he himself went down from Cerdylion and into Amphipolis. He did not go out in a regular line of march for pitched battle, because he was anxious concerning his own equipment, believing his men to be inferior, not in numbers—the numbers were about equal—but in quality, for the real Athenians had come out on this expedition and the best of the Lemnians and Imbrians. Brasidas, therefore, devised a trick attack. For if he was going to show the enemy both the number and the scanty armor of his troops,[4] he thought he would not be more likely to prevail than he would without the Athenians seeing his men beforehand, and not as a result of Athenian contempt for his true situation."

When construed in this way, 5. 8. 3 no longer conflicts with Brasidas' reflections before battle on the number and quality of his troops as compared to those of Cleon. In the past, students of Greek history have found Brasidas' reflections inconsistent and finally, therefore, merely confusing.[5] But it may be that 5. 8. 3

3. Τοῦ *ὄντος* is an objective genitive that defines the phrase *μὴ ἀπὸ . . . καταφρονήσεως*; *μὴ* rather than *οὐ* because a condition is implied. Cf. R. C. Jebb ad Soph. *Ant*. 23 (3d ed., Cambridge, 1900), who paraphrased *ἄνευ προόψεως . . . αὐτῶν* with *εἰ μὴ προΐδοιεν αὐτούς*. For the sense of *ἀπὸ καταφρονήσεως*, see LSJ[9], s.v. *ἀπό* III, 6.

4. I take this to mean, if Brasidas was going to take his troops out of Amphipolis at all that day and commit them to battle (*pace* Gomme, ad loc.).

5. See, e.g., Gomme, 3:643: "Together with the contradictory hints about Brasidas' numbers (§§ 2, 4), the difficulties of this sentence make the whole chapter extremely puzzling."

was the principal cause of confusion. Readers who were uncertain how the sentence should be understood could not be confident with related sentences. In any case, a coherent account of Brasidas' reasoning can now be attempted.

Cleon had 1,500 Athenians (1,200 hoplites plus 300 mounted troops), 30 ships, and more than 1,500 allies (5. 2. 1). At Scione, he added hoplites from the garrison there to his own number (5. 2. 2). At Torone, he left a garrison and sailed toward Amphipolis (5. 3. 6). Inasmuch as we do not know how many troops he added at Scione, or how many he left at Torone, or how many more than 1,500 allies he had, we cannot put an exact number on his total force. At Eion, he sent emissaries to Perdiccas, who was to bring an army, and to Polles, in an effort to bring as many Thracian mercenaries as possible to his aid (5. 6. 2).

Brasidas had 1,000 peltasts from Myrcinos and Chalcis, in addition to those in Amphipolis. His total hoplite force came to about 2,000, plus 300 Greek mounted troops. Of these,[6] he had 1,500 with him on Cerdylion. The rest of his troops were stationed in Amphipolis with Clearidas (5. 6. 4–5). We never learn whether the Thracians and Edonians Brasidas was summoning arrived in time for the battle. Presumably they did not. As in the case of Cleon, we cannot give an exact figure for Brasidas' forces: the peltasts (?) or Myrcinian horse (?) in Amphipolis, however many they may have been, are not counted in the 3,300 troops which Thucydides explicitly mentions.[7]

When, therefore, Thucydides has Brasidas estimate that Cleon's forces and his own are about equal in number (5. 8. 2), we must be content with approximations. On the one side there are 1,500 Athenians plus more than 1,500 Lemnians and Imbrians (and, in addition, the unknown number of troops from Scione, less those left as a garrison at Torone). On the other side there are Brasidas' 3,300 plus some unknown number.[8]

Now it is time to present a summary of Brasidas' comparisons in order. At 5. 6. 3 Brasidas can expect Cleon to despise his numerical strength: Brasidas has only 1,500 of his troops on Cerdylion, and Cleon therefore will think he has more than twice the number of Brasidas' troops. At 5. 8. 2 Brasidas reckons that Cleon's forces no longer outnumber his; Brasidas has by this time gone down from Cerdylion to rejoin Clearidas and the others in town. His perspective has changed, for the numbers now are about equal.

Why then should Brasidas regard his troops as inferior? Why should he think that Cleon might be contemptuous first upon looking at his partial force of 1,500 troops on Cerdylion, but then upon his total force as well? The answer lies in the kinds of troops that make up those numbers and their inferior armor. Cleon has troops of the best quality to pose against an enemy force of comparable size, one-third of which is peltasts. Brasidas (and almost any other Spartan) knows that these light-armed troops are inferior to hoplites and cavalry.

Brasidas' troops therefore need a special advantage. One possible advantage is that, if Cleon sees the enemy troops, he may become contemptuous and hence

6. Whether the antecedent of τούτων is "hoplite force" or "hoplites and peltasts" does not affect the present argument in any essential way.

7. J. Kromayer, *Antike Schlachtfelder*, vol. 4 (Berlin, 1931), pp. 203–4, refers only to peltasts. See Classen–Steup and Gomme, ad loc., on the possibility of textual corruption here.

8. Kromayer, *Schlachtfelder*, 4:203–4, estimates 4,000 to a side.

overconfident. But Brasidas decides no. If he is going to commit his troops, he has a better chance with a staggered surprise attack. He accordingly eschews the putative benefits of making his enemy contemptuous (5. 8. 3). Also, he assumes or knows that Cleon expects reinforcements.[9] Brasidas will accordingly attack before any reinforcements can arrive. This will be the sense in which Cleon's troops are μεμονωμένους at 5. 8. 4.

Finally, when Brasidas, addressing his troops before the battle (5. 9. 3), alludes to Athenian contempt, he is again back in the context of the Athenian view of him and his 1,500 troops on Cerdylion, when the Athenians did not have any means of forming an accurate estimate of his troop strength.[10] They never do, in fact, until too late, when Clearidas bursts out of the Thracian Gate in the second phase of Brasidas' successful battle plan.[11]

To sum up, Thucydides does not lose his way when he tells us what Brasidas is thinking. Whether Brasidas is soliloquizing or addressing troops, his assessment at each point of the narrative is in accordance with what it should be at the time and place stipulated. Thucydides, as he writes, seems to put himself inside Brasidas, a position from which he can gauge how Brasidas would change responses as position and circumstances changed. It is such attention to detail that distinguishes the best writers.

ALAN L. BOEGEHOLD
Brown University

9. Βρασίδας δὲ πυνθανόμενος ταῦτα . . . (5. 6. 3).

10. The phrase ἀπὸ τοῦ ὄντος καταφρονήσεως at 5. 8. 3 stipulates contempt arising from the true situation (τοῦ ὄντος) because, as 5. 9. 3 shows, Brasidas can also encourage his troops with the hope that Cleon will be contemptuous out of a false notion of Brasidas' strength.

11. It is by no means a necessary inference from 5. 10. 2 that Cleon, who was outside the city, could count all of Brasidas' troops in the city.

AN UNNOTICED RULE OF PLAUTINE METER

In a regular lyric meter in Plautus whose normal form contains two consecutive *longa*, if the verse is syncopated by omitting one of these *longa*, then (*a*) the syllable omitted will be the second of the two, and (*b*) a word break will occur at that point. The rule has two unequivocal applications, one in cretic and one in bacchiac systems. Most cretics in Plautus come in tetrameters:

— ∪ — | — ∪ — || — ∪ — | — ∪ —
nam secun- | dum patrem | tu's pater | proxumus. [*Capt.* 239]

There is a diaeresis between the two halves of the verse; otherwise, word breaks may occur, or fail to occur, at any point. Occasionally we meet a shortened form, in which only one *longum* occurs at the juncture of the third and fourth feet:

— ∪ — | — ∪ — || — ∪ — ∪ —
uox uiri | pessumi | me exciet foras. [*Pseud.* 1285]

This is the most common syncopated verse form in Plautus, and it has been mentioned by those who have discussed Plautine meter.[1] Although nobody has commented on the fact, these lines almost always show a word break before the next-to-last syllable. Out of sixty-one such lines, at least fifty-five[2] have such a break, a circumstance whose random probability is less than one in a trillion.[3]

In bacchiacs we find, rather less commonly, a form in which the next-to-last foot has one *longum* rather than two:

⏑ — — | ⏑ — — | ⏑ — | ⏑ — —
adaeque miser :: ludo ego hunc facete; [*Cas.* 685]

According to our rule, such lines should show a diaeresis before the last foot: eleven of thirteen cases do so.[4] There are other shortened forms of cretics and bacchiacs: — ⏑ ⏑ ⏑ —, ⏑ — — — —, and ⏑ — — ⏑ —, to mention the most common. To none of them would our rule apply, and none shows any obligatory word break.

All of the exceptions to the rule may be plausibly explained or emended. Four of them have, instead of a word break, a juncture between a separable prefix and the root: *ad-uenis*, *red-didi*, *ac-cubat*, *im-peratum est*,[5] and we may perhaps add *op-pido*,[6] if the *op-* was felt to be a prefix. For two more, Lindsay had already proposed emendations which would remove them from our list,[7] and the last could also be "fixed" by a trifling correction,[8] though I do not think it is necessary: Plautus was anything but a rigid versifier.

1. In English, W. M. Lindsay, *Early Latin Verse* (Oxford, 1922; repr. 1968), pp. 293–94. In current handbooks, J. W. Halporn, M. Ostwald, and T. G. Rosenmeyer, *The Meters of Greek and Latin Poetry* (Indianapolis and New York, 1963), p. 88; and D. S. Raven, *Latin Metre* (London, 1965), p. 127. Lindsay scanned — ⏑ | — ⏑ —, and others have suggested — ⏑ | — ⏑ | — ∧. In view of the rule here noted, I presume that the correct scansion is — ⏑ — | ⏑ —.

2. *Bacch.* 26, 621, 622, 643, 645, 650, 663–65, 667, *Cas.* 873, 942, 952–53, *Curc.* 117, *Ep.* 169, *Most.* 109, 133, 134, 141, 337, 338, 343, 345, 690–92, 694, 695, 698–701, 707–11, 714, 717, *Pseud.* 258, 261–63, 1109, 1112, 1280*a*, 1285, 1287, 1288, 1291, 1294, 1300, *Truc.* 116–18 (my list is based on Lindsay's text and analysis). The six exceptions are *Amph.* 242, *Capt.* 836, *Most.* 113, 136, *Pseud.* 1309, 1311.

3. The probability—lest I be accused of inventing the figure—is

$$\sum_{n=55}^{61} \binom{61}{n} (.45)^n (.55)^{61-n},$$

taking the probability of such a break as .45 on the basis of a random sampling of some six hundred lines from the *Epidicus* and the *Menaechmi*.

4. *Bacch.* 1121*a*, 1139, 1140*a*, *Cas.* 662, 673–74, 685, 695, 702, *Men.* 763*a*, *Rud.* 287, 289. The two exceptions are *Most.* 314 and 796.

5. *Capt.* 836, *Pseud.* 1309, 1311, *Most.* 314.

6. *Most.* 136.

7. *Conspicatust* for *conspicatus est*, *Amph.* 242; *hasc' uenum dedisse* for *hasce uendidisse*, *Most.* 796.

8. For *iam est usus* (*Most.* 113), one might read *iám* | *usus est*, giving an unsyncopated cretic. There are also sixteen cases where the sequence — ⏑ — ⏑ — appears either alone or as the first half of a line; of these ten (*Bacch.* 621, 643, 645, *Cas.* 942, *Cist.* 16, *Pseud.* 1112, 1280*a*, 1292, 1308, 1310) have a diaeresis before the penultimate syllable; three (*Pseud.* 1109, 1293, *Rud.* 231) have a separable prefix there; one is an uncertain reading (*Pseud.* 1308*a*, where the reading of the Ambrosian palimpsest, *tactus est Ballio*, would remove it from our list), and two are halves of lines that do not appear to be cretic at all (*Epid.* 67 and 68*a*, where the first shows a morpheme break any-

I am certain that Plautus never dreamed of a rule such as I have formulated. Why, then, did he observe it? There hardly seems to have been any need to break up the cretic tetrameter, which was already short and split in half by a diaeresis. Nor can the word break have been heard as part of a regular system, for these syncopations do not generally come in groups, but are rather occasional sports in longer, more or less regular, cretic and bacchiac systems.

But these "systems" were songs sung to a tune. It is at least possible to suggest that, where our text is predominantly cretic or bacchiac, the tune was even more regularly so, so that even syncopated lines might be sung to the tune of an *un*-syncopated tetrameter,[9]

♩ ♪♩ ♩ ♪ ♩ ♩♪♩ ♩ ♪ ♩
uox uiri pessumi me͡ exciet foras.

It would surely be awkward to have a single word straddling the one-*longum* rest; and this will be why Plautus regularly avoided such a thing. Had he placed the pause at the end of the third foot, rather than the beginning of the fourth, he would have left a short syllable before the pause: such a syllable would probably not be short at all, but an *anceps*, which would have no place in the middle of the line. In musical terms, I should think that the singer would either have to cut the syllable unnaturally short before the pause, or let it carry over inelegantly into the next note. Where the second *longum* is omitted rather than the first, the inelegance is avoided.[10]

DAVID SCHAPS
Bar-Ilan University

way). Two of our exceptions here, and another two in the first list (n. 2), belong to the drunken Pseudolus; I do not think this is accidental.

9. Some syncopations are too extreme for this explanation; there the tune must surely have changed.

10. My thanks to Professor G. P. Goold for introducing me to the labyrinth of Plautine metrics, and to much else in Latin letters.

THE CHRONOLOGY OF PRISCUS FRAGMENT 6

O. J. Maenchen-Helfen has conclusively demonstrated that the great Hun War mentioned in fragments 3 and 5 of Priscus occurred in 447.[1] The Peace of Anatolius mentioned in fragment 5 must therefore be dated to the same year. E. A. Thompson mistakenly dates the Peace of Anatolius to 443, and assigns fragment 6 to the following year (444).[2] I contend that fragment 6 is to be dated to 441 and not to either 444 or 447, in spite of the fact that fragment 6 follows fragment 5 in the *Excerpta de legationibus gentium*.

Priscus says in fragment 6 that after a certain treaty with the Romans the Huns sent repeated embassies to Constantinople on the pretext of demanding the

1. *The World of the Huns* (Berkeley, 1973), pp. 111–25.
2. *A History of Attila and the Huns* (Oxford, 1948), pp. 87–88.

return of fugitives but actually to extort more money from the Romans. Because of other military problems that they faced the Romans invariably yielded. These military problems were: (*a*) the Persians were preparing for war; (*b*) the Vandals were harassing the seacoast; (*c*) Isaurian bandits were disturbing Anatolia; (*d*) the Saracens were overrunning the East; and (*e*) Ethiopian tribes were threatening the Nile frontier.

The disturbance in the Sudan was evidently not serious enough to have left its mark in any extant source other than Priscus. The other incidents, however, can be dated to 441 but not to a later year. The only war which the Romans fought with the Persians in this period began in 441.[3] It is therefore accurate to describe the Persians as preparing for war in 441 but hardly in 444 or 447, when the war was either still going on or finished. There are even more compelling reasons for believing that Priscus' comment about the Vandals can refer only to 441. The Romans and the Vandals had been at war since Geiseric seized Carthage in 439. But a treaty had concluded this war in 442.[4] Geiseric sent embassies to both Valentinian III and Theodosius II. No source specifically states that the Vandals violated the treaty, and there is every reason to believe that they did not. As part of the agreement of 442, Huniric, Geiseric's son, was sent to Ravenna as a hostage. This should certainly have deterred Geiseric from any piratical attacks against the Empire. There is even evidence that relations between the Vandals and the Romans became friendly. In connection with the treaty or shortly thereafter, Huniric was engaged to Eudocia, the daughter of Valentinian III.[5] In such circumstances it seems incredible that the Vandals would continue to attack the Empire. Finally, the Isaurians and the Saracens are known to have disturbed the peace in 441.[6] About later attacks there is not a word in any source. The treaty with the Huns discussed in fragment 6, then, would be the one-year treaty of 441 mentioned by Count Marcellinus.[7]

An additional conclusion can be drawn from this discovery. Thompson and several other scholars claim that the treaty which concluded the Persian War of 441 was only a one-year truce.[8] Unfortunately, none of them gives a reference for this statement, and none of the ancient sources that discuss the Persian War mentions it. Presumably they have inferred that this was the case from Priscus' statement in fragment 6 that the Persians were preparing for war. But, if this event is dated to 441, the unattested "one-year truce" vanishes. Priscus is really referring to conditions before the outbreak of the Persian War.

WILLIAM N. BAYLESS
Rutgers University

3. Marcell. comes, s.a. 441. 1 (ed. Mommsen, *Chron. min.*, 2:80).
4. Prosper 1347 (ed. Mommsen, *Chron. min.*, 1:479); Victor Vitensis 1. 13 (ed. Halm, *MGH:AA*, 3:4); Procopius *BV* 1. 4. 13–14; and, wrongly, Theophanes, A.M. 5941 (p. 101 De Boor). Prosper dates the treaty to 442. Procopius tells us that Huniric was sent as a hostage.
5. Merobaudes *Carm.* 1. 7–8. This interpretation is doubted (with insufficient reason) by T. D. Barnes, "Merobaudes on the Imperial Family," *Phoenix* 28 (1974): 314–19. It is true that it is not strictly proper to refer to Huniric as *exul opes*, but this is easily understood as rhetorical hyperbole. Moreover, Barnes' suggestion, Tibatto, can hardly be covered by the term *novus*.
6. Marcell. comes, s.a. 441. 1.
7. Ibid.
8. *History*, p. 87; see also A. Güldenpenning, *Geschichte des oströmischen Reiches unter den Kaisern Arcadius und Theodosius II* (Halle, 1885), p. 348; C. D. Gordon, *The Age of Attila* (Ann Arbor, 1960), p. 69.

A NEW MS OF THE *VATICANUS PARADOXOGRAPHUS*

The history of the editions of the small collection—largely but not entirely derived from similar collections—of paradoxa known as the *Vaticanus Paradoxographus* (*vel Rohdii*) has not been happy. The *editio princeps*, by Erwin Rohde,[1] was like its successors based on a single MS, V = Vat. Gr. 12, foll. 212^{r}–215^{v}. This edition was full of errors, which are to be explained only partly, one assumes, by the physical condition of the MS: the paper and pen were of poor quality (to the extent that it is now impossible to divine what the scribe intended in one instance: cf. line 64). The next editor, O. Keller,[2] corrected some of Rohde's errors, preserved others, and added more of his own. The last editor, A. Giannini,[3] was justly critical of his predecessors, but his own edition is not so free of fault that one can confidently accept what he reports, where that report differs from those of Rohde and Keller.[4]

There is, moreover, another MS which contains part of the work and which I refer to as D(ecurtatus).[5] In what follows, I print the readings of D (where they differ from Giannini's text) and V (where they have been misreported, in text or apparatus, or omitted by Giannini).

2 *φησιν*: *φασιν* V   3 *μέλλωσιν*: *μέλλουσιν* D   4 *ἀγνίσασαν* D, corr. Rohde   6 *διαπεραιῶνται* D, corr. Rohde, *διαπερεῶνται* V   9 *Δαλίων*: *Θαλία* D   10 *κροκότταν*: *κρότταν* D   17 *σφῆκαν*: *σφῆκα* D   20 *Ἄναιμα*: *Ἔναιμα* D (E a rubricatore)   20 *πλείους*: *πλείω* D   22 *ἰχθῦες*: *ἰχθῦς* DV   22 *διό, ἐὰν*: *δι' ὃν καὶ ὅταν* DV   22 *διώκηται* D, corr. Rohde   22 *ὁ* om. D   26 *τὰ* om. D   29 *κἂν*: *ἐν* DV   30 *Γάγγῃ*: *σάγγη* D   30 *μεδίμνας*: *μεδίμνους* D   31 †*πληόις* †*ὡς*: *πλοίοις καὶ* D, *πλείοις καὶ* V[6]   35 *τὸ μὲν ἐν*: *τὸ μὲν* D^{ac} *τὸ ἐν* D^{pc} *τὸ ὣν ἐν* V   36 *πέσσεσθαι*: *πήσσεσθαι* DV   37 *Λυγκήσταις*: *λυγγίσταις* D (ut V)   37 *τι εἶναι*: *εἶναι* D *εἶναι* V[7]   46 *εὑρίσκεσθαι*: *εὑρίσκεται* DV   50 *φυλλῶν*: *φύλλων τούτων* V   58 *εἰ δ' οὐ*: *εἰ δ' οὖν* V[8]   59 *Πέρινθος*: *Πείρινθος* V   63 *Μαρσύας*: *Μαρσίας* V   64 *ἤν πως*: *η πω* (?)

1. "Isigoni Nicaeensis de rebus mirabilibus breviarium e codice Vaticano nunc primum edidit," *Acta Societatis philologicae Lipsiensis* 1 (1871): 25–42. Cf. A. Nauck, "Kritischc Bcmerkungen VI: Zu Isigonus Nicaeensis," *Bulletin de l'Académie impériale des sciences de St.-Pétersbourg* 17 (1872): 262–63, several of whose emendations of Rohde's text are actually in V.

2. *Rerum naturalium Scriptores Graeci minores*, vol. 1 (Leipzig, 1877), pp. 106–15.

3. *Paradoxographorum Graecorum reliquiae* = *Classici Greci e Latini* (Milan, 1965), pp. 331–51. In his review (*Mnemosyne*, ser. 4, 23 [1970]: 91), D. Holwerda was able to correct three mistaken readings from the page reproduced in Giannini.

4. I use throughout Giannini's line numbering.

5. It is the final folium (284^{rv}) of Vat. Gr. 1144, a "Mischhandschrift" of saec. xiv/xv. The text extends to line 49 *ἀμειφθῆναι*. D and V are descended from a common ancestor: both, for example, have intrusive *φησί* at 39 (Giannini) or 40 (Rohde, Keller). There are no errors which qualify as separative, but D > V seems excluded by 9 *Θαλία* D, *Δαλίων* V. V > D is, I think, excluded by the number of errors in V.

6. There is no doubt about the text of V here. The letter which Giannini interprets as *η* cannot be that, since the right hasta of this scribe's *η* regularly descends to or below the line (see the plate after p. 342, lines 2 and 5). The abbreviation which Giannini interprets as *καί* is *ὡς* (the same abbreviation at line 36), but *ὡς* should be retained as an emendation.

For discussion and other emendations (rendered unnecessary by the reading of D), see E. K. Borthwick, "Lucretius' Elephant Wall," *CQ* 23 (1973): 292 and n. 3.

7. The squiggle over *ειναι* in V probably represents breathing and accent. It cannot be *τι*.

8. The reading of V may be due to a *lapsus oculi* from 56: *εἰ δ' οὖν*, corrected there to *εἰ δ' οὐ* by Rohde.

V 65 Μαρσύου: Μαρσίου V 70 ψυχρὸς: Ψυχρὸς V[9] 79 Ἴβηρσιν: Ἴβερσιν V 81 ὑφήνασαι sic V[10] 86 τοῦτο τῷ: τούτων τῷ V 89 κτάνωσι: κτείνωσι V 93 τινας: τινα V 96 γυνὴ 'κγίνεται: γυνὴ γίνεται V 110 δῆτα βαίνει: διαβαίνει V 118 ἀποσπασθεῖσαν: ἀποσπασθεῖσα V 119 Σκύλλαιον: Σκύλαιον V 121 ἐκεῖνο: ἐκείνου V 124 Γέτας: Γαίτας V 124 ἐπιτυμπανίζειν: ἀποτυμπανίζει V 157 πείθονται: πύθονται V 166 δὲ: τε V 175 ταῖς παρθένοις: ταῖς lac. παρθένοις 177 ἐπινοήσῃ: ἐπινοήσει V 179 βίον: βίου V 180 ἀφίενται: ἀφεῖνται V 186 χεῖρα ἢ ὀφθαλμὸν: χείρᾳ ἢ ὀθφαλμῷ V[11] 192 στρατεύσωνται: στρατεύωνται V 204 ἀνύοντες sic V 207 κατακρημνίζουσιν: κατακρυμνίζουσιν V 215 ἑαυτῶν sic V 220 τῶν non hab. V.

JOHN J. KEANEY
Princeton University

9. A proper noun is intended: these are regularly signaled, as here, by a suprascript stroke.
10. The MS is damaged here, but ὑφη[ν]άσαι is beyond doubt.
11. Iotas subscript, used here, are comparatively rare in this MS.

REVIEW ARTICLE

THE LOEB MANILIUS*

Time was, as W. M. Calder III lately reminded us, when eminent scholars were but seldom seen contributing to the Loeb Classical Library. Mediocrity or worse proliferated in the red and green ranks, though not to the exclusion of such meritorious achievements as Colson's Philo and Anderson's Sidonius. *Sed haec prius fuere.* Of latter years some of the best-known names in contemporary classical scholarship have given their services, and it is no longer unusual for an outcoming volume to deserve serious professional attention. But Goold's long-awaited Manilius is a special case. It offers the first complete translation into English prose[1] of perhaps the most ingenious, though certainly not the most generally enjoyable, of Latin poets. Also it is the first text to appear since Housman's *editio minor* of 1932, except for a recent regrettable incident in Italy known to me only by report. The editor and translator is a distinguished Latinist, deeply versed in celestial lore. For the first time the *Astronomica* has become accessible to those who cannot or will not cope with Housman's commentary.

In a Loeb edition the translation is usually what matters most. Goold's deserves high praise.[2] Manilius' often strained and cryptic utterance is faithfully conveyed in a style both lucid and elegant. Full use has been made of Housman, who rarely ignores a serious difficulty and hardly ever misdirects. Goold is very seldom significantly at variance with Housman's interpretations, but he accepts W. Bühler's views at 4. 442 and 5. 410, and I flatter myself that "Maniliana," *CQ* 6 (1956): 81–86, will have encouraged him to avoid Housman's mistake at 4. 370–71. Other admonitions have been overlooked or disregarded. At 2. 871–74 Manilius is still made "nugas nugatorie exornare," though Goold's interpretation of the untenable paradosis differs from Housman's. At 4. 682 Goold adheres to a false interpretation of *taurumque resolvit* (= "fecit ut tauri formam exueret"), "and gave the bull release," in spite of "Maniliana," p. 85 and *Propertiana* (Cambridge, 1956), p. 211. At 4. 294 "sed nihil in semet totum valet," his rendering ("but no sign has exclusive control over itself") coincides with mine (except that I wrote "undivided power"), but it requires my conjecture *solum*, which Goold ignores. Another ancient error is upheld at 4. 523 (see p. 167). At 2. 13–14 Housman (and Garrod) give faulty guidance: "orbemque sub illo / infantem" does not mean "the childhood of the world beneath its [Chaos'] sway," but "hard after it [Chaos] the childhood of the world" (cf. 2. 187–88 "te, Capricorne, sub ipso / promittit"; Virg. *Aen.* 5. 323); once the elements were separated, Chaos vanished (1. 125–27; Ov. *Met.* 1. 5–68).

Manilius: "Astronomica." Edited and translated by G. P. Goold. Loeb Classical Library. Cambridge, Mass.: Harvard University Press; London: William Heinemann, Ltd., 1977. Pp. cxxii + 387 + 8 + frontispiece (map) + 2 folding charts (star-charts); 24 figs. + 7 tables in text. $8.50.

1. H. W. Garrod translated Book 2 in his edition (Oxford, 1911).

2. A debt is acknowledged to Percival Vaughan Davies, who handed over his own version, covering about two-thirds of the text, with license to use at will.

Since newcomers to Manilius are sure to rely on this translation, it seems useful to point out lapses, not including minor liberties like "lore" for *sacra* in the first sentence of the poem. Considering the difficulty of the original, they are commendably few.

1. 10 "inspires my design": *das animum* surely means "gives me courage." 1. 59 *proprias sedes* = "their old positions" (as when first observed), not "their customary positions"; and *reddita* means "assigned by the observers," not by fate. 1. 84 *commentum* cannot mean "communicated" (text doubtful). 1. 312 "quae [*sc.* astra] quia dissimilis, qua pugnat, temperat aer" = "because the heterogeneous atmosphere tempers them inasmuch as it is in conflict [with itself]," not "since [they] are tempered by an atmosphere which is unlike its neighbours in so far as it is at variance with them." 1. 482 "so sure in all its ways" (*tam vice certum*): *vice* = *ordine*. 1. 512 "fatis Asiae iam Graecia pressa est" means that Greece has been crushed by Asia's destiny, i.e., by Rome, not as Goold's note explains, displaced from the primacy of the world. 1. 726–27 "qui deinde sequitur verborum strepitus meum captum superat" (Housman). Goold too (reading a conjecture of his own) is for once unintelligible. 1. 839 "ball" is an unfortunate rendering of *glomus*, which Bentley substituted for *globus* just because this type of comet is not round. 1. 876 "for the fires . . .": the Latin has no equivalent for "for," which disrupts the sequence. So does "yet" at 2. 7. 1. 898 "in foreign parts, when" should read "when in foreign parts" (with a comma before *ut*, as in Housman's text).

2. 28 *et* seems to have been misunderstood. 2. 31 "her disguise" is a slip for "his disguise." 2. 161–62 "when destiny hangs in the balance, the signs that are accompanied have power to decide for good or ill" (similarly Garrod). Manilius means: "are powerful for good or ill, dispensing doubtful destinies." 2. 292 *laevă* seems to be rendered instead of *laevā*. 2. 677 "notwithstanding the vast space between": for "notwithstanding," which interferes with the sense, read "across" (Garrod). 2. 751 "now it is enough to teach new principles by demonstrating their uses": "suos ignota per usus" = "non per suos usus nota," "facts not [yet] known in their application" (cf. 2. 769–71, 2. 900, 3. 156–59); Garrod too is wrong here.

3. 427 *superatur* could not in any case mean "is held in excess"; but see "Maniliana," pp. 83–84. 3. 523 *motus* = "movements," not "influences."

4. 139 *seque sua . . . vendere laude* = "to commend itself by its own praise," not "to sell itself for praise." 4. 406 *quid caelo dabimus?* = "what shall we give *to* heaven [in exchange for heaven]?" not "*for* heaven." 4. 537 "heedless of father and sons alike": *reus* = "answerable to," i.e., "guilty in respect of" (cf. Housman, "eorum postulationibus obnoxius").

5. 10 *semel* = "once for all," as in the Lucretian source (6. 47), not "but once." 5. 83 *meta currere acuta* must, if the text is sound, be taken as "drive round the pointed turning-post," not "sharply on the inside graze the turning-post." 5. 546 "weeping, she is adorned," not "she is tearfully adorned." 5. 637 *rector* = "horseman," not "commander."

Besides numerous helpful notes accompanying the translation, there are 112 pages of introduction, largely devoted to seriatim summary and exposition of the poem's content. Housman has no such introduction to Book 1, but for the rest

Goold follows in Housman's footsteps, with occasional dissent[3] and some impressive original matter (as on pp. lxiv f. and lxxxi ff.). Diagrams are plentiful; note also a colored frontispiece, "The world of Manilius," and two decorative star-charts—all prepared by the editor's brother, Kevin Goold. The introduction also contains sections on the poet, the manuscripts, "editorial principles," and a select bibliography which commendably includes ancient astronomical and astrological sources. Add a good index. This wealth of ancillary matter, unprecedented in a Loeb text, greatly increases the book's usefulness.

Goold's text has a particular interest for those conversant with Housman's masterpiece. Admirable as it generally is, the cause and nature of its excellence do not appear on the surface and seem indeed to be partially unrealized by the editor himself, who writes in his preface as follows:

> Whilst the text and the interpretation given in this edition represent my own judgement of what the poet wrote and meant . . . my obligation to former editors and scholars in this field is practically total. But to none is it greater than to Housman. There cannot be a page of this book untouched by his influence.[4] I differ from him more than I should once have thought reasonable, but if time has opened my eyes to his fallibility, it has also brought me a fuller awareness of his scholarship, for which my respect has grown and not diminished. Where I have asserted independence I have not done so lightly.

Housman was explicitly aware of the fallibility of human reason *in rebus criticis*. But in his mature work his nods were singularly infrequent. "Easy also to forget how often the giants stumbled. What proportion of Markland's or Madvig's or the early Housman's conjectures would be printed above an unknown name in the modern *Classical Quarterly*?"[5] For the early Housman a fair answer might be "at least half"; for the later Housman, "practically the lot." An editor less scrupulous and intelligent than Goold who wished to assert his independence would have no problem. He would only need to restore to the text a sufficient quantity of manuscript readings which Housman had replaced with conjectures. He would thus find himself translating nonsense, but the kind of editor I have in mind would

3. As on the authenticity of 2. 732–34 (pp. liii f.). Goold may be right in condemning these lines, but goes too far when he says: "Their composition was good enough to deceive Housman, though it is exposed as a fake by the anapaest *reliquis;* cf. Lachmann on Lucretius 5. 679." Lachmann tells us that among classical versifiers only Lucretius and Phaedrus use *rĕlĭcŭus*, whereas *rĕlĭquus* first occurs in Persius (this passage apart). That is suggestive, but hardly conclusive. Goold's generally laudable fidelity to his great precursor has landed him in an awkward inconsistency with respect to 4. 548–52, for which Housman is not blameless. In the introduction to his first volume (pp. lxix–lxxii) Housman held that these lines, which concern an emperor born under Libra, must refer to Tiberius and not Augustus because the latter's natal sign was Capricorn. Later he altered this opinion in consequence of an article by J. G. Smyly. A man, it seems, could be credited with two natal signs, the one rising at the time of birth (ascendant or horoscope) and the one occupied by the moon; and it is the dead Augustus, whose ascendant was in Libra, whom Manilius means in 4. 548–52. Housman set forth his new position in "Manilius, Augustus, Tiberius, Capricornus, and Libra," *CQ* 7 (1913): 109–14 (= *Classical Papers* [Cambridge, 1972], pp. 867–72); and his commentary ad loc. and on 4. 773–77 reflects it. But he did not see fit to point out that the new doctrine invalidated the old. Goold's introduction (p. xii) follows Housman's introduction, and his notes on both passages follow Housman's notes.

4. In fact, to speak only of Housman's emendations, the 180 pages of Goold's text contain over 280 of them. And they form the tip of the iceberg.

5. "Bentley and Horace," *Proceedings of the Leeds Philosophical Society* 10 (1963): 105.

make a poor hand at translating Manilius anyway. Mumpsimus-fanciers[6] would approve. They get no such comfort from Goold. Out of 236 conjectures[7] of his own (not including many repunctuations) which Housman read in his *editio minor* Goold accepts all but fourteen, and two of these latter he replaces by other conjectures of Housman. That implies fallibility of a remarkable order, especially when we remember that Housman was dealing with a text already winnowed by Scaliger, Bentley, and a multitude of lesser men.

It is true that Goold's text differs from Housman's in 167 places, spelling apart, and perhaps a few more which I have failed to notice. In a poem of over 4,200 verses, with manuscripts as corrupt as Manilius', that is no very large number; but it is the character of the differences, not the quantity, that counts.

Forty-five readings not mentioned in Housman's *editio maior*[8] are listed separately. Five are supplementary verses added by Goold where Housman marked a lacuna. Five are conjectures of Housman's taken from the *editio minor*. Eleven are conjectures by Bentley and others which Housman may be supposed to have overlooked. The remaining twenty-four are conjectures subsequently published, by the following: Goold (twelve, seven of them not previously published), Shackleton Bailey (six, including one repunctuation), Gain (three), Alton (two), Flores (one). Of Goold's conjectures I particularly like those at 1. 227, 3. 269, 4. 467, and 5. 87. Most of the others are at least plausible.

The other divergences consist almost entirely in the substitution of conjectures for manuscript readings, many of which are obelized in the *editio minor* (Goold never uses the obelus). About half of these conjectures are Housman's! Housman explained in his preface that he had dropped some conjectures which had appeared in the text of the *editio maior*, not in most cases because his opinion had changed, but "because the text is now no longer accompanied by discussion and justified by argument, and because in this cheaper and handier form it will be purchased or consulted by new readers whose scope is not the same and who may fairly expect consideration." A good Loeb editor, however, naturally favors a text he can translate,[9] and it is entirely appropriate that Goold should reinstate conjectures from the text of the *editio maior* and accept others from its commentary. Most of those in the latter category, if not Housman's own, are mentioned by Housman with some degree of approval. I have found only two places, 1. 260 and 5. 615, where Goold has returned to the paradosis.

Conjectural readings in Goold's text are indicated as such by the corresponding manuscript readings reported below, except that "minute and obviously correct conjectures, made not later than the sixteenth[10] century and universally accepted,

6. See G. V. Sumner, rev. of *Two Studies in Roman Nomenclature*, *CP* 73 (1978): 164.

7. I do not claim absolute accuracy for these figures, which in any case would vary slightly according to the *modus numerandi*.

8. *Fugiens* for *iuvenis* at 2. 566 is not on the list. I have not traced it in the *editio maior*, where *lugens* is suggested "verbi causa," or anywhere else except in Garrod's note, which says that Housman wrote it. But Garrod (pp. 159–61) does not include it in his list of post-Scaligerian emendations.

9. "Of the principle of *difficilior lectio* I pragmatically take no account," wrote one of them, Maurice Platnauer.

10. In practice, the seventeenth. A few later ones have gone unnoticed, including eleven of Bentley's and one of Housman's. Let me add here that misprints and the like are very hard to find in this book. I have noticed only *propias* in 1. 59, erroneous verse-numberings in the text of 2. 124–45 and 5. 453–61, and *artu* for *actu(s)* in the critical note on 4. 797.

are ignored." But the names of their authors are suppressed. Thus to treat some of the finest triumphs of divinatory genius is *lèse-majesté*. It also has the effect of hiding the preponderance of the three giants, Scaliger, Bentley, and, most conspicuously, Housman. Perhaps as General Editor of the series Goold felt impelled to set an example of austerity in this matter. I hope it will not be followed. It is also a pity that no conjectures are mentioned other than those read in the text.

Here then we have virtually the text of the *editio minor*, incorporating a few items which Housman overlooked or predated, and modified, sparingly, judiciously, and mostly in accordance with Housman's expressed views, to suit the special purposes of this edition. So far, so good; and nobody is ever likely to get much further. But neither is the final word ever spoken.

1. 343–44 tum magni Iovis ales fertur in altum,
assueta evolitans gestet ceu fulmina *mundi*.

adsueta Housman, *adsudet* M, *assueto* GL *evolitans* Ellis, *et uol-* M, *uol-* GL

The otiose *mundi* is poorly protected by *fulmen caeli* in Lucretius 1. 489. In this text *fulmina* already has an epithet, and the addition is not only needless but offensive in that it gets in the way of the main idea—the constellation rising aloft like an ordinary thunderbolt-carrying eagle on its way up to Jupiter. Nor are thunderbolts happily described as "of heaven" *before* they reach the celestial arsenal. I would therefore advocate the dismissal of *mundi* as a stopgap and its replacement by (*assueto volitans*) *nisu*, which *ex hypothesi* fell out after *-mina;* cf. Horace *Odes* 4. 4. 1–8 "qualem ministrum fulminis alitem . . . insolitos docuere nisus." Silius seems to have had these lines in mind in the two passages cited by Housman (addenda), 12. 58–59 *assuetis fulmina ferre / unguibus* and 15. 404–5 *ceu . . . gestet . . . fulmina*.

1. 392–400 at caput *Orion* excelso immersus Olympo
per tria subducto signatur lumina vultu.
[non quod clara minus sed quod magis alta recedant
hoc duce per totum decurrunt sidera mundum.
subsequitur rapido contenta Canicula cursu,
qua nullum terris violentius advenit astrum
nec gravius cedit. nunc horrida frigore surgit,
nunc vacuum soli fulgentem deserit orbem:
sic in utrumque movet mundum et contraria reddit.

394 del. Housman

I have the feeling that something more distinct than *subducto vultu* ("with his countenance remote") is needed to tell us that the stars which mark out Orion's head are hardly visible (ἀμαυρούς in Housman's citation from Eratosthenes), especially as *signatur* might give a different impression. Also Orion's name, which has occurred earlier in the sentence (387 "cernere vicinum Geminis licet Oriona"), is conspicuously uncalled-for. Putting these two items together we might reconstruct: "at caput excelso ⟨vix ille⟩ immersus Olympo." The interpolated line then becomes an explanation of *vix signatur*. It looks to me as though the interpolator had been busy again in verse 400, a singularly flat and needless summary of what precedes. He will have made it up with the help of 406 "sic movet, ut vidit, mundum."

1. 415–16 cui proximus Anguis
squamea dispositis imitatur *tergora* flammis

In his *editio maior* Housman wrote, "*tergora* Bentley, *lumina* libri ridicule: flammae non imitantur squamea lumina sed ipsae lumina sunt et imitantur squamas" (nonetheless he restored *lumina* in the *editio minor*). Bentley compared 1. 433 *squamea terga;* add 1. 614 *squamosaque tergora Ceti*. No notice seems to have been taken of Breiter's casual observation: "näher läge doch *tegmina*." Perhaps that was because *tegmen* is not usually applied to the skin of a living animal (cf., however, Lucan 9. 770–71 "sine ullo / tegmine poples erat"). But the Snake in the sky is hardly alive, and, more important, there is a certain aptness in calling a *snake's* skin, which is sloughed, a "covering." Or perhaps the plural offends, as would *cutes* or *pelles*. But *tegmina* = *tegmen* is quite natural; cf. Cicero *In Pisonem* 12 *frontis . . . integumentis* (but *Red. sen.* 16 *frontis . . . integumento*).

1. 797–99 et Cato fortunae victor, *fictorque* sub armis
miles Agrippa *suae*, Venerisque ab origine proles
Iulia.

Fictorque for *matrisque*, proposed in the addenda to Housman's *editio maior* but not mentioned in the *editio minor*, makes perfect sense, though I do not feel sure that so rumbustious an assonance would have suited Manilius' taste. But why should *matris* have come in to fill the gap? I suppose Housman would have blamed *Veneris*, but since this does not appear very plausible, I prefer my semantically equivalent *meritusque . . . suam*. I put this and eight other conjectures into "Maniliana" (p. 86) without discussion because of the editors' refusal to print the article at its original length.

1. 829–30 alter nocte dies esset, *Phoebusque* rediret,
immersum et somno totum deprenderet orbem.

Phoebusque Goold, *caelumque* codd. *immersum* Scaliger, *immensum* codd. *totum*] *positum* Housman

If comets did not vanish so quickly, there would be another daytime in the night. "The corruption of *febus* to *celum* is neither great nor improbable" (Goold). Perhaps not, but that of *somni* to *somno* is easier. Punctuate as formerly:

caelumque rediret
immersum, et somni totum deprenderet orbem.

"The [daytime] sky, sunk [below the horizon], would return and catch the whole world in the thrall of sleep." For the genitive, cf. Varro Atacinus' line "omnia noctis erant placida composta quiete," which in Ovid's opinion should have come to a halt with *omnia noctis erant* (Sen. *Contr.* 7. 1. 27); also Housman on Lucan 5. 572. *Totum orbem*, says Goold, is used exactly as the French *tout le monde*.

2. 203–4 nec te praetereat nocturna diurnaque signa
quae sint perspicere et propria *deducere* lege.

It surprises me that Goold should reject *diducere* (also in "Maniliana," p. 86) here, while reading it on Scaliger's conjecture in 2. 294 "sic licet in totidem partes diducere cuncta." In such cases manuscript authority hardly counts and there can be no doubt which of the two verbs belongs here. Manilius is not asking his readers to deduce anything; he is about to *tell* them which signs are nocturnal and which diurnal. *Propria* means "appropriate," i.e., relevant, not "true."

2. 211 and 2. 550 rabidique Leonis

In the former place *rapidique* is read by two of the three significant manuscripts, in the latter by all of them. Housman and Garrod were equally confident of its impossibility; but see *Propertiana*, p. 317, as directed in "Maniliana," p. 86, n. 1. One thing I had overlooked. In Lucan 6. 337 Housman read *rapidique Leonis* and explained it briefly but correctly, making no mention of Manilius. Five years later *rabidique* still stood in his *editio minor*.

2. 337–41 et, quiscumque quater iunctis favet angulus usque,
quaeque loca in triplici signarit linea ductu
cum sinuata viae linquet dispendia recta
his natura dedit communi foedera lege
inque vicem adfectus et mutua iura favoris.

These verses disrupt their context and should perhaps be placed after 2. 395.

2. 383–84 sic, *quamquam* alternis, par est natura figuris,
et cognata iacent generis sub legibus astra.

quamquam Bentley, *quicquam* codd. *alternis* ς′
alterius codd. *par est* anon., *paret* codd.

Alternate signs have the same gender: and why not, pray? If six males and six females are to be arranged in some kind of order, the most natural way is to make them alternate. I think we should consider *quisque* (= *quibusque*, as in Lucr. 4. 798), even though I have no precise parallel for *alterna quaeque* = *tertia quaeque*. The admissibility of the expression is implied by Pliny *Natural History* 33. 52 *annis quibusque* = "every year."

2. 469–70 conversaque quaedam [*sc.* astra]
in semet proprio ducuntur *plena* favore.

Proprio plena favore rings false. Read *prona* (cf. Tac. *Ann.* 2. 73 "favore in Pisonem pronior," *Hist.* 1. 6 "non in unum aliquem prono favore," *Hist.* 1. 13 "prona in eum aula Neronis"; Phaedr. 5. 5. 1 "prono [vv. ll. prauo, paruo] favore labi mortales solent"; Sen. *Dial.* 1. 4. 5 "si te . . . pronus favor sequitur").

2. 475–80 quod deus, in leges mundum cum conderet omnem,
affectus quoque divisit variantibus astris,
atque aliorum oculos, aliorum contulit aures,

iunxit amicitias horum sub foedere certo,
cernere ut inter se possent audireque quaedam,
diligerent alia et noxas bellumque moverent

Lines 479–80 cover the four categories (*videntia*, *audientia*, *amantia*, *insidiantia*), thus answering 477–78. But 477–78 have unaccountably omitted the fourth. That is to say, a line has fallen out after 478, such as "illis perpetuas statuit discordibus iras."

2. 898–900 sub corde sagaci
conde locum numenque *dei* nomenque potentis,
quae tibi posterius magnos revocentur ad usus.

What god? Manilius is writing of the fifth "temple" (astrological house), which, as he tells us, is called "Daemonie" by Greeks, a name which has no Latin equivalent (in fact, our sources call it ἀγαθὴ τύχη). *Dei* should refer to its planetary "lord" (cf. 2. 967 "effectusque loci per se cuiusque deosque") but cannot, because in this instance the poet has omitted to tell us who he, or rather she, was, information supplied by Firmicus (2. 19. 6): Venus. Breiter explains "Daemonie": "ist selbst als *numen dei* und *nomen* zu fassen." But a "temple" is not a god, or a goddess, though as a determinant of destiny it may properly be said to have *numen;* cf. 4. 56 *sine numine fati*. *Dei* must go. Read *loci*.

3. 112–14 fundentem verba patronum
pendentemque reum lingua *nervisque* loquentis
impositum

nervisque Housman, *rostrisque* codd.

In the *editio minor* the manuscript reading is obelized without mention of the conjecture, which should yield to *labrisque;* cf. Cicero *De oratore* 3. 138 "cuius in labris veteres comici . . . leporem habitasse dixerunt."

3. 376–77 neque enim circumvenit illum
recta acies, mediaque tenus *distinguitur* alvo.

Illum = *mundum*. As Housman says, "distinguit medium mundum horizon," but "mundus media tenus alvo distinguitur" is nonsense. I suggest *distenditur* [sc. *acies*]. *Aciem intendere* is the usual expression, but cf. Lucan 4. 140 "medios pontem distendit in agros." Another probable example of the corruption can be diagnosed in *Anthologia Latina* 132. 5 (ed. Riese); see *Towards a Text of "Anthologia Latina"* (Cambridge, forthcoming).

3. 500–502 quaque ille sub astri
parte cadet, credas illam cum corpore natam
esse hominis pariterque orbem vidisse per *ignes*.

There is nothing wrong with 497 "haec erit exoriens et pars et forma per ignes," since the figures of zodiacal signs *are* produced by their stars. But how a single degree of a sign beholds the earth through its stars I do not see. *Ignes*, from 497, will have replaced *umbras* (Manilius is here dealing with nocturnal nativities).

3. 525–27 idcirco tanta est rerum discordia in aevo
et subtexta malis bona sunt lacrimaeque sequuntur
vota nec *inconstans* servat fortuna tenorem.

inconstans Goold, *in cunctos* codd.

The conjecture is attractive, but I am not sure that any conjecture is necessary. Can we not understand "et in cunctos fortuna tenorem non servat [i.e., mutat]"? Cf. 4. 24–25 "Troia sub uno / non eversa [i.e., conservata] viro" and the note on 2. 751 above (p. 159). *Totum Caesarem non novi* in Cicero *Ad familiares* 6. 7. 4 (Caecina) means "Caesar is an utter stranger to me," not "I don't know Caesar thoroughly."

3. 637–40 parte ex adversa brumam Capricornus inertem
per minimas cogit luces et maxima noctis
tempora, producitque diem tenebrasque resolvit,
inque vicem nunc damna *legit*, nunc tempora supplet.

"Capricornus in priore sui parte diebus subtrahit quod nocturno tempori adiciat, in posteriore vicissim noctium damnis dies auget"; cf. Goold, "by turns it now steals time from day and now repairs day's loss." In other words, "nunc tempora legit, nunc damna supplet," which, however, is not what Manilius wrote. Read *regit* (= *gubernat*). Capricorn controls the losses of day, i.e., apportions them according to natural law, until the turning point of the winter solstice; cf. 4. 338–39 "pariterque regentem / noctes atque dies," 3. 681–82 "nec defuit auctor / qui primae [*sc.* parti] momenta daret frenosque dierum."

4. 53 cum te iam posses alium componere Magnum

te iam scripseram, *iam etiam* codd.

This conjecture was explained as follows ("Maniliana," p. 84): " 'when you might have made from yourself another Magnus,' i.e., 'when your achievements were such that, if divided among two men, they would have earned the name of "Great" for both.' " *Te* = *ex te;* cf. Pliny *Natural History* 15. 31 "suis herbis componunt inter Cappadociam et Galatiam quod Selgiticum vocant [oleum]." Goold, however, translates, "when you could now represent yourself as another styled the Great," with reference to Alexander. I accept the involvement of Alexander, though not the rest. Pompey could have made out of himself another Magnus to stand beside himself and Alexander. Thus *alium* does not have to stand for *alterum*, as in my earlier interpretation or Goold's.

4. 343 Centauri *tertia* summa est.

That is to say, Libra's third decan (segment consisting of ten degrees) belongs to Sagittarius; cf. 4. 321 "Centauri tertia pars est," 4. 332 "sub Geminis pars tertia fertur." Manilius sometimes uses *summa* for *numerus*, but nobody has explained how *summa* can stand for *pars*. Read "Centauri portio summa est"; cf. 4. 353 "summas partes et Virginis esse," 4. 357 "summas [*sc.* partes] Centaurus retinet." On the final *-o*, shortened as in Juvenal 9. 128, see Housman on 3. 423.

4. 404–5 luxuriae quoque militia est, vigilatque ruinis
venter et, ut pereant, *suspirant* saepe nepotes.

Bühler ("Maniliana," *Hermes* 87 [1959]: 484) correctly pointed out that *suspirant* cannot mean "sigh for" because Manilius is here saying that people *toil* for objects which do them harm and therefore should be willing to work even harder for the benefits of astrology. But his explanation, " 'keuchen' (zu ergänzen: bei der Beschaffung der Luxusgüter)," seems verbally impossible. I suggest that *suspirant* came from *sperant*, which came from *operantur* (*operant'*). Work is the last thing that *nepotes* would do from choice. If this emendation is right, it is the first occurrence of *operari*, as distinct from *operatus*, before the elder Pliny; see *OLD*, s.v. *operor*.

4. 523–24 accedunt et ruris opes, propriaque iuvencum
dote per inversos exornat vomere campos.

In Latin a person born under Taurus is not "a Taurus," nor yet a steer or a heifer. As pointed out in "Maniliana," p. 85, *iuvencum* is genitive plural, a form used by Virgil and Statius. The passage (4. 518–24) should read:

at, quos prima creant nascentis sidera Tauri,
feminei incedunt (nec longe causa petenda est,
si modo per causas naturam quaerere fas est:
aversus venit in caelum divesque puellis,
Pleiadum parvo referens glomeramine sidus).
accedunt *sqq.*

Exornat [sc. *eos*] (cf. 5. 113).

4. 615–17 hinc penitus iuvenisque *fretum* mersaeque puellae
truditur invitum, faucesque Propontis aperto
Euxino iniungit ponto Maeotis et undis

hinc Bentley, *hic* codd. *penitus* Jacob, *pontus* codd.
Propontis aperto Housman, *propontidis apto* codd.

The passage is still in trouble. Housman cites Pliny *Natural History* 6. 1, where the narrowness of the Hellespont and Bosporus is said to show that the penetrations of the sea occurred *invitis terris*. But nobody would say that the Hellespont is thrust deep (into the Propontis) against its will. That statement could properly be made of the sea (*mare*, 4. 606), which remains the subject (*pontus . . . invitus* is discountenanced by *ponto* in 617). *Fretum* must be changed to *freto*, "by means of the channel."

5. 112–14 in vulnus numquam virtus sed saepe libido
impellit, turpisque emitur vel morte voluptas;
et minimum cecidisse malum est, quia crimine *vincunt*.

vincunt Housman, *victum* codd., *victus* Jacob ("quod quid significet quove referatur, nescio" Housman)

I am not sure just what sort of combat Housman had in mind ("quia victoria eorum stupro constat"). *Iunctum,* proposed necessarily without explanation in "Maniliana," p. 86, is paleographically better (= *uīctum*) than *vincunt* and easier to understand. If the libertine is cut down in the pursuit of his desires, that is a trifling evil because it is conjoined with another and great evil—guilt. Note that the guilt involved is the same whether the *stuprator* lives or dies.

5. 216–17 tantus per sidera fervor
funditur atque uno *censentur* lumine cuncta.

censentur lumine Garrod, *ceu sunt in flumine* codd.

My conjecture *cessant in lumine* gives a simpler sense than Garrod's, which is not to say that it is more Manilian. Is the idea of rating the light of the rest of the stars by that of the Dog a little too artificial even for that poet? *Iudicent docti.*

5. 248–49 annonae quoque vectigal mercesque sequetur
praecipue quas umor alit nec *deserit unda.*

"Merces quas unda non deserit" is a strange expression, and I find it hard to identify these wares which water does not forsake as distinct from those which moisture fosters. Read *nec deseret undam.*

5. 414–15 et quisquis verove favet culpamve perodit
proditur atque alto qui iurgia pectore tollat.

". . . and the man to remove dissensions from the depth of the heart." It is the umpire's business to settle disputes (cf. 3. 115 *solventem iurgia*), but to remove them from the hearts of the disputants will not always, or even often, be in his power. I think *alto pectore* has to be understood as "with profound intelligence"; cf. Valerius Maximus 8. 12 ext. 1 *Platonis . . . eruditissimum pectus;* Silius 16. 338–39 *prudentia circi / altior;* Statius *Silvae* 2. 6. 51 *altis . . . consiliis.*

5. 664–66 luctantur corpora nodis
exspectantque novas acies ferroque necantur,
inficiturque suo permixtus sanguine pontus.

Dormitant Homeri. Housman takes *novas acies* as *novum discrimen* ("Manilii interpretes nova thynnorum agmina adnatantia intellegere iam facile mihi credetur"), an incredible sense for the noun. Goold renders "new assaults"; the fish had not been assaulted. And why should they, as they struggle against the net, be *waiting* for fresh trouble? They were not waiting for it, they got it: *exceptantque;* cf. Silius 9. 368–69 "per pectora saevas / exceptat mortes [i.e., cuspides]." The sharp edges of the weapons were a novelty to the fish. Copyists are naturally prone to confuse the rare *exceptare* with *expectare;* the *Thesaurus* has examples.

Goold expresses the hope that many who use this edition will be stimulated to go on to Housman's. Amen. It is sad that so few classicists know Housman's commentary or have any idea what they are missing: "ardua dum metuunt, amittunt vera viai." To read it closely, intelligently, and completely is more than a unique intellectual experience. For a second time[11] I resort to the Cambridge historian Herbert Butterfield, who so admirably expressed, mutatis mutandis, what is in my mind (emphasis added):

> It is not always realised that, apart from the pleasure which can be added to history by the imagination of the literary man, there is an exquisite loveliness that can arise within the realm of historical technique itself. *The peak is reached when it is out of the actual scientific procedures of the authentic student that we gain our aesthetic moments,* and the artistry is not an additional adornment but lies in the historical thought itself, like the beauty which a piece of mathematics can possess.
>
> [*George III and the Historians* (London, 1957)]

D. R. SHACKLETON BAILEY
Harvard University

11. The first time was in a review of Housman's *Classical Papers* (*Cambridge Review* 94 [1973]: 189–90).

BOOK REVIEWS

Livius und Polybios. By HERMANN TRÄNKLE. Basel and Stuttgart: Schwabe und Co. Verlag, 1977. Pp. 254. Fr./Mk. 60.

A renaissance in Livian scholarship seems at hand. The last two decades have witnessed an outburst of activity: new texts, commentaries, and a variety of interpretative studies. Changed attitudes and interests begin to emerge. *Quellenforschung* as a scholarly obsession in this field is now, happily, outmoded. Nissen laid its foundations more than a century ago in his careful dissection of Polybian and "annalistic" layers in the fourth and fifth decades. Arguments mounted for three generations about Livy's annalistic sources and their reliability, and about the extent of his dependence on Polybius, arguments that culminated in A. Klotz's classic, *Livius und seine Vorgänger* (Leipzig, 1941). Livy, for the most part, did not come off well: a compiler who mindlessly followed where his sources led, a colorful writer but not a critical historian, prone to error, patriotic distortions, and oversimplification. More recent scholarship provides increasingly positive assessments. E. Burck's *Die Erzählungskunst des T. Livius* (Berlin, 1934) set the standard for examining Livy's narrative techniques. P. G. Walsh offered a general study, balanced and circumspect, *Livy: His Historical Aims and Methods* (Cambridge, 1961), though he found greater merit in Livy's literary competence than in his historical acumen. The historian's "Roman ideology" as superimposed on his Polybian material is the subject of E. Pianezzola's *Traduzione e ideologia* (Bologna, 1969). In the past several years the design and structure of the *Ab urbe condita* have received growing attention, especially in G. Wille's *Der Aufbau des Livianischen Geschichtswerks* (Amsterdam, 1973) and T. J. Luce's fine new study, *Livy: The Composition of His History* (Princeton, 1977). We now possess a keener appreciation of Livy's own contribution and of the quality of his mind.

Livy acquires greater stature still in Hermann Tränkle's work. T. treads a somewhat different path from those noted above. He is little concerned with *Quellenkritik*, with narrative methods, style, or Latinity, with ideology, overall design, or general appraisal. The approach owes more to the pioneering article of K. Witte, "Über die Form der Darstellung in Livius' Geschichtswerk," *RhM* 65 (1910): 270–305, 359–419, who analyzed with care a number of parallel Polybian and Livian passages to illuminate the compositional technique of the Latin historian. But while Witte found that Livy enhanced the Polybian narrative at the expense of historical truth, T. is at pains to save the Roman's historical incisiveness as well as his literary sensitivity. His close comparison of Livy's presentation with the Polybian originals provides the most systematic and thoroughgoing treatment we possess on the subject.

The bulk of the book naturally concerns itself with the fourth and fifth decades, where the Polybian material is richest for comparison. T. steers a middle course between Nissen and Mommsen on the question of Livy's reliance upon Polybius in portions where Polybian excerpts are sparse. For T., the Roman did follow Polybius, but in no mechanical way, adding his own flavor and interpretation.

So, for example, Livy's elaboration (39. 53. 2–8) on the narrative of Demetrius' return to Macedonia (Polyb. 23. 7)—drawn from Polybius but designed both to show that Roman actions met with the favor of the Macedonian populace and to foreshadow the ultimate fate of Demetrius (pp. 40–43). The general conclusions here are sound (pp. 32–44).

Livy's conflation of Polybian with annalistic material, on the other hand, receives less discussion than one might expect. T. acknowledges the chronological tangles to which this occasionally leads, but dismisses them as "exceptions" (pp. 46–54). He also soft-pedals the "contamination" of Polybius' account with annalistic additions: the spurious terms appended to the peace treaty of 196 B.C. (cf. Polyb. 18. 44 with Livy 33. 30) do not reflect normal practice (pp. 60–62); other accretions, like the multiplication of embassies not found in Polybius or the altered picture given of Lepidus' ultimatum to Philip in 200 (cf. Polyb. 16. 34 with Livy 31. 18), stem from Livy's conscientious effort to reconcile discrepancies in the sources before him (pp. 65–71). Those are unusually charitable judgments.

When Livy abbreviates his Greek source, the purposes, so T. argues, are intelligible and intelligent. The Latin historian omits many details, reduces discussion of circumstances and surrounding events, avoids Polybian excursuses and historiographical comments, and softens the emphasis on τύχη. Instead, he highlights certain themes, stressing major events and dramatic episodes, without doing violence to historical fact. In the confrontation of Rome and Antiochus the Great, Livy abridges Polybius' account to place greater emphasis on the threat to the West than on the "freedom of the Greeks." He adapts the material on Achaean affairs in the 180s to presage the eventual Achaean rebellion of 146. He shortens military narrative and dwells on negotiations during the Antiochene and Aetolian wars in order to place Scipio's role in the center. His briefer version of the encounter between Popillius Laenas and Antiochus Epiphanes in 168 underlines the manifestation of Roman power, in contrast to Polybius' analysis of specific preliminaries and consequences. And so on. These are but a few of the numerous illustrations employed by T. to point out the differences between Polybius' and Livy's interests and to establish the purposeful character of Livian reductions (pp. 73–98).

The same holds for instances where Livy has expanded on his model. He amplified rather than invented, with clear aims in mind: to heighten drama and lead readers into more intimate contact with historical personages, to bring broader themes into view, to build suspense, or to set the stage for future events. As examples T. notes the scenes of Perseus' council of war and the meeting of Manlius Vulso and Moagetes, where Livy supplies an immediacy and vividness lacking in the Polybian original; the private talks between Scipio and Antiochus, which both underscore the Roman general's character and look ahead to his trial; the speech of the Rhodians in 189, a vehicle to convey the idea of a Roman *patrocinium* in the East. When Livy chose to rework the material at hand, he knew exactly what he was doing. Such, at least, is T.'s operative principle (pp. 98–131).

Did Livy distort the historical picture by introduction of patriotic considerations, thereby to whitewash Roman motives or actions? The accusation is a common one. T., for the most part, denies the charge. He observes, quite justly, that Livy transmits a considerable amount of Polybian narrative unflattering to the Romans: e.g., discreditable episodes in Manlius' Galatian campaign, the harshness of Popillius Laenas, Marcius Philippus' duplicity, the victimization of Greece after Pydna (pp. 132–35). Elsewhere, when Livian omissions or changes seem to cover up Roman misdeeds, T. offers different explanations: Livy genuinely preferred the treatment of certain episodes by his Roman sources to that of Polybius, whether because they conformed better to his own conception of his countrymen's behavior (as with Roman-Rhodian relations after the Third Macedonian War [pp. 157–61]) or because they offered simpler explanations than Polybius' involved account (as in the misunderstanding between Glabrio and the Aetolians on the meaning of *deditio* [pp. 170–77]). T. admits with some reluctance that Flamininus receives consistently more favorable treatment from Livy than from Polybius. But the Roman historian (so it is suggested) perhaps sought only to provide a clearer and more coherent picture of Flamininus—or indeed to supply corrective to Polybius, who was misled by Greek attitudes (pp. 144–54, 162–65)! Not too many will embrace that conclusion.

T. deals swiftly and smartly with Livian mistranslations and misunderstandings of Polybius' Greek. The errors are few and mostly minor. Many concern technical terms or constitutional matters, as onc might expect. Some can, in fact, be explained by textual corruption, without indicting Livy. And where there is haste or oversight, the fault is forgivable in a work of the size and scope produced by Livy (pp. 178–91). On this issue T.'s remarks are judicious and plausible.

The final portion of the book addresses an old and much disputed subject: to what extent did Livy use Polybius in the third decade? T. explores carefully those few episodes for which Polybian fragments are available for comparison. The findings, expressed with due caution, are not new: that Livy made little or no direct use of Polybius in Books 21–30. But T. employs to good effect the results of his research on the fourth and fifth decades, making quite clear that the divergences between Polybius and Livy in the third decade are of a scale well beyond anything discoverable in the later books (pp. 196–241). The case is unprovable. But T.'s argument is as strong a one as we are likely to get on that side of the issue.

T.'s Livy is an estimable writer and historian, conscientious in following his Greek source, intelligent in abbreviating or expanding upon it, occasionally critical of it, and even improving on it for the sake of clarity and consistency. Perhaps too good to be true. Certainly T.'s generosity toward his subject often leans to the extreme. His assertion that Livy's chronology is never chaotic (p. 49) will surprise those who have grappled with the doublets and confusion in the account of preliminaries to the Third Macedonian War. If the addition of spurious terms to the peace of 196 shows no more than Livy's desire to combine annalistic and Polybian evidence (pp. 60–62), one may well question at least his judgment if not his scholarly integrity. T.'s attempt to explain away Livian omission of discreditable motives and actions as "exceptions" or "correctives to Polybius" is special pleading. One thinks particularly of the senate's treatment of Attalus in 167 (cf. Polyb. 30. 3 with Livy 45. 20), Flamininus' devious calculations in the peace negotiations of 197 (cf. Polyb. 18. 9–10 with Livy 32. 36), and private conversations with Demetrius that encouraged him to seek the Macedonian throne (cf. Polyb. 23. 3 with Livy 39. 47). In each of these instances Livy makes small but telling changes in the Polybian account—and for none of them do T.'s explanations suffice (pp. 144–47, 151–53, 155–57).

In short, a stimulating book, insightful, at times ingenious. The apologia for Livy goes too far and the strained argumentation will not win universal assent. But T. takes a worthy place among those engaged in a welcome, ongoing process: the rehabilitation of Livy.

Erich S. Gruen
University of California, Berkeley

Studies in Aulus Gellius. By BARRY BALDWIN. Lawrence, Kansas: Coronado Press, 1975. Pp. x + 130. $6.50.

Since the highly influential essay of Nettleship published in 1883, very little has been written in English specifically on the *Noctes Atticae* of Aulus Gellius to deal with the more general literary and intellectual aspects of the work. Recent decades have seen much excellent work in French by R. Marache, but the English-speaking student still cannot be directed to anything in any way comprehensive in his own language. It is presumably to meet this general need that Professor Baldwin has produced the present set of *Studies*. The titles of the various chapters speak for themselves: "The Career of Gellius"; "Friends and Enemies"; "Literary Opinions"; "Scholarly Interests"; "Miscellaneous Facts and Contemporary Themes"; "The Antonine Intellectual Scene." There is nothing new here, but that is not the point: the book is designed as a general introduction for the student coming to the second century for the first time. It is regrettable that B. deliberately decided against a bibliography, simply referring us to "the usual sources" and Marache's survey of the scholarly literature for the period 1938–64 (*Lustrum* 10 [1965]: 213–45). A great pity this, as the beginner could surely profit from a judicious selection of reliable works: even an older book like M. D. Brock's *Studies in Fronto and His Age* (Cambridge, 1911) still has much to offer. It is also surprising to see Fronto cited from the antiquated edition of Haines in the Loeb Classical Library instead of the infinitely superior 1954 text of Van den Hout. This is not just a matter of convenience: Haines is so often simply wrong. The style of the book is light and often engaging, but it will hardly improve a student's English to be faced with sentences such as: "An article on some legal abstrusity may be postluded by a tirade against charlatan philosophers" (p. 89).

As for the scholarship involved, there is, unfortunately, much to provoke disagreement. A few examples must suffice.

Fundamental to B.'s view of Gellius is the constantly repeated belief that the scenes created in the *Noctes Atticae* are to be taken as having literally happened. Thus we read: "Gellius was essentially honest; he does not go in for large scale suppression of authorities' names, if only because . . . the ancient freedom in matters of copyright precluded any great need for dissembling" (p. 85). While it may be healthy to react against various nineteenth-century attempts to isolate *the* source of each chapter, this complete reversal seems much worse. It rests upon the belief that an artistic setting for what is in origin a purely literary discussion would constitute "plagiarism" (pp. 10, 66). This is to misunderstand an ancient literary convention. Are we to imagine, for example, that contemporary readers berated Macrobius for "plagiarism" when he used the dialogue form to enliven his *Saturnalia?* It must also be observed that to deny literal truth to many of the scenes in the *Noctes Atticae* is not to deny their verisimilitude or their value as evidence with which to reconstruct the life of Gellius.

In discussing the date of birth of Gellius (p. 15), B. inevitably has to face the problems posed by the reference to Erucius Clarus (13. 18. 2): "qui praefectus urbi et bis consul fuit." This is surely a general "obituary notice" looking back over Clarus' career. B., however, wants to resuscitate the old heresy that *bis* here equals *iterum*, in order to introduce a specific reference to the early months of A.D. 146. He is uneasy about allowing this linguistic usage in Gellius (as well he might be), but clutches desperately at a compromise: "Perhaps the words had become interchangeable in officialese, and Gellius was wittingly or unwittingly quoting this new usage." No evidence. We are even invited to believe that this interchangeable usage, which does occur later in the *Historia Augusta*, is there because "the biographer, or his source, has been reading and transcribing Gellius." No evidence, of course, of any such influence.

The discussion of Taurus' berating a young man for his conversion to philosophy (p. 37) completely misses the point. It was not the conversion itself which provoked Taurus, but the motive, which incurs the censorious adverbs *inhoneste* and *improbe* (10. 19. 1).

The analysis of "archaism" in Gellius and the second century in general (chapter 3) falls far short of the precision so complicated a subject demands. A hideous confusion is introduced in the references to the word *insolens*, as quoted by Gellius 1. 10. 4 from Caesar's *De analogia:* "ut tamquam scopulum, sic fugias inauditum atque insolens uerbum." Here it clearly means "unfamiliar." But it is absurd to put this side by side with Fronto (Haines, 2:80, alas): "Dicet aliquis: 'tu igitur praeter ceteros nimirum uerbis pulchris et insignibus uteris?' Ego immo uulgaribus et obsoletis." Here the word *obsoletis* means exactly the opposite of what *insolens* does in Caesar and Gellius, and no theory can be built upon such a coincidence.

Is this book a success? If it leads the beginner to explore at first hand the literature of the second century, then it has much value. But in itself it is far too treacherous a guide for the unwary.

P. K. Marshall
Amherst College

A History of Greek Philosophy, vol. 4: *Plato: The Man and His Dialogues: Earlier Period.* By W. K. C. GUTHRIE. Cambridge–London–New York–Melbourne: Cambridge University Press, 1975. Pp. xviii + 603. $34.50.

Professor Guthrie has chosen the path of Taylor in preference to that of Grube and has devoted this first Plato volume of his *History* mainly to a "description and discussion of the dialogues." (Later he remarks that "each dialogue has a life of its own.")

In the case of all dialogues except the *Republic*, description, which includes an extremely bald summary, precedes discussion. These summaries seem to me to be the only unsatisfactory feature of the book. They have been made too colorless to attract the reader who does not know the dialogue in question, and they are not really helpful to those who do know it, since the references given are to fairly lengthy sections rather than to particular, distinctive passages. It is a relief when G., rightly perceiving that the *Republic* is too long for this type of treatment, alters his method to one of combined summary and comment. The *Republic* section is certainly the best.

In his discussion of the early dialogues, G. is sufficiently candid to show that he has likes and dislikes. The *Lysis* "is not a success" (p. 143), and of the *Hippias Minor* he writes that "to read through this little dialogue without a growing sense of irritation at its manifest absurdities calls for a strong historical imagination" (p. 195). The *Hippias Major*, on the other hand, is described as "a racy little work" (p. 185), and even as "a considerable work of art" (p. 183). I happen not to agree with any of the above (which shows, I suppose, that I have likes and dislikes, too), but I applaud the author's recognition of the fact that books on Plato reveal the writer as well as the subject.

A review of a book of this size could easily become very long: in my remaining space I shall sacrifice connected exposition to a listing of points that seem to me particularly striking or worth comment.

P. 25: On Plato's motives in going to Sicily, G. writes: "But more than anything else Plato was moved by that pathetic and mistaken shame which the naturally theoretical and contemplative spirit feels at failing to meet a challenge to action for which it is, in fact, entirely unsuited." (A sensitive comment, producing immediate conviction.) *P. 34:* It may be true that there is "no trace of irony" in Socrates' reference to Parmenides at *Theaetetus* 183E, but it still remains the case that the descendants of Parmenides caused Plato a great deal of philosophical trouble, and I believe that this fact is referred to in the same passage. *P. 62:* The whole discussion of Plato's attitude toward his own dialogues is excellent; we are advised, for instance, that "we can think differently of his remark (*Phaedrus* 277E) that nothing ever written in verse or prose is worth taking very seriously when we know that he applied exactly the same phrase to the whole field of human action." *Pp. 70 etc.*: In the discussion of the *Apology*, *Crito*, and some other early dialogues, G. relies quite heavily on cross-references to volume 3. This is a bit awkward but perhaps inevitable in view of the plan of the series. *P. 116:* On the theory of Forms: "in the 'two-world' dialogues the language of 'transcendence' never supersedes altogether the language of 'immanence.' " *Pp. 130, 363:* In spite of some quite harsh remarks on the obsessive desire of scholars to discover the *Hauptzweck* of each individual dialogue, G. appears not to be without comparable desires himself. Thus he writes that "whatever people may say, the *Phaedo* is about the immortality of the soul, and the posthumous blessedness of the wise and good," and "essentially . . . the *Republic* is not a piece of political theory but an allegory of the individual human spirit, the *psyche*." (I value his comments of this kind more than I would deprecate his inconsistency.) *Pp. 232–33:* On hedonism in the *Protagoras:* Plato is arguing from Protagoras' premises, with the intention of showing them at their best. Well, perhaps, but is it a very good best? Plato believed too firmly that God, not man, was the measure of all things (*Laws* 716C) to give Protagoras much of a run, I should say. *P. 241:* On *Meno* 81A, G. is probably right to say that here "one might almost detect the very moment when Plato first deliberately goes beyond the historic Socrates. . . ." *P. 345:* G. is inclined to doubt that Plato, in mentioning "the equals themselves" in the *Phaedo*, had in mind "any class of 'intermediates' between Forms and Sensibles." I agree with this and also with his defence of the Forms as final as well as formal causes

(p. 351). Incidentally, it strikes me as odd of Aristotle to complain that the Forms lack efficient causality when the Forms are objects of love and his own Unmoved Mover moves *hōs erōmenon.* (G. comes close to saying this in his discussion of *erōs* in the *Phaedrus* on p. 421.) *P. 356:* G.'s treatment of *Phaedo* 103A–C in terms of Aristotle's concept of substratum is most enlightening, as is the reminder (p. 362) that in *Meteorology* 355b33 ff. Aristotle "criticized Plato's account of rivers and seas [*Phaedo* 111C ff.] as a serious scientific theory." *Pp. 396–97:* On the *Phaedrus*: Plato's critics "do not always see connexions where he did." Further, "the novelty of the method of collection and division has been exaggerated." *Synagōgē* should not, however, be looked for at 246B–C; the faculty mentioned here is "a mark of our common humanity" (p. 427). (Again Aristotle is relevant [p. 428], this time *Posterior Analytics* 100a13, b4.) *P. 436:* G. is absolutely right in stating that an attempt to separate the descriptive from the prescriptive in the *Republic* "would lead to a caricature of Plato." I can't quite agree, however, when he says (in commenting on Book 1) that "the fallacy of equating *technai* and virtues was shown up by Critias in the *Charmides*" (p. 440). I would rather say something like: "by equating virtues with *technai* like carpentry and cobbling, Plato shows that virtues are *technai* of a higher order." *P. 455:* The passage 408D ff., in which Plato says that the doctor should experience illness in himself but the judge injustice only in others, is described as "an odd little note." I think, rather, that it has considerable significance for the problem of the knowledge of evil by good. *Pp. 457–58:* To the question of *pseudos* G. takes a medical approach and also quotes an illuminating passage by Gouldner on the clash between commitment to truth and attachment to a given society. (Plato, in any case, is more an "impractical theorist" than a "totalitarian monster" [p. 469].) *P. 477:* G. is particularly good on the tripartite soul, stating (with implications for the *Phaedo* and *Phaedrus*) that "it is only association with the body that calls for the virtues connected with the lower parts of the soul." *P. 474:* On the implementation of the ideal state, G. does well to remind this materialistic age that, for Plato, practice is *less* real than theory. *Pp. 490; 524, n. 1:* Other views that G. sensibly knocks on the head are: inconsistency between the *Meno* and the *Republic* on the objects of *doxa* (resemblance is the clue) and "the accepted opinion that Plato . . . advocates doing away with visual observation" of the heavenly bodies.

To end with some more general remarks: Guthrie's particular strengths are in classics and the history of philosophy, rather than in philosophy proper. Some will find his book overly conservative in terms of recent discussions, particularly of logical issues. (G. Vlastos' review, *TLS*, 12 December 1975, pp. 1474–75, should be consulted.) But for his learning, humanity, and sanity, as well as for his willingness to undertake this tremendous task, Guthrie must surely command our unqualified respect.

Rosamond Kent Sprague
University of South Carolina

Studies in Presocratic Philosophy, vol. 2: *The Eleatics and Pluralists.* Edited by R. E. ALLEN and DAVID J. FURLEY. ("International Library of Philosophy and Scientific Method.") Atlantic Highlands, N.J.: Humanities Press, 1975. Pp. viii + 440. $23.75.

We now have Allen and Furley 1975 to complete Furley and Allen 1970. The earlier volume contained some general essays and also covered individual thinkers up through Heraclitus. The present volume covers the Eleatics and Pluralists, in the following proportions: Zeno 119 pages (Fränkel, Owen, Vlastos); Anaxagoras 106 pages (Cornford, Vlastos, Strang); Parmenides 101 pages (Fränkel, Owen, Long); Empedocles 54 pages (Solmsen, Furley); Democritus 28 pages (Vlastos).

The editors have performed a great service by translating Fränkel's "Parmenidesstudien." Quite apart from its striking use of literary parallels (a respect in which the volume as a whole is rather weak), the paper lays down some important general principles. We "should not reconstruct the philosophies of this peculiar epoch from testimonia about them," and "we must always be prepared to be brave and give up completely." After all, Fränkel tells us, there are only four great preclassical figures who "can be reasonably well understood by us": Hesiod, Anaximander, Heraclitus, and Parmenides.

The other two Parmenides papers deal with the status of the cosmogony, and the two authors are in general agreement. According to Owen, the view that the cosmogony might have "some measure of truth or reliability in its own right" is "demonstrably false"; its purpose is "wholly dialectical." According to Long, "the cosmogony gives a totally false picture of reality." Neither writer makes it clear how long he supposes the cosmogony to have been. Diels estimated that we possess only a tenth, as opposed to nine-tenths, of the Way of Truth. A cosmogony ten times the length of the existing fragments might call for a different view. Owen, in fact, shows a certain uneasiness when he writes, first, that the goddess' account "is not introduced as a contribution to science," and then, in the next breath, that "this is not of course to deny that it was the most complete and plausible system its author knew how to produce." My own view of the cosmogony would be that of the *deuteros plous* or return to the Cave.

Papers on Zeno always, to my shame, fill me with a certain ennui. I therefore record my gratitude to Fränkel for the suggestion, austerely rejected by Vlastos, that Zeno intended, at least in part, to be *funny*.

Empedocles next: Solmsen argues quite convincingly for a single rather than a dual cosmogony; his strongest points are those based on the undeniably creative powers of Love. Furley makes good sense of the clepsydra, characterizing it as a "persuasive analogy" rather than an experiment.

The three excellent papers on Anaxagoras' theory of matter filled me with something like despair; all are so careful, so sweetly reasonable, and, finally, so incompatible. When Cornford writes "[corn] does not nourish silver or rubies, so why should it contain particles of these?" common sense breathes a sigh of relief. But then Vlastos' elegant and more general theory of powers makes a strong appeal to reason—at least until convincingly rejected by Strang. I take some comfort in Fränkel's omission of Anaxagoras from the list of philosophers "who can be reasonably well understood by us."

The atomists are represented by only one paper, Vlastos' "Ethics and Physics in Democritus," but the choice is happy. The subject is fresh and the implications are important. This is the paper from which I learned most.

My general reaction to the volume is that it is worthy but a little stodgy. Mourelatos' volume in the Anchor series (which costs only $5.95!) is a much livelier collection.

Rosamond Kent Sprague
University of South Carolina

Glossarium Epicureum. By HERMANNUS USENER. Lessico Intellettuale Europeo (Centro di Studio del C. N. R.), 14. Edendum curaverunt M. GIGANTE et W. SCHMID. Rome: Edizioni dell'Ateneo & Bizzarri, 1977. Pp. xlviii + 873.

This is Usener's own index, which he made to help him in his work. The editors have added only a modern bibliography and an index to the *Gnomologium Vaticanum* by I. F. Fabiano.

Scholars have profited from this index, by private arrangement, during the years since it was lodged in the Seminar at Bonn, and the editors and publishers have produced an extremely accurate and handsome volume. But was it right to publish it now, ninety years after U.'s *Epicurea* (Leipzig, 1887)?

In that work U. wrote: "Epicuro ut operam darem, non philosophiae Epicureae me admiratio commovit, sed ut accidit homini grammatico, librorum a Laertio Diogene servatorum obscuritas et difficultas" (p. v). With great learning and imagination, he emended the text until it was easier to read. His edition brought together a rich collection of Epicurean material, which enabled and stimulated scholarship to progress. U.'s text has been studied and analyzed during the last ninety years—and it has been frequently rejected. P. von der Mühll (Leipzig, 1922), C. Bailey (Oxford, 1926), G. Arrighetti (Turin, 1960; 2nd ed., 1973), and Jean Bollack and his collaborators (Paris, 1971–) all differ widely from U.

But *Glossarium Epicureum* is an index to U.'s Epicurus. It indexes more material than was published in *Epicurea*, since it takes note of the papyrus fragments of Epicurus' Περὶ φύσεως published in *Voluminum Herculanensium collectio prior* and *Collectio altera*, and some other material. In the case of the crucial material from Diogenes Laertius, however, the *Glossarium* follows U.'s text, and in many instances there is no warning that a reading is a doubtful choice from varying manuscript readings or even that it is based wholly on conjecture. The following examples are all taken from the *Letter to Herodotus* (line numbers as in Bollack's edition).

37. 3: ἐνέργημα F, Usener, Mühll, Bailey, Arrighetti; ἐνάργημα BP, Bollack, defended at length by K. Kleve, "A Textcritical Note on Epicurus *Letter to Herodotus* 37 (Diog. Laert. 10)," *Symb. Oslo.* 46 (1971): 90–95. Only ἐνέργημα is indexed, without warning (however, hesitation between ἐνεργείας and ἐναργείας at 48. 12 and at 52. 3 is scrupulously noted under both words).

65. 5: ὄξυ codd., Bollack; ἕξει Usener, Bailey; σῴζει Mühll, Arrighetti. Only ἕξει is indexed, without warning (note that Arrighetti's index has only σῴζει, without warning).

67. 11: διαλαμβάνει codd., Bollack; διαλαμβάνομεν Mühll, Arrighetti; διαλαμβάνεται Bailey; συμβαίνει Usener. Only συμβαίνει is indexed, without warning.

69. 7: μεγεθῶν codd., Mühll, Bailey, Arrighetti, Bollack; μερῶν Schneider, Usener. Only μερῶν is indexed, without warning.

72. 7: περιφέροντες codd., Mühll, Arrighetti, Bollack; ἐπιφέροντες Usener; ἐπιφέροντας Bailey. Only ἐπιφέροντες is indexed, without warning.

73. 6: πάλιν codd., Mühll, Bailey, Arrighetti, Bollack; πάντα Usener. Only πάντα is indexed, without warning.

80. 9: παραδιδόντων codd., Bailey, Arrighetti, Bollack; παριδόντων Usener, Mühll. Only παριδόντων is indexed, with the MS reading in parenthesis.

81. 6: καὶ codd., Bollack; ἀεὶ Usener, Bailey; ἢ Mühll, Arrighetti. Ἀεὶ is indexed without warning.

So the situation in which the Epicurean researcher now finds himself is this. He has the "Indice delle parole principali" in Arrighetti's *Epicuro* (preferably the 1973 edition, since Arrighetti changed nearly all of his numeration between the two editions). This indexes all of Diogenes Book 10, the *Gnomologium Vaticanum*, and a selection of fragments of the lost books, including—most usefully—all the papyrus fragments of any length from the Περὶ φύσεως.

The researcher also has two books from the Bollack team (with the *Letter to Pythocles* shortly to be added): *La lettre d'Épicure* (*Letter to Herodotus*) and *La pensée du plaisir* (*Letter to Menoeceus, Kyriai Doxai, Gnomologium Vaticanum*, and select passages from Diogenes' doxography). Each volume is indexed scrupulously and fully, although always following Bollack's preferred readings, without mention of variants. Since Bollack almost always follows a manuscript reading, these indexes are an excellent guide to the manuscript tradition. But they omit the papyrus fragments and citations from authors other than Diogenes Laertius.

Using the *Glossarium Epicureum* has three advantages over the combination of Arrighetti and Bollack. It indexes a richer stock of material, since it includes all of U.'s fragments (but it omits the recently edited Herculaneum papyrus 1413 = Arrighetti², no. 37). It includes a much greater proportion of the words than Arrighetti, although it is less complete than Bollack for the works indexed by Bollack. And it prints out the whole phrase for each occurrence of the word indexed (a great time-saver, where the text is reliable).

The *Glossarium* has four disadvantages. It is based on a text of the main works that no one now accepts. It does not distinguish between conjecture and undoubted tradition—and so the fact that it prints the whole of the phrase for each entry becomes a positive danger for anyone who tries to save time by not checking the passage and its apparatus criticus for every entry. It gives all references to the Περὶ φύσεως in the old nineteenth-century editions of *Volumina Herculanensia*, except that it uses Gomperz' edition of the book on free will; the attempt to convert any of these references in order to look up a more recent text in Arrighetti's edition defeats all rational procedures (e.g., the *Glossarium* reference "*nat. inc.* VH² VI 87 col. 9, 6" converts to Arrighetti² "36. 16. 6"—you cannot determine this without looking up a key word in Arrighetti's index). Finally, the price (over one hundred dollars) is shocking.

David J. Furley
Princeton University

Scholia Graeca in Homeri "Iliadem" (*Scholia Vetera*), volumen tertium scholia ad libros Κ–Ξ continens. Recensuit HARTMUT ERBSE. Berlin: Walter de Gruyter & Co., 1974. Pp. xxxv + 685 + 2 + 4 pls. Mk. 380.

Once again we have reason to admire the speed with which Erbse's splendid new edition of the *Iliad* scholia moves to its completion. And again we note with admiration that this volume, like its predecessors, is beautifully printed.

In a short preface E. restates some of the principles he adopted. He also thanks his publishers for being willing to print again the more than twenty pages of bibliographical materials dealing with works which are cited in abbreviated form in the body of the book. We continue to marvel at how up to date the bibliographical materials are. E.'s preface is dated August 1972. Yet the bibliography lists C. J. Herington's *Older Scholia on the "Prometheus Bound"* (Leyden, 1972), and the testimonia cite the edition of Posidonius' fragments by L. Edelstein and I. G. Kidd (Cambridge, 1972). The reader may note with some surprise occasional references to "Gladstone" in the testimonia; he has appeared in all three volumes. This is indeed the Victorian prime minister, and one does not ordinarily connect his Homeric writings with the sort of problems dealt with in these books. E.'s references are to what is apparently a German translation (published in Breslau in 1878) of the chapter "Homer's Perceptions and Use of Colour" which formed part of volume 3 of Gladstone's *Studies on Homer and the Homeric Age* (Oxford, 1858).

As in the previous volumes, E.'s text differs now and then from the texts of Dindorf and of Maass, especially from the text of Maass. Probably the most obvious difference is that E. has frequently supplied or augmented lemmata. As before, he has printed few conjectures in the text, though he occasionally suggests one in his notes. Conjectures printed by others are sometimes rejected. References are given to collections of fragments not available to earlier editors (e.g., R. Berndt's edition of the fragments of the grammarian Nicias in *BPhW* for 1910). Scholia previously attached to the wrong lines are put into their proper place. The rich collection of testimonia continues to add to the value of this edition. Van der Valk's researches on the scholia and on Eustathius are often noted, and E. fairly often disagrees with Van der Valk's conclusions or suggestions. At the end of the A scholia on *Iliad* 10. 110, was the article before *naustathmou* omitted through inadvertence?

Erbse deals with a few scraps of papyrus, giving an elaborate commentary and illustrating them on four plates. One of these papyri, treating four lines in Book 14, is here published for the first time. Finally, we are given five pages of corrections to the text (a number of them only corrections of accents) and additions to the apparatus criticus of all three volumes.

Frederick M. Combellack
University of Oregon

BOOKS RECEIVED

[Not all works submitted can be reviewed, but those that pertain to the subject matter of this journal are regularly listed under "Books Received." Offprints from periodicals and parts of books will not be listed unless they are published (sold) separately. Books submitted are not returnable.]

Acta omnium gentium ac nationum conventus Latinis litteris linguaeque fovendis: A die XXX mensis Augusti ad diem IV mensis Septembris A.D. MDCCCCLXXIII. Volumen edendum curavit EDUARDUS COLEIRO. Malta: In aedibus Universitatis Melitensis, 1976. Pp. 625. £M6 (paper).

ADAMIETZ, JOACHIM. *Zur Komposition der "Argonautica" des Valerius Flaccus.* Zetemata, vol. 67. Munich: Verlag C. H. Beck, 1976. Pp. vii + 128. DM 23 (paper).

BERGREN, ANN L. T. *The Etymology and Usage of "peirar" in Early Greek Poetry: A Study in the Interrelationship of Metrics, Linguistics and Poetics.* American Classical Series, no. 2. State College, Pa.: The American Philological Association, 1975. Pp. xi + 208. Order from Interbook Incorporated, 545 Eighth Avenue, New York, N.Y. 10018.

BLEICKEN, J.; MEIER, CHR.; STRASBURGER, H. *Matthias Gelzer und die römische Geschichte.* FAS: Frankfurter Althistorische Studien, vol. 9. Kallmünz Opf.: Verlag Michael Lassleben, 1977. Pp. 100 + 2 pls. (portraits).

BRADFORD, ALFRED S. *A Prosopography of Lacedaemonians from the Death of Alexander the Great, 323 B.C., to the Sack of Sparta by Alaric, A.D. 396.* Vestigia: Beiträge zur Alten Geschichte, vol. 27. Munich: Verlag C. H. Beck, 1977. Pp. x + 499. DM 45.

BRIGHT, DAVID F. *"Haec mihi fingebam": Tibullus in His World.* Cincinnati Classical Studies, new series, vol. 3. Leyden: E. J. Brill, 1978. Pp. xv + 275. Fl. 39.

BUDÉ, ANDRÉ WINAND ANTOINE MARIE. *De hypotheseis der Griekse tragedies en komedies: Een onderzoek naar de hypotheseis van Dicaearchus.* Diss., Nijmegen. The Hague: Drukkerij J. H. Pasmans, 1977. Pp. 220. Available from the author: A. W. A. M. Budé, Mendelssohnstraat 1, Lichtenvoorde.

BUTTERWORTH, CHARLES E. (ed. and trans.). *Averroës' Three Short Commentaries on Aristotle's "Topics," "Rhetoric," and "Poetics."* Studies in Islamic Philosophy and Science. Edited and translated by CHARLES E. BUTTERWORTH. Albany: State University of New York Press, 1977. Pp. xi + 206. $30.00.

CHERNISS, HAROLD. *Selected Papers.* Edited by LEONARDO TARÁN. Leyden: E. J. Brill, 1977. Pp. ix + 575 + 1 pl. (portrait).

DAWE, R. D. *Studies in the Text of Sophocles*, vol. 3: *"Women of Trachis"–"Antigone"–"Philoctetes"–"Oedipus at Colonus."* Leyden: E. J. Brill, 1978. Pp. vi + 152. Fl. 88.

Dionysiaca: Nine Studies in Greek Poetry by Former Pupils Presented to Sir Denys Page on His Seventieth Birthday. Edited by R. D. DAWE, J. DIGGLE, P. E. EASTERLING. Cambridge, 1978. Pp. xiv + 203 + 1 pl. (portrait). £3.50, $8.00. Published by The Editors, Classical Faculty Library, Mill Lane Lecture Rooms, Mill Lane, Cambridge.

DRAKE, GERTRUDE C., and FORBES, CLARENCE A. (eds. and trans.). *Marco Girolamo Vida's "The Christiad."* A Latin–English Edition. Edited and Translated by GERTRUDE C. DRAKE and CLARENCE A. FORBES. Carbondale and Edwardsville: Southern Illinois University Press; London and Amsterdam: Feffer & Simons, Inc., 1978. Pp. ix + 285. $9.85.

ENGELS, DONALD W. *Alexander the Great and the Logistics of the Macedonian Army.* Berkeley–Los Angeles–London: University of California Press, 1978. Pp. xiv + 194; 8 tables + 16 maps in text. $15.00.

GOLDMAN, NORMA, and NYENHUIS, JACOB E. *Latin via Ovid: A First Course.* Detroit: Wayne State University Press, 1977. Pp. xxviii + 495.

HAVELOCK, ERIC A. *The Greek Concept of Justice: From Its Shadow in Homer to Its Substance in Plato.* Cambridge, Mass., and London: Harvard University Press, 1978. Pp. ix + 382. $16.50.

HEINRICHS, ACHIM DIETER. *Sejan und das Schicksal Roms in den "Annalen" des Tacitus.* Diss., Philipps–Universität Marburg/Lahn. Marburg/Lahn, 1976. Pp. iii + 199.

HOLWERDA, D. (ed.). *Scholia in Aristophanem*, pars I: *Prolegomena de comoedia; Scholia in "Acharnenses," "Equites," "Nubes,"* fasc. III 1 continens scholia vetera in *Nubes*. Edidit D. HOLWERDA, cum duabus appendicibus, quas subministravit W. J. W. KOSTER. Groningen: Bouma's Boekhuis B. V., 1977. Pp. xxxix + 296 + 2 pls. Fl. 185.

KATSOURIS, ANDREAS G. *Hē parexēgēsē stēn tragōdia kai stēn kōmōdia.* Iōannina: The University, 1976. Pp. 96.

LATACZ, JOACHIM. *Kampfparënese, Kampfdarstellung und Kampfwirklichkeit in der "Ilias," bei Kallinos und Tyrtaios.* Zetemata, vol. 66. Munich: Verlag C. H. Beck, 1977. Pp. viii + 267 + 1. DM 67 (paper).

Lexikon des Mittelalters, vol. 1, fasc. 1: *Aachen–Ägypten.* Munich and Zurich: Artemis Verlag, 1977. Pp. 112 (coll. 224). DM/SFr. 32 (in subscription) (paper). *Lexikon des Mittelalters:* 5 Bände zu je 1128 Seiten plus Registerband. Jeder Band: 10 Lieferungen à 112 Seiten und eine Titelei. Subskriptionspreis [pro Lieferung] (gültig bis zum Abschluss des 1. Bandes) DM/SFr. 32,—. Einbanddecke in Leinen je Band ca. DM/SFr. 18,—.

LINDBERG, GERTRUD. *Studies in Hermogenes and Eustathios: The Theory of Ideas and Its Application in the Commentaries of Eustathios on the Epics of Homer.* Lund, 1977. Pp. x + 350 + 1 loose sheet of corrigenda. Kr. 40 (paper). Privately published and obtainable from the author at Lagerbrings väg 4 C, S–223 60 Lund, Sweden.

LINKE, KONSTANZE; HAAS, WALTER; NEITZEL, SUSANNE (eds.). *Die Fragmente des Grammatikers Dionysios Thrax.* Herausgegeben von KONSTANZE LINKE. *Die Fragmente der Grammatiker Tyrannion und Diokles.* Herausgegeben von WALTER HAAS. *Apions Glōssai Homērikai.* Herausgegeben von SUSANNE NEITZEL. Sammlung griechischer und lateinischer Grammatiker (SGLG), vol. 3. Berlin and New York: Walter de Gruyter, 1977. Pp. v + 328. DM 218.

LOSEMANN, VOLKER. *Nationalsozialismus und Antike: Studien zur Entwicklung des Faches Alte Geschichte 1933–1945.* Historische Perspektiven, 7. Hamburg: Hoffmann und Campe Verlag, 1977. Pp. 283 + 5. DM 48 (paper).

Lyne, R. O. A. M. (ed.). *"Ciris": A Poem Attributed to Vergil.* Cambridge Classical Texts and Commentaries, 20. Cambridge–London–New York–Melbourne: Cambridge University Press, 1978. Pp. xii + 332. $45.00.

Magno, Pietro. *Marco Pacuvio.* Milan: Edizioni Pegaso, 1977. Pp. 130. L. 3500 (paper).

Malkiel, María Rosa Lida de. *La tradición clásica en España.* Letras e Ideas, Maior, 4. Esplugues de Llobregat (Barcelona): Editorial Ariel, 1975. Pp. 437 + 2.

Manfredini, Mario, and Piccirilli, Luigi. *Plutarco: La "Vita di Solone."* A cura di Mario Manfredini e Luigi Piccirilli. N.p. [Milan?]: Fondazione Lorenzo Valla, Arnoldo Mondadori Editore, 1977. Pp. liv + 299 + 5. L. 10,000.

McGushin, P. C. *Sallustius Crispus: "Bellum Catilinae"; A Commentary.* Mnemosyne, suppl. 45. Leyden: E. J. Brill, 1977. xii + 317. Fl. 80 (paper).

Mertens, J. *Ordona,* V: *Rapports et Études.* Études de Philologie, d'Archéologie et d'Histoire Anciennes publiées par l'Institut Historique Belge de Rome, vol. 16. Présentés par J. Mertens. Brussels: Rue de Ruysbroeck, 2–6; Rome: Academia Belgica, 1976. Pp. 188 + 61 pls. + 4 plans (loose, in end-pocket); 27 figs. in text.

Il mito greco: Atti del Convegno Internazionale (Urbino 7–12 maggio 1973). Università degli Studi di Urbino, Centro Internazionale di Semiotica e Linguistica, Istituto di Filologia Classica; Quaderni Urbinati di Cultura Classica, Atti di Convegni, 1. Rome: Edizioni dell'Ateneo & Bizzarri, 1977. Pp. xii + 426. L. 14,000 (paper).

Momigliano, Arnaldo. *Essays in Ancient and Modern Historiography.* Middletown, Connecticut: Wesleyan University Press, 1977. Pp. x + 387. $20.00. Published in Great Britain by Basil Blackwell Oxford, 1977.

Nichols, Roger, and McLeish, Kenneth. *Through Roman Eyes: Roman Civilisation in the Words of Roman Writers.* Compiled, translated and introduced by Roger Nichols and Kenneth McLeish. Cambridge–London–New York–Melbourne: Cambridge University Press, 1976. Pp. viii + 136; numerous ills. in text. $10.95 (cloth), $4.95 (paper).

Nisbet, R. G. M., and Hubbard, Margaret. *A Commentary on Horace: "Odes," Book II.* Oxford: Clarendon Press; New York: Oxford University Press, 1978. Pp. xvi + 355. £12.50 (in U.K.), $29.95.

Noussan-Lettry, Luis. *Spekulatives Denken in Platons Frühschriften: "Apologie" und "Kriton."* Alber-Broschuren zur Philosophie aus Forschung und Lehre. Freiburg and Munich: Verlag Karl Alber, 1974. Pp. 246 + 2.

O'Connell, Richard (trans.). *More Epigrams from Martial.* Philadelphia: Atlantis Editions, 1977. Pp. 27 (unnumbered). $2.00 (paper).

O'Loughlin, Michael. *The Garlands of Repose: The Literary Celebration of Civic and Retired Leisure; The Traditions of Homer and Vergil, Horace and Montaigne.* Chicago and London: The University of Chicago Press, 1978. Pp. xix + 326. $23.00.

Pallottino, Massimo. *The Etruscans.* Revised and enlarged edition. Translated by J. Cremona. Edited by David Ridgway. Harmondsworth: Penguin Books,

Ltd.; New York: Penguin Books, 1978. Pp. 317 + 48 pls.; 6 figs. in text. £2.95, $7.95 (paper). Revised edition, based on the sixth Italian edition (1968, 1973), published by Allen Lane 1975; published in Pelican Books 1978.

PAPAÏOANNOU, VAGGOS. *Loukianos, ho megalos satirikos tēs archaiotētos: Symbolē stēn parousiasē tēs epochēs tou biou kai tou ergou tou.* Thessaloniki, 1976. Pp. xvi + 328. Distributed by Konstantinidis Bros., 25 Egnatia Street, Thessaloniki, Greece.

PILTZ, ANDERS (ed.). *Studium Upsaliense: Specimens of the Oldest Lecture Notes Taken in the Mediaeval University of Uppsala.* Acta Universitatis Upsaliensis: Skrifter rörande Uppsala universitet, C: Organisation och historia, 36; Skrifter utgivna till Uppsala-universitets 500-årsjubileum, I: Texter, 2: Urkunder till undervisningens historia. Critically edited, with an introduction, a description of the MMS., a list of abbreviations, and indices by ANDERS PILTZ. Uppsala, 1977. Pp. 382. Kr. 91 (paper).

Proceedings of the 3rd International Humanistic Symposium at Athens and Pelion September 24–October 2, 1975 (*Topic: "The Case of Objectivity"*); *Praktika tou G' Diethnous Anthrōpistikou Symposiou 24 Septembriou–2 Oktobriou 1975* (*Thema: "Hē dynatotēs tēs antikeimenikotētos"*). Hellenic Society for Humanistic Studies, International Centre for Humanistic Research, second series: Studies and Researches, 29; Hellēnikē Anthrōpistikē Hetaireia, Diethnes Kentron Anthrōpistikōn Klassikōn Ereunōn, seira deutera: Meletai kai Ereunai, 29. Athens, 1977. Pp. 521 + 6.

Quaderni Urbinati di Cultura Classica, Quadrimestrale N. 26 (1977) degli "Studi Urbinati," Università di Urbino. Università degli Studi di Urbino, Istituto di Filologia Classica. Rome: Edizioni dell'Ateneo & Bizzarri, 1977. Pp. 164. L. 3500 (per fascicolo), 10,000 (abbonamento annuale) (per l'Italia); L. 5000 (per fascicolo), 15,000 (abbonamento annuale) (per l'Estero).

RAMAGE, EDWIN S. (ed.). *Atlantis: Fact or Fiction?* Edited by EDWIN S. RAMAGE. Contributors: J. RUFUS FEARS, S. CASEY FREDERICKS, JOHN V. LUCE, EDWIN S. RAMAGE, DOROTHY B. VITALIANO, HERBERT E. WRIGHT, JR. Bloomington and London: Indiana University Press, 1978. Pp. xiv + 210; 3 maps + 4 figs. in text. $10.95.

Ramus: Critical Studies in Greek and Roman Literature, vol. 6, no. 2. Berwick, Victoria, Australia: Aureal Publishers, 1977. Pp. iv + 81–164. Price per single issue: $6 (Australian) for individuals, $8.50 (Australian) for institutions and libraries (plus postage and packing charges) (paper).

REA, J. R. (ed. and trans.). *The Oxyrhynchus Papyri*, vol. 46: nos. 3267–3315 (*Graeco-Roman Memoirs*, no. 65). London: Egypt Exploration Society (for The British Academy), 1978. Pp. xvi + 127 + 8 pls.

RIJLAARSDAM, JETSKE C. *Platon über die Sprache: Ein Kommentar zum "Kratylos."* Mit einem Anhang über die Quelle der Zeichentheorie Ferdinand de Saussures. Utrecht: Bohn, Scheltema & Holkema, wetenschappelijke uitgeverij, 1978. Pp. viii + 350.

RIST, JOHN M. (ed.). *The Stoics.* Major Thinkers Series. Berkeley–Los Angeles–London: University of California Press, 1978. Pp. viii + 295. $18.00 (cloth), $4.75 (paper).

Rocha-Pereira, Maria Helena (ed.). *Pausaniae "Graeciae descriptio,"* vol. II: *Libri V–VIII*. Bibliotheca Scriptorum Graecorum et Romanorum Teubneriana. Edidit Maria Helena Rocha-Pereira. Leipzig: BSB B. G. Teubner Verlagsgesellschaft, 1977. Pp. v + 338. Mk. 56.

Sandbach, F. H. *The Comic Theatre of Greece and Rome*. Ancient Culture and Society. New York: W. W. Norton & Company, Inc., 1977. Pp. 168 + 4 pls.; 2 figs. in text. $9.95.

Schmeling, Gareth L., and Stuckey, Johanna H. *A Bibliography of Petronius*. Mnemosyne, suppl. 39. Leyden: E. J. Brill, 1977. Pp. xi + 239 + frontispiece; 14 ills. in text. Fl. 96 (paper).

Schrader, Carlos. *La paz de Calias: Testimonios e interpretación*. Introducción de C. L. Murison; Epílogo de A. E. Raubitschek. Barcelona: Universidad de Barcelona, Instituto de Estudios Helénicos, 1976. Pp. xv + 217.

Schwartz, Jacques, et al. (eds.). *Papyrus grecs de la Bibliothèque Nationale et Universitaire de Strasbourg, Nos 601 à 640*. Publications de la Bibliothèque Nationale et Universitaire de Strasbourg, V–1-2. Publiés par Jacques Schwartz et ses élèves de l'Institut Paul Collomp de l'Université de Strasbourg II. Strasbourg, 1976. Pp. 60.

Smith, Ole Langwitz. *Scholia metrica anonyma in Euripidis "Hecubam," "Orestem," "Phoenissas."* Opuscula Graecolatina (Supplementa *Musei Tusculani*), vol. 10. Edited with Prolegomena, Critical Apparatus, Appendix and Index by Ole Langwitz Smith. Copenhagen: Museum Tusculanum, 1977. Pp. xxvi + 69. Kr. 25 (Kr. 15 for subscribers to Museum Tusculanum) (paper).

Teodorsson, Sven-Tage. *The Phonology of Ptolemaic Koine*. Studia Graeca et Latina Gothoburgensia, 36. Lund, 1977. Pp. 278. Distributors: Acta Universitatis Gothoburgensis, Box 5096, S–402 22 Göteborg 5, Sweden. Kr. 150 (cloth), 125 (paper).

Thalmann, William G. *Dramatic Art in Aeschylus's "Seven against Thebes."* Yale Classical Monographs, 1. New Haven and London: Yale University Press, 1978. Pp. viii + 193. $12.50.

Väänänen, Veikko. *"Ab epistulis . . . ad Sanctum Petrum": Formules prépositionelles latines étudiées dans leur contexte sociale*. Annales Academiae Scientiarum Fennicae, ser. B, tom. 197. Helsinki: Suomalainen Tiedeakatemia, 1977. Pp. 54. Mk. 30 (paper). Distributor: Akateeminen Kirjakauppa (The Academic Bookstore) 00100 Helsinki 10.

Viveros, Germán (trans.). *P. Terenti Afri "Comoediae" Sex; Publio Terencio Africano: Comedias*, Tomo I: *"La Andriana," "El Eunuco," "El Atormentador de Sí Mismo."* Biblitheca Scriptorum Graecorum et Romanorum Mexicana. Introducción, traducción y notas de Germán Viveros. Mexico: Universidad Nacional Autónoma de México, 1975. Pp. i–xliv (Introducción) + double pp. 1–181 + pp. xlvii–xcv (notas).

Waiblinger, Franz Peter. *Senecas "Naturales Quaestiones": Griechische Wissenschaft und römische Form*. Zetemata, vol. 70. Munich: Verlag C. H. Beck, 1977. Pp. viii + 124. DM 35 (paper).

Wallach, Luitpold. *Diplomatic Studies in Latin and Greek Documents from the Carolingian Age*. Ithaca and London: Cornell University Press, 1977. Pp. xiii + 398 + 7 pls. $30.00.

WARRINGTON, JOHN. *Everyman's Classical Dictionary, 800 B.C.–A.D. 337*. Everyman's Reference Library. London–Melbourne–Toronto: J. M. Dent & Sons, Ltd., 1978. Pp. xxxviii + 537. £3.50 (net U.K. price), $7.95. First published 1961; second edition revised 1965; third edition revised 1969; reprinted 1970, 1978. J. M. Dent & Sons, Ltd. c/o Biblio Distribution Center, 81 Adams Drive, Totowa, New Jersey 07512.

WEEBER, KARL-WILHELM. *Das 4. Properz-Buch: Interpretationen zu seiner Eigenart und seiner Stellung im Gesamtwerk*. Diss., Ruhr-Universität Bochum. Bamberg: aku-Fotodruck GmbH, 1977. Pp. ii + 289. DM 25 (paper). Obtainable from Dr. K.-W. Weeber, Osterfeldstr. 26, D–5802 Wetter 4.

WILLETTS, R. F. *The Civilization of Ancient Crete*. Berkeley and Los Angeles: University of California Press, 1977. Pp. 279 + 23 pls.; frontispiece + 25 ills. in text. $22.75.

WYCHERLEY, R. E. *The Stones of Athens*. Princeton, N.J.: Princeton University Press, 1978. Pp. xviii + 293; 78 ills. in text. $25.00 (cloth), $12.50 (paper).

Yale Classical Studies, vol. 25: *Greek Tragedy*. Edited for the Department of Classics by T. F. GOULD and C. J. HERINGTON. Cambridge–London–New York–Melbourne: Cambridge University Press, 1977. Pp. ix + 350. $24.95.

CLASSICAL PHILOLOGY

A Quarterly Journal devoted to research in the Languages, Literatures, History, and Life of Classical Antiquity

VOLUME 74 NUMBER 3

July 1979

THE UNIVERSITY OF CHICAGO PRESS

Editorial correspondence: The Editor, *Classical Philology*, Box I, Faculty Exchange, The University of Chicago, Chicago, Illinois 60637. N.B. To be considered for publication, all material submitted must be typewritten, with texts, quotations, and footnotes double-spaced, and on stout paper with ample margins.

Classical Philology (ISSN 0009-837X) is published in January, April, July, and October. Subscription rates, U.S.A.: institutions, 1 year $24.00, 2 years $43.20, 3 years $61.20; individuals, 1 year $18.00, 2 years $32.40, 3 years $45.90; students, $14.40 (with signature of faculty member). Other countries add $1.50 for each year's subscription to cover postage. Single copy rates: institutions $6.50; individuals, $5.00. Back volumes available from 1965 (vol. 60). Single issues and reprinted volumes through 1961 (vols. 1–56) available from Walter J. Johnson, Inc., 355 Chestnut Street, Norwood, New Jersey 07648. Volumes available in microfilm from University Microfilms, 300 North Zeeb Road, Ann Arbor, Michigan 48106; in microfiche from J. S. Canner & Co., 49–65 Lansdowne Street, Boston, Massachusetts 02215. Checks should be made payable to CLASSICAL PHILOLOGY, The University of Chicago Press, 5801 Ellis Avenue, Chicago, Illinois 60637.

Claims for missing numbers should be made within the month following the regular month of publication. The publishers expect to supply missing numbers free only when losses have been sustained in transit and when the reserve stock will permit.

Subscribers are requested to notify the Press and their local postmaster immediately of change of address. All changes of address should provide *both* the old and the new address. *Please allow four weeks for the change.* Postmaster: send address changes to *Classical Philology*, 5801 Ellis Avenue, Chicago, Illinois 60637.

The articles in this journal are indexed in the *Humanities Index*.

Second-class postage paid at Chicago, Illinois.

CLASSICAL PHILOLOGY

VOLUME 74, NUMBER 3

July 1979

REFRAIN IN AESCHYLUS: LITERARY ADAPTATION OF TRADITIONAL FORM, *Helen E. Moritz* 187

ARISTOTLE'S CRITICISM OF EUDOXAN HEDONISM, *Roslyn Weiss* 214

A NATIVITY POEM OF THE SIXTH CENTURY A.D., *Averil Cameron* 222

A NOTE ON THEOCRITUS *Idyll* 18, *David Konstan* 233

THE THREE HUNDRED AT THASOS, 411 B.C., *Harry C. Avery* 234

Curuca AND JUVENAL *Satire* 6, *Mechtilde O'Mara* 242

POET OR PLATO IN PLUTARCH?, *Robert Renehan* 244

NOTES ON THE *Dialogus* OF TACITUS, *Charles E. Murgia* 245

REVIEWS IN THIS ISSUE 250

B. C. DIETRICH: *The Origins of Greek Religion*, and E. T. VERMEULE: *Götterkult* (Jameson).—J. J. POLLITT: *The Ancient View of Greek Art: Criticism, History, and Terminology* (Price).—P. CASTRÉN: *Ordo populusque Pompeianus: Polity and Society in Roman Pompeii* (Morgan).—P. A. L. GREENHALGH: *The Year of the Four Emperors* (Bradley).—A. MEHL: *Tacitus über Kaiser Claudius: Die Ereignisse am Hof* (Shotter).—J. W. BINNS (ed.): *The Latin Poetry of English Poets* (Russo).—S.-T. TEODORSSON: *The Phonemic System of the Attic Dialect 400–340 B.C.* (Wyatt).—A. H. SOMMERSTEIN: *The Sound Pattern of Ancient Greek* (Nagy).

MANUSCRIPT ACCEPTANCE POLICY

While it is our policy to require the assignment of copyright on most journal articles, we do not usually request assignment of copyright for other contributions. Although the copyright to such a contribution may remain with the author, it is understood that, in return for publication, the journal has the non-exclusive right to publish the contribution and the continuing right, without limit, to include the contribution as part of any reprint of the issue and/or volume of the journal in which the contribution first appeared by any means and in any format, including computer assisted storage and readout, in which the issue and/or volume may be reproduced.

COPYING BEYOND FAIR USE

The code on the first page of an article in this journal indicates the copyright owner's consent that copies of the article may be made beyond those permitted by Sections 107 or 108 of the U.S. Copyright Law provided that copies are made only for personal or internal use, or for the personal or internal use of specific clients and provided that the copier pay the stated per-copy fee through the Copyright Clearance Center Inc. Operations Center, P.O. Box 765, Schenectady, New York 12301.

To request permission for other kinds of copying, such as copying for general distribution, for advertising or promotional purposes, for creating new collective works, or for resale, kindly write to the publisher.

If no code appears on the first page of the article, permission to reprint may be obtained only from the author.

REFRAIN IN AESCHYLUS: LITERARY ADAPTATION OF TRADITIONAL FORM

HELEN E. MORITZ

NUMEROUS studies have shown that recurrent themes and images in Aeschylean tragedy are often controlled mechanisms by which the poet emphasizes and develops significant aspects of the dramatic action.[1] Thus far, however, scant attention has been paid to Aeschylus' use of a poetic form which is inherently recurrent, the lyric refrain. Critics have confined themselves to historical observations, attributing Aeschylean refrains, often imprecisely, to supposed ritual or other "primitive" antecedents of drama.[2]

It is easy to see why. For each refrain in Aeschylus, there is a precedent in nondramatic ritual, either in substance or in context. The triple refrain in the parodos of the *Agamemnon* (121, 139, 159 αἴλινον αἴλινον εἰπέ, τὸ δ' εὖ νικάτω) begins with an antique cry which is identical to the "Linos song" (Λίνον) attested in Homer (*Il.* 18. 570); the prayer for good with which the refrain concludes seeks to avert the evil implications of an omen, and is analogous to the apotropaic paean in *Iliad* 1. 473.[3] The celebration of the Eumenides' goodwill which closes the *Oresteia* employs two other refrains. Celebrants are summoned, subject to the usual ritual caution (*Eum.* 1035, 1038 εὐφαμεῖτε; cf. *Il.* 9. 171), to raise the same cry of exultation which was uttered by Eurycleia in the *Odyssey* (22. 408, 411): ὀλολύξατε νῦν ἐπὶ μολπαῖς (*Eum.* 1043, 1047). Functions of magic, lamentation, and necromancy are fulfilled by the remaining refrains in Aeschylus' extant plays. The "binding song" of the Furies is a magical incantation consigning Orestes to the Underworld (*Eum.* 328–33 = 341–46). Lamentation and necromancy combine in the conjuring of Darius by the Persian elders, the reverse process of the Furies' magic (*Pers.* 663, 671). The Danaids alternately lament and pray for deliverance from evil in the ephymnia of the parodos of the *Suppliants* (117–21 = 129–33, 141–43 = 151–53, 162–67, repeated after 175;

1. E.g., O. Hiltbrunner, *Wiederholungs- und Motivtechnik bei Aischylos* (Freiburg, 1934); J. Dumortier, *Les images dan la poésie d'Eschyle* (Paris, 1935); R. D. Murray, Jr., *The Motif of Io in Aeschylus' "Suppliants"* (Princeton, 1958); A. Lebeck, *The "Oresteia." A Study in Language and Structure* (Cambridge, Mass., 1971); for additional bibliography, see n. 7.

2. E.g., W. Kranz, *Stasimon* (Berlin, 1933), pp. 127–33; R. Arnoldt, *Der Chor im "Agamemnon" des Äschylus* (Halle, 1881), p. 23; M. Croiset, *Eschyle* (Paris, 1928), pp. 66, 93–94, 248; E. T. Owen, *The Harmony of Aeschylus* (Toronto, 1952), p. 116. Cf. P. Masqueray, *Théorie des formes lyriques de la tragédie grecque* (Paris, 1895), pp. 107–10; M. Horneffer, *De strophica sententiarum in canticis tragicorum responsione* (Bonn, 1914), p. 14.

3. M. Alexiou, *The Ritual Lament in Greek Tradition* (Cambridge, 1974), pp. 57 and 218, nn. 8, 10. In effect, the chorus repeat Calchas' paean, *Ag.* 146–54; cf. G. Méautis, *Eschyle et la trilogie* (Paris, 1936), p. 135; Owen, *Harmony*, p. 67; J. A. Haldane, "Musical Themes and Imagery in Aeschylus," *JHS* 85 (1965): 38. Unless noted, the text is the OCT of D. Page (1972).

0009-837X/79/7403-0001$01.65

cf. 889–92 = 899–902, esp. *φοβερὸν ἀπότρεπε*). These functions, too, have a much older origin. Formal lamentation is accompanied by refrain in Hector's funeral (*Il.* 24. 725–45). Refrain in necromancy may be implicit in Circe's instructions to Odysseus for evoking the spirits of the dead (*Od.* 10. 521).[4] Repeated language is in any case turned to magical purpose at least as early as the Dirae of Teos, a series of curses from the early fifth century B.C. which inveigh against wrongdoers who would harm the state: "let him perish, both himself and his race."[5] The intent of these curses is identical to that of the Furies in their "binding song."

It is not surprising, then, that critics of Aeschylean refrain find the requirements of exegesis served if reference is made to traditional, nondramatic occurrences of similar forms. Contexts which demand a refrain regularly also determine its content. In the literary form of tragedy, however, the poet retains control of the material. Recent studies have shown how Aeschylus actively refashions tradition in matters of plot construction and characterization.[6] One suspects that the received forms of liturgical and magical refrain may be transformed by the same creative artistry. Aeschylus has also been proven a master at establishing powerful motifs which pervade the dramatic action.[7] The themes of sacrifice and of blood on the ground become fixed in the reader's mind whatever the mode in which the poet introduces them, visual or verbal, dialogue or lyric.[8] The emphasis of verbatim repetition in refrain might, a fortiori, be expected to focus attention on major themes, that is, in a sense, to create motifs.

That the poet does more with the refrain than merely transcribe traditional phrases has been maintained. For example, Kranz observes, without elaboration, that Aeschylus "hat es [the refrain] seinem künstlerischen Willen untertan gemacht und zu einem kraftvollen Mittel seines dramatischen Stiles gestaltet."[9] Other scholars have noted the thematic importance of individual refrains. The *αἴλινον* phrase in the parodos of the *Agamemnon* has been recognized as an intimation of the tragic conflict in the *Oresteia;* the *ὀλολύξατε* refrain has been perceived as a symbolic expression of its resolu-

4. "Invoke them *many* times," *πολλὰ δὲ γουνοῦσθαι*. For a different view, see S. Eitrem, "The Necromancy in the *Persai* of Aischylos," *Symb. Oslo.* 6 (1928): 5.

5. A. Kirchhoff's estimate of the date (*Studien zur Geschichte des griechischen Alphabets*[3] [Berlin, 1877], pp. 12–13). For the inscription, see H. Röhl (ed.), *Inscriptiones Graecae antiquissimae praeter Atticas in Attica repertas* (Berlin, 1882), no. 497 (pp. 135–36) and E. Ziebarth, "Der Fluch im griechischen Recht," *Hermes* 30 (1895): 65–66.

6. G. Else, *The Origin and Early Form of Greek Tragedy* (Cambridge, Mass., 1965), esp. ch. 4, "Aeschylus: The Creation of Tragic Drama" (pp. 78–102); C. J. Herington, "The Influence of Old Comedy on Aeschylus' Later Trilogies," *TAPA* 94 (1963): 113–25.

7. F. Zeitlin, "The Motif of Corrupted Sacrifice in Aeschylus' *Oresteia*," *TAPA* 96 (1965): 463–508; eadem, "Postscript to Sacrificial Imagery in the *Oresteia* (*Ag.* 1235–37)," *TAPA* 97 (1966): 645–53; Lebeck, "*Oresteia*"; J. J. Peradotto, "Some Patterns of Nature Imagery in the *Oresteia*," *AJP* 85 (1964): 378-93; cf. G. S. Rousseau, "Dream and Vision in Aeschylus' *Oresteia*," *Arion* 2 (1963): 101–36.

8. Zeitlin, "Corrupted Sacrifice," passim; R. F. Goheen, "Aspects of Dramatic Symbolism: Three Studies in the *Oresteia*," *AJP* 76 (1955): 115–26.

9. *Stasimon*, p. 127. For other general appreciations of Aeschylus' transforming artistry, see R. Hölzle, *Zum Aufbau der lyrischen Partien des Aischylos* (Ph.D. diss., Freiburg, 1934), p. 5; Croiset, *Eschyle*, pp. 33, 35–36.

tion.[10] These isolated observations have not, however, led to a systematic analysis of programmatic significance in Aeschylus' refrains.

I shall investigate Aeschylus' use of the form on two levels. First, I shall seek to demonstrate the extent to which Aeschylean refrain is more than mechanical in its immediate context, to show—whatever its ritual function—how far the refrain is integrated into its dramatic setting. Second, and more important, I shall examine the function of the refrain's components in the play as a whole, the extent to which they indicate major themes for the larger context.

One result of the investigation will be anticipated here, by way of explaining the manner of presentation. Previous studies have found the thematic force of a motif continuous throughout a drama, whether its most prominent statement occurs in lyric or in trimeter;[11] similarly, the motifs identified by refrain pervade all portions of a play. The refrain as such operates only in its immediate ritual context of incantation, lament, or religious ceremony. Its programmatic aspect, however, is developed freely in the drama, as its verbal components are employed in motific permutations and combinations which could not have been predicted from the refrain itself.

This study is limited to Aeschylus' single-line refrains, the *αἴλινον* and celebratory expressions in the *Oresteia* and the conjuring cry in the *Persians*. The brevity of the single-line phrase permits a more thorough analysis than would be possible for longer refrains like those in the *Suppliants* and the *Eumenides*. Moreover, the emphasis of repetition is exaggerated in a pithy, easily remembered phrase, and so it is preeminently the short refrains that can be expected to highlight important ideas.[12] Accordingly, I shall first examine the conjuring cry of the *Persians*—the Aeschylean refrain closest to its ritual roots—and then, in conjunction with one another, the refrains which begin and end the *Oresteia*.

REFRAIN IN THE "PERSIANS"

At first inspection, *βάσκε πάτερ ἄκακε Δαριάν· οἴ* (663, 671), the refrain in the ode which conjures Darius, appears entirely straightforward, its simple meaning all on the surface: "Come, father without harm, Darius, Oh!" Each element of the cry has been uttered repeatedly throughout the ode.[13]

10. On *αἴλινον*, see E. Fraenkel, *Aeschylus: "Agamemnon,"* vol. 2 (Oxford, 1950), pp. 146–47; Owen, *Harmony*, pp. 67, 105–7; Méautis, *Eschyle et la trilogie*, pp. 135–36. On *ὀλολυγμός*, see Owen, *Harmony*, p. 130; Goheen, "Three Studies," pp. 124–25; Peradotto, "Nature Imagery," p. 393; Zeitlin, "Corrupted Sacrifice," p. 507.

11. The lion imagery of the *Agamemnon* receives principal focus in the second stasimon; cf. B. Knox, "The Lion in the House," *CP* 47 (1952): 17–25. The male-female conflict in the *Oresteia*, introduced in the watchman's trimeters (*Ag.* 10–11), recurs in Cassandra's lyrics (esp. *Ag.* 1125–26) and in choral lyric (*Ag.* 1470–71, *Ch.* 594–601); cf. R. P. Winnington-Ingram, "Clytemnestra and the Vote of Athena," *JHS* 68 (1948): 130–47.

12. Preliminary investigations of these longer refrains indicate that Aeschylus uses them much as he does the shorter ones; see my "Patterns of Repetition in the Choral Odes of Aeschylus" (Ph.D. diss., Chicago, 1976), pp. 61–89, 246–51.

13. Repetitiveness within the ode receives ample notice in commentaries on the passage; see the summary in H. D. Broadhead (ed.), *The "Persae" of Aeschylus* (Cambridge, 1960), p. 171 (ad 657–63).

Βάσκε is part of a litany of summons, first to the overseers of the Underworld (644 πέμπετε δ' ἄνω, 649 ἀνίει[14]), then to Darius himself (658–59 ἴθι ἱκοῦ, ἔλθ', 666 φάνηθι). The insistence of these requests actually led one scholar to "restore" Δαρεῖ' ἄνει from Δαριάν· οἴ, so as to complete a second triad of imperatives (βάσκε—ἄνει—φάνηθι) parallel to ἴθι ἱκοῦ, ἔλθ'.[15]

Πάτερ is one in a series of epithets by which the late king is addressed, epithets which allude to all phases of his career: as present divinity while alive—ἰσοδαίμων βασιλεὺς (634), Περσᾶν Σουσιγενῆ θεόν (643), θεομήστωρ (654–55); as king—βασιλεὺς (634), ἀνάκτορα (651), βαλὴν (657), δυνάστα (675); as individual—φίλος ἀνήρ (647); and as shade—ψυχὴν (630), ὄχθος (647), [ὁ] θανὼν (674). The transition here from formal address by royal title to the greater intimacy of a term of family relationship is paralleled in the addresses of the chorus to Atossa and may reflect Persian practice.[16] At the queen's first entrance the elders greet her with a full panoply of honorific epithets, and she is called "mother" only with reference to her royal son: ὦ βαθυζώνων ἄνασσα Περσίδων ὑπερτάτη, / μῆτερ ἡ Ξέρξου γεραιά, χαῖρε, Δαρείου γύναι (155–56). But when Atossa has revealed the anxiety caused her by an ominous dream about Xerxes, the chorus, in a more intimate tone of counsel, use the title "mother" in their own right (215 οὔ σε βουλόμεσθα, μῆτερ). In the present song, too, the term "father" is employed only at the culmination of the appeal, after due respect has initially been paid, and when, in the image of Darius' tiara appearing over the tomb (661–62), there is a sense that the incantation has been effective. The cry thus comes at a moment of high emotion, when the chorus may be regarded as acting on instinct rather than protocol.

Darius' record as victorious king and general is implied by the next term of the refrain, ἄκακε; compare in the same ode ἦ φίλος ἀνήρ . . . οὐδὲ γὰρ ἄνδρας πώποτ' ἀπώλλυ πολεμοφθόροισιν ἄταις (647–53). It is the very different military record of Xerxes, epitomized by the contrasting alpha-privatives in the last line of the ode (680 ἄναες ἄναες), which necessitates the invocation of Darius' spirit. But the epithet ἄκακε may be proleptic as well, suggestively drawing an omen for the future from Darius' past record. The elders had entreated the nether powers for the king's release on the ground that he alone might know a "remedy of evils," κακῶν ἄκος (631), a phrase which plays on the sounds in ἄκακε. Finally, the term may serve an apotropaic function. The raising of the dead was a dreadful task; this is clear in the cautionary statements by queen and chorus that they make libation with kindly intention (609 πρευμενεῖς χοάς) and expect kindly return from Darius (610 ἅπερ νεκροῖσι μειλικτήρια) and from the gods below (625–27 αἰτησόμεθα . . . πομποὺς εὔφρονας). It is significant that at his appearance Darius allays that particular anxiety almost at once: χοὰς δὲ πρευμενὴς ἐδεξάμην (685). All these connotations of the concept "absence of evil" as

14. Reading with Broadhead and Murray (1955 OCT); Page accepts Brunck's ἀνείης.
15. See Broadhead, "*Persae*," p. 171.
16. Cf. Eitrem, "Necromancy," p. 14; Kranz, *Stasimon*, p. 88.

associated with Darius are present in the song itself, and all coalesce in the repeated epithet, ἄκακε.

The clustering of the king's name with a mourning cry (Δαριάν· οἴ) has also been anticipated earlier in the song: ἀνάκτορα Δαριᾶνα· ἠέ (651). This cry of Δαριᾶνα· ἠέ closes one strophe (β, 647–51), the Δαριάν· οἴ of the refrain two others, the result being a litany of lamenting invocations of the late king. Further, if the text is sound, the unique spelling of "Darius" in this song (final -αν or -ανα instead of -ον, as elsewhere[17]) may represent a magical design in which the name of the man invoked enhances the efficacy of the ritual, as its sound seemingly compels the former "lord" (ἄναξ; cf. 651 ἀνάκτορα, 647 ἀνήρ) to "ascend" (644 ἄνω; cf. 649 ἀναπομπὸς ἀνίει). The -αν ending of Darius' name echoes not only the ἄναξ and ἀνά terms, but other -αν sounds which are surprisingly frequent in the ode: παναίολ' αἰανῆ . . . παντάλαν' ἄχη (636–38), αἰνέσατ' . . . Περσᾶν (643), ἄνδρας (652), βαλήν, ἀρχαῖος βαλὴν (657), δέσποτα δεσποτᾶν φάνηθι (666), and νᾶες ἄναες ἄναες (680). There is also a high incidence of α and ν sounds in other combinations in the stasimon; to cite only a few, γύναι (623), forms of δαίμων (628, 634), 'Αιδωνεύς (649–50), ἀείρων (660), δυνάστα δυνάστα (675). As may be seen, the -αν sounds often occur in mournful contexts or in words denoting grief or wretchedness (e.g., αἰανῆ, παντάλαν'). Thus, even Darius' name is made to participate in an onomatopoetic representation of mourning which is reinforced at intervals by exclamations of grief: οἴ (663, 671), ἠέ (651, 656), αἰαῖ αἰαῖ (673).[18]

Sound is not the only means by which the effect of lamentation is created. Standard features of lament for the dead include interjectional cries, commands, and some form of address. A general address, like "my child," is frequent; address by name, extraordinary. "Among primitive peoples, it was believed that mention of the dead man's name would cause the return of his spirit, and it was therefore avoided."[19] In the present instance it is precisely the spirit's return which is desired, and both forms of address are found—the general term of relationship, πάτερ, and the king's own name, Δαριάν. Though cries, commands, and forms of address are plentiful throughout the song, it is significant that all are collected in the one line which is repeated as refrain.

The refrain, then, not only contains the elements which characterize ritual lament and incantation, it also captures the salient features of the tragic stasimon in which the ritual is embedded—the grief, anxieties, and childlike trust of the Persian elders who are called upon to raise the spirit of their dead king in the hour of defeat. Moreover, beyond the present

17. Eitrem, "Necromancy," p. 11, says the unique form may have been coined in order to comply with the magical requirement of using the true name of the person conjured.

18. The entire ode is a good illustration of W. Porzig's concept of the "lyric value" of sound: important words are "resolved" into their components and in this form permeate the whole (*Aischylos. Die attische Tragödie* [Leipzig, 1926], pp. 74–81). The αι-sound, which Porzig (p. 84) declares to have the absolute "gestural" value of expressing pain, is also frequent in this song.

19. Alexiou, *Ritual Lament*, p. 232, n. 14; see also pp. 131–37.

scene, in the wider framework of the play, nearly every term of the refrain has important multiple associations.

Of the connotations carried by *ἄκακε* in the conjuring song, the one with the widest application in the rest of the play is that Darius brought no harm to his people. The chorus raise that theme twice elsewhere in lyric: Darius is remembered as *ἀβλαβής* at the first report of the disaster at Salamis (555, first stasimon) and as *ἀκάκας* after the descent of his shade (855, third stasimon).[20]

Πάτερ suggests the wisdom of age and experience as a factor in Darius' success, and the late king is repeatedly described as "old" or otherwise connected with "ancient" splendor. Recalling that Darius never led his army into defeat, the chorus cry to him as *ἀρχαῖος βαλήν* (657); when his shade appears, they ascribe their reluctance to speak to a respect which springs from "ancient dread" (696 *ἀρχαίῳ περὶ τάρβει*). The connection between age and success becomes most explicit in the chorus' outburst of nostalgia following the descent of the shade (852–57):

ὢ πόποι ἦ μεγάλας ἀγαθᾶς τε πο-
λισσονόμου βιοτᾶς ἐπεκύρσαμεν, εὖθ' ὁ γεραιὸς
πανταρκὴς ἀκάκας ἄμαχος βασιλεὺς
ἰσόθεος Δαρεῖος ἆρχε χώρας.

More precisely, however, *πάτερ* is a term of human relationship, and although it may have been Persian practice so to address their kings—Kranz observed that "Vater" was a "typische Beiname des Kyros"[21]—Darius was in the simplest sense the father of Xerxes. Thus, *πατὴρ ἄκακος* used of Darius suggests for Xerxes the analogue *παῖς κακός*, and indeed Aeschylus' insistence on bracketing Darius' age with success and wisdom, and Xerxes' youth with evil and folly, has often drawn fire from critics as unhistorical.[22]

Although the contrast runs throughout the play, it is seen most vividly where references to father and son are juxtaposed. Their names occur together, for example, in the lyric passage just mentioned (548–57, first stasimon): *Δαρεῖος . . . ἀβλαβής* (554–55) stands as foil to the triple incrimination *Ξέρξης μὲν ἄγαγεν, ποποῖ, Ξέρξης δ' ἀπώλεσεν, τοτοῖ, Ξέρξης . . .* (550–52). The implications of *πάτερ ἄκακε*, however, are indicated more clearly in two passages in which the terms of relationship are themselves juxtaposed. In her speech preceding the conjuring scene, Atossa contrasts the current evils (606 *τοία κακῶν ἔκπληξις*) with times in which evil is unimagined (601–2), subtly avoiding associating either with the male members of her family. But the dissimilarity of the men's careers is implicit in the very need for the ritual at hand, and in describing her part in it Atossa sets the

20. In all three cases the epithet "harmless" is used in close conjunction with Darius' name.

21. *Stasimon*, p. 88.

22. E.g., Broadhead, "*Persae*," pp. xvii–xviii; H. D. F. Kitto, *Greek Tragedy: A Literary Study* (London, 1960), pp. 36–37; H. W. Smyth, *Aeschylean Tragedy* (Berkeley, 1924; repr. New York, 1969), pp. 82–83; Croiset, *Eschyle*, pp. 95–96; but cf. Hdt. 7. 7–19.

kinship terms side by side: "I come," she says, "bearing kindly libations to the father of [my] child" (609–10 παιδὸς πατρὶ πρευμενεῖς χοὰς / φέρουσ'). The divergence between father and son is still more strongly suggested in the language used by Atossa to report her ill-omened dream (197–99):

πίπτει δ' ἐμὸς παῖς, καὶ πατὴρ παρίσταται
Δαρεῖος οἰκτίρων σφε· τὸν δ' ὅπως ὁρᾷ
Ξέρξης, πέπλους ῥήγνυσιν ἀμφὶ σώματι.

The contrast between the two men is triply emphasized by the word order; the personal names introduce successive trimeters, and παῖς and πατήρ are not only juxtaposed but constitute the inner terms in a striking chiasmus: "there falls the son, but the father stands [by]."

Atossa's dream, unfortunately, proves all too true. If Darius' age had been proof against harm, Xerxes' youth has become inextricably bound up with evils. In her speeches following news of the disaster, Atossa uses κακά repeatedly—three times in the instructions for the incantation (598–622), twice in the six-line description of Xerxes succumbing to evil counselors (753–58), and twice as she announces that she will prepare fresh clothes for her returning son (845–51). In the first and third of these passages, Atossa explicitly uses παῖς of Xerxes (609, 847, 850). In the second, Atossa reports that Xerxes' advisors sought to provoke a fresh campaign by playing on the disparity between the two royal generations in prosperity (τέκνοις πλοῦτον, πατρῷον ὄλβον) and mettle (αἰχμῇ, αἰχμάζειν) (754–56):

λέγουσι δ' ὡς σὺ μὲν μέγαν τέκνοις
πλοῦτον ἐκτήσω σὺν αἰχμῇ, τὸν δ' ἀνανδρίας ὕπο
ἔνδον αἰχμάζειν, πατρῷον δ' ὄλβον οὐδὲν αὐξάνειν.

If Atossa expresses regret over the evils into which her son has fallen, Darius judges more harshly: Xerxes has not fallen victim to evil, but has brought it upon himself. In two separate passages the old king links the current evil with the *youthful* rashness of his *child*, and with the failure of the son to keep the commands of his father. Thus, lines 743–44:

νῦν κακῶν ἔοικε πηγὴ πᾶσιν ηὑρῆσθαι φίλοις·
παῖς δ' ἐμὸς τάδ' οὐ κατειδὼς ἤνυσεν νέῳ θράσει,

and 781–83 (Darius is speaking):

ἀλλ' οὐ κακὸν τοσόνδε προσέβαλον πόλει.
Ξέρξης δ' ἐμὸς παῖς νέος ἐὼν νέα φρονεῖ,[23]
κοὐ μνημονεύει τὰς ἐμὰς ἐπιστολάς.

We see, then, that the address πάτερ ἄκακε, in itself and in its implied converse παῖς κακός, adumbrates a major contrast developed in the play. The theme of the παῖς κακός is enunciated mainly in the familial setting where mother and father meet at the central point of the play. The connection of youth and woe with Xerxes, however, pervades the drama from

23. Keeping the MS reading.

first to last. Already in line 13 the chorus (whose guardianship was granted in virtue of their age, κατὰ πρεσβείαν [4]) allude to the youth of the army's commander (νέον δ' ἄνδρα).[24] Again, in the final antiphonal lament, the chorus castigate Xerxes so insistently for the evils (κακά) he has caused that at one point they virtually recite the word's declension: κακοφάτιδα βοάν, κακομέλετον ἰάν (936), κακὰ πρόκακα λέγεις (986), δόσιν κακὰν κακῶν κακοῖς (1041). The language in which Xerxes acknowledges their charges reinforces the connection between the present miseries, youth, and dangerous novelty (1010 νέα νέα δύα δύα), and the young king himself draws the contrast with his father Darius (932–34):

> ὅδ' ἐγὼν οἰοῖ αἰακτός,
> μέλεος γέννᾳ γᾷ τε πατρῴᾳ
> κακὸν ἄρ' ἐγενόμαν.[25]

We come at length to the word with which the refrain begins, βάσκε. In context, it is the mere equivalent of the numerous other injunctions to the king's spirit to "come," such as ἴθι ἱκοῦ. But the rarity of the word, coupled with its emphatic position, may hint at greater significance than is immediately apparent. As a Homeric form, βάσκε lends the dignity of the heroic past to the ancient Darius. Further, in Homer βάσκε is used exclusively to exhort an immortal—Iris, Hermes, or the false dream of Agamemnon (*Il.* 24. 144, 24. 336, 2. 8)—to undertake a mission on earth; the shade of Darius, itself divine (cf. 643 Περσᾶν Σουσιγενῆ θεόν), is similarly exhorted to appear among men. Because of the different vantage point of the individuals here pronouncing the imperative, however, the sense of the word is subtly altered; Zeus dispatches messengers with βάσκε, the Persian elders summon Darius. Although testimonia for the word are scanty, the meaning "come" is found only in this Aeschylean passage.[26]

Thus, βάσκε strikes the ear as somewhat strange, and its prominent position reinforces the strangeness. Elsewhere in the play words for "go" are fearfully ambivalent: in the very first line, Περσῶν τῶν οἰχομένων has the intended meaning, "the Persian army is not here," but contains the foreboding that "the army has been destroyed"; οἴχομαι is similarly used at lines 13 and 60. In such a context the synonym βαίνω must also presage disaster (cf. 18 προλιπόντες ἔβαν). The negative meaning of these expressions is realized in the words of the messenger who announces the defeat at Salamis, echoing a metaphor from the parodos: τὸ Περσῶν δ' ἄνθος οἴχεται πεσόν (252; cf. 59–60). That the army is "gone" in this disastrous sense is

24. Reading νέον with the MSS. Page reads ἐὸν δ' ἄνδρα βαΰζει; he posits a lacuna following line 13 which would have supplied a subject like *mulier desiderans* for βαΰζει, citing 63, 134, 288, and 541 as analogies. In both the anapaests and lyrics of the parodos, however, the chorus describe first the Persian army's triumphant departure and then the sorrow of the desolate relatives; the two topics are not combined. It is βαΰζει which is troublesome, not νέον. For a discussion of the attempts to explain this passage, see Broadhead, "*Persae*," pp. 249–50; cf. D. Korzeniewski's remark in his review of Page's OCT (*Gymnasium* 81 [1974]: 240).

25. Defeat has perverted Xerxes' role as leader (cf. ἄναξ, ἄνακτος); he is now αἰακτός.

26. The sense in which LSJ, s.v. βάσκω, takes βάσκ' ἄλαστε (*Mim. Oxy.* 413. 60) is unclear. "*Go*, wretch," seems most likely, without further context.

repeated in the closing *kommos* between Xerxes and the chorus, but here it is βαίνω, not οἴχομαι, which is picked up from the parodos (1002–3):

Ξε. βεβᾶσι γὰρ τοίπερ ἀγρέται στρατοῦ.
Χο. βεβᾶσιν, οἴ, νώνυμοι.[27]

Hence the unusual term used to summon the king's spirit in the conjuring ritual contributes to an ambivalence which attaches to the concept of absence throughout the play. At this moment of desperation, the chorus' words harbor an unintentional irony: Darius' shade may return for a moment, but the prosperity of the father's reign is lost as irrevocably as is the host at Salamis.[28]

This deceptively simple refrain in the *Persians*, then, contains the effective elements of the incantation ritual and suggests, allusively, the important themes of the stasimon and of the whole tragedy. Major dramatic motifs are similarly highlighted by the refrains in the *Oresteia*.

REFRAIN IN THE "AGAMEMNON" AND THE "EUMENIDES"

The refrain which punctuates the opening triad of the *Agamemnon* parodos (121, 139, 159 αἴλινον αἴλινον εἰπέ, τὸ δ' εὖ νικάτω) has elicited more critical comment than other Aeschylean refrains, both for its traditional elements and for its programmatic significance. Although this refrain, unlike the one in *Persians*, is not set in a religious ceremonial, the αἴλινον cry has ritual parallels and the precautionary wish, "may good come of it," is a standard coda to prayer.[29] Because the refrain is prominent in the opening chorus of the trilogy, scholars have observed that its conflicting strains of good and ill prefigure the ambivalence which dominates the dramatic action.[30]

Critics have also seen that the summonses to celebration which close the *Oresteia* (*Eum.* 1035, 1038 εὐφαμεῖτε δέ, χωρῖται [πανδαμεί]; 1043, 1047 ὀλολύξατε νῦν ἐπὶ μολπαῖς) are the culmination, now divinely sanctioned, of the many tainted and premature cries of triumph which resound earlier in the trilogy. But we should recognize, too, that the opening and closing refrains are analogs of one another: εὐφαμεῖτε and ὀλολύξατε joyously reverse the grief of αἴλινον and proclaim the fulfillment of the prayer, τὸ δ' εὖ νικάτω.[31]

27. Cf. Broadhead, "*Persae*," pp. 236 (ad 1002–4), 38 (ad 1), who denies sinister significance to οἴχομαι and βαίνω in the parodos (13, 18, 60). Since the terms deliberately echo Phrynichus' *Phoenissae* and the outcome is known, these emphatically repeated words carry more than "factual" significance.

28. A chiastic juxtaposition in the third antistrophe (νεολαία . . . κατὰ πᾶσ' ὄλωλεν. βάσκε πάτερ) reinforces the notion: the beloved old monarch and the flower of youth are alike gone.

29. Cf. nn. 34–36 (αἴλινον), 41 (εὖ).

30. Arnoldt, *Der Chor im "Agamemnon,"* pp. 10–11, 17, 20–24, assumes that each αἴλινον refrain was first delivered as a recitative, then repeated by the chorus or one of its divisions. Such repetition, if true, reinforces the idea of refrain as emphatic theme statement.

31. For criticism of the programmatic significance of the αἴλινον refrain and resolution in the final ὀλολυγμός, see n. 10. J. T. Sheppard, "The Prelude of the *Agamemnon*," *CR* 36 (1922): 5; Goheen, "Three Studies," p. 125; Haldane, "Musical Themes," pp. 37–38, all note the general counterpoint of lament and triumph in the trilogy.

The significance of the refrains extends to still finer detail. The dominant terms, *εὖ* and *νικᾶν*, and ritual cries of joy and sorrow recur pointedly throughout the *Oresteia*. In varying guises and definitions "good" and "victory" are the prayer and boast of all participants in the tragic conflict and its resolution; contrasting exclamations of disappointment and satisfaction mark all stages of the struggle. In this section I will show how Aeschylus has adapted the ritual forms of these two refrains to his dramatic purposes while retaining much of their traditional force, and trace the themes implicit in the refrains through the course of the trilogy.

AMBIVALENCE AND THE RITUAL ELEMENTS

The first refrain, a repeated cry of sorrow followed by a wish for good, reflects an ambivalent situation in which the proportion of good to evil remains uncertain, and any good will almost certainly come at the price of some ill. In the opening triad which it punctuates, therefore, the refrain responds admirably to the ambivalence in the omen of eagles and hare, in Calchas' interpretation of the omen, and in his prediction of its possible consequences.

In the strophe, where the omen is described, good (*τὸ εὖ*) is found in the sudden appearance of the eagles, "king of birds to the kings of ships" (*Ag.* 114), sorrow (*αἴλινον*) in the plight of the pregnant hare, "stayed from her last running" (119–20).[32] The omen's double character appears also in the distinction between the two eagles, one dark, one bright (114–15). In the antistrophe it is the seer's interpretation which is ambivalent, telling of assured success (*εὖ*) at Troy (126), shadowed (*αἴλινον*) by the chance of pollution and the threat of Artemis' anger (131–32). In this stanza the dissimilar eagles of the omen are mirrored in the Atreidae themselves, *δύο λήμασι δισσοὺς Ἀτρεΐδας* (122–23). The epode concentrates on the baneful aspects of the omen: bad weather may hinder embarkation (147–48); the remedy for unfavorable winds may create trouble for the future (154–55). But here, too, both sides of the omen find a place. Calchas mixes his fearful predictions (*αἴλινον*) with great goods (156 *ξὺν μεγάλοις ἀγαθοῖς*), and the apparitions are both favorable and not (145). The chorus explicitly select a refrain to accord with the ambivalence of the omen when they sing: *τοῖς δ' ὁμόφωνον αἴλινον αἴλινον εἰπέ, τὸ δ' εὖ νικάτω* (158–59).

But it is clearly the element of sorrow, indicated by the position of *αἴλινον* and its emphatic repetition, which predominates in the chorus' response to the events they describe; "the good" (*τὸ εὖ*) is present only as the object of fervent prayer.[33] Were they reacting merely to the potential evil which the

32. Reading *βλαβέντα* with the codices. On Page's *βλάψαντε*, cf. W. B. Stanford's remarks on "improvements" in his review of the 1972 OCT (*Hermathena* 117 [1974]: 87).

33. Athen. 14. 619C reports that *αἴλινος* may express good fortune as well as grief, but his source, Aristophanes of Byzantium, has misunderstood Eur. *HF* 348–49. Athenaeus has been quoted uncritically by Wilamowitz, *Euripides "Herakles,"* vol. 2[2] (Berlin, 1895), p. 84 (in a long note which is otherwise useful), and more recently by Alexiou, *Ritual Lament*, p. 218, n. 10, who (surely in haste) describes *αἴλινον* in our *Agamemnon* passage as "a cry of joy or victory"! F. A. Paley, *Euripides*, vol. 3[2] (London, 1880), p. 33 (ad *HF* 348–49), notes the misrepresentation of the Euripides passage in Athenaeus. According to Athenaeus, *λίνος δὲ καὶ αἴλινος οὐ μόνον ἐν πένθεσιν, ἀλλὰ καὶ ἐπ' εὐτυχεῖ μολπῇ κατ' Εὐριπίδην*; Euripides, however, states, *αἴλινον μὲν ἐπ' εὐτυχεῖ*

portent announces, the elders' note of despair would seem excessive and premature. They sing, though, remembering also how that evil was realized in the sacrifice of Iphigeneia, and that further wrongs were destined to follow on that deed. Ten years after the omen at Aulis, its evil is very apparent to the elders, its good, the taking of Troy, still to come.

Αἴλινον is a standard cry of woe, but it has specific associations which contribute to its appropriateness in context. The cry imitative of wailing was early rationalized as αἲ Λίνος,[34] and Linos was identified as a god of the Adonis type, associated with agriculture and so inevitably with death in the fullness of youth.[35] Linos is elsewhere described as the son of Urania, killed by Apollo out of jealousy for his musical ability—a type, according to Plumptre, "of life prematurely closed and bright hopes never to be fulfilled."[36] In either case, the Linos image is one of youthful life cut short and, as such, suits Calchas' prophecy well: Artemis hated the destruction of the young. It suits Iphigeneia even better, cut down in the flower of her maidenhood (*Ag.* 229, 245); in fact, a musical Iphigeneia, who sang at her father's libations (*Ag.* 243–47).

Stripped to its essentials, the Linos story signifies ritual death, as reflected in the "Linos song" which accompanies the grape harvest on the shield of Achilles (*Il.* 18. 570). Linos and his mythical equivalents are associated with the problematic sacrificial aspect of the harvest and the offering of firstfruits. The cutting of the crop, or of its symbolic representative, is seen as necessary, even as desired by the gods, but also as a violent act requiring propitiation.[37] The cry αἴλινον, which connotes the ambivalence of sacrifice, is therefore particularly apposite to the offering of Iphigeneia (herself in a sense the firstfruits of the victory at Troy; cf. *Ag.* 227 προτέλεια ναῶν[38]), inasmuch as her sacrifice was simultaneously demanded and hated by Artemis. The cry also fits the imagery of dying vegetation and bitter harvest in the *Agamemnon*: αἴλινον is an apt lament for the withering of the

μολπᾷ Φοῖβος ἰαχεῖ ("Hard on the paean triumphant-ringing / Oft Phoebus outpealeth a mourning song," in the Loeb translation of A. S. Way [1912]). Here as in the *Agamemnon*, though αἴλινον itself is sorrowful, its context is of mixed good and evil.

Apparently the only other support for a positive emotion in αἴλινον is another passage in Athenaeus (14. 618D), where it is said to be the song of workers at the loom: ἡ δὲ τῶν ἱστουργούντων ᾠδὴ αἴλινος, ὥς φησιν Ἐπίχαρμος, ἡ δὲ τῶν ταλασιουργῶν ἴουλος. As these designations are assigned to the comedian Epicharmus, we must surely understand a pun. The loom workers cry "αἶ, the linen!" as they lament their hard work (cf. Gulick's note in the Loeb Athenaeus [1937]); the spinners (ταλασιουργῶν) are "wretched workers" by definition, and their song is merely the cry ἰοῦ. (G. Kaibel, *CGF* 93, interprets Athenaeus as attributing only the αἴλινος phrase to Epicharmus, but the ἴουλος statement is of similar stripe, transferring a standard hymn to Demeter to a new and punning context.)

34. Cf. Wilamowitz, "*Herakles*," 2²:85.

35. Ibid., 2²:84–85. Sheppard, "Prelude," p. 8, paraphrases, "Woe for youth dead." Cf. Alexiou, *Ritual Lament*, p. 57, and Hdt. 2. 79; G. Thomson (ed.), *The "Oresteia" of Aeschylus*, vol. 2 (Cambridge, 1938), p. 17; E. H. Plumptre (trans.), *Aeschylus' Tragedies and Fragments*, pt. 2 (Boston, 1901), p. 16, n. 1.

36. Plumptre, *Aeschylus' Tragedies and Fragments*, pt. 2, p. 16, n. 1. For the killing of Linos by Apollo, see Paus. 9. 29. 6–7.

37. J. P. Guépin, *The Tragic Paradox* (Amsterdam, 1968), pp. 63–67, 184–90 (without serious assessment of the explanation of the *Heracles* passage in Athenaeus).

38. Cf. Zeitlin, "Corrupted Sacrifice," pp. 464–67.

"bloom of the Argives" at Aulis which is described in the parodos (197–98); it could appropriately be extended to the murder of Agamemnon, which Clytemnestra regards as a sacrifice and describes with an agricultural metaphor (1390–92).[39] That "victim," however, Clytemnestra dispatches with a different ritual cry, one which more nearly reflects her view of the deed, the ὀλολυγμός.[40] Of this, more later.

Τὸ δ' εὖ νικάτω reflects standard liturgical practice; such a wish was regularly included in prayer.[41] Indeed, it recurs two more times in the present song—in Agamemnon's εὖ γὰρ εἴη upon his decision to sacrifice Iphigeneia (217) and in the chorus' closing words, "may success attend upon these things" (255).[42]

In all three cases the wish for good is associated with some danger which it seeks to turn aside.[43] In the opening triad the danger lies in the evil augured by the appearance of eagles and hare. Recalling that omen, the elders seek to reverse its negative effects with a positive prayer for good, τὸ δ' εὖ νικάτω, just as Calchas, interpreting the portent, had deprecated its evil side with a paean (146–54).[44]

Agamemnon's prayer echoes that of the chorus even more closely. The double cry of sorrow, αἴλινον αἴλινον, finds its counterpart in the king's βαρεῖα . . . βαρεῖα, as he weighs the alternatives open to him: "dreadful not to yield, dreadful to kill my child" (206–8). But the elders, lacking confidence, at least pray for good without guile. When Agamemnon elects to proceed with the sacrifice, arguing distortedly that it must be θέμις (214–17), his attempt to avert pollution with an εὖ γὰρ εἴη (217) can be nothing more than deliberate self-delusion.[45]

The final prayer for good issue in the parodos (255 πέλοιτο δ' οὖν τἀπὶ τούτοισιν εὖ πρᾶξις) is a counsel of despair. The chorus acknowledge that the prophecies of Calchas are not idle (249). Therefore, since the "untasted, unmusical sacrifice" has been exacted, the "fearful, child-avenging μῆνις" must also come (cf. 151–55). Yet the chorus ignore the clear implications of their own words, as if to obviate their significance. "Before it happens, let it go," they say (252), "may good come of it."

In the αἴλινον refrain the almost formulaic "may it be well" has unusual urgency. The chorus' prayer for good is intimately bound up with the aspirations of prophet, king, and Argive army, although its juxtaposition with the mournful αἴλινον indicates apparent hopelessness. In the first play

39. See Peradotto, "Nature Imagery," pp. 379–81.

40. Cf. Zeitlin, "Corrupted Sacrifice," p. 496; eadem, "Postscript," p. 652.

41. Cf. H. J. Rose, *A Commentary on the Surviving Plays of Aeschylus*, vol. 2 (Amsterdam, 1958), pp. 13–14 (ad 121). Thomson, "*Oresteia*," 2:28–29, and Fraenkel, "*Agamemnon*," 2:126, give parallels in connection with Agamemnon's prayer, εὖ γὰρ εἴη (217; 226–27 in Thomson).

42. See Fraenkel's remarks on the echo ("*Agamemnon*," 2:146–47).

43. A spot check of Thomson's tragic parallels for the phrase suggests that such a verbal "knock-on-wood" is standard practice when potential evil is mentioned. Most contexts are clearly dangerous or negative: Aesch. *Supp.* 974, "The world tends to reproach foreigners, but may all be well"; Pheres to Alcestis after her death (Eur. *Alc.* 627), "Even in the House of Hades may good befall you"; at Eur. *Hec.* 902, Agamemnon wishes the old queen luck in her attempt to harm Polymestor.

44. Cf. Herodas 4. 85: a priestess prays, ἰὴ ἰὴ Παίηον· ὧδε ταῦτ' εἴη, the other character seconds her, εἴη γάρ, ὦ μέγιστε. See also n. 3.

45. Cf. Zeitlin, "Corrupted Sacrifice," pp. 493–95.

of the *Oresteia* it is indeed the pessimistic expectations of the chorus which are fulfilled. In time, however, the oft-repeated prayer has its own efficacy, even if the "good issue" of the trilogy is not one the elders could have foreseen.

THE STRUGGLE FOR SUCCESS

We see, then, how the refrain's ritual features enhance the literary context. More than that, the refrain as a whole incorporates an ambivalence which characterizes all of the tragic action in the *Oresteia*. Fraenkel has already observed a connection between refrain and dramatic structure; for him the disharmony between αἴλινον and εὖ is resolved in the trilogy by the progressive fulfillment of the will of Zeus, as expressed in the law which, however distressing when applied to individuals, ultimately prevails as the standard of order: Δίκα δὲ τοῖς μὲν παθοῦσιν μαθεῖν ἐπιρρέπει (*Ag.* 250–51).[46]

So cosmic a resolution, however, is concealed from the mortals of the drama. The refrain reveals the cruder human perspective on life—hope of change for the better, an ambition to triumph against great odds. As such it furnishes a model for the fears and hopes of individuals throughout the trilogy, but a model which is inevitably inadequate to the needs of society. Human aspirations tend to be narrow, a fact well expressed in the unusual formulation of the chorus' wish for good; the elders do not simply say, "may all be well," but rather, "may good [success?] win the victory." Satisfaction can be imagined only as the result of conflict, the dominance over another which victory implies; but human victory is never secure and dominance seems to exist only to invite further challenge.

"Victory" is, nevertheless, a recurrent battle cry in the trilogy. The setting of the tragic action against the background of the Trojan War makes νίκη an obvious metaphor for the ambitions of the characters, and in the judicial contest in the *Eumenides* νίκη is good Athenian idiom for winning one's case.[47] But the goals of victory and domination are adopted in turn by each of the principals in the *Oresteia*: Agamemnon, Clytemnestra, Orestes and Electra and their supporters, the Furies, Apollo, and finally Athene. Until the ultimate resolution each claim of triumph elicits a counter-challenge which prolongs the struggle and negates the prior claim. Only when Athene, as the mouthpiece of Zeus, demonstrates that one man's victory may be achieved without another's loss can a lasting settlement be reached.

What is τὸ εὖ for which the elders cry? It admits the meaning "moral good," but the chorus also seek fulfillment of the specific good augured by the omen—military success pure and simple. Even the definition of morality varies infinitely with circumstance and point of view. The prayer for τὸ εὖ, like that for victory, echoes throughout the trilogy, indiscriminately cloaking in respectability a great diversity of mutually exclusive desires. Only at the

46. Fraenkel, "*Agamemnon*," 2:147.
47. For "victory" as a law term, see LSJ, s.vv. νικάω, I. 5, IIb; νίκη, I. 3.

trilogy's end will personal fortune and moral right be integrated in a resolution which is simultaneously conducive to social and cosmic harmony.

In the refrain the chorus first cry αἴλινον, then pray for success, and hence implicitly desire also to exchange their sighs of grief for the vaunt of triumph, the ὀλολυγμός. As the action unfolds, intermittent peals of the ὀλολυγμός seem to signal fulfillment of the elders' hopes, but on each hallelujah follows another groan of woe. This alternation of the tones of joy and sorrow is the necessary consequence of the restricted perceptions of characters who struggle to realize conflicting visions of success; it can cease only when the nature of "good victory" is permanently established by one whose vision transcends human limitations. The lament was uttered in a context of prayer, and the exultation will likewise find its lasting and proper expression only in a divinely sanctioned setting in which the peal of celebration resonates in genuine harmony with an admonition to piety.

Independent of the ritual forms and motific ambivalence in the refrain, therefore, the words of the refrain are themselves thematically important. This will emerge more clearly in an examination of the expanding significance in the *Oresteia* of νικᾶν and its cognates and of the substantive εὖ and its principal compounds such as εὐτυχεῖν and εὔφρων. The development of these themes can then be related to the antiphony of joy and sorrow, and especially to the final summons, εὐφαμεῖτε and ὀλολύξατε, which together announce the long-awaited consonance of piety and victory.

VICTORY

Aeschylus has described each of the major conflicts in the *Oresteia* in the language of victory. The fact and nature of Agamemnon's conquest of Troy, the success of Clytemnestra's plot to kill her husband and assume his throne, that of Orestes' plot to kill his mother at Apollo's direction, the conflicting claims of the parties in the trial in Athens—all find expression in the terms νίκη and νικᾶν. Even apparently casual or metaphorical uses of the words have applications to one or more of these four themes.[48] When one character's victory is contended by another, that, too, is reflected in the language. Although the struggles in the trilogy have varying implications, all the principals share at base a competitive orientation.[49] And, indeed, each act of vengeance requires the active contest, the almost martial strife, implicit in the term νίκη.

In the *Agamemnon* the frequency of νίκη and νικᾶν in Clytemnestra's speeches indicates an unequaled drive for dominance. Moreover, by carefully manipulating her words, the queen strives to turn the gods' grant to her husband of victory at Troy into a guarantee, even a justification, of success in her plot against him. In this play Clytemnestra controls the use of

48. On the other hand, "victories" outside these contexts are described by other terms; cf. *Ag.* 935, *Eum.* 728.

49. Winnington-Ingram, "Clytemnestra," pp. 130–40, sees the νίκη-terms as part of the battle between the sexes for power (κράτος, ἀρχή, νίκη), but that theme, however pervasive, is only one dimension of the broader struggle for νίκη which is developed "consistently and importantly" (Zeitlin's criteria, "Corrupted Sacrifice," pp. 463–64) throughout the trilogy.

"victory" language, and the words of other characters play against her own.

Reporting that the Trojan War is won, Clytemnestra assigns a share in that victory to the "runners" whose beacon relay brought word of it home to Argos: νικᾷ δ' ὁ πρῶτος καὶ τελευταῖος δραμών (314). If the news has arrived, the Greek troops themselves have yet to follow. The triumphant flight of the beacons would have been impeded had the watchers not resisted sleep (290–91 οὐδ' . . . ὕπνῳ νικώμενος); just so, the army's victorious return might be hindered by sacrilegious greed. The queen deprecates this possibility, making an omen of verbal repetition: ἔρως δὲ μή τις πρότερον ἐμπίπτῃ στρατῷ / πορθεῖν ἃ μὴ χρή, κέρδεσιν νικωμένους (341–42).

More ominous for being unconscious, however, is a further echo by the herald who arrives to confirm the beacons. He seems to tarnish the triumph of his message when, weighing the pain of war against the joy of final success, he expresses his conclusion, νικᾷ τὸ κέρδος (571). At this point, when the loss of the fleet is still unknown, the herald's very presence refutes the dangerous *kledon*,[50] and the chorus, professing to be "conquered" by his words (583), accept his evaluation of the Trojan campaign. Thus far νίκη and νικᾶν have applied exclusively to the discussion of the victory, which Agamemnon, returning, formally claims and prays to stabilize: νίκη δ', ἐπείπερ ἕσπετ', ἐμπέδως μένοι (854).

Agamemnon's wish will not be granted, for victory begins to shift to Clytemnestra's camp. By recalling the phrase she used to describe the watchful beacon "runner" (cf. 290–91), the queen reveals her intention of duplicating the success of the signal relay in her plot against Agamemnon. Of the "celebrations" in honor of his homecoming she says, "A concern not conquered by sleep (912 οὐχ ὕπνῳ νικωμένη) will tend to them." In the carpet scene Clytemnestra's aspirations to victory become transparent (941–43):[51]

> Κλ. τοῖς δ' ὀλβίοις γε καὶ τὸ νικᾶσθαι πρέπει.
> Αγ. ἦ καὶ σὺ νίκην τήνδε δήριος τίεις;
> Κλ. πιθοῦ· κρατεῖς μέντοι παρεὶς ἑκὼν ἐμοί.

Agamemnon's incredulity at his wife's insistence on gaining the upper hand does not engender caution. He succumbs. After the murder, Clytemnestra denies the elders any authority to criticize her except from the same position of power she has obtained: ἀπειλεῖν ὡς . . . ἐκ τῶν ὁμοίων, χειρὶ νικήσαντ' ἐμοῦ ἄρχειν (1422–24).[52]

In time her challenge is met, not by the Argive elders, but by her own children. The vulnerability of the victories of both Agamemnon and Clytem-

50. An apparently casual utterance interpretable as an omen; cf. J. J. Peradotto, "Cledonomancy in the *Oresteia*," *AJP* 90 (1969): 1–21, esp. 11–12; Lebeck, "*Oresteia*," p. 215, n. 11.

51. Reading with Murray and Fraenkel. See Fraenkel, "*Agamemnon*," 2:426–27 (ad loc.); cf. Goheen, "Three Studies," pp. 129–30; Winnington-Ingram, "Clytemnestra," pp. 133–34.

52. Thomson, "*Oresteia*," 2:138, argues for Wilamowitz' νίκη τέλειος at *Ag*. 1378 over Heath's νείκης παλαιᾶς (or MS νίκης παλαιᾶς). Although Wilamowitz' reading necessitates greater change of the MS, it makes better sense and echoes two important concepts from the carpet scene. Eager for νίκη, after Agamemnon enters the house, the queen prays, Ζεῦ Ζεῦ τέλειε (973–74). Similarly, Winnington-Ingram, "Clytemnestra," p. 134, n. 45.

nestra is pointed up by verbal similarity. In the first play the queen had sought to assure herself the prerogative of punishing Agamemnon by praying that the return of the Greeks from Troy not be forestalled by any "ἔρως to do what they must not, conquered (νικωμένους) by gain" (341–42). That "conquering passion" had prevailed, in the sack of the Trojan temples (527), but had not deprived Clytemnestra of her own victory. The chorus of the *Choephoroi*, seeking a precedent for Clytemnestra in natural and human horrors, unwittingly revert to her own language of destructive ἔρως and distorted victory: θηλυκρατὴς ἀπέρωτος ἔρως παρανικᾷ κνωδάλων τε καὶ βροτῶν (600–601).[53]

The campaign for νίκη is now taken up by the royal children. The idea figures prominently in Electra's appeal for vengeance to her father's spirit (*Ch.* 147–48 ἡμῖν δὲ πομπὸς ἴσθι . . . σὺν . . . δίκῃ νικηφόρῳ) and in the chorus' similar appeals to the chthonic powers (477–78 πέμπετ' ἀρωγὴν παισὶν προφρόνως ἐπὶ νίκῃ) and to Zeus (868 εἴη δ' ἐπὶ νίκῃ).[54] Orestes, like Clytemnestra in the *Agamemnon*, is so obsessed with victory that he fashions favorable omens from events leading up to the stroke of retribution. Telling the false tale of his own death, Orestes speaks as if Clytemnestra's acceptance of the urn for burial in Argos would symbolize victory (683 εἴτ' οὖν κομίζειν δόξα νικήσει φίλων); and he accepts Pylades' advice, to regard anyone his enemy rather than the gods (902), as "victorious," that is, as insuring his own ability to overcome Clytemnestra's appeal to her motherhood (903 κρίνω σε νικᾶν, καὶ παραινεῖς μοι καλῶς).[55]

Because each apparent victory is met with a further challenge, there is a recurring confusion about the roles of conqueror and conquered. As Clytemnestra confronts Agamemnon, she induces him to walk on the tapestries by arguing that a victor should be great enough to submit on occasion: τοῖς δ' ὀλβίοις γε καὶ τὸ νικᾶσθαι πρέπει (*Ag.* 941). Orestes, in turn, before the encounter with his mother, reminds Agamemnon's spirit that his defeat may yet be reversed, and pleads, "Grant your aid, εἴπερ κρατηθεὶς γ' ἀντινικῆσαι θέλεις" (*Ch.* 499). On the point of facing Orestes, Clytemnestra is much more direct: εἰδῶμεν εἰ νικῶμεν ἢ νικώμεθα (*Ch.* 890).

The second play, like the first, sees the erstwhile victor defeated. But Orestes, unlike Clytemnestra (cf., e.g., *Ag.* 1388–92), experiences no exultation. He finds the victory polluted (*Ch.* 1017 ἄζηλα νίκης τῆσδ' ἔχων μιάσματα)[56] and himself overcome almost immediately by fear and frenzy (1023–24 φέρουσι γὰρ νικώμενον φρένες δύσαρκτοι). An assurance by the chorus that he has succeeded magnificently (1052 μὴ φοβοῦ, νικῶν πολύ) is of no avail. Ultimate victory in this conflict remains an illusion.

In the *Eumenides* the struggle for domination continues, this time between Orestes and his mother's Furies. Here the contest is openly avowed rather

53. See Winnington-Ingram, "Clytemnestra," p. 138, n. 76, for fuller analysis.

54. Similarly, Electra invokes Κράτος as ally (244–45) and prays for εὔμορφον κράτος (490).

55. Winnington-Ingram, "Clytemnestra," p. 140, sees Apollo as the victor here, and the δαίμων as the victor in the *Agamemnon* (p. 136, n. 59); ultimately, however, the victories of these divinities are no more permanent than those of the human actors.

56. Cf. Zeitlin, "Corrupted Sacrifice," pp. 496–97.

than secretly plotted; played out in an arena of reason, not violence; and ultimately resolved in a draw, with each contender a winner, in the transcendent victory of Zeus and of mankind as symbolized by Athens.

The fight continues to be described in the language of victory. Both parties are warned against any weakness in the preliminary skirmishes that might preclude victory in the direct encounter; Apollo, echoing the chorus of the *Choephoroi* (cf. 1052), counsels Orestes, μὴ φόβος σε νικάτω φρένας (88); Clytemnestra urges the Furies, μή σε νικάτω πόνος (133).[57] Athene monitors the conditions for the ensuing struggle. She insists on a consideration of motives, not permitting a decision based on an oath which merely stipulates whether the deed was done: ὅρκοις τὰ μὴ δίκαια μὴ νικᾶν λέγω (432). Undaunted, both sides share absolute conviction that they will prevail, the Furies threatening blight on the state should they be defeated (477 μὴ τυχοῦσαι πράγματος νικηφόρου),[58] Apollo arrogantly enunciating his expectation as fact (722 νικήσω δ' ἐγώ).

In the event, Athene and her newly established court of Athenian citizens adjudicate the matter in a way unmatched in the trilogy—in a victory which does not involve a corresponding defeat. Aeschylus formulates this precisely. As the final ballots are deposited, Athene announces the minimum condition of Orestes' acquittal: νικᾷ δ' Ὀρέστης κἂν ἰσόψηφος κριθῇ (741). For the disappointed Furies she draws a paradoxical conclusion from the same facts: Orestes won, but they did not lose; on the contrary, they were honored: οὐ γὰρ νενίκησθ', ἀλλ' ἰσόψηφος δίκη / ἐξῆλθ' ἀληθῶς οὐκ ἀτιμίᾳ σέθεν (795–96). The goddess makes good her statement by a promise of glorious precincts and steadfast respect from the citizens of Athens (804–7).

Since Athene's elegant solution to the dilemma is dependent on the jury's absolute impartiality, it is appropriate that both parties to the dispute accord the Athenians themselves a share in the victory.[59] Orestes, as soon as the vote tally proclaims his acquittal, promises friendship between Argos and Athens, and prays victory for Athens over her enemies (776–77 πάλαισμ' . . . δορὸς νικηφόρον). A "worthy victory" is also what the Furies are instructed to invoke for Athene's city when the goddess has convinced them of their own success in the trial. "What magical incantations do you bid us make?" the Furies ask (902); ὁποῖα νίκης μὴ κακῆς ἐπίσκοπα (903) is the reply. Athene's similar and final injunction to the Eumenides also redeems the notion of "profit" which had spoiled the Trojan victory (cf. *Ag.* 341–42, 571) by transferring it to the common good: τὸ δὲ κερδαλέον πέμπειν πόλεως ἐπὶ νίκῃ (1008–9). In both cases the spirits comply.

Orestes in his acquittal, the Eumenides in their cult, the Athenians in a new political alliance and in the special care of the Eumenides—all are victors in some sense. But the ultimate victory Athene ascribes to Zeus,

57. Clytemnestra continues, μηδ' ἀγνοήσῃς πῆμα μαλθαχθεῖσ' ὕπνῳ (134). It must particularly gall the ever-alert Clytemnestra (*Ag.* 912; cf. 290) that *her* Furies were "conquered by sleep."

58. Athene's prediction, but accurate; cf. 780–87 = 810–17. The Furies anticipate general anarchy if Orestes wins, i.e., εἰ κρατήσει δίκα . . . τοῦδε μητροκτόνου (491–92).

59. Cf. Winnington-Ingram, "Clytemnestra," p. 146: the Athenians are "pioneers and beneficiaries of the new order."

Zeus and an altered concept of success and the good: ἀλλ' ἐκράτησε Ζεὺς ἀγοραῖος, / νικᾷ δ' ἀγαθῶν / ἔρις ἡμετέρα διὰ παντός (973–75).[60] In this statement we come full circle from the Argive elders' attribution of victory to Zeus in their hymn to that god in the *Agamemnon* parodos: Ζῆνα δέ τις προφρόνως ἐπινίκια κλάζων / τεύξεται φρενῶν τὸ πᾶν (174–75). The Argive chorus alluded principally to Zeus's mysterious but permanent victory over his immortal predecessor; Athene extends Zeus's triumph, both on the cosmic level, in the settlement with the Erinyes, and in the human sphere, in the institution of a revised charter of human relationships and human justice.

THE GOOD

Characters who echo the Argive elders' prayer τὸ δ' εὖ νικάτω in the *Oresteia* often reveal morally questionable goals of success (εὐτυχεῖν, εὖ πράσσειν), limited self-interest, or futile hopes. For these characters the prayer is dangerous or gratuitous, its apparent fulfillment a delusion. The Furies introduce a new context for good—fear, τὸ δεινόν. Again, it is Athene who lays the groundwork for the prayer's genuine fulfillment with her redefinition of good in terms of society.

The transformation of the Furies is a crucial factor in the goddess' achievement. In the new dispensation they become εὔφρονες (*Eum.* 992, 1030), a demonstration that true good is inseparable from good intention. Before this point in the trilogy εὔφρων and its synonyms ironically share the qualifications and imperfections of τὸ εὖ itself.

Like those for "victory," the terms for "good," "success," and "goodwill" accompany and provide commentary on the principal conflicts in the tragedy and on their resolution.

Mortals in the *Oresteia* usually pray for good in circumstances which offer little chance of its realization. Faced with alternatives of sacrificing his daughter or abandoning the Trojan expedition, Agamemnon finds neither course unobjectionable (*Ag.* 211 τί τῶνδ' ἄνευ κακῶν), and yet prays εὖ γὰρ εἴη (217). The chorus break off their description of that sacrifice to pray that all be well (255). The refrain itself, τὸ δ' εὖ νικάτω, punctuates the telling of the double-edged omen and its fearful interpretation. Beyond hope, all these prayers at first seem granted. Troy is taken.

Clytemnestra's announcement of the victory, however, almost instantly renews the need for prayer. As the queen speculates on conditions in the captured city, she dwells on the potential for evil which is still present. Thus, in the cry with which she concludes her narrative, τὸ δ' εὖ κρατοίη μὴ διχορρόπως ἰδεῖν (349), the idiom is that of the elders, but her goodwill is not equally beyond question (cf. 271); although she deprecates uncertainty in the issue, it is not clear what issue she intends. Ostensibly Clytemnestra prays that the Greek troops will resist the temptation to plunder temples

60. The Furies earlier recognized Zeus as παγκρατής (918); cf. Winnington-Ingram, "Clytemnestra," p. 145. For the victory of Zeus, see Haldane, "Musical Themes," p. 38; Méautis, *Eschyle et la trilogie*, pp. 282–83.

at Troy, the moral victory (341–42 μὴ . . . κέρδεσιν νικωμένους—"good" and "victory" appear close together here) being necessary to insure their safe return.[61] Agamemnon's homecoming, however, will only deliver him into Clytemnestra's murderous arms. The queen's next words hint obscurely at a personal request for vengeance underlying her prayer for τὸ εὖ (345–47):

> θεοῖς δ' ἀναμπλάκητος εἰ μόλοι στρατός,
> ἐγρηγορὸς (εὐηγορὸς?) τὸ πῆμα τῶν ὀλωλότων
> γένοιτ' ἄν, εἰ πρόσπαια μὴ τύχοι κακά.[62]

The dark and disputed syntax so multiplies and confuses the conditions under which Agamemnon could enjoy a clear triumph that his ability to extricate himself from all possible dangers is cast into serious doubt. Whether the "pain of the dead" be hypothetically "roused" or "smoothed over," that πῆμα is clearly a factor with which to reckon. And who are "the dead"? Clytemnestra dissembles with the plural: a few lines earlier she masked her obsessive eagerness for Agamemnon's return with a wish for the safety of the whole army (338–45),[63] and here she is thinking first and foremost of Iphigeneia's death.[64] The effect of the speech, therefore, is to preclude realization of the prayer. In the light of the potential dangers Clytemnestra has enunciated, the good seems impossible of attainment; in the light of her hidden intentions, the goal seems only questionably good.

Elsewhere, too, the context works against the hope of good issue. The watchman in the *Agamemnon* seeks good fortune for himself in the beacon which will announce his master's return (20 εὐτυχὴς γένοιτ' ἀπαλλαγὴ πόνων); by a repetition of the πόνος-root, however, he associates his own pains with those of the royal household (18–19 οἴκου τοῦδε . . . διαπονουμένου); and, in fact, that house, its former excellence already diminished (19 οὐχ ὡς τὰ πρόσθ' ἄριστα), will only sink deeper into trouble when the king returns.[65] The Argive elders later conclude an ode which recounts the people's resentment at the loss of loved ones for the sake of a faithless woman with the prayer εὖ γὰρ πρὸς εὖ φανεῖσι προσθήκη πέλοι (500). The herald appends the wish γένοιτο δ' ὡς ἄριστα (674) to the tale of Menelaus' disappearance.

The next wishes for "good" are grouped just before the crisis in the *Choephoroi*. Orestes' old nurse echoes the herald's wish for Menelaus in a situation which is similarly hopeless. Agreeing to an apparently pointless ruse which will bring Aegisthus to the palace unattended, and in despair at news of Orestes' death, she prays, γένοιτο δ' ὡς ἄριστα σὺν θεῶν δόσει (782).

61. Fraenkel "*Agamemnon*," 2:178 (ad 348–49) connects this prayer, which concludes the speech, with the future in general, not the return voyage alone; certainly, however, any future presumes that voyage.

62. Thomson, "*Oresteia*," 2:42 (ad [his] 357–59 [εὐήγορον]), and Fraenkel, "*Agamemnon*," 2:177 (345–47 [παρηγορεῖν]) argue for a word of favorable meaning. But see J. D. Denniston and D. Page, *Aeschylus' "Agamemnon"* (Oxford, 1957), p. 100, for a good explanation of the passage.

63. Similarly, Clytemnestra uses the plural in referring to the need to respect Troy's temples (338–42); but the herald connects Agamemnon alone with their sacking, in a vivid ring composition (522–31: ἥκει—ἄναξ—Τροίαν—βωμοί, ἱδρύματα—Τροίᾳ—ἄναξ—ἥκει).

64. Cf. *Ag.* 865 and Winnington-Ingram, "Clytemnestra," p. 132.

65. Cf. Winnington-Ingram, "Clytemnestra," p. 137, n. 70, on a possible reminiscence in *Ag.* 1673.

The handmaids, with more reason for confidence, continue the prayer: good fortune for the house (808 εὖ δὸς ἀνιδεῖν δόμον ἀνδρός) and for themselves the privilege of raising the cry of triumph (824 πλεῖ τάδ' εὖ).[66] "Good" is the expected result of the murders of Clytemnestra and Aegisthus; yet when those murders are accomplished, the chorus' first word is στένω (931).

Although so often the object of prayer, the good is elusive, its nature unclear. Even the apparent attainment of good fortune is not wholly satisfying. Agamemnon's herald pronounces the Trojan War a success (*Ag.* 551 εὖ γὰρ πέπρακται), but in his very next words the old ambiguity of the omen at Aulis comes again to the surface (552–53 τὰ μὲν . . . εὐπετῶς ἔχειν, τὰ δ' αὖτε κἀπίμομφα; cf. 145). Agamemnon sadly realizes that few men endure a friend's good fortune with equanimity (832–33 φίλον τὸν εὐτυχοῦντ' ἄνευ φθόνων σέβειν) and that success (846 τὸ καλῶς ἔχον) must actively be safeguarded against inevitable threats (847 ὅπως εὖ μενεῖ βουλευτέον). For Cassandra, a life of success is an illusion, a shadow, preferable to misfortune but equally evanescent (1327–29):

> εὐτυχοῦντα μὲν
> σκιᾷ τις ἂν πρέψειεν, εἰ δὲ δυστυχῇ,
> βολαῖς ὑγρώσσων σπόγγος ὤλεσεν γραφήν.

At the end of the *Choephoroi* Orestes cannot rest in the success the chorus attribute to him (1044 ἀλλ' εὖ γ' ἔπραξας), but flees into exile pursued by the Furies (cf. 1042–43, 1048–50). The chorus see him off with a prayer that he might yet fare well (1063 ἀλλ' εὐτυχοίης), but sink at once into despair over the fortunes of the house (1065–76).

For all these characters success has its shortcomings—contamination with evil, impermanence, and envy. For the chorus of the *Agamemnon* success contains the threat of another danger, impiety. Pondering the news of the victory at Troy, the Argive elders become apprehensive: too much acclaim (εὖ κλύειν) is dangerous (468–69). Yet human appetite for success is insatiable (1331 τὸ μὲν εὖ πράσσειν ἀκόρεστον ἔφυ), a universal truth the elders readily apply to Agamemnon (1335 καὶ τῷδε). This passage intimates a tendency to hybris in the successful man; man acknowledges no surfeit of success, never shuts the doors of his overflowing house against it (1332–34). The chorus had earlier associated such excess (κόρος) with injustice and impiety (381–84; cf. 374–78):

> οὐ γὰρ ἔστιν ἔπαλξις
> πλούτου πρὸς Κόρον ἀνδρὶ
> λακτίσαντι μέγαν Δίκας
> βωμὸν εἰς ἀφάνειαν.

The connection between hybris and success adumbrated in the *Agamemnon* is made explicit in the *Choephoroi*. In the parodos the chorus of maid-servants describe a city in which success has displaced all other values,

66. Kirchhoff's reading maintains the nautical weather imagery; cf. Peradotto, "Nature Imagery," pp. 386–87.

divine as well as human: τὸ δ' εὐτυχεῖν, / τόδ' ἐν βροτοῖς θεός τε καὶ θεοῦ πλέον (59–60).

By the time the matter is referred to Athene in the *Eumenides*, the need for a new conception of the good is undeniable. Against the self-serving and contradictory human definitions, the Furies advance a view which is at least less narrow. In the second stasimon (490–565) they claim that *they* are the good, since by virtue of their dire offices fear of retribution inhibits wrongdoing and reckless sinners are punished (517 ἔσθ' ὅπου τὸ δεινὸν εὖ). Athene concurs, to a degree; she adjures her citizens "not to cast dread (τὸ δεινόν) entirely from their city" (698), for justice cannot survive without some measure of fear (699).

But the goddess' vision is more comprehensive. The Furies must be incorporated into the city, but with a new orientation to their task. Henceforth, in addition to controlling evil, they must reward and foster good. By so doing, the Furies will gain a share of honor in Athene's "most god-beloved land," εὖ δρῶσαν, εὖ πάσχουσαν, εὖ τιμωμένην (868–69). Athene's assignment of good here is like her assignment of victory described earlier: it is shared by all parties. Under the old system, one man's victory meant another's defeat, success involved corresponding failure, the good was inseparable from evil. Athene rejects such destructive contests. For her, as for Zeus (973), the victory lies in a "rivalry in good": νικᾷ δ' ἀγαθῶν ἔρις ἡμετέρα διὰ παντός (974–75).

In the final scenes of the play the abstract τὸ εὖ is replaced by concrete benefits (ἀγαθά), and the Eumenides, who truly embody τὸ εὖ, compete with Athene in inaugurating the new dispensation wherein good may be common to all. The Furies wish the Athenians a harmonious exchange of joy and affection (984–85 χάρματα δ' ἀντιδιδοῖεν κοινοφιλεῖ διανοίᾳ). Athene, foreseeing victory (1009) and justice (992–95) from the Eumenides' good offices in the city, instructs her citizens in the responsibility to reciprocate: they must requite the Furies' benefactions with benevolence (1012–13 εἴη δ' ἀγαθῶν ἀγαθὴ διάνοια πολίταις) and return goodwill (εὔφρονες) to the spirits of goodwill (992 τάσδε εὔφρονας).[67]

From the vantage point of the resolution, where the spirits of vengeance become "Eumenides" or, in Aeschylus' term,[68] εὔφρονες, we can see that the compounds which express "kindly intention" undergo a development in the trilogy inseparable from that of the Furies and parallel to that of τὸ εὖ. Before Athene establishes conditions which can produce genuine good, these εὖ-compounds often cloak intrigue in the murder plots or indicate points at which appearance diverges from reality. In most of these passages we can unveil a latent truth by substituting "Erinys-like," in the primitive sense of "vengeful," for εὔφρων or εὐμενής.

67. Word repetition also suggests reciprocity in the love of Athene and her citizens (999 παρθένου φίλας φίλοι), mutuality of goodwill between Furies (1030 εὔφρων ἤδ' ὁμιλία) and citizens (1034 ὑπ' εὔφρονι πομπᾷ).

68. The term Εὐμενίδες does not occur in the surviving text. G. Hermann posits a lacuna after *Eum.* 1027, in part to allow for the expected term (*Aeschyli Tragoediae*², vol. 2 [Berlin, 1859], p. 645 [ad loc.]).

A few examples will illustrate. The Argive elders, not suspecting guile, greet the queen's contorted prayer for the return of Agamemnon with approbation (*Ag.* 351 εὐφρόνως λέγεις). Agamemnon's herald invokes the city's gods who sent them forth to receive propitiously (*Ag.* 516 εὐμενεῖς) the remnant of the host. Coming in disguise to the royal house, Orestes professes to regret that his unhappy news must preclude entertainment in so prosperous a house—"for what is more friendly (*Ch.* 703 εὐμενέστερον) than a guest to his hosts?" In truth, Clytemnestra in her wish for Agamemnon's return, the gods in their welcome of the king, and Orestes in return for the "unexpected" hospitality act, rather, "like Erinyes."[69]

Aeschylus has even contrived a link between one of these compounds and the Furies' genealogy. Deviating from Hesiod's account of the Furies' origin in the castration of Ouranos (*Theog.* 178–85), Aeschylus makes their sole parent Night, Νύξ, or, euphemistically, εὐφρόνη.[70] The spirits of vengeance themselves do not call their mother by this gentle name (cf. *Eum.* 321–22, 416, 745, 791–92, 844, 1034). Nonetheless, in the *Oresteia* εὐφρόνη refers almost exclusively to a single night, that on which Paris' theft of Helen was finally redressed by the capture of Troy. In the pointed use of εὐφρόνη for that particular "night," we can recognize the mentality which greets brutal vengeance, paradoxically, as though it were an act of benevolence. Not surprisingly, then, the term is a favorite with Clytemnestra and appears three times in her announcement of the sack of Ilium; the irony is heaviest in her opening words, in which the maternity of Night is also explicit: εὐάγγελος μέν, ὥσπερ ἡ παροιμία, / ἕως γένοιτο μητρὸς εὐφρόνης πάρα (*Ag.* 264–65; cf. 279, 337). If Clytemnestra's prayer is answered, a welcome "dawn child" will bring vengeance to Agamemnon, just as its "kindly" mother, Night, brought retribution to Troy. The king's herald ironically describes Agamemnon as he comes from his vendetta as "he who lights up the kindly time" (*Ag.* 522 φῶς ἐν εὐφρόνῃ φέρων). Aegisthus' first words play on the same ideas; addressing the day which sees Agamemnon in the web of the Erinyes (*Ag.* 1580 ἐν πέπλοις Ἐρινύων), he cries, "Oh light of good will!" (*Ag.* 1577 ὦ φέγγος εὖφρον; cf. 1581 φίλως ἐμοί).[71]

Human agents of vengeance may rejoice in their task, but they do not perform it with "kindly disposition." The necessity for human agency is disregarded by the Furies when they argue (*Eum.* 517–37) that their function of vengeance (τὸ δεινόν) both demonstrates goodwill and promotes "right-mindedness" by imposing a healthy restraint on men's minds (φρενῶν ἐπίσκοπον) which rewards them with prosperity (ἐκ δ' ὑγιείας φρενῶν . . . ὄλβος). The contradictions involved in this disquieting interconnection of εὐφρόνη, vengeance, and kindliness are alleviated somewhat when Athene transfers the vengeance function of the Furies to the Areopagus; the salutary fear which the court inspires, she says, will prevail by day and by

69. Cf. *Ag.* 950–52, 1434–36, *Ch.* 109, *Eum.* 631–32.

70. For some implications of this genealogy, see F. Solmsen, *Hesiod and Aeschylus* (Ithaca, 1949), pp. 179–83, 203–5; cf. G. Thomson (ed.), *The "Oresteia" of Aeschylus*, vol. 2^2 (Amsterdam, 1966), pp. 56–57; Lebeck, "*Oresteia*," pp. 43, 64, and 184, n. 21.

71. Cf. Peradotto, "Nature Imagery," p. 390.

night (*Eum.* 692 καὶ κατ' εὐφρόνην ὁμῶς). Night can henceforth truly be "kindly." By quoting their warning of the necessity of dread (696–99), Athene confirms that the Furies fulfill a beneficial function in society.[72] It is only when an individual mortal presumes to usurp that function that the designation εὔφρων becomes bitterly ironic.[73]

Nonetheless, like εὖ, the εὔφρων terms do not wholly assume their proper significance until the Furies personally take a part in the new order. When in addition to deterring and punishing crime they undertake to foster well-being in Athens, the daughters of Εὐφρόνη fully inherit the "kindliness" of their mother.[74] In the closing pageant Night and her children are genuinely illuminated by torches which conduct the transformed spirits to their new abode; in the accompanying celebration of mutual good will the salient terms are juxtaposed for the last time (1029–34):

> Αθ. καὶ τὸ φέγγος ὁρμάσθω πυρός,
> ὅπως ἂν εὔφρων ἥδ' ὁμιλία χθονὸς
> τὸ λοιπὸν εὐάνδροισι συμφοραῖς πρέπῃ.
> Προπομποί. βᾶτε δόμῳ μεγάλαι φιλότιμοι
> Νυκτὸς παῖδες ἄπαιδες ὑπ' εὔφρονι πομπᾷ.

As the Furies become εὔφρονες and their benevolence is reflected in human society, the elders' prayer, τὸ δ' εὖ νικάτω, is realized at last.

THE FINAL REFRAINS

The refrains εὐφαμεῖτε δέ, χωρῖται [πανδαμεί] (*Eum.* 1035, 1038) and ὀλολύξατε νῦν ἐπὶ μολπαῖς (*Eum.* 1043, 1047) have both a liturgical purpose in the sacred installation of the Eumenides and a broader significance which arises from the resolution of the trilogy.

In context, εὐφαμεῖτε is a ritual admonition to piety required by the solemn ceremonies inaugurating the new cult.[75] The imperative also captures the "euphemism" of the closing scene in the etymological sense; it echoes on the human level the compliments and good feeling exchanged moments before by Athene and the Eumenides. The exuberant religious confidence in ὀλολύξατε is at home in the closing pageant as nowhere else,[76] for the Eumenides have promised Athens eternal good fortune in return for the establishment of the cult (1018–20; cf. 1031), and the goddess Athene looks benignantly on.

As the trilogy comes full circle, the final refrains also signify the complete satisfaction of the terms of the Argive elders' original prayer, τὸ δ' εὖ νικάτω.

72. Cf. Solmsen, *Hesiod and Aeschylus*, p. 198.

73. Since virtually every other character has at one point or another acted as a "child of Night," i.e., as an Erinys or spirit of vengeance, it may be significant that the drafter of the resolution of the conflict, Athene, is in no sense a child of darkness, as Apollo declares (*Eum.* 665): οὐκ ἐν σκότοισι νηδύος τεθραμμένη. Cf. Peradotto, "Nature Imagery," pp. 388–93 (on "Light and Darkness").

74. Peradotto, "Nature Imagery," pp. 392–93; cf. Lebeck, "*Oresteia*," p. 22.

75. Εὐφαμεῖτε here (*pace* LSJ, s.v., II. 1) clearly belongs to the category of ritual injunctions barring impious speech, and is so taken, e.g., by Goheen, "Three Studies," p. 124, n. 25; Thomson, "*Oresteia*," 2^{2}:233 (ad 1035).

76. Zeitlin, "Corrupted Sacrifice," p. 496.

In εὐφαμεῖτε, "sing εὖ," the Athenians celebrate the combination of advantage with morality which only Athene was able to effect; the inclusiveness of the summons (χωρῖται, πανδαμεί) shows that Athene's settlement is at last a good (τὸ εὖ) for all society. In ὀλολύξατε they celebrate the joy of a victory beyond the Argive elders' imagination, the victory of Zeus proclaimed by Athene when the Furies acquiesced in the new order (973).[77]

Scholars have noted that this ὀλολυγμός is the only fully vindicated cry of triumph in the series of such cries throughout the trilogy.[78] But the final ὀλολυγμός is at the same time an answer to the αἴλινον of the opening refrains. It substitutes a different set of ritual assumptions and replaces the original mood of despair with exultation. Moreover, the contrast between these cries, which bracket the *Oresteia*, is emblematic of the alternation of grief and joy in the trilogy and of the eventual predominance of joy.

The sacrificial nuances of αἴλινον were noted earlier. The problematic ritual aspects of the harvest are embodied in the tale of a beautiful human, Linos, whose death, like the cutting of the crop, is mourned in the cry. As the crop must be "killed" to be utilized by humans, so must an offering be destroyed to be consecrated to the gods; in each case there is destruction of objects of value which must be compensated, mystically, by ritual lament.[79] Thus, αἴλινον is an expression of anxiety amid the uncertainty of divine approval, and it is especially appropriate in the Argive elders' response to the unholy sacrifice of Iphigeneia.

The ὀλολυγμός expresses a different emotion associated with sacrifice, the exhilarated release of tension when the victim is struck or the offering otherwise irreversibly committed to the gods.[80] The ritual enthusiasm of the ὀλολυγμός is seen especially in the cry of the Pylian women when Nestor sacrifices a gilded cow to Athene in the *Odyssey* (3. 449–52). Its almost involuntary peal may sometimes reflect a magical attempt to bind φθόνος, but the tone of this early, inarticulate form of prayer is generally positive. The sacrificial connotations of the ὀλολυγμός apparently derived from a more elemental signification: the cry was fundamentally a spontaneous expression of strong emotion. One such emotion was joy, and in particular the joy of victory.[81]

All these elements, relief, joy of victory, prayer, deprecation of divine envy, ring in the ὀλολυγμός of the Argive women as they celebrate the imminent return of their men from Troy (*Ag.* 594–97, esp. 595–96 ὀλολυγμὸν . . . ἔλασκον εὐφημοῦντες[82]). Elsewhere in the trilogy, however, the emotions of

77. For ὀλολυγμός in the joy of victory, cf. L. Deubner, *Ololyge und Verwandtes*. Abhand. der Preuss. Akad. der Wiss., Phil.-hist. Kl., no. 1 (Berlin, 1941), p. 12. In hailing Zeus victor, Athene's citizens exhibit the soundness of mind once defined by the chorus of the *Agamemnon* (174–75; cf. *Eum.* 1034).

78. See the references in n. 10, esp. Zeitlin, "Corrupted Sacrifice," p. 507; eadem, "Postscript," pp. 652–53.

79. Guépin, *Tragic Paradox*, pp. 165, 181–90.

80. Ibid., pp. 164–65; Deubner, *Ololyge*, pp. 5, 21–22.

81. Deubner, *Ololyge*, pp. 17–18 (magic), 18–23 (prayer), 12 (strong emotion), 10–12 (joy), 6, 12, (joy of victory).

82. The combination of piety and triumph reflected in the juxtaposition of ὀλολυγμός and εὐφημεῖν is genuine in the Argive women and in the beacon watchman (cf. *Ag.* 28), but it is not achieved by the main characters until the conclusion of the trilogy; cf. n. 75.

sacrificial enthusiasm and joy of victory do not combine so felicitously in the ὀλολυγμός. Clytemnestra's ululation (*Ag.* 587), though spontaneous enough, celebrates more the anticipation of her own victory over Agamemnon than his conquest of Troy. The queen also regards the murder as a sacrifice, but Cassandra shows Clytemnestra's cry of triumph, like that of the Furies in the household (*Ag.* 1117–18), to be sacrilegious mockery (*Ag.* 1235–38).[83]

The chorus of the *Choephoroi* pray (386–89) to raise the ὀλολυγμός of victory over the bodies of Aegisthus and Clytemnestra; since this vengeance is divinely prescribed and to some extent socially sanctioned, they pray with a truer heart than Clytemnestra. Nonetheless, when the anticipated moment comes, the chorus' spontaneous reaction is στένω (931); the ἐπολολύξατ' ὦ comes more deliberately, after they remind themselves that Apollo had enjoined the deed (942–45; cf. 939–41). But the vacillation of the handmaids about the bloodshed endemic in the house (cf. 466–78) requires the anxious αἴλινον, not the exuberant spirits of the ὀλολυγμός. Orestes and Electra themselves raise no shout of triumph.[84]

Only when Athene proclaims Zeus the ultimate victor (*Eum.* 973–75) and prescribes solemn rites in honor of the Erinyes/Eumenides (1007 σφαγίων τῶνδ' ὑπὸ σεμνῶν) do joy of victory, confidence in sacrifice, and piety once more unite in the ὀλολυγμός.

In addition to its ritual connotations, αἴλινον is a general exclamation of sorrow; this is clear from the mournful sound αἶ in the expression itself.[85] In the *Oresteia* its opposite is found in the ὀλολυγμός, which invariably signifies joy.[86] Joy is implicit in the watchman's greeting to the beacon, which will give rise to the first ὀλολυγμός in the drama (*Ag.* 22 χαῖρε; cf. 27–29), and in his irresistible impulse to dance (*Ag.* 31). It sounds again in the farewells of Athene and the Eumenides (*Eum.* 996, 1003, 1014 χαίρετε) and bursts out in the song of the celebrants in the exodos (*Eum.* 1043, 1047 ἐπὶ μολπαῖς; cf. 1042 τερπόμεναι). Clytemnestra explicitly avows the joy of her own exultation (*Ag.* 587 ἀνωλόλυξα . . . χαρᾶς ὕπο).

The antithetical refrains αἴλινον and ὀλολυγμός, then, represent the sorrow and joy which mark the stages of competition for νίκη and τὸ εὖ in the trilogy. At each victory or defeat, gain or loss of "good," the exclamations of characters and chorus modulate from woe to joy and back again until the end. A strophe in the second stasimon of the *Agamemnon* is paradigmatic: the Trojans' jubilant wedding song for Paris and Helen (707 ὑμέναιον) gives way in a moment to lament (711 πολύθρηνον μέγα), when the true significance of Helen's marriage becomes clear.

Just so with reactions to the taking of Troy. Clytemnestra's joy in it

83. Deubner, *Ololyge*, pp. 12, 21–22; Zeitlin, "Postscript," 647–53.
84. Zeitlin, "Corrupted Sacrifice," pp. 496–97.
85. Porzig, *Aischylos*, p. 84.
86. For ὀλολυγμός as the reverse of αἴλινον, see the parallel in Euripides' *Orestes*, a play which shares some plot elements with the *Oresteia*. Orestes and Pylades plan the crafty murder of a woman, Helen, expecting their deed to be met with a cry of triumph: ὀλολυγμὸς ἔσται, πῦρ τ' ἀνάψουσιν θεοῖς, κτλ. (1137–39; with πῦρ τ' ἀνάψουσιν θεοῖς, also cf. *Ag.* 594–97). Instead, a Phrygian slave of the household reacts with αἴλινον αἴλινον ἀρχὰν θανάτου βάρβαροι λέγουσιν, αἰαῖ (1395–96).

(*Ag.* 266 χάρμα) is soon overpowered by the grief and anger (445 στένουσι, 456–57 βαρεῖα φάτις, δημοκράντου ἀρᾶς) of the Argive citizens. Agamemnon's herald at first reports it with satisfaction (574 πολλὰ χαίρειν συμφοραῖς), but then is forced to reveal the πῆμα of the army's loss at sea (629, 638, 643; cf. 571–73); in the midst of the city's good fortune (647 χαίρουσαν εὐεστοῖ) he had hesitated to mix good with ill (648 κεδνὰ τοῖς κακοῖσι). The Greeks' triumphant capture of an enemy city is to Cassandra the mournful loss of a homeland (1167 ἰὼ πόνοι πόνοι πόλεος ὀλομένας τὸ πᾶν).

To Clytemnestra Agamemnon's death is also a source of joy (*Ag.* 1391 χαίρουσαν) in which she invites the chorus to join (1394 χαίροιτ' ἄν, εἰ χαίροιτ'); to the elders, it brings inexpressible grief (e.g., *Ag.* 1489–90, 1513–14 ἰὼ ἰὼ βασιλεῦ βασιλεῦ, πῶς σε δακρύσω;), as it does to Agamemnon's children (*Ch.* 333 πολυδάκρυτα πένθη). The handmaids of the *Choephoroi*, in turn, expect joy in the death of the usurpers (387 ὀλολυγμός; cf. 819–24), but Aegisthus' death is sorrow to his servant (875 οἴμοι πανοίμοι δεσπότου) and his mistress (893 οἲ 'γώ, τέθνηκας); and, when Orestes murders his mother, even the chorus falter, both before (931 στένω) and after (1008, 1019 αἰαῖ αἰαῖ) delivering the victory cry they had anticipated (942). The Furies would deprive Orestes eternally of joy (*Eum.* 423 ὅπου τὸ χαίρειν μηδαμοῦ νομίζεται); but, when the verdict is rendered, it is not Orestes, but they, who grieve (e.g., 791–92, 821–22 ἰὼ μεγάλατοι κόραι δυστυχεῖς Νυκτὸς ἀτιμοπενθεῖς) until Athene promises a happy abode (893 πάσης ἀπήμον' οἰζύος) and rejoicing becomes general.

These are but the clearest examples of the conflicting emotions which accompany the principal events in the trilogy. For individuals, the pattern is always that of the Trojan singers at Helen's wedding: first joy, then grief. For the *Oresteia* and society as a whole, however, the succession is that of the opening and closing refrains, and of the αἴλινον refrain itself: initial sorrow replaced ultimately by victory, good, and joy.

The trilogy's first song (*Ag.* 106 μολπαί) rehearsed the dangerous omen at Aulis and was punctuated with cries of despair (αἴλινον). From the watchman's vigil for the beacon signal, even before the elders' prayer τὸ δ' εὖ νικάτω, mortals had longed for an end of woes (*Ag.* 20) and a good in which they could rejoice (cf. *Ag.* 28 ὀλολυγμὸν εὐφημοῦντα). Impiety and narrow self-interest had belied early claims of achieving that goal, a goal which required nothing less than the transcendent victory of Zeus. When good became the shared concern of society under divine auspices, only then could true piety (εὐφαμεῖτε) and genuine joy (ὀλολύξατε) combine, and song become part of the general rejoicing: εὐφαμεῖτε δὲ πανδαμεί, ὀλολύξατε νῦν ἐπὶ μολπαῖς. The stages of progression toward this resolution are clearly marked, not least by the poet's use throughout the *Oresteia* of the terms which dominate its refrains—victory, good, ritual cries.

In conclusion, the refrains in the *Persians* and the *Oresteia* exhibit both a primitive aspect, in the use of ritual and traditional elements, and an artistic sophistication, in the adaptation of these elements to their context and in the use of repetition to emphasize key ideas. We may go a bit farther. The choruses of Argive and Persian elders are locked in the past, and the refrains they sing reflect the old order, the benevolent paternalism of Darius, a system of honor inseparable from a destructive vendetta. Within the refrains, however, are concepts which are not so fixed. The association of departure and death, the suggestion of youthful folly as the antithesis of ancient wisdom: these themes pervade and partly define the tragedy in the *Persians* quite independently of the dramatic role assigned to the play's chorus. In the economy of the *Oresteia*, νίκη and τὸ εὖ of the elders' prayer take on a life of their own, to be realized, ultimately, in a way that would have exceeded those elders' imperfect understanding. The joy and confidence of the final *Eumenides* refrains, on the other hand, are tied to the image of divine intervention in the progress of human affairs. These refrains, then, anchored in tradition, are at the same time submissive to the poet's creative will.[87]

University of Santa Clara

87. I wish to express my appreciation to Professor Anne Burnett for her encouragement and expert direction of the dissertation from which this article was derived; I am grateful also to the anonymous *CP* reader for suggestions which strengthened this paper. All remaining defects are my own responsibility.

ARISTOTLE'S CRITICISM OF EUDOXAN HEDONISM

ROSLYN WEISS

In the final book of the *Nicomachean Ethics*,[1] Aristotle reveals his view of the nature of the chief good, εὐδαιμονία. He presents this view as the only reasonable and acceptable alternative to the untenable opinions of his opponents. Having already dispensed with many of these views—notably Plato's belief in one universal form, the Good, common to all good things, and Speusippus' doctrine that the good is certainly not pleasure, for all pleasure is evil—Aristotle faces a new adversary, Eudoxus, for whom pleasure is not simply good, but is, in fact, *the* good.

It must be noted that the Eudoxan view is the only one that Aristotle does not specifically treat in his discussion of pleasure in Book 7. There Aristotle criticizes negative views about pleasure so harshly (including the mildly negative view that, even if some pleasures are good, pleasure cannot be the supreme good) that he comes dangerously close to committing himself to the position that pleasure is indeed the supreme good. He goes so far as to say that (1153b7–15),

> And if certain pleasures are bad, that does not prevent the chief good from being some pleasure, just as the chief good may be some form of knowledge though certain kinds of knowledge are bad. . . . Thus the chief good would be some pleasure, though most pleasures might perhaps be bad without qualification. And for this reason all men think that the happy life is pleasant and weave pleasure into their ideal of happiness—and reasonably too . . .

It is true that in Book 1 Aristotle characterizes those who identify the good with pleasure as vulgar men who prefer a life suitable to beasts. But even this seemingly harsh denunciation is tempered with the phrase "not without some ground," οὐκ ἀλόγως (1095b15). Already in Book 1, then, it is apparent that Aristotle will encounter difficulties in his investigation of pleasure; he can neither praise nor condemn it without qualification.

Even discounting Book 7's favorable remarks about pleasure (on the improbable assumption that Aristotle did not write it),[2] his ambivalent feelings toward pleasure are still apparent. Very early in the *Ethics* Aristotle admits that pleasure is a necessity for the happy life. In fact, Aristotle says in Book 1 that the man who does not take pleasure in virtuous actions is not even good (1099a17–18) and that the happy life is thus also the most pleasant (1099a24–25). Therefore, when he attempts to refute the Eudoxan view that pleasure is the good, Aristotle faces greater difficulties than he did in

1. I have used the Greek edition of I. Bywater (London, 1920) and the English translation of W. D. Ross (London, 1931) throughout.

2. See, e.g., A. Grant (ed.), *The "Ethics" of Aristotle*, 2 vols. (London, 1855), 1:34, 38, 145, who attributes Book 7 to Eudemus (not accepted by most authorities).

0009-837X/79/7403-0002$00.75

his refutation of Speusippus. His greatest difficulty, no doubt, lies in the striking similarity between arguments he uses elsewhere in the *Ethics* and arguments he presents as constituting Eudoxus' proof for pleasure as the chief good.

The first argument (1172b9–15), which may be a direct quotation of Eudoxus,[3] begins with the premise that all things—both rational and irrational—aim at, and choose, pleasure. Since each thing chooses what is good for it, if there is one good which all things choose, it must be good for all. That which is most chosen, that at which all things aim, is thus the greatest good; since pleasure is that thing, pleasure is the greatest good.

At this point Aristotle injects the superfluous comment that Eudoxus' arguments were accepted, not for their own value, but because of the excellence of his character: although Eudoxus argues that pleasure is the good, he is himself remarkably self-controlled. This comment has been variously interpreted. Surprisingly, some critics consider this passage merely a tribute to Eudoxus' character.[4] It seems evident, however, that this same tribute also serves as a device for belittling Eudoxus' argument. Why did Aristotle prefer an ad hominem to a straightforward argument?

Apparently Aristotle simply could not refute the Eudoxan argument. In fact, in Book 7 he uses Eudoxus' first argument to support the same conclusion (except for a qualifying "somehow," πῶς). He writes, "And indeed the fact that all things, both brutes and men, pursue pleasure is an indication of its being somehow the chief good" (1153b25–26). This passage has generated much discussion because it is inconsistent with Aristotle's refutation elsewhere of precisely this view.[5] We need not, however, read as far as Book 7 to find Aristotle using this Eudoxan argument, for the very first paragraph of the *Nicomachean Ethics* defines the good along the same lines: "Every art and every inquiry, and similarly every action and pursuit, is thought to aim at some good; and for this reason the good has rightly been declared to be that at which all things aim" (1094a1–3). For Aristotle, then, as for Eudoxus, the fact that all things aim at some one thing is an indication that that thing is, in fact, the good.[6]

3. Aristotle never uses ἔλλογα (1172b10) for λόγον ἔχοντα; see J. Burnet (ed.), *The "Ethics" of Aristotle* (London, 1900), p. 442; Grant, *"Ethics,"* 2:316.

4. E.g., Grant, *"Ethics,"* 2:316. Since in Book 1 Aristotle characterizes as most vulgar (φορτικώτατοι) those who identify the good with pleasure, this tribute to Eudoxus' character is unexpected. There is, however, another respectable sort of man introduced in connection with pleasure, ὁ σπουδαῖος, mentioned at 1176a16 and again at 1176b25. I do not think, however, that Eudoxus and ὁ σπουδαῖος have much in common for a number of reasons: (*a*) the specific virtue of Eudoxus, namely, his σωφροσύνη, is not attributed to ὁ σπουδαῖος; (*b*) the distinguishing mark of ὁ σπουδαῖος, his reliability as a gauge of the authenticity of particular pleasures, is not applied to Eudoxus; (*c*) popular opinion is apparently unswayed by ὁ σπουδαῖος—it is far more impressed with the lifestyle of those ἐν δυναστείαις (1176b16–17)—but, if we are to believe Aristotle, it readily accepts the philosophical position of the temperate Eudoxus; and (*d*) in the case of Eudoxus, though certainly not in the case of ὁ σπουδαῖος, Aristotle links excellence of character to mediocrity of argument.

5. See, e.g., W. D. Ross, *Aristotle* (London, 1953), p. 227; G. E. R. Lloyd, *Aristotle: The Growth and Structure of His Thought* (Cambridge, 1968), pp. 235–36; cf. W. F. R. Hardie, *Aristotle's Ethical Theory* (Oxford, 1968), p. 294.

6. Ross (on the first page of his translation), Burnet (*"Ethics,"* p. 442), and M. Ostwald (*Aristotle: "Nicomachean Ethics"* [New York, 1962], p. 3) think Aristotle may be referring specifically to Eudoxus here.

Eudoxus' second argument (1172b18–20) reasons that, since pain is an object of aversion to all things, and since pleasure is its opposite, pleasure must be the object of choice for all things. Once again Aristotle offers a similar argument in Book 7. He establishes pain as that which is to be avoided, and continues, "the contrary of that which is to be avoided, *qua* something to be avoided and bad, is good" (1153b3–4).

The argument in Book 10 does not quite establish that pleasure is the good, for that conclusion requires the further claim that being most desirable[7] is a sufficient condition for being the good. This, of course, is the claim of the first argument, but, according to Aristotle, Eudoxus believes that it is οὐχ ἧττον . . . φανερὸν (1172b18)—"no less clear"—from the second argument than from the first that pleasure is the good. Surely, however, this is not so; the second argument establishes only that pleasure is most desirable. (The argument in Book 7, on the other hand, does make the connection between being an object of choice and being a good, but does not make the strong claim that pleasure is most desirable and therefore that it is the chief good.) Aristotle does not comment upon this second argument until later (1176a6–13), when he actually defends it.

Nor does Aristotle fault the third argument (1172b20–23).[8] This argument, which maintains that pleasure is most worthy of choice since it is desirable in itself and not for the sake of some further good, approximates Aristotle's own view of pleasure. Aristotle actually concedes to Eudoxus here, and declares most emphatically elsewhere,[9] that pleasure is good and desirable in itself.

Nevertheless, Aristotle and Eudoxus (at least as he is represented here) do differ. For it seems that Eudoxus accepts the quality of being an object of choice "in itself" as somehow a sufficient condition for being most desirable. For Aristotle, however, since many things are good in themselves (for example, health, honor[10]), this criterion alone could not possibly determine the unique supreme good.[11]

Indeed, there is little justification for identifying the phenomenon of being an object of choice in itself with that of being most desirable. And one begins to wonder if Eudoxus really intended such an identification. We certainly have no reason to suppose that Eudoxus believed pleasure to be the only thing good in itself; and, if Eudoxus accepted the plurality of things

7. This is a standard translation of the τὸ μάλιστα which appears at 1172b11 as the superlative of τὸ αἱρετόν. Ross's rendering, "most the object of choice," is perhaps more accurate, but it is too cumbersome to be used more than once.

8. Some commentators regard this argument as part of the previous one; cf. H. H. Joachim, *Aristotle: The "Nicomachean Ethics"* (Oxford, 1951), p. 263. Others regard it as distinct; cf. Grant, *"Ethics,"* 2:316.

9. Aristotle claims that pleasure is good in itself in Book 1 (1096b16–20), objecting to Plato's view that the form of the Good is the only thing truly good in itself.

10. Despite Aristotle's trenchant refutation of honor as τἀγαθόν at 1095b22–30, he later states unequivocally (1096b16–19 and esp. 1097b2–4) that honor is among those goods that are good in themselves.

11. For Aristotle, the sufficient condition for being the good is being the ultimate end of all human action. Although pleasure, honor, and health, for example, are desired for themselves, they are also desired for the sake of εὐδαιμονία. Εὐδαιμονία alone is desired for itself and not for any further good (1097a28–1097b6).

good in themselves, then for him, as for Aristotle, the criterion of being good in itself is insufficient to identify the chief good.[12]

In the fourth and final argument (1172b23–25) confusion regarding the goal of Eudoxus' argumentation appears once again. The argument states that a good can only be improved by the addition of something good and that the addition of pleasure to goods such as justice and temperance renders them more desirable. Aristotle notes that this argument proves, not that pleasure is the chief good, but merely that it is good or a good;[13] he neglects to tell us whether Eudoxus insisted that it is meant to prove more. Perhaps Aristotle himself did not know. Is it not therefore possible that Eudoxus himself did not specify what this last argument, or indeed any of the previous ones, sought to prove? Is it unreasonable to suppose that Aristotle was responsible for supplying the specific conclusions of all or some of the Eudoxan arguments?

Of course, Aristotle is our main authority on Eudoxus. But, if all he really knew is that Eudoxus believed that pleasure is the good and that he offered the four arguments just discussed to support his view, it is conceivable that Aristotle's presentation of these arguments constitutes only an imperfect interpretation of them. Even if Aristotle is quoting the arguments themselves,[14] the order in which he chooses to present them and his opinion as to what they are intended to prove may be mistaken.[15]

It is interesting that the order of the points in a non-Aristotelian account of the argument for the supremacy of pleasure found in Alexander of Aphrodisias' *Commentaria* on Aristotle's *Topics* is not the same as it is in the *Ethics*. Alexander discusses the view that pleasure is the highest good, but in presenting the argument he says *first* that pleasure is good in itself (δι' αὑτό) and hence is an ἀγαθὸν τέλος, and *second* that pleasure is desired by all things, both rational and irrational, and hence is μάλιστα κατὰ φύσιν τελικώτατον.[16]

12. A parallel case occurs in Book 1, where Aristotle says: "Eudoxus also seems to have been right in his method of advocating the supremacy of pleasure; he thought that the fact that, though a good, it is not praised indicated it to be better than the things that are praised, and that this is what God and the good are; for by reference to these all other things are judged" (1101b27–31). Here Aristotle appears to accept the claim that pleasure is not praised and that it is therefore better than things that are praised, but he nevertheless rejects the absolute supremacy of pleasure. Eudoxus, like Aristotle, may have believed that the quality of not being praised is a criterion for the relative superiority of pleasure but not for its absolute superiority.

13. The weakness of this argument (if indeed it is meant to prove the stronger claim that pleasure is the good) caused L. von Spengel (*Aristotelische Studien*, vol. 1 [Berlin, 1863], p. 50) to interpret the Eudoxan argument quite differently. He thought that Eudoxus argued that the addition of pleasure to any good thing, however small, makes that good thing better than any other good thing, however great.

14. In the third argument there is reason to believe that the direct quotation from Eudoxus begins *after* the identification between being an object of choice in itself and being most desirable is made—probably at οὐδένα γὰρ ἐπερωτᾶν (1172b22); see Burnet, "*Ethics*," p. 442. Unless this is a direct quotation, it is difficult to account for the redundancy of the argument. On the other hand, if it is a direct quotation, there is a basis and justification for Aristotle's previous interpretation of Eudoxus' position.

15. Aristotle here excludes one of Eudoxus' arguments, which he cites in Book 1 (1101b27–31), apparently because it suits his purpose to do so.

16. M. Wallies (ed.), *Alexandri Aphrodisiensis in Aristotelis "Topicorum" libros octo commentaria*

Surely this order is more acceptable than Aristotle's because, unless it is first established that a given thing is good in itself, there is no point in claiming that it is the chief good. In fact, if we rearrange the individual Eudoxan arguments cited by Aristotle, it becomes easy to form a coherent and complete proof for pleasure as the good. The last argument (Aristotle is correct in saying that it proves that pleasure is a good but not the good) should be first, not last. Before pleasure can be established as the chief good, it must first be shown to be good. The next step is to show pleasure to be good, not solely for the sake of some further good, but rather in itself. Now that it is a strong candidate for chief good, pleasure can be shown to be most choiceworthy (as the argument from the opposition of pleasure to pain is designed to show). Finally, it must be proved that the most choiceworthy thing is the chief good. This order is precisely the reverse of that provided by Aristotle.

Let us return now to the text. Regardless of whether Eudoxus intended his last argument (that pleasure, when added to any good, makes that good better) to prove that pleasure is the chief good or simply that pleasure is a good, Aristotle uses a similar, Platonic argument to show that pleasure is not the good. According to Aristotle (1172b28–34), Plato argues that, since the pleasant life is more desirable with wisdom than without, pleasure cannot be the good. Aristotle, convinced that this is true of pleasure and that anything whose value can be increased by the addition of some good is not the chief good, insists that pleasure is not the good, which must accordingly be sought elsewhere.

This is Aristotle's first attempt to refute a Eudoxan argument, but it seems rather strained. A perfectly natural observation—that pleasure makes good things more desirable and thus must itself be good—is countered by the awkward suggestion that pleasure is improved by wisdom. Pleasure may certainly be said to "accompany" something, but it is odd to speak of wisdom "accompanying" pleasure.

Aristotle tries to impute this suggestion to Plato, but it is really his own. In the *Philebus* Plato does try to prove that pleasure is not the good, and it is perhaps also true that he does so, as Aristotle says, *τοιούτῳ δὴ λόγῳ* (1172b28), that is, by an argument similar to Eudoxus'; but it is certainly false that he does so by precisely the argument that Aristotle presents here. For, although Aristotle initially represents Plato faithfully, by the end of his statement of Plato's argument and its ramifications he has in effect substituted his own argument.

Plato's view is roughly as follows: if pleasure is the good, then the pleasant life is the best life. If, however, the pleasant life can be improved by something else, then the pleasant life is not the best and hence pleasure is not the good. Since the pleasant life can be improved by knowledge, reason, memory, true judgment, and the power of calculation (these enable one to be aware of, to remember, and to anticipate the pleasant experiences of one's

(Berlin, 1891), p. 6 (lines 2–11). Burnet, "*Ethics*," p. 442, quotes Alexander's second point as a parallel to Aristotle's opening argument of Book 10, chapter 2, but does not mention the first point.

life), the purely pleasant life is not the best life and pleasure is not the good (*Phlb.* 19E–21D).

Aristotle moves so smoothly from Plato's argument into his own that he blurs the real, and significant, distinction between them. Whereas Plato says that the life of pleasure, but not pleasure itself, can be rendered more desirable by the addition of some other good,[17] Aristotle does not mention the pleasant *life* in his discussion at 1172b31–34. Moreover, unlike Plato, Aristotle cannot allow his argument to work at the level of the pleasant life and to move from there to a refutation of pleasure as the good. Plato is attacking the general hedonist position; Aristotle, an explicitly formulated argument in favor of that position. And, since the particular argument under attack makes no mention of the effect of pleasure on good *lives*, but rather states simply and directly that the addition of pleasure ὁτῳοῦν τῶν ἀγαθῶν (1172b24) makes that ἀγαθόν more desirable, Aristotle's attack must be similarly direct. He, too, must say simply, with no mention of lives, that pleasure is not the good οὐδενὸς γὰρ προστεθέντος αὐτῷ τἀγαθὸν αἱρετώτερον γίνεσθαι (1172b31–32), the understood premise being that pleasure is made more desirable by the addition of something else (presumably wisdom).

Aristotle's use of this Platonic argument is particularly objectionable because, within just a few pages of its use, Aristotle himself defines pleasure in terms of its "accompanying" function. There is, he maintains, a pleasure corresponding to (κατά) each sense as well as to thought and speculation, and each of these pleasures perfects (τελειοῖ) the activity to which it corresponds (1174b20–23).

It is interesting to observe some of the words Aristotle employs to describe the relationship between pleasure and activity. Aristotle says that pleasure perfects activity ὡς ἐπιγινόμενον (1174b33), that it accompanies or attends it (1175a5–6 ἕπεται γὰρ τῇ ἐνεργείᾳ, 1176a26 ταύταις γὰρ ἕπονται αἱ ἡδοναί), but, most important, συναύξει γὰρ τὴν ἐνέργειαν ἡ οἰκεία ἡδονή (1175a30–31). Συναύξει is reminiscent of αὔξεσθαι, which Aristotle used in the statement of the final Eudoxan argument to describe the effect of pleasure on other good things (1172b25). Aristotle, then, also sees pleasure as the perfecter, the accompanier, the bloom (1174b33 ὥρα), the augmenter of activities, and not as that which is perfected, accompanied, or augmented.

Regardless of whether it is proper to speak of pleasure as augmented by other goods, there is no reason to suppose that Eudoxus would have been forced to concede to Plato and Aristotle that pleasure can be made more desirable by the addition of other good things. For Eudoxus, the making-more-desirable relation was probably asymmetrical, working from pleasure to other goods but not vice versa.

Aristotle's refutation of the final Eudoxan argument is the only refutation he directs specifically at any Eudoxan argument. As mentioned earlier,

17. *Phlb.* 11D4–6, 11D11–12A1, 20E1–2, 21A8–9, 21B3–4, 21C6–7, 22A9–22B2, 60C6–9. Plato does say (60D) that no one would choose pleasure without memory, intelligence, knowledge, and true opinion, but this statement is in the context of his evaluation of the corresponding life of pleasure (60C).

Aristotle actually defends Eudoxus' second argument, and, as we are about to see, his first and primary one as well. According to Aristotle, anyone who would seriously object to Eudoxus' first argument on the ground that it posits an unwarranted connection between a thing's universal desirability and the notion that this thing is good is talking nonsense (1172b36–1173a1). If only irrational creatures aimed at this thing, it might not necessarily be good, but, as it is, rational creatures do so as well. It might even be possible, he adds, that irrational creatures have within themselves a natural good which aims at the goods appropriate to them. Aristotle, then, believes that Eudoxus is correct in establishing a connection between being desired by all and being good. Furthermore, Aristotle himself makes the connection between being desired by all and being *the* good both in Book 7 and in the first sentence of Book 1 (1094a1–3).

With regard to the second argument (that from the opposition of pleasure to pain), Aristotle insists that it is not the case that both pleasure and pain are evil simply because they are opposed to each other and to the neutral state as well. For, if pleasure were evil, it would be an object of aversion just as pain is; in fact, pleasure is not an object of aversion (1173a5–13). Once again Aristotle reinforces the criterion of desirability for determining goodness.

Aristotle is clearly less than successful in his criticism of the view that pleasure is the supreme good. Having conceded the commonsense notion that there is an intimate connection between goodness and desirability, and between being desired by all and being the chief good, Aristotle is committed to the acceptance and appreciation of the important role of pleasure in the good life for man. Indeed, pleasure is quite significant in Aristotle's presentation of his own view of *εὐδαιμονία*. Since Aristotelian *εὐδαιμονία* consists of contemplation (*θεωρητική*), which is an activity, it necessarily contains an element of pleasure as well—the pleasure that accompanies contemplation. Aristotle even maintains that the life of contemplation is the most pleasant (1177a23 *ἡδίστη*).

This is not to say that Aristotle's philosophy is hedonistic. Pleasure is never assimilated to activity,[18] and this justifies Aristotle in offering as his chief good an alternative to *ἡδονή* which nevertheless includes it.[19] Nonetheless, since he allows—indeed emphasizes—the criterion of desirability by all in determining the good, and since he supports three of Eudoxus' argu-

18. It is true that Aristotle seems to equate *ἐνέργεια ἀνεμπόδιστος* with *ἡδονή* when he says that the activity which constitutes happiness, when unimpeded, is probably the most desirable thing there is (1153b12 *τοῦτο δ' ἐστὶν ἡδονή*). If Aristotle is here really attributing to pleasure the status of activity, this passage will constitute his most serious commitment to hedonism. But the real purpose of this passage (1153b7–25) is to reject the view that pleasure is *ἐνέργεια* and to assert that it is the unimpeded nature of activity. For, whereas it is an error to equate *τὸ ἄριστον* with a particular pleasure, it is correct (*εὐλόγως*) to include pleasure in the happy life: no one, no matter how good, can be happy in misfortune. Furthermore, if *εὐτυχία* (which substitutes for *ἡδονή* in the latter part of this passage), when excessive, impedes activity, it is a fortiori not itself activity; *πρὸς γὰρ τὴν εὐδαιμονίαν ὁ ὅρος αὐτῆς* (1153b24–25).

19. Aristotle has no trouble disqualifying *παιδιά* (and *σωματικαὶ ἡδοναί* and *διαγωγαί*) as the good (1176b9–1177a11), but *ἡδονή* is another matter.

ments and is unsuccessful in the attempted refutation of the fourth, he has not satisfactorily eliminated *ἡδονή* as a candidate for the good. Unfortunately, Aristotle's futile efforts in this direction lead him to undermine Eudoxus and prematurely to declare: *τὰ μὲν οὖν λεγόμενα περὶ τῆς ἡδονῆς καὶ λύπης ἱκανῶς εἰρήσθω* (1174a11–12).

University of Delaware

A NATIVITY POEM OF THE SIXTH CENTURY A.D.

AVERIL CAMERON

The Latin poem of twenty-four lines which I shall discuss not only opens up questions of the development of Marian themes and imagery in Greek and Latin poetry of the sixth century A.D., especially in relation to the iconography of the Virgin, but also allows us to glimpse once again the intimate contacts which existed at high levels of society between Rome and Constantinople. In this case, as so rarely happens, it is actually possible to demonstrate a personal connection, with implications for a community of ideas between East and West that we sometimes tend to underestimate. The poem brings us into the world of Gregory the Great and his friendships within the court circles of Constantinople in the 580s, and especially with those highborn Roman émigrés whose presence in Constantinople in the later sixth century was still to make the Eastern capital seem like a cosmopolitan city.[1]

But first, there are textual problems to be discussed. The best version of the poem currently available is by Riese:[2]

Virgo parens hac luce deumque virumque creavit
  Gnara puerperii, nescia coniugii.
Obtulit haec iussis uterum docuitque futuros,
  Sola capax Christi quod queat esse fides.
Credidit et tumuit: verbum pro semine sumsit.
  Clauserunt magnum parvula membra deum.
Conditor extat opus, servi rex induit artus
  Mortalemque domum vivificator habet.
Ipse sator semenque sui matrisque creator,
  Filius ipse hominis, qui deus est hominum.
Adfulsit partus, lucem lux nostra petivit,
  Hospitii linquens ostia clausa sui.
Virginis et matris servatur gloria consors:
  Mater das hominem noscere, virgo deum.
Unius colitur duplex substantia nati:
  Vir, deus, haec duo sunt; unus utrumque tamen.
Spiritus huic genitorque suus sine fine cohaerent,
  Triplicitas simplex simplicitasque triplex.
Bis genitus, sine matre opifex, sine patre redemptor,
  Celsus utroque modo, celsior unde minor.

1. For a good counter to conventional views of the separation of East and West, see P. Brown, "Eastern and Western Christendom in Late Antiquity: A Parting of the Ways," *Studies in Church History* 13 (1976): 1–23. I am grateful to Professor Thomas Gelzer for helpful comments and suggestions.
2. *Anth. Lat.* 1. 2. 494*c* Buecheler–Riese (Leipzig, 1906).

0009-837X/79/7403-0003$00.80

Sic voluit nasci, domuit qui crimina mundi,
  Et mortem iussit mortuus ipse mori.
Nostras ille suo tueatur numine vitas;
  Protegat ille tuum, Rusticiana, genus.

In Riese's edition the poem is headed *Andreae oratoris*. The heading is given in A, the Antwerp MS of Sedulius, no. 126, of the tenth century, which Riese cites in his apparatus.[3] Although Riese appears at first sight to have revised his edition of the poem in the light of C. Caesar's article on this manuscript, on closer inspection his reporting in the apparatus criticus turns out to be seriously misleading. Caspar Barth printed a text of this poem in his *Adversaria*,[4] "ex codice ignoto, cum A faciens," as Riese reports. Thus Barth's testimony would seem to have independent value. But the very article cited by Riese shows clearly that Barth was not using a manuscript at all, but derived his knowledge of the poem entirely from Poelmann's edition of Prosper of Aquitaine, which appeared in 1560.[5] In this edition our poem appears between Prosper's epigrams and his *De providentia*. Poelmann found this poem in the same Sedulius manuscript (our A) which contained the works of Prosper, and edited it along with them. When Riese attributes to Barth the testimony that our poem is *Andreae oratoris de Maria virgine ad Rusticianam carmen*, he implies that Barth had found these words in an independent manuscript. The truth is that Barth copied them from Poelmann's edition, where they were used by Poelmann as a heading for the poem.[6] Thus the words *de Maria virgine* have no manuscript authority, but are merely a composition by the first editor based on the poem itself. We shall find that this is relevant for the interpretation of the poem, and we should not be misled by Poelmann's facile assumption that it is a poem about the Virgin.

There is in fact a different version of the last line which we must now consider. J.-B. de Rossi also edited this poem—but from Vaticanus Palatinus 833, where it belongs to a collection of inscriptional poems from the city of Rome.[7] In this version the last line reads: *Protegat ille tuum Gregori presule genus*. The clumsy and unmetrical *Gregori presule* immediately looks like a substitution for the metrically perfect reference to Rusticiana, and De Rossi, knowing the Rusticiana version from Barth but unaware of the Antwerp manuscript of Sedulius in which it is included, himself realized that the Rusticiana version must have been the original, and that our poem must have been used again for a different person.[8] In its context in Vaticanus Palatinus 833 the Gregory version is clearly pre-seventh century, and I

3. Riese refers to the discussion of this MS by C. Caesar, "Die Antwerpener Handschrift des Sedulius," *RhM* 56 (1901): 247–71; the MS was not used in Huemer's 1885 edition of Sedulius (*CSEL* 10), which also contains the epigrams of Prosper of Aquitaine and some short poems, including the one under discussion.

4. *Adversaria* 56. 16 (Frankfurt, 1624; 2nd ed., 1628).

5. See Caesar, "Sedulius," p. 264.

6. Ibid., p. 265. Caesar conveniently quotes the relevant passage in Barth which proves the connection.

7. *ICUR*, 2.1. 63 (p. 109).

8. Ibid. (note).

think that De Rossi was undoubtedly right to assume that the Gregory named as *praesul* can only be Pope Gregory the Great (590–604).[9] If, then, the poem was adapted for Gregory I from an existing version, two different versions of it were in existence already in the sixth century; as Caesar observed,[10] this can be clearly seen in the existing manuscript tradition, for different manuscripts vary according to whether they derive from the Rusticiana version, which I shall argue is Constantinopolitan, or from the Gregory version, which is Roman. Such readings or headings as individual manuscripts may have must then be interpreted in the light of this dual tradition. Thus Vaticanus Palatinus 487, which contains only the last two lines, has them in the Rusticiana version. On the other hand, a twelfth-century MS in Trinity College, Cambridge,[11] clearly stems from the later adaptation, as we shall see.

This manuscript deserves more attention than it has had so far. Riese cites it only on line 24, and it is clear from his preface and apparatus criticus on *Anthologia Latina* 786*b* that he had not seen the MS himself.[12] The last line of this version is perhaps an even clumsier attempt to mend the meter: *Protegat ille tuum genus Gregorie praesul.* Its textual affinity is clearly with Vaticanus Palatinus 833, although in this later version the text is disturbed by the omission of lines 15 and 16 and the displacement of lines 17 and 18 after lines 19 and 20.[13] For our purposes, however, the heading of the poem in this MS is of more interest than the text presented, for before the text itself are written in red the words *Versus beati pape Gregorii*, and then a heading which reads: *In diem natalem Christi.* Several points can be made. First, the poem is here detached from its context of Christian inscriptions. In this manuscript it is the last of seventeen short poems, mostly unattributed and without titles, of which all the rest are about calendars or planets and signs of the zodiac. The first twelve are about the twelve months of the year. Some attempt has surely been made in the heading to give the poem a title which will make clear its association with the others in the group, and the connection is precisely that it is about a specific day—Christmas Day. The author of the headings, whoever he was, was in no doubt that the poem referred to Pope Gregory the Great, or that it was a poem not primarily about the Virgin (as Poelmann and Barth thought), but actually about the birth of Christ. This is a valuable clue in the exposition of the poem, and one that will lead us to reject De Rossi's assumption, based on his acceptance of the characterization of the poem as being *de Maria virgine*, that it was written perhaps as an inscription to accompany a picture of the Vir-

9. Ibid.; nothing in De Rossi's collection dates from a later period.
10. "Sedulius," p. 266.
11. Cantabrig. Tr. 0. 2. 24.
12. See pp. iv, 266 (vol. 1, pt. 2).
13. My thanks to the Librarian of Trinity College, Cambridge, for allowing me to consult this MS, and for subsequently providing me with a photograph. See M. R. James, *The Western MSS. in the Library of Trinity College, Cambridge*, vol. 3 (Cambridge, 1902), pp. 116–17. Readings in common with Vat. Pal. 833 are *saepserunt* (6), *Fit fabricator* (7), *pater* (10), *dans* (14).

gin holding the child Jesus.[14] Our poem found its way into this twelfth-century MS collection of miscellaneous grammatical and technical works, many of them by medieval authors (Charlemagne, Alcuin, Bede), not as an epigram accompanying an icon of the Virgin, but as a poem concerned with a date—the date of the birth of Christ.

Before we can take this argument further, the Rusticiana mentioned in the original version must be identified. The attribution to Andreas *orator* given in A is not much help. No suitable Andreas seems to emerge from the files of the second volume of *PLRE*. As for Rusticiana, De Rossi assumed that she was the wife of Boethius, whose sufferings after the Gothic capture of Rome in 546 are described by Procopius.[15] Forced to beg for her bread, she was saved from the enmity of the Goths by Totila himself.[16] The daughter of Symmachus, she was the mother of the consuls of 522, themselves called Boethius and Symmachus.[17] But after 546 there is no further evidence. Another Rusticiana died in 538,[18] but nothing more is known about her. But there is a third, the granddaughter of Boethius, called by the same name as her grandmother.[19] This lady moved from Rome to Constantinople toward the end of the sixth century, and was there one of the circle of Westerners around the court of the Emperor Maurice.[20] We are still in the world of the great families who could span both Rome and Constantinople. Boethius belonged to the Anicii; thus this Rusticiana was one of the clan that had been such a factor in the politics of the first half of the century.[21] So far the Western aristocrats in Constantinople at the end of the sixth century have received less study, but their influence must still have been considerable, and Rusticiana the younger was a leading member of the group. We do not know exactly when she moved to the East, but her daughter married Apion III of Oxyrhynchus, probably early in the 590s.[22] She would then surely have been in Constantinople when Gregory,

14. See the discussion in *ICUR*, 2.1. 63 (p. 109): "Epigramma fortasse appictum imagini Virginis puerum Iesum gestantis."

15. *BG* 3. 20. 27.

16. *BG* 3. 20. 29–31.

17. See *PLRE* 2, s.v. "Rusticiana" 1.

18. *CIL*, 6. 32042, described as *inl(ustris) f(emina)*.

19. See J. Sundwall, *Abhandlungen zur Geschichte des ausgehenden Römertums* (Helsingfors, 1919), pp. 102–3.

20. We await a study by T. S. Brown which will illuminate this circle. In the meantime see F. Homes Dudden, *Gregory the Great. His Place in History and Thought*, vol. 1 (London, 1905), pp. 154–55; E. Stein, *Histoire du Bas-Empire*, vol. 2 (Amsterdam, 1968), p. 618, n. 1. P. Goubert, *Byzance avant l'Islam*, vol. 2.2: *Rome, Byzance et Carthage* (Paris, 1965), pp. 148–52, uses the evidence of Gregory's letters, but without reference to Rusticiana.

21. See A. Momigliano, "Cassiodorus and Italian Culture of His Time," *PBA* 41 (1956): 207–45; idem, "Gli Anicii e la storiografia latina del VI sec. d. C.," *Rendiconti Accademia dei Lincei*, Classe di scienze morali, storiche e filologiche, ser. 8, 11–12 (1956): 231–54 (both in *Secondo contributo alla storia degli studi classici* [Rome, 1960], pp. 191–254).

22. See Sundwall, *Abhandlungen*, p. 104. Despite E. R. Hardy, *The Large Estates of Byzantine Egypt* (New York, 1931), p. 37, further developed (with detailed discussion of the careers of Strategius and Apion II under Justinian) in idem, "The Egyptian Policy of Justinian, *DOP* 22 (1968): 23–41, esp. p. 35 ("after two generations of prominence in the imperial court the family seems to have retired to its native province"), it is clear from Gregory's letters that the Apiones of the late sixth century spent a good part of their time in Constantinople.

the future pope, was there as *apocrisiarius* from 579 to 586; it must have been then that the two met and laid the foundations of the friendship that was to continue until the first years of the seventh century.[23]

Sundwall was surely right in identifying the Rusticiana of our poem with this great lady.[24] During his years in Constantinople Gregory met a whole group of people with whom he continued to correspond after his return to Rome as pope. They included the empress herself, the emperor's sister, two ladies called Italica and Dominica, Leander of Seville, Anastasius the ex-patriarch of Antioch, and Cyriacus the future patriarch of Constantinople.[25] Given such a network, it is overwhelmingly likely that the two versions of our poem somehow reflect the close connection between Gregory and the younger Rusticiana. Gregory wanted her to come to Rome in A.D. 598—he says he cannot understand her liking for Constantinople and her neglect of Rome[26]—but, though "everyone" wanted to see her again, she apparently did not return. In 601 Gregory thanked her for sending a gift of a pair of curtains to St. Peter's; they had not been installed with the exact ceremony she requested because Gregory was ill with gout, and the messenger (a Symmachus) bearing Rusticiana's letter with full instructions had delayed it out of consideration for the pope's health.[27] In the same letter Gregory mentions another gift from Rusticiana, to the monastery of St. Andrew. The last letter dates from February 603;[28] when he wrote it, Gregory evidently did not yet know of the murder of Maurice.[29] But in May he was writing an official letter to the new emperor Phocas,[30] and in June he wrote to Rusticiana's daughter Eusebia, wife of Apion, urging her to forget the troubles of the *regia civitas* by keeping her mind on spiritual matters.[31] We might be tempted to suppose that Rusticiana had suffered in the debacle that struck Maurice and his family, but this is unlikely, for in his letter to her daughter Gregory only mentions the general woes of the city and Eusebia's own concern for her possessions (*divitiae*). At any rate, after this we hear no more of Rusticiana, and Gregory's correspondence ends in the following year.

It is not at all surprising that a lady such as Rusticiana living in Constantinople might have commissioned a poem in Latin, or found a poet capable of writing it for her. As Gregory's letters show, Latin was still in

23. Greg. *Epist.* 2. 27 (A.D. 592), 4. 44 (594), 8. 22 (598), 11. 26 (601), 13. 26 (603).

24. *Abhandlungen*, p. 104.

25. Homes Dudden, *Gregory the Great*, 1:154–55; Stein, *Histoire du Bas-Empire*, 2:618, nn. 1–2.

26. *Epist.* 8. 22.

27. *Epist.* 11. 26. Such was Rusticiana's deferential attitude toward Gregory that in this letter he asks his old friend to refrain from calling herself his *ancilla*. Seven or eight years earlier (encouraged by Gregory) she had been on a pilgrimage to Mt. Sinai (*Epist.* 2. 27, 4. 4). Later Rusticiana and Gregory were able to commiserate with each other when she, too, was afflicted with gout (*Epist.* 11. 26, 13. 26).

28. *Epist.* 13. 26.

29. Maurice and his sons were killed on November 26 or 27, 602: Theophylact 8. 113; *Chron. Pasch.*, 1:694 Bonn; Theophanes, p. 290 De Boor. See A. Stratos, *Byzantium in the Seventh Century*, vol. 1 (Amsterdam, 1968), p. 52; J. B. Bury, *History of the Later Roman Empire from Arcadius to Irene (395 A.D. to 800 A.D.)*, vol. 2 (London, 1889), pp. 91–92.

30. *Epist.* 13. 34.

31. *Epist.* 13. 35.

regular use not only in the imperial bureaus, but also for communication between members of the upper classes, not all of them Westerners.[32] The fact that Gregory's knowledge of Greek continues to be disputed at least shows that there were still many in Constantinople who understood Latin.[33] Rusticiana had children and grandchildren living in Constantinople, frequent recipients of Gregory's good wishes and prayers,[34] and apparently still had friends and members of her family in Rome.[35] Quite apart from these personal connections, it is becoming clear that in general there was more Latin surviving in Constantinople even at the end of the sixth century than is commonly supposed, and there must certainly still have been some professional poets or rhetoricians capable of composing Latin works to order.[36] I suggest, therefore, that our poem was commissioned by Rusticiana for her own purposes, probably to inscribe on or beside some picture which she set up herself; subsequently, perhaps, she gave this picture to Gregory, who took it to Rome, where the epigram was freshly inscribed, either in Gregory's house or elsewhere, but with a suitably (and not very skillfully) altered ending. It is possible that the poem could have been composed in Rome before Rusticiana moved to the East, but it is prima facie much more likely that it belongs to the period of her residence in Constantinople. I shall argue that the content and style of the poem very much supports such an Eastern context. Fuller consideration of Corippus' panegyric on Justin II has revealed how completely the Latin language could be made a vehicle for sentiments and subject matter belonging wholly to Constantinople,[37] and I would suggest that in this poem we have another example of the continued use of Latin. But if our poem is basically an Eastern poem, we must be very cautious about using it to illustrate the development of Marian imagery or iconography in the West.

Despite lines 1–14, this poem is not, in its total effect, about the Virgin, even though the first half does, as we shall see, contain imagery and language parallel to other contemporary Marian texts. At line 15, the writer

32. E.g., *Epist.* 1. 4 (to the patriarch John of Constantinople), 1. 5 (to Theoctista, the sister of Maurice), 1. 7 (to Anastasius of Antioch)—merely a random sample.

33. Recently, J. M. Peterson, "Did Gregory the Great Know Greek?" *Studies in Church History* 13 (1976): 121–34.

34. Her daughter, Eusebia, married Apion III; she also had a son, Eudoxius, whose wife was called Gregoria. Eusebia and Apion III had daughters (unnamed) and the son Strategius, frequently mentioned by Gregory. All of these people seem to have been living in Constantinople; see *Epist.* 4. 44, 11. 26, 13. 26, 13. 35. *PLRE* 3 will eventually make it possible to demonstrate the deep penetration of the aristocracy of Constantinople by Westerners, at the end of the sixth century no less than at the beginning. Rusticiana and her family were, after all, related to the descendants of the great Anicia Juliana, who intermarried not merely with the surviving line of the Emperor Anastasius but also with the imperial family in the reigns of Justinian and Justin II. See Alan Cameron, "The House of Anastasius," *GRBS* 19 (1978): 259–76.

35. Perhaps the Symmachus mentioned in *Epist.* 11. 26 was her brother. See also *Epist.* 8. 22.

36. Coripp. *Iust.* 4. 154 mentions Latin panegyrics as still normal. Latin in Constantinople: I. Ševčenko, "A Late Antique Epigram and the So-Called Elder Magistrate from Aphrodisias," *Synthronon. Bibliothèque des cahiers archéologiques* 2 (1968): 32–33; G. Dagron, "Aux origines de la civilisation byzantine: langue de culture et langue d état," *Rev. hist.* 241 (1969): 23–56. A series of Western ambassadors were present in Constantinople throughout the sixth century.

37. See my edition (with commentary and translation), *In laudem Iustini Augusti minoris, libri IV* (London, 1976).

leaves the Virgin and concentrates on her Son. The theme of the second half of the poem is actually Christ incarnate, and the prayer with which it ends is a prayer, not to the Virgin, but to Christ. De Rossi's supposition that it accompanied a picture of the Virgin and Child at least gives due weight to both halves of the poem, and it is well known that not until the very end of the sixth century do we even begin to find representations of the Virgin alone.[38] But I would suggest a different explanation. *Hac luce* in the first line gives a clue: why "this day"? Such a use of *hac* is typical of ekphrastic poetry, where the poet's aim is to invoke a visual scene with the most vivid language possible. He will point out individual elements in the picture, as though the reader is standing before it himself.[39] The effect is complete if the ekphrastic poem is inscribed beside or upon the work of art it describes.[40] Since the Gregory version of our poem appears in a collection of inscriptions preserved in manuscript but taken from their original sites, we can say that this second version *was* written up beside its subject, though it was clearly soon copied into book collections. As for the original poem, written for Rusticiana in Constantinople, we have no way of knowing whether it was inscribed on a wall or panel for her, too, or simply composed as an ekphrastic poem. That version, if it was inscribed, was evidently also copied out either then or later into manuscript, where it was attributed (at an unknown date) to Andreas *orator*. But whether inscribed or not, our poem is clearly ekphrastic: take, for example, the language of lines 11–12, with the vivid use of *adfulsit* of the birth of Christ. Then in line 14 the poet addresses the subject of the picture;[41] then we have *haec* in 16 and *huic* in 17.[42] *Sic voluit nasci* (21) gives us the answer, if we still need it: this is a poem about a Nativity scene. The ekphrastic pointers bring out the moment in time which the scene represents—the very birth of Christ, as indeed the scribe of the Trinity College MS or his model realized in heading the poem *In natalem diem Christi*. If the poem was inscribed on a wall in Rome, objects such as gems or medallions, which we know to have had Nativity scenes during this period,[43] are ruled out. But

38. Perhaps first in the Rabbula Gospels (A.D. 586); see G. A. Wellen, "Das Marienbild der frühchristlichen Kunst," in *Lexikon der christlichen Ikonographie, allgemeinen Ikonographie*, vol. 3 (Freiburg, 1971), s.v. "Maria" (p. 159).

39. For the manner of Byzantine *ekphrasis*, see H. Maguire, "Truth and Convention in Byzantine Works of Art," *DOP* 28 (1974): 113–40; C. Mango, "Antique Statuary and the Byzantine Beholder," *DOP* 17 (1963): 65–66; G. Downey, s.v. "Ekphrasis," *RAC* 4 (1959): 921–44; C. Mango, *The Homilies of Photius* (Cambridge, Mass., 1958), p. 290; C. Mango and E. J. W. Hawkins, "The Apse Mosaics of St. Sophia at Istanbul," *DOP* 19 (1965): 115–48, 142–43.

40. The first poem of Merobaudes, describing a mosaic of the imperial family, provides a good comparison. See F. M. Clover, *Flavius Merobaudes. A Translation and Historical Commentary*, Transactions of the American Philosophical Society, vol. 61, pt. 1 (Philadelphia, 1971), pp. 16–17, 18, n. 28 (deictic pronouns). There are many problems associated with this poem; see recently T. D. Barnes, "Merobaudes on the Imperial Family," *Phoenix* 29 (1974): 314–19. But even ekphrastic poems inscribed alongside the works they described did not always describe the works realistically; see Maguire, "Truth and Convention," pp. 113–40.

41. As commonly in ekphrastic poems; cf. Merobaudes *Carm.* 1. 23 *o felix. . . .* For *topoi* of realism in *ekphraseis*, see Maguire, "Truth and Convention," pp. 125–26.

42. Cf. Merobaudes *Carm.* 1. 11 *hic ubi . . .* , 1. 17 *hac de prole . . .* , 1. 19 *en . . . iam*, 1. 21 *putares. . . .*

43. As, for example, the splendid late sixth-century gold encolpium at Dumbarton Oaks, perhaps struck for the baptism of the Emperor Maurice's son Theodosius in A.D. 584 (M. Ross, *Cata-*

it could well have accompanied a painted panel or conceivably even an ivory. Whatever the exact object, I would suggest that the younger Rusticiana in Constantinople may well have sent it as a Christmas gift to her friend Gregory, together with a copy of the poem describing it, which Gregory in turn caused to be inscribed in his house.

The poet's treatment of the subject still needs comment, however. For, despite his ekphrastic demonstratives, the poet does not describe the scene pictorially. There are no shepherds, no animals, no baby.[44] On the contrary, the treatment is doctrinal. The poem divides into two sections, the first focusing on the Virgin, the second on the Child, and in each the entire emphasis is on the theological implications of the Incarnation. At the close of the poem the emphasis is on the Child, who is the recipient of the poet's prayer to bless the family of the donor or patron. The naming of Rusticiana/Gregory is the literary equivalent of the portrayal of the donor in contemporary donor mosaics, but it is the Child, in His full theological realization, who will bless them. This recalls the doctrinal implications of the apse mosaics of the sixth century which portray an enthroned Virgin with the Child on her lap; there, too, the focus is on the Child, and the Virgin's role is that of the "vessel of the Incarnation," so that she is less there in her own right than as the way by which Christ was able to come into the world. Closer examination of our poem will make this point even more clearly. In the first fourteen lines, we have a miniature exposition of the theological significance of the Virgin. In lines 7–10, and even in lines 11–14, there is less focus on the Virgin than on the Father and the Son. In the parts that do especially concern the Virgin, two things are emphasized: first, her submission, which is the type of faith (*nescia, obtulit, fides, credidit*) and, second, the paradox of the birth (2 *gnara . . . nescia*, 5–6 *credidit et tumuit . . . clauserunt magnum parvula membra deum*). Thus the Virgin's function is as instrument; she is not accredited with any personal qualities but appears only in a symbolic role. The poem fits perfectly into the context of the development of Marian cult and literature in the late sixth century. It belongs to a time when the later characteristic aspects of the Virgin were as yet present in only the most rudimentary forms, if at all, a time when her chief representation was still basically doctrinal, as one of the central elements in the demonstration of orthodoxy. The large number of churches dedicated to the Virgin which Justinian erected in outlying or wavering

logue of the Byzantine and Early Medieval Antiquities in the Dumbarton Oaks Collection, vol. 2 [Washington, D.C., 1965], no. 36). A seventh-century marriage ring also at Dumbarton Oaks carries a Nativity scene (no. 47.15), and the theme was common on objects such as pyxides and censers, and also on ampullae from the Holy Land of the late sixth and early seventh centuries. One might think of an ivory diptych, bearing in mind the five-part diptych of which the central part, with Nativity scene, is in the John Rylands University Library, Victoria University, Manchester. But if the epigram really was inscribed on a wall, and the picture in question transported from Constantinople to Rome, we should have to envisage a portable image, in fact an icon. Speculation about the iconography of such an image is tempting, though there is little in the poem to help us; on the basis of the John Rylands diptych, however, and others of the objects mentioned, it could well have depicted an enthroned Virgin holding the Child, with a miniature Nativity representation below.

44. For other *ekphraseis* of Nativity scenes, cf. Maguire, "Truth and Convention," pp. 116, 118, 136.

parts of the empire as well as in major cities had exactly this function—to reinforce orthodoxy, not to boost the cult of the Virgin as such.[45] Justin II was also primarily concerned with the definition of orthodox belief.[46] When he sent a piece of the True Cross to Poitiers, his action was represented by the poet Venantius Fortunatus as illustrative of the concern for orthodoxy which the new emperor had evinced already in other actions.[47] The Cross of Justin II, now in the Vatican, shows Justin and his empress Sophia in a composition indicative of Trinitarian symbolism, with the Lamb of God in the center of the Cross.[48] When the poet Corippus wished to compliment Justin's order inserting the Creed of Constantinople into the liturgy of all churches, he did so by an elaborate evocation of Trinitarian symbolism,[49] followed by a paraphrase of the Creed itself. Our poem fits very well, therefore, into such a context.

It so happens that it was the Emperor Maurice, whose court was the meeting place for Gregory and Rusticiana, who made the Dormition of the Virgin into an official feast,[50] certainly an important step in the process leading to the spectacular recognition of the Virgin as savior and future protectress of the city of Constantinople during and after the siege of the city in A.D. 626.[51] But that recognition, and the enormous efflorescence of Marian devotion and Marian hymnography and homiletic which it produced, was still in the future when our poem was composed. We can, however, find still other parallels from the later sixth century for our poem's treatment of the theme. Undoubtedly there are earlier parallels in Western Latin poetry for the wordplays used in the first part of the poem, notably in Merobaudes' *De Christo* and the *De Salvatore* attributed to Claudian.[52] But the closest parallels, totally understandable if the poem was written in Constantinople, come from the prayer to the Virgin included in Corippus'

45. E.g., Procop. *Aed.* 6. 2. 20. Procopius tells us that Justinian himself wished the churches of the Theotokos to be given priority in the panegyric (*Aed.* 1. 3. 1). Other churches of the Virgin built by Justinian: *Aed.* 2. 10. 24, 3. 4. 12, 5. 6. 1, 5. 7. 5, 5. 9. 23, 6. 4. 4, 6. 5. 9, 6. 7. 16. The great church of the Virgin in Jerusalem (the Nea—*Aed.* 5. 6. 1) has now been discovered; see N. Avigad, "A Building Inscription of the Emperor Justinian and the Nea in Jerusalem," *Israel Exploration Journal* 27 (1977): 145–51. In Justinian's theological writings the Virgin plays the same role; cf. E. Schwartz, *Drei dogmatische Schriften Iustinians*², ed. M. Amelotti, R. Albertella, and L. Migliardi (Milan, 1973), pp. 16, 96–97, 114.

46. See Averil Cameron, "The Early Religious Policies of Justin II," *Studies in Church History* 13 (1976): 51–67; A. de Halleux, "Trois synodes impériaux du VIe siècle dans une chronique syriaque inédite," in *A Tribute to Arthur Vööbus*, ed. R. H. Fischer (Chicago, 1977), pp. 302 ff. (I owe this reference to Professor H. J. W. Drijvers).

47. *Ad Iustinum et Sophiam Augustos* (*MGH:AA*, 4:275–78).

48. J. Beckwith, *The Art of Constantinople*² (London, 1968), pl. 55. See A. Grabar, *L'iconoclasme byzantin* (Paris, 1957), pp. 19, 25.

49. *Iust.* 4. 292–93. Creed: 4. 299–311.

50. Niceph. Call. *HE* 17. 28.

51. For this process, see Averil Cameron, "The Cult of the Theotokos in Sixth-Century Constantinople: A City Finds Its Symbol," *JTS*, n.s. 29 (1978): 79–108; N. Baynes, "The Supernatural Defenders of Constantinople," *Analecta Bollandiana* 67 (1949): 165–77 (= *Byzantine Studies and Other Essays* [London, 1955], pp. 248–60); S. MacCormack, "Roma, Constantinopolis, the Emperor," *CQ* 25 (1975): 149.

52. For the authenticity of the *De Salvatore* (Claud. *Carm. min.* 32), see W. Schmid, s.v. "Claudianus" 1, *RAC* 3 (1957): 158–59. For Merobaudes, see S. Gennaro, *Da Claudiano a Merobaude* (Catania, 1959). T. Birt cites earlier parallels (*MGH:AA*, 10:330).

Latin panegyric for Justin II, composed in Constantinople in 566.[53] There is the same emphasis on Mary as the type of faith, the same paradoxes, the same vocabulary. In line 13, our poet picks up Corippus' *gloria matrum*,[54] and, in line 5, the conception of the Word *pro semine* (associated also with faith—*credula*). Both use the famous and much quoted phrase from Philippians 2: 7 (*μορφὴν δούλου λαβών*).[55] Nine lines from Corippus are in point:

> Virgo, *creatoris genetrix* sanctissima mundi,
> excelsi regina poli, specialiter una
> vera *parens* et virgo manens, *sine semine* patris
> quam deus elegit matrem sibi, *credula verbum*
> *concipiens* nostram genuisti feta salutem.
> o *pietas* miranda dei dictuque tremenda!
> *caelorum factor dominus deus*, unica patris
> forma dei, verae sese velamine carnis
> *induit*, et *servi formam* de virgine *sumpsit*.[56]

I have italicized the words and phrases recalled by our poem. Now the background for Corippus' phraseology, as I have tried to show elsewhere,[57] is Greek and contemporary—the Greek hymns and homilies on the Virgin current in Constantinople in the sixth century. The present poem has the same background, and its writer must have been as much influenced as Corippus by the *kontakia* of Romanos and others; like Corippus, our poet writes in Latin, in his case for Latin-speaking patrons, but he draws on the theology and imagery of the Eastern capital in which he lived.

It is hard to find Western poems of the same period which will provide similar parallels,[58] but there is one major poem which offers itself for comparison, namely, the *In laudem Mariae* attributed to Venantius Fortunatus.[59] This is a long poem (360 lines), which from a very early date was included with the poems of Venantius; it has certain infelicities which have led some scholars to be very sure that it is not authentic.[60] My own view is that it probably is by Venantius, and belongs to the 590s;[61] even if it was not written by Venantius, it could hardly be dated much later. Some linguistic similarities have been detected between this poem and the Corippus passage just quoted, though they are not as close as those between Corippus and our poem.[62] The interest of the *In laudem Mariae* for the present study,

53. For fuller discussion of this passage, see Cameron, "Cult of the Theotokos," pp. 82–85.

54. *Iust.* 2. 62; cf. Proclus of Constantinople, *PG*, 65:680.

55. This was a text expounded in favor of Chalcedon by Justinian; see Schwartz, *Drei dogmatische Schriften Iustinians*, pp. 16, 96.

56. *Iust.* 2. 52–60; for full discussion, see my commentary, pp. 152–54.

57. "Cult of the Theotokos," pp. 86–87.

58. The fourth-century Latin poem on a Barcelona papyrus, supposed formerly to be a poem about the Virgin, is rather about God the Father, and in any case not at all similar; see A. Emmett, "The Subject of Psalmus Responsorius: P. Barc. 149b–153," *Museum Philologicum Londiniense* 2 (1977): 99–109. Nor is the hymn to the Virgin by Ennodius (*Carm.* 1. 19 *Hymnus S. Mariae*), except in some inescapable details.

59. Ed. Leo, *MGH:AA*, 4:371–80.

60. Ibid., p. xxiv.

61. "Cult of the Theotokos," pp. 91–96.

62. M. Manitius, "Zu spätlateinischen Dichtern," *Z. öst. Gym.* 37 (1886): 250–54.

however, is that, although it is a poem about the Virgin, one of its themes is the association of the Virgin with the definition of orthodoxy—exactly as we have it in our inscriptional poem, but on a bigger scale and with a more literary treatment.[63] There are many places in the *In laudem Mariae* where the poet uses the same terminology and ideas of the Virgin as we find both in Corippus and here,[64] but for our purposes the emphasis on Mary as a means to defining orthodoxy gives an excellent context for our poem.

In treating the theme of the Nativity in such a depersonalized and theological manner, our unknown poet has given us not only a small but precious addition to the collection of evidence illustrating the growing cult of the Virgin at the end of the sixth century, but also, and perhaps more pertinent for the circumstances in which he was writing, a document of complete Chalcedonian orthodoxy. The Virgin gave birth to "God and man" together (1); Christ had a *duplex substantia* (15); the Trinity is in existence *sine fine* (17). For *triplicitas simplex simplicitasque triplex* (18) we may again compare Venantius, this time the poem of thanks which he wrote to Justin II when the emperor sent his gift to Poitiers: *persona triplex, substantia simplex* (3). *Triplicitas* in our poem may be the first use of the word—it is the only example cited by Du Cange—but compare Sedulius *Carmen Paschale* 1. 298, also of the Trinity, "quod simplex triplicet quodque est triplicabile simplex." Again Venantius *Carmen* 5. 5. 41–42: "est deus, alta fides, unus trinus et trinus unus: / personis propriis stat tribus unus apex." The notion of *bis genitus* in line 19 is very striking, but again we have similar (though indeed not exactly parallel) plays of "mother" and "father" in, for example, Venantius *In laudem Mariae* 37–38. There, too, the idea that the Son became *minor* through his Incarnation is expressed (line 20 in our poem). Finally, our poet ends this section with a play on the idea of redemption, a theme which is found both in Corippus' Trinitarian section and in Venantius.[65]

So we have it: a small contribution to the corpus of sixth-century *ekphraseis*, to our sense of the developing cult of the Virgin, to our knowledge of contacts between the upper classes, both lay and ecclesiastical, of Rome and Constantinople. The culture of late sixth-century Constantinople is in urgent need of investigation, and texts like this, especially those without a direct imperial connection, will have a large part to play.

Institute for Advanced Study and
King's College London

63. Cf. *In laudem Mariae* 29–30, 251–52. Note 47 "sed redeo qua virgo trahit mihi laude canenda"; the Trinitarian material here is a conscious artistic digression.

64. E.g., 43 *induit artus*, 46 *formam servi*, 122 *concipiente fide*, 203 *vincens super omnia matres*, 210 *hospitium vitae*, 248–49 *inscia coniugio feta negante viro. / accipis et nescis*.

65. *Iust.* 4. 298, 4. 307–8; *In laudem Mariae* 123–24.

NOTES AND DISCUSSIONS

A NOTE ON THEOCRITUS *IDYLL* 18

> When at last in the war's ninth year he faced Paris in single combat, it was purely for the sake of form. "I don't ask why she went with you," he paused to say. "But tell me, as I spear you: did Helen ever mention, while you clipped and tumbled, how she happened to choose me in the first place?"
>
> [John Barth, "Menelaiad"]

In his wedding song to Helen and Menelaus, Theocritus has introduced a subtle vein of humor or irony in the contrast between the divine stature of Helen, whose praises occupy the middle thirty lines of the chorus (19–48), and the rather hapless figure which Menelaus cuts as the butt of several sallies.[1] Menelaus is first rebuked for being too tired or sluggish to attend to his wife on their wedding night (9–15). Then, his success in wooing her is attributed to a lucky sneeze (16–17). A stroke of wit at the end of the poem completes the picture of a groom himself amazed to have the divine Helen as his wife. The joke is subtle and has been obscured by misguided commentary. I shall attempt to recover it.

In lines 56–57, the chorus promise to return at dawn, "when the first songster raises his gaily-feathered neck from sleep to crow." The translation is A. S. F. Gow's, and is inspired, like all other versions of these lines, by the interpretation of the scholiast: ἅμα ὄρθρῳ καὶ ἡμεῖς ἐλευσόμεθα ὅταν ἀλεκτρυὼν ᾄσῃ (p. 333 Wendel). Despite Gow's lengthy defense of this interpretation in his commentary, it should be noted that the scholiast ignores the ambiguities of the original: ἐπεί κα πρᾶτος ἀοιδός / ἐξ εὐνᾶς κελαδήσῃ ἀνασχὼν εὔτριχα δειράν. For example, where Gow has "songster," we should properly read "singer." "Songster" carries the specific suggestion of a songbird, while ἀοιδός ordinarily denotes a human minstrel, and nowhere (outside of the present passage) means "rooster," as Gow points out. Second, εὐνή can refer to a nest, as it does in a vivid simile at Sophocles *Antigone* 424, and is also occasionally used for the lairs of mammals; but it is difficult, in the context of an epithalamium, to suppress its common significance of "marriage-bed" (LSJ, s.v., 4), which it bears, for example, at line 11 of this poem. Κελαδέω is perhaps neutral: it can refer to the chirping of birds or to the act of singing a hymn or other song (LSJ, s.v., I. 2; cf. II. 1, the transitive usage). On the other hand, "gaily-feathered" specifies εὔθριξ far too narrowly. Εὔθριξ may also be applied to human hair, as the root θρίξ is generally, and by extension to the manes of horses (always in the *Iliad*) or the wool or fur of other mammals (LSJ, s.v.). While Gow cites three other instances of θρίξ or its compounds referring to birds, one of these involves a deliberately striking metaphor (Bacchyl. 5. 28 λεπτότριχα . . . ἔθειραν, of an eagle), and in any case the usage is obviously rare. Finally, it may be pointed out that

1. "Middle thirty lines" indicates my conception of the structure of the poem: eight lines of introduction, with the following song divided ten–thirty–ten. Despite Dover's recent arguments for a different arrangement (*Theocritus: Select Poems* [Basingstoke and London, 1971], p. 231), I believe that change of addressee as well as verbal responsions guarantee the symmetry of the chorus.

πρᾶτος need not mean "first" in the sense of "earliest"; taken predicatively, it can also signify "for the first time," as it does in lines 43 and 45 of this same poem.

Taken together, these observations suggest a plausible version of 56–57: "when a minstrel for the first time raises his well-tressed neck from the marriage-bed and crows." Strange way to describe a rooster. But another subject presents itself when we recognize in εὔτριχα at 57 (the final line of the poem, apart from the conventional invocation to Hymen) an echo of ξανθότριχι πὰρ Μενελάῳ in the first verse. Thus, the strained periphrasis for "rooster" conceals a witty comment on Menelaus' exuberant pride in the consummation of his marriage to the divine Helen—he tosses his mane and howls aloud (a reference to his famous war cry?) as though he had just learned to sing.[2]

The comic treatment of Menelaus may conform to a Fescennine convention, although there is no certain evidence for such a convention in Greek epithalamia. Nowhere, moreover, is the groom presented as sluggish or reluctant. He is more likely, in what survives of Sappho's epithalamia, to be the subject of extravagant praise (frags. 111, 115). In the poem which by all accounts is thematically closest to Theocritus *Idyll* 18 (Sappho frag. 44, on the wedding of Hector and Andromache), the bride and groom are both likened to gods (vv. 21, 34). I suggest that the disparity between the lovers conveyed by the epithalamium for Helen and Menelaus is rather in keeping with Theocritus' treatment of love in several other idylls, such as those devoted to Polyphemus and Galatea, or the third on Amaryllis and her enamored goatherd. I am inclined to venture an additional interpretative point. Theocritus has refrained from anything more than a hint at Helen's future elopement: the hint occurs at 37 τᾶς πάντες ἐπ' ὄμμασιν ἵμεροι ἐντί. Dover, following Gow, explains that " 'on whose eyes are all desires' means 'whose eyes kindle a desire surpassing all others.' "[3] Surely, however, the phrase—for which there is no precise parallel—is ambiguous, and also suggests Helen's passions. Perhaps, too, the contrast between bride and groom intimates the denouement. When Menelaus, astonished at his good fortune, bellows after possessing the divine Helen, the reader may be entitled to suspect that Helen, idealized and transcendent, must ultimately exceed and elude him.

DAVID KONSTAN
Wesleyan University

2. Shall we also retain the scholiast's interpretation and treat the verse and a half as an elaborate play on words? I tend to think we should, although I do not feel confident about the matter.
3. *Theocritus*, p. 235.

THE THREE HUNDRED AT THASOS, 411 B.C.

The overthrow in 411 B.C. of democracy and the establishment of the oligarchy of the Four Hundred in Athens were accompanied by simultaneous plots—carried out in conjunction with local collaborators—to set up oligarchies elsewhere in the Athenian empire. The Athenian conspirators apparently reasoned that they could rule oligarchically at home and at the same time preserve the empire by establishing cooperating oligarchies in the allied states (Thuc. 8. 48. 5; cf. 8. 91. 3). Thucydides, our main source for these events, characteristically tells us less than we would like to know about the happenings in allied cities, concentrating instead on the train of events in Athens. The information he does provide, however, is of great interest, especially the brief chronicle of events on Thasos, where the conspirators met with success (8. 64. 2–4).[1] Thucydides says,

> They [i.e., the Athenian oligarchic conspirators on Samos] also sent Dieitrephes, who had been elected to command in the Thracian district but who was then in the neighborhood of Chios, to his command. When he arrived at Thasos, he overthrew the democracy. Within two months of his departure, however, the Thasians began to wall their city on the grounds that they no longer wanted aristocracy in association with the Athenians and that they were in daily expectation of freedom coming from the Lacedaemonians. They felt this way because a group of Thasians, exiled by the Athenians, were in the Peloponnese and were, in collaboration with their friends in the city, exerting every effort to send ships and effect the revolution of Thasos. Thus these Thasians realized the goal they most desired: the establishment of their state on a proper foundation with no danger and the destruction of the democracy which would have opposed them.[2]

Thucydides tells us no more about this oligarchy, but we know from other sources that these events triggered a turbulent period in Thasian history when there were violent conflicts within the state. Oligarchy appears to have remained the form of government until 407 B.C., at which time the state was brought back into the Athenian alliance.[3] Several inscriptions discovered at Thasos are generally agreed to pertain to this period of oligarchic rule, but their exact place in the history of these years is still unsettled.

The key document is an inscription seen and copied by Cyriacus of Ancona in the fifteenth century and rediscovered by the French excavators of Thasos.[4] This inscription records a list of the six men, four from Thasos and two from Neapolis on the mainland opposite Thasos, whose property was confiscated and dedicated

1. In addition, Thucydides describes at some length the failure to subvert democracy on Samos (8. 73. 1–6); he tells us that attempts to substitute oligarchy for democracy occurred in an unspecified number of other cities (8. 64. 1, 5); he provides material to render reasonably certain the inference that such attempts succeeded at Andros, Tenos, Karystos, and Aegina (8. 64. 1; 65. 1; 69. 3). Diodorus 13. 47. 8 allows us to add Paros to this list.

2. It should be no cause for concern that Thucydides does not use the word oligarchy to describe the form of government which succeeded the overthrow of democracy. Since he explicitly states (8. 64. 1) that the Athenian oligarchic conspirators planned to establish oligarchies in the subject states, and since Dieitrephes' mission was part of this plan, it is certain that an oligarchy was set up at Thasos. That Thucydides calls the type of government rejected by Thasian oligarchs aristocracy indicates that that term had been employed by Dieitrephes and his supporters as a propaganda device in order to put the best possible interpretation on the dissolution of democracy (cf. J. Classen and J. Steup [eds.], *Thukydides: Achter Band*[3] [Berlin, 1922], ad 8. 64. 3; and A. Fuks, *The Ancestral Constitution* [London, 1953], pp. 11–12). In this regard it is significant that Theramenes, one of the chief oligarchic movers in Athens (Thuc. 8. 68. 4), later used the term aristocracy to describe the oligarchy of the Thirty (Xen. *Hell.* 2. 3. 47).

3. Xen. *Hell.* 1. 4. 9 and Diod. 13. 72. 1. The reference to Thasos at Xen. *Hell.* 1. 1. 32 appears to be mistaken: see A. Andrewes, "The Generals in the Hellespont, 410–407 B.C.," *JHS* 73 (1953): 7, n. 21 (but for arguments in support of the received text, see F. Chamoux, "L'île de Thasos et son histoire," *REG* 72 [1959]: 355, n. 1). For an account of this period, see R. Meiggs, *The Athenian Empire* (Oxford, 1972), pp. 574–78.

4. *IG*, 12.8. 263; cf. *IG*, 12, supp., p. 151, and J. Pouilloux, *Recherches sur l'histoire et les cultes de Thasos*, vol. 1: *De la fondation de la cité à 196 avant J.-C.*, Études thasiennes, 3 (Paris, 1954), p. 145 and n. 3, pl. 13, no. 4.

to Apollo "at the behest of the Three Hundred" (κατὰ τὸν ἄδον τῶν τριηκοσίων). One of the proscribed, Apemantus son of Philon, is widely regarded as the same individual whose name appears on an Attic inscription of the early fourth century B.C. as the father of five men who had been granted *proxenia* sometime before the oligarchy of the Thirty in Athens.[5] The original stele had been destroyed at the time of the Thirty, and the grant was inscribed anew on the extant stone at the expense of one of the sons. Another son, Amytor, almost certainly appears in another document, dated to 390–385 B.C.,[6] which awards tax benefits to Thasians exiled from their native land for Athenian sympathies.[7] The confluence of names on these three inscriptions makes it extremely probable that the six men in the first were proscribed for loyalty to Athens and that this event took place during the period of oligarchic rule on Thasos.

Three other Thasian epigraphical documents have been tied to the proscription list because they also refer to groups of three hundred individuals in judicial or administrative contexts. The first, dated much earlier in the fifth century,[8] mentions a group of three hundred in regard to regulations for the wine industry. The other two, inscribed on the same stone and usually dated late in the fifth century, offer rewards for information about plots against the state. In cases where two informers appear, a jury of three hundred is to render judgment.[9] J. Pouilloux, on the basis of the four documents mentioning groups of three hundred, has argued that the Three Hundred were the oligarchic instrument of government for the period 411 to 407 and that the oligarchs had at that time looked to their own history for the precedent which they followed in regard to the number of participants in the oligarchy. It has been pointed out, however, that Pouilloux's argument is seriously, perhaps fatally, flawed by the fact that, whereas the list of proscribed refers to *the* Three Hundred, the other three documents refer merely to a three hundred, with no article.[10] The absence of the article breaks the connection which Pouilloux sought to establish between the group which ordered the proscriptions and those mentioned in the other documents, with the result that the regulations about wine become less relevant to our period and the two laws on informers are less securely moored to the period of the oligarchy. We are left, however, with the Three Hundred of the proscription list, which is fairly firmly set in our period. Who were these Three Hundred?

In order to answer this question we must first make certain distinctions which to my knowledge have not been made in regard to the Thasian oligarchy established in 411 B.C. Although our information (primarily Thuc. 8. 64. 2–4) is too sparse to allow the establishment of many details, it permits us to infer that the oligarchy did go through three separate and distinct phases in the first nine months of its

5. *IG*, 2². 6 (= Tod, 2. 98), line 10.

6. *IG*, 2². 33, line 26; for the date, see Chamoux, "L'île de Thasos," p. 358, who argues convincingly against Pouilloux's attempt (*Thasos*, pp. 195–204) to place it earlier.

7. *IG*, 2². 33, lines 6–7: [ἐπ' 'A] / ττικισμῶι. Meiggs, *Athenian Empire*, p. 576 (cf. pp. 219, 365) erroneously implies that this phrase appears in *IG*, 12.8. 263

8. Pouilloux, *Thasos*, pp. 37–40, no. 7. The date is uncertain: cf. Pouilloux, *Thasos*, p. 38, and L. H. Jeffery, *The Local Scripts of Archaic Greece* (Oxford, 1961), pp. 302–3.

9. Pouilloux, *Thasos*, pp. 139–42, no. 18 (= R. Meiggs and D. Lewis, *Greek Historical Inscriptions* [Oxford, 1969], no. 83). Pouilloux discusses the historical setting of these laws on pp. 142–62.

10. Chamoux, "L'île de Thasos," pp. 352–54; Meiggs-Lewis, *GHI*, p. 254.

existence.[11] The first phase, lasting from one to two months, began when Dieitrephes overthrew democracy and helped establish oligarchic government in April 411.[12] During this period the oligarchic government was loyal, ostensibly at least, to Athens or, more precisely, to the Athenian oligarchic planners who were at that time implanting oligarchies in other allied states and who were conspiring to establish an oligarchy in Athens itself. Since the Thasian oligarchy was set up in order to keep the state within the Athenian empire, we may assume that Dieitrephes chose as participants in the oligarchy those he thought would remain loyal to Athens. At the same time it is reasonable to suppose that he would have excluded those who were loyal to Athens but hostile to oligarchy. The first phase ended in the second month after Dieitrephes' departure.[13] At this time the Thasians[14] began to wall their city, rejected Athenian control of their oligarchy, and awaited outside help.

At this point, sometime between mid-May and mid-June, the second phase began. During this period the Thasian oligarchs were particularly vulnerable, for, having frankly signaled their rebellious intent by rebuilding their walls, they were open to attack until their walls were completed. Since the old walls probably had not been taken down altogether (Thuc. 1. 101. 3) but had only been breached (cf. Xen. *Hell.* 2. 2. 15 and Lys. 13. 8), this period of extreme danger was relatively brief. But even afterward Thasos remained exposed because it had no ships. Happily for the Thasian oligarchy, the Athenian fleet was occupied elsewhere during this period; and the first indication we have of Athenians in Thasian waters is in the late winter or early spring of 410 (Xen. *Hell.* 1. 1. 12), after the Thasians had received help from their friends abroad. We do not know how different the oligarchic government in the second phase was from that in the first, but there must have been a change in at least one respect. The basis on which the oligarchy was initially established, loyalty to Athens and Athenian oligarchs, was abandoned. This decision must have caused some internal dissension and struggle among the oligarchs set in place by Dieitrephes, and it probably resulted in the

11. There may have been other disruptions and phases afterward, but the evidence is very uncertain; see n. 3.

12. I arrive at this date (on which depend the dates for the oligarchy's second phase) by the following process. The oligarchic revolution in Athens took place in Thargelion of Callias' year (Arist. *Ath. Pol.* 32. 1–2), that is, in the late spring or early summer—June—of 411. Therefore, Peisander and his fellow envoys must have arrived in Athens toward the end of May to set in motion the final events leading to the establishment of the Four Hundred (cf. G. Busolt, *Griechische Geschichte*, vol. 3.2 [Gotha, 1904], p. 1476). Since Peisander and his colleagues set up oligarchies in a number of cities on their way from Samos to Athens (cf. n. 1), I calculate that they left Samos in early April. Dieitrephes was dispatched to Thasos at about the same time Peisander left Samos, but went directly and appears to have set about instituting an oligarchic government immediately on his arrival (Thuc. 8. 64. 1–2). Accordingly, the event probably occurred in April.

13. One may assume that Dieitrephes left Thasos as soon as the new political system was in place, since his duties extended to the whole Thracian district.

14. I agree with H. W. Pleket, "Thasos and the Popularity of the Athenian Empire," *Historia* 12 (1963): 74–76, that Thucydides is obscure here, seeming to give the impression that he is referring to all the Thasians. But inasmuch as he has already said that democracy was overthrown and mentions two sentences later that the demos was hostile toward those who had rejected Athenian control, it is clear that he means the oligarchic government of Thasos, not the city as a whole. For similar usage in an Athenian official document, see *IG*, 1^2. 298 (= Meiggs–Lewis, *GHI*, no. 81), recording transactions of the Treasurers of Athena during the oligarchy of the Four Hundred. Though the oligarchs are in charge (lines 2, 14–15), the expenditures are made in the name of Athenians collectively (line 1: if the generally accepted restoration is correct, as I believe it is).

removal from power of those individuals who wished to remain loyal to Athens. But the disruption cannot have been very great because the success of the oligarchs in establishing independence from Athens in the face of a hostile demos argues a high degree of unity among them. For these reasons, I believe that the number of ruling oligarchs during the second phase was reduced because of the loss of Athenian loyalists, but not by a substantial number. Although Thucydides gives us no indication how long this second stage lasted, we do find help elsewhere. The Oxyrhynchus historian tells us (7[2]. 4; cf. schol. Aeschin. 2. 31) that the Corinthian admiral Timolaus brought about the defection of Thasos from the Athenians. It is usually, and probably correctly, assumed that Timolaus commanded the ships raised by Thasian exiles in the Peloponnese that Thucydides mentions. Since the Oxyrhynchus historian was a continuator of Thucydides,[15] an event recounted by him must have taken place after the end of Thucydides' narrative in the late fall of 411 B.C. We cannot be certain when Timolaus arrived at Thasos (except that it was before the events of 396–395 recorded in the London papyrus), but it is very likely that the event took place before the end of the year.[16] The main argument for this position is the vulnerability already mentioned. It seems reasonable to suppose that in this hazardous situation the exiles in the Peloponnese would have pressed hard for the dispatch of help as soon as possible. Timolaus probably left before the advent of bad weather; and, given that he sailed north with only two triremes, it is unlikely that he delayed on the way. We may reasonably assume that the second phase lasted about six months, from, say, early June to about the beginning of December.

The third stage began when Timolaus and the Thasian exiles entered the city, and it lasted, so far as we know, until the recapture of Thasos by the Athenians in 407 B.C. This period would have seen the tightest oligarchic control of the state and probably the bitterest internal conflicts resulting in the miserable situation mentioned by Xenophon (*Hell.* 1. 4. 9). During this time the number of oligarchs participating in the government must have been considerably larger than in the first phase (and—if our arguments are correct—larger than in the second phase). This view is based on the assumption that most, if not all, of the exiled Thasians would have returned home with Timolaus and that they would have participated in the government they had helped put on a firm foundation (cf. Thuc. 8. 64. 4). Though we have no means of assessing the number of returning oligarchs, it seems reasonable to suppose that the group was fairly large, especially if it consisted of all Thasians exiled during the years of Athenian control.

Having distinguished among the three phases of oligarchic government on Thasos, we may now consider the identity of the Three Hundred of *IG*, 12.8. 263. It is my contention that this group constituted the instrument of government in the first phase, but not in the second, when the number of participants was smaller,

15. See I. A. F. Bruce, *An Historical Commentary on the "Hellenica Oxyrhynchia"* (Cambridge, 1967), pp. 3–4.

16. Not, however, for the reason often cited (see, e.g., E. Meyer, *Theopomps "Hellenika"* [Halle, 1909], pp. 47–48, n. 2), namely, that the island had a Spartan harmost in 410 B.C. The evidence for this view (Xen. *Hell.* 1. 1. 32) is very doubtful; cf. n. 3.

or in the third, when it was larger.[17] In support of this position there are three main arguments.

First, let us take up the source for the figure three hundred as the number of ruling oligarchs. Pouilloux, as we have seen, sought it in earlier Thasian history, but he was unable to establish the earlier existence of a specific governing body of three hundred, merely the existence of a group of three hundred exercising a judicial or administrative function. A more probable source is near to hand. The Samian conspirators who failed to overthrow democracy on Samos in 411 B.C. numbered three hundred (Thuc. 8. 73. 2, 6), and it is a fair assumption that, had they succeeded, they would have constituted an oligarchy of three hundred. Thucydides does not tell us the origin of this number on Samos, but his narrative makes it abundantly clear that the Athenian oligarchic conspirators played the dominant role in instigating, in planning, and even in attempting to execute the Samian coup d'etat (8. 63. 3, 73. 2–5). On the other hand, the Samian magnates who collaborated with the Athenians appear to have had no particular political or emotional bias in favor of oligarchy. Just one year earlier these same individuals had emerged as leaders of the revolution which had overthrown the previous government, probably oligarchic, and established a democracy loyal to Athens (Thuc. 8. 21; cf. *IG*, 1^2. 101). In view of this and of the need for Peisander and his fellow Athenian conspirators to exhort and persuade the Samians to undertake the coup,[18] it does not seem imprudent to suppose that the figure three hundred arose, not from local Samian conditions or traditions, but from an appraisal by the Athenian oligarchic planners of the figure which would constitute a suitable oligarchy, sufficient to control the situation in Samos and at the same time circumscribed enough to be regulated by the oligarchic government in Athens.[19] Dieitrephes himself could not have been party to these negotiations, for he was occupied in Chios at that time (Thuc. 8. 64. 2). It is clear from Thucydides' account, however, that, although the abortive revolution at Samos may have taken place after the establishment of oligarchy in Thasos, the plans were decided upon before Dieitrephes left for Thrace. It is also plain that Dieitrephes received his instructions about how to proceed on Thasos after the details of the oligarchic revolutions in Samos and other allied cities had been worked out by the Athenian planners (Thuc. 8. 63. 3–64. 2). Under these circumstances it seems reasonable to suggest that Dieitrephes' instructions specified the number of Thasians to be included in the newly established oligarchy and that this figure—if the considerations in regard to Thasos were analogous to those operating at Samos—would have been three hundred.

17. One might argue that the ruling body continued to be called the Three Hundred even when the number of participants was larger or smaller than three hundred, on the analogy of the Four Hundred and the Thirty in Athens: both bodies retained their original designations after their numbers had been reduced by death or defection. But would the Thasian oligarchs have wished to preserve the name and number imposed upon them by the Athenians from whom they had revolted?

18. Thuc. 8. 63. 3 προυτρέψαντο, 8. 73. 2 πεισθέντες.

19. If the government in Samos before the democratic revolution of 412 consisted of six hundred members (Thuc. 8. 21; cf. G. E. M. de Ste. Croix, *The Origins of the Peloponnesian War* [London, 1972], p. 42), then the new oligarchy would have been much more restricted—probably at the insistence of the Athenian conspirators.

Second, I believe that we can determine with greater precision than heretofore the date of *IG*, 12.8. 263. The original stele recording the award of *proxenia* to the five sons of Apemantus was destroyed during the rule of the Thirty in 404/403 B.C.[20] We cannot be certain why the stele was destroyed or whether such destruction was widespread;[21] but it is at least possible—perhaps even probable—that, in view of the deep commitment to oligarchic theory and practice on the part of the Thirty,[22] the stele in question was pulled down by the oligarchs on doctrinal grounds, that is, because its existence was somehow offensive to oligarchic sentiments and sensibilities.[23] What in this particular inscription gave offense? The answer would seem to be that the persons honored by the Athenian democracy were viewed with hostility by the Thirty. On what grounds? We know nothing about the activities of Apemantus' sons before they were awarded *proxenia*, but it is usually—and in my view correctly—assumed that the sons shared the father's political coloration and that they suffered his fate in 411: confiscation of property and probable exile from Thasos by the Thasian oligarchs. We have seen that there was a significant change in the relationship between Athens and the Thasian oligarchs in the course of the oligarchy: the oligarchs in Thasos were pro-Athenian in the first phase and anti-Athenian in the two succeeding phases. Thus, if Apemantus' property was confiscated and his family exiled in either the second or third phase, we would have indications of their Athenian sympathies but no grounds for animosity against them by the Thirty. For, had Apemantus and his family been punished in the second or third stage, they must, at the least, have acquiesced in the overthrow of democracy and the establishment of oligarchy by

20. *IG*, 2^2. 6, lines 11–13: ἐπειδὴ καθηιρέθη / ἡ στήλη [ἐ]πὶ τῶν τριάκοντ / α.

21. For a highly uncertain restoration indicating that a second stele suffered the same fate, see *IG*, 2^2. 9; cf. *IG*, 2^2. 52.

22. See, e.g., Critias' epitaph, 88 A 13 D.-K. (= schol. Aeschin. 1. 39); and Xen. *Hell.* 2. 3. 25–26.

23. The possibility that the earlier stele was destroyed accidentally, not deliberately demolished by the Thirty, cannot be ruled out; but the following considerations make it extremely remote. The first decree honoring the sons of Apemantus was in all probability set up on the Acropolis where the extant stone was found (cf. *IG*, 1^2. 118 [= Meiggs–Lewis, *GHI*, no. 90], lines 20–24 for the practice of placing honorary decrees there). Though the Spartan garrison supporting the Thirty was stationed on the Acropolis (Lys. 12. 94, 13. 46; Isoc. 15. 319; Arist. *Ath. Pol.* 37. 2; Plut. *Lys.* 15. 5; cf. Xen. *Hell.* 2. 3. 13–14, 20, 42; Aeschin. 2. 77; and Diod. 14. 4. 3–4), there is no indication that it caused damage there. Furthermore, we know of no warfare or rioting on the Acropolis or in its vicinity during the time of the Thirty. The procession mentioned at Xen. *Hell.* 2. 4. 39 could well have involved considerable commotion and perhaps some accidental damage, but that event took place, strictly speaking, after the rule of the Thirty. Use of the temple on the Acropolis by the Thirty to store confiscated arms (Xen. *Hell.* 2. 3. 20) suggests that the common citizen might not have had free access to the sanctuary during the Spartan occupation. Thus, there appears to be no basis for violent but accidental destruction. On the other hand, accidental destruction unaccompanied by violence seems highly improbable in view of the durable material on which the document was inscribed. Moreover, since the Acropolis was holy ground, it is unlikely that any private agent would have demolished the stele. The most probable alternative, therefore, seems to be deliberate destruction, carried out at the command of the government in power, the Thirty, perhaps by the Spartan garrison.

The Thirty are said (Arist. *Ath. Pol.* 35. 2) to have "taken down" (καθεῖλον) the laws of Ephialtes and Archestratus from the Areopagus. The exact meaning is uncertain: see J. E. Sandys, *Aristotle's "Constitution of Athens"*[2] (London, 1912), ad loc.; A. Fuks, *The Ancestral Constitution*, pp. 22, 77; and J. Day and M. Chambers, *Aristotle's History of Athenian Democracy* (Berkeley and Los Angeles, 1962), pp. 128–29. It seems clear, however, that the Thirty had both the power and the will to overthrow official documents of the Athenian state. For the hypothesis that they also erased part of the newly inscribed law code, see A. Fingarette, "A New Look at the Wall of Nikomakhos," *Hesperia* 40 (1971): 330–35.

Dieitrephes. In that case, the Thirty ought to have deemed the family well disposed to their cause, with the consequence that their animus would remain inexplicable. If, however, the confiscations took place during the first stage of the oligarchy, then Apemantus and his family would have been at odds with the Thasian oligarchs during the pro-Athenian phase. Since the family was honored by the Athenian democracy, it is justifiable to assume that they could not have opposed the pro-Athenian aspect of the new government imposed by Dieitrephes. They must, then, have stood in opposition to the overthrow of democracy and the establishment of oligarchy. It follows that, when the sons were awarded *proxenia* (had the father died before their arrival in Athens?) in the years before the establishment of the Thirty, they were honored not merely because they were friendly to Athens—as indeed they must have been—but more particularly because they had opposed oligarchy and stood loyal to democracy. In this case the Thirty would have had ample grounds for considering the family anathema to the cause of oligarchy and for wishing to destroy the visible monument on the Acropolis to the family's loyalty to democracy—both Thasian and Athenian. The restored democracy, for its part, would also have had cause to renew the honors and to fete Eurypylus, one of the sons, in the Prytaneion. If these arguments are cogent, then the circumstances behind the destruction of the predecessor to *IG*, 1^2. 6 seem to preclude the possibility that the confiscations recorded in *IG*, 12.8. 263 occurred during the second or third phase of the Thasian oligarchy, with the result that the document must be dated to the first phase. Placing it in the first phase helps to corroborate our contention that the Athenian oligarchs established an oligarchy of three hundred on Thasos, since in this document we see the Three Hundred in action.

Third, Pouilloux has noted that *IG*, 12.8. 263 is written in Attic script (as are other documents dated to this time), whereas the two laws offering rewards to informers are written in the local Parian script.[24] This anachronistic recrudescence of localism has been attributed to a "burst of patriotic insularity," and this may well have been the case. But if it is, the relationship developed by Pouilloux between the act of confiscation and the laws about informers seems somewhat odd. Pouilloux believes that the laws were promulgated first and that the confiscations came about as a result of denunciations arising from them. In order to support this position, he is forced to posit a distinction between "more official" documents and other, less official, ones which were not touched by the wave of local pride. But this distinction appears arbitrary in view of the official nature of the act of confiscation, which begins with a list of the three *theoroi* for the year in question.[25] A simpler hypothesis is to ascribe the document written in Attic script to the first stage of the oligarchy, when Athenian domination was still recognized. The two laws could then be placed, with Pouilloux, in one of the later phases (most likely the third), when pride of independence from Athens would provide a plausible setting for them. If this line of reasoning is sound, it gives us another indication that *IG*, 12.8. 263 records an action taken in the first month or two of the oligarchy.

Our discussion leads to the following conclusions: that the oligarchy established

24. *Thasos*, pp. 139–47, 440; Jeffery, *Local Scripts*, p. 303.

25. These same magistrates are listed in the official catalog of *theoroi: IG*, 12.8. 277, lines 81–83 = Pouilloux, *Thasos*, p. 262, cat. 1, col. 5, lines 26–28. Note, too, that Carl Fredrich, the editor of *IG*. 12.8, places 263 among the decrees of state.

by Dieitrephes at Thasos in 411 B.C. consisted of three hundred members, that this number was imposed by Athenian oligarchic planners, that the nature and composition of the oligarchy changed within two months of its inception, and that *IG*, 12.8. 263 is to be dated to the period before the Thasian oligarchs cut their ties with Athens.[26]

HARRY C. AVERY
University of Pittsburgh

26. I wish to thank two anonymous referees for helpful criticism and comments.

CURUCA AND JUVENAL *SATIRE* 6

Modern editors of Juvenal adopt the following version at *Satire* 6. 276: "tu tibi tunc, uruca, places fletumque labellis."[1] Manuscripts show two main variants: *uruca* appears in P and its closest kin, *curuca* in the majority of other manuscripts. I propose that *curuca* be restored to the text.[2] The nature of the variants makes it likely that the original was *tum curuca*. Since scribes tended to change *tum* to *tunc* before a guttural,[3] the change from *tum curuca* to *tunc uruca* was an easy step.

The sense of neither *curuca* nor *uruca* is securely established in classical Latin. Scholia attached to both readings indicate that neither word was common and that the scholiasts were not agreed on the meaning of *uruca*, for which three glosses have been provided.[4] One of these scholiastic interpretations, that *uruca* denotes a worm or caterpillar, has been adopted in most recent translations. This definition of *uruca*, however, has little evident relevance to the poem as a whole or to the section in which the word appears. *Curuca*, on the other hand, is well suited to the imagery of the poem. Its meaning is found in texts of the medieval period, which have the advantage of being consistent and definite. Without citing his sources, Papias (fl. 1053–1063) writes opposite *currucula:* "est avicula: quae alterius filios educat. haec dicitur linosa vel cucula eo quod cuculus dum eius ova sorbeat sua relinquit quae curruca tam diu fovet; donec extracti pulli eam comedant."[5] Alan of Lille (ca. 1116–1202), whose reputation for extensive learning makes his witness especially valuable, seems not to have been noted previously in discussions of the word. His *Liber de planctu naturae* states: "Illic curruca novercam exuens, materno pietatis ubere, alienam cuculi prolem adoptabat in filium; quae tamen capitali praemiata

I should like to thank Professor G. P. Goold for constructive criticism of an earlier version of this paper.

1. E.g., W. V. Clausen (ed.), *A. Persi Flacci et D. Iuni Iuvenalis "Saturae"* (Oxford, 1959); A. E. Housman (ed.), *D. Iunii Iuvenalis "Saturae"*[2] (Cambridge, 1931); U. Knoche (ed.), *D. Iunius Juvenalis "Saturae" mit kritischem Apparat* (Munich, 1950).

2. It was removed by O. Jahn (ed.), *D. Iunii Iuvenalis "Saturarum" libri V* (Berlin, 1851), p. 58.

3. Housman, *"Saturae"*[2], p. xxi, n. 1.

4. P. Wessner (ed.), *Scholia in Iuvenalem vetustiora* (Leipzig, 1931), p. 91; for additional glosses and commentaries on the line, see idem, *Corpus Glossariorum Latinorum*, vol. 1, ed. G. Goetz (Leipzig, 1923), p. 389; C. F. Heinrich (ed.), *D. Iunii Iuvenalis "Satirae,"* vol. 2 (Bonn, 1839), pp. 244–46; L. Friedlaender (ed.), *D. Junii Juvenalis "Saturarum" libri V*, vol. 1 (Leipzig, 1895), p. 316.

5. *Papias Vocabulista* (Venice, 1496), p. 83. The definition extends beyond the relevant scholia: Wessner, *Corpus Glossariorum Latinorum*, 1:389. *Curruca* is a common variation in spelling for *curuca;* the contexts in which the two words appear show that they designate the same species of bird regardless of the spelling.

stipendio privignum agnoscens, filium ignorabat."[6] Alan's use of *curuca* in this context gives the reader a clear understanding of the peculiar nature of a bird whose nest was robbed of its young when the cuckoo deceived the owner and left its egg to be hatched and its young to be reared by the *curuca* as its own.[7] Theodorus of Gaza (ca. 1450), who avers in his preface that he names the various species according to the practice of the best ancient authors, employs *curuca* to translate Aristotle's ὑπολαΐς, referring to a bird whose nest the cuckoo invades.[8] Interest in ornithology during Juvenal's lifetime is evident from the writings of the elder Pliny.[9] Latin translations of Greek works on birds are known to have existed in the early Middle Ages and are thought to have been used by Fathers of the Church as the basis for allegorical teachings on faith and morals.[10] Authors of the sixteenth century agree with Alan and Theodorus in their definitions of *curuca*.[11]

To judge from the content of the poem as a whole, its imagery, and Juvenal's characteristic style, *curuca* is intrinsically more probable than *uruca* as an address to the groom in line 276. The poet, in a dramatic, last-minute attempt to dissuade Postumus from marrying, insists that his hope of begetting a legitimate son is doomed because of the bride's infidelity. His view of woman's basic tendency is disclosed through words and images reflecting her likeness to birds;[12] other birds are explicitly mentioned or are suggested through literary allusion.[13] Given the prominence of birds in this satire and the meaning of *curuca* consistently attested, *curuca* fits line 276 with admirable point: it is directed to Postumus precisely as a husband allowing himself to be betrayed by an adulterer. Such vivid particularity is characteristic of Juvenal's diction.

In summary, *curuca* is the common reading of the "interpolated" manuscripts of Juvenal at *Satire* 6. 276. The word is used by Alan and is employed in translations from Greek and in original late Latin works to describe a bird having the characteristics outlined by Alan and attributed to a bird called ὑπολαΐς by Aristotle and Theophrastus. It is probable that the meaning of *curuca* given in Papias and assumed by writers of the medieval and Renaissance periods is consistent with the meaning of the word in Juvenal's day. It is likely also that *curuca* had a life independent of Juvenal, thereby making it a vivid addition to a unifying system of

6. *PL*, 210:436C.

7. The existence of such a bird called ὑπολαΐς by the Greeks is attested by Arist. *HA* 564a2, 618a8; Theophr. *Caus. pl.* 2. 17. 9; Pliny *NH* 10. 11. 26. See also D. W. Thompson, *A Glossary of Greek Birds*[2] (Oxford, 1936), p. 295. As victim-host the bird bears a general resemblance to the cuckolded husband.

8. *Aristotelis libri omnes, ad animalium cognitionem attinentes*, vol. 6 (Venice, 1562), ad 6. 7 (564a2) and 9. 29 (618a8).

9. *NH* 10; cf. 8. 41, 11. 79, 11. 102, 11. 112, 17. 6, 18. 87, 29. 13, 29. 24–26, 29. 38; see also E. Stresemann, *Ornithology from Aristotle to the Present*, trans. H. and C. Epstein, ed. G. W. Cottrell (Cambridge, Mass., 1975), p. 7.

10. M. Wellman, *Der Physiologus. Eine religionsgeschichtlich-naturwissenschaftliche Untersuchung*, Philologus, Suppl. 22 (Leipzig, 1930).

11. R. Stephanus, *Dictionarium seu Latinae Linguae Thesaurus* (Paris, 1536), p. 387; W. Turner, *Avium praecipuarum, quarum apud Plinium et Aristotelem mentio est brevis et succincta historia* (Cologne, 1544), D iiii v; C. Gesner, *"Historiae animalium" liber III, qui est de avium natura* (Zurich, 1555), p. 355

12. E.g., lines 88, 165, 197–98, 226, 398.

13. E.g., lines 8, 39, 63, 518, 540, 549, 551, 644, and line 6 of the Oxford fragment.

comparison which operates throughout *Satire* 6. For these reasons *curuca* is to be preferred to the reading of P and its kin.

MECHTILDE O'MARA
St. Michael's College,
University of Toronto

POET OR PLATO IN PLUTARCH?

ἔοικε γὰρ ὄντως χαλεπὸν εἶναι φωνὴν ἐχούσῃ πόλει καὶ μοῦσαν ἀπεχθάνεσθαι. καὶ γὰρ ὁ Μίνως ἀεὶ διετέλει κακῶς ἀκούων καὶ λοιδορούμενος ἐν τοῖς Ἀττικοῖς θεάτροις κτλ.

[Plut. *Thes.* 16. 3]

Lindskog and Ziegler in their Teubner edition pose a question here: "φωνὴν—μοῦσαν ex aliquo poeta petitum?" Scholars have recognized that in this passage Plutarch has in mind the *Minos*, one of the spurious dialogues in the Platonic corpus; see 320D–321B, especially 320E: . . . μηδέποτε ἀπεχθάνεσθαι ἀνδρὶ ποιητικῷ μηδενί. οἱ γὰρ ποιηταὶ μέγα δύνανται εἰς δόξαν . . . ἢ εὐλογοῦντες ἢ κακηγοροῦντες. ὃ δὴ καὶ ἐξήμαρτεν ὁ Μίνως. In 321A tragedy is mentioned: ἐν ᾗ δὴ καὶ ἐντείνοντες ἡμεῖς τὸν Μίνων τιμωρούμεθα (Socrates is the speaker).

Nothing in the *Minos* can be the source of φωνὴν ἐχούσῃ πόλει καὶ μοῦσαν. The collocation φωνὴ . . . καὶ μοῦσα is, in fact, an unusual and elevated one, and it is proof of a certain *Stilgefühl* to have perceived this.[1] But the language is borrowed, not from a lost work of poetry, but from Plato. At *Laws* 667A we read: . . . ἔχομεν μοῦσαν τῆς τῶν χορῶν καλλίω καὶ τῆς ἐν τοῖς κοινοῖς θεάτροις. . . . There is a twofold correspondence: ἔχομεν μοῦσαν answers to Plutarch's ἐχούσῃ . . . μοῦσαν, and ἐν τοῖς κοινοῖς θεάτροις to ἐν τοῖς Ἀττικοῖς θεάτροις. (The change from κοινοῖς to Ἀττικοῖς was necessitated by the change of context; Plutarch, in contrast to Plato, had to refer specifically to the Athenian theater.) These two correspondences, of themselves, are perhaps not decisive. What clinches the case is that in this same passage of the *Laws*—and apparently nowhere else—we find the same collocation of φωνή and μοῦσα: ποίαν δὲ ἤσουσιν[2] οἱ ἄνδρες φωνὴν ἢ μοῦσαν; (666D). This gives us a tantalizing glimpse of Plutarch the stylist at work; he has here blended together phrases from the *Minos* and the *Laws*. Ἀπεχθάνεσθαι comes from the *Minos*, but in place of ἀνδρὶ ποιητικῷ (*Minos*) Plutarch substitutes φωνὴν ἐχούσῃ πόλει καὶ μοῦσαν. The latter phrase contains elements taken from two separate sentences in the same passage of the *Laws* (666D, 667A). In Plutarch's next sentence, ἐν τοῖς . . . θεάτροις comes from one of the same two sentences (667A).

The story does not end here. At *Laws* 666D the unusual combination φωνὴν ἢ μοῦσαν has troubled scholars. Burnet placed a full stop after φωνὴν and began a new sentence with ἢ μοῦσαν [ἢ] κτλ.; England took a similar approach. Wilamowitz went so far as to delete φωνὴν ἢ μοῦσαν as "zwei Ergänzungsversuche." I have dis-

1. Whether Lindskog or Ziegler made this observation is unclear. The title page of the 1969 edition states that ". . . recensuit Konrat Ziegler . . . ," whereas the 1914 edition reads ". . . recensuit Cl. Lindskog. . . ." It was more probably Lindskog who remarked, "ex aliquo poeta petitum?" but it cannot be absolutely excluded that his fellow editor Ziegler made the suggestion to him.

2. ἤσουσιν Porson, Cobet: ᾄσουσιν MSS. The future active of ᾄδω is a barbarism in Attic Greek. See my *Studies in Greek Texts*, Hypomnemata, vol. 43 (Göttingen, 1975), pp. 140–42.

cussed these proposals elsewhere and attempted to defend the reading of the MSS, *φωνὴν ἢ μοῦσαν*, taken *coniunctim*.[3] The imitation in Plutarch's *Theseus*, which has now been detected, guarantees the correctness of the transmitted Plato text.

ROBERT RENEHAN
University of California, Santa Barbara

3. Ibid.

NOTES ON THE *DIALOGUS* OF TACITUS

In a recent review article criticizing the OCT of M. Winterbottom and R. M. Ogilvie,[1] I presented evidence indicating that, of the extant MSS of the *Dialogus*, the family known as ζ,[2] represented by the codices EV, is basically independent of the consensus of the other two families, whose main representatives are codices B and C. The following stemma represents the basic relationships of these codices.

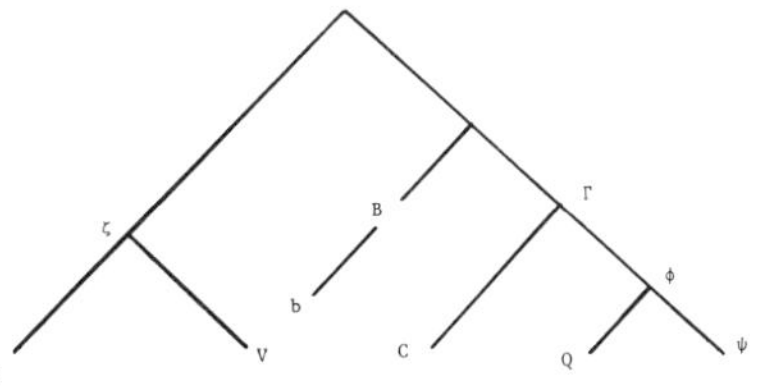

The siglum φ is given by Winterbottom to represent the consensus of codex Q with ψ, a family made up of a group of contaminated MSS. The family φ is itself, despite Winterbottom, probably also contaminated.[3] Winterbottom believed that

1. "The Minor Works of Tacitus: A Study in Textual Criticism," *CP* 72 (1977): 323–43. The discussion of the MSS of the *Dialogus* is on pp. 335–38. Winterbottom edited the *Dialogus*.

2. I use the sigla adopted by Winterbottom for his OCT (1975), which should be consulted for their expansion. All of the MSS descend eventually from a lost Hersfeldensis of the ninth century, but through a Renaissance archetype (see my "Minor Works of Tacitus," p. 336). The Hersfeldensis is extant for one quaternion in the *Agricola* (codex Aesinas lat. 8, published in facsimile by R. Till, *Handschriftliche Untersuchungen zu Tacitus "Agricola" und "Germania"* [Berlin–Dahlem, 1943]).

3. M. Winterbottom, "The Transmission of Tacitus' *Dialogus*," *Philologus* 116 (1972): 123, states: "It is, I am sure, by inherited resources that φ can avoid the following omissions of C: 12. 3. 18 *illud;* 14. 2. 16 *defendi*. . . ." But it is more likely that *illud* was already omitted by Γ; otherwise we might expect Γ's characteristic error, *id* (see "Minor Works of Tacitus," p. 336; Winterbottom, "Transmission," pp. 127–28). In 14. 2, for *poetas defendi*, B reads *poetas defendi poetas*, and C reads simply *poetas*. In all probability, then, the common source of BΓ had B's reading, and C's omission resulted when the scribe's eye skipped from the first *poetas* to the second. In both examples, probabilities favor φ's supplying an inherited omission through contamination. Other explanations can be given, but confidence in φ's purity is clearly misplaced. The examples do not indicate the source of the contamination, but the lack of shared omissions which Winterbottom's apparatus attributes to Cφ as the fault of Γ indicates that there was some contamination. At least I do not believe that, though C, Q, and the others have many omissions, Γ omitted nothing but one monosyllable: 37. 5. 5 *in*.

Omitted from the stemma are codices c and Δ. Winterbottom believes that these codices descended from a close ancestor of C, after that ancestor had been corrected from ζ. R. P. Robinson (ed.), *The "Germania" of Tacitus* (Middletown, Conn., 1935), p. 187, believed something similar, except that he thought that the ancestor had already been corrected from ζ before C was copied from it, with C simply ignoring most of the corrections. I would not try to resolve so delicate a matter without seeing the codices.

ς, B, and Γ were all independent witnesses to the archetype, and that the agreement of any two of them should normally establish the archetypal reading. With the above stemma, however, it should be obvious that the solitary witness of ς is the equal of the consensus of the other codices. In the review article, I pointed out a number of places where the witness of ς must be judged to transmit the archetypal reading more accurately than the consensus of BC or BΓ.[4] I wish here to examine a few more readings, particularly readings of ς that have up to now been casually dismissed by editors in the mistaken belief that they have, by themselves, little or no authority.

17. 4 nam ipse ego in Britannia vidi senem qui se *fateretur* ei pugnae interfuisse qua Caesarem inferentem arma Britanni arcere litoribus et pellere adgressi sunt.

fateretur BCψ, *fatentur* Q, *fatebatur* ς

Whether the subjunctive *fateretur* is explained as consecutive, characteristic, or potential, it is rhetorically inferior to the indicative. Aper is claiming that a man may live to be one hundred and twenty. As evidence he claims to have seen a man who himself claimed to have fought against Caesar: cf. 17. 4. 23 "qui armatus C. Caesari restitit." The subjunctive weakens the value of the evidence. Read *fatebatur*. It might be thought that a scribe would more easily convert a subjunctive into an indicative than vice versa, but this would be difficult to prove from the performance of Renaissance scribes in copying the extant archetype (the ninth-century Hersfeldensis) in the *Agricola*. At *Agricola* 31. 1. 2, the Hersfeldensis reads clearly and with perfect sense *effugerunt*. The scribe of codex A, the illustrious Pomponio Leto, wrote *effugiant*, and, despite its inferior sense, the reading went unchallenged until the archetypal reading was revealed in this century. For other examples of change to the subjunctive, see *Germania* 2. 1. 6 (*quod . . .*) *est*] *sit* Γ; 3. 2. 4 (*quod . . .*) *incolitur*] *incolatur* ς; 4. 19 *adsueverunt*] *assueuerint* B^{v}Em; *Dialogus* 1. 1. 4 *appellamus* S *appellemus* BΓςN; 23. 3. 3 *consequuntur*] *consequantur* ψ; 25. 1. 7 *constat*] *constaret* E; 25. 4. 21 *differunt* Halm *differant* BΓς. In MSS of the minor works, movement toward the subjunctive is more common than the reverse.

Note that I do not claim that the subjunctive is impossible. Examples can be found in the Latin of Tacitus' day of relative clauses in which the subjunctive is attested where the indicative might be expected, and vice versa (see Leumann–Hofmann–Szantyr, *Lateinische Grammatik*, vol. 2 [Munich, 1965], pp. 560–61). But a choice must be made, and an assumption that the subjunctive is the *difficilior lectio* does not accord with the observable performance of the scribes of the minor works. That Tacitus would use an imperfect indicative in such a clause can be demonstrated from a very similar sentence which closely follows: 17. 5 "ipsi vidistis plerosque senes qui se a divo quoque Augusto semel atque iterum accepisse congiarium narrabant." This should be strong enough evidence to support *fatebatur* even for those who believe it to be a conjecture.

23. 4 prope *abest* ab infirmitate in quo sola sanitas laudatur.

abest BΓ, *est* ς

4. In "Minor Works of Tacitus," I cite 11. 1. 21 *parant enim quid*, 21. 4. 23 *illae*, 10. 8. 17 *necesse sit expressit* (pp. 336–37); 41. 3. 4 *obscurior* (p. 341); I also list the omission of *est* at 37. 5. 5 (p. 343).

Since *abest ab* is the normal idiom, the simple *est* is the *difficilior lectio.* It is supported by the only other example in Tacitus of *prope* meaning "near": *Histories* 1. 10. 1 "tam prope ab exule fuit quam postea a principe," where the simplex is also used. Another possible parallel is *Germania* 30. 3. 5–6 *cunctatio propior constantiae est*, where *propior constantiae* is the reading of B, ς reads *propriora constantiae*, C has *propiora constantiae*, and Robinson conjectured *propior a constantia* (with greater transcriptional probability).

27. 2 "Non sum" inquit "offensus Apri mei disputatione, nec vos offendi decebit si quid forte aures vestras *perstringit*, cum sciatis hanc esse eius modi sermonum legem, iudicium animi citra damnum adfectus proferre." "Perge" inquit Maternus . . .

perstringit ςφ, *perstrigit* C, *perstringat* B, *perstringet* Lips.

If Tacitus is using his words carefully (and he always does), *perstringit* should not be right. Mesalla is not asking that his audience not be offended by what has already been said, but rather that they not be offended by what he is going to say. Either B's conjecture *perstringat* or Lipsius' *perstringet* should be read. The latter is more likely to have been corrupted to *perstringit*, and should be preferred.

29. 1 horum fabulis et erroribus [*et*] *virides* [*teneri*] statim et rudes animi inbuuntur

et secl. Knaut, om. b² *virides* B(b), *uides* ςφ, *uires* C, om. b² *teneri* codd., secl. Knaut

Basically three approaches have been taken to this text. One attitude is that *teneri* is in origin a gloss or variant for *virides*, and is wrong (so Knaut, followed by Winterbottom). Although this interpretation fits the juxtaposition of *virides* and *teneri*, it fails as an explanation of *et*. The attachment of *et* to *virides* shows rather that the words were originally a marginal variant for *et rudes*. The *et* was prefixed to the variant in order to make clear the word in the text (*rudes*) for which *virides* (or *vides*) was a variant. The extant Hersfeldensis on the *Agricola* provides several examples of this method of locating the reference of the variant by including a word for which there is no variation: 21. 1. 16 *et otio* E^v *in otio* E;[5] 22. 1. 28 *ad taum* E^v *ad tanaum* E; 35. 3. 11 *quo ceteri* E *quo steteri* E^v.[6]

The other two approaches are therefore closer to the truth: that *virides* is a variant for *rudes* and wrong (so Halm following b²), and that *virides* is a variant for *rudes* and correct (so Gudeman). The MSS of the minor works offer ample evidence of conflated variants, with the doublets often separated from each other by a word

5. Ogilvie reports *et otio* as the reading of E², when his usual practice would require attribution to E^{2m}. Hence there is a slight error in my statistics in "Minor Works of Tacitus": on p. 330, line 15, change "six times" to "seven times" and list 21. 1. 16 *quieti et otio* E^vAB *quieti in otio* E *qui et in otio* T—probably T's reading reflects a conflation of E^v and E (*quieti et in otio*) followed by haplography of *eti*. On p. 330, line 32, the citation of 44. 4. 25 should be omitted (A^v has it), and the figures adjusted accordingly.

6. Ogilvie's apparatus is misleading here. Where Ogilvie prints Bekker's *agmen in aequo ceteri*, E has *agminae quo ceteri*. E² in the margin has the variant *quo steteri* for *quo ceteri*.

or more.[7] Gudeman[8] cites a number of passages that show *teneri et rudes* to be a consecrated collocation: Cicero *De legibus* 1. 17. 47 *teneros et rudes;* Quintilian 1. 11. 2 *tenerum . . . et rudem;* Seneca *Epistle* 50. 4 *teneri et rudes animi. Rudis* is a frequent word in Tacitus in passages of sense analogous to the current one. From Gerber and Greef's *Lexicon Taciteum* (Leipzig, 1903) we find that it is used three times modifying *animi* (as here),[9] another three times of age (modifying *aetas* or *annis*),[10] and three times as the second element in a pair.[11] Gudeman's reaction to such evidence was to prefer *virides*, on the ground that no one would gloss *rudes* by *virides*, but could easily do the reverse. Although it is true that *rudes* would not be so glossed, the words are close enough in appearance that one could easily be a simple slip for the other. The variants of the Hersfeldensis are, for the most part, not glosses, but readings which the corrector found in another MS.[12] Further, it is not even clear that the archetypal reading was *virides*. The reading is found only in B and its copy, b. Unless there was an archetypal variant (a variant, then, on a variant), the reading which we would have to reconstruct as archetypal is *uides*, which is found on both sides of the tradition, and which cannot even be sensibly construed (that is, it is the *difficilior lectio*). The other readings, *virides* and *vires*,[13] make enough sense for them to be attempts at correcting *uides:* with *virides*, "even though vigorous, tender and untrained minds are promptly tainted"; with *vires*, "even their strengths, their tender and untrained minds," etc. It is unlikely that a scribe who knew *virides* or *vires* would deliberately choose to write *vides*. I concede that, if I wished to defend *virides*, I would argue for an archetypal variant (either $\overset{ir}{\textit{uides}}$ or $\overset{id}{\textit{uires}}$ to explain the variation between B and C).[14] There is no example in the extant part of the Hersfeldensis of such superscribed letters above a marginal variant. The superscription, then, if it existed, probably appeared first in a Renaissance exemplar in which the marginal variant of the Hersfeldensis had already intruded as a conflation in the text. If so, the intrusive reading could easily have

7. In the *Agricola* we find 10. 4. 4 *sed transgressis*] *est transgressis sed* AB, where *est* and *sed* were in origin variants. In the *Dialogus* there are many examples, including 16. 7. 3 *sed fama*] *et fama sed* ς.

Conflation is characteristic of the descendants of the Hersfeldensis (see "Minor Works of Tacitus," p. 336), but not of the Hersfeldensis itself, to whose original text a slightly later corrector (E^2 or E^v) has added hundreds of corrections and marginal variants. The lack of conflation in the original text of the Hersfeldensis supports the belief that the corrector excerpted from an exemplar different from the first scribe's source (see also "Minor Works of Tacitus," p. 330, n. 8).

I hope that the reader perceives beneath my arguments an underlying principle: though for any given error usually more than one explanation can be given which is logically satisfying, preference should go to the explanation which fits the known circumstances of transmission and the transmission's demonstrable effects on the text.

8. *P. Cornelii Taciti "Dialogus de Oratoribus"* (Boston, 1894), p. 284.

9. *Ann.* 1. 31, 3. 26, 6. 3.

10. *Ann.* 4. 8, 13. 16, 15. 13.

11. *Agr.* 21. 1. 16 *ut homines dispersi ac rudes; Dial.* 5. 7. 3 *inexercitatam et . . . rudem Helvidii sapientiam; Dial.* 19. 2. 15 *populus ut imperitus et rudis.*

12. See "Minor Works of Tacitus," p. 330, n. 8, and supra, n. 7.

13. Codex c is reported to have *uiles*, which is, I am sure, another attempted emendation, though it is not clear what the scribe thought it meant.

14. The latter is Winterbottom's suggestion ("Transmission," p. 125, n. 30), and the more likely, since for the former we would expect $\overset{ri}{\textit{uides}}$.

been *uides* or *uires*, with *uirides* a Renaissance conjecture.[15] The only other example of *viridis* in Tacitus (*Agr.* 29. 4. 1 *viridis senectus*) is a Renaissance conjecture for *uiris* (*ui*^{di}*ris* by Stefano Guarnieri, the Renaissance corrector of the Hersfeldensis). In short, although I suspect that in *Dialogus* 29. 1. 16 the Renaissance archetype had *et uides teneri*, we cannot be certain whether the marginal variant of the Hersfeldensis was *uirides* or simply *uides*. If the latter, it could be a slip for *rudes* through miscombination of the minims. If the former, it is still close enough to *rudes* to be an accidental slip (psychologically influenced by *teneri* for a scribe thinking of vegetation). The choice between *virides* and *rudes*, then, should be made on the basis of appropriateness, and not on the supposition that only one could have led to the other.

Not only is *rudes* supported by Tacitean vocabulary, and the combination *teneri et rudes* by the consecration of the phrase,[16] but both words are supported by parallels in sources of similar sentiment. Gudeman cites several examples:[17] (*a*) [Plut.] *Moralia* 3E εὔπλαστον γὰρ καὶ ὑγρὸν ἡ νεότης καὶ ταῖς τούτων ψυχαῖς ἁπαλαῖς ἔτι τὰ μαθήματα ἐντήκεται—here ψυχαῖς ἁπαλαῖς is the equivalent of *teneri animi* and ἐντήκεται of *inbuuntur;* (*b*) Seneca *Dialogi* 12. 18. 8 "altius praecepta descendunt quae teneris imprimuntur aetatibus"; and (*c*) Quintilian 1. 1. 5 "natura tenacissimi sumus eorum quae rudibus annis percepimus." To these may be added: (*d*) Vergil *Georgics* 2. 272 "adeo in teneris consuescere multum est"; and (*e*) Quintilian 1. 1. 36 "Prosequitur haec memoria in senectutem et impressa animo rudi usque ad mores proficiet." The last passage, together with the three examples of *rudes animi* in Tacitus, provide good support for the *rudes animi* of this passage. When in the *Agricola* Tacitus talked of "green old age," he used a familiar[18] and appropriate image, which contrasts with old age's usual "whiteness." I am less than charmed with the image of "green minds," though in combination with *teneri* it is tolerable.[19] For the Romans, the normal connotations of *viridis* were of vigor,[20] rather than of impressionableness. We should follow b^2 in reading simply *teneri statim et rudes*.[21]

CHARLES E. MURGIA
University of California, Berkeley

15. *Vides* would, in this context, prompt such conjecture more readily than *uires*.

16. Gudeman, "*Dialogus*," p. lv, cites fifteen examples of familiar pairs of words used in the *Dialogus:* that is, the employment of well-worn pairs is characteristic of the style of the *Dialogus*.

17. Ibid., p. 284. Gudeman (pp. xcix–cii) argues that Pseudo-Plutarch, Quintilian, and Tacitus all use Chrysippus' lost treatise on the education of children. Quint. 1. 1. 4 cites Chrysippus by name. R. Güngerich, "Der *Dialogus* des Tacitus und Quintilians *Institutio Oratoria*," *CP* 46 (1951): 159–64, has proved that among Tacitus' sources was Quintilian himself.

18. E.g., Verg. *Aen.* 6. 304.

19. Sen. *Epist.* 66. 1 uses *viridem animo ac vigentem* of an old friend who was still young and vigorous of mind.

20. This is the only connotation (besides youth) recognized in Lewis and Short; so also Ae. Forcellinus, *Lexicon totius Latinitatis*, vol. 4 (Padua, 1940), p. 1008: "II.) Translate ¶1. Generatim refertur ad juventam, vigorem, robur." No examples are cited illustrating the common English meaning of "green" as "inexperienced."

21. I am indebted to Professors R. F. Renehan and R. H. Rodgers for reading and criticizing this paper.

BOOK REVIEWS

The Origins of Greek Religion. By B. C. DIETRICH. Berlin and New York: Walter de Gruyter, 1974. Pp. 345. $51.20.

Götterkult. By EMILY TOWNSEND VERMEULE. "Archaeologia Homerica," Band III, Kapitel V. Aus dem Englischen übersetzt von MARIA und HANS-GÜNTER BUCHHOLZ. Göttingen: Vandenhoeck & Ruprecht, 1974. Pp. 179 + 14 pls.

Here are two studies that promise to bring us up-to-date on the sources of Classical Greek religion. In the past thirty years there has been much progress in archaeological discovery, the decipherment of prehistoric Greek texts, fuller and more informed use of comparative material from the ancient Near East and elsewhere, and, not least, in our understanding of early Greek society. The subject of Dietrich's book is described as the debt of Greek religion to prehistoric and foreign sources, and the work of M. P. Nilsson is claimed as a model and the scholar himself as a spiritual guide. Vermeule's is a "chapter" (translated from an English manuscript) in a rather uneven encyclopedia of Homeric archaeology being published in fascicles; the manuscript was completed in 1963 and, although bibliographical additions have been made up to 1971, the author fears the text may seem "old-fashioned and naive." That is far from being the case. Her concise and modest volume provides the best summation of the evidence, guide to further study, and individual interpretation yet published. To make it more widely available we must agitate for its separate publication, in its original language as well as in translation, and with a supplement to take into account more recent developments (if only to satisfy the author's conscience). By contrast, Dietrich's much more ambitious book is extremely disappointing.

V. owes her success in part to sure control of the indispensable archaeological evidence (line drawings and plates are well chosen) and to careful attention to the differences in time and place, both marked and subtle, that the archaeological evidence reveals. She lays stress on the local character of Greek and prehistoric religion and makes us think about such problems as how the Mycenaean Greeks would have had contact with and so been influenced by the religion of Crete. She sees the Greeks taking over certain locally tied cults rather than a unified religion. Rustic shrines, apparently not characteristic of Mycenaean Greece, are less likely than the cults of the palace centers to have impinged on the mainland. Minoan religion is to be thought of as no less rich and complex than Minoan culture itself. Contrasts are drawn between the palatial and post-palatial periods, and between Crete and Mycenaean Greece, where, she believes, cult was less tied to special, separate places, more surely centered on animal sacrifice, and less concerned in its art with nature and more with man and, increasingly, with fantasy. But the limitations of art as a source for religion are made clear; for example, the importance of the male element among divinities as seen in the Pylos tablets could not have been deduced from contemporary artistic representations.

D.'s emphasis is on unity, of the Aegean with the Near East, of Crete with Mycenae ("the modern habit of strictly dividing Cretan from Mycenaean religion has gone too far" [p. 137]), of the Bronze Age with Classical Greece. Of the last he says specifically that "religious values had remained fundamentally the same" (p. 237). By avoiding distinctions, minimizing change, slighting and misunderstanding archaeological evidence (there is not a single illustration in the 345 pages of this expensive book), D. reduces early religion to a pallid blur in which everything can be, and usually is, identified with everything else. Thus the use of the caves of Crete at different periods for habitation, cult, and burial is seen as a single phenomenon, confirming the goddess' role in death as well as in life. Under the various names and types of representation there is only one goddess, known to the Mycenaeans also as Potnia and Wanassa. The evidence of the tablets is presented in as derivative and shaky a manner as that of excavation: Apollo is and is not to be found in the tablets (pp. 264, 309; he is not attested, at least by that name); Demeter, it is granted, is "not present beyond a doubt" (the name is not attested).

For V., the period of transition to historical Greece, the "Dark Ages" of ca. 1150–1000 B.C., with its movement of people, is seen as a challenge to the gods closely tied to place. This is a crucial time for the development of later mythical and religious traditions. V.'s economical and comprehensive analysis of Homeric evidence for gods and cult is matched by a review of the evidence of monuments and representations into the seventh century B.C. By itself the issue of continuity between the Bronze Age and the Classical world has little meaning. V. rightly is concerned rather with the effect of profound social and economic changes on religious conceptions and practice as they can be detected through art, excavations, and poetry. She confronts the disconformity between Homer and the monuments (the poet, for example, pays less heed to the great goddesses of the eighth- and seventh-century cult centers and ignores flourishing Olympia) and suggests that he may have seemed radical in some respects to his contemporaries and that his world knew no rigid hierarchy of deities. The poems, however, also reveal common grounds of belief in Homer's society, notably an objectivity about the individual's ability to control his own fate. The procedures of cult provided a mechanism for mediating between the individual and what controlled his fate. V. concludes by reminding us of the millennium of development that lies behind the sudden, contemporaneous appearance of rich poetic and archaeological evidence and warns, as she does throughout her study, against oversimplification.

D.'s goal allows him less space for Homer and requires that he continue through the Archaic period. For him, any trace of later occupation on a prehistoric site proves continuity of society and hence of cult ("uninterrupted settlement presupposes enduring cult" [p. 226]). Continuity of cult, in turn, requires continuity of social organization; the clans (D.'s unexamined translation of γένη) and phratries that recent historians have seen as the product of Archaic Greece must go back to the Bronze Age. Indeed, Indo-European *genos* and the specialized "brotherhood" that eliminated the stem's ordinary use as a kinship term must be old, but why should we suppose that their forms and functions were immutable? Otherwise D.'s last chapter owes much to Nilsson, whose conception of Archaic Greek society was never unassailable. The book ends with three appendices: on the Minoan peak cult (similarities with other Minoan cults stressed), Delphic Apollo (D. implies that the *Homeric Hymn* derives the god from Crete, but the poem has only Apollo's priests coming from there), and on Mycenaean mythology.

Trying to make up for my obvious lack of sympathy with D.'s approach, I would point to his recognition of the importance of the bull in Minoan iconography and presumably cult, all the more striking if, against Nilsson, one dissociates the bull from animal sacrifice of the usual Greek type. D. is also surely right in seeing more evidence for cult in Bronze Age burial customs than is commonly allowed, although I do not know that his notion of "a promise of new life" is a less anachronistic explanation of the disregard for the bones of earlier burials than Mylonas' escape of the soul with the decay of the flesh. And his observations of similarities between different forms of cult, for instance, between Minoan peaks and palaces, would be helpful if they were balanced by a fair appreciation of the differences.

V.'s study, admirable as it is, allows room for disagreement, too—it would be less original and intriguing if it did not. To my mind, V. does not give enough weight to the immeasurable but inescapable contribution of the pre-Indo-European culture of the mainland to the religion of the Middle and Late Bronze Age. She draws probably more inferences than are warranted from the tablets. Peleia the "Dove Goddess" (D. has her, too) is apparently *Pe-re-swa;* cf. Perse? (M. Ventris and J. Chadwick, *Documents in Mycenaean Greek*[2] [Cambridge, 1973], p. 463). I am skeptical of the notion that Poseidon was more prominent than Zeus at Pylos on the basis of the tablets (where his consort is Posidaeia, not Posideia) and the *Odyssey*. On the other hand, Tn 316 seems to refer to a number of separate shrines, and this conflicts more with the general picture V. draws than she admits. The attribution to goddesses of early buildings at Olympia and Delos is also arguable. Her work is so firmly founded, however, that the decade that elapsed between writing and publication should cause no alarm to author or reader. Even if one proposition after another has to be modified or abandoned because of new discoveries, this edition will not lose its value. A new edition will want to take more account of the new evidence, not yet fully published, for the area of the citadel house and Tsountas' house at Mycenae.[1] Have we a cult center for the town as opposed to the palace? Are shrine, fresco, and idols late and of Cretan derivation, as V. seems inclined to think? D., without reference to this site, sees the influence flowing in the other direction. Or are we seeing house shrines, essentially, of a type that would be more common if we had more foundations of the larger Mycenaean houses? There is now an interesting house shrine on the *Unterburg* of Tiryns. On Crete, Hermes Kedrites and his previous Minoan incarnations will add much to our knowledge of "tree cult" in both the Bronze and Iron Ages.[2] As for the series itself, the bibliographies are splendid but ungraded. A Michelin star system would be helpful. The concept of "Homeric Archaeology" is ambiguous (V. does not address the problem of locating the Homeric world in history), but, for the time being, the brilliance of this section of the enterprise silences doubts.

Michael H. Jameson
Stanford University

1. Add to V.'s bibliography on p. 32, n. 68, reports in *To Ergon tēs Archaiologikēs Hetaireias* (1941–75) and G. E. Mylonas, *Mycenae. A Guide to Its Ruins and History* (Athens, 1976), p. 23 and fig. 34.

2. See A. Lebessi, "A Sanctuary of Hermes and Aphrodite in Crete," *Expedition* 18, no. 3 (1976): 2–13; see also the entries "Κρήτη. Σύμη Βιάννου" in *To Ergon* (1973, 1975) and "Κρήτη. Ἱερὸν Σύμη Βιάννου" in *To Ergon* (1976); cf. G. Daux, "Notes de lecture," *BCH* 100 (1976): 211–13.

The Ancient View of Greek Art: Criticism, History, and Terminology. By J. J. POLLITT. Yale Publications in the History of Art, 25. New Haven and London: Yale University Press, 1974. Pp. xiv + 464. $25.00.

J. J. Pollitt was already known in the field of art history from his books, *The Art of Greece: 1400–31 B.C.* (Englewood Cliffs, N.J., 1965) and *The Art of Rome: 753 B.C.–337 A.D.* (Englewood Cliffs, N.J., 1966), both in the series "Sources and Documents in the History of Art" edited by H. W. Janson. This book, much more ambitious than the other two, was begun as a doctoral dissertation, "The Critical Terminology of the Visual Arts in Ancient Greece" (Columbia University, 1963), and it fills an important gap in the bibliography of Greek art. Pollitt belongs to the generation of ancient art historians who can study the ancient authors in the original languages; what he has given us here is a discussion of the critical terminology of the ancients, written from the point of view of an art historian rather than of a philologist. Even Greekless students of art will profit from this book, since the ancient passages are translated and the commentaries are detailed and explicit.

The book is divided into three parts. Part 1, "Art Criticism in Antiquity," distinguishes four traditions of ancient criticism, connected respectively with artists, philosophers, rhetoricians, and common people. Part 2, "Art History in Antiquity," discusses ancient writing on the history of the arts, as it may be recovered from Pliny, Quintilian, Cicero, and their sources. The third and largest portion of the book is a glossary of Greek and Latin terms (like *eurhythmia, symmetria, typos*) which were regularly used in describing and evaluating works of art. P. describes these terms as "semantic crystals solidified out of the molten material of Greek aesthetic experience" (p. 2). (For the nonspecialist there is available an abridged edition of the book containing only samples from this glossary.)

As he explains in the prologue, P.'s objective is to see ancient art as ancient critics saw it, so far as the fragmentary evidence permits, and to assess the evidence without letting his own aesthetic experience interfere. The modern sensibility, he argues, has been strongly influenced by idealism and naturalism, the two major critical attitudes toward Greek art which have been popular since the Renaissance, and which, as he observes, were not entirely unknown among the ancients. P.'s study of ancient critical concepts ranges roughly from the time of the Homeric epics in the eighth century B.C. to the lifetime of Callistratus in the fourth century after Christ. But his emphasis is on the classical and Hellenistic periods, for which there is more extant evidence and wider interest.

In Part 1, after an introduction which discusses our sources for ancient art criticism,[1] P. deals first with the professionals: painters, sculptors, and architects who wrote treatises about their art. Polyclitus' *Canon* is lucidly discussed, and his concept of symmetry is related to contemporary Greek philosophical thought, Pythagorean number theory, and Eurytus' pebble diagrams. P. suggests that Polyclitus' notion that symmetry in sculpture achieves "the good" or "the beauti-

1. One work which ought to be mentioned in this context, but which was perhaps not yet available when P.'s manuscript was being written, is G. Schwarz, *Die griechische Kunst des 5. und 4. Jahrhunderts v. Chr. im Spiegel der "Anthologia Graeca"* (Vienna, 1971).

ful" was derived from Pythagorean thought.[2] From the evidence about other professional treatises, he elicits the terminology which was developed for art criticism. Values implicit here he relates to more universal habits of Greek thought and culture—for example, the tendency "to view the specific in the light of the generic" (p. 26). But P. also calls attention to changes between the classical period, with its emphasis on reality (expressed as *aletheia* and *akribeia*), and the Hellenistic period, with its interest in appearance and illusion (*opsis*, *phantasia*) and in the representation of character and emotion (*ethos* and *pathos*).

He next surveys the contribution of the philosophers. P. describes the development given to the concept of *techne* by the Sophists, who included under it the "intellectual and emotional activities by which a man practiced 'virtue' or 'excellence' in his society" (p. 34), and finally by Aristotle, who defined it as "a purposive process that produces a final form out of preexisting matter" (pp. 35–36). A second crucial term is *mimesis*, which leads P. to discuss the philosophers' preoccupation with the effects of art on human character. Much attention is given to Plato, who condemns art in the tenth book of the *Republic* as mere imitation twice removed from the Ideas; P. raises the possibility that there is the glimmering of a distinction between "good" and "bad" imitation in Plato's separation of art into *eikastike*, which produces images "that are other than but like what they imitate," and *phantastike*, which produces images "that appear to be like what they imitate but are in reality quite unlike it" (p. 46). This section on the philosophers as critics of art deals also with Gorgias' praise of art as persuasive deception (*apate*); with Zeno's theory of the *kataleptike phantasia* and its role in perception; with the later development of what P. calls the "*phantasia* theory"—"the view that the great artists of the Classical period had been inspired seers, visionaries of a sort, who had been able to grasp the nature of divinity and convey it to their fellow men through the medium of the visual arts" (p. 52); and finally with the attitudes toward art which are evident in Plotinus' *Enneads*, including the "incipiently medieval" notion that "beauty in the sensible world was only of value to the extent that it pointed the way to transcendental experience" (pp. 56–58).

In a shorter section on rhetorical and literary criticism, P. shows how, after rhetoricians had begun to distinguish characteristic "virtues" (*aretai*) of literary style and to classify orators accordingly, a similar effort was made to classify painters and sculptors. Alongside canons of writers appear canons of artists, in which Phidias regularly has pride of place. Two more short sections follow, one summarizing the strain of "popular" criticism, which judged works of art in terms of their realism, miraculous qualities, and costliness, and a final section on late manifestations of Hellenistic theory in Roman writers; here P. deals especially with Vitruvius and what he calls the "*decor* theory," that the form of a work of art should be "appropriate" (pp. 68–69).

Part 2, "Art History in Antiquity," surveys first the tradition of art history

2. P. is wrong, however, in thinking that the paper by Iversen to which he refers (p. 88, n. 4) was able to "prove beyond any reasonable doubt that canons did exist in Ancient Greece." No actual marks have been found on unfinished Greek figures, as marks have been found on Egyptian ones, and Iversen himself admits that there is great flexibility in the proportional systems of the works he studied. It is more likely that there were no consistent and rigid digital canons, like those observed by Egyptian sculptors, but simply different systems of proportions and symmetry which varied with the artist, district, period, and fashion.

represented by Books 34–36 of Pliny's *Natural History*. Relying on the bibliographical information which Pliny preserves about his sources, P. reconstructs the influence of a Sicyonian school with an evolutionary theory of artistic development. "This theory envisions a gradual evolution of Greek sculpture and painting toward a stage of perfection which was finally achieved in the late fourth century by the foremost sculptor and the foremost painter—Lysippus and Apelles—of the Sicyonian school" (pp. 74–75); this interpretation is traced ultimately to Xenocrates. Apart from Xenocrates and Pliny's other Greek sources, P. emphasizes the influence on the *Natural History* of Marcus Terentius Varro, who was responsible for transmitting a great deal of Greek art criticism, and who offered Pliny a model for writing systematically about art. A different, less evolutionary approach to art history is preserved in Quintilian's *Institutio oratoria* (12. 10. 3–9) and Cicero's *Brutus* (70); in this tradition, the formation of which is unclear, Phidias represents the culmination of Greek art.[3]

In sum, by elucidating certain cultural attitudes of the Greeks, the first two parts of the book help us to appreciate the place of the visual arts in relation to the literary arts in ancient times. P. effectively brings out how widespread was the appreciation of the visual arts among literary men and, in a different way, among common people. His survey is useful for classical scholars who are not specialists in ancient art, and for both modern and ancient art historians. Since the conclusions he draws in the epilogue may serve as a basis for the study of art criticism in subsequent eras, they will bear repeating here (p.85):

> [There was] a gradual shift from objectivity toward subjectivity in the rendering of critical judgments; from the preoccupation of the professional artist with form and the means of controlling form toward the connoisseur's preoccupation with his reactions to art and the philosopher's interest in evaluating its extrinsic meaning; from an interest in perfecting a product . . . toward an interest in the personality and the state of mind of the man who produced it. . . . [By the late Hellenistic period] "aesthetics" in the academic sense became divorced once and for all from the problems of professional technique and replaced professional interests as the leading force in the criticism of the visual arts. . . . Popular criticism probably ran as an inconspicuous current parallel to all of these developments, and in the time of Callistratus, when the impetus that had prompted more ambitious traditions of criticism was spent, this type of criticism was all that remained.

Almost three-quarters of the book (pp. 113–449) is taken up by the glossary, which lists the principal terms of Greek art criticism and the Latin terms that were used to translate them. Although P. says that this material could be arranged by categories (the nature and methods of artistic representation, the nature of the artist, the nature of the work of art), he has preferred to arrange the terms alphabetically. After each entry, the relevant testimonia are set out, both in the original and in translation, and a detailed and very helpful commentary follows.

For the problem of the sources, only tentative solutions are usually possible. When a term such as *akribeia* appears in a discussion of Phidias by Aristotle, and

3. Since in this section P. has occasion to deal with the rendering of Greek terms in Latin, it may be worth asking here why Pliny and others use the Greek term *toreutike* (= metal work, embossed work) as a general word for sculpture. The reason is probably that the Greek sources used it for artists like Phidias, who was a *toreutes* as well as a sculptor.

later also in writers like Demetrius, Plutarch, Lucian, and Pausanias, one can conclude that it was probably a classical conception handed down through Hellenistic sources. In the case of the term *haplotes* (simplicity), however, which does not appear before Dionysius of Halicarnassus in the first century B.C., it may be legitimate to hypothesize Platonic influence, as P. does. But it is equally possible that the appreciation of simplicity in art is a spontaneous reaction of the late Hellenistic period, when people grew tired of the complex and elaborate. The history of any given term is difficult to reconstruct because the evidence from the late Hellenistic and Roman periods is much richer than from earlier periods. It is perhaps for this reason that P. has not on the whole been able to conclude which qualities were most admired in each period. But despite the fragmentary nature of the evidence, and the disputes surrounding the significance of certain terms (e.g., *to axiomatikon*), P.'s glossary of the critical terminology is an important instrument that brings alive, more than anything else, the aesthetic values and approaches of the Greeks. His translations in the glossary (and in the first two parts of the book) are generally clear and accurate, and only rarely somewhat unsatisfactory (as for example in his rendering of Posidonius on p. 102, n. 41).

The book is nicely produced; it has an elegant terracotta-colored cloth binding, and the dust jacket has scenes from a red-figure *kylix* by the Foundry Painter, which show the progress of work in a metal sculptor's workshop. There is no select bibliography, which would have been useful, but there are detailed references in the notes. I should like to add that Dr. Doreen Innes of St. Hilda's College, Oxford, has written for her doctoral dissertation a commentary on half of the work of Demetrius; she is currently working on the other half, and will eventually publish the whole. Also of interest is a recent article on Ammianus Marcellinus, an Antiochene Greek writing in Latin for the Roman aristocracy, who viewed art not from an aesthetic, but from an illustrative and ethical point of view: M. A. Tomei, "Fonti per la storia dell'arte antica: Ammiano Marcellino," *ArchClass* 24 (1972): 75–95.

I noticed a few typographical errors, e.g., p. 45, line 35, read "Plato's" for "plato's"; p. 49, line 26, the accent on σημεία should be circumflex; p. 144, line 7, read τηλικοῦτοι for τηλικοῦτος; line 25, read Ὁμήρου for Ὁηήρου; p. 152, line 2, Ἐρωτας requires an accent; p. 196, line 17, εἶδους should have an acute accent; in the index on p. 461, κολόσσος should have the accent on the last syllable; in the index of ancient authors, after Ammianus Marcellinus the passage should be 30. 9. 4, not 30. 94.

The Ancient View of Greek Art is a comprehensive study, clearly written and carefully annotated. It will be most useful for teachers and students of ancient art. As Pollitt says near the beginning, the task he undertook was so laborious and required the use of so many disciplines that anyone would naturally shy away from it—as many scholars have done until Pollitt. We are grateful that he had the courage to take up and complete this work.

Theodora Hadzisteliou Price
Naperville, Illinois

Ordo populusque Pompeianus: Polity and Society in Roman Pompeii. By PAAVO CASTRÉN. Acta Instituti Romani Finlandiae, vol. 8. Rome: Bardi Editore, 1975. Pp. 296.

Pompeii was never a particularly important town in the Roman world, and perhaps for this reason the plentiful evidence on its political, social, and economic setup long failed to attract the quality of scholarship it merits (see Castrén's discreet remarks on pp. 27–37). At last, however, the tide has begun to turn, and Castrén's book may be placed alongside J. Andreau's *Les affaires de Monsieur Jucundus* (Rome, 1974) as a fundamental, indeed invaluable, contribution to our knowledge.

C.'s aim, briefly, is to set out and evaluate the epigraphical evidence on the citizens of Pompeii, the best attested of whom are inevitably those from the leading families, and the core of his book is the prosopographical index, containing more than 5,000 names under 479 *gentilicia* (pp. 125–244). This material is preceded by a historical introduction devoted to the pre-Roman period (pp. 37–46), an account of the establishment and the administration of the Roman colony (pp. 49–82), and an attempt to sketch the ups and downs of the leading families between 80 B.C. and A.D. 79 (pp. 82–124). A bibliography, two appendixes (on *cognomina* and lists of magistrates), and three indexes complete the work.

Although the most important part of the book is undoubtedly the prosopographical index, the third section on the nature of municipal life in Pompeii will probably draw the widest readership, and here some problems arise. C. maintains, for example, that the inscriptions give us the names of more than half the municipal magistrates (a minimum of 50.8%, according to p. 84). But this estimate depends on arguments like the assertion that "many of the persons whom we know only as candidates must have been elected" (p. 85). If the elections at Pompeii were contested at all vigorously, as they seem to have been, there is no knowing how many candidates stood for a particular office at any one time (cf. p. 79). So when we come upon a man who is the only attested bearer of his *gentilicium* in the town, and we have only one or two election notices to tell us that he was a candidate for office (thus, e.g., C. Aburius on p. 129, L. Cordius on p. 157, or L. Ovidius Veiento on p. 201), it may be an act of faith to reckon him a member of the Pompeian establishment.

This problem becomes especially acute when the evidence consists almost exclusively of election notices, as it does for the later Julio-Claudian and Flavian periods (p. 83; cf. pp. 113–14); and yet this is a period when C. argues for a fundamental change in the nature of political life in Pompeii, with old families being pushed or withdrawing into the background and new families taking over (p. 121). The argument may be correct; it is not without a certain plausibility. But consider this statement: "The Lollii seem not to have entered the group of magisterial families until the last period, having previously been represented in Pompeii only by a *minister Augusti* in the year A.D. 1" (p. 119). As consultation of the index will show (p. 183), the evidence consists only of election notices, all alike referring to candidates for the lowest office of all, the aedileship (cf. pp. 62–64); and it is far from clear (*a*) whether we are talking of two, three, or four Lollii, (*b*) whether any of them were elected, and (*c*) whether these men would have been induced by a common *gentilicium* to cooperate politically with one another at or after election time.

If these criticisms suggest a need for caution in accepting Castrén's views about the nature of political life in Pompeii, it should not be thought that they detract from the overall importance of his work. If Castrén had not assembled the evidence so painstakingly, it would not be possible to carp at all.

M. Gwyn Morgan
University of Texas at Austin

The Year of the Four Emperors. By P. A. L. GREENHALGH. New York: Barnes and Noble Books (a division of Harper and Row Publishers, Inc.), 1975. Pp. xv + 271 + 17 pls.; 6 maps in text. $17.00.

Any modern account of the year of the four emperors must of necessity be dominated by Tacitus' *Histories*. Greenhalgh's useful and very readable version, mostly narrative, relies heavily on Tacitus indeed, not just for the record of events but in matters of style as well. One of the author's stated intentions is to convey to the reader the spirit of the *Histories*, and he is often successful; the descriptions of the two battles of Bedriacum and of the siege of Cremona are fine examples of how Greenhalgh can capture the pace, excitement, and suspense of the original. It is largely because of such paraphrases that the book never loses interest throughout.

G.'s other intentions, however, are not so successfully fulfilled. He has written for two types of audience: "the general reader" and "the student of this period" (p. xii). But the needs of neither are met adequately. The latter is not presented with any scholarly apparatus (footnotes, bibliography, etc.) by which the formulation of G.'s judgments can be checked, and the former is at times misled on matters of historical substance. The first chapter, for instance, on Nero's loss of power in 68, is full of conventional stuff from the literary tradition on the Julio-Claudian emperors and devoid of any penetration beyond it. Equally trustworthy, apparently, are the speeches of the *Histories*, which G. frequently presents as historically accurate, both in the sense that they were actually made at the points Tacitus inserts them and that their content is accurately reported by him. The general reader is no more than indirectly led to understand that Tacitus' speeches may have been fabricated for literary effect, and that their inclusion is governed essentially by the conventions of ancient historiography. And the student will not accept, without qualification, that Claudius was "senile" (p. 4), that Nero was nothing more than "a Greek virtuoso" (p. 6), or that Nero's last years were an unmitigated reign of terror.

After such dependence on the literary sources, it comes as something of a surprise to find that G. insists on deflating the traditional picture of Vitellius as simply cruel, debauched, and gluttonous. G. points to the success of his pre-imperial career, his constitutionalism as emperor, his clemency, his reform of the "civil service," and his ability to inspire loyalty to the last. This "careful sifting of all the evidence" finds that the tradition is based on Flavian "revisionist propaganda" (pp. 115–17). But the case is overargued. It should not require such emphasis that a man who usurped the imperial power has to be taken seriously in his own right no matter what the tradition; and, on a point of detail, Domitian's later unpopularity for repeated tenure of the consulship ought to offset G.'s view that Vitellius' perpetual consulship was "more likely to have delighted than dismayed the constitutionalists" (p. 118).

There is little else with which the serious student can come to grips. But he will notice that Ti. Iulius Alexander was not procurator of Egypt (p. 69), that Calvia Crispinilla was not Nero's mistress (p. 9), that (more importantly) Thrasea Paetus was not removed solely on the basis of an "unguarded outburst" (p. 118), and that Vespasian cannot have been so seriously out of favor with Nero and for so long as G. suggests (p. 125). The notion of Gallic nationalism, introduced for the rebellion of Civilis (p. 192 ff.), is not the same as Gallic separatism, and the difference should be pointed out.

The eruption of civil war in 68–69 produced the most serious crisis faced by the principate up to that point in its history. The system survived the test, but the fact of military monarchy assumed a more blatant aspect than before, while the material damage inflicted by the process of war was a costly price to pay for the eventual establishment of a new dynasty. G. has not concerned himself with any discussion of these or related topics—the problem of the transfer of power, the reasons that the principate survived when its precariousness as a system of government had been exposed, and so on. Instead, he has concentrated on providing a well-written narrative for the most part. So perhaps the most suitable audience for the "story" will be students coming to the events for the first time, who will be able to enjoy the lively and exciting presentation but must be warned of the misleading features mentioned above. At seventeen dollars, the book is unfortunately overpriced.

K. R. Bradley
Stanford University

Tacitus über Kaiser Claudius: Die Ereignisse am Hof. By ANDREAS MEHL. Studia et Testimonia Antiqua, vol. 16. Munich. Wilhelm Fink Verlag, 1974. Pp. 199 + 1.

Tacitean scholarship has failed to lavish upon the Claudian books of the *Annales* the attention and ingenuity employed upon those dealing with Tiberius. Partly no doubt this lesser regard is due to the defective nature of the transmitted text, which leaves us with a climax, but without the buildup to it—although Mehl observes that the picture of Claudius in the missing books is unlikely to have differed much from his presentation in what survives (cf. R. Syme, *Tacitus* [Oxford, 1958], 1:259–60). Partly, too, the lack of attention paid to the Claudian books has itself contributed to the notion that the books lack interest—"never perhaps an enigma to be scrutinized and penetrated. Mere oddities palled, and the lack of dignity became an offence" (Syme, *Tacitus*, 1:319).

The idea that the narration of Claudius, even in its present truncated form, is without interest is well dispatched by M.'s new study which (it is promised in the concluding pages) is to be the precursor of others on Claudius. For this service, M.'s book is a welcome addition to the corpus of Tacitean scholarship.

M.'s subject is Tacitus' treatment of the *domus regnatrix*; all events are causally connected in the context of the entourage—an interpretation mirrored in the two major subdivisions of the book, chapter 1, "Triumph und Sturz Messalinas" (pp. 13–95), and chapter 2, "Aufstieg und Triumph Agrippinas" (pp. 96–181). These subdivisions also mirror the book's major thesis, that Tacitus had no high opinion of Claudius as an initiator, in which M. echoes I. S. Ryberg's observation that Claudius is rarely the subject of an active verb ("Tacitus' Art of Innuendo," *TAPA* 73 [1942]: 404).

Claudius' principate is dominated by others. In contrast to Suetonius and Cassius Dio (and, one infers, many of the emperor's contemporaries), Tacitus does not hold Claudius responsible for the *saevitia* of his reign, and to that extent Claudius fails to fit the "Tyrannenschema" which is recognizable in Tacitus' account of Tiberius, Nero, or Domitian. Yet the assumption that Tacitus has taken over the main features of the rhetoricians' stock tyrant, though often invoked in M.'s discussion, is less than convincing; indeed, M.'s view of the individuality of the Tacitean Claudius would rather argue against a stereotyped approach on the historian's part to the history of the early principate.

Although M. is clearly right to emphasize Claudius' subservience to others in court politics, his concentration on the *domus principis* may be responsible for producing a regrettable imbalance; for the exclusion in this book of those areas of imperial policy in which Claudius had ideas (sometimes of great consequence) removes what in one sense is an important counterweight to the dominated Claudius, although in another sense it might be argued that the disparity would only accentuate Claudius' domestic weaknesses still further.

The *saevitia* which is absent from Claudius is present in full measure in others, particularly Messalina and Agrippina. The great political ambition of Agrippina has long been recognized, although M. sees additional elements in Tacitus' portrayal of the mother of Nero. On the other hand, M. shows that Tacitus also recognized the political ambitions which were present alongside the *lascivia* of Messalina; Tacitus alone perceived more in the bigamous marriage with Silius than a simple erotic diversion.

Like most writers on Tacitus, M. puts some emphasis on the historian's power of dramatic composition. He argues against the idea that Claudius' stupidity lessens the sense of drama, for, as he justly insists, antagonism exists between the freedmen and the womenfolk. M. even believes that the historian's interest in dramatic portrayal leads him into inaccuracies, for example, concerning Narcissus' attitude toward Agrippina and Messalina—though one might say that Narcissus' attitude is perfectly credible in the context of his adherence to the house of Claudius and particularly to Britannicus.

In general M. finds that Tacitus has set out to heighten the dramatic intensity of his narrative by emphasizing the behavior of all those striving for power. Yet surely this is not a motif imposed from outside, as M. sometimes seems to think. Rather it is a theme which Tacitus discovered as he reenacted events in the writing of his history, and which he saw was fundamental to Claudius' principate, particularly in the area of domestic affairs. On the other hand, M. will certainly not provoke disagreement when he argues that Tacitus' account has a deeper penetration into the realities of power than either Suetonius' or Cassius Dio's.

The book's weaknesses are two. First, it tends to view Tacitus' "dramatic technique" as an artificial imposition on an otherwise intelligible picture. Second, although M. admits that Claudius' domestic situation did indeed impinge upon other aspects of his principate, the decision not to treat those aspects in the final analysis precludes a balanced view of the emperor's work and of the view which Tacitus took of it.

Despite these flaws, the book can be recommended for its lucid and readable treatment and for its orderly indication of the themes under discussion. The themes are carefully keyed by extensive references to the text, which allow the book to be used as a running commentary on Tacitus' narrative. Finally, among scholarly writings on this period, M.'s work is welcome too for its positive evaluation of Tacitus' individuality.

Mehl may not strike total accord among Tacitean scholars. But he will certainly stimulate them to think again about Tacitus' treatment of an emperor who did pose an enigma: "quippe fama spe veneratione potius omnes destinabantur imperio quam quem futurum principem fortuna in occulto tenebat."

D. C. A. Shotter
University of Lancaster

The Latin Poetry of English Poets. Edited by J. W. BINNS. London and Boston: Routledge & Kegan Paul, 1974. Pp. x + 198. $15.50.

J. W. Binns, who has edited this addition to Routledge's "Greek and Latin Studies" series, properly sets forth the questions to consider in the Latin poetry of English writers. "What is its significance, and its relation to their work in English? Can we interpret their English poems in the light of their achievement in Latin? How is our judgment of a poet altered by an awareness of his Latin works?" The six essays on Thomas Campion, John Milton, Richard Crashaw, George Herbert, Vincent Bourne, and Walter Savage Landor deal most successfully with the significance of the Latin poems, and our understanding of the poets generally is to that degree improved. The relationship between the Latin and the English poetry in most cases is, however, left largely for the reader to pursue on his own.

Edmund Waller's challenge in his *Of English Verse* becomes ironic whenever it is quoted:

> Poets that lasting marble seek
> Must carve in Latin, or in Greek;
> We write in Sand; our language grows,
> And like the tide, our work o'erflows.

Perhaps the metaphorical confusion in the last two lines conceals some uncertainties, but Pope expresses similar fears in the "Preface" to his collected *Works* in 1717. Nevertheless, if neo-Latin poetry did not fare well in the seventeenth century or afterward, there were many poets who committed themselves to it with distinction. Pope himself learned from them, as Johnson remarks: they were "a class of authors whom Boileau endeavoured to bring into contempt, and who are too generally neglected." Johnson even toyed with the idea of writing their history in 1734. The practice of Latin poetry had not yet become "the pastime of scholars and the eccentricity of unusual undergraduates." So concluded Leicester Bradner, who wrote the comprehensive *Musae Anglicanae: A History of Anglo-Latin Poetry* (London, 1940).

The English poets frequently produce Latin lines of striking beauty, but they are lines and not poems. For example, Herbert's on the death of his mother, the renowned Magdalen celebrated by Donne in *The Autumnall:*

> Parvam piamque dum lubenter semitam
>   Grandi reaeque praefero,
> Carpsit malignum sydus hanc modestiam
>   Vinumque felle miscuit.

The shift between the quiet opening *parvam piamque* and *carpsit* catches that turbulence characteristic of Herbert's inner debates. Or the often praised lines from Milton's *Mansus*, in which he mentions his hope of writing an epic on King Arthur and his knights:

> Aut dicam invictae sociali foedere mensae,
> Magnanimos heroas, et (O modo spiritus adsit)
> Frangam Saxonicas Britonum sub Marte phalanges.

Or Bourne's on the memory of a Cambridge servant whom he now imagines directing river traffic in the Stygian gloom as expertly as once he did on the Cam:

> Prospice, si crassam fors exploraveris umbram.

Herbert's epigrams in *Musae Responsoriae* expose his strong animus against the Puritan movement. In these poems Herbert attacks Andrew Melville, the Scots Presbyterian minister whose *Anti-Tami-Cami-Categoria* was a reply to the Oxford and Cambridge men angered by the Puritan Millenary Petition of 1603. W. Hilton Kelliher handles his analysis tactfully and informatively. But he is right in preferring as Herbert's Latin masterpiece the *Memoriae Matris Sacrum*. Here Herbert creates a personal tone and makes the Latin idiom, potentially a distancing factor, "serve his own immediate needs rather than merely . . . fulfill a literary ideal."

J. W. Binns skillfully relates Campion's amatory verses to their Ovidian models in exhaustive detail. Not only does Campion borrow the vocabulary of love, but also the tone, the mythological figures, the very landscapes. Campion's bizarre epyllion *Umbra*, however, which spans his career, offers a mythological story with no discoverable analogue. Since it is his finest Latin poem, one is prepared for a more probing account of it. The story, briefly, is this: Apollo has drugged Iole, then raped her in her sleep. She gives birth to Melampus, who is black but for the image of the sun on his breast. Later, Morpheus, the god of sleep, falls in love with the youthful Melampus but cannot attract him even with various transformations. At length Morpheus journeys to the underworld to find the shades of the most beautiful women and to fashion, like Zeuxis, a composite form of ideal feminine beauty. Returning to the sleeping Melampus, he appears disguised in this ravishing form. Melampus falls in love with the vision, but dawn breaks and the vision vanishes. As Binns concludes, "*Umbra* is a strange poem."

Milton is the major writer of neo-Latin poetry in English. For students of English literature today, he is the only poet whose Latin verses attract regular notice, because they frequently refer to his English poems or to his personal life. The fifth and sixth elegies, the *Ad Patrem* and the *Mansus*, and the elegant *Epitaphium Damonis*, on the death of his friend Diodati, are essential to our understanding of Milton. R. W. Condee studies each with care. He argues insightfully on the development of the personae, father and son, in the *Ad Patrem*, where the clash between them makes the central element in the poem. How can the young poet's high conception of his art be reconciled with his father's deprecation? "Milton solves this aesthetic [but surely not just aesthetic] problem essentially by the use of two ideas—by repeated praise of the old man's 'dona,' and by skilfully stressing the old man's accomplishments as a musician and therefore also as a protégé of Phoebus."

Kenneth J. Larsen develops an ingenious dating system for Crashaw's *Epigrammata Sacra*, written during his tenure at Pembroke Hall, Cambridge, in 1631–35. The liturgical key is discovered in the second lesson of the morning prayer. (Larsen thus makes a substantial contribution to the dating procedures advanced by Austin Warren and Sister M. S. Milhaupt.) Armed with a chronology, we may follow Crashaw through these crucial years; he proceeds from championing a justification of faith along Puritan lines

> Quae nec in externos modo dextera profuit usus,
> Certe erit illa tuae jam *manus* & *fidei*.

to extolling the virtue of love and its salvific implications:

> Absint, quo ficto simulant pia pectora vultu,
> Ignea quos luteo pectore lingua beat.
> Hoc potius mea vota rogant, mea thura petessunt,
> Ut mihi sit mea mens ignea, lingua luti.

The Puritan preachers are finally rejected; the incense-bearing poet embraces the Laudian liturgy; and Crashaw has made a large step toward conversion to Rome.

The little known Bourne (1695–1747) was the beloved Latin master of William Cowper at Westminister, though Cowper portrays him as indolent and slovenly. Lamb commends his Latin verses: ". . . his diction all Latin and his thoughts all English. Bless him!" Bourne's popular collection, *Carmina Comitialia Cantabrigiensia*, appeared in 1721—the poems were not all his own—and Mark Storey places it and later work in the context of Latin verses written as a pastime for the educated. In judicious asides Storey gives criticism by Johnson, Gildon, and Beattie; and he compares Cowper's translations of Bourne to their originals. Bourne falls victim to an abuse of the high neoclassic mode exemplified in Henry Felton's *Dissertation on Reading the Classics and Finding a Just Style* (London, 1713)—the title reveals the problem all too clearly. Felton praises Catullus for the "Softness and Delicacy" of his style but is shocked by the "Coarseness of his Thoughts too immodest for chaste Ears to bear." As Johnson writes, the "sonorous magnificence of Roman syllables" is frequently used to conceal "penury of thought" and "want of novelty"—both from the public and the author.

But if Bourne is not the Latin Prior, as Lamb would have wished, he is shown by Storey to have his own distinctively light-hearted jeu d'esprit. With Landor, on the other hand, we have a body of Latin poetry that in scope and quality approaches Milton's. Landor was the last English poet of stature to write a substantial amount of his poetry in Latin. In an excellent essay by Andrea Kelley we observe that Landor's Romantic tastes show themselves strongly, and that he revives as his models Ovid, Catullus, and Lucretius, all of whom had endured a century of relative neglect. Landor's fierce republicanism leads him to attack, with virulence and in none-too-marmoreal Latin, most of the sovereigns of Europe (e.g., the mock epitaph for George IV, "Heic. jacet, / Qui. ubique. et. semper. jacebat."). But is there any line among the Latin poems equal to Landor's masterful sound in "Past ruined Ilion Helen lives," where the order of each word is so decisively set, with "lives" commenting powerfully on "ruined Ilion?" I doubt it. Nonetheless, the *Ad Robertum Fratrem* of 1806 is touching and the *Daphne Suaveolens in Vase Fictili* graceful:

> Daphnen odoram quae tuis natalibus
> Florere gaudet, accipe.

I should add that all the Latin selections in Binns's collection have English translations in parentheses below them, a most convenient procedure, especially since the book will be useful to students of English literature who have little Latin. The index could have been enlarged and made topical.

John Paul Russo
Camden College, Rutgers University

The Phonemic System of the Attic Dialect 400–340 B.C. By Sven-Tage Teodorsson. Studia Graeca et Latina Gothoburgensia, vol. 32. Göteborg: Acta Universitatis Gothoburgensis, 1974. Pp. 326.

The heart of this book (pp. 75–162) consists of a catalog of spelling variations found on Attic inscriptions from earliest times down to about 200 B.C. Each variation is described in terms of the spelling norm, the phoneme which it can tentatively be assumed to represent, and the spelling variant. Thus the first entry deals with the variant ⟨I⟩ for expected ⟨E⟩/⟨EI⟩ corresponding to tentative /e:/, as in ἰς πόλιν. Each example within the entry is keyed as to the source, the date, the factors (phonetic or otherwise) possibly influencing the spelling, and the degree of control the author had over the inscription (e.g., through autopsy or photograph). Though one can quibble with various of the keys, or with the inclusion of a given example in the corpus, Teodorsson has performed his task admirably.

A collection of data, however, remains just that unless it is interpreted, and the author's purpose is "to reconstruct the phonemic system of the dialect spoken by the majority of the population living in the province of Attica, Greece, during the period 400–340 B.C." (p. 13). In order to reconstruct the dialect one must inspect the phonetic record, and that phonetic record consists of misspellings found on inscriptions, hence the data. For the most part (not surprisingly) T.'s conclusions match those of others (e.g., W. S. Allen, *Vox Graeca*[2] [Cambridge, 1974]). In the long vowel and diphthongal systems, however, he comes to remarkably different conclusions; for he thinks that by 350 B.C. all *i*-diphthongs had already been monophthongized and all distinctions of vowel quantity had already been lost. Hence for him Attic possessed only the eight phonemes /i, e, ϵ, a, ɔ, o, u, y/, though the traditional spelling remained more or less consistent for some time with purely conventional ι, ει, η, ηι, υ, and υι all representing /i/. Allen, on the other hand, allows fifteen phonemes and phoneme sequences, and assumes that in all cases save α, ι, and υ, a graphic symbol or sequence of symbols corresponds to a phoneme or sequence of phonemes.

Clearly we are here faced with different approaches to the same data. Allen and most others before him have assumed that Greek writing was essentially a phonemic transcription, and that change in the phonemic system is signaled only by fairly massive and systematic misspellings. T. believes that all spelling is conventional, more or less independent of the underlying phonetic reality, and that spelling may remain unchanged even though the phonetic (and phonemic) substance has shifted markedly. It is from this assumption that T. derives his Principle 1, the principle which informs the entire investigation: "The more fixed the orthographic norm, the greater is the phonetic evidence of each fully valid instance of an orthographic variant" (pp. 50 and 165). And, since Attic spelling conventions were quite rigid (p. 32), even a few cases of spelling uncertainty indicate phonetic uncertainty or even phonemic merger. Allen derives his conclusions from the orthographic norm, T. from the orthographic variant.

And yet T. is not completely consistent in his application of Principle 1. His Neutralization 1 (pp. 175–78) deals with the following four variations (number of examples in parentheses).

(*a*) ⟨I⟩ instead of ⟨E⟩/⟨EI⟩ for /e:/ (77)
(*b*) ⟨E⟩/⟨EI⟩ instead of ⟨I⟩ for /i:/ (24)
(*c*) ⟨E⟩/⟨EI⟩ instead of ⟨I⟩ for /i/ (32)
(*d*) ⟨I⟩ instead of ⟨E⟩ for /e/ (41)

From the first two of these variations he concludes that /i:/ and /e:/ had merged in /i:/ by 400 B.C. (Allen assumes that it happened ca. 350). But from the second two, which should indicate a merger also of /i/ and /e/, he fails to assume merger, even though the number of examples is approximately the same. It is his Principle 5 which justifies this divergent conclusion: "The more reliable our knowledge is of the development of a phonemic system during periods later than the one investigated, the more positive phonemic conclusions may be drawn from orthographic data from that period" (p. 283). Since modern Greek still distinguishes /e/ and /i/, the two phonemes cannot have merged in 350 B.C. Principle 5, though applied rarely, destroys the validity of Principle 1: either the data lead us to the facts or they do not. Since they do not directly, and since new principles can be appealed to, one feels justified in appealing to other principles as well to resolve uncertainties, for example, the fact that quantitative poetry continued to be written in Greek for many years after 350 B.C.

Because of the above inconsistency I am unwilling to accept the validity of Principle 1 and with it the extreme conclusions to which it leads. On the other hand, Teodorsson's data are impressive; they do indicate that phonetic change (and hence phonemic uncertainty) was occurring earlier than had been previously thought: perhaps some—though certainly not many—speakers of Attic even in 350 B.C. spoke in the way he imagines. Furthermore, his discussion of the uses of secondary evidence (pp. 243 ff.) is valuable and well worth reading. I shall continue to follow Allen, but shall want often to consult Teodorsson both for details and for intelligent comment.

William F. Wyatt, Jr.
Brown University

The Sound Pattern of Ancient Greek. By ALAN H. SOMMERSTEIN. Publications of the Philological Society, no. 23. Oxford: Basil Blackwell, 1973. Pp. viii + 215. £4.50.

This book was not meant as an alternative to W. S. Allen's *Vox Graeca* (Cambridge, 1968). Rather, as the title itself suggests, it serves as an answer to *The Sound Pattern of English* by N. Chomsky and M. Halle (New York, 1968), a treatise that tried to do away with morpheme structure rules in its generative approach to the phonology of English. Using the evidence of Attic Greek, Sommerstein seeks to show that generative phonology cannot do without morpheme structure rules.

As such, S.'s book is concerned more with the theory and praxis of generative phonology than with the actual sound pattern of Greek. For the latter, the *Vox Graeca* of Allen (who has been one of the author's teachers) remains the definitive book. Nevertheless, *The Sound Pattern of Ancient Greek* can serve as a case-in-point introduction to the techniques of generative phonology. Of course, there are many general introductions available, and it is worth noting that the two most eminent exponents of generative phonology are Chomsky and Halle themselves!

The author's apparatus is forbidding, but the reader will find himself acclimated after the first few pages of slow reading. A word of consolation: only a decade ago, when generative grammarians were still using acoustics rather than articulation as the main criterion for setting up phonological features, the same book would have been even more difficult.

It remains to ask what this generative approach adds to our understanding of Attic phonology. Perhaps the most important contribution is S.'s demonstration that the article has no accent (see esp. p. 139), with his ingenious use of "Porson's Law" as a criterion. At times, however, the generative approach seems to offer nothing beyond what is already known by way of the historical approach. There are even instances where it may be better to dispense with the generative explanation altogether: for instance, the discussion of πατήρ and its declension (pp. 64–65) seems useless.

In this connection I have a general criticism. The book assumes the make-believe posture that the historical approach does not exist. That much is justifiable. But then the author should not have used concepts that can only be developed from the historical approach, such as *Ablaut*. We see the concept already at work on pages 8–9, although a formal definition is offered only on page 70.

The author also has some problems with other kinds of descriptive linguistics as distinct from historical linguistics. It is, I think, not his fault but rather a deficiency in the generative approach itself. For instance, S. struggles valiantly with the Prague School concept of an opposition between productive and unproductive categories (see esp. pp. 9, 44, 59–60, 71), but the results are altogether unsatisfying.

These criticisms, however, are not meant to overshadow the praises that the book deserves. The author has given us a conscientious and honest demonstration of generative grammar at work. He has drawn upon a powerful mode of approach in his study of the Greek language.

Gregory Nagy
Harvard University

BOOKS RECEIVED

[Not all works submitted can be reviewed, but those relating to the subject matter of this journal are regularly listed under "Books Received." Offprints from periodicals and parts of books will not be listed unless they are published (sold) separately. Books submitted are not returnable.]

ADAMS, ROBERT M. *The Roman Stamp: Frame and Facade in Some Forms of Neo-Classicism.* Berkeley–Los Angeles–London: University of California Press, 1974 (paperback edition 1978). Pp. vii + 254 + 20 ills. on 16 pls. $6.95 (paper; also available in cloth, $13.95).

ALBERT, KARL (ed. and trans.). *Hesiod: "Theogonie."* Texte zur Philosophie, vol. 1. Herausgegeben, übersetzt und erläutert von KARL ALBERT. Kastellaun: A. Henn Verlag, 1978. Pp. 137. DM 14.80 (paper).

ALBRECHT, MICHAEL VON. *Römische Poesie: Texte und Interpretationen.* Heidelberg: Lothar Stiehm Verlag, 1977. Pp. 368 + 3. DM 59.

ALEXIS, LOUIS E. M. *School of Nero: Europe's first Christian ruler identified and excerpts edited from his literary heirs: Silius Italicus, Papinius Statius, Valerius Flaccus.* With Textual Notes, Commentaries, Illustrations, etc. Sevenoaks, Kent, England: Sevenoaks School, 1975. Pp. xi + 112; 6 ills. in text. All enquiries about this book to the author at Sevenoaks School, Kent (L. E. M. Alexis, 22 Camden Road, Sevenoaks, Kent, England).

ALLEN, W. SIDNEY. *Vox Latina: A Guide to the Pronunciation of Classical Latin.* 2nd ed. Cambridge–London–New York–Melbourne: Cambridge University Press, 1978. Pp. xiv + 132. $11.95.

Ancient and Modern: Essays in Honor of Gerald F. Else. Edited by JOHN H. D'ARMS and JOHN W. EADIE. Ann Arbor: Center for Coordination of Ancient and Modern Studies, The University of Michigan, 1977. Pp. xv + 234 + 1 pl. (portrait).

The Ancient World, vol. 1, no. 1 (March 1978). Chicago: Ares Publishers, Inc., 1978. Pp. iv + 1–64 + 4. *The Ancient World* is published by Ares Publishers, Inc., 612 North Michigan Avenue, Suite 216, Chicago, IL 60611, USA at the subscription rate of $10.00 per 4 issues.

ANDRÉ, JACQUES. *Les mots à redoublement en latin.* Études et Commentaires, 90. Paris: Éditions Klincksieck, 1978. Pp. 121 + 3.

ATHANASSAKIS, APOSTOLOS N. (trans.). *The Life of Pachomius (Vita Prima Graeca).* Society of Biblical Literature, Texts and Translations 7, Early Christian Literature Series 2. Translated by APOSTOLOS N. ATHANASSAKIS. Introduction by BIRGER A. PEARSON. Missoula, Montana: Scholars Press (for The Society of Biblical Literature), 1978 (copyright 1975). Pp. xi + 201. $4.00 (members' price), 6.00 (nonmembers' price) (paper).

——— (ed. and trans.). *The Orphic Hymns: Text, Translation and Notes.* Society of Biblical Literature, Texts and Translations 12, Graeco-Roman Religion 4. Missoula, Montana: Scholars Press, 1977. Pp. xiv + 146.

AUGELLO, GIUSEPPE. *Studi apuleiani: problemi di testo e loci vexati delle "Metamorfosi."* Letteratura Classica, no. 5. Palermo: Palumbo, 1977. Pp. 261. L. 6500 (paper).

BABINIOTIS, GEORGE (ed.). *Bibliographical Bulletin of the Greek Language for the Year 1974; Deltio Bibliographias tēs Hellēnikēs Glōssas gia to Etos 1974*, vol. 2. Athens: Department of Linguistics of the University of Athens, 1976. Pp. 62. Orders should be addressed to: A. Kardamitsa, "Institut du Livre," Hippokratous 8, Athens 143, Greece.

BAGG, ROBERT (trans.). *The "Bakkhai" by Euripides*. Translated by ROBERT BAGG. Amherst: University of Massachusetts Press, 1978. Pp. ix + 82. $8.50 (cloth), 3.95 (paper).

BAGNALL, ROGER S., and WORP, K. A. *The Chronological Systems of Byzantine Egypt*. Studia Amstelodamensia ad Epigraphicam, Ius Antiquum et Papyrologicam Pertinentia, 8. Zutphen, Holland: Terra Publishing Co., 1978. Pp. xii + 150.

BARCHIESI, MARINO. *La "Tarentilla" rivisitata: Studi su Nevio comico*. Università degli Studi di Pisa, Istituti per le Scienze dell'Antichità, Biblioteca degli Studi Classici e Orientali, 12. Pisa: Giardini Editori e Stampatori, 1978. Pp. v + 171. L. 10,000 (estero $15) (paper).

BAUER, WALTER. *A Greek-English Lexicon of the New Testament and Other Early Christian Literature: A translation and adaptation of the fourth revised and augmented edition of Walter Bauer's "Griechisch-Deutsches Wörterbuch zu den Schriften des Neuen Testaments und der übrigen urchristlichen Literatur."* Second Edition, revised and augmented by F. WILBUR GINGRICH and FREDERICK W. DANKER from Walter Bauer's Fifth Edition, 1958. Chicago and London: The University of Chicago Press, 1979. Pp. xl + 900.

BENNER, MARGARETA, and TENGSTRÖM, EMIN. *On the Interpretation of Learned Neo-Latin: An Explorative Study Based on Some Texts from Sweden (1611–1716)*. Studia Graeca et Latina Gothoburgensia, 39. Göteborg: Acta Universitatis Gothoburgensis, 1977. Pp. iv + 112 + 2. Kr. 60 (paper). Distributors: Acta Universitatis Gothoburgensis, Box 5096, S–402 22 Göteborg 5, Sweden.

BLÁZQUEZ, J. M. *Economía de la Hispania Romana*. Bilbao: Ediciones "Najera," 1978. Pp. 725; numerous maps, tables, and ills. in text.

BOEFT, J. DEN. *Calcidius on Demons (Commentarius CH, 127–136)*. Philosophia Antiqua, vol. 33. Leyden: E. J. Brill, 1977. Pp. ix + 70. Fl. 30 (paper).

BÖHM, RICHARD GREGOR. *Gaiusstudien VIII/IX*. Freiburger Beiträge zur Papyrusforschung und antiken Rechtsgeschichte, vols. 8 and 9. Freiburg im Breisgau: Selbstverlag, 1975. Pp. xiv + 469. DM 233 (paper). Zu bestellen nur direkt beim Autor: D–7800 Freiburg i. Br., Universitätsstrasse 11, Deutschland (West).

BOER, W. DEN. *Progress in the Greece of Thucydides*. Mededelingen der Koninklijke Nederlandse Akademie van Wetenschappen, Afd. Letterkunde, Nieuwe Reeks–Deel 40–No. 2. Amsterdam–Oxford–New York: North-Holland Publishing Company, 1977. Pp. 59. $10.95, Fl. 25.00 (paper).

BOLLACK, JEAN, and LAKS, ANDRÉ (eds.). *Cahiers de philologie*, vol. 1: *Études sur l'Épicurisme antique*. Lille: Centre de Recherche Philosophique de l'Université de Lille III, 1976. Pp. vi + 367.

BOLLACK, MAYOTTE. *La raison de Lucrèce: Constitution d'une poétique philosophique avec un essai d'interprétation de la critique lucrétienne*. Le Sens Commun. Paris: Les Éditions de Minuit, 1978. Pp. xliv + 630 + 3. Fr. 82 (paper).

BONIFAZ NUÑO, RUBÉN (trans.). *Sexti Propertii "Elegiarum" Libri Quattuor; Sexto Propercio: "Elegías."* Bibliotheca Scriptorum Graecorum et Romanorum Mexicana. Introducción, versión rítmica y notas de RUBÉN BONIFAZ NUÑO. Mexico: Universidad Nacional Autónoma de México, 1974. Pp. i–lxiii (introducción) + double pp. 1–132 (textos latino y español) + pp. lxvii–ccvii (notas).

BOSWINKEL, E., and PESTMAN, P. W. *Textes grecs, démotiques et bilingues* (*P. L. Bat. 19*). Papyrologica Lugduno-Batava, vol. 10. Édités par divers auteurs et publiés par E. BOSWINKEL et P. W. PESTMAN. Leyden: E. J. Brill, 1978. Pp. x + 286 + 28 pls. + 1 folding chart. Fl. 240 (paper).

BOWMAN, A. K. et al. (eds. and trans.). *The Oxyrhynchus Papyri*, vol. 45 (Graeco-Roman Memoirs, no. 63): Nos. 3209–3266. Edited with Translations and Notes by A. K. BOWMAN, M. W. HASLAM, S. A. STEPHENS, M. L. WEST. With Contributions by M. A. H. EL-ABBADI, E. LOBEL, J. R. REA, M. E. WEINSTEIN. London: Egypt Exploration Society (for The British Academy), 1977. Pp. xviii + 173 + 8 pls.

BOYER, BLANCHE B., and MCKEON, RICHARD (eds.). *Peter Abailard: "Sic et Non": A Critical Edition*, fascs. 3–7. Chicago and London: The University of Chicago Press, 1977. Pp. 193–288, 289–384, 385–480, 481–575 + 1 loose sheet of corrigenda et addenda, vii + 576–714. $14.00 each (paper).

BRADEN, GORDON. *The Classics and English Renaissance Poetry: Three Case Studies*. Yale Studies in English, 187. New Haven and London: Yale University Press, 1978. Pp. xv + 303.

BRONEER, OSCAR. *Isthmia: Excavations by the University of Chicago under the Auspices of the American School of Classical Studies at Athens*, vol. 3: *Terracotta Lamps*. Princeton, N. J.: American School of Classical Studies at Athens, 1977. Pp. xii + 112 + 41 pls. $25.00.

BRUWAENE, M. VAN DEN. *Cicéron: "De Natura Deorum," Livre II*. Collection Latomus, vol. 154. Brussels: Latomus, Revue d'Études Latines, 1978. Pp. 224 + 6 pls. Fr. 700 (paper).

Bulletin de l'Association Guillaume Budé trimestriel, 2 (1978). Paris: Société d'Édition "Les Belles Lettres," 1978. Pp. 117–228. Cotisation 1978: France et Étranger: 45 F par an.

CALBOLI, GUALTIERO (ed.). *Marci Porci Catonis Oratio "Pro Rhodiensibus": Catone, l'Oriente greco e gli imprenditori romani*. Edizioni e Saggi Universitari di Filologia Classica, 18. Bologna: Pàtron Editore, 1978. Pp. xv + 376. L. 15,000.

CASERTANO, GIOVANNI. *La nascita della filosofia vista dai Greci* (*Morte o rinascita della filosofia?*). Naples: Edizioni "Il Tripode" S. r. l., 1977. Pp. 130. L. 3000 (paper).

CHANTRAINE, PIERRE. *Dictionnaire étymologique de la langue grecque: Histoire des mots*, Tome IV—1: P–Y. Paris: Éditions Klincksieck, 1977. Pp. iv + 963–1164.

CLARK, R. T. RUNDLE. *Myth and Symbol in Ancient Egypt*. New York: Thames and Hudson, Inc., 1978. Pp. 292 + 18 pls.; 1 map + 40 line drawings + 1 chart in text. $7.95 (paper). Copyright 1959 Thames and Hudson, Ltd., London; originally published in the United States of America in 1960 by The Grove Press, first paperback edition 1978.

COLLI, GIORGIO. *La sapienza greca*, 2: *Epimenide—Ferecide—Talete—Anassimandro—Onomacrito—Teofrasto, "Opinioni dei fisici"* 1. Milan: Adelphi Edizioni, 1978. Pp. 356. L. 32,000.

COPLEY, FRANK O. (trans.). *Lucretius: "The Nature of Things."* Translated by FRANK O. COPLEY. New York: W. W. Norton & Company, Inc., 1977. Pp. xxi + 177. $1.95 (paper).

DAHLMANN, HELLFRIED. *Über Helvius Cinna.* Akademie der Wissenschaften und der Literatur, Abhandlungen der Geistes- und Sozialwissenschaftlichen Klasse, Jahrgang 1977, Nr. 8. Mainz: Akademie der Wissenschaften und der Literatur; Wiesbaden: Franz Steiner Verlag GmbH (in Kommission), 1977. Pp. 50 + 2. DM 13 (paper).

DAVIES, J. K. *Democracy in Classical Greece.* Fontana History of the Ancient World. Hassocks, Nr. Brighton, Sussex: The Harvester Press, Ltd.; Atlantic Highlands, New Jersey: Humanities Press, Inc. (In Association with Fontana), 1978. Pp. 284 + 8 pls.; 6 maps in text. $19.50 (cloth). Published simultaneously in paperback in Great Britain by Fontana Books (London): £1.75.

DAVIS, JOHN T. *Dramatic Pairings in the Elegies of Propertius and Ovid.* Noctes Romanae: Forschungen über die Kultur der Antike, vol. 15. Bern and Stuttgart: Verlag Paul Haupt, 1977. Pp. 125. SFr./DM 28 (paper).

D'IPPOLITO, GENNARO. *Trifiodoro e Vergilio: il proemio della "Presa di Ilio" e l'esordio del libro secondo dell' "Eneide."* Palermo: Università di Palermo, Istituto di Filologia Greca, 1976. Pp. 29.

DOVER, K. J. *Greek Homosexuality.* Cambridge, Mass.: Harvard University Press, 1978. Pp. x + 244 + frontispiece + 56 pls. $22.50.

DRAKE, H. A. *In Praise of Constantine: A Historical Study and New Translation of Eusebius' "Tricennial Orations."* University of California Publications: Classical Studies, vol. 15. Berkeley–Los Angeles–London: University of California Press, 1976 (reissued in the California Library Reprint Series 1978). Pp. xiv + 191. $11.75.

DREW-BEAR, THOMAS. *Nouvelles inscriptions de Phrygie.* Studia Amstelodamensia ad Epigraphicam, Ius Antiquum et Papyrologicam Pertinentia, 16. Zutphen, Holland: Terra Publishing Co., 1978. Pp. xii + 128 + 40 pls.

Étrennes de septantaine: Travaux de linguistique et de grammaire comparée offerts à Michel Lejeune par un groupe de ses élèves. Études et Commentaires, 91. Paris: Éditions Klincksieck, 1978. Pp. 238 + 1 pl. (portrait).

FEHLING, DETLEV. *Amor und Psyche: Die Schöpfung des Apuleius und ihre Einwirkung auf das Märchen, eine Kritik der romantischen Märchentheorie.* Akademie der Wissenschaften und der Literatur, Abhandlungen der Geistes- und Sozialwissenschaftlichen Klasse, Jahrgang 1977, Nr. 9. Mainz: Akademie der Wissenschaften und der Literatur; Wiesbaden: Franz Steiner Verlag GmbH (in Kommission), 1977. Pp. 110 + 2. DM 28 (paper).

FENIK, BERNARD C. (ed.). *Homer: Tradition and Invention.* Cincinnati Classical Studies, New Series, vol. 2. Leyden: E. J. Brill, 1978. Pp. ix + 90. Fl. 24.

FONTENROSE, JOSEPH. *The Delphic Oracle: Its Responses and Operations with a Catalogue of Responses.* Berkeley–Los Angeles–London: University of California Press, 1978. Pp. xviii + 476 + frontispiece; 2 figs. in text. $25.00.

FRAME, DOUGLAS. *The Myth of Return in Early Greek Epic*. New Haven and London: Yale University Press, 1978. Pp. xii + 178. $15.00.

FUCHS, JACOB (trans.). *Horace's "Satires" and "Epistles."* Translated by JACOB FUCHS. Introduction by WILLIAM S. ANDERSON. New York: W. W. Norton & Company, Inc., 1977. Pp. xiv + 105. $1.95 (paper).

GARRISON, DANIEL H. *Mild Frenzy: A Reading of the Hellenistic Love Epigram*. Hermes Einzelschriften, vol. 41. Wiesbaden: Franz Steiner Verlag GmbH, 1978. Pp. x + 97. DM 26 (paper).

GAUTHIER, PHILIPPE. *Un commentaire historique des "Poroi" de Xénophon*. Centre de Recherches d'Histoire et de Philologie de la IVe Section de l'École Pratique des Hautes Études, III: Hautes Études du Monde Gréco-Romain, 8. Geneva and Paris: Librairie Droz, 1976. Pp. xiv + 289.

GERSH, STEPHEN. *From Iamblichus to Eriugena: An Investigation of the Prehistory and Evolution of the Pseudo-Dionysian Tradition*. Studien zur Problemgeschichte der antiken und mittelalterlichen Philosophie, vol. 8. Leyden: E. J. Brill, 1978. Pp. xii + 365. Fl. 140.

GIANCOTTI, FRANCESCO. *Il preludio di Lucrezio e altri scritti lucreziani ed epicurei*. Biblioteca di Cultura Contemporanea, 63. Messina and Florence: Casa Editrice G. D'Anna, 1978. Pp. vii + 595. L. 10,500 (paper).

GJERSTAD, EINAR. *Greek Geometric and Archaic Pottery Found in Cyprus*. Acta Instituti Atheniensis Regni Sueciae, series in 4°, XXVI. By EINAR GJERSTAD in collaboration with YVES CALVET, MARGUERITE YON, VASSOS KARAGEORGHIS and J. P. THALMANN. Stockholm, 1977. Pp. 86 + 5 + 113 pls. Kr. 175.

GRIFFITH, MARK. *The Authenticity of "Prometheus Bound."* Cambridge Classical Studies. Cambridge–London–New York–Melbourne: Cambridge University Press, 1977. Pp. xii + 419. $24.95.

GRILLONE, ANTONINO (ed.). *Hygini qui dicitur "De metatione castrorum" liber*. Bibliotheca Scriptorum Graecorum et Romanorum Teubneriana. Edidit ANTONINO GRILLONE. Leipzig: BSB B. G. Teubner Verlagsgesellschaft, 1977. Pp. xxiii + 28. Mk. 13 (paper).

GRIMAL, PIERRE. *Le lyrisme à Rome*. Paris: Presses Universitaires de France, 1978. Pp. 304.

GUARIGLIA, OSVALDO NORBERTO. *Quellenkritische und logische Untersuchungen zur Gegensatzlehre des Aristoteles*. Studien und Materialien zur Geschichte der Philosophie, Kleine Reihe, vol. 4. Hildesheim and New York: Georg Olms Verlag, 1978. Pp. v + 131 + 3. DM 39.80.

GUNDERT, HERMANN. *Pindar und sein Dichterberuf*. Utrecht: H & S (HES Publishers), 1978. Pp. 151 + 23. Photomechanischer Nachdruck der Ausgabe Frankfurt, 1935, erweitert mit drei spätere Artikel des Verfassers.

HANDFORD, S. A. (trans.). *Caesar: "The Conquest of Gaul."* Penguin Classics. Harmondsworth: Penguin Books, Ltd.; New York: Penguin Books, 1976 (reprint). Pp. 283 + 3; 1 map in text. 75p (U.K.). $1.95 (paper). This translation first published 1951, reprinted 1953, 1956, 1958, 1960, 1963, 1965, 1967, 1970, 1972, 1974, 1976.

HANFMANN, GEORGE M. A., and RAMAGE, NANCY H. *Sculpture from Sardis: The Finds through 1975*. Archaeological Exploration of Sardis, Report 2. Cambridge,

Mass., and London: Harvard University Press, 1978. Pp. xxi + 322; 472 figs. in text.

HAY, JOHN. *"Oedipus Tyrannus": Lame Knowledge and the Homosporic Womb.* Washington, D.C.: University Press of America (division of R. F. Publishing, Inc.), 1978. Pp. vii + 159. $7.25 (paper).

HENGEL, MARTIN. *Crucifixion: In the ancient world and the folly of the message of the cross.* Translated by JOHN BOWDEN from the German *"Mors turpissima crucis:* Die Kreuzigung in der antiken Welt und die 'torheit' des 'Wortes vom Kreuz,'" published in *Rechtfertigung, Festschrift für Ernst Käsemann zum 70. Geburtstag . . . 1976*, with substantial later additions by the author. Philadelphia: Fortress Press, 1977. Pp. xii + 99. $4.50 (paper).

HENRY, ALAN S. *The Prescripts of Athenian Decrees.* Mnemosyne, suppl. 49. Leyden: E. J. Brill, 1977. Pp. xiv + 120. Fl. 60 (paper).

HERRERA ZAPIÉN, TARSICIO (trans.). *Albii Tibulli aliorumque "Elegiarum" Libri I–III; Albio Tibulo y su círculo: "Elegías" Libros I–III.* Bibliotheca Scriptorum Graecorum et Romanorum Mexicana. Introducción, versión rítmica y notas de TARSICIO HERRERA ZAPIÉN. Mexico: Universidad Nacional Autónoma de México, 1976. Pp. i–cix (introducción) + double pp. 1–69 + pp. clxxi–ccxxviii (notas).

HOPKINS, KEITH. *Conquerors and Slaves.* Sociological Studies in Roman History, vol. 1. Cambridge–London–New York–Melbourne: Cambridge University Press, 1978. Pp. xvii + 268 + 4 pls.; 1 map + 11 tables + 3 figs. in text. $22.50.

HORST, P. W. VAN DER. *The Sentences of Pseudo-Phocylides.* Studia in Veteris Testamenti Pseudepigrapha, vol. 4. With Introduction and Commentary by P. W. VAN DER HORST. Leyden: E. J. Brill, 1978. Pp. xii + 295. Fl. 76.

HORSTMANN, AXEL. *Materialien für griechische Sprachkurse an theologischen Ausbildungsstätten: Kurzgrammatik und Lehrbuch.* Forum Linguisticum, vol. 16. Frankfurt am Main–Bern–Las Vegas: Peter Lang, 1978. Pp. vii + 116.

HUZAR, ELEANOR GOLTZ. *Mark Antony: A Biography.* Minneapolis: University of Minnesota Press, 1978. Pp. x + 347 + 8 pls. + 1 folding chart + 1 map (repeated) on endpapers; 1 ill. + 5 maps in text. $20.00.

Illinois Classical Studies, vol. 3 (1978). Urbana–Chicago–London: University of Illinois Press, 1978. Pp. x + 274 + 1 pl. (portrait).

JIMÉNEZ DELGADO, JOSÉ, C. M. F. *Latine scripta: Disquisitiones ad humaniorum litterarum cultum.* Madrid, 1978. Pp. v + 420 + frontispiece (portrait) + 4 pls. Pesetas 1300 (paper), 1500 (cloth). To be purchased from the author: Pasaje Lóriga, 10, Madrid–2, Spain.

JONES, C. P. *The Roman World of Dio Chrysostom.* Loeb Classical Monographs. Cambridge, Mass., and London: Harvard University Press, 1978. Pp. viii + 208; 1 map in text. $15.00.

JONES, CHARLES W. *Saint Nicholas of Myra, Bari, and Manhattan: Biography of a Legend.* Chicago and London: The University of Chicago Press, 1978. Pp. ix + 558 + 1 map (repeated) on endpapers. $28.00.

JONES, TOM B. *In the Twilight of Antiquity.* The R. S. Hoyt Memorial Lectures (1973). Minneapolis: University of Minnesota Press, 1978. Pp. x + 146; 2 maps in text. $15.00.

KAGAN, DONALD (ed.). *The End of the Roman Empire: Decline or Transformation?* The Problems in European Civilization Series. 2nd ed. Edited and with an introduction by DONALD KAGAN. Lexington, Massachusetts, and Toronto: D. C. Heath and Company, 1978. Pp. xiii + 188; 1 map in text.

KAIMIO, MAARIT. *Characterization of Sound in Early Greek Literature.* Commentationes Humanarum Litterarum, 53 (1977). Helsinki: Societas Scientiarum Fennica, 1977. Pp. 285. Mk. 60 (paper). Sale: The Academic Bookstore, P. Box 10 128, Helsinki 10.

KAMMERBEEK, J. C. *The Plays of Sophocles, Commentaries,* Part III: *The "Antigone."* Leyden: E. J. Brill, 1978. Pp. xiv + 212. Fl. 96.

KASTEN, HELMUT (trans.). *Cicero: Staatsreden,* part 3: *"Die Philippischen Reden."* Schriften und Quellen der Alten Welt, vol. 28. Lateinisch und Deutsch von HELMUT KASTEN. 2., unveränderte Auflage. Berlin: Akademie-Verlag, 1977. Pp. 348. Mk. 32.

KESSELS, A. *Stellenregister zu: E. Bruhn, Anhang zu: "Sophokles" erklärt von F. W. Scheidewin und A. Nauck.* Utrecht: HES Publishers, 1977. Pp. 64 (unnumbered). Fl. 20 (paper).

KEULS, EVA C. *Plato and Greek Painting.* Columbia Studies in the Classical Tradition, vol. 5. Leyden: E. J. Brill, 1978. Pp. xv + 154 + 4 pls.; 2 figs. in text. Fl. 54.

LACEY, W. K. *Cicero and the End of the Roman Republic.* New York: Barnes & Noble Books (a division of Harper & Row Publishers, Inc.), 1978. Pp. viii + 184; 1 map in text. $16.50.

LAZENBY, J. F. *Hannibal's War: A Military History of the Second Punic War.* Warminster, England: Aris & Phillips, Ltd., 1978. Pp. xiii + 340 + 9 pls. + 1 map (repeated) on endpapers; 21 maps + plans in text. £8.75.

LEACH, JOHN. *Pompey the Great.* London: Croom Helm, Ltd.; Totowa, N. J.: Rowman and Littlefield, 1978. Pp. 265 + 4 pls.; 1 table + 9 figs. in text. $13.50.

LEFKOWITZ, MARY R., and FANT, MAUREEN B. *Women in Greece and Rome.* Toronto and Sarasota: Samuel Stevens, 1977. Pp. xiv + 225; 11 ills. in text. $3.95 (paper), 10.00 (cloth).

†LENZ, FRIEDRICH WALTER, and BEHR, CHARLES ALLISON (eds.). *P. Aelii Aristidis Opera quae exstant omnia,* Volumen primum Orationes I–XVI complectens, Fasciculus secundus Orationes II et III (partim) continens et Fasciculus tertius Orationes III (continuatur), IV–VIII continens. 2 vols. Orationes I et V–XVI edidit FRIDERICUS WALTHARIUS LENZ†. Praefationem conscripsit et Orationes II, III, IV edidit CAROLUS ALLISON BEHR. Leyden: E. J. Brill, 1978. Pp. 141–396; 397–624. Fl. 154; 112 (paper).

LLOYD, G. E. R., and OWEN, G. E. L. (eds.). *Aristotle on Mind and Senses: Proceedings of the Seventh Symposium Aristotelicum.* Cambridge Classical Studies. Cambridge–London–New York–Melbourne: Cambridge University Press, 1978. Pp. x + 362. $24.50.

LLOYD-JONES, HUGH. *Myths of the Zodiac.* Sculptures by MARCELLE QUINTON. New York: St. Martin's Press, 1978. Pp. 95; 15 ills. in text. $14.50.

LOLOS, ANASTASIOS. *Die dritte und vierte Redaktion des Ps.-Methodios.* Beiträge zur klassischen Philologie, vol. 94. Meisenheim am Glan: Verlag Anton Hain, 1978. Pp. 94 + 2. DM 24 (paper).

MACK, SARA. *Patterns of Time in Vergil.* Hamden, Connecticut: Archon Books, 1978. Pp. vii + 120. $12.50.

McDONALD, MARIANNE. *A Semilemmatized Concordance to Euripides' "Alcestis."* Costa Mesa, California: TLG Publications, Inc., 1977. Pp. 135 (unnumbered).

———. *A Semilemmatized Concordance to Euripides' "Andromache."* Costa Mesa, California: TLG Publications, Inc., 1978. Pp. 153 (unnumbered).

———. *A Semilemmatized Concordance to Euripides' "Cyclops."* Costa Mesa, California: TLG Publications, Inc., 1978. Pp. 96 (unnumbered).

McLEISH, KENNETH. *Food and Drink.* Greek and Roman Topics, 7. London–Boston–Sydney: George Allen & Unwin, 1978. Pp. 64; 29 ills. in text. $2.95 (paper).

NORTH, HELEN F. (ed.). *Interpretations of Plato: A Swarthmore Symposium.* Mnemosyne, suppl. 50. Edited by HELEN F. NORTH. Leyden: E. J. Brill, 1977. Pp. vii + 112.

NUSSBAUM, MARTHA CRAVEN (ed. and trans.). *Aristotle's "De motu animalium."* Text with Translation, Commentary, and Interpretive Essays by MARTHA CRAVEN NUSSBAUM. Princeton: Princeton University Press, 1978. Pp. xxiii + 430. $30.00.

OGILVIE, R. M. *The Library of Lactantius.* Oxford: Clarendon Press; New York: Oxford University Press. 1978. Pp. x + 121. $19.50.

OLECHOWSKA, ELŻBIETA M. (ed. and trans.). *Claudii Claudiani "De bello Gildonico."* Roma Aeterna, 10. Texte établi, traduit et commenté par ELŻBIETA M. OLECHOWSKA. Leyden: E. J. Brill, 1978. Pp. xv + 212. Fl. 144.

OLSEN, STEIN HAUGOM. *The Structure of Literary Understanding.* Cambridge–London–New York–Melbourne: Cambridge University Press. 1978. Pp. xi + 235. $19.95.

O'NEIL, EDWARD N. (ed. and trans.). *Teles (The Cynic Teacher).* Society of Biblical Literature, Texts and Translations 11, Graeco-Roman Religion 3. Missoula, Montana: Scholars Press (for The Society of Biblical Literature), 1977. Pp. xxv + 97.

ORTH, WOLFGANG. *Königlicher Machtanspruch und städtische Freiheit: Untersuchungen zu den politischen Beziehungen zwischen den ersten Seleukidenherrschern (Seleukos I., Antiochos I., Antiochos II.) und den Städten des westlichen Kleinasien.* Münchener Beiträge zur Papyrusforschung und antiken Rechtsgeschichte, vol. 71. Munich: Verlag C. H. Beck, 1977. Pp. viii + 209 + 2. DM 56 (paper).

PANESSA, G. *Bibliografia topografica della colonizzazione greca in Italia e nelle isole tirreniche* diretta da G. NENCI e G. VALLET, I: *Opere di carattere generale (1537–1975).* A cura di G. PANESSA. Pisa: Scuola Normale Superiore; Rome: École Française de Rome, 1977. Pp. xxxi + 377.

PETERSMANN, HUBERT. *Petrons urbane Prosa: Untersuchungen zu Sprache und Text (Syntax).* Österreichische Akademie der Wissenschaften, Philosophisch-Historische Klasse, Sitzungsberichte, vol. 323. Vienna: Verlag der österreichischen Akademie der Wissenschaften, 1977. Pp. 319. DM 90.

PFISTER, FRIEDRICH (trans.). *Der Alexanderroman mit einer Auswahl aus den verwandten Texten.* Beiträge zur klassischen Philologie, vol. 92. Übersetzt von FRIEDRICH PFISTER. Meisenheim am Glan: Verlag Anton Hain, 1978. Pp. xii + 191 + 1. DM 48 (paper).

PICONE, GIUSTO. *L'eloquenza di Plinio: Teoria e prassi.* Letteratura Classica. Palermo: Palumbo, 1978. Pp. 211.

RAWSON, BERYL. *The Politics of Friendship: Pompey and Cicero.* Sources in Ancient History. Sydney: Sydney University Press, 1978. Pp. vi + 217. $9.00 (paper). Exclusive Distributor: ISBS, Inc., Post Office Box 555, Forest Grove, Oregon 97116.

REINHOLD, MEYER. *The Golden Age of Augustus.* Aspects of Antiquity. MEYER REINHOLD with the assistance of PAUL T. ALESSI. Toronto and Sarasota: Samuel Stevens, 1978. Pp. xvi + 281; 8 ills. in text. $9.95 (cloth), 3.95 (paper).

RIST, ANNA (trans.). *The Poems of Theocritus.* Translated with Introductions by ANNA RIST. Chapel Hill: The University of North Carolina Press, 1978. Pp. xi + 249. $16.00.

ROTHE, CHRISTIAN. *Humanitas, Fides und Verwandtes in der römischen Provinzialpolitik: Untersuchungen zur politischen Funktion römischer Verhaltensnormen bei Cicero.* Schriften zur Geschichte und Kultur der Antike, 12. Berlin: Akademie-Verlag, 1978. Pp. 107. Mk. 18 (paper).

SPEAKE, GRAHAM. *A Collation of the Manuscripts of Sophocles' "Oedipus Coloneus."* Greek, Roman and Byzantine Monographs, no. 8. Durham, North Carolina: Duke University, 1978. Pp. vi + 53. $4.00 (paper).

SPRAGUE, ROSAMOND KENT. *Plato's Philosopher-King: A Study of the Theoretical Background.* Columbia, South Carolina: University of South Carolina Press, 1976. Pp. xvii + 129. $9.95.

STOESSL, FRANZ. *C. Valerius Catullus: Mensch, Leben, Dichtung.* Beiträge zur klassischen Philologie, vol. 85. Meisenheim am Glan: Verlag Anton Hain, 1977. Pp. vii + 264.

STUMP, ELEONORE (trans.). *Boethius's "De topicis differentiis."* Translated, with notes and essays on the text, by ELEONORE STUMP. Ithaca and London: Cornell University Press, 1978. Pp. 287. $18.50.

SUSSMAN, LEWIS A. *The Elder Seneca.* Mnemosyne, suppl. 51. Leyden: E. J. Brill, 1978. Pp. xiv + 187. Fl. 52 (paper).

SYNODINOU, KATERINA. *On the Concept of Slavery in Euripides.* Panepistēmion Iōanninōn, Epistēmonikē Epetēris Philosophikēs Scholēs, parartēma ar. 7. Iōannina, 1977. Pp. 135.

TARÁN, LEONARDO. *Anonymous Commentary on Aristotle's "De Interpretatione" (Codex Parisinus Graecus 2064).* Beiträge zur klassischen Philologie, vol. 95. Meisenheim am Glan: Verlag Anton Hain, 1978. Pp. xlvii + 122. DM 34 (paper).

THOMSON, D. F. S. (ed.). *Catullus: A Critical Edition.* Edited and Introduced by D. F. S. THOMSON. Chapel Hill: The University of North Carolina Press, 1978. Pp. xvi + 206.

THRAEDE, KLAUS. *Der Hexameter in Rom: Verstheorie und Statistik.* Zetemata, vol. 71. Munich: Verlag C. H. Beck, 1978. Pp. xi + 168. DM 46 (paper).

TODD, MALCOLM. *The Walls of Rome.* Totowa, New Jersey: Rowman and Littlefield, 1978. Pp. 91; 41 figs. in text. $14.50.

TÖCHTERLE, KARLHEINZ. *Ciceros Staatsschrift im Unterricht: Eine historische und systematische Analyse ihrer Behandlung an den Schulen Österreichs und Deutschlands.* Commentationes Aenipontanae, vol. 24. Innsbruck: Universitätsverlag Wagner, 1978. Pp. 170. ÖS 492/DM 490.

TORRANCE, ROBERT M. *The Comic Hero*. Cambridge, Mass., and London: Harvard University Press, 1978. Pp. xv + 346.

VAN SICKLE, JOHN. *The Design of Virgil's "Bucolics."* Istituto di Filologia Classica, Università di Urbino; Filologia e Critica, 24. Rome: Edizioni dell'Ateneo & Bizzarri, 1978. Pp. 258. L. 10,000 (paper). Distributor in North America: Scholars Press, PO Box 5207, Missoula, MT 59806.

WACHER, JOHN. *Roman Britain*. London, Toronto and Melbourne: J. M. Dent & Sons, Ltd., 1978. Pp. 286 + 72 pls.; 52 figs. in text. £6.95 (Net U. K. Price), $15.00. J. M. Dent & Sons, Ltd., c/o Biblio Distribution Center, 81 Adams Drive, Totowa, New Jersey 07512.

WADDELL, HELEN (trans.). *Mediaeval Latin Lyrics*. New York: W. W. Norton & Company, Inc., 1977. Pp. viii + 342. $12.95. First published in 1929, revised edition 1948, reprinted 1977.

WALBANK, MICHAEL B. *Athenian Proxenies of the Fifth Century B. C.* Toronto and Sarasota: Samuel Stevens, 1978. Pp. xvi + 552 + 65 pls. $15.00.

WALCOT, PETER. *Envy and the Greeks: A Study of Human Behaviour*. Aris & Phillips Classical Studies. Warminster, England: Aris & Phillips, Ltd., 1978. Pp. vi + 120.

WEBER, FRANZ JOSEF (ed.). *Platonos Apologia Sokratous*. Uni-Taschenbücher, 79. Mit einer Einführung, textkritischem Apparat und Kommentar herausgegeben von FRANZ JOSEF WEBER. 2., überarbeitete Auflage. Paderborn: Ferdinand Schöningh, 1978. Pp. 151. DM 9.80 (paper).

WEBSTER, GRAHAM. *Boudica: The British Revolt against Rome A.D. 60*. Totowa, New Jersey: Rowman and Littlefield, 1978. Pp. 152 + 16 pls.; 8 maps + diagrams in text. $12.50.

WEINBROT, HOWARD D. *Augustus Caesar in "Augustan" England: The Decline of a Classical Norm*. Princeton, New Jersey: Princeton University Press, 1978. Pp. xi + 270. $15.00.

WENDER, DOROTHEA. *The Last Scenes of the "Odyssey."* Mnemosyne, suppl. 52. Leyden: E. J. Brill, 1978. Pp. ix + 83.

WILLCOCK, M. M. (ed.). *The "Iliad" of Homer, Books I–XII*. Edited with Introduction and Commentary by M. M. WILLCOCK. Basingstoke and London: Macmillan Education Limited; New York: St. Martin's Press, 1978. Pp. xxx + 328. $12.95.

WILLIAMS, FREDERICK. *Callimachus: "Hymn to Apollo": A Commentary*. Oxford: Clarendon Press; New York: Oxford University Press, 1978. Pp. ix + 113. $19.50.

CLASSICAL PHILOLOGY

A Quarterly Journal devoted to research in the Languages, Literatures, History, and Life of Classical Antiquity

VOLUME 74 NUMBER 4

October 1979

THE UNIVERSITY OF CHICAGO PRESS

Editorial correspondence: The Editor, *Classical Philology*, Box I, Faculty Exchange, The University of Chicago, Chicago, Illinois 60637. N.B. To be considered for publication, all material submitted must be typewritten, with texts, quotations, and footnotes double-spaced, and on stout, noncorrasable paper with ample margins.

Classical Philology (ISSN 0009-837X) is published in January, April, July, and October. Subscription rates, U.S.A.: institutions, 1 year $24.00, 2 years $43.20, 3 years $61.20; individuals, 1 year $18.00, 2 years $32.40, 3 years $45.90; students, $14.40 (with signature of faculty member). Other countries add $1.50 for each year's subscription to cover postage. Single copy rates: institutions $6.50; individuals, $5.00. Back volumes available from 1965 (vol. 60). Single issues and reprinted volumes through 1961 (vols. 1–56) available from Walter J. Johnson, Inc., 355 Chestnut Street, Norwood, New Jersey 07648. Volumes available in microfilm from University Microfilms, 300 North Zeeb Road, Ann Arbor, Michigan 48106; in microfiche from J. S. Canner & Co., 49–65 Lansdowne Street, Boston, Massachusetts 02215. Checks should be made payable to CLASSICAL PHILOLOGY, The University of Chicago Press, 5801 Ellis Avenue, Chicago, Illinois 60637.

Claims for missing numbers should be made within the month following the regular month of publication. The publishers expect to supply missing numbers free only when losses have been sustained in transit and when the reserve stock will permit.

Subscribers are requested to notify the Press and their local postmaster immediately of change of address. All changes of address should provide *both* the old and the new address. *Please allow four weeks for the change.* Postmaster: send address changes to *Classical Philology*, 5801 Ellis Avenue, Chicago, Illinois 60637.

The articles in this journal are indexed in the *Humanities Index*.

Second-class postage paid at Chicago, Illinois.

HOMERIC METAPHOR

CARROLL MOULTON

METAPHOR is a comparatively neglected feature of Homeric imagery. Scholars and critics have focused attention on the extended similes that are so prominent in the *Iliad* and *Odyssey;* discussion of Greek metaphor, on the other hand, has almost invariably concentrated on lyric and tragedy.[1] Furthermore, previous appraisals of Homeric metaphor have given rise to some influential misconceptions. The purpose of this essay is to reaffirm the vitality of metaphor as a significant poetic device in the language of the epics, particularly the *Iliad.* We will start with a summary sketch of previous analyses, and proceed to examine a selection of examples. The metaphors in the analysis have been chosen specifically to illustrate the range and sophistication of figurative language in Homer, and to invite comparison with the survey of previous analyses. We will conclude with some suggestions for further research.

W. B. Stanford's definition of metaphor is useful: "the process and result of using a term (X) normally signifying an object or concept (A) in such a context that it must refer to another object or concept (B) which is distinct enough in characteristics from A to ensure that in the composite idea formed by the synthesis of the concepts A and B and now symbolized in the word X, the factors A and B retain their conceptual independence even while they fully merge in the unity symbolized by X."[2] Stanford was far readier than A. L. Keith or Milman Parry to allow the presence of a number of imaginative, striking metaphors in the epics. But his main thesis, that words in Homer's time lacked precise definitions and that therefore the poet was deliberately cautious in using metaphor because he ran the risk of sacrificing clarity, will not survive serious scrutiny.[3] C. H.

1. E.g., A. L. Keith, *Simile and Metaphor in Greek Poetry* (Chicago, 1914), p. 33, declared, "The most striking difference that the metaphors of the *Iliad* present as distinguished from the similes is the almost universal lack of deep feeling." W. B. Stanford, *Greek Metaphor* (Oxford, 1936), pp. 135, 143, felt that the partial overlap in material between similes and metaphors (e.g., νέφος πεζῶν at *Il.* 4. 274 and the simile of the cloud at 4. 275–79) could be explained by Homer's desire to clarify possibly confusing metaphors through extended similes employing the same image. A recent study which focuses on the metaphors of the lyric and tragic poets (though not quite to the exclusion of Homer) is the interesting book of M. S. Silk, *Interaction in Poetic Imagery* (London and New York, 1974).

2. *Greek Metaphor,* p. 101. The definition is adopted with approval by W. K. Wimsatt, *The Verbal Icon* (Lexington, Ky., 1954), p. 128.

3. *Greek Metaphor,* pp. 118 (n. 1), 121. The hypothesis that words themselves lacked precise definitions in Homer's time is vulnerable to the results of numerous recent studies of Homeric vocabulary. See, e.g., A. Parry, "Have We Homer's *Iliad?*" *YCS* 20 (1966): 177–216; idem (ed.), *The Making of Homeric Verse* (Oxford, 1971), pp. ix–lxii, an excellent critical survey; Anne Amory Parry, *Blameless Aegisthus* (Leyden, 1973); M. Nagler, *Spontaneity and Tradition* (Berkeley, 1974); N. Austin, *Archery at the Dark of the Moon* (Berkeley, 1975), pp. 11–80 ("The Homeric Formula");

0009-837X/79/7404-0001$01.02

Whitman, on the other hand, has claimed that the formulas themselves function as a type of metaphor; while perhaps true at one basic level, this theory is too generalized to be really useful.[4]

Keith and Parry are together responsible for the principal theories about Homeric metaphor which must claim our attention; Parry's judgments have been especially influential.[5] Four contentions are particularly significant. (1) Few metaphors in Homer are sustained beyond the single word; it is thus impossible to determine with the majority if the poet had the notion of metaphor in mind.[6] (2) Metaphor in Homer is a "casual poetic device," seldom used to heighten emotion or a crucial narrative incident.[7] (3) A large number of the extended metaphors are vague and problematic in meaning.[8] (4) Many metaphors are used so often that they retain no force greater than that of the ordinary word. These phrases are "fixed" metaphors in their context; although they may possess decorative charm, their semantic force becomes eroded to the extent that it is "felt" rather than "understood."[9] Parry was scrupulous in his emphasis on the contributions of mood and propriety which traditional diction, including the fixed metaphor, had made to the poems.[10] Nevertheless, we are inescapably left with the impression that the vast majority of metaphors in the *Iliad* and *Odyssey* are "fixed," and consequently devoid of meaning.

In the decades since Parry, the criticism of an oral Homer has demonstrated that repetition, by itself, does not automatically act to deprive a phrase of meaning; recent studies have inclined more to the hypothesis

---

A. L. T. Bergren, *The Etymology and Usage of* ΠΕΙΡΑΡ *in Early Greek Poetry* (State College, Pa., 1975); P. Vivante, "On Homer's Winged Words," *CQ* 25 (1975): 1–12.

Despite the disappointing quality of Stanford's more general arguments, he performed a considerable service in classifying Homeric metaphors "according to the degree of their imaginative force" (p. 129), and his description and appreciation of some individual phrases are instructive and observant (e.g., pp. 136–37 on ἔπεα πτερόεντα and ἄπτερος μῦθος).

4. See *Homer and the Heroic Tradition* (Cambridge, Mass., 1958), pp. 102–27. Whitman shows credibly enough how certain metaphors in the poems have their counterparts in action sequences; e.g., the image at *Od.* 5. 383, κατέδησε κελεύθους, is literally part of the scene at *Od.* 10. 19–27, when Aeolus binds the winds. In such cases, the distinction between action and image breaks down; by way of further illustration, Whitman provides a brief analysis of the mingling of literal and figurative clouds in *Iliad* 16–17 (pp. 151–53). But when he speaks of words such as σάκος or ἀσπίς as "metaphors," or as "symbolic of all that a heroic shield should be" (p. 126), Whitman's rhetoric merely embellishes the fact that Homeric heroes usually wield good shields competently. He is forced, then, to see the shield of Achilles as a "tremendous expansion . . . a metaphor of the whole heroic world" (p. 126). The last part of this statement may be true. But the shield of Achilles stands out precisely because it is *not* like any other shield at all (cf. 20. 262–72); its description at 18. 478–608 is thoroughly differentiable from all other shields in the poem and cannot usefully be related to the supposed "metaphorical" qualities of such shields.

5. See Keith, *Simile and Metaphor*, passim. Parry's arguments were first published in an abstract, "The Homeric Metaphor as a Traditional Poetic Device," *TAPA* 62 (1931): xxiv, reprinted in idem, *Making of Homeric Verse*, p. 419. His contentions were argued more fully in "The Traditional Metaphor in Homer," *CP* 28 (1933): 30–43 = *Making of Homeric Verse*, pp. 365–75. References below will be to the pagination in *The Making of Homeric Verse*.

6. See Keith, *Simile and Metaphor*, p. 33; Parry, *Making of Homeric Verse*, p. 373.

7. Parry, *Making of Homeric Verse*, p. 419.

8. Ibid.

9. Ibid., pp. 419, 371–73.

10. Although the fixed metaphor was devoid of specific meaning, according to Parry's thesis, it was far from lacking in charm: it becomes "an incantation of the heroic" (*Making of Homeric Verse*, p. 375).

that the poet is the master of the traditional phrase, rather than its prisoner, and that meter and meaning may be fully compatible.[11] Our selection of texts from the *Iliad* will attempt to gauge the effectiveness of repeated metaphors, as well as to assess the contributions of unique phrases. The specific illustrations have been chosen both for their intrinsic interest and for their value as responses to one or more of the theories that we have outlined. In addition, these texts have been largely ignored in commentaries and in the critical literature. Collectively, they comprise an argument for the poetic vitality of Homeric metaphor. Limitations of space will permit us to consider only a small fraction of the metaphors in the *Iliad*, but the selection is diverse enough to represent the images' considerable variety and importance.[12]

We begin with a group of brief metaphors which are restricted to single phrases and which occur only once in the *Iliad:*

1. 81 εἴ περ γάρ τε χόλον γε καὶ αὐτῆμαρ καταπέψῃ

1. 170–71 οὐδέ σ' ὀΐω
ἐνθάδ' ἄτιμος ἐὼν ἄφενος καὶ πλοῦτον ἀφύξειν.

1. 231 δημοβόρος βασιλεύς, ἐπεὶ οὐτιδανοῖσιν ἀνάσσεις

1. 243–44 σὺ δ' ἔνδοθι θυμὸν ἀμύξεις
χωόμενος ὅ τ' ἄριστον Ἀχαιῶν οὐδὲν ἔτεισας.

Parry, who analyzed the metaphors of *Iliad* 1, comments, "[They] may, for a while, keep the force of their metaphor because they are not elsewhere found in Homer. But because there is nothing outside the word to show the reader that Homer had the notion of metaphor in his mind, and because he soon ceases in reading Homer to look for any active force in such single words, they too finally become for him simply epic words with no more meaning than the usual term would have."[13]

But in all these cases there is sufficient evidence of the literal usage of terms elsewhere in the poems to establish the phrases as metaphorical. For example, compare with καταπέψῃ at 1. 81 the literal meaning of πέσσω at *Odyssey* 7. 119 (= ripen).[14] With ἀφύξειν at 1. 171, compare ἀφύσσω at *Iliad* 1. 598 (= draw off a liquid). For the metaphor in ἀμύξεις at 1. 243, we may note ἀμύσσω at *Iliad* 19. 284 (= lacerate). Finally, with respect to the compound δημοβόρος at 1. 231, Homer has two other literal compounds of δῆμος: δημιοεργός at *Odyssey* 17. 383 and 19. 135 (= public worker) and δημογέρων at *Iliad* 3. 149 and 11. 372 (= elder of the people); compare also the verb καταδημοβορέω at *Iliad* 18. 301. The presumption is certainly

11. Cf. the studies cited in n. 3

12. Stanford, *Greek Metaphor*, p. 120, acknowledges that metaphors "far outnumber" similes in the epics, but provides no comprehensive listing. As a rough indication of the frequency of metaphor, consider the following statistics for three diverse narrative segments of the *Iliad*. Book 6 has thirty-one metaphors in 529 lines (vs. five similes), Book 11 has fifty-two metaphors in 847 lines (vs. thirty-three similes), and Book 24 has thirty-nine metaphors in 804 lines (vs. twelve similes).

13. *Making of Homeric Verse*, p. 373.

14. Cf. also χόλον θυμαλγέα πέσσει (*Il.* 4. 513).

that the phrase δημοβόρος βασιλεύς, employed in an excited context and parallel to other figurative terms of abuse (cf. *Il.* 1. 225), is metaphorical.[15]

Thus, contrary to contention (1) in the list of theories, it is often possible to establish the metaphorical character of a single phrase by examining lexical usage elsewhere in the poems. Even in cases where we may encounter difficulties, that is, with phrases involving terms whose precise meaning is debatable, or terms with a considerable range of meaning, close analysis is useful for arriving at a balance of probabilities. For example, however we regard the Homeric concept of θυμός, it seems clear that such phrases as θυμολέων (*Il.* 5. 639, 7. 228), ἔρις θυμοβόρος (*Il.* 7. 210), θυμὸν κατέδων (*Il.* 6. 202), and πᾶσιν δὲ παραὶ ποσὶ κάππεσε θυμός (*Il.* 15. 280) are all metaphorical. We face similar problems in applying a definition of metaphor to phrases with φρένες, for example, with φρένες . . . μέλαιναι (*Il.* 1. 103; cf. 17. 83). Yet it is likely that a phrase such as δάκε δὲ φρένας Ἕκτορι μῦθος (*Il.* 5. 493) is metaphorical.[16] Compare also τὸν δ' ἄχος ὀξὺ κατὰ φρένας τύψε βαθεῖαν (*Il.* 19. 125). In both of these latter instances, we are aided by literal usages of δάκνω and τύπτω elsewhere in the poems. But even when we do not possess the "control" of a term's literal usage, we may safely categorize certain brief phrases as metaphorical; consider, for example, ἀνεμοτρεφὲς ἔγχος at *Iliad* 11. 256.[17]

These illustrations confirm that, even when an image is not extended beyond the single word, we may identify metaphor through analysis of usage. Let us turn now to assess the claim that metaphor in Homer is a casual poetic device, seldom used to heighten emotion or a crucial narrative incident.

3. 54–57 οὐκ ἄν τοι χραίσμῃ κίθαρις τά τε δῶρ' Ἀφροδίτης,
ἥ τε κόμη τό τε εἶδος, ὅτ' ἐν κονίῃσι μιγείης·
ἀλλὰ μάλα Τρῶες δειδήμονες· ἦ τέ κεν ἤδη
λάϊνον ἕσσο χιτῶνα κακῶν ἕνεχ' ὅσσα ἔοργας.

There are two striking metaphors in this passage, the conclusion of Hector's first reproach of Paris. The only parallel to the phrase at 3. 55, ὅτ' ἐν κονίῃσι μιγείης, is a verse used for the deaths of Dolon in the *Iliad* and Leodes in the *Odyssey:* φθεγγομένου δ' ἄρα τοῦ γε κάρη κονίῃσιν ἐμίχθη (*Il.* 10. 457 = *Od.* 22. 329). Μίσγω, of course, is frequently used in a variety of formulas for sexual intercourse (cf. ἐμίγην φιλότητι καὶ εὐνῇ at *Il.* 3. 445). Given the prominent erotic motifs of *Iliad* 3, it is surely possible to argue for an ambiguous, ironic significance in Hector's expression: he implies, metaphorically, that Paris will clutch at the ground, as in lust.[18]

The unparalleled expression λάϊνον ἕσσο χιτῶνα at 3. 57, which almost

15. Parry, *Making of Homeric Verse*, p. 371, n. 1, denied that the insults in *Il.* 1. 225 were metaphorical; I cannot agree. For wealth as a liquid at *Il.* 1. 171, cf. the phrase of Eumaios, ῥυδὸν ἀφνειοῖο, at *Od.* 15. 426.

16. Cf. θυμοδακὴς γὰρ μῦθος (*Od.* 8. 185).

17. The only analogue to this phrase is also metaphorical, at *Il.* 15. 624–25: ὡς ὅτε κῦμα θοῇ ἐν νηῒ πέσῃσι / λάβρον ὑπαὶ νέφεων ἀνεμοτρεφές.

18. Cf. the apparently neutral usage by Hector at *Il.* 3. 48: μιχθεὶς ἀλλοδαποῖσι γυναῖκ' εὐειδέ' ἀνῆγες.

certainly refers to execution by stoning,[19] may be linked to the emphasis on Paris' appearance in the speech as a whole; compare εἶδος at 3. 39, 45, 55. Aphrodite later draws attention to the Trojan's physical handsomeness and to his clothes at 3. 390–94; compare particularly κάλλεΐ τε στίλβων καὶ εἵμασιν at 392. Thus, ironic reference to a garment, χιτῶνα, at 3. 57 is not to be ruled out. The metaphor itself is probably related in conception to others which picture shame as a garment; compare ἀναιδείην ἐπιειμένε (ἐπιειμένος) at *Iliad* 1. 149 and 9. 372. Both of Hector's images, at the climax of his speech, combine to emphasize the forceful tone of outrage, tinged with irony, of the reproach.

6. 327–31 λαοὶ μὲν φθινύθουσι περὶ πτόλιν αἰπύ τε τεῖχος
μαρνάμενοι· σέο δ' εἵνεκ' ἀϋτή τε πτόλεμός τε
ἄστυ τόδ' ἀμφιδέδηε· σὺ δ' ἂν μαχέσαιο καὶ ἄλλῳ,
ὅν τινά που μεθιέντα ἴδοις στυγεροῦ πολέμοιο.
ἀλλ' ἄνα, μὴ τάχα ἄστυ πυρὸς δηΐοιο θέρηται.

This passage also shows Hector reproaching Paris. The metaphor of battle and the war cry "blazing" around the city is certainly to be related to a group of images with the simple verb δαίω: μάχη ἐνοπή τε δεδήει (*Il.* 12. 35), στέφανος πολέμοιο δέδηε (*Il.* 13. 736), ἔρις πολέμοιο δέδηεν (*Il.* 17. 253), μάχη πόλεμός τε δέδηε (*Il.* 20. 18). The metaphor, with the verb in the same position in the verse, is also used of rumor (*Il.* 2. 93 μετὰ δέ σφισιν Ὄσσα δεδήει) and of Hector's eyes in battle (*Il.* 12. 466 πυρὶ δ' ὄσσε δεδήει).[20] Virtually all the contexts are martial, and the notion of the metaphor is to be compared with the repeated, short simile, ὣς οἱ μὲν μάρναντο δέμας πυρὸς αἰθομένοιο (*Il.* 11. 596, 13. 673, 18. 1). But whereas the simile is a brief, summarizing image employed in transition passages, all but one of the metaphors of "blazing war" occur in speeches of apprehension and urgency. These emotions are especially evident in Hector's speech in *Iliad* 6, where the verbal structure of the image differs most markedly from the norm (note the enjambement), and where the hero's fear for Troy, expressed in the last verse (331), transfers the motif of fire from imagery to narrative. The rhetorical power of the metaphor is thus reinforced by its context.

11. 241 ὣς ὁ μὲν αὖθι πεσὼν κοιμήσατο χάλκεον ὕπνον

This phrase, employed for the death of Iphidamas at the hands of Agamemnon, is unique in the poems, although the epithets χάλκεος and πολύχαλκος are used in other metaphorical contexts. In the nominative, χάλκεος alternates with ὄβριμος when Ares is to receive an epithet in the adonic segment of the verse; compare *Iliad* 5. 704, 859, 866, 7. 146, 16. 543. It is scarcely surprising, then, that the majority of the epithet's figurative uses occur in martial contexts. In the invocation to the Catalog of Ships, the poet imagines an unbreakable voice and a heart of bronze (*Il.* 2. 490 φωνὴ δ' ἄρρηκτος, χάλκεον δέ μοι ἦτορ ἐνείη). Achilles shouts at the trench with a brazen voice

19. Cf. W. Leaf, *The "Iliad,"* vol. 1² (London, 1900), ad loc.
20. Cf. *Od.* 6. 131–32, 20. 353.

(*Il.* 18. 222 ὄπα χάλκεον).[21] At *Iliad* 17. 424–25 the noise of battle rises to the brazen sky: ὣς οἱ μὲν μάρναντο, σιδήρειος δ' ὀρυμαγδὸς / χάλκεον οὐρανὸν ἷκε δι' αἰθέρος ἀτρυγέτοιο· Here the clash of metal on metal is perhaps suggested by the twin metaphors, χαλκεὸν οὐρανόν and σιδήρειος ὀρυμαγδός.[22] Finally, in related usages, the sky is described as πολύχαλκος at *Iliad* 5. 504 and *Odyssey* 3. 2.[23] Only in the last instance is there no battle context. At *Iliad* 11. 241 the image of bronze sleep for death is particularly striking. Agamemnon's slaying of Iphidamas is considerably elaborated: in ring composition, we are first given details of the warrior's background and marriage (221–28), then the combat scene, and finally a pathetic close, which focuses on the bereaved wife (242–45). The finality of Iphidamas' encounter with Agamemnon is accentuated by the unique metaphor for his death.

15. 694–95 . . . τὸν δὲ Ζεὺς ὦσεν ὄπισθε
χειρὶ μάλα μεγάλῃ, ὤτρυνε δὲ λαὸν ἅμ' αὐτῷ.

These lines occur just before Hector takes hold of the ship of Protesilaus and calls for fire at the end of Book 15 (cf. 716–25). The action has reached a climax. The context is plainly the apogee of the glory granted to Hector by Zeus (cf. the prophecy at *Il.* 11. 192–94). Leaf (ad loc.) calls the passage an "anthropomorphic metaphor": we need not suppose that Zeus is present in person on the battlefield. He then compares *Iliad* 13. 358–60 as "the nearest parallel in Homer." But the context there is one of even battle, and seems scarcely analogous to the present situation. Here the "intervention" of Zeus may be compared to the literal intervention of Apollo at *Iliad* 16. 791–92: στῆ δ' ὄπιθεν, πλῆξεν δὲ μετάφρενον εὐρέε τ' ὤμω / χειρὶ καταπρηνεῖ, στρεφεδίνηθεν δέ οἱ ὄσσε. In view of the close narrative connection between Hector's drive to the ships and Patroclus' entrance into battle, and the thematic links that relate Hector's limited success, Patroclus' death, and Hector's mortality, these unusual passages are appropriately taken together. But there is a fine shading of differences: Apollo intervenes as a hostile god, and with immediate consequences; Zeus intervenes ostensibly as the patron of Hector, but there is something ominous about his standing behind the Trojan, pushing him on to achievements that are perhaps beyond him, and limiting his grant of glory to a brief period, which will expire at sunset.[24] There can be no doubt that Apollo is literally present in the battle in Book 16; the physical effects of his action are described. In the absence of such details, the strong presumption is that the passage at 15. 694–95 is metaphorical. The image of Zeus's intervention, with its under-

21. The simile which directly precedes this verse and compares Achilles' voice to a trumpet (219–21) is possibly to be associated with the metaphor.

22. The epithet σιδήρειος also has a variety of metaphorical usages; cf. *Il.* 22. 357, 23. 177, 24. 205 ≈ 521; *Od.* 4. 293, 5. 191, 12. 280, 15. 329 = 17. 565, 23. 172. Both χάλκεος and σιδήρειος (σιδήρεος) are applied to οὐρανός and ἦτορ.

23. Dolon is described as πολύχρυσος πολύχαλκος at *Il.* 10. 315.

24. Zeus's plan and Hector's doom are recalled shortly before our passage at 15. 610–14.

currents of ambiguity and foreboding, is placed at a major turning point in the narrative.

18. 107–10 ὡς ἔρις ἔκ τε θεῶν ἔκ τ' ἀνθρώπων ἀπόλοιτο,
καὶ χόλος, ὅς τ' ἐφέηκε πολύφρονά περ χαλεπῆναι,
ὅς τε πολὺ γλυκίων μέλιτος καταλειβομένοιο
ἀνδρῶν ἐν στήθεσσιν ἀέξεται ἠΰτε καπνός.

Achilles' words on anger occur in his meeting with Thetis. Parry compared the passage with the metaphor used of Nestor at *Iliad* 1. 249: τοῦ καὶ ἀπὸ γλώσσης μέλιτος γλυκίων ῥέεν αὐδή. He argued that the latter image was "the one active metaphor of the first *Iliad*," but found it deprived of any significant poetic effect since it recurs at Hesiod *Theogony* 83–84 and 96–97. Parry then adduced the more complex phrase of Achilles to show "clearly how little Homer felt its force, unless one should wish to make Homer mix metaphors with all the ruthlessness of an Elizabethan."[25] But the recurrence of the image at *Iliad* 1. 249 in Hesiod does not automatically deprive it of poetic effect, unless one clings rigidly to the theory that repetition of a phrase cancels its semantic force. More important, Achilles' image, far richer and more concentrated than the bare comparison of soothing speech to honey, should be appreciated for its psychological insight. The attractiveness of anger and the sweet satisfaction with which it is nursed over time fuse in the image with the notions of danger and emptiness, conveyed by the brief, internal simile ἠΰτε καπνός. The two vehicles of honey and smoke, taken together, produce a sense of clash which is in turn mitigated by the appropriateness of each separate image. As a whole, the complex description of anger is just what we might expect from a character so familiar with that emotion; the graphic images of honey and smoke, correlated by the antithesis of καταλειβομένοιο and ἀέξεται, are produced by a character of singular imagination.[26]

The last five examples of Homeric metaphor have suggested that figurative language may indeed be employed in the *Iliad* to heighten emotion or to underline the importance of a particular narrative incident. The following three analyses illustrate the poetic significance of complex or extended metaphors.

19. 221–24 αἶψά τε φυλόπιδος πέλεται κόρος ἀνθρώποισιν,
ἧς τε πλείστην μὲν καλάμην χθονὶ χαλκὸς ἔχευεν,
ἄμητος δ' ὀλίγιστος, ἐπὴν κλίνῃσι τάλαντα
Ζεύς, ὅς τ' ἀνθρώπων ταμίης πολέμοιο τέτυκται.

Odysseus' description of war as a reaper who cuts down much straw and gathers a mean harvest comprises a dense fusion of images: satiety in warfare, the bronze which scatters the straw, the poor harvest, Zeus poising his scales, the god as the steward of warfare (19. 224 = 4. 84). Leaf aptly compares the simile at *Iliad* 11. 67–71, which likens the Greeks and Trojans to reapers:

25. *Making of Homeric Verse*, p. 374.
26. Achilles' entire speech at *Il.* 18. 98–126 is rich in metaphor; cf. 102, 104, 114, 117.

οἱ δ', ὥς τ' ἀμητῆρες ἐναντίοι ἀλλήλοισιν
ὄγμον ἐλαύνωσιν ἀνδρὸς μάκαρος κατ' ἄρουραν
πυρῶν ἢ κριθῶν· τὰ δὲ δράγματα ταρφέα πίπτει·
ὣς Τρῶες καὶ 'Αχαιοὶ ἐπ' ἀλλήλοισι θορόντες
δῄουν, οὐδ' ἕτεροι μνώοντ' ὀλοοῖο φόβοιο.

Yet the simile is less complex and suggestive than the passage in Book 19. The former presents one principal point of comparison, with little detail, whereas Odysseus' metaphor is far more unusual.[27] It occurs in the context of his exhortation to Achilles to allow the army time to eat before it goes into battle; the soldiers will thus be better prepared to endure hardship (cf. 19. 155–70, 225–29). Thus the images of satiety, harvest, and stewardship are aptly contrived for the context. Leaf (ad loc.) interprets Odysseus' principal metaphor to mean that hard work in battle outweighs a small reward, just as the straw in the field is greater than the grain that is harvested; therefore, the soldiers require food to be strengthened for their task. M. M. Willcock partially concurs: the thin harvest "indicates that the armies have great labor but little reward." He interprets the straw, however, as a metaphor for the bodies of the dead.[28] Willcock is surely right; the bronze (222 χαλκός) is to be understood figuratively as the weapon which slays in battle.[29] The straw (καλάμην) is thus to be interpreted as the dead; compare Odysseus' use of the word to mean an old, worn-out man, battered by sorrow (*Od.* 14. 214). The thin harvest should be equated with the men who are left alive, rather than merely with the reward of battle. Zeus's poising of the scales (223–24) always occurs in the *Iliad* in contexts of deliberation between life and death (cf. 8. 69, 16. 658, 22. 209), and Odysseus proceeds in this passage to draw a contrast between the numerous dead warriors (226) and those who escape the battle alive (230). The metaphor thus becomes more of a generalizing comment than Leaf's interpretation would suggest. Satiety in warfare (i.e., rushing to battle without proper preparations) is said to result in the grim debacle of a tiny harvest (i.e., few survivors); the antithesis of κόρος (221) and ὀλίγιστος (223) emphasizes Odysseus' pointed contrast. The repetition of ἀνθρώποισιν (221) in ἀνθρώπων (224) helps to unify the entire metaphorical statement through a type of ring composition.[30]

27. For additional comment on the simile, and on the interesting phrase ἀνδρὸς μάκαρος at *Il.* 11. 68, see C. Moulton, "Similes in the *Iliad*," *Hermes* 102 (1974): 390–91.

28. *A Companion to the "Iliad"* (Chicago, 1976), p. 219.

29. Cf. the use of αἴθωνι σιδήρῳ in the simile for the death of Simoeisius at *Il.* 4. 485.

30. With the metaphor at *Il.* 19. 221–24 one may compare Aeschylus' famous image of Ares as a gold changer, who converts men's bodies in war to the ashes held by funeral urns (*Ag.* 438–44): ὁ χρυσαμοιβὸς δ' Ἄρης σωμάτων / καὶ ταλαντοῦχος ἐν μάχῃ δορὸς / πυρωθὲν ἐξ 'Ιλίου / φίλοισι πέμπει βαρὺ / ψῆγμα δυσδάκρυτον, ἀντ- / ήνορος σποδοῦ γεμί- / ζων λέβητας εὐθέτους. [εὐθέτους Auratus: εὐθέτου FTri.]. Here, too, there is a metaphor for the presiding deity (ὁ χρυσαμοιβὸς δ' Ἄρης σωμάτων / καὶ ταλαντοῦχος ἐν μάχῃ δορός); cf. Zeus as the steward of war who poises his scales. Living men become ashes in Aeschylus' image; the passage in the *Iliad* likens them to straw cut down by bronze. There are no Aeschylean counterparts for the notions of satiety (κόρος) and harvest (ἄμητος) in the Homeric passage. It is fair to say that the verses from the *Iliad* are just as complex and rich in imagery as the lines from the *Agamemnon*. E. Fraenkel, *Aeschylus: "Agamemnon"* (Oxford, 1950), ad 438, denies any reminiscence of Homer in the Aeschylean passage; but cf. A. Sideras, *Aeschylus Homericus* (Göttingen, 1971), p. 211.

16. 745–50 ὢ πόποι, ἦ μάλ' ἐλαφρὸς ἀνήρ, ὡς ῥεῖα κυβιστᾷ.
εἰ δή που καὶ πόντῳ ἐν ἰχθυόεντι γένοιτο,
πολλοὺς ἂν κορέσειεν ἀνὴρ ὅδε τήθεα διφῶν,
νηὸς ἀποθρῴσκων, εἰ καὶ δυσπέμφελος εἴη,
ὡς νῦν ἐν πεδίῳ ἐξ ἵππων ῥεῖα κυβιστᾷ.
ἦ ῥα καὶ ἐν Τρώεσσι κυβιστητῆρες ἔασιν.

This passage, the vaunt of Patroclus over Cebriones, is the only truly extended metaphor in the *Iliad*, and resembles many of the similes in its structure. Its ironic effect, however, sets the speech apart from the similes. Patroclus' sustained pretense of discerning an acrobatic tumbler or diver in the dying Cebriones has little in common, for example, with the poet's elaborate comparison of Ajax with an acrobatic horseman at *Iliad* 15. 679–84. The speech, too, is clearly distinct from the short diver simile that precedes it at 16. 742 (ἀρνευτῆρι ἐοικώς).[31] The verb κυβιστάω is used at *Iliad* 21. 354 (of fish leaping out of the water), and the noun κυβιστητήρ recurs in literal contexts at *Iliad* 18. 605 = *Odyssey* 4. 18. Patroclus' metaphor is organized through ring composition (cf. ῥεῖα κυβιστᾷ at 745, 749); the elaboration of the diving image contains a contrast between the grim situation of the narrative and a constructive activity (here, diving for food); there is the addition of a gratuitous detail (748 εἰ καὶ δυσπέμφελος εἴη). All these features are typical of similes in the *Iliad*. But perhaps the closest analogue to the passage's tone is the heavily ironic speech of Achilles to Lycaon in Book 21.

21. 54–63 ὢ πόποι, ἦ μέγα θαῦμα τόδ' ὀφθαλμοῖσιν ὁρῶμαι·
ἦ μάλα δὴ Τρῶες μεγαλήτορες, οὕς περ ἔπεφνον,
αὖτις ἀναστήσονται ὑπὸ ζόφου ἠερόεντος,
οἷον δὴ καὶ ὅδ' ἦλθε φυγὼν ὑπὸ νηλεὲς ἦμαρ,
Λῆμνον ἐς ἠγαθέην πεπερημένος· οὐδέ μιν ἔσχε
πόντος ἁλὸς πολιῆς, ὁ πολέας ἀέκοντας ἐρύκει.
ἀλλ' ἄγε δὴ καὶ δουρὸς ἀκωκῆς ἡμετέροιο
γεύσεται, ὄφρα ἴδωμαι ἐνὶ φρεσὶν ἠδὲ δαείω
ἢ ἄρ' ὁμῶς καὶ κεῖθεν ἐλεύσεται, ἦ μιν ἐρύξει
γῆ φυσίζοος, ἥ τε κατὰ κρατερόν περ ἐρύκει.

No explicit metaphor is sustained here. The speech is carefully structured around the notion of "holding in check," "restraining" (59, 62, 63 ἐρύκω). Like Patroclus at *Iliad* 16. 745–50, Achilles opens with a cry of ironic surprise (ὢ πόποι): the Trojans are indeed courageous if, once slain, they can return from the dead (54–56). This is hyperbole, since Lycaon was not in fact slain, but rather sold into slavery on Lemnos by Achilles on a previous occasion. But Achilles equates him with one of the dead: now he has come back, since the sea journey has not deterred him (57–58). Let him have a taste of Achilles' spear, so that the latter may know for certain if Lycaon can perform a second miracle and come back from *there* (κεῖθεν), or if the

31. On the simile, which is employed with greater effectiveness at *Il.* 12. 385 and *Od.* 12. 413, see B. C. Fenik, *Typical Battle Scenes in the "Iliad,"* Hermes Einzelschriften, 21 (Wiesbaden, 1968), p. 215.

fertile earth will deter him and hold him in check for good (60–63). The literal "restraint" of the sea in the first half of the speech is transformed into a metaphor in the second portion: the idea is that Lycaon, once he has been killed by Achilles, may yet be struggling to "return from the earth." The grim rhetoric is enhanced by Achilles' illogical, but effective, assimilation of Lycaon to the dead in the first place (55–57 Τρῶες . . . οὕς περ ἔπεφνον / αὖτις ἀναστήσονται ὑπὸ ζόφου ἠερόεντος, / οἷον δὴ καὶ ὅδ' ἦλθε). The speech itself is highly metaphorical in individual phrases, for example, ὑπὸ ζόφου ἠερόεντος, νηλεὲς ἦμαρ, δουρὸς ἀκωκῆς ἡμετέροιο γεύσεται. But the overall conception, which is that of killing Lycaon for the second time, is a suppressed metaphor which dominates the entire passage, making all the more pathetic Lycaon's own recollection of his previous capture and ransom.[32]

Let us pass now to the issue of "fixed" metaphor. Here we will discuss a number of images that occur more than twice in the *Iliad* in either identical or slightly varied form. A fair assessment of Parry's theory—that these metaphors are deprived of meaning through repetition—may concede at the outset that certain phrases appear to lack much distinctive color and seem to have been repeated numerous times as decorative, metrical "fillers." For example, an inspection of the metaphor ποιμένι/α λαῶν (repeated fifty-six times, always in the adonic segment of the verse) shows that the phrase is applied to a wide variety of characters, with little discrimination. On the other hand, a recent examination of the numerous occurrences of ἔπεα πτερόεντα (123 times by Parry's count) has defended the phrase's vitality and the appropriateness of its placement.[33] Careful analysis of such repeated metaphors on an individual basis is called for, if we are fairly to evaluate their effectiveness as poetic devices. In particular, we should probe the relationships of a group of metaphors to variations of the same image; we must study features of context which may act to reinforce the rhetorical intensity of any given occurrence of a repeated metaphor; and we should investigate instances of "clustering," or the grouping of similar or identical metaphors within a distinct narrative segment. As illustrations of such analysis, let us consider the following passages.

11. 574 (τά τε δοῦρα . . .)
ἐν γαίῃ ἵσταντο, λιλαιόμενα χροὸς ἆσαι.

This phrase typifies the frequent personifications of weapons in the *Iliad*.[34] It recurs at 15. 317 and, with a slight alteration, at 21. 168. One may compare as well 21. 69–70 (ἐγχείη . . . ἐνὶ γαίῃ / ἔστη, ἱεμένη χροὸς ἄμεναι

32. With respect to the speech of Patroclus at *Il.* 16. 745–50, whose ironic tone resembles that of Achilles, it is interesting that the juxtaposition of death in the narrative and diving for fish in Patroclus' image is refracted at *Il.* 21. 126–27 in the vaunt of Achilles over Lycaon: Achilles says that a fish will jump to break the surface of the water as it feeds on the body of the slain Trojan (cf. νηὸς ἀποθρῴσκων at 16. 748 with θρῴσκων at 21. 126). Achilles does not employ metaphorical language here, however.

33. See Vivante, "On Homer's Winged Words," pp. 1–12.

34. For other examples, see Stanford, *Greek Metaphor*, pp. 138–39. Aristotle seems especially to have admired the vivid personifications of the battle narrative; for his comments on Homeric metaphor, see *Poet.* 1459a4, *Rhet.* 1411b31.

ἀνδρομέοιο) and a related expression, containing an even more grotesque image, at 5. 289 = 20. 78 and 22. 267 (αἵματος ἆσαι Ἄρηα ταλαύρινον πολεμιστήν). In the *Iliad*, one can have one's fill of mourning (23. 157, 24. 717) or of war (19. 402). But to speak of sating Ares with blood, or of spears eager to glut themselves with flesh, is obviously a figurative transformation of eating (cf. the literal ὄψου τ' ἄσαιμι at *Il.* 9. 489 or the grim feasting of dogs pictured at *Il.* 11. 818 and 24. 211). It is noteworthy that, although our phrase and its cognates are repeated, metaphors involving the verb ἄω come gradually to be concentrated on Achilles in the last books of the *Iliad*; compare 19. 402 (Achilles' speech to his horses), 20. 78 (his hatred for Hector), 21. 69–70 (the capture of Lycaon), 21. 168 (the encounter with Asteropaeus), 22. 267 (Achilles' refusal to treat with Hector), 23. 157 (his speech to Agamemnon). This cluster of metaphors is in turn linked with Achilles' literal abstention from food (cf. ἄω at *Il.* 19. 307) and with the themes of grief and revenge in the last books.[35] The metaphor with which we started (11. 574) must thus be viewed as part of a system, which is manipulated with increasing intensity as the narrative builds to its climax.[36]

3. 212 . . . μύθους καὶ μήδεα πᾶσιν ὕφαινον

This is a key metaphor in the *Odyssey*, although it is important in the *Iliad* as well. The literal usage of ὑφαίνω (= weave at the loom) is clear enough at *Iliad* 3. 125, 22. 440, *Odyssey* 2. 94 = 24. 129, 15. 517, 19. 139. Our metaphorical phrase never recurs exactly, but to be compared are ὑφαίνειν ἤρχετο μῆτιν (*Il.* 7. 324 = 9. 93), δόλον ἄλλον ὕφαινε (*Il.* 6. 187), μή τίς μοι ὑφαίνῃσιν δόλον αὖτε (*Od.* 5. 356), δόλους καὶ μῆτιν ὕφαινον (*Od.* 9. 422), μῆτιν ὕφαινον (*Od.* 4. 678; cf. *Od.* 4. 739, 13. 303, 386). Of the six Odyssean usages, four are directly concerned with Odysseus at suspenseful crises in the narrative: the landing on Scheria (5. 356), the escape from the Cyclops (9. 422), and the meeting with Athene on Ithaca (13. 303, 386). All these scenes are described in elaborate detail, and in two of them other rhetorical features combine to underline the importance of μῆτις; compare the puns at 9. 410 and 414 and the repetitions of the word or its compounds at 13. 293, 299, 311, and 382. The other two Odyssean usages occur in the narrative of the suitors' plot to kill Telemachus: the first is used of the suitors (4. 678), the second of Laertes by Penelope (4. 739). The Iliadic usages are distributed as follows: the plot of Proetus to ambush Bellerophon (6. 187), and the attempts of Nestor to counsel the Greek chiefs, first to build the wall and the ditch (7. 324), and then to send the embassy to Achilles (9. 93). The metaphor at 3. 212, in Antenor's account of Odysseus, also concerns an embassy. The point of this elaborate speech (the longest in the Teicho-

35. I am grateful here to Julia Heskel, who, in an unpublished essay entitled "Banqueting in the *Iliad:* A Study of Homeric Metaphor," has analyzed in impressive detail this group of images and its links to important narrative themes.

36. There is no reason a priori to believe that such ordering of imagery is inconsistent with the oral theory, whatever the processes of composition or the circumstances of performance. For this question and detailed discussion of the ordering of similes in the poems, see C. Moulton, *Similes in the Homeric Poems* (Göttingen, 1977), esp. pp. 13–14.

skopia) is to describe Odysseus' wondrous rhetorical powers. Although both Odysseus and Menelaus are said to "weave words and counsel" for the assembly, it is clear that Odysseus surpasses Menelaus (cf. 3. 223). Shortly before the metaphor (200), and shortly afterward (216), Odysseus is given the epithet *πολύμητις*, exclusively reserved for him in the *Odyssey* and, with but one exception, in the *Iliad* also (eighteen times).[37] On the whole, the metaphors involving *ὑφαίνω* occur at suspenseful points in the narrative of both poems, where they underscore the evolution of particularly momentous (or treacherous) plans by the characters. At *Iliad* 3. 212, the suspense inheres in the assembly's recognition of Odysseus' true powers, barely suspected from his appearance, but revealed as extraordinary when he speaks (cf. the contrast of the simile at 219, *ἀΐδρεϊ φωτὶ ἐοικώς*, with the simile at 222, *ἔπεα νιφάδεσσιν ἐοικότα χειμερίῃσιν*). The "weaving of words and counsels" results in a dramatic reversal of expectation.

4. 274–75 *τὼ δὲ κορυσσέσθην,*[5] *ἅμα δὲ νέφος εἵπετο πεζῶν.*
ὡς δ' ὅτ' ἀπὸ σκοπιῆς εἶδεν νέφος αἰπόλος ἀνήρ

The metaphor in 4. 274 is part of a remarkably flexible system. After the penthemimeral caesura, 4. 274*b* is repeated with the slight change of *μετὰ* for *ἅμα* at 23. 133*b*. At 17. 755 we find *τῶν δ' ὥς τε ψαρῶν νέφος ἔρχεται ἠὲ κολοιῶν* as the start of a simile. At 16. 66 we have *εἰ δὴ κυάνεον Τρώων*[7] *νέφος ἀμφιβέβηκε*. The second half of this expression, in turn, resembles 16. 350 (≈ *Od*. 4. 180): *πρῆσε χανών·*[3] *θανάτου δὲ μέλαν*[7] *νέφος ἀμφεκάλυψεν*. The cloud of death is virtually interchangeable with the cloud of war, except for the different syntactical requirements of the similar verse at 17. 243: *καὶ σῇ, ἐπεὶ*[3] *πολέμοιο νέφος περὶ πάντα καλύπτει*. The omission of the metaphor's second term results in a lexical variation and enjambement at 20. 417–18: *γνὺξ δ' ἔριπ' οἰμώξας,*[5] *νεφέλη δέ μιν ἀμφεκάλυψε / κυανέη, κτλ.* This expression is loosely analogous to the metaphor at 17. 591 (= 18. 22; *Od*. 24. 315): *ὣς φάτο,*[2] *τὸν δ' ἄχεος*[5] *νεφέλη ἐκάλυψε μέλαινα*. In every case, the cloud is associated with death or extreme danger. The metaphor is extended beyond the single word so often that the figurative meaning cannot be in doubt. The last three examples occur at highly emotional moments: the death of Hector's special companion Podes (cf. *Il*. 17. 575–96), the announcement of Patroclus' death to Achilles, and the point at which Laertes gives up hope for news of Odysseus.[38]

The verbs *τείνω* and *τανύω* are employed metaphorically in the *Iliad* in contexts of evenly matched battle (cf. 11. 336, 12. 436 = 15. 413, 13. 359, 14. 389, 16. 662, 20. 101.)[39] These verbs are also used of Zeus's sending of

37. The exception is at *Il*. 21. 355 *πολυμήτιος Ἡφαίστοιο*. In Antenor's speech, note the repeated emphasis on words and counsel (cf. *μήδεα πυκνά* at *Il*. 3. 208, *οὐ πολύμυθος / οὐδ' ἀφαμαρτοεπής* at *Il*. 3. 214–15); cf. Helen's reference to *μήδεα πυκνά* at *Il*. 3. 202.

38. At *Il*. 4. 274–75, the metaphor is followed by an ominous extended simile involving a cloud; the same technique appears at *Od*. 19. 205–9, where the simile of melting snow precedes the image of Penelope's cheeks "melting" (208). Cf. also *Od*. 19. 136, 263–64, and H. Fränkel, *Die homerischen Gleichnisse* (Göttingen, 1921), p. 33.

39. On 13. 359 (*πεῖραρ ἐπαλλάξαντες ἐπ' ἀμφοτέροισι τάνυσσαν*), see Bergren, *Etymology and Usage of* ΠΕΙΡΑΡ, pp. 45–57.

the whirlwind and of night (cf. *Il.* 16. 365 and 567). It is in *Iliad* 17, the single episode of the fight over Patroclus' body, that such metaphors are concentrated.

The first striking occurrences of τανύω are literal usages in the famous simile of the oxhide. The image is placed squarely in the center of the *Leichenkampf*, and serves as a grotesque emblem for it (17. 384–95):

> τοῖς δὲ πανημερίοις ἔριδος μέγα νεῖκος ὀρώρει
> ἀργαλέης· καμάτῳ δὲ καὶ ἱδρῷ νωλεμὲς αἰεὶ
> γούνατά τε κνῆμαί τε πόδες θ' ὑπένερθεν ἑκάστου
> χεῖρές τ' ὀφθαλμοί τε παλάσσετο μαρναμένοιιν
> ἀμφ' ἀγαθὸν θεράποντα ποδώκεος Αἰακίδαο.
> ὡς δ' ὅτ' ἀνὴρ ταύροιο βοὸς μεγάλοιο βοείην
> λαοῖσιν δώῃ τανύειν, μεθύουσαν ἀλοιφῇ·
> δεξάμενοι δ' ἄρα τοί γε διαστάντες τανύουσι
> κυκλόσ', ἄφαρ δέ τε ἰκμὰς ἔβη, δύνει δέ τ' ἀλοιφὴ
> πολλῶν ἑλκόντων, τάνυται δέ τε πᾶσα διαπρό·
> ὣς οἵ γ' ἔνθα καὶ ἔνθα νέκυν ὀλίγῃ ἐνὶ χώρῃ
> εἵλκεον ἀμφότεροι· κτλ.

The repeated τανύω (390, 391, 393) is closely associated with the soldiers' dragging of the body to each side (393 ἑλκόντων, 395 εἵλκεον). The narrative proceeds to emphasize the expectations of each army, Greek and Trojan; the battle was so savage that not even Ares and Athene could have scorned it. The poet then reintroduces τανύω, this time in a metaphorical usage, as if to remind us of the image of the oxhide (17. 400–401):

> τοῖον Ζεὺς ἐπὶ Πατρόκλῳ ἀνδρῶν τε καὶ ἵππων
> ἤματι τῷ ἐτάνυσσε κακὸν πόνον· κτλ.

One may note the specific touches which are added to the phrase here: the mention of Patroclus' name (400) and the enjambed verse (401), with the expression ἤματι τῷ.

After the episode of Achilles' horses and Automedon's short *aristeia*, the poet returns to the main action with a metaphorical usage of τείνω; this expression, too, is fuller than usual (17. 543–44):

> ἂψ δ' ἐπὶ Πατρόκλῳ τέτατο κρατερὴ ὑσμίνη
> ἀργαλέη πολύδακρυς, κτλ.

Shortly after these verses, Athene's descent to the battlefield to stir up Menelaus is described in an unusual simile, where τανύω is employed for Zeus's "stretching" of the rainbow (17. 547–52):

> ἠΰτε πορφυρέην ἶριν θνητοῖσι τανύσσῃ
> Ζεὺς ἐξ οὐρανόθεν, τέρας ἔμμεναι ἢ πολέμοιο,
> ἢ καὶ χειμῶνος δυσθαλπέος, ὅς ῥά τε ἔργων
> ἀνθρώπους ἀνέπαυσεν ἐπὶ χθονί, μῆλα δὲ κήδει,
> ὣς ἡ πορφυρέῃ νεφέλῃ πυκάσασα ἓ αὐτὴν
> δύσετ' Ἀχαιῶν ἔθνος, ἔγειρε δὲ φῶτα ἕκαστον.

The notion of Zeus extending the rainbow from the sky may be compared to his sending of night at *Iliad* 16. 567 and his creation of the tempest at *Iliad* 16. 365. But, as commentators have noticed, there is a curious merging in the simile of image and narrative reality; since Athene wraps herself in the purple cloud (17. 551), her journey to earth is associated with a physical transformation into a rainbow, before she takes on her disguise as Phoenix.[40] The ominous *νεφέλῃ* at 551 is to be noted within the context of Books 16 and 17, where there is a strikingly effective interaction between literal clouds or darkness and cloud imagery.[41] The passage is thus particularly suggestive: the simile itself becomes an omen of evil in the narrative, associated with the prominent cloud imagery of the episode (cf. 17. 243, 591, and 755 for metaphorical clouds, and 17. 269, 368, 594, 645 for literal clouds or mist), and also linked through *τανύω* with the motif of the stretching of battle at 543–44.[42]

The final occurrence of the metaphor in Book 17 comes at the point when Menelaus and Meriones lift the body of Patroclus: a furious battle ensues. Here too the passage is immediately followed by a simile, although there is no connection of motifs (17. 735–37):

> ὣς οἵ γ' ἐμμεμαῶτε νέκυν φέρον ἐκ πολέμοιο
> νῆας ἐπὶ γλαφυράς· ἐπὶ δὲ πτόλεμος τέτατό σφιν
> ἄγριος ἠΰτε πῦρ, κτλ.

It is noteworthy that all the metaphorical usages of *τείνω*/*τανύω* in Book 17 occur in the second half of the episode, after the unsuccessful attempts of Menelaus and Ajax to defend the body. Perhaps the poet wished to reserve the intensity of evenly matched battle on a general scale for the climactic stages of his long narrative of the *Leichenkampf*.[43] The initial confrontations of Menelaus with Euphorbus, and of Ajax with Hector and the Trojans, give way to a more general battle scene about the midpoint of the episode; compare the speeches of anonymous warriors at 415 and 421. It is interesting, too, that the literal usages of *τανύω* occur first—in the context of the oxhide simile. That unusual image conditions our response to the ensuing metaphors: each recurrence of the phrase for the stretching of battle reinforces the grotesque, literal struggle on the battlefield for the possession of Patroclus' corpse.[44] Thus this particular metaphor, closely

40. Cf. the simile at *Il.* 4. 75–79, where Athene appears to be transformed into a shooting star, also a *τέρας* for mortals, before she completes her mission to earth in the guise of Laodocus (4. 86–88). On both passages, see Fenik, *Battle Scenes*, pp. 182–83.

41. For a summary analysis, see Whitman, *Homer and the Heroic Tradition*, pp. 151–53.

42. A similar connection is to be observed in Book 16; note that Zeus's sending of night at 567 (*νύκτ' ὀλοὴν τάνυσε*) and his "stretching of strife" at 662 (*ἔριδα κρατερὴν ἐτάνυσσε*) both occur within the context of a *Leichenkampf*, this time the struggle over Sarpedon.

43. Indeed, at the culmination of the episode (17. 722–61) the narrative is virtually recounted through the imagery of five full similes and their applications; see Moulton, *Similes in the Homeric Poems*, pp. 75–76.

44. This is not tantamount to asserting with Stanford (*Greek Metaphor*, p. 135) that simile "clarifies" metaphor. Both the oxhide simile at 17. 389–93 and the metaphor for the stretching of labor that follows it at 400–401 are equally intelligible on their own terms; the close juxtaposition serves to make each image more powerful. Such reinforcement is also the case in the juxtaposition of the metaphor at 543 with the simile at 547 (*τείνω*/*τανύω* common to both passages); but the principal vehicle of the second passage, the rainbow, differs in content from the metaphor. Another

allied to formulaic phrases in other passages of the *Iliad*, acquires considerable poetic force in Book 17. Through repetition, slight variation, and skillful placement, the poet is able to employ metaphor for a powerful, sustained effect.[45] At least in this instance, neither repetition nor formulaic composition seems to have deprived a metaphor of meaning. Indeed, these factors, combined with the concentration of an image in a particularly appropriate context, contribute to the cumulative force of a single metaphor.

The examples and discussions in this essay are intended to convey the range and variety of Homeric metaphor, and also to respond to the contentions and theories that have tended to dismiss its significance in the epics. Much remains to be done, and the analysis here can only claim to be a prolegomenon. Specifically, as our insights into Homeric vocabulary become more precise, we need detailed exploration of problematic phrases, for example, μέλπεσθαι Ἄρηϊ (*Il.* 7. 241) or ἐντυπὰς ἐν χλαίνῃ (*Il.* 24. 163), which can be apprehended as striking images but which are decidedly curious in meaning.[46] We surely stand in need of more discussion of the "fixed" metaphors and their variants. And a review of the distribution of images, with a comprehensive list, would aid further analysis considerably. How does the poet of the *Iliad* apportion metaphors among speeches and narrative? And does the distribution in speeches indicate significant differences in the characterization of the heroes? The latter question is particularly interesting, given the evidence that other poetic devices (e.g., similes, apostrophe) are occasionally employed to individualize character in both poems.[47] Finally, a comparison of metaphor in the *Iliad* and the *Odyssey*, in which the role and characteristics of similes display important differences, would be informative. For the present, the evidence assembled here should confirm that metaphor is a vital, significant part of the language of Homer.[48]

Emory University

variation of the technique appears in the relationship of metaphor at 736 with simile at 737–39. Here, two images in rapid succession emphasize the ferocity of the battle, and thus may be said to reinforce each other; but there is no overlap whatever between them in content or diction.

45. One may compare the metaphors with ἄω used of Achilles; cf. p. 289 on *Il.* 11. 574.

46. A recent example is Bergren's *The Etymology and Usage of* ΠΕΙΡΑΡ *in Early Greek Poetry*.

47. On the similes used, e.g., of Menelaus, see Fenik, *Battle Scenes*, p. 161. For apostrophe, see A. Parry, "Language and Characterization in Homer," *HSCP* 76 (1972): 1–22, esp. 9–21. With regard to metaphor in speeches, one might compare, e.g., Antinous and Eurymachus in the *Odyssey*. That the characters are doublets, and yet subtly individualized in a variety of ways, has been demonstrated by B. Fenik, *Studies in the "Odyssey,"* Hermes Einzelschriften, 30 (Wiesbaden, 1974), pp. 198–205. Antinous speaks more often than his comrade (twenty-three speeches for 212 lines vs. Eurymachus' thirteen speeches for 126 lines). Yet even allowing for this disparity, there is a wide discrepancy in metaphorical content between their speeches: Antinous is made to employ nineteen images, with two unique expressions (cf. *Od.* 16. 389, 17. 448), whereas Eurymachus speaks only three metaphors, all of them with many parallels. The significance of this differentiation is probably related to the typical conduct of the two chief suitors. In the main, Eurymachus is deceptively friendly, hypocritical, and smooth; Antinous, on the other hand, is direct, boastful, violent: his language is exaggerated and colorful (cf. *Od.* 16. 379, 17. 377, 446, 448, 18. 79, 21. 88, 299, 302).

48. It is a pleasure to acknowledge the helpful suggestions of M. W. Edwards and S. D. Atkins, and of the referees of *CP*. I am also grateful for the assistance of a grant from the National Endowment for the Humanities.

PUBLIC AND PRIVATE IN THREE PLAYS OF EURIPIDES

GEORGE B. WALSH

Aristophanes depicted Euripides as the poet of petty household worries, and more gracious critics have praised him for his fine observation of the individual's inner experience. Nevertheless, the private life in Euripidean drama is an elusive thing; scarcely one of his dramatic characters lives beyond the range of public concerns or entirely by his own inner imperatives. We may eavesdrop briefly when Medea raves within her house; but, as soon as she steps out upon the stage, she begins to conceal her feelings to make herself acceptable to the women of Corinth. The expectations and demands of the public world impose themselves upon the dramatic character and sometimes even appear to change him, as they transform the retiring, pitiable Iphigenia into a heroine. Thus, if we wish to discover what is private in Euripidean drama, we must seek it within another, public realm.

We may begin by defining the private life negatively, as something different from the dramatic character's public role. If his public role is imposed by society which demands service and accords approval and honor, or blame, he plays a private role when he does not aim at service to society or at winning its approval, and a privately motivated action is most sharply marked when the hero contemplates doing something that will damage society's interest or win him shame in its eyes. Achilles in *Iliad* 9 might be described in these terms. He rejects honor from the Achaeans because he has enough from Zeus (607–8), and he seems to offer a rudimentary definition of the alternative to public endeavor: he would please himself rather than Agamemnon and set the enjoyment of riches before winning more at Troy (398–409), life and a family before glory and an early death (414–15, 398–99).

Hector faces a more complicated decision in Book 6, but it can be formulated in similar terms, as a choice between chiefly private well-being and public honor. Andromache, who regards him as father, mother, brother, and husband at once, pleads for the preservation of the οἶκος (429–30); she asks him to fight defensively (431–34) and fears most that he may die (406–13). Hector, on the other hand, wishes to avoid shame and win glory in the Trojans' eyes (440–46), and so chooses to fight among the front ranks, inviting death and his family's ruin, although he foresees that the reputation for bravery he wins now will make Andromache's slavery harder to bear in the future (459–61).

Since Achilles must relinquish glory if he is to rejoin his father at home, and Andromache sets the preservation of her home against Hector's honor, the ties of family seem to inhibit distinction, and the private life seems to

0009-837X/79/7404-0002$01.40

be incompatible with heroic action. This may explain why, when honor is at stake in the plays discussed below, Euripides gives prominence to the feelings between parents and children and makes the action turn upon the children's deaths.

We shall seek, first, to mark the boundaries between the dramatic character's public and private roles; this is most easily done in the *Medea*, where the two stand in irreconcilable conflict. We shall then follow the attempts of Euripides' characters in the *Iphigenia at Aulis* and the *Madness of Heracles* to reconcile public and private claims upon them.

When Medea first enters the stage, she suggests that her current difficulties stem from the failure of the public accurately to assess individual character, since those who live quietly, as she claims to do, win a bad reputation (218 δύσκλεια). The public, before it judges, should know a man's inner qualities, his internal organs, where feelings reside (220 σπλάγχνον); these are the real determinants of character, for one cannot judge properly from appearances (219 δίκη γὰρ οὐκ ἔνεστ' ἐν ὀφθαλμοῖς βροτῶν). But since Medea's public position as a foreigner at Corinth is especially weak (255 ἔρημος ἄπολις), she must exert herself to repair her reputation and adapt herself to society (222 χρὴ δὲ ξένον μὲν κάρτα προσχωρεῖν πόλει). Medea's speech makes two points that will be critical for the play's treatment of public and private roles: first, that the two roles differ, since there is a "quiet" life distinct from life in society and an emotional life distinct from public image; second, that there is a public dimension to Medea's predicament. She has sacrificed her father's home and her family to be Jason's wife (257–58), one private life for another which may be narrowly defined as εὐνή (cf. 265). When Jason rejects her and abandons their οἶκος, he forces her out of the private and into the public realm; Medea finds that she is vulnerable to public opinion, which she had earlier neglected, and without allies. For this reason, she attempts to win the chorus' aid and to repair her public image with an argument based upon the shared private miseries of women (230–51). She will, if she can, bring public perception into line with her experience.

As the play continues, a conflict between public and private roles develops, first between the heroine and Jason, and then within Medea herself. Jason seems aware of little but the public dimension of his relationship to Medea, and he regards marriage not as a benefit in itself but as a means for obtaining material prosperity. He will marry the king's daughter not ἱμέρῳ πεπληγμένος (556) but ὡς . . . μὴ σπανιζοίμεσθα (559–60), and he desires her wealth not so that he may enjoy it but to enhance his social status (cf. 542–44): his family will live according to its rank (562 ἀξίως δόμων ἐμῶν), and he will prevent the defection of his φίλοι (561). By a public standard, Jason has satisfied his marital obligation toward Medea and returned favor for favor by bringing her to Greece, where she has acquired universal renown for her wisdom (540 δόξαν ἔσχες). Even her passion, in his view, is not a personal feeling that must be reciprocated in kind but a divine and impersonal force (526–31).

Jason characteristically speaks of the ends he seeks as a kind of profit that may be won with reason and moderation:

ἐμοί τε λύει τοῖσι μέλλουσιν τέκνοις
τὰ ζῶντ' ὀνῆσαι . . . [566–67]

λήξασα δ' ὀργῆς κερδανεῖς ἀμείνονα. [615]

When Medea insists upon expressing her hatred to please herself, Jason accuses her of folly (457, 614 *μωρία*, cf. 600), but she rejects his notion of reason, as she does his plan to marry for profit: feeling must be the criterion of prosperity (598–99),

μή μοι γένοιτο λυπρὸς εὐδαίμων βίος
μηδ' ὄλβος ὅστις τὴν ἐμὴν κνίζοι φρένα.

Thus, Medea insists upon what Jason denied, that the emotions must be counted in assessing their duties to one another. Since personal feeling is opposed here to Jason's social ambition, as it was to public opinion in Medea's first speech, it seems a characteristic feature of the nonpublic and, therefore, of the private life.[1] Medea, who posits a distinction between public and private roles, has sought in her first speech to bring the public into line with the private. Jason, on the other hand, acknowledges no distinction between the two roles, and he manipulates for public ends what Medea would regard as private relationships.

Gradually, however, the differences between Jason and Medea become less apparent, until Medea entirely assumes Jason's principles and negates the position she had taken against him earlier. As Jason seeks to enhance his status at Corinth by abandoning Medea, Medea's decision to punish Jason also turns upon the issue of status.[2] At each key point of planning and resolve, her desire for vengeance is described not as aimed at emotional satisfaction or the restitution of justice, although these are both important themes, but as a means for throwing off the public onus of the victim's role and for rehabilitating herself in the eyes of society as potent and dangerous. To win vengeance, Medea must dissemble and control her anger, and the hatred she feels for Jason takes shape in calculation. In the process, she abandons her initial attempt to reconcile public judgment with private feeling, for circumstance requires that feeling be violated or denied.

What Medea fears most is ridicule, especially by her enemies. She will not risk a direct attack upon the palace because, if she is caught and killed, *θήσω τοῖς ἐμοῖς ἐχθροῖς γέλων* (383). When she first explains her plan to kill the children, she opposes her maternal grief to the preservation of her dignity, which is now revealed as the stronger motive (791–96):[3]

1. *θυμός* (1079) seems to represent another sort of feeling, which favors Medea's pursuit of honor, but it need not be taken as signifying feeling in general; see E. Schlesinger, "Zu Euripides' *Medea*," *Hermes* 94 (1966): 29–30.

2. The problem is raised as one concerning women generally by Medea (236–37) and by the chorus (410–20).

3. Medea's final decision to murder the children is similarly motivated: *βούλομαι γέλωτ' ὀφλεῖν / ἐχθροὺς μεθεῖσα τοὺς ἐμοὺς ἀζημίους; / τολμητέον τάδ'* . . . (1049–51), and, as she explains her-

ᾤμωξα δ' οἷον ἔργον ἔστ' ἐργαστέον
τοὐντεῦθεν ἡμῖν· τέκνα γὰρ κατακτενῶ
τἄμ' . . .
οὐ γὰρ γελᾶσθαι τλητὸν ἐξ ἐχθρῶν, φίλαι.

The feeling that binds together kin cannot be reconciled with the demands of honor.

In seeking to avoid the laughter of enemies, Medea subscribes to a common heroic sentiment,[4] and the obligation she feels to preserve her honor derives, like Jason's desire for wealth, from a sense of high rank that must be maintained (404–6):[5]

οὐ γέλωτα δεῖ σ' ὀφλεῖν . . .
γεγῶσαν ἐσθλοῦ πατρὸς Ἡλίου τ' ἄπο.

Ridicule, for such a person, is best avoided and renown most easily won by a demonstration of power—the power to hurt one's enemies and, should the occasion arise, to help one's friends.[6] Thus Medea expresses her sense of the murder of Jason's bride (807–10):[7]

μηδείς με φαύλην κἀσθενῆ νομιζέτω
μηδ' ἡσυχαίαν, ἀλλὰ θατέρου τρόπου,
βαρεῖαν ἐχθροῖς καὶ φίλοισιν εὐμενῆ·
τῶν γὰρ τοιούτων εὐκλεέστατος βίος.

Among Medea's φίλοι, however, her children should take first place[8] (1250 φίλοι γ' ἔφυσαν); and, since her plan for achieving vengeance entails her murdering them, it evidently excludes the possibility that she will be εὐμενῆ φίλοισιν. In this failure to fulfill her obligations to help, or at least to do no harm to her friends, Medea repeats Jason's offense, φίλους κακῶς δράσαντ' (470).[9]

Medea's plan also causes her more grief than it does her enemy (1046–47):

τί δεῖ με πατέρα τῶνδε τοῖς τούτων κακοῖς
λυποῦσαν αὐτὴν δὶς τόσα κτᾶσθαι κακά;

By so constructing Medea's situation, the playwright has clearly opposed

self to Jason at the end of the play, σὺ δ' οὐκ ἔμελλες τἄμ' ἀτιμάσας λέχη / τερπνὸν διάξειν βίοτον ἐγγελῶν ἐμοί (1354–55).

4. Cf. Soph. *Aj.* 367, 382; for the pleasure of laughing at enemies, *Aj.* 79. See also A. P. Burnett, "Medea and the Tragedy of Revenge," *CP* 68 (1973): 22; B. Knox, "The *Medea* of Euripides," *YCS* 25 (1977): 198–99.

5. Cf. *Med.* 562, *Hcld.* 507–10; Soph. *Aj.* 472.

6. For this reason suicide is ruled out by Ajax (Soph. *Aj.* 466–69).

7. Cf. *HF* 585–86.

8. Cf. *Med.* 16, where τὰ φίλτατα for Jason are his wife and children, and the words describe their family relationship rather than affection: the point is that he owes them loyalty. Cf. A. W. H. Adkins, "Homeric Gods and the Values of Homeric Society," *JHS* 92 (1972): 12; idem, " 'Friendship' and 'Self-sufficiency' in Homer and Aristotle," *CQ*, n.s. 13 (1963): 33.

9. Medea also deserves to be treated well as a φίλος because of the favors she conferred upon him (476–87).

the heroic code to what is most natural[10]—the protection of offspring—and what privately would please the heroine best.[11] Medea's plan of vengeance sets her concern with status above personal pleasure (598–99), so that she comes to value what she had complained of in Jason's plan, a sort of profit that brings with it emotional pain (1362 λύει δ' ἄλγος, ἢν σὺ μὴ 'γγελᾷς). What Jason offered (598) and what Medea now does is λυπρός (1037), and so her vengeance exacts the same price from her that Jason's new marriage would have done.

Medea justifies killing the children with another argument that sets public and impersonal values over private and emotional ones. She kills them, she says, not only to punish Jason, but to save them from an enemy's insult (781–82):[12]

> οὐχ ὡς λιποῦσ' ἂν πολεμίας ἐπὶ χθονὸς
> ἐχθροῖσι παῖδας τοὺς ἐμοὺς καθυβρίσαι.

As she sends them into the palace, she promises (1060–61),

> οὔτοι ποτ' ἔσται τοῦθ' ὅπως ἐχθροῖς ἐγὼ
> παῖδας παρήσω τοὺς ἐμοὺς καθυβρίσαι.

This argument[13] strikes the modern reader as so peculiar that he cannot resist asking why, if Medea can flee in the Sun's chariot, the children cannot also, and why the life Aegeus promises Medea at Athens, guaranteed by solemn oaths to be secure from attack by Medea's enemies (734–53), should not be safe enough for them.[14] In other words, if Medea kills the children to preserve their honor as an extension of her own, why can she not save them as an extension of herself? The anomaly in Medea's reasoning underscores the significance of her decision, which is entirely consistent with her motives as they emerge elsewhere in the play.

The murder of the children is not an act of hatred against them, any more than Medea's wish to live means that she looks forward to pleasure in life: both arise from impersonal motives, their purpose defined principally in terms of the judgment they may elicit from society. The children's death, like her survival, is necessary to cause her enemies pain, and in this way to win the greatest renown for her power,[15] but Medea is not interested in saving the children's lives, because she is not truly interested in saving her own.

10. Medea's resentment may be a natural feminine trait, but the murder of the children surely does not represent "the power of sacred φύσις," as W. Arrowsmith suggests ("A Greek Theater of Ideas," in *Ideas in the Drama*, ed. J. Gassner [New York and London, 1964], p. 20).

11. Ajax in Sophocles' play must also make a choice between preserving his honor and protecting his family, but he clearly prefers his honor. Euripides' use of a female protagonist enables him here to formulate the choice in more sharply antithetical terms.

12. Cf. Megara in the *Madness of Heracles* (below, p. 305) and Phaedra in the *Hippolytus* (p. 299).

13. Cf. Medea's motive in burying the children herself, ὡς μή τις αὐτοὺς πολεμίων καθυβρίσῃ (1380).

14. Schlesinger, "Zu Euripides' *Medea*," p. 32.

15. Medea also wins a terrible sort of distinction because her action is almost unique: cf. 1282 and, for the text, D. Page (ed.), *Euripides' "Medea"* (Oxford, 1938), ad loc. For disinterest in life linked to concern for honor, cf. *Hcld.* 443–44.

We may see in Medea's disinterest in life for its own sake an extension of the impulse toward suicide that she expresses early in the play.[16] Medea's first thought of killing the children stems from her feeling that she is hateful herself (112–14),

ὦ κατάρατοι
παῖδες ὄλοισθε στυγερᾶς ματρὸς
σὺν πατρί, καὶ πᾶς δόμος ἔρροι,

and from an urge toward self-destruction (97 πῶς ἂν ὀλοίμαν;). She reconciles herself to the murder with the thought that her own life is worthless (798 τί μοι ζῆν κέρδος;), and so her victory over Jason is also an act of despair.[17] Medea's vengeance is also like a suicide in that both sorts of action are aimed at saving face, by sacrificing a life regarded as impossible to preserve honorably. By killing oneself one avoids the abuse suffered by the homeless and despised (*HF* 1285–90; cf. *Hcld.* 303), and the higher one's rank the greater one's obligation to die well and to deny one's enemies an occasion for glee.[18] Phaedra, in the *Hippolytus*, kills herself to save her own and her children's honor (715–21; cf. 419–23, 687–88), and also to deny Hippolytus any sense of superiority to her in her distress (728–30).

Thus, Medea's early impulse to kill herself has been not so much abandoned as transformed into a plan of vengeance. Vengeance saves her honor much more effectively than suicide would,[19] but it serves a similar purpose, and in the *Medea* it exacts a price from the avenger not unlike the loss of life. To a fifth-century thinker like the sophist Antiphon, who regarded the natural and the conventional as exclusive categories and the natural by definition as that which promotes the preservation of life,[20] suicide might seem the most social and least natural of acts. By extension, Medea's murder of her children may be regarded as an act of complete socialization, designed to win respect from society but inimical to her instinctive role as a mother.[21] The dramatic point of the murder depends partly upon its failure to achieve precisely the intended social effect, for the public whose respect Medea seeks must surely feel as much horror at her violation of natural ties as esteem for her ability to avenge herself (cf. 846–65); while Medea has come to set public motives against private ones, the chorus does not.

Abandoning her role as a mother and accepting emotional distress, Medea chooses to elevate herself over her enemy, and so to make of herself

16. Cf. Schlesinger, "Zu Euripides' *Medea*," pp. 34, on the version of Anouilh ("So ist auch hier vielleicht der Selbstmord Medeas die richtige Deutung des eigentlichen Gehalts der euripideischen Tragödie"), and 53, on Medea's revenge ("die ihren eigenen Untergang als Mensch bedeutet").

17. Medea's words are typically those of a suicide: cf. *HF* 1301–2 (τί δῆτά με ζῆν δεῖ; τί κέρδος ἕξομεν / βίον γ' ἀχρεῖον ἀνόσιον κεκτημένοι;); Soph. *Aj.* 475.

18. *Or.* 1060–63, *HF* 287–92; Soph. *Aj.* 479–80.

19. One avoids by killing oneself a fate over which one has no control, and so suicide is a confession of ἀπορία; at best it will succeed only in saving some shred of one's former dignity. The suicide hides in death (*HF* 1155–60; cf. 1199–1201) to escape δύσκλεια (*HF* 1152). Vengeance, on the other hand, can do more than repel δύσκλεια—it can create εὔκλεια (*Med.* 807–10).

20. Diels-Kranz[8] (Berlin, 1956), 87B44 frag. A col. 3, 25–col. 4, 8.

21. Cf. *HF* 636, *Phoen.* 356.

an entirely public figure. Her triumph consists not so much in Jason's pain as in his humiliation and his recognition of her power, and in this respect Medea's vengeance resembles an act of divine punishment. Like Dionysus' coolly executed public humiliation of Pentheus in the *Bacchae*, the punishment of Jason completes the avenger's plan to win honor, and the plan succeeds because the avenger can act, when necessary, without feeling. For this reason, among others, Medea's godlike[22] escape in the machine seems appropriate.

The *Medea* presents public and private roles in a dialectic that develops through the conflicts of the dramatic characters and shapes the meaning of the dramatic action; the action gives the dialectic a concrete form, in which the audience may test its own values. The play does not, however, simply reflect what one might expect to be the conventional judgment of its audience, nor does it offer its own single point of view. Its discoveries are paradoxical and inconclusive: Medea's heroic bid for public honor isolates her completely, for in abandoning natural feeling she offends conventional sensibility. But Medea perhaps represents a special case, because she takes her public life in hand only when Jason's debased ambition has begun the destruction of her *οἶκος*. Embodied for other characters in another kind of dramatic plot, the dialectic may take a different form.

The conflict in the *Medea* between public and private motives for action also characterizes Euripides' treatment of self-sacrifice, or acquiescence in a death imposed by enemies or the gods. Vengeance and self-sacrifice both serve to fulfill the demands of the heroic code which requires aid to friends and harm to enemies—self-sacrifice aims chiefly at the first, and vengeance at the second—and, since both sorts of heroic action enhance one's stature in the eyes of society, both may be regarded as located within the public sphere.

Vengeance and self-sacrifice differ, however, in two ways. First, society can be more intimately concerned in an action of self-sacrifice, for it is not only the arbiter and audience of the hero's success, but may also be his beneficiary.[23] Menoeceus' self-sacrifice in the *Phoenician Women*, for example, aims clearly at public benefit (1012 *ἐλευθερώσω γαῖαν*) as well as public approval (1005 *ὅπου δ' ἂν ζῶ, κακὸς φανήσομαι*), to the dismay of his closest kin, his father Creon (963–67). Creon's reluctance and Menoeceus' readiness to complete the sacrifice points to a second difference between the dramatic treatments of vengeance and self-sacrifice. Menoeceus experiences no internal conflict like Medea's, engendered by the opposed claims of public and private roles. The case for the sacrificial victim's private ties to

22. Cf. Knox, "The *Medea* of Euripides," p. 206; M. P. Cunningham, "Medea ΑΠΟ ΜΗΧΑΝΗΣ," *CP* 49 (1954): 152, 158–59.

23. Not all actions of self-sacrifice are inspired by their social utility: Polyxena's death in the *Hecuba* helps no one but Achilles' ghost and her enemies the Greeks, and so may be called public only because it saves Polyxena herself the shame of cowardice and slavery (346–78); Alcestis and Phaedra intend by dying to benefit principally members of their own family, although Phaedra wishes also to set an example as a wife (stated negatively, *Hipp.* 409–12); Macaria, in the *Children of Heracles*, dies less to help Athens than her kin (500–34).

family must be made by his family, which must then itself face a conflict between its own desires and society's.[24]

The interplay of rank and personal desire, public and private roles, pervades the *Iphigenia at Aulis*, Euripides' final and most complete statement of this theme. The role of the sacrificial victim has been much expanded,[25] but every other character also contributes to the elaboration of the theme, by eliminating each area of common ground between public and private motives and finally by isolating Iphigenia as the only wholehearted representative of the public interest. Only she achieves what she desires; others, who would arrange public life so that it reflects personal priorities, or who reject the demands of honor entirely in favor of family feeling, fail. In the prologue and the first episode, Agamemnon and Menelaus prepare the way for what follows by establishing between them that their own public and private roles cannot be reconciled and that the public demand for Iphigenia's death must inevitably be satisfied.

Agamemnon first raises the question of public life as he debates with an old servant the meaning of social position. He envies the servant (16–19) and his own honor pains him (23), because his position has imposed upon him now the duty to sacrifice his daughter;[26] but the old man rebuffs him, warning that everyone, at every social level, must accept his rank.

Menelaus has no trouble doing this at first, because the common goals of the Greek expedition coincide with his own personal desire (330 ὅτι τὸ βούλεσθαί μ' ἔκνιζε), and he accuses Agamemnon of having dissembled a similar self-interest in seeking command (338). Agamemnon, he feels, has now failed to live up to the position he has won, having abandoned his public role as soon as it ceased to satisfy his personal desire. As a result, all of Greece now suffers the fate Medea sought to avoid, the laughter of its enemies, and it excites Menelaus' sympathy (366–75). As a spokesman for public duty,[27] Menelaus criticizes Agamemnon's self-indulgence in terms similar to those invoked by Jason against Medea: Agamemnon, by implication, lacks νοῦς and ξύνεσις (374–75),[28] the most important qualities in a leader. In both the *Medea* and the *Iphigenia* terms for wisdom and intelligence seem to denote a type of practicality that is hard to distinguish from social ambition and opposed to the impracticality of indulging one's emotions.

Agamemnon responds by redefining intelligence: the divine is not ἀσύνετον (394*a*), and so does not make binding oaths taken κακῶς and under compulsion (395). Similarly, the bonds of birth are to be regarded only if they

24. The internal conflict, if there is one, falls upon the parent of the victim, who must perform or sanction the sacrifice: see below on Agamemnon in the *Iphigenia at Aulis* (pp. 301–2).

25. Cf., e.g., Macaria in the *Children of Heracles* or Menoeceus in the *Phoenician Women*.

26. Cf. E. Fraenkel, *Aeschylus: "Agamemnon,"* 3 vols. (Oxford, 1950), ad 212, on Agamemnon's social obligation in Aeschylus.

27. F. M. Wasserman, "Agamemnon in the *Iphigenia at Aulis:* A Man in an Age of Crisis," *TAPA* 80 (1949): 177, identifies Agamemnon as an introvert, Menelaus as an extrovert.

28. Cf. *Med.* 457, 614 on Medea's μωρία; 548–49 on Jason's σοφία and σωφροσύνη; 600 on the desirability of Medea's becoming σοφωτέρα.

enforce good sense (406–7):

Με. δείξεις δὲ ποῦ μοι πατρὸς ἐκ ταὐτοῦ γεγώς;
Αγ. συνσωφρονεῖν σοι βούλομ', ἀλλ' οὐ συννοσεῖν.

Thus, according to Agamemnon, Menelaus' definition of intelligence is purely formal and social; intelligence in essence, on the contrary, does not depend upon society's judgment, even society's interest, but upon the individual. The relationship of φίλοι and the common interest of Greece take second place to Agamemnon's own perception of comfort (409 μὴ λυπῶν ἐμέ) and moral correctness defined apart from society (411 Ἑλλὰς . . . σὺν σοὶ . . . νοσεῖ).

But Agamemnon cannot maintain his position: he realizes that once Iphigenia has arrived at Aulis she must be sacrificed, and that she cannot be saved by his σοφίσματα because the daemon is σοφώτερος (444–45) and so overturns his personal definition of wisdom. This inspires another discourse on the conflict between his public and private roles. Once again, he deplores his high position: ἡ δυσγένεια δ' ὡς ἔχει τι χρήσιμον (446); ὄγκος constrains both his speech and his tears (447–50), so that the well-born is a slave to the mob. The constraints of Agamemnon's position forbid his weeping at Iphigenia's fate, but he also feels the compulsion of personal misfortune urging him to weep despite the mob; caught between these two pressures, he does not know what to do (451–53):

ἐγὼ γὰρ ἐκβαλεῖν μὲν αἰδοῦμαι δάκρυ,
τὸ μὴ δακρῦσαι δ' αὖθις αἰδοῦμαι τάλας,
ἐς τὰς μεγίστας συμφορὰς ἀφιγμένος.

Coincidentally, as Agamemnon confronts the defeat of his personal desire, Menelaus reverses himself. Speaking to Agamemnon ἀπὸ καρδίας . . . / καὶ μὴ 'πίτηδες μηδέν (475–76), he cancels his earlier δεινοὶ λόγοι (477–80, 500); he no longer desires Helen, because pity and love inspired by his relationship by blood to Iphigenia (492 συγγένειαν ἐννοουμένῳ) and to Agamemnon (501–2 τὸν ὁμόθεν πεφυκότα / στέργων) have proved the stronger feelings. Since his own desire no longer requires what he regarded before as the public interest, he contemplates breaking up the expedition with equanimity (495), and so incurs the charge he levelled against his brother, that he supported public causes only when they satisfied his private wants (337–62).

Although Menelaus now adopts a personal position like Agamemnon's, the public necessities they reject can no longer be resisted: Odysseus, who is ambitious for honor (527 φιλοτιμίᾳ)[29] and in league with the mob (526 τοῦ ὄχλου μέτα), will force the sacrifice. The Greek army must proceed against Troy, although neither Agamemnon nor Menelaus wishes it.

The pattern of the first episode, in which Agamemnon's reasoning and Menelaus' abrupt conversion to feeling together fail to save Iphigenia, is repeated when Achilles' plan of reasoned persuasion and Iphigenia's emo-

29. The term appears frequently in the *Iphigenia at Aulis* with negative connotations: cf. 342, 385, 520, 527.

tional appeal also fail. Achilles presents reason and moderation as his chief virtues and the means to stop the sacrifice (922–23, deleted by some editors):

λελογισμένοι γὰρ οἱ τοιοίδ' εἰσὶν βροτῶν
ὀρθῶς διαζῆν τὸν βίον γνώμης μέτα.

He suggests to Clytemnestra that they may make Agamemnon *βέλτιον φρονεῖν* (1011), and he prefers λελογισμένως πράσσοιμι μᾶλλον ἢ σθένει (1021), claiming that *οἱ λόγοι γε καταπαλαίουσιν λόγους* (1013).[30]

Achilles' difficulty in acting as Iphigenia's protector, however, arises principally from his commitment to the public interest and public opinion. Although Clytemnestra tells him that she feels no shame in doing anything that may aid so vital a purpose as saving her daughter (900–902), and so clearly sets private values over public ones, her appeal for help is based upon Achilles' honor. She holds before him the prospect of ill-repute if his pretended bride should be slaughtered (906–8); and, since it is his name, she says, that has destroyed her, she calls upon him to defend it (910). Clytemnestra appears to believe that Achilles' obligation to behave well derives specifically from the rank he inherits from his divine mother,[31] and she self-consciously treats him as a god although she knows he is mortal (900–901), calling him an altar at which she seeks sanctuary (911). Achilles promises to become the god he appears, to make real this external aspect of himself (973–74):

θεὸς ἐγὼ πέφηνά σοι
μέγιστος, οὐκ ὤν· ἀλλ' ὅμως γενήσομαι.

His own quarrel with Agamemnon is purely formal—his name was available to trap Iphigenia had the king requested it (962–63)—and he seems even now committed to the common good (967 *τὸ κοινόν*), as Menelaus was before pity taught him otherwise (cf. 370), and to salvaging his position among the chieftains (968–69), as Agamemnon was when he first planned Iphigenia's death (356–60). Achilles is afraid that he may incur the army's blame by indiscreetly taking Clytemnestra's part (1020); he wishes to preserve her reputation as well as his own (1030–32), and he has been uneasy about speaking to her since they first met (830 *αἰσχρὸν δέ μοι γυναιξὶ συμβάλλειν λόγους*).

By contrast, until she changes her mind and accepts the sacrifice, Iphigenia seems the perfect representative of private values, disinclined toward reason and careless of honor. She has none of Achilles' rational arguments (*λόγοι*) to plead her case (1211–14), and instead of wise words she offers tears to persuade Agamemnon. To give pleasure, she is willing to make no sense (654 *ἀσύνετά νυν ἐροῦμεν, εἰ σέ γ' εὐφρανῶ*), and to enjoy pleasure she easily sets aside glory (1250–52 *τὸ φῶς τόδ' ἀνθρώποισιν ἥδιστον βλέπειν* . . .

30. Although Clytemnestra expects little from this approach (1014), she accuses Agamemnon of lacking *νοῦς* (1139) and argues from the same premise that Agamemnon invoked against Menelaus, the intelligence of the gods (1189; cf. 349*a*).

31. This is suggested by the train of thought of 909–10 *πρὸς μητέρος—/ ὄνομα γὰρ τὸ σόν μ' ἀπώλεσ', ᾧ σ' ἀμυναθεῖν χρεών.*

κακῶς ζῆν κρεῖσσον ἢ καλῶς θανεῖν).[32] But Iphigenia fails to save herself, because there is a higher harmony of public necessity and personal feeling: the collective passion of the mob (1264), which achieves what no individual dramatic character could in reconciling public and private motives, and carries all individuals before it. It defeats Achilles' rational pursuit of honor and Iphigenia's personal appeal to the emotions. Even Agamemnon, who is "intelligent in pity" (1255), and so, in this curious phrase, combines reason and feeling, cannot resist. Public passion is a divine force (1264).

Iphigenia responds to this impasse by identifying herself with the forces that destroy her—reason, honor, and the public good—and she decides to offer herself freely at the altar.[33] Like Achilles, she is now conscious of herself as the object of public scrutiny (1378), and she has become concerned with winning a good reputation (1375–76 τοῦτο δ' αὐτὸ βούλομαι / εὐκλεῶς πρᾶξαι, cf. 1383 κλέος and *Hcld.* 534); therefore, she wins Achilles' approval (1407–9). Iphigenia conflates the normally sexual and private ἀρετή of women (569) with its masculine counterpart, the glorious destruction of cities: her children and her marriage will be the expedition against Troy (1398–99 ταῦτα γάρ μνημεῖά μου / διὰ μακροῦ, καὶ παῖδες οὗτοι καὶ γάμοι καὶ δόξ' ἐμή). Her identity merges with that of the goddess to whom she is sacrificed, and she requires no tomb but Artemis' altar (1444). She now defines her very existence as public, admonishing her mother, πᾶσι γάρ μ' Ἕλλησι κοινὸν ἔτεκες, οὐχὶ σοὶ μόνῃ (1386; cf. *Phoen.* 996 πατρίδος ἥ μ' ἐγείνατο).

Iphigenia has no stake like Medea's in the result of her action, nothing to fear but the sacrifice itself; she does not avoid the laughter of enemies because she was never threatened by it. The *Iphigenia* presents a new and extended version of the plot of sacrifice, in which the victim does not die for her family, like Macaria in the *Children of Heracles*, or even her city, like Menoeceus in the *Phoenician Women*, but for her entire society. Greece as a whole is to enjoy the honor won by Iphigenia's death, and it is to Greece that she feels obligated to act honorably.

By setting the interest of Greece against the life of the girl, the playwright gives the dialectic of public and private a form different from the *Medea*. The two realms are as sharply distinguished, but when Iphigenia chooses public goals, and subverts her οἶκος by setting her parents at odds (cf. 1171–79), she takes all of Greece in its place (1386), and so escapes Medea's isolation. Iphigenia's attachment to public honor also differs from Achilles', and this explains why he does not fully grasp the vigor of her resolve (1430). Iphigenia at the last combines the emotional directness of her first appearance in the play with patriotism, and thus she reflects the overwhelming

32. Cf. 1218. For the generalization and the value Iphigenia places upon common human qualities, cf. Demophon (*Hcld.* 413) and Heracles (*HF* 633–36); her wish to live reverses Soph. *Aj.* 479–80 ἢ καλῶς ζῆν ἢ καλῶς τεθνηκέναι / τὸν εὐγενῆ χρή.

33. On the language in which her decision is expressed, cf. Knox, "The *Medea* of Euripides," p. 198, and *Med.* 822, 1236. The abruptness of Iphigenia's conversion to public values and of Menelaus' to private ones emphasizes the separation of the two realms: cf. Arrowsmith, "A Greek Theater of Ideas," p. 19, who sees it as explained by the heroine's function as a "specification of the shaping ideas of the play." Both conversions come as the result of reflection (492 συγγένειαν ἐννοουμένῳ, 1374 ἐννοουμένην).

power of the army's collective feeling. Like the army, Iphigenia attains a harmony of personal and public motives that is not possible for Achilles, who thinks of public life only as an arena in which honor is won with calculation.

When Iphigenia forbids Achilles to defend her and chooses death because she believes that a woman's life is worth less than a man's (1392–94), she resolves the dialectic of public and private with a new sort of feminine, acquiescent heroism modeled neither upon the old-fashioned, fearsome and uncompromising type Medea emulates nor the ungenerous pragmatism of Jason and Achilles. The *Madness of Heracles*, by placing at center-stage the chief exemplar of male ἀρετή and generous service, casts the dialectic of roles in a third and different form, which encompasses the attempts of one character at the start and another at the end to come to terms with the demands of honor.

The first action is occasioned by a coup d'etat at Thebes, where Heracles' family has remained while he completes his labors for Eurystheus; the new tyrant Lycus plans to kill Heracles' wife Megara and his children to forestall any vengeance they might seek for the death of Megara's father, the former ruler of the city. Megara's predicament seems worse than Medea's or Iphigenia's: she and her children are threatened with shameful death at the hands of an enemy, with no protector in view, no power of their own, and no divine mechanism like a sacrifice through which salvation may be won with honor. Like Medea, Megara is concerned most with avoiding the laughter of enemies (285 ἐχθροῖσιν γέλων) and the ignominy of cowardice, and for her children the humiliation of exile (303–4 τόδ' ἄθλιον, / πενίᾳ σὺν οἰκτρᾷ περιβαλεῖν σωτηρίαν, 291); she feels that her rank, derived from the fame of Heracles and his nominal father Amphitryon, obliges her to behave honorably (287 δόκησις . . . εὐκλεής, 290 εὐκλεὴς πόσις). Megara's plan for preserving honor calls for surrendering her children from the sanctuary of the altar at which they have taken refuge, so that they may die willingly and with good grace (cf. *Hcld.* 550–51); thus, despite their defeat and the loss of Heracles' wealth, their name will remain (338 τὸ δ' ὄνομ' ἔσθ' ἡμῶν ἔτι). She is brought to this decision not by any lack of feeling for her children, for like Medea she embarks upon what she thinks is a heroic course against the pressure of her own emotions (485–89). Her inability to act against her enemies forces her to choose a kind of honor that violates personal ties, and so she fails through weakness to reconcile public and private roles.

Heracles is paired with Megara by contrast, and his approach to the conflict between public and private roles, completed at the end of the play, balances and corrects hers at the beginning.[34] He arrives in time to save his family from Lycus, but the danger they have faced is enough to make him reject his past achievements because they distracted him from

34. Amphitryon also serves as a foil for Megara: he values honor less than the lives of the children and vainly offers his own life in despair of saving theirs (317–18). Cf. A. P. Burnett, *Catastrophe Survived* (Oxford, 1971), pp. 161–62, for another view of Megara's error; for the opposite approach, H. H. O. Chalk, "Ἀρετή and Βία in Euripides' *Herakles*," *JHS* 82 (1962): 12, who suggests that Megara represents a valid sort of ἀρετή. A. W. H. Adkins, "Basic Greek Values in Euripides' *Hecuba* and *Hercules Furens*," *CQ*, n.s. 16 (1966): 212, disputes Chalk.

the safety of his home, his good deeds because they have won no return, and his status because it commanded no palpable honor or reward (575–82 *χαιρόντων πόνοι . . . οὐκ ἄρ' Ἡρακλῆς ὁ καλλίνικος ὡς πάροιθε λέξομαι*). What matters most matters regardless of distinction, honor, or wealth (632–36):

> *καὶ γὰρ οὐκ ἀναίνομαι*
> *θεράπευμα τέκνων. πάντα τἀνθρώπων ἴσα·*
> *φιλοῦσι παῖδας οἵ τ' ἀμείνονες βροτῶν*
> *οἵ τ' οὐδὲν ὄντες· χρήμασιν δὲ διάφοροι·*
> *ἔχουσιν, οἱ δ' οὔ· πᾶν δὲ φιλότεκνον γένος.*

In this preference for universal and instinctive protection of his family, Heracles seems to confute Megara's concern for their public stature and her decision to let the children die.

The central action of the play, however, ruins Heracles precisely in the personal realm for which he has just expressed his preference, and it forces him to reconsider his carelessness of public stature. He distinguishes himself heroically with one more victory by killing Lycus, but then he is driven mad and kills the children whose safety he now values above everything. In his madness, Heracles thinks that he has merely continued the attack upon his enemies (938 *ἔργον μιᾶς μοι χειρὸς εὖ θέσθαι τάδε*, cf. 1279, where the murder is described as another of his toils), and this represents a real connection between his vengeance and the murder of the children: like the rest of his labors, his vengeance is achieved at the expense of the family whom he left undefended, and, like Megara, Heracles can win victory only by violating his role as a parent.

With the loss of his children Heracles has lost the focus of his private life, and he has nothing left to contemplate but a minimal public advantage—to escape ill-repute (1152 *δύσκλεια*) and the humiliations of exile (1285–90) made worse by the eminence he once enjoyed as the son of Zeus. His position now resembles Megara's at the start of the play, but his response differs. Megara thinks it *δειλία* not to die voluntarily (289), Heracles *δειλία* not to live (1347–48), and he apparently sees a standard of heroic behavior that extends beyond what Megara envisions, that makes demands upon the hero other than *καλῶς ζῆν ἢ καλῶς θανεῖν*.

Heracles does not arrive at the decision to live immediately, and its meaning may be deduced from the manner in which it is made. At first he wishes to die (1256–57) because, like Megara, he sees himself in the grip of external forces—a necessity that has made him commit involuntary murder (1262 *ἀνάγκῃ δυστυχεῖν*, cf. Megara at 282–83 *τῷ δ' ἀναγκαίῳ τρόπῳ / ὃς ἀντιτείνει σκαιὸν ἡγοῦμαι βροτόν*), imposed both by his human father's crimes and by the hatred of his divine father's wife (1258–64), and the results of the murder, which make another sort of necessity (1281 *ἥκω δ' ἀνάγκης ἐς τόδ'*), including pollution, exile, and public humiliation.

To these externally imposed conditions Theseus applies public, external, "non-moral"[35] remedies—purification for Heracles' pollution (1324), and

35. Cf. A. W. H. Adkins, *Merit and Responsibility* (Oxford, 1960; repr. Chicago, 1975), pp. 90–91, on pollution.

honors and a place to live in his exile (1325). He argues, too, that Heracles' crime, like the immorality of the gods, reflects a universal condition of which one should not complain (1321), and this part of Theseus' prescription reinforces the other, for, if the gods' crimes relieve Heracles of responsibility for the murder, nothing remains of it but the physical stain that purification may remove.

Heracles rejects both these notions[36] and yet obliquely arrives at the decision to which Theseus wished to bring him, to persevere in life. Noting that the topics Theseus addresses are irrelevant to his misery (1340), Heracles nevertheless feels impelled to refute him on one point: the gods do not commit crimes, do not enjoy illicit love (1341–46). Thus, he deprives himself of a consolation and an excuse for having murdered his family, and so must bear a kind of responsibility for it that Theseus cannot remove when he purifies him physically of pollution. He accepts the Athenian's offer of honors and asylum (1351–52), but such things cannot cure his misery since they are remedies only for the public ills of humiliation and exile, and his decision to live goes beyond what Theseus urges, for it entails not merely a continuation of his heroic past (cf. 1250, 1252) but bravery of a different sort, the acceptance of grief that the hero never tasted in all his toils (1356).

To endure to live Heracles requires something different from what Theseus offers, a point of view that will break the helpless passivity he feels at first before the necessity of his misfortune. Theseus' notion that crime is universal merely reinforces his own belief, that the gods have made him suffer (cf. 1303–10), for both excuse his crime only by making him a victim of the inevitable. Perhaps Theseus' consoling speech encourages Heracles to live precisely because it does not address his greater need, and so provokes him to meet it himself: his change of heart, for some time already in motion (1347), is completed immediately after he refutes the claim that the gods are criminal, and so, because he acknowledges his own responsibility for misfortune, he comes to see that he can endure it. He must accept what he has done not as a helpless victim of ἀνάγκη but as a servant of fortune (1357 τύχη), and this leaves room for an active courage radically different from Megara's acquiescence in death. Misfortune and life are enemies that must be withstood like opponents in battle (1349–51).

Heracles overcomes two obstacles in deciding to live, the first, with Theseus' help, his public shame, exile, and pollution, the second a permanent grief that cannot be washed away. In overcoming both shame and grief, Heracles undertakes a combined public and private enterprise, which is figuratively embodied in the weapons with which he has won renown and killed his children.[37] The arms must be kept for a conventional heroic

36. Heracles and Theseus differ as Phaedra and her nurse do in the *Hippolytus*. When the nurse urges that the gods' licentiousness excuses Phaedra's, Phaedra condemns her arguments as the bane of society (451–58, 486–87); and, when she asks whether Phaedra's hands are stained with blood, as if that were the worst she could suffer, Phaedra replies that her pollution lies within herself, in the heart (316–17). Cf. Adkins, *Merit and Responsibility*, p. 114, n. 29, on the latter passage.

37. Cf. J. C. Kamerbeek, "Unity and Meaning of Euripides' *Heracles*," *Mnemosyne*, ser. 4, 19 (1966): 6; Chalk, " Ἀρετή and Βία," p. 14.

reason, to save him from shameful death at the hands of his enemies (1382–84):

> ἀλλὰ γυμνωθεὶς ὅπλων
> ξὺν οἷς τὰ κάλλιστ' ἐξέπραξ' ἐν Ἑλλάδι,
> ἐχθροῖς ἐμαυτὸν ὑποβαλὼν αἰσχρῶς θάνω;

But, since they are the instruments of his children's death, they also remind Heracles of his terrible crime (1379–81) and the grief he must endure as a concomitant of his heroic dignity (1385 ἀθλίως δὲ σῳστέον). By choosing to live and to retain his weapons, Heracles accepts his public role as a hero who cannot allow himself to be discovered a coward or weaker than his enemy. At the same time, he is fully conscious of the personal cost of maintaining this role, and of the magnitude of his loss.

Theseus' tendency to see only public shame and public heroism makes him impatient of Heracles' grief, and blind to the personal side of his endurance. For Theseus, Heracles' wish to linger near the corpses of his children and to embrace his father ill suits his heroic past (1410);[38] grief is a disease, which makes Heracles a woman and no longer the hero he was before (1412–14 εἴ σ' ὄψεταί τις θῆλυν ὄντ', οὐκ αἰνέσει . . . ὁ κλεινὸς Ἡρακλῆς οὐκ εἶ νοσῶν). But Heracles insists that he is the same man, no worse than Theseus himself (1415–17).[39] He will not, like Agamemnon at Aulis, feel shame for his grief, or sacrifice family feeling for the sake of public appearance.

Caught between the conflicting claims of his sentiment as a father and his public role, Agamemnon becomes incapable of choice or action; Iphigenia chooses and acts, but only by relinquishing the persona we first encountered on stage and by putting on another, more abstract, ideally heroic one; Medea in pursuit of honor appears to shed human form. Heracles, on the other hand, by choosing to live a life of honor and grief, extends the dialectic of roles so that it defines a new kind of heroism, which differs both from Iphigenia's patriotic surrender to the passion of the group and from Medea's savage isolation. He clings, as no other Euripidean character seems able, to his place in a human οἶκος, as the son of Amphitryon, as well as to the distinction he won as the son of Zeus;[40] he seems at the last to have made Theseus his family, following his ally as his children once followed him.[41]

38. LP ascribe 1412 to Amphitryon, P 1414 and 1416 as well. Amphitryon's sentiments noted earlier (n. 34) support the distribution of lines given by Murray. For the meaning of the passage, cf. Chalk, "Ἀρετή and Βία," p. 13.

39. Since society judges public actions and the individual himself his private ones, public and private roles differ as shame and guilt do: cf. Gouldner's concise definition of these terms, *Enter Plato* (New York and London, 1965), pp. 81–90. Heracles now seems to reject the old standard of shame as mere failure: cf. Adkins, *Merit and Responsibility*, p. 33, on τὸ αἶσχρον. What matters instead is his response to failure, and it is tempting to see in this the emergence of an internalized standard of success. Adkins, "Basic Greek Values," pp. 218–19, however, would object that Heracles can win no success here and seeks only to avoid worse dishonor.

40. See now J. Gregory, "Euripides' *Heracles*," *YCS* 25 (1977): 259–75, on the significance of the double heritage.

41. 1424 Θησεῖ πανώλεις ἑψόμεσθ' ἐφολκίδες, cf. 631 ἄξω λαβών γε τούσδ' ἐφολκίδας χεροῖν, / ναῦς δ' ὣς ἐφέλξω. A connection between the two passages is noted by Wilamowitz, *Euripides "Herakles"*[2], 2 vols. (Berlin, 1895), ad 1424.

Medea, Iphigenia, and Heracles cannot represent directly the values of Euripides' audience, for each engages the dialectic of public and private in a different way, and consequently discovers within it a different sort of heroic stature. The conflict itself, however, is not new, only sharper than before, as the code of social behavior has progressively become more abstract and depersonalized, while coincidentally the human personality emerges as a counterforce of richer complexity. In the first of these developments, Menelaus conceives of defending the honor of Greece as a hero like Ajax does of defending himself; from the second grows Euripides' penchant for psychological characterization. The familiar fifth-century opposition of *φύσις* and *νόμος* also helps to separate public and private more decisively. While a man acting privately attempts to win recognition of his superior or unique qualities, and so to distinguish himself from other men, personal motives will be shared by all members of the human species, and so make the man acting privately indistinguishable from others; social distinctions in the public realm are often regarded as conventional (Eur. frag. 52 Nauck^2, for example), the common, private motives of the species, among which Heracles ranks family ties first (*HF* 632–36), as natural.[42] In such a formulation, public action may be natural, and so penetrate the private realm, only when it arises from collective passion, as it seems to do in the *Iphigenia*, although even in this case it may collide with competing individual impulses.

Euripides' characters must therefore reconcile the immediate experience of their emotions with abstract or conventional claims upon their loyalty, or with their need to maintain their position in a society that often fails to reward instinctive behavior. Thus, the individual personality's scope for action is diminished, or subordinated to some greater force. Those who would reject public pressures, like Menelaus after his change of heart, or Clytemnestra, will find their private desires frustrated by circumstance; Heracles' initial conversion to private values is thwarted by god-sent madness; emotionally vital figures such as Medea and Iphigenia transform their private distress and public vulnerability into public success, but they are transformed themselves. Private life has been made a foil for the social values these Euripidean characters profess and for the public figures they become.[43]

University of Chicago

42. For instinct and the family, cf. Arist. *EN* 1162a7 *ἄνθρωπος γὰρ τῇ φύσει συνδυαστικὸν μᾶλλον ἢ πολιτικόν, ὅσῳ πρότερον καὶ ἀναγκαιότερον οἰκία πόλεως, καὶ τεκνοποιία κοινότερον τοῖς ζῴοις.*

43. I owe much to the generous advice of Anne Burnett, Michael Murrin, and the journal's referees.

THE TEXTUAL TRADITION OF DONATUS' COMMENTARY ON TERENCE

MICHAEL REEVE

Only two manuscripts of Donatus' commentary on Terence antedate the fifteenth century, and together they contain less than half of it. The other thirty-odd manuscripts, almost all written in Italy, derive from lost manuscripts discovered by humanists, one at Mainz in 1433 (the Maguntinus), one at Chartres in the late 1440s (the Carnotensis), and perhaps others of which there is no report. Two lost manuscripts survived in northern Europe long enough to improve the editions of Stephanus (Paris, 1529) and Lindenbrog (Paris, 1602; Frankfurt, 1623). Despite the labors of Sabbadini and Wessner at the turn of the century and Zwierlein in a recent monograph,[1] the relationships of these witnesses remain obscure, partly because they change in the course of the commentary and can only be established by more collation than anyone has undertaken, partly because the historical evidence, though fairly copious, never quite sheds enough light on them.

Elsewhere I have tried to show that the Maguntinus and the Carnotensis can be made to account for the whole of the Italian tradition. After examining either in the original or from reproductions all but two of the manuscripts known to me, I still maintain the soundness of this conclusion, but no longer accept my way of achieving it.[2] Rather than risk having to change my mind again, I shall concentrate in this article on the relation-

1. Sabbadini's contributions were "Storia e critica di alcuni testi latini: Donato Terenziano," *Mus. ital. di ant. class.* 3 (1890): 381–468; "Il commento di Donato a Terenzio," *Studi ital. di fil. class.* 2 (1894): 1–134; "Gli scolii Donatiani ai due primi atti dell'*Eunuco* di Terenzio," *Studi ital. di fil. class.* 3 (1895): 249–363; sections 1 and 2 of "Biografi e commentatori di Terenzio," *Studi ital. di fil. class.* 5 (1897): 289–303; "Spogli Ambrosiani latini: commento di Donato a Terenzio", *Studi ital. di fil. class.* 11 (1903): 185–201; "Quintiliano, il *Commentum Terenti* e Cicerone in Francia nel secolo XIV," *Riv. fil.* 39 (1911): 541–43. Many of these studies are reprinted or summarized in Sabbadini's *Storia e critica di testi latini* (Catania, 1914), itself reprinted as *Medioevo e umanesimo*, vol. 11 (Padua, 1971), the edition cited in this paper. Before publishing his edition, *Aeli Donati quod fertur "Commentum Terenti,"* 2 vols. (Leipzig, 1902–5), Wessner had written "Die Überlieferung von *Aeli Donati Commentum Terentii,*" *RhM* 52 (1897): 69–98. O. Zwierlein, *Der Terenzkommentar des Donat im Codex Chigianus H VII 240* (Berlin 1970), made numerous improvements to the text with the aid of the Chigianus and discussed the place of the Chigianus in the tradition, unfortunately without consulting other manuscripts (except O).

2. The results of my earlier research will appear shortly in *Hermes*. Much of the present work was carried out on a grant from the Wolfson Foundation, to which I express my warmest thanks. I am also indebted to the Institut de Recherche et d'Histoire des Textes (IRHT), to the libraries that supplied microfilms of BDEGILMNQRSTVY, Magl. VII 1210, and part of U, and to Professor Zwierlein, who very kindly arranged for me to borrow his film of K from the Mittellateinisches Seminar of the Freie Universität Berlin. The manuscripts that I have ignored are both copies of Calphurnius' edition: Vat. Urb. Lat. 354 (Wessner, "*Commentum,*" 1: xxiii–xxiv) and the missing Gandavensis (ibid., 1: xxxv), now Genoa Bibl. Durazzo A VII 13, on which see P. Kristeller, *Iter Italicum*, 2 vols. (Leyden, 1963–67), 1:247, 2:523.

0009-837X/79/7404-0003$01.10

ships of extant manuscripts and lost manuscripts easily reconstructed from them. The number of contributions to the classification of these manuscripts should outweigh the absence of a wider perspective and a grand conclusion. Historical evidence will be introduced where it confirms or supplements my inferences.

A word about the system of reference employed here. The title of a play refers throughout to Donatus' commentary on it, which I cite mostly by volume, page, and line of Wessner's edition (e.g., 2: 373. 7), but occasionally, where that would be too precise or less helpful, by play, act, scene, and verse (e.g., *Ad.* 2. 4. 13)—admittedly an outdated convention for Terence, but some references of this kind have acquired familiarity in the literature on manuscripts of Donatus. Wessner's symbols for the manuscripts are used, with these additions:[3]

S	Ambros. L 53 sup. (init.–1: 37. 6)
K	Vat. Chig. H VII 240
Q	Cors. 43 E 28
W	Cors. 43 G 13
Y	Cors. 43 G 23
p	Vat. Pal. Lat. 1629 (a. 1474)
H	Mus. Brit. Add. 11906
J	Mus. Brit. Burn. 171
I	Mus. Brit. Add. 21083 (*Eunuchus*, *Phormio*)
h	Matrit. Reg. 2 B 4
U	Esc. E III 3
e	editio princeps (Venice ca. 1471)

I previously divided the text into eight sections, Zwierlein's seven with the fourth split at *Hec.* 5. 1. 2 and the end of the first moved forward from the beginning of *Andria* to the end of the prologue. It will be necessary to alter some of these sections, but I will first set them all out unaltered:

(1) *Vita–An.* prol.
(2) *An.* 1. 1–*Ad.* 2. 4. 13
(3) *Ad.* 2. 4. 13–*Hec.* 3. 5. 8
(4) *Hec.* 3. 5. 8–5. 1. 2
(5) *Hec.* 5. 1. 2–fin.
(6) *Phorm.* praef.–1. 2. 45
(7) *Phorm.* 1. 2. 45–2. 1. 50, 5. 2–fin.
(8) *Phorm.* 2. 1. 50–5. 2.

Eunuchus here follows *Andria*, and there is no commentary on *Hautontimorumenos*.

3. On S, see Sabbadini, "Spogli Ambrosiani latini," pp. 185–99, and Wessner, "*Commentum*," 2: iii–vi; on KQWYp, M. Warren, "On Five New Manuscripts of the Commentary of Donatus to Terence," *HSCP* 17 (1906): 31–42; for a detailed study of K, Zwierlein's monograph; on JHI, my previous article. I have examined the ed. Rom. 1472 (Paris B.N. Rés. gr. Yc 212) and am certain that it was printed from e. Calphurnius' edition conflates e and a manuscript like f; cf. Wessner, "*Commentum*," 1: xxxiv.

Two of the boundaries in this division, the end of section 1 and the end of section 6, deserve initial consideration. Both are defined by the behavior of the same manuscript, and the exact determination of each brings with it an elimination.

Section 1 ends when KV desert TC and join forces with A (s. xi). I said that this happens at 1: 49, and more precisely it happens between 48. 12 *quasi* A *quaeso* TCKV and 49. 1 *in* TC om. AKV. It cannot be a coincidence that in K the second hand takes over from the first at 49. 1 *ABITE*. As V behaves like K but with no change of hand, there is a strong probability that it derives from K. Without actually broaching the question, Zwierlein offers contrary evidence,[4] but all of his "Sonderlesarten von K" in the introductory treatises, apart from an omission caused by loss of leaves, are recorded by Wessner from V^1, and so are most of those in *Andria* and *Ad.* praef.–2. 4. 13. Accounting for the implied divergences would be a waste of time, because V does indeed derive from K. At 2: 3. 4–5 and 46. 6–7, V^1 omitted for no obvious reason *cum sit . . . Terentius* and *EGOMET . . . desperationis*, which both occupy a line in K. At 1: 132. 15, where all the manuscripts except V and K have *intelligeret Pamphilus*, V has *intelligere potuisset Pamphilus* and K *intelli Pamphilus* with *intelli* at the end of f. 18v and *Pamphilus* at the beginning of f. 19r; clearly, the scribe of K neglected to complete the unfinished word, and V completes it reasonably but wrongly. So far as I can see, the derivation holds good in section 1 and the rest of *Andria*, in *Ad.* praef.–2. 4. 13, in a small part of *Eunuchus*, and in sections 4 and 5. In *Phormio* and the rest of *Adelphoi*, *Eunuchus*, and *Hecyra*, it does not. More later about V.

As for the end of section 6, Zwierlein showed that, after differing at the beginning of *Phormio*, KR and CO come into agreement somewhere near 1. 2. 45. In fact, Wessner's apparatus, checked in appropriate places,[5] reveals that the transition occurs between 2: 373. 7 *custos cui* CO (1. 2. 37) and 373. 17 *illi loco* KRCO (1. 2. 38),[6] and it so happens that a marked change comes over the script of K after 373. 16 *EXADVERSVM:* the scribe remains the same, but he seems to have changed his pen, as he might on returning to work after an interval. Up to that point R derives from K. The *Sonderfehler* of K that Zwierlein inferred from Wessner's report of R prove illusory on collation of R, and the appearance of K accounts for several *Sonderfehler* of R, for example, 346. 5 *rex*, 372. 11 *prodiit* (*-ite* altered to *-itus* in K looks like *-iit*, and the compendium could be taken for either *per-* or *pro-*), 373. 15 *fieri* (*fig.* K, with an easily misinterpreted *g*). Evidently K had not gone beyond 373. 16 when R was copied from it. After 373. 16, K has errors not shared by R, for example, abbreviated forms of the citations from Virgil in 377. 24–378. 3, 378. 11 *dixerunt* after 10 *ignem*.

Another descendant of K is a manuscript of the commentary on *Adelphoi*, Magl. VII 1210. It omits in the middle of a page a passage omitted by K

4. *Terenzkommentar*, pp. 90–92, 135–36.
5. At 2: 373. 18, "*vel* CO" should read "*vel* KRCO."
6. The two omissions of CO between these points could have occurred independently through homoeoteleuton.

in turning from one page to another, 2: 175. 18–183. 14 *PARERE HAEC . . . Terentius*, and the part written by the first of its three scribes contains numerous errors induced by the transalpine hand that wrote *Adelphoi* in K.

The unequal skill of its scribes shows that Magl. VII 1210 is not just a descendant of K but a direct copy.[7] No such demonstration presents itself for V or R, but equally none to the contrary. The assumption that all three are direct copies of K fits several pieces of historical evidence. In my previous article I surmised that Magl. VII 1210 might have been owned by Pierfilippo Pandolfini of Florence, to whom Sabbadini attributed R, and I am now certain that it was. Two hands wrote R,[8] and Sabbadini was right to see the first in Ricc. 647, which has an *ex libris* of Pandolfini.[9] It is identical with the third hand in Magl. VII 1210.[10] R and Magl. VII 1210, then, were written at Florence; but on the authority of Dr. de la Mare I previously disclosed that V is Neapolitan. If copies were taken from K both at Florence and at Naples, K need not have been written in either place. A third possibility is Rome. Aurispa was at Rome in January 1451, when he promised a manuscript to Panormita in Naples, and Jacopo Ammannati was at Rome in October 1451, when Donato Acciaiuoli wrote from Florence in request of one.[11] Aurispa's hand is known,[12] and I am not aware of having come across it in any manuscript of Donatus. When I asked De la Mare about Ammannati's hand, however, the article to which she referred me showed at once that he was the first scribe of K—the one who organized its production, the only one of the four who could cope with Greek, and the one whose transcript of *Phormio* was copied by Pandolfini before completion.[13] The other three scribes escape identification; the

7. It must have been written before K was bound and foliated, because it has the correct order where K inverts ff. 37–38.

8. Wessner wrongly denies this ("*Commentum*," 1: xii). The first three words of the gathering that follows the change of hand and the blank space on f. 152 were written by the *manus prima* (*m*[1]). Presumably *m*[1] began at the beginning and simultaneously set *m*[2] to work on another portion; *m*[2] finished first, whereupon *m*[1] said, "all right, just finish off this bit."

9. The manuscript has two parts, ff. 1–20 (16–20 blank) and ff. 21–36 (33v–36 blank), and old foliation in the second part shows that it was originally separate; two bifolia were prefixed to the combination, and the *ex libris* occurs on the first verso of the second. Only the first part was written by the hand under discussion.

10. Ff. 1–26 *m*[1], ff. 27–46 *m*[2], ff. 47–50 *m*[3]; three seniones, one quinio, one binio. On f. 26v the last eight lines are crammed in and the text ends in the middle of a line. F. 33v, inadvertently left blank, was filled up before the scribe reached the foot of f. 34r; a note on f. 33v draws attention to the error. Moisture has rendered the tops of many leaves of Magl. VIII 1210 and R illegible; both manuscripts have roughly the same format and watermark.

Quite by chance I came across other manuscripts owned by Pandolfini in the library of the Società Colombaria, Florence. Manuscript 241 has a partially erased *ex libris*, 235 an *ex libris* in the same hand as the text (more formal than elsewhere); the note on f. 61v of 241 may also have been written by Pandolfini, and the hand of 239 is not much different. These manuscripts all belong to the Fondo Pandolfini, named after an eighteenth-century Pandolfini. It doubtless contains more of his ancestor's manuscripts, but I ordered 235 and 241 only for their content and had no time to pursue the matter further. According to the librarian, someone in Florence is working on Pandolfini.

11. For the historical material in the rest of this paragraph, see Sabbadini, *Storia e critica*, pp. 163–64, and idem, *Carteggio di Giovanni Aurispa* (Rome, 1931), pp. 126, n. 1, 133.

12. Sabbadini, *Carteggio*, plate opposite p. 3.

13. F.-R. Hausmann, "Armarium 39, tomus 10 des Archivio Segreto Vaticano," *Quellen und Forschungen aus italienischen Archiven* 50 (1971): 112–80 and plates after p. 128; plate V is closest. Hausmann remarks (p. 118) that the identification of Ammannati's hand could be "überliefe-

second was probably German,[14] the fourth probably Florentine.[15] Donato Acciaiuoli's letter illuminates the circumstances in which K was produced by taking up what Ammannati had told him:

> VIII° Kal. Octobris reddite sunt mihi litere tue, quibus certior sum factus commentarium Donati ceptum esse a te scribi ea mente ut non diffideres posse absolvi, deinceps permultis occupationibus te impediri eisque ita quotidie premi ut nil temporis tibi superesse possit quod ad reliquum scribendum conferas; quod profecto tibi evenire existimo, non ignarus et tempus et commoditatem eis semper deesse quibus alieno arbitrio vivendum sit et occupatissimis dominis serviendum. Verum cum id a te expleri non possit et ego omnino habere exoptem, vellem ipsum ad me Florentiam mitti; nam cum primum ipsum suscepero, paucis diebus transcribi faciam idque ad te confestim remittam.[16]

If by chance Ammannati's letter survives, it may reveal more; but the manuscript that Acciaiuoli was so eager to lay hands on, whether in the original or in Ammannati's transcript, can hardly have been any other than the one promised to Panormita by Aurispa, his newly acquired copy of the Carnotensis. Though I have found no evidence that Ammannati was closely associated with Aurispa in 1451, Aurispa commended him to Panormita by letter when he went to Naples in July 1453 on the staff of Capranica. Perhaps he took K with him, and perhaps it had already been to Florence.

Zwierlein's monograph on K established its importance, but it has proved to be more important still. Further manuscripts derive from it, but, as I do not know where all of them were written, I postpone discussion momentarily. One more thing should be said about K, however. KA alone put *Adelphoi* before *Eunuchus*, and in my previous article I suggested that the Carnotensis was responsible for this order in K and for the text of *An.* 1. 1–fin. and *Ad.* praef.–2. 4. 13 in KV. That suggestion I see no reason to retract, though I have simplified it by eliminating V and must modify it by substituting *Ad.* 1. 1. 40, where A breaks off, for 2. 4. 13, where nothing happens in K. How much of K after *Ad.* 1. 1. 40 derives from the Carnotensis becomes one of the main problems in the tradition. Unable to solve it yet, I pass to other manuscripts.

Besides descendants of K, two manuscripts used here and there by Wessner, LP, and their relatives, cdk, can be eliminated. They all derive from Y.[17] I have found no errors in Y that they do not share, and some of their errors can be put down to Y's appearance, for example, 1: 37. 18

rungsgeschichtlich bedeutsam" and in a footnote mentions Donato Acciaiuoli's letter. I sent him specimens from K, and he kindly tells me that he accepts the identification.

14. He sometimes writes *gw* for *gu* and *v* for *f* or the converse; cf. Zwierlein, *Terenzkommentar*, pp. 9–11, who draws no inference.

15. He resembles Piero Cennini.

16. Magl. VIII 1390 f. 34v. De la Mare very kindly filled out the lacuna in Sabbadini's quotation for me.

17. Y consists of 296 leaves, all quiniones except ff. 131–36; *Eunuchus* ends on f. 136r, and f. 136v is blank.

ipse . . . totus om. k, unam lineam efficit in Y; 1: 5. 10–11 *ascribere* k, *ascribitur* in ras. c, *ascrib'r* Y. Single words omitted by the whole family tend to be omitted by Y at the end of a line, for example, 1: 8. 8 *filiam*, 9. 4 *-que*, 39. 9 *non*. It may be that k is a direct copy, but errors shared by Lc and Pd demand intermediaries: 1: 3. 9 *capto* and 5. 4 *utinam* for *autem* Lc, 3. 12 *pulchritudine* for *gratia*, and 3. 13 *docet* for *arguit* Pd. Codices c and d are Florentine, and L, though apparently decorated in Ferrara,[18] was written by the scribe of d. Another manuscript that Y perhaps eliminates for much of the text is N; at least in the *Vita*, however, N generally follows Wessner's *meliores*.

Now to some manuscripts that deserve more attention than they have received. In my previous article, three groups in section 6 were distinguished. As further acquaintance with the manuscripts does not raise the number of groups, I need only enumerate the members of the first two, since the rest with one exception[19] belong to the third: the first consists of KQGHJ[20] and a vexing manuscript (about which more in a moment), the second of CFO. The first, however, may really be two, because, though KQGHJ share errors (e.g., 2: 346. 5 *lepos*, 349. 16 *Nausistrata eque*), they are neither numerous nor hard to correct; certainly QGHJ agree in many errors against K and the rest,[21] and K has lacunae that QGHJ and the rest are free from. Here Δ will denote the source of QGHJ, Θ the source of CFO, and Λ the source of the rest.[22] My immediate concern is with Δ, for much of *Phormio* an unknown but valuable witness.

In section 7, defined by the coalition of KRCFO,[23] Δ often outdoes not only Θ but Λ, too. Particularly noteworthy are its agreements with Stephanus' edition, the lost but certainly medieval Cuiacianus used at second hand by Lindenbrog, and the excerpts in a manuscript of Terence, Ricc. 528 (s. xi). I confine myself to a few examples:

18. "Vine-stem initials look Ferrarese," according to De la Mare.

19. U conflates a text akin to K with one akin to CFO; it is the only manuscript besides K(R) that quotes Ennius at the end of the prologue. In section 5, U has *deletum propter vetustatem* in the text at 2: 334. 2–3, followed by the missing words, which do not fill the space left for them. In section 1 it introduces at 1: 3. 6–7 a transposition found only in K(V), ⟨*natus sit*⟩ *et ad initium tertii* [*natus sit et*] *mortuus*. In *Phorm*. 2. 3 it has a *redactio* only partly *confusa*. Worthless though it may be for the constitution of the text, U could convey something useful about its history. In De la Mare's opinion, the hand is probably Neapolitan or Spanish.

20. As I state in *Hermes*, the ed. Mediol. 1476 is a hybrid of this group and e. Wissowa's suspicion that its source was q (Wessner, "*Commentum*," 1: xviii, xxxiv) must have rested on woefully inadequate evidence. G would be a more promising candidate; but in section 4, whose absence from e leaves the ed. Mediol. pure, G has omissions of its own.

21. In my previous article I reported these readings at 347. 2: *actionem* R *ire actionem* HJ *narrationem* cett. Q, too, has *ire actionem*, G *ne actionem*. More important, I have now collated Gronovius' collation of Pithoeus' lost collation of the lost Cuiacianus, Leid. 759 C 16, which gives *ne actionem* al. *narrationem*.

22. Y stands apart from the other descendants of Λ: 345. 8 *fiscus* KΔY *filii* Θ *festus* Λ, 347. 22–348. 1 *advenisset et eam vellet* KΔΘY *venisset et vellet eam* Λ, 348. 8 *mutato consilio dum* KΔΘ *mutato consilio* Y *dum mutato consilio* Λ, 348. 10 *Nausistratae* ⟨*est*⟩ *et* Λ om. KΔΘY, 349. 9 *errorem* ⟨*et*⟩ *Phormio* KΔY om. ΘΛ, 349. 14 *ita ut* KΔΘ *quae cum ita ut* Y *quae cum ita* Λ. Contamination may be responsible.

23. I do not always include F alongside C merely because of its absence from Wessner's apparatus and my collection of microfilms.

393. 12 *non esuris aut* Cuiac., Δ: *ut* cett.
394. 2 *agimus* Ricc., Δ: *habemus* KR, C mg.: *amamus* CΛ: *habemus amamus* O
476. 1 *sine arte aliqua* Steph.: *sine arte* Δ, recte: *arte aliqua* cett.
478. 5–6 *ex arca sine* Steph.: *ex arcas ne* Δ: *exactis ne* cett.
482. 10 *tu deomenu* (i.e., τοῦ δεομένου) *fecit* Δ: *actu deficit* (*-fec-* RO) ΘV: *** *fecit* Λ
484. 9 *ioco solatam* Δ: *hic consolatam* (*-ativam* V) cett.: *hic omnino sublatam* Steph.: *hic consedatam* Wessner: fort. *ioco sublatam*

Both Δ and Λ have 2. 1. 4–19, which Θ omits. Full attention to Δ in section 7 will not make a vast difference to the text, because many of its advantages over Θ are reported by Wessner from other sources; but Δ has the merit of being continuous, which the Cuiacianus and Ricc. 528 are not, and largely pure and honest, which Λ and Stephanus' edition are not.

Section 8 is defined by the independent and often virtuous behavior of O, which Zwierlein rightly or wrongly attributed to the Carnotensis.[24] Codex O is matched and sometimes surpassed in this section by Δ, which continues to agree with Stephanus or the Cuiacianus against the rest of the tradition. First, an example that makes an important difference to the text:

432. 17–19 *TENE ASYMBOLVM VENIRE VNCTVM ATQVE LAVTVM E BALNEIS haec non ab Apollodoro sed de *** translata sunt omnia: "quippe . . ."* (there follows a long quotation in senarii)
sed de sexto salis *** Λ: *sed de cen* *** V: *redeas* Θ: lac. O: *sed e sexto satirarum Ennii* Steph.

Wessner and Vahlen mistrusted Stephanus despite the *vetustum exemplar* given to him by Ascensius; but the descendants of Δ have these readings:

Q *se de sextos aɫ rarum est mi*
G *se de sextos alias rarum est* ***
H *se de sextos rarum est*
J *se desertos aɫr rarum mi*

It does not take much ingenuity to extract precisely what Stephanus gives (*est mi* < ēnni). At one stroke, then, the ascription to Ennius is confirmed and Stephanus vindicated. GHJ, I cannot resist pointing out, are three of the seven manuscripts that, according to Wessner, "nullius omnino pretii ad crisin factitandam aut sunt aut esse videntur";[25] he did not know Q. Here are more good readings (again just a few examples):

447. 4–5 *illi crimina de* Steph., OΔ: *illa criminandi* cett.
453. 18 *stat* Steph., OΔ: om. cett.
455. 26 *convenientiae* Cuiac., OΔ: *veritatis* ΘΛ²: *conventionis* VΛ
465. 12 *furtim* Cuiac., Δ: *ferrum* O: *separatim* cett.

These examples appear in Wessner's apparatus (without, of course, the

24. *Terenzkommentar*, pp. 111–12. His derivation of CO from the Carnotensis in section 6, which I challenged in my previous article, has now been overturned by my proof that the change at the end of section 6 occurs not in CO but in KR. His other contention about the Carnotensis in *Phormio*, that it lacked section 7, can stand if K derives from the Carnotensis in section 6.

25. "*Commentum*," 1: xxiii; Wessner continues, "ex parte *enim* minus mihi innotuerunt, quam ut certam de eis proferam sententiam" (emphasis added).

reading of Δ), but others can be found:

445. 3–5 *capere dicimus cum id quod in nobis* ⟨*non*⟩ *est assumimus*
assumimus RCV, ⟨*non*⟩ Karsten: *assumemus* K: *assumamus* Λ: [*cum*] . . . *an sumamus* OΔ

457. 14–15 *artificiose personam* ⟨*non*⟩ *reprehendit sententiam reprehensurus*
reprehendit ΘVΛ, ⟨*non*⟩ Sabbadini: *deprehendit* O: *defendit* Steph., Δ

464. 10 *volup* Steph.: *volupe* OΔ: *voluptatis* cett.

In this section, O does not derive from Δ, which has a *redactio confusa* in 2. 3. It is uncertain whether any errors unite OΔ against ΘVΛ.

At this point an apology is owed to a manuscript mentioned in my previous article, codex I. It contains *Eunuchus* and *Phormio* in different hands, and I said that *Phormio* was garbled almost beyond recognition. Garbled it is. It skips passages, and its wording often bypasses points where the other manuscripts disagree; small disturbances in the order suggest that it may have been put back together from marginal citations in a manuscript of Terence.[26] Nevertheless, it quite clearly has the original *redactio distincta* in 2. 3 (the second sequence is simply absent), it preserves a good deal of Greek (not written simultaneously with the Latin),[27] and it has numerous readings of merit. In it can be recognized a source akin to Δ but not so corrupt:

369. 15 *necessaria fabulae praestructio* (*per-* Δ) *ad fabulae* περίστασιν (*perifrasin* Δ) *avaritia Demiphonis* IΔ: *necessaria est* (om. CO) *ad fabulae* (*-am* CO) *per istas in* (*peristasim* Λ) *avaritia Demiphonis* cett.

370. 2 *solum* IΔ: *solos* cett.

352. 27 *praetermisit* IKΘΛ: *pertransit* Δ

Indeed, codex I is less corrupt, or better emended, than all the other fifteenth-century witnesses in a surprising number of places:

§6 356. 13–14 *loco motus* schol. Bemb. (s. vi): *motus loco* I: *locus motus* cett.

367. 17 *a coniectura·cui* ⟨*bono*⟩ Schoell: *a coniectura quae dicitur cui bono* I

§7 397. 9 *sustinet* Cuiac., I: *fuit tenet* Δ: *suae tenet* cett.

408. 9 *gravem* Steph., I: *gratam* cett.

§8 428. 1 *litis molimen* Bentley: *molimen litis* I: *militis molimen* ΘO: *vulgus molimen* ΔVΛ

430. 2 κυριολογία Bentley, I: *acyrologia* vel sim. VΛ: lac. Δ: om. ΘO

433. 17 *latratoriis* Schoell, I: *latratoris* KC: *latraturis* Λ: *latratoribus* OV: *latranuibus* QR: *latrantium* G

448. 10 *minores aetate* Sabbadini, I: *minores aetates* O: *minoris aetatis* cett.

458. 21 *amant iungi* Cuiac., I: *amantium g.* G: *amantium* Q: *amantum* O: *amanti* V: *amanti* *** Λ: deest Θ

463. 7 *ferre* Steph., I: *prae* ΘG: *per* VΛQ: *parere* O

470. 2 *horia autem est locus in quo* Cuiac., I: *hara autem est in qua* OΔ: *har(r)a autem in qua* cett.

26. A speaker in Angelo Decembrio's *Politia Litteraria* says, "Terentium habeo . . . in locis difficilioribus expositionibus Donati circumscriptum"; cf. Sabbadini, "Il commento di Donato," p. 20, n. 1. Manuscripts like this are probably lying undiscovered, because no one looks at late copies of Terence; cf. n. 45.

27. The Greek that e offers in *Eunuchus* and *Phormio* came from codex I or a relative.

§7	478. 5	*ex arca sine* Steph.: *ex area sine* I: *ex arcas ne* Δ: *exactis ne* cett.
	481. 3	*lurcones* Nonius, I, G^2: *laucones* Δ: *claucones* (*gl-* V) cett.
	484. 2	*delata* Steph.: *dilata* I: *illata* ΔΛ: *dicta* ΘV

As I do not doubt I's kinship with Δ, some of these readings are likely to be conjectures, especially where the other manuscripts agree; conjecture may also be expected in excerpts, which serve little purpose unless they make sense. Even so, conjectures seem to be in the minority.

Fortunately, codex I has an interesting text of *Eunuchus*, too, and it is not garbled. The manuscripts of *Eunuchus* fall into the following groups. As elsewhere in the commentary, TCF have omissions from which the rest of the manuscripts are free, for example, 1: 272. 12 *paulatim*, 298. 19 *et depravatam*, 350. 7 *amatorie*. Other omissions, such as 307. 17 *bene*, 324. 21–22 *VOCABVLA . . . accipimus*, 352. 9 *hortative*, are shared by the manuscripts that adopt the interpolations listed by Wessner (1: xxxi); since these manuscripts almost all derive from Λ in section 6, they presumably do so here. There remain BKV, which do not constitute a group, and IEQHe,[28] which do: 266. 3 *nunc* for *noster*, 292. 18 *erratum* for *mirum*, and omission of 302. 9 *nigram*, 309. 23–24 *ideo . . . probavit*, 331. 2–4 *quod . . . perdidit*, to name a few errors from many. Within the group contamination has run riot:

271. 17	*quibus* IE: *quidvis quibus* e: *quidvis* QH cett.
275. 18	*in illo* IEQH: *nulla* e cett.
275. 21	*ipse* IE: *rem* QHe cett.
275. 21–22	⟨*quia*⟩ *qui . . . verba* ⟨*deceptus est*⟩ QHeΛ: *qui . . . verba* IEBKVΘ
276. 6	*translatam* om. EQH: hab. Ie cett.
279. 12	*non si* EQHe: *sed* I cett.
306. 21	*ancilla* ⟨*figurate illi*⟩ e, *ancilla* ⟨*figurative illi*⟩ Λ: *ancilla* IEQH cett.

The process of contamination has left its mark in e at 271. 17; QH have been in contact with Λ at 275. 21–22, e at 306. 21, wherever the interpolations originated. The simplest assumption, therefore, is that E and I are the pure members of the group, the former being more corrupt than the latter. It deserves notice, however, that QH in *Phormio* descend from Δ. In *Phormio* Δ stands for the common source of QGHJ, and in that sense it can only be traced from the beginning of section 4, *Hec.* 3. 5. 8; its errors include 281. 22 *conclamatione per totam* in section 4 and 319. 9–10 *quod immisit sit quod me vocat* in section 5. Nevertheless, it is highly probable that QH derive from it in *Eunuchus*.

What, then, was the source of these valuable manuscripts, Δ and I? Q, though it does not in general excel the other descendants of Δ in sections 4–8, preserves a subscription that distinguishes Δ from all the other fifteenth-century witnesses: "Aelii Donati v.c. oratoris urbis Rome commentarium in Terentii Phormione explicit." Compare the subscriptions in A (s. xi), "Apli Donati $\overline{\text{vc}}$ oratoris urbis Rome commentum Terentii . . . ," and in the Cuiacianus, "Aelii Donati v.c. oratoris urbis Romae commentum Terenti

28. G sometimes follows IEQHe, but not consistently enough to deserve serious attention.

Phormionis explicit." Warren observed the resemblance,[29] but it has won Q no friends, and certainly it fails to betray the source of Δ. If either Δ or I antedated 1450, when a copy of the Carnotensis arrived in Italy, the source could not have been the Carnotensis; but Donatus seems to have attracted self-effacing scribes, and the earliest of the few dated manuscripts was written in 1459. In fact, codex I could well antedate 1450, and for two reasons I do not think Δ can have derived from the Carnotensis. I shall not press these reasons here, however.

Sections 4 and 5 are the best place to start discussing the rest of the Italian manuscripts. In place of section 4 Oare have nothing, xp a lacuna, mn an interpolation. In section 5 they agree in, for example, the following errors: 2: 320. 16 *obsequentem*, 322. 25 *tantam et* for *quantumque*, 325. 14 *quasi* for *quam*, 325. 24–26 *HIS . . . ANIMVM* om. (homoeoteleuton), 329. 22–24 *ut . . . permittente* om. (homoeoteleuton). These recur in DMsqtfWh, which do not omit section 4;[30] D and M, however, show signs of having gone elsewhere for it.[31] Evidently all eight reinstate the defective source at 5. 1. 2. It must have been Λ, the source in section 6 of all sixteen witnesses except O, because z, which agrees with them in *Hecyra* up to 3. 5. 8, has this note at the bottom of the page that includes 3. 5. 8 (f. 146r): *ἰστεον ὅτι ἀπὸ ἐδῶ ἕως τὸ τέλος αυτῆς τῆς κωμωδίας ἐξ ἄλλον ἀθιβοίλιον ἔγραψεν ὁ μαρτινος.* The note implies that *ὁ μαρτινος* returned to his original exemplar at the beginning of *Phormio*, where z derives from Λ. Two other manuscripts that do the same as z are V and Y.[32] All three derive in sections 4 and 5 from K; corrections by the first hand of K appear in their text at, for example, 325. 8 *gratum* BCK[1] *segregatum* K[2]VYz, and they omit, for example, 284. 23 *hoc tantopere* and 323. 4 *tarde*, omitted by K in embarking on a new page and a new line, respectively. I have not tried to determine the sources used by all the descendants of Λ that remedy the omission of section 4, but M conflates manuscripts like K and Δ (283. 4 *dixit* MΔ for *dictum*, 284. 23 *hoc tantopere* om. MK) and W manuscripts like D and Δ (281. 22 *conclamatione* WΔ, 285. 2 *hunc* for *hic autem* WD); I should expect sqtf to do the same as M.[33]

Most of the manuscripts that derive from Λ in sections 5 and 6 agree in errors and interpolations throughout the commentary. The tradition can be best surveyed by indicating which manuscripts do not derive from Λ. Those that nowhere derive from it are ABSTCFKRIE, roughly Wessner's *meliores;* I called the source of CFO in section 6 Θ, and I will use the symbol throughout for the source of CF and their kin.[34]

N derives from Θ in the *Vita;* QJ up to the end of *An.* praef.; O and

29. "Five New Manuscripts," p. 32.

30. The microfilm of h that I consulted at the IRHT had no pretension to completeness, and I may be wrong to infer from its behavior in sections 1 and 2 that it does not share the omission; but I should be surprised if h did not belong to this group.

31. Cf. Wessner, "*Commentum*," 1: xix, xxi.

32. Yz already agree closely in section 1—1: 6. 9 *areore* Y *artore* z for *auctore*.

33. So close are tf throughout the commentary that one may well be a copy of the other. The same applies to mn.

34. I have already done this for simplicity on p. 315, where Θ stands variously for the source of CFO, KRCFO, and KRCF. I do not think that the ambiguity vitiates any of my arguments.

presumably amn, which share its distinctive interpolations in section 1, up to some point between 1: 65. 10 and 66. 8; q until the hand changes after three seniones at 1: 190. 11 *hic paulo / sapientior inducitur* (*An.* 3. 3. 20).

QHe desert Λ for something else in *Eunuchus*; MsqtfWh for other things in section 4; Yz for K in sections 4 and 5; QGHJ for Δ in sections 4–8; O for Θ in sections 6 and 7 and for something like Δ in section 8; codex a for Θ when the first hand returns at *Phorm.* 1. 4. 21 *ex metu* (2: 401. 23) and then for the same thing as O in section 8;[35] D for Θ in section 4 and after *Phorm.* 2. 3. 4; W for Δ where the hand changes at *Phorm.* 2. 3. 1 *QVAESO* | *interim* (439. 16).[36]

V derives from Λ only in *Ad.* 2. 4. 13–*Hec.* 3. 5. 8 and at the beginning of *Phormio* (though V² derives from it where V derives from something else).

My knowledge of U is limited, but I have mentioned its behavior in *Phormio*.

All the Italian manuscripts, U and V apart, have now been classified throughout the commentary in as much detail as an editor is ever likely to need. Before discussing the remaining parts of V, let me set out the available sources section by section. The old section 2 must go, not only because the elimination of V in *Ad.* praef.–2. 4. 13 leaves *Ad.* 2. 4. 13 insignificant, but also because AK invert *Eunuchus* and *Adelphoi*, within which the behavior of K may change. In order not to cause confusion by inventing a completely new division of sections, I will exclude *Eunuchus* and *Adelphoi* from the sequence and understand by section 2 merely the rest of *Andria* from 1: 49. 1 and by section 3 merely *Hec.* praef.–3. 5. 8. Manuscripts that do not cover a whole section are in brackets.

(1) *Vita–An.* 1. 1. 1 (1: 3. 1–49. 1 *AVFERTE*) Θ, Λ, A, [S]
(2) *An.* 1. 1. 1–fin. (1: 49. 1 *ABITE*–261. 17) Θ, Λ, AK, [B]
Eunuchus (1: 265. 1–497. 6) Θ, Λ, [B], K, V, IE
Adelphoi (2: 3. 1–185. 19) Θ, Λ, [A]K
(3) *Hec.* praef.–3. 5. 8 (2: 189. 1–271. 8 *dicere*) Θ, Λ, [B], K
(4) *Hec.* 3. 5. 8–5. 1. 2 (2: 271. 8 *an*–319. 8 *servatus*) Θ, B, K, Δ
(5) *Hec.* 5. 1. 2–fin. (2: 319. 9 *NEC POL*–342. 5) Θ, Λ, [B], K, Δ
(6) *Phorm.* praef.–1. 2. 38 (2: 345. 1–373. 16 *EXADVERSVM*) Θ, Λ, K, Δ, I
(7) *Phorm.* 1. 2. 38–2. 1. 47/49 (2: 373. 17–ca. 418), 5. 1. 19/29–fin. (2: 472–484. 9) Θ, Λ, [V], Δ, I
(8) *Phorm.* 2. 1. 47/49–5. 1. 19/29 (2: ca. 419–472) Θ, Λ, V, Δ, Oa, I.

35. Neither Sabbadini nor Wessner observed that codex a is written in two hands.

36. Though D and W are close relatives, D seems not to have switched at exactly this point: 435. 20 *dicitur Phormionem* ΘΔW *Phormionem dicitur* ΛD. W confirms that the home of D was Bologna (cf. Wessner, "*Commentum*," 1: xix) by adding on f. 53v the *alter exitus* of *Andria* together with the following note: "hic textus ex antiquissimo Terentio Sancti Domenici de *** [*ras. 7 litterarum*] habitus est, quem tamen non arbitror esse Teren *** [*ras. 7 litterarum*] neque stillus neque sententiae superioribus congruunt." At first sight the gaps are annoying, but the second can easily be filled by conjecture (*-tii nam*) and the first by reference to Prete's edition of Terence (Heidelberg, 1954), p. 111, where a manuscript that he cites for the *alter exitus* has this note: "hanc scenam nusquàm alibi vidi praeterquam in codice Terentii qui est in catenis apud S. Dominicum Bononiae."

No manuscript is more of a hodgepodge than V. In *Eunuchus* and sections 7 and 8 it derives from neither K nor Λ, but even within *Eunuchus* one passage, roughly 1: 308. 11–332. 17, was taken straight from K. This curiosity came to my attention while I was scanning Wessner's apparatus in order to find out something not revealed in his introduction, how much of the Greek in V was written at one stretch with the Latin. The point is important, because a scribe who includes the Greek in some passages and leaves gaps for it in others unwittingly says something about his sources. In *Andria* and *Ad.* praef.–2. 4. 13, where its exemplar K has no Greek, V has none either, apart from later additions in *Ad.* 1. 2. 62–2. 1. 33 (2: 34. 1–42. 24). In most of *Eunuchus* the Greek was there from the start, but not in the brief passage I mentioned. Why V should have switched to K for this passage is unclear; I do not know whether it switched back because K omits 333. 7–339. 13 *vitiasse . . . formarum*. V also has Greek at six points in *Hec.* praef.–2. 1[37] and then regularly from 2. 2. 6 (2: 236. 20 *ἀνακόλουθον*) to the end of the commentary. From 2. 2. 6 on, all V's Greek in *Hecyra* came from K, even between 2. 2. 6 and 3. 5. 8, where all the Latin derives from Λ. In K, the first hand (the only one that copies Greek) returns at 2. 2. 3 (236. 3), and a comparison of the Greek in K and V puts the matter beyond question; at 254. 4, for instance, εχ- in V is a misreading of a very curly χ- in K. In sections 4 and 5, as I have said, V is a straightforward copy of K. At the beginning of *Phormio* it derives from Λ, but other parts of *Phormio*, and the Greek throughout, do not derive from K, Λ, Θ, or Δ.

What accounts for the independence of V in unadjacent plays, *Eunuchus* and *Phormio?* Probably its Neapolitan origin. Well before Aurispa acquired a copy of the Carnotensis in 1450, his copy of the Maguntinus had supplied Panormita at Naples with an unspecified part of the commentary,[38] and Valla had used *Eunuchus* in his *Elegantiae*, which he almost certainly wrote at Naples.[39] Codex I, it will be remembered, contains *Eunuchus* and *Phormio*, albeit in different hands and different states; unfortunately, I could find no watermarks. There is further evidence that *Eunuchus* circulated either alone or at the head of other plays. E contains nothing else, and De la Mare has pointed out to me that the Venetian scholar Lauro Quirini lent a manuscript of *Eunuchus* alone to Maffeo Vallaresso in the early 1450s (Vat. Barb. Lat. 1809 ff. 283, 304, 314–15).[40] QMr originally began

37. 2: 190. 9, 191. 3, 193. 12, 193. 17, 199. 5, 230. 5.

38. In an undated letter ("1442?" Sabbadini, *Storia e critica*, p. 161; "1439?" idem, *Carteggio*, p. 96) Aurispa tells Panormita that "cupidissimi codicum novorum et doctissimi" have kept his Donatus, of which "Karolus [Marsuppini] solum id transcripsit quod tu habes."

39. Sabbadini, "Il commento di Donato," p. 19, n. 1; A. Casacci, "Gli *Elegantiarum libri* di Lorenzo Valla," *Atene e Roma*, n.s. 7 (1926): 188; F. Adorno, "Di alcune orazioni e prefazioni di Lorenzo Valla," *Rinascimento* 5 (1954): 193, 194, n. 2. In a letter assigned by Sabbadini ("Il commento di Donato," p. 18, n. 4) to March 1441, Valla says explicitly that he had seen only *Eunuchus*.

40. Vallaresso's phrase "tam preciosum antiquitatis monumentum" in the last letter probably refers to the text rather than the manuscript. On Quirini's life up to the 1450s, see V. Branca (ed.), *Lauro Quirini umanista* (Florence, 1977), pp. 11–13; he seldom left Venice or Padua but did visit Florence in 1441.

with it,[41] and the inventory of Aurispa's library at his death in 1459, just published,[42] opens with the following entry: "1. . . . Donatus in Terentium, scriptus in carta bombicina mezana quaternorum vigintiduorum, qui incipit: Hic masculini generis; explicit: fermo, non inquaternatus."[43] This manuscript might have saved a lot of trouble by surviving, especially since it cannot quite be taken for granted that *fermo* is a version of *Phormio*.[44]

So much for the Italian manuscripts. Broadly, three connected problems remain: the extent of the Carnotensis, the value of Λ, and the stemma in each section. I could say something about all of them now; but, having already written one article that is largely out of date, I prefer to say more at another time. I will therefore finish by dealing with the only fifteenth-century *meliores* that I have not yet had occasion to discuss—S, namely, the Ambrosian excerpt owned by Fr. Pizolpasso († 1443), and Leid. B.P.L. 191BF.

The Leidensis, a manuscript of Terence probably written near the lower Rhine, is every bit as vexing as codex I. It has introductory matter and marginal annotations that include fairly faithful excerpts from the introductory treatises and prefaces of Donatus;[45] and the text it drew on was a good one, because at 1: 20. 4 it had *vilitatem*, omitted by all the other manuscripts except AS, and it did not follow Λ in 1: 37. 11 ⟨*eam sibi*⟩ *petebat*, 2: 3. 16 *autem* ⟨*et*⟩, or 2: 4. 18 *lenis*. It seems closer to Θ than to anything else, though the evidence (all from the first volume of Wessner) is not concordant:

9. 5	*nobis* AS: om. Θ: *certe* K: *scenae* O: *populi* JΛ: *semper* Leid.
27. 8	*relatus* AΛ: *sic latus* SΘ: *simulativus* Leid.
27. 14	*quod* ASΘ: *quia* Λ Leid.
38. 4–5	*et Philomena* Θ: *Philomena vero* Λ Leid.: deest A
268. 3	*se non ante* BKVIEΛ: *non ante se* Θ Leid.

The simplest explanation of the agreement between the Leidensis and Λ in

41. In Q, *Andria* ends in the middle of a gathering (f. 57v) and *Eunuchus* begins on the next (f. 61r). On M, see Sabbadini, "Il commento di Donato," pp. 50–51. Ff. 1–148 of r consist entirely of quiniones except for one quaternio, ff. 51–58; *Andria* ends on f. 58v, most of which is blank. Admittedly these facts will bear another construction: while the scribes of QMr were beginning on *Eunuchus*, other scribes were beginning on *Andria* from the same exemplars. The scribe of Y began on *Adelphoi* (cf. n. 17), and I attach no significance to that.

42. A. Franceschini, *Giovanni Aurispa e la sua biblioteca* (Padua, 1976).

43. The other entries for Donatus or what may be Donatus are these: "288. item Donatus in Terentium, in papiro"; "336. item Donatus in Terentium, in membranis quaternorum sedecim non inquaternatis, quem dominus Joannes donare promisit domino Malatestae Novello"; "387. item Donatus in Terentium, in papiro, sine albis"; "391. item comentum Terentii, in papiro, sine albis"; "577. item Donatus in Terentium, novus, in membranis vigintiquattuor quinternionum, depaginatus." I can identify only the last, which is either L or d. 336 looks at first sight like M, but the gatherings do not square.

44. Might not the manuscript have ended with, e.g., 2: 424. 28 *sermo?*

45. While inspecting a snippet of miscellaneous and inadequately labelled film from Madrid at the IRHT, I noticed Donatus' argumentum to *Eunuchus* in another manuscript of Terence (7804?), but it came from e. The extracts in Vindob. Scot. 212, part of which I saw on microfilm at the IRHT, might be interesting if their date were really 1452, because they derive from Λ; but I doubt this date.

38. 4–5, though it will not serve at 27. 14 against the unanimity of ASΘ, is that they are correct.

Sabbadini, who discovered S, denied that it had any connection with either the Carnotensis or the Maguntinus,[46] even though in 1436 the Maguntinus went through Pizolpasso's hands; but, so far as the Maguntinus is concerned, Sabbadini apparently had no better reason than that its presumed descendants, TCF, have errors absent from S. This reason would have satisfied C. H. Beeson, who maintained that certain errors peculiar to T or C could only have been caused by abbreviations in a manuscript older than the fifteenth century and therefore to be identified with the Maguntinus itself;[47] but I think he underestimated the varieties of fifteenth-century script. Perhaps one day the watermark in S will help;[48] the hand is French, but Frenchmen visited Italy. Meanwhile I can safely say that the stemma of the passage covered by S (at any rate up to 1: 23 or thereabouts) is this:

FIGURE 1

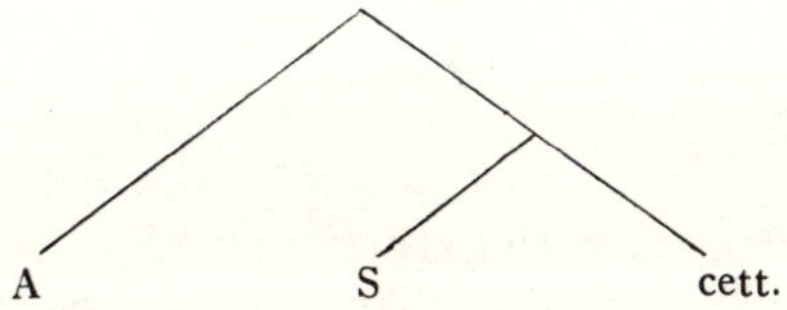

All the manuscripts except A are united by the omission of 1:14. 10 *prior(um)*, 15. 1 *ad*, 15. 15–16 *consistens nunc* (homoeoteleuton), 18. 13 *tollerent*, 19. 7 *egerunt*,[49] 20. 9 *non aut*, and all except AS by the omission of 7. 11 *non*, 8. 8 *post*, 9. 5 *nobis*, 9. 7 *item*, 20. 4 *vilitatem*, 23. 9 *morum*, to say nothing of other errors. If the scribe of S had copied out the whole commentary, editing it would be far less arduous.

That a new edition is called for has already been shown by Zwierlein's study of K. Now, however, K has turned out to eliminate parts of three manuscripts used by Wessner, VRL; two more witnesses of consequence have emerged, Δ and I; and V has been exposed as a veritable edition in itself. There is a further point, one that I am reluctant to make, because I know what collating this long and tiresome text is like. In the first sixteen pages of *Hecyra* that I examined, I found three serious errors in Wessner's edition: 270. 18 *uxori* (*amori* codd. omnes), 322. 13 *reclamavit meretrix et* (*reclamavit meretrix statim et* codd. omnes), 323. 4 *longe* B ex silentio *longum*

46. "Spogli Ambrosiani latini," p. 197.

47. "The Text Tradition of Donatus' Commentary on Terence," *CP* 17 (1922): 300–301.

48. James Butrica, who has very kindly examined it, writes: "Unfortunately, it is one of the difficult ones, three mounts in a circle surmounted by a cross; it seemed to me to be closest to B. 11869 (Palermo 1413, var. Nieuwport, Belgium, 1417)."

49. As Rufinus (s. v?) cites the passage without *egerunt* (*GLK.*, 6: 554. 7), either the division between A and S cett. goes back to Rufinus' time, which no one now believes, or *egerunt* is an interpolation, which disqualifies it from appearing in the list. I cannot believe, however, that every reading in the list is an interpolation.

CV (*longum* BCV). At 2: 410. 21 Wessner's conjecture *cogitaturae* appears in all the manuscripts, and D is misreported five other times on the same page in spite of having been collated by Vahlen, Dziatzko, and Wessner himself (1: xix). Room, then, for elementary improvement, too.

POSTSCRIPT ON THE CUIACIANUS AND CODEX I

Before the Cuiacianus (Cujas' manuscript) disappeared, one of the brothers Pithoeus had collated it. The collation has also disappeared, but Lindenbrog used it for his edition (Paris, 1602; Frankfurt, 1623) and Gronovius transcribed it.[50] As these sources show that the Cuiacianus often had a better text than the surviving witnesses (e.g., Greek where they pass over it), every effort must be made to recover its readings.

On which edition did Pithoeus collate the Cuiacianus, and which did Lindenbrog take as his foundation? Gronovius reports readings that would not have needed recording on any edition earlier than Stephanus' of 1541, for example, 2: 206. 23 *persuasit* (sic codd., Steph. 1529, 1536: *suasit* 1541). The same edition served Lindenbrog, as I established by comparing his second edition with Stephanus' first and then seeing whether Stephanus' later editions accounted for any of the differences.[51] The coincidence makes it possible that Gronovius transcribed not Pithoeus' collation itself but Lindenbrog's copy, and possibility becomes probability in the light of Lindenbrog's statement in the preface to his second edition: "DONATI duo exemplaria habuimus, et illa [like two copies of Terence] Pithaeorum accurata diligentia ad MSS. codd. Antonii Contii et Iacobi Cuiacii Antecessorum Bituricensium collata." Fr. Pithoeus lent him, that is, separate collations of A and the Cuiacianus; yet neither he nor Gronovius distinguishes them. One expects better of Gronovius; but, if Lindenbrog's copy lay before him and Lindenbrog had run them together, to do better was not in his power. That Lindenbrog's copy lay before Gronovius would also explain 1: 36. 12 "γρ. aut canticis" and 83. 23 "ἴσως nervis," which Lindenbrog puts forward as conjectures of his own. If, therefore, only Lindenbrog's copy of Pithoeus' collation of the Cuiacianus can be reconstructed, the two editions whose differences may yield other readings of the Cuiacianus besides those that appear in Gronovius' transcript or Lindenbrog's notes are Lindenbrog's and the one Lindenbrog used, Stephanus' of 1541. For comparison I chose Lindenbrog's second edition rather than his first because the second would have had to be collated anyway for its emendations. I then checked my list of differences against his first. Most of them already occur there, and for none of the rest can his copy of Pithoeus' collation be proved responsible.

The editions relevant to the Cuiacianus, then, are Stephanus' of 1541 and Lindenbrog's of 1602. After comparing them and collating Gronovius' transcript, I have three conclusions to offer, one of them disturbing.

50. Cf. Wessner, "*Commentum*," 1: xvi, xxxv–xxxvi.

51. The edition of 1541 deserves the credit for several emendations that Wessner ascribes to Lindenbrog, e.g., 2: 240. 6 *auctivum*, 364. 20 *dictum*.

The first, deducible from Wessner's apparatus, is that very few readings of the Cuiacianus have been preserved in *Eunuchus* and next to none in the part of the commentary covered by A, namely, the introductory treatises, *Andria*, and *Ad.* praef.–1. 1. 40. It would be rash to draw inferences from this about a manuscript accessible only at three removes.

The second conclusion is that, though Lindenbrog felt free to touch up quotations from extant authors, Terence included, most of his other alterations unquestionably derive from a manuscript. The following, for instance, recur in K—2: 43. 4 ⟨*et*⟩ *inimicum*, 57. 22 *gaudens*, 64. 2 *dixerat*, 71. 23 *o tempora o mores*, 76. 18 ⟨*mire*⟩ *interponitur*, 77. 1 *amet*, 82. 18 *impurus* ⟨*autem*⟩, 86. 8 *in physicum*, 99. 5 *novum* (for *vitium*), 191. 4 *addiscat*, 205. 13 ⟨*id est claudus*⟩, 224. 18 *augmenta*.[52] Of Lindenbrog's alterations, therefore, even those that cannot be shown to derive from a manuscript may well do so.

"A manuscript"—and therein lies the disturbing point. The readings that I cited from codex I in *Phormio* included one in which it agreed strikingly with the Cuiacianus: 2: 470. 3 *horia autem est locus in quo* I, Cuiac.: *har*(*r*)*a autem* (*est*) *in qua* ΘΔΟΛ. If, as I maintained, codex I has a close affinity with Δ, a grouping like this should not occur. Here are more places where it nevertheless does occur (with a fuller treatment of the passage just cited):

469. 14 *observatum* I, Lind. in textu et adnot.: *obstetricum* ΘΔΛ: *obstrictum* O

469. 18–19 *ponatur. imitabantur aspirationem in exhalando* I, *ponatur. an quod imitabantur aspirationem in exhalando* Lind. in textu: *mutabantur in exhalando* O: *mutabantur* (*imit-* Θ) *an ab halando* ΘΔΛ

470. 2–3 *in qua inclusa servatur. horia autem est locus in quo pecora concluduntur* I, . . . *horia autem est locus in quo inclusa servantur* Lind. in adnot.: *in qua* (*quae* Θ) *concluditur et* (*ob-* OR^1, *ab-* R^2K, *ad-* C) *servatur. har*(*r*)*a autem* (+ *est* ΔO) *in qua pecora includuntur* (*con-* O) ΘΔΟΛ

470. 4 *mysticus* . . . *haruga* I, Lind. in adnot.: *rusticus* (*mist-* O) . . . (*h*)*ar*(*r*)*a* ΘΔΟΛ

474. 10 ⟨*et habet primam longam. quando autem significat aliud, primam brevem habet*⟩ I post 9 *statu* (omisso 9–10 *Plautus . . . signa*), post 10 *signa* Lind. in textu

475. 7 *quasi omnis cena prout in se lactatur insultat* I, *qui in omni scena prout in se iactatur insultat* Lind. in textu: *quasi omnis senatus* (*scena* *** Θ, *** Λ) *provenisse* (*prout in se* $Θ^2$) *laetatur* (*-etur* Δ) ΔΘΛ: *senatus* saltem Gron., Lind. in adnot.

475. 13 ⟨*senibus leno ob fallaciam mire exultat*⟩ I inter 7 et 14 ceteris omissis, ⟨*SENIBVS ob fallaciam mire exultat*⟩ Lind. in textu post 13 *superiore*

479. 17 *alteros alteri* I, *alteri alteros* Lind. in textu et adnot.: *alter* (*altus* RKO) *alterum* ΘΛ: *latera alterius* Δ

482. 4 τῆς ⟨συγγνώμης καὶ⟩ I, Lind. in textu

482. 6 *alias partes addidit ad* I, *alias partes adducit ad* Lind. in adnot.: *praestes eos* (*praesto* $ΘΛ^2$) *addidit* ΘΔΛ

52. As Wessner either ignores these readings of Lindenbrog or takes them for conjectures, they do not appear in Zwierlein's list of agreements between K and the Cuiacianus (*Terenzkommentar*, pp. 132–33).

484. 5 *facilius* I, Lind. in adnot.: *facetius* ΘΔΛ
484. 8 *paternarum deliciarum vindex* I, Lind. in textu: *censor paternarum deliciarum* ΘΔΛ
484. 9 *ioco solatam* IΔ, *hic ioco sublatam* Lind. in textu (*hic omnino sublatam* Steph.): *hic consolatam* ΘΛ

The readings cited here from Lindenbrog's edition all have one thing in common, whether printed in his text or ascribed to "MS." in his notes: they are absent from Gronovius' transcript. This would not be significant if Gronovius' failure to alter Lindenbrog's text confirmed that it derived from Lindenbrog's copy of Pithoeus' collation; but Gronovius often records a reading already adopted in Lindenbrog's text by underlining it and writing *v.c.* in the margin (some compensation for his unhappy choice of edition). As he does not do so in any of the relevant passages listed above, nor records any of the readings I have cited from Lindenbrog's notes, Lindenbrog surely used another source besides Pithoeus' collation. A second reason for thinking so is the nature of the differences between Lindenbrog's reading and the reading of ΘΔ(O)Λ: whereas guaranteed readings of the Cuiacianus, or at any rate of Lindenbrog's copy of Pithoeus' collation, tend either to support one branch of the extant tradition or to account for corruptions in its various branches, the readings under discussion do neither. Their source, granted that it was not the Cuiacianus, comes immediately to hand—codex I or something very like it.[53] It does not seem to have been used throughout *Phormio:* I have found no significant agreement with codex I against other manuscripts and Gronovius' transcript before 2: 469. 14.[54] The disturbing point is not Lindenbrog's use of such a source but his complete silence about it in the preface and his indiscriminate use of "MS." in the notes. Be that as it may, unburdening the Cuiacianus of its readings appreciably lightens the task of assessing both the Cuiacianus and codex I.

Dr. T. S. Pattie of the British Library kindly tells me that nothing is known about the history of codex I before it was sold as lot 1559 in the auction of H. Drury's library (1827).

Exeter College, Oxford

53. 2: 481. 11 *gnaviter* Lind. in adnot., *graviter* cum cett. I, perhaps tells against codex I.

54. The only possibilities are 466. 17 *definitivum* Lind. in textu et fort. I (mendose scriptus), *definitum* cett., and 463. 1 *μόνος* Lind. in textu et I, *μόνος γε* ed. Stephani 1541.

NOTES AND DISCUSSIONS

THUCYDIDES 1. 74. 1 AND THE USE OF 'ΕΣ WITH NUMERALS

THUCYDIDES 1. 74. 1

At Thucydides 1. 74. 1 some Athenian ambassadors speaking to a meeting of the Peloponnesian League at Sparta in 432 are made to boast of the outstanding contribution their city had made to the repulse of Xerxes:

> *τρία τὰ ὠφελιμώτατα ἐς αὐτὸ παρεσχόμεθα, ἀριθμόν τε νεῶν πλεῖστον καὶ ἄνδρα στρατηγὸν ξυνετώτατον καὶ προθυμίαν ἀοκνοτάτην. ναῦς μέν γε ἐς τὰς τετρακοσίας ὀλίγῳ ἐλάσσους τῶν δύο μοιρῶν, Θεμιστοκλέα δὲ ἄρχοντα . . . προθυμίαν δὲ καὶ πολὺ τολμηροτάτην ἐδείξαμεν. . . .*[1]

Gomme, in his note on this passage, raised three questions regarding the numerical justification here offered of the claim that Athens contributed "the largest number of ships" to the war effort. (1) If the speaker (i.e., Thucydides) had in mind Herodotus' figure (8. 43–48 and 82), namely, a total of 378 Greek ships at Salamis, of which 200 (180 manned by Athenians and 20 lent to the Chalcidians) were Athenian, is it too much of an exaggeration for an orator to say that the Athenians contributed "a little less than two-thirds" of the whole fleet (given in round figures as 400 ships)?[2] (2) Should it concern us that Thucydides gave the total as

1. All quotations from Thucydides not otherwise attributed are from H. S. Jones's OCT, emended and augmented by J. E. Powell (1942).

2. The variant reading *τριακοσίας* appears in some manuscripts; see J. Classen and J. Steup (eds.), *Thukydides*, 8 vols. (Berlin, 1892–1922), and A. W. Gomme, A. Andrewes, and K. J. Dover, *A Historical Commentary on Thucydides*, 4 vols. (Oxford, 1945–70), ad loc. If that is what Thucydides wrote, then he was following the Aeschylean (see n. 3) rather than the Herodotean tradition. There is no conclusive paleographic argument to decide the question: if Thucydides wrote *τριακοσίας*, the variant *τετρακοσίας* will have arisen from an editor who wanted to make him agree with Herodotus; if the original reading was *τετρακοσίας*, one can assume that an editor corrected this to *τριακοσίας* to agree with Aeschylus and the authors who followed him. Note, however, that if Thucydides' orator thought that the total number of ships was 300, then his description of the Athenian contingent as *ὀλίγῳ ἐλάσσους τῶν δύο μοιρῶν* of this total makes sense only if he excluded the 20 ships lent to the Chalcidians, thus reducing the Athenian contribution to only 180. That an orator in a mood of patriotic exaggeration should have neglected to include every ship that Athens could possibly claim seems unlikely, and decisive in favor of *τετρακοσίας*.

Herodotus' figures have provoked much discussion in themselves, because the first four contingents are the same in the lists for both Artemisium and Salamis (8. 1 and 8. 43–48) and because of the discrepancy in the latter passage between the sum of the individual contingents detailed (366) and the total given by Herodotus (378); see R. W. Macan (ed.), *Herodotos: The Seventh, Eighth & Ninth Books* (London, 1908), ad loc., for possible solutions to this problem. Dispute has also focused on whether Aeschylus, who gave 310 as the size of the whole Greek fleet at Salamis (*Pers.* 338–40; see n. 3), is to be believed in preference to Herodotus. C. Hignett, *Xerxes' Invasion of Greece* (Oxford, 1963), pp. 209–10, and A. R. Burn, *Persia and the Greeks* (London, 1962), pp. 441–43, are both inclined to accept the suggestion of W. W. Tarn, "The Fleet of Xerxes," *JHS* 28 (1908): 219, that the figures in the list at Hdt. 8. 43–48 are "*campaign* totals, the sum total of the individual ships of each state commissioned during the summer of 480 B.C." If this is correct, then Aeschylus' 310, which Tarn, Hignett, and Burn all calculate to be approximately correct on other grounds, can be accepted without hesitation as the total for the Greek fleet at Salamis. The orator in Thucydides, who was speaking in general terms, naturally referred to Herodotus' campaign total (378) rather than to the figure (310) attached specifically to Salamis by Aeschylus.

400 ships, while Aeschylus, Demosthenes, and Nepos gave it as 300?[3] (3) What exactly is the construction of *ναῦς . . . ἐς τὰς τετρακοσίας ὀλίγῳ ἐλάσσους τῶν δύο μοιρῶν?*

Gomme argued that neither (1) the degree of exaggeration in this statement (200 is only 53 percent of 378) nor (2) the existence of another, lower, figure in some accounts was sufficient reason to doubt the correctness of the text. The grammatical question (3), however, he found problematic. In fact, he pronounced the text on this ground unacceptable, and suggested two possible emendations. His comment shows that he took ἐς τὰς τετρακοσίας to modify ναῦς, a reading that causes confusion, as he says, by frustrating the reader's expectation that the first accusative will be the direct object of the verb (παρεσχόμεθα, understood from the previous clause). Another difficulty is that, if one takes ἐς as qualifying the numeral (τετρακοσίας) in the sense of "about," nothing remains to indicate the relationship between the two accusatives (ναῦς . . . ἐς τὰς τετρακοσίας and ὀλίγῳ ἐλάσσους ⟨ναῦς⟩ τῶν δύο μοιρῶν).

Gomme's difficulty clearly stemmed from a misconstruction of ἐς. The clause reads satisfactorily if one takes ἐς not as qualifying τετρακοσίας ("about 400 [ships]") but in its basic meaning of "to" (". . . [we supplied] a little less than two-thirds of the ships *to* the 400 [ships] that constituted the Greek fleet . . ."). This interpretation has been advocated by several editors,[4] and must be correct. Others besides Gomme, however, have misconstrued this passage,[5] and it is worth trying to identify what in its wording should have led people astray. One major problem is the ambiguity of ἐς when closely followed by a numeral, since in many such cases ἐς appears to be used, like περί, or ὡς, or μάλιστα, to qualify the numeral, in the sense of "about" or "approximately." And the fact that the figure which follows ἐς here (400) was a round approximation of the actual figure (378) made many scholars look for some qualifying word to signal this imprecision. Second, the proportional designation (ὀλίγῳ ἐλάσσους τῶν δύο μοιρῶν) attached to the Athenian contingent of the fleet generates an expectation of a partitive genitive specifying the whole fleet.[6] Why did Thucydides not fulfill this expectation by writing ναῦς (or νεῶν) μέν γε τῶν τετρακοσίων ὀλίγῳ ἐλάσσους τῶν δύο μοιρῶν (sc. παρεσχόμεθα)? Partly, no doubt, because he felt that such an accumulation of genitives would be con-

3. For the variant reading τριακοσίας in Thucydides, see n. 2. Aeschylus' total for Salamis (*Pers.* 338–40) may be either 300 or 310, depending on whether the squadron of ten is taken as part of the 300 or as an addition to it. H. J. Rose, *A Commentary on the Surviving Plays of Aeschylus*, vol. 1 (Amsterdam, 1957), p. 116, argues for the latter interpretation; H. D. Broadhead, *The "Persae" of Aeschylus* (Cambridge, 1960), ad loc., for the former. Demosthenes (18. 238) and Nepos (*Them.* 3. 2) both state that Athens contributed 200 of a total of 300 Greek ships.

4. See J. J. Owen (ed.), *Thucydides I–III* (New York, 1858), p. 314; Classen–Steup, *Thukydides*[5], ad 1. 74. 1. The occurrence of the definite article between ἐς and the numeral (ἐς τὰς τετρακοσίας) is another indication that ἐς here does not qualify the numeral: the definite article does not appear in this position in any of the twenty-six cases of qualifying ἐς in Thucydides (listed below, n. 14).

5. Both H. Stephanus, *Thesaurus Graecae Linguae ab Henrico Stephano constructus*, vol. 3, ed. C. B. Hase, G. Dindorf, and L. Dindorf (Paris, 1863), cols. 294–95, and A. Matthiae, *Ausführliche griechische Grammatik* (Leipzig, 1807), p. 845, cited this passage as an example of ἐς meaning "about." LSJ[9], s.v. εἰς, III. 2, list Thuc. 1. 74. 1 separately, not as an instance of εἰς meaning "about"; but they group it with Thuc. 1. 100. 1, which surely is an instance of qualifying εἰς. T. Arnold, *The History of the Peloponnesian War by Thucydides* (Oxford and London, 1868), ad 1. 74. 1, argued that ἐς with numbers never means "about" but always "up to" or "as many as," translations which are no less inappropriate in this passage than "about," since they, too, are expressions normally used to qualify numerals (see n. 13).

6. Cf. Thuc. 2. 98. 4, where there is no other genitive to complicate the syntax.

fusing.[7] But he was doubtless influenced also by the run of the previous sentence (τρία τὰ ὠφελιμώτατα ἐς αὐτὸ παρεσχόμεθα . . .), where παρέχεσθαι is completed by ἐς αὐτό.[8]

Two other passages in Thucydides where ἐς introduces a numeral without qualifying it (6. 8. 1 and 8. 29. 2) provide an interesting comparison. In these passages, too, the prepositional phrase appears to have been used for greater clarity to replace a simple genitive or dative of the noun. In both cases the obscurity that motivated this change of construction was caused by the word μισθός, which can generate dependent genitives and datives of several types (as, e.g., to denote the recipient of the payment, or the task or the period of time for which he was paid).[9] But in spite of this similarity of construction, 6. 8. 1 and 8. 29. 2 lack the same possibility of confusion as 1. 74. 1, for in neither of them is the figure known to be rounded, and therefore felt to require qualification, nor is the noun to which the figure applies omitted.[10]

ἐς AS A NUMERAL QUALIFIER

The confusion evident in the comments of editors and grammarians on the construction and meaning of ἐς at 1. 74. 1 prompts a more general investigation of how ἐς functions in passages where most would interpret it as qualifying the numeral. First, some general remarks about qualification. A numeral qualifier can be defined as an expression (consisting of one or more words) attached to a figure to indicate that that figure is something other than the precise figure which applied (or applies, or will apply) to any one actual case of the phenomenon described. Qualifiers are of two main types, "approximating" and "comparative," the former naming a figure as being in the neighborhood of the precise actual figure, the latter specifying that the figure mentioned lies above or below the precise actual figure. Thus, if "about 500" people are said to have died in an earthquake, the speaker is expressing the belief that the exact figure lies within a range extending not too far on either side of 500; the extent of the range is not defined, but varies, in practice, with the size of the number mentioned. If, on the other hand, the casualties are said to number "more than 500" or "somewhat less than 500," this comparative qualification signifies that the exact figure is believed to lie within a certain distance of 500, but only on one side of that figure. The simplest cases to interpret of both kinds of qualification are those where the speaker is clearly mentioning one figure (qualified) as a compromise among several different figures, as when he gives an average figure (e.g., that for the

7. This was Classen–Steup's explanation. Gomme, while denying that Thucydides would have taken such steps to avoid two genitives (on the rather insufficient ground that he did not do so at 1. 75. 1), apparently agreed that he would have expected a partitive genitive here.

8. Αὐτό has no definite antecedent, but refers generally to the Greek victory over Xerxes. Other examples of παρέχεσθαι ἐς (or εἰς) with a noun denoting the group to which something was supplied are Thuc. 6. 83. 1 (another Athenian orator alludes to the same episode in Athens' history in very similar terms, substituting "the Greeks" for "the 400 ships" as the object of ἐς) and Xen. *Anab.* 6. 2. 10 (. . . μηδεμίαν δύναμιν παρεχόμενος εἰς τὴν στρατιάν—the closest parallel to Thuc. 1. 74. 1).

9. Cf. Thuc. 1. 143. 2 and 8. 97. 1 for other solutions to the same problem. For other passages where Thucydides seems to have altered his syntax to avoid piling up genitives or datives, see Dover's notes ad 7. 28. 3 and 6. 4. 6 (citing 5. 33. 1, where Gomme–Andrewes had not suggested this possibility, 6. 18. 6, and 7. 71. 5).

10. There are problems of text and arithmetic at 8. 29. 2, but they do not affect this argument.

tribute received by Athens annually; at Thuc. 2. 13. 1, ὡς ἐπὶ τὸ πολύ is an approximating qualifier) or mentions the highest or lowest figure ever reached in a certain circumstance (e.g., the estimate of the maximum time for which people predicted that Athens might withstand Peloponnesian invasions; at Thuc. 7. 28. 3, οὐδεὶς . . . πλέον is a comparative qualifier). Less straightforward, though more common, are cases where the reference in the speaker's mind to more than one figure is implied rather than stated. He may be indicating the range within which several possible figures in a single instance are felt to lie (e.g., at Thuc. 5. 74. 3, περί names 500 as the midpoint in the range of figures considered possible for the Lacedaemonian dead; and at 4. 72. 1, οὐκ ἔλασσον names 6,000 as the lower limit of the range of possible figures for Brasidas' hoplite troops) or a nodal point near which the exact but uneven figure is known to lie (e.g., at Thuc. 1. 118. 2, μάλιστα names 50 years as the midpoint of a range of periods within which the exact figure, probably 48 or 49 years, lies).[11]

Most qualifying expressions, in English or in Greek, belong to one of these two major types. Thus, "about," "in the neighborhood of," περί, μάλιστα are approximating qualifiers, whereas "at least," "a maximum of," "almost," οὐκ ἐλάσσους, πλείους are comparative qualifiers.[12] If we ask, however, to which type the preposition ἐς belongs, we find ourselves in a difficulty. Ἐς is, of course, a very common preposition, which has many uses; but the one that comes closest to its use as a numeral qualifier is that in which it designates a limit of some kind (e.g., Hdt. 1. 52 ἐς ἐμέ, "down to my time"; Thuc. 1. 51. 3 ἡ ναυμαχία ἐτελεύτα ἐς νύκτα, "the sea-battle drew to an end toward nightfall").[13] If ἐς were used to qualify numerals in this "limiting" sense, it would have much the same force as those comparative expressions which name the upper rather than the lower limit of a certain numerical range (like οὐ πλείους or ἐλάσσους). In some passages this is fairly clearly the case, but in others it seems at least doubtful. Furthermore, this interpretation runs counter to the equation that is often assumed between ἐς as a numeral qualifier and words like μάλιστα, ὡς, and περί, which are approximating rather than comparative qualifiers. What are we to make of this apparent contradiction? In order to suggest a solution it will be necessary to examine the twenty-six passages in Thucydides (apart from the three already discussed, 1. 74. 1, 6. 8. 1, and 8. 29. 2) where ἐς occurs in combination with a numeral,[14] and to compare the use of ἐς here with that of approximating qualifiers such as μάλιστα, ὡς, and περί.

There is one passage where ἐς makes sense only if taken in that limiting sense which resembles comparative qualification. At 4. 118. 3, Thucydides quotes a clause of a truce between the Athenian and Peloponnesian alliances stipulating

11. The passages cited in this paragraph are more fully discussed in my paper, "Qualification of Numerals in Thucydides," forthcoming in *AJAH* 3 (1978).

12. See the paper cited in the preceding note.

13. Cf. R. Kühner and B. Gerth, *Ausführliche Grammatik der griechischen Sprache*, vol. 2.1 (Hannover and Leipzig, 1890), p. 469, on εἰς used to qualify numerals: "zur Angabe des *quantitativen* Zieles, *bis auf*, bes. bei ungefähren Zahlangaben." The translations proposed by Arnold, *History of the Peloponnesian War*, ad 1. 74. 1, of qualifying εἰς, "up to" and "as many as," are of this limiting type.

14. The twenty-six passages are the following: 1. 100. 1, 1. 115. 4, 3. 20. 2, 3. 70. 6, 3. 85. 1, 3. 107. 3, 3. 111. 4, 3. 114. 4, 4. 48. 1, 4. 80. 4, 4. 118. 5, 4. 124. 1, 5. 3. 4, 5. 6. 5, 6. 67. 2, 7. 1. 5, 7. 19. 3, 7. 30. 3, 7. 32. 2 (2 cases), 7. 33. 1, 8. 10. 3, 8. 21. 1, 8. 32. 2, 8. 44. 4, 8. 73. 2.

that the latter shall use oared ships only "up to a burden of 500 talents." This framing of a prescription to apply to all cases of a certain activity for some future period naturally requires neither an exact figure ("500 T"), which would be inappropriately precise, nor an approximate figure ("about 500 T"), which would be inappropriately vague, but a maximum limit, defining a permissible range of figures. A comparative qualifier ("not more than 500 T") would have served equally well. In a second passage ἐς has generally been glossed with a comparative qualifier. At 4. 124. 1, the qualifying expression is ὀλίγου ἐς, a combination of words that seems not to occur as a numeral qualifier elsewhere in Thucydides or any other author, but which most editors have interpreted as equivalent to ὀλίγῳ ἐλάσσους.[15] In these two passages, then, ἐς functions more like a comparative than an approximating qualifier.

In the other twenty-four passages the use of ἐς is harder to categorize. First, there are a number of passages where the figure introduced by ἐς appears to be specified as the total obtained by adding together several groups of people or ships. At 8. 10. 2–3 this is particularly clear because the prepositional phrase, ἐς ἑπτὰ καὶ τριάκοντα, makes sense only if taken adverbially to express the result of the action described in the participle (". . . the Athenians later manned other ships in addition, to a total of 37 . . ."), instead of adjectivally as modifying ἄλλας (sc. ναῦς). In this sentence the substitution of a simple approximating qualifier (e.g., περὶ ἑπτὰ καὶ τριάκοντα) would necessitate the adjectival interpretation of the prepositional phrase, which would change the meaning completely.[16] In seven passages (1. 100. 1, 3. 107. 3, 4. 124. 1 [discussed earlier], 5. 34, 6. 67. 2, 7. 19. 3, and 7. 30. 3) the figure introduced by ἐς modifies a list of two or more nouns, which are summed up by a collective word (e.g., 3. 107. 3 λοχίζει . . . ὁπλίτας καὶ ψιλοὺς ξυναμφοτέρους ἐς τετρακοσίους).[17] Although such summary figures are sometimes given elsewhere in Thucydides either absolutely (e.g., 7. 1. 5 Ἱμεραίους δὲ ὁπλίτας καὶ ψιλοὺς ξυναμφοτέρους χιλίους . . .) or qualified by another word (e.g., 8. 100. 3 διακομίσαντες ἔκ τε τῆς Κύμης προσεταιριστοὺς ὁπλίτας ὡς πεντήκοντα καὶ τῶν ἐκ τῆς ἠπείρου μισθωσάμενοι, ξύμπασιν ὡς τριακοσίους . . .[18]), it does seem reasonable to regard the seven passages cited as extensions of that adverbial use of summary ἐς at 8. 10. 2–3 which is not found with any other qualifier. In three other passages (3. 70. 6, 7. 1. 5, 8. 21. 1) either the enumeration of the constituents of the group or the collective word is absent, but a similar summary motivation may perhaps still be inferred for the use of ἐς.[19]

15. See LSJ[9], s.v. ὀλίγος, IV, and Classen–Steup, *Thukydides*[3], ad loc.

16. Most of the manuscripts omit ἐς in this passage, although it is found in one papyrus (see the OCT apparatus criticus). Most editors have preferred to take the omission as a scribal error (an easy haplography after προσπληρώσαντες) because the attachment of the number to ἄλλας, which would result from the omission of ἐς, as also from its replacement by περί, would produce a second constituent of thirty-seven ships in addition to those already manned by the Athenians, instead of a total fleet of thirty-seven ships. The smaller total accords better with the other information supplied in these chapters about naval resources on both sides; see Classen–Steup, *Thukydides*[3], ad 8. 10. 2–3.

17. At 1. 100. 1, ἐς διακοσίας summarizes not two nouns but the objects of two verbs (εἷλον . . . καὶ διέφθειραν), which are collected by the adjective, τὰς πάσας.

18. Perhaps the use of ὡς to qualify another figure earlier in this sentence prompted Thucydides to repeat it later in the summary situation.

19. Classen–Steup, *Thukydides*[3], ad 7. 1. 5, observe that the 1,000 Sicels here mentioned must be the total obtained by adding together several small contingents from different places, perhaps differently armed.

There are three passages in which ἐς qualifying a number occupies a syntactical position used by Thucydides for no other approximating qualifier. In these passages (3. 114. 4, 7. 33. 1, and 8. 44. 4) ἐς introduces not just a numerical adjective, but an adjective plus a noun, and the whole phrase stands in loose apposition to another noun of more general meaning, which it amplifies or further specifies. Thus, at 3. 114. 1, ἐς τριακοσίους ὁπλίτας gives more information about the φυλακή sent out by the Corinthians; at 7. 33. 1, ἐς πέντε ναῦς similarly describes the ναυτικόν of the Geloans; and at 8. 44. 4, ἐς δύο καὶ τριάκοντα τάλαντα specifies the amount of the χρήματα collected by the Peloponnesians.[20] Here, then, it seems likely that ἐς was used primarily because it made possible the addition of numerical information to a statement that would have been syntactically complete without it, though more general in import.[21] I suggest that this use of ἐς is an extension of its "summary" function (detected earlier, p. 331, at 8. 10. 2–3, and with less certainty in a slightly different kind of situation in ten other passages).

There are five passages where a figure is qualified by a second qualifying word in addition to ἐς.[22] At 3. 20. 2, 7. 30. 3, and 7. 32. 2, we find ἐς . . . μάλιστα, and at 3. 111. 4 and 8. 21. 1, ἐς . . . τινας.[23] Such combinations of two independent qualifiers occur only eight times altogether in Thucydides, the three cases not involving ἐς being 3. 98. 4, 4. 8. 6 (both περὶ . . . μάλιστα) and 1. 18. 1 (μάλιστα . . . καὶ ὀλίγῳ πλείω). One would like to be able to explain why Thucydides qualified these eight figures doubly and what made him favor ἐς as the first of the two qualifiers in five of the cases. As regards the second question, it is clear that the normal function of a qualifier in a sentence (i.e., whether it is a preposition, an adverb, or an adjective, and whether it can stand at the beginning of a phrase) will determine generally which qualifiers can be conveniently combined; the combinations found tend to be of a preposition (ἐς or περί) with an adverb (μάλιστα) or an adjective (τις—note that both μάλιστα and τις are postpositive words). But these grammatical considerations do not explain why Thucydides used ἐς more often than περί, in the prepositional position, or why only ἐς is paired with τις. Some light can perhaps be shed on this by a scrutiny of the five cases where ἐς is coupled with another qualifier. Did Thucydides double his qualifiers in order to define with extra

20. At 3. 114. 4, the numeral seems to come rather as an afterthought, at the end of the sentence. At 7. 33. 1 and 8. 44. 4, it appears that Thucydides put first the general word (ναυτικόν or χρήματα), to which the numerical detail was then attached by ἐς, because he wanted to have a balanced contrast between two or more elements in the sentence. In the former passage ναυτικόν τε balances ἀκοντιστὰς . . . καὶ ἱππέας; in the latter there is a larger contrast between χρήματα μὲν ἐξέλεξαν and τὰ δ' ἄλλα ἡσύχαζον. Thus, in both these cases the balanced structure of the sentence, once established, dictated the use of a qualifier like ἐς, which could attach a phrase consisting of numeral + specific noun (namely, ναῦς, τάλαντα) to a more general noun.

21. Thuc. 4. 48. 1 somewhat resembles the three passages just discussed; it, too, has ἐς introducing a noun as well as a numerical adjective, and the sentence seems to require a similar degree of syntactical independence in the prepositional phrase. If, for example, περί were substituted for ἐς, the phrase would attach itself closely to τοὺς ἐν τῷ οἰκήματι, in which case this whole group of words would logically have to be taken as the object only of the participles ἐξαγαγόντες καὶ διαφθείραντες; thus, in translation, "[The Corcyraeans] escaped notice when they took out and put to death in this way about 60 men of those inside the building." As the sentence stands, however, while ἐς . . . ἄνδρας ἑξήκοντα must refer to those killed, τοὺς ἐν τῷ οἰκήματι can be taken with both ἔλαθον and its participles: "[The Corcyraeans] escaped the notice of those inside the building when they took out and put to death in this way up to 60 men [from among them]."

22. Thuc. 4. 124. 1 (see p. 331), where the unique expression ὀλίγου ἐς appears, is hardly a parallel case, since ὀλίγου is nowhere found as an independent qualifier.

23. On τις used to qualify numerals, see Classen–Steup, *Thukydides*³, ad 3. 68. 3, 7. 34. 5.

precision the degree and/or the type of uncertainty or rounding he was attaching to the figure in question?

The doubly qualified figure at 3. 20. 2 refers to an episode in the siege of Plataea, a section of Thucydides' *History* exceptionally rich in detail of all kinds, including numbers. By putting together all the figures that relate to the garrison at Plataea (2. 78. 3, 3. 20. 2, 3. 24. 2, and 3. 68. 2) and paying careful attention to how they are qualified, one can infer that Thucydides probably obtained firm figures only for (*a*) the initial strength of the garrison (400 Plataeans + 80 Athenians—these are absolute, and should be precise, figures), (*b*) those who escaped to Athens, and those who were captured, in the mass breakout during the siege (212 escaped and 1 was captured—these numbers have obviously not been rounded), and (*c*) the number of Athenians executed by the Peloponnesians after the city surrendered to them (an absolute 25; contrast the qualified, apparently rounded figure for the Plataeans who were executed, οὐκ ἐλάσσους διακοσίων). For the rest, he had the more general recollection of those who escaped to Athens that "a few" had turned back in the attempt. That "roughly half" of those in Plataea withdrew from the escape attempt at the last minute may be Thucydides' own or his informants' estimate. If this is right, then the statement that ἐς . . . ἄνδρας διακοσίους καὶ εἴκοσι μάλιστα actually left Plataea on the way to Athens is Thucydides' calculation from the 212 + 1 + "a few" (= a minimum of 215) known to him from various sources. In that case, it seems probable that he thought 220 the maximum possible number who initially went over the walls of Plataea, and used ἐς therefore in its limiting sense to mean "up to" or "to a maximum of" (the usage at 4. 118. 3 and possibly also at 4. 124. 1). He added μάλιστα to show that the figure was arrived at by his own calculations, instead of being supplied directly by an informant.[24] As an additional reason for thinking that the figure 220 is the product of a fairly precise calculation, one may note that it is the only one of the twenty figures greater than 100 qualified by ἐς which is not a multiple of 100.

It may be significant that the figure qualified by ἐς . . . μάλιστα at 7. 30. 3 is a relatively small one (20), which is therefore unlikely to be much rounded. In this case (the figure refers to the Thebans and others who were killed attacking the Thracian raiders who had sacked Mycalessus) we have no information about the size of the group from whom the casualties fell. But since such a low number is bound to be relatively precise, one might guess that here, too, ἐς is used in its limiting sense to name what Thucydides regards as a maximum figure, and μάλιστα once again marks the figure as his own calculation. The other three cases of ἐς coupled with another qualifier (3. 111. 4, 7. 32. 2, and 8. 21. 1) do not lend themselves to such analysis, for the figures concerned cannot be argued to be especially precise, nor do we have sufficient information to infer how Thucydides might have made his calculations. 3. 111. 4 is interesting, however, for another reason, since the group of casualties among the Ambraciotes and their Peloponnesian allies referred to there by Thucydides himself as ἐς διακοσίους . . . τινας is alluded to a few pages further on, at 3. 113. 3, by an Ambraciote herald, as numbering διακοσίους μάλιστα: the same figure is cited, but the qualifier is changed. Did Thucydides

24. For this implication of μάλιστα, see Dover, *Commentary*, ad 7. 42. 1, where the figure qualified (73) is so obviously unrounded as to rule out any straightforward approximating interpretation. See also the paper cited in n. 11.

intend to convey a difference of nuance? One cannot tell. Since no obvious reason for such a difference of view between the historian and the Ambraciote herald leaps to mind, one is inclined to think this may be more a case of literary variation, and to deduce from it that ἐς . . . τινας and μάλιστα here have much the same force.[25] Finally, we may note that two of these passages (7. 30. 3 and 8. 21. 1) have been discussed earlier (p. 331) as cases where ἐς appears to perform a summary function. Thus, the nuance expressed by the double qualification may not be precisely the same in all cases.

It is useful to compare the general profile of the qualifier ἐς in Thucydides with the profiles of the most common expressions of the approximating and comparative types (μάλιστα, ὡς, περί, and οὐκ ἐλάσσους, ὀλίγῳ ἐλάσσους, ὀλίγῳ πλείους). It will be clear that, although in many respects the three major expressions of each type diverge too much to permit the extrapolation of a "typical" approximating word or a "typical" comparative word with which ἐς could be compared, the comparison of ἐς with various particular expressions of both types is nonetheless illuminating in many ways.

Take first of all frequency of employment. In general, approximating qualifiers are used three times as often as comparative qualifiers (the total for approximating expressions, excluding ἐς, is 121 cases, as compared to forty of comparative type), and this generally higher frequency of approximating qualifiers is naturally reflected in the higher frequency of individual expressions of this type. 'Ες, used twenty-six times, falls between μάλιστα (47) and ὡς (19), while the commonest comparative expression, οὐκ ἐλάσσους, occurs eighteen times; the remaining figures are: περί (12), ὀλίγῳ ἐλάσσους (6), ὀλίγῳ πλείους (5).

Second, in range of employment, it is not surprising that the most general comparative expression, οὐκ ἐλάσσους, is used with the largest range of figures (from 25 to 150,000); this is presumably due to the tendency of such comparative expressions to be used rhetorically, as a means of emphasizing the magnitude of the figure qualified.[26] The more specific expressions, ὀλίγῳ ἐλάσσους and ὀλίγῳ πλείους, are used, as one would expect, with a much more restricted range of figures (from 50 to 1,000 and from 30 to 1,000, respectively). Among the approximating words, μάλιστα has by far the most extended range (from 2 to 6,000); by contrast, περί is rarely used with large numbers (range: from 13 to 5,000; but all cases except 7. 42. 1 are below 1,000), and ὡς appears with no figure higher than 300 (range: from 6 to 300). These differences in the range of figures with which μάλιστα, περί, and ὡς are employed can be explained to some extent by Thucydides' apparent preference for one word or another in qualifying different sorts of numerical information. Thus, μάλιστα is the only approximating word used to qualify figures of all three main types (those relating to time, distance, and groups of fighting men or ships); περί is used only once (in combination with μάλιστα at 4. 8. 6) of distance, while ὡς is never used of time. I suggest that Thucydides generally

25. E. C. Marchant, *Thucydides III* (London and New York, 1965), ad 3. 20. 2, cites Andoc. 1. 37 as a case where "εἰς τριακοσίους is presently repeated in the form μάλιστα τριακοσίους." In fact, μάλιστα (1. 38) is an insertion into the text made on the basis of a quotation of this passage by Galen; see D. MacDowell (ed.), *Andokides "On the Mysteries"* (Oxford, 1962), ad loc. (app. crit.). If the emended text is correct, this wouid be a clear instance of ἐς and μάλιστα being used more or less interchangeably.

26. On this point, see the paper cited in n. 11.

avoided qualifying distance figures with περί and time figures with ὡς because of the possibility of confusion with other common spatial uses of περί and temporal uses of ὡς. Ἐς corresponds most closely to μάλιστα in the range of its figures (from 5 to 2,000), although a much smaller proportion of the figures with ἐς fall in the lower range of the scale (in only two cases does ἐς qualify figures of 20 or less, as compared to fourteen cases for μάλιστα; these figures represent, respectively, 7 percent and 30 percent of the totals for each word). It is significant that thirteen of the fourteen cases of μάλιστα with very low numbers relate to time or distance, types of figures which Thucydides never qualifies with ἐς, no doubt because of the ambiguities that might be generated by the common occurrence of ἐς in a non-qualifying sense in these contexts (cf. his avoidance of περί for distance and ὡς for time, pp. 334–35). Thus, the distribution of figures qualified by ἐς corresponds most closely to the distribution of the μάλιστα figures excluding those relating to time and distance. It appears that, when qualifying figures between 21 and 100 relating to groups of fighting men or ships, Thucydides had a strong preference for ὡς (10 cases); compare μάλιστα (3), ἐς (3), and περί (2). Thus, Thucydides did not use all the approximating words in his repertoire interchangeably, but made his selection in each case with regard to some fairly subtle differences of connotation between them. Ἐς appears here to correspond more closely to the pattern of approximating than of comparative qualifiers; but it, too, has its own distinctive pattern.

This same picture, of a general difference between most approximating qualifiers and most comparative qualifiers, but still a considerable variation in the employment of individual approximating words, among which ἐς seems to fall, emerges from a study of the degree to which the figures qualified by different expressions cluster at a few points on the scale, and the tendency of certain particular figures to occur very frequently with certain qualifiers. One can obtain a "cluster index" for any qualifier by dividing the number of different figures that appear with it by the total number of occurrences of that qualifier: a low figure will indicate a high degree of clustering, and a high figure the converse. This calculation produces high figures for the three comparative qualifiers, signifying very little clustering (οὐκ ἐλάσσους—17 figures in 18 cases = 94.4; ὀλίγῳ ἐλάσσους—5 figures in 6 cases = 83.3; ὀλίγῳ πλείους—4 figures in 5 cases = 80.0). The approximating qualifiers show greater variation, ranging from περί, with the highest index (11 figures in 12 cases = 91.6), through μάλιστα (31 figures in 47 cases = 65.9), to ὡς, with the lowest index (9 figures in 19 cases = 47.3); and, if one looks at the cases of ὡς, one finds in fact that over half of them (10 of 19) involve just two figures, namely, 50 and 300. It thus appears that figures qualified by approximating expressions tend to cluster considerably more than those qualified by comparative expressions. This may reflect only the generally greater frequency of approximating qualifiers (especially as περί, the one approximating word whose cluster index falls in the same range as those of the comparative expressions, is also the least frequently used), or it may show a greater tendency (in Thucydides or his informants) to think in certain stereotyped round numbers when laboring under a general uncertainty or imprecision. Ἐς has a cluster index of 61.5 (16 figures in 26 cases), which puts it closest to μάλιστα (65.9), and clearly among the approximating rather than the comparative expressions. A look at the list of figures that occur more than once with each approximating qualifier discovers very little overlap between them: the only figures qualified more than once by each of two or more qualifiers are 60 (twice each by μάλιστα and ἐς), 120 (twice each by μάλιστα and ἐς), and 300 (twice each by μάλιστα and ἐς, and five times by ὡς). And each qualifier appears to have its own "favorite" figures: μάλιστα appears four times with 40, three times each with 7 and 400; ὡς appears five times each with 50 and 300; ἐς appears four times with 200 and three times with 500. Some of these patterns can be partly explained by Thucydides' preference for using certain qualifiers with certain types of information: thus, the three cases of 7 and the four cases of 40 qualified by μάλιστα all involve time or distance figures, and μάλιστα is by far the commonest qualifier used with figures of these types. But no such explanation will account for his apparent preference for ἐς rather than ὡς, περί, or μάλιστα with groups of 200 soldiers or ships. One wonders whether euphonic considerations generated by the rhythm and order of words in a particular sentence did not play a part here.

To sum up, a study of the passages where Thucydides uses ἐς to qualify a number finds two (4. 118. 3 and 4. 124. 1) where ἐς definitely has comparative force, and a few others (e.g., 3. 20. 2, 7. 30. 3) where it may have comparative force. In another group of passages (8. 10. 3 and the ten others cited on p. 331) it seems reasonable to discern another facet of the original "limiting" sense of ἐς, by which it performs a summary function (meaning something like "to a total of"). So used, although the connection with the comparative use remains clear, ἐς comes closer in force to an approximating qualifier. It seems, however, that in such summary cases, as well as in cases where the phrase containing the qualified numeral was added almost as an afterthought to an already syntactically complete sentence (3. 114. 1, 7. 33. 1, and 8. 44. 4), Thucydides preferred to use ἐς rather than a more straightforward approximating qualifier, such as ὡς, περί, or μάλιστα. Similarly, he apparently liked using ἐς as the first of two qualifiers attached to the same number. But there remain many cases where one can discern no difference in meaning or construction between ἐς and ὡς, περί, or μάλιστα. These passages tend to support the common assumption that ἐς is in many respects merely another approximating qualifier.

More support for this assumption is provided by the comparison of the figures qualified by ἐς with those qualified by the three commonest approximating qualifiers (μάλιστα, ὡς, περί) and the three commonest comparative qualifiers (οὐκ ἐλάσσους ὀλίγῳ ἐλάσσους, ὀλίγῳ πλείους). In frequency of use, range and distribution of figures qualified, and tendency of figures to cluster, ἐς stands clearly among the approximating rather than the comparative qualifiers. In addition, however, this general survey of the profiles of different qualifiers makes it plain that no two expressions even of the same type are exactly alike in usage. This confirms the conclusion suggested by the study of particular instances of ἐς, that Thucydides did not use all the approximating expressions available to him absolutely interchangeably but that a variety of considerations, including differences of connotation, grammatical function, and rhythm, probably influenced his choice in any given passage. The unique idiosyncrasy of ἐς, however, remains—that its usage overlaps that of comparative qualifiers (like οὐκ ἐλάσσους) at one end, and blends at the other into that of approximating qualifiers (like μάλιστα). This helps to explain why editors and lexicographers have often had trouble in elucidating its meaning and use in particular passages.[27]

CATHERINE REID RUBINCAM
Erindale College
University of Toronto

27. This paper was written with the support of a Canada Council Leave Fellowship. I am grateful to Joan Bigwood for reading and commenting on an earlier version of this paper, and to the journal's referees for some useful suggestions toward improving the argument.

THEOCRITUS, CALVUS, AND *ECLOGUE* 6

Of the six unconnected lines surviving from Calvus' epyllion, none is better known than the neoteric exclamation addressed to Io herself (Serv. Dan. ad *Ecl.* 6. 47 = Calvus frag. 9 Morel):

a virgo infelix, herbis pasceris amaris.

We are indebted to Servius Danielis; for, as has been noted,[1] it can be seen that in *Eclogue* 6 Virgil drew from Calvus' line to produce an acknowledgment of previous literary expression. Stewart observes that at *Eclogue* 6. 47 ("a, virgo infelix, quae te dementia cepit!") Virgil combined the first half of Calvus' line with the second half of a verse from *Eclogue* 2 (69 "a Corydon, Corydon, quae te dementia cepit"), a line whose antecedent is Theocritus *Idyll* 11. 72 (ὦ Κύκλωψ Κύκλωψ, πᾷ τὰς φρένας ἐκπεπότασαι;). *Eclogue* 6. 47, then, is a recognition of the poet's literary predecessors, molded into a single Virgilian line.

But what of line 52 of the same poem?

a! virgo infelix, tu nunc in montibus erras.

Virgil does not lightly repeat himself, and we may ask why this line, with the alteration of the second half, reappears after five verses. It is true that there is a structural purpose to the repetition: lines 47–52 are, in fact, a self-contained panel.[2] But why the change in the second half ("tu nunc in montibus erras")? The motif of wandering is common in the *Eclogues*, particularly in *Eclogue* 6.[3] For the moment, however, instances outside this poem will be important. First, *Eclogue* 2. 21:

mille meae Siculis errant in montibus agnae.

As Servius recognized, Virgil drew from, but altered, Theocritus (again the Cyclops poem) at this point:

1. Z. Stewart, "The Song of Silenus," *HSCP* 64 (1959): 190.
2. Briefly noted, together with other panels, by F. Skutsch, *Aus Vergils Frühzeit* (Leipzig, 1901), p. 13.
3. J. P. Elder, "*Non Iniussa Cano*," *HSCP* 65 (1961): 118–19, points to the numerous instances of *erra-* in the *Eclogues*, particularly 6. 40, 52, 58, and 64. Is there significance in the distribution —an interval of twelve lines followed by two of six?

MILLE MEAE SICULIS ERRANT I. M. A. Theocritus ⟨XI 34⟩ βοτὰ χίλια βόσκω errant autem cum securitate pascuntur.

Again, on *Eclogue* 1. 9–10:

ERRANT pasci ut ⟨II 21⟩ mille meae Siculis errant in montibus agnae.

The discrepancy in verbs between Theocritus and Virgil seemed significant to Servius, as it should to us, for Virgil clearly had *Idyll* 11 constantly before him while writing *Eclogue* 2. When he wrote *errant*, he intended his reader to recall the Theocritean verse and to supply *pascuntur*. Nor is Servius alone in seeing this approximation. Pseudo-Acron, on Horace *Epode* 2. 12 ("prospectat errantis greges"), notes:

ERRANTES GREGES libere pascentes ut ⟨Virg. *Ecl.* 1. 9⟩ ille meas errare boves.

Thus, Virgil creates a parallel between grazing and wandering: *errare* and *pasci* can imply the same activity.

Let us return to *Eclogue* 6. When Virgil repeated Calvus' exclamation at line 52, but ended the line differently ("tu nunc in montibus erras"), he intended his reader to consider the model again, this time, however, the second half of Calvus' line as well as the first:

a virgo infelix, herbis pasceris amaris.

Keeping in mind the equivalent meaning possible for *pasci* and *errare* (as established at *Ecl.* 2. 21), we will see exactly what *Eclogue* 6. 52, seemingly anticlimactic after its allusive counterpart five lines earlier, represents: a restatement, in Virgilian terms, of the complete line of Calvus—in this context, *pasceris* and *erras* are virtually interchangeable. Pasiphae's actions, then, are those of Io. Virgil, it seems, gives an additional indication of his source by alluding, two lines later (in the same metrical position, and in the same word order—verb enclosed by noun and adjective), to Calvus' half line ("pallentis ruminat herbas").

In the poetic genealogy of *Eclogue* 6 Virgil appears to have played further on this connection. He makes Linus the shepherd (67 *pastor*)[4] hand the pipes of Hesiod to Gallus, who is wandering (64 *errantem*) on the banks of the Permessus. Of course, *errare* here has only its conventional sense; but, since the verb is applied to Linus as *pastor*, its appearance does seem significant when we consider Virgil's earlier approximation of *errare* to *pasci*.

This leads to other considerations. *Pasci* obviously has a central place in pastoral poetry. Wandering, as noted, is also a prominent feature of the *Eclogues*. In particular, it can be the activity of the elegiac lover. In *Eclogue* 6 Virgil had placed Gallus, the author of the *Amores*, in this situation, just as Propertius, in the first poem of the *Monobiblos*, was to describe (the Gallan) Milanion, stricken by love:

4. Virgil elsewhere shows an interest in words derived from *pasco: Ecl.* 6. 4–5 "pastorem, Tityre, pinguis / pascere oportet ovis," *G.* 2. 435–36 "pastoribus . . . pabula," *G.* 3. 339–42 "pastores . . . pascua . . . pascitur." For an elaborate development of this feature of Virgilian poetry, together with further etymological allusion, see David O. Ross, Jr., *Backgrounds to Augustan Poetry* (Cambridge, 1975), pp. 155–56 (on Tib. 2. 5. 25–30). Ross (pp. 21–23) also discusses the significance of Linus' role as *pastor*.

"nam modo Partheniis amens errabat in antris" (1. 1. 11).[5] So Virgil makes Pasiphae, who is subject to frustrated love, wander in the mountains. *Errare* is thus appropriate in this sense at *Eclogue* 6. 52, as well as in the sense established in *Eclogue* 2.

We can go no farther, for without the poetry of Calvus and Gallus the full significance of Virgil's construct is lost. If, from a single line, it is possible to detect Virgil's reshaping of his poetic antecedents, we can only regret once again the loss of those earlier works.

RICHARD F. THOMAS
Harvard University

5. Cf. H. Tränkle, *Die Sprachkunst des Properz und die Tradition der lateinischen Dichtersprache*, Hermes Einzelschriften, 15 (Wiesbaden, 1960), p. 13, for the tradition of *amens errabat*, and Ross, *Backgrounds*, pp. 61–64, for the demonstration that this phrase, together with the entire Milanion exemplum, reflects a Gallan archetype.

REVIEW ARTICLE

LATIN TEXTUAL CRITICISM*

As a *cri de coeur* against conservatism in textual criticism, Willis' *Latin Textual Criticism* both succeeds and fails; it fails because the author, committed almost on principle to conjectural criticism, is therefore committed to a bias, the very reverse of the bias against which he clamors. I limit the following remarks to chapters 5–25, the "practical" section of the book.[1] In these chapters there is something to be learned, but the tone is polemical. The presentation is marred by a pervasive dogmatism; variations of "nihil certius hac emendatione" frequently usurp, as in a primer they should not, the place of thorough and careful argumentation. Willis' mind, in his examples at least, is not always "nimble, flexible, empty of prepossessions and alert for every hint" and, if his mind is not, why should those of his readers be? His readers, professedly tiros, are encouraged to be bold in new suspicion and conjecture. About the obelus, or even the risk of cutting into sound matter, they hear not a word. Nor is any clear distinction drawn between text and apparatus—when a conjecture belongs in the one, when in the other, or when in neither. No need here for Professor Goodyear's maxim "inter tot uerisimilia latet uerum"; here *uerisimilia* do not even compete—with Willis it is always *the* conjecture, never *which*. Well for him, then, if the readings advocated in his examples exhibited a tolerably uniform degree of probability. But they do not. Add that they sometimes ignore formal criteria, sometimes retail reckless assertions. In a real sense therefore—to borrow a turn from Housman—the only readers who can use a number of them with safety are those whose knowledge and judgment extend beyond Willis'. In this regard his reviewers have failed to fault him. Dr. J. Diggle complained justly that "instead of leading his reader by the hand towards the truth he prefers to give him an impatient shove" (impatient, yes, but not, as I hope to show, invariably toward the truth), but he dissented from Willis in only two of his examples.[2] Professor E. J. Kenney dissented in none and even stated that "the examples are nearly all well chosen and cogent,"[3] an especially charitable judgment because in many of them Willis had attempted to dispossess readings holding a place in Kenney's own OCT of Ovid. Of these I now consider four.

> Desine mirari, posito quod candida uino
> Atracis ambiguos traxit in arma uiros.
>
> [Ov. *Amor*. 1. 4. 7–8 (p. 59)]

* *Latin Textual Criticism*. By JAMES WILLIS. Illinois Studies in Language and Literature, 61. Urbana–Chicago–London: University of Illinois Press, 1972. Pp. x + 237.

1. For certain fundamentals and for Willis' treatment of the Middle Ages, see E. J. Kenney, review of *Latin Textual Criticism* by J. Willis, *CR*, n.s. 23 (1975): 302–3. "On the Middle Ages," Kenney concludes, Willis is " 'like nothing so much as an ill-bred child interrupting the conversation of grown men.' "
2. Review of *Latin Textual Criticism* by J. Willis, *JRS* 65 (1975): 242–43.
3. Review of Willis, p. 302.

I quote Willis' discussion at length: "Thus Ovid . . . bids his mistress cease to wonder that the Centaurs fought over Hippodamia. He follows by an *argumentum a minore:* he (Ovid) is no wild creature of the woods, compounded of man and stallion, but even he can hardly keep his hands off her. All would be well in this passage if only there were room to suppose that the young woman was thinking about Centaurs, or that Ovid was able to read her thoughts. Douza's *desino*, approved by Bentley and excluded from Kenney's apparatus, very properly makes Ovid's own feelings the subject of the distich." Douza's *desino* was excluded not only from Kenney's apparatus; Merkel, Brandt, Bornecque, and Lenz also excluded it. No sooner, in fact, had it appeared in the apparatus of Munari's first edition than Eduard Fraenkel, in the words of Professor G. P. Goold, "issued an imperious veto against [its] resurrection from Orcus (even as far as the apparatus criticus)." Yet grant that *desino* might be correct: it would not be so for the reason Willis gives. Ovid does not have to "read her thoughts," nor does she have to be "thinking about Centaurs" for him to say *desine*. Here, where the imperative introduces an exemplum, R. Renehan acutely detects a topos; he adduces inter alia Archilochus fragment 74. 6D μηδεὶς ἔθ' ὑμέων εἰσορῶν θαυμαζέτω (note ἔθ' and the fantastic exempla which follow). Willis himself seems to be peddling one of Goold's arguments.[4] As usual, however, Willis has told his readers too little. Why, for instance, does he refrain from telling them about the prosodic license in *desinŏ?* On prosody he might even have founded his *ratio corruptelae*. Goold appeals, for what he regards as the couplet's purely masculine realization, to Propertius 2. 2. 4 "Iuppiter, ignosco pristina furta tua." For this topos, a different one, Renehan adduces Theognis 1345–46 and Callimachus *Epigram* 52 (53) Pfeiffer. In further support of *desino* Goold thinks he can cite Cicero *De oratore* 2. 59 "illud iam mirari desino." If he can cite that, for *desine* I can cite Catullus 69. 10 *admirari desine*, Martial 6. 89. 8 *desine mirari*, Horace *Carmen* 3. 29. 11 *omitte mirari*.[5] But let that pass. Come now to a difficulty which both Goold and Willis failed to apprehend. Neither scholar quotes in his lemma verse 11 "quae tibi sint facienda tamen cognosce." To what is this *tamen cognosce* to be referred, if not to *desine?* "No longer marvel . . . *but all the same* learn" is a sequence; "*I* cease to marvel . . . nevertheless *you* learn" is not. For a similar linkage of two imperatives, compare 13–14 "ante *ueni* quam uir . . . *sed tamen* ante *ueni*." For *desine* followed by a negative and first person pronoun, as here in 9–10 "*nec mihi* silua domus *nec* equo *mea* membra cohaerent: / uix a te *uideor* posse tenere manus," compare *Amores* 3. 11(10). 31–32 "*desine* blanditias et uerba potentia quondam / perdere: *non ego* sum stultus, ut ante fui."

fortia nam posito sumpserat arma colo
[Ov. *Ars am.* 1. 702 (p. 104)]

Thus Kenney's OCT; but Willis, presently absorbed in internal rhyme as a source of corruption, is not to be denied his misgivings. "Examples of *colus* masculine are few and far between." Yet consider Ovid himself: should one of Willis' readers open the concordance, he would find eight instances of *colus*, four in which the

4. "*Amatoria Critica*," *HSCP* 69 (1965): 19–21.
5. Arguably part of the topos; see Mart. 8. 36. 7 "Regia pyramidum, Caesar, miracula *ride*" (E. Fraenkel, *Horace* [Oxford, 1958], p. 225, n. 3).

gender can be determined. In three of these instances, counting the passage in hand, *colus* is represented as masculine. MSS vary and editors waver, it is true, in these three passages. Yet at *Amores* 2. 6. 46 Kenney does print *uacuo . . . colo* (*uacuo* PSs: *uacua* ω)—what strikes Willis dumb here, MS authority?—and at *Heroides* 3. 76 certain editors have printed *plenos . . . colos* (*plenos* P¹E: *plenas* G cett.). This should come as no surprise. The gender of *colus* in particular is known to fluctuate, and Latin poets in general are known to avail themselves, quite consciously, of a less usual gender. Catullus, for example, had written "*laeua colum* molli lana retinebat *amictum*, / *dextera* tum leuiter deducens fila supinis / formabat digitis" (64. 311–13). When later Propertius set himself to write "non sunt a *dextro* condita fila *colo*" (4. 1. 72), was he perhaps recalling, in the light of the Catullian *laeu- . . . dexter-*, the Catullian gender of *colus?* His subject too was the Fates. Notice also Propertius 4. 9. 48 "officia et *Lydo* pensa diurna *colo*" and Seneca *Hercules Oetaeus* 1084–85 *consumptos . . . colus* (EA).

Turpe reos empta miseros defendere lingua;
quod faciat magnas, turpe tribunal, opes.
[Ov. *Amor*. 1. 10. 39–40 (p. 107)]

Willis begins: "That *facere opes* is possible Latin for 'to make money' I gravely doubt." Possible! The merest glance at Lewis and Short (s.v. *facio*), the *Oxford Latin Dictionary*, or *TLL* (6:94. 32–52) reveals that, of all verbs lending themselves to contexts of money, *facere* must be the most frequent and the most flexible. Such is its range of direct objects (e.g., *pecuniam, lucrum*) that, even if *opes* were not spotted among them, the combination could be defended by analogy. No need, however: compare Livy 1. 9. 3 "magnas opes sibi magnumque nomen facere" and Sallust *Oratio Lepidi* 26 "non fuit consilium priuatas opes facere." "Even if it were," he proceeds, "the sentiment is odd. Cicero somewhere says that 'mercatura, si tenuis est, sordida habenda est; sin est admodum ampla et quaestuosa, non est adeo uituperanda,' and that is indeed the common judgment of the world." What Willis has thus misquoted is *De officiis* 1. 151 "mercatura autem, si tenuis est, sordida putanda est: sin magna et copiosa, multa undique apportans, multisque sine uanitate impertiens, non est admodum uituperanda." Where in this is the crucial *quaestuosa*? And does not "multisque sine uanitate impertiens" appreciably alter the thought? "But Ovid," he concludes, "seems to be saying the reverse: for a court to make big profits is base, but a little profit, or a moderate . . . ? Clearly Ovid has no notion of saying this at all; he is not concerned with the size of the fee, but with any fee's being demanded at all. Ovid of course wrote

quod faciat magni turpe tribunal opes,

('a court which attaches importance to money is a disgrace'). Since this conjecture was made long ago by Riese, Mr. Kenney should not have put his readers to the trouble of making it for themselves." Strained logic. But suppose we strain it in the opposite direction. Suppose, for the sake of argument, we choose to hold that Willis' paraphrase conceals a potential objection to Riese's *magni*. For why does he not write ". . . attaches *great* importance . . ."? Is it because he would thereby have invited the inference "great as opposed to what—little, or moderate . . ."? Neither this logic nor Willis' logic need be applied. The transmitted *magnas* need do no more than intensify the disgrace. Nothing, moreover, is to be gained by forcing *faciat* to mean, as with *magni* it must, "regard" or "consider"; the whole tenor of the passage favors its meaning, literally, to "make money."[6]

> "Da reditum puero, senis est si gratia uilis;
> si non uis puero parcere, parce seni."
> Dixerat haec; sed et haec et multo plura licebat
> diceret, egressus non dabat ille uiro.
>
> *dicere et* Aω: *dicere* Rα *egressus* RAω: *progressus* r: *regressus* Itali, α, edd.
>
> [Ov. *Ars am.* 2. 29–32 (p. 146)]

Here Willis pours scorn on the conjecture *diceret, egressus.* Its proposer, the late Alan Ker, he even forbears to name. Touching but superficially on the *ductus litterarum,* he altogether ignores the tangible reason that induced it—that "Ovid never uses *licet* concessively except with the subjunctive."[7] Moreover, he ignores the scansion. Kenney has written, "Mr. Ker's simple and elegant correction ought to command instant assent. My reason for repeating it here is to add an argument not mentioned by Mr. Ker himself . . . , which ought to weigh heavily: that his correction at last abolishes the unexampled scansion *rēgressus. . . .*"[8] Then again, "The scansion *rēprensa* is highly improbable in a classical poet [here Grattius] . . . , especially given the more dactylic alternative [i.e., Sannazarius' conjecture *reprehensa*]."[9] *Re-* lengthened in "positio debilis," though indeed rare, occurs in Lucretius 4. 703 *rēfrigescit; Aetna* 440 *rēfrixit;* Virgil *Georgics* 2. 175 *rēcludere, Aeneid* 11. 140 *rēplet,* 11. 380 *rēplenda;* Horace *Carmen* 3. 24. 29 *rēfrenare;* Ovid *Metamorphoses* 8. 41 *rēcludere;* Valerius Flaccus 4. 231 *rēclusa* and 4. 35 *rēclinem.*[10] In itself, then, the weight of the scansion is slightly less heavy than Kenney at first reckoned. And yet who would be unhappy, if it goes with the breach in style, to see the scansion go? But to return to Willis: ". . . the attentive reader," he asserts, "will have no difficulty in recognizing the variants as proceeding from attempts to make metre out of *dicere gressus.*" The attentive reader will rather ask why, if R's *dicere egressus* is such an attempt, it happens not to make meter. As for context, from Daedalus' point of view it may be a *reditus* (cf. 29 "da reditum puero," a factor contributing to *regressus?*), but from Minos' and Ovid's and the reader's it is more naturally an *egressus.*

Our confidence in Willis' exegesis is in fact shaken by the very first error he selects to expose. "It is," he states, "a remarkable infirmity of a noble mind that makes Lachmann read *defleuimus* with OQ at Lucr. 3,907."

> Tu quidem, ut es leto sopitus, sic eris aeui
> quod superest, cunctis priuatus doloribus aegris.

6. For a list of expressions of commerce and finance in verses 17–49, see L. C. Curran, "Ovid *Amores* 1. 10," *Phoenix* 18 (1964): 315–16.

7. A. Ker, "Notes on Some Passages in the Amatory Poems," in *Ovidiana,* ed. N. Herescu (Paris, 1958), p. 225.

8. "Notes on Ovid: II," *CQ,* n.s. 9 (1959): 254.

9. "Grattiana," *CR,* n.s. 15 (1965): 14.

10. See also E. J. Kenney, review of *Gli epigrammi attribuiti a L. Anneo Seneca* by C. Prato, *CR,* n.s. 15 (1965): 188, n. 1 (citing N. M. Horsfall); E. Courtney, "A New Text of the *Aetna,*" *CR* n.s. 16 (1966): 50, n. 1.

At nos horrifico cinefactum te prope busto
insatiabiliter *defleuimus*, aeternumque
nulla dies nobis maerorem e pectore demet.

[Lucr. 3. 904–8 (p. 58)]

Quite the contrary: it is a remarkable strength. Editors have followed Lachmann here not because they regard the *codices interpolati*—and thus *deflebimus*—with Lachmann's "frantic hatred," but because, presumably, they judge OQ's *defleuimus* to be the better reading. What charge does Willis bring against it? "The perfect not only interrupts the series of future tenses, but is nonsense in itself: have the speakers finished weeping? Then their weeping was not insatiable. Are they still weeping? Then with what right do they use the perfect tense?" Not so fast. *Deflere*, first of all, is almost a *uox technica* for *lamentatio*. Mark too the word order, "te . . . busto . . . / insatiabiliter defleuimus"; surely *busto* localizes and defines, as technically it should, the activity of *defleuimus*. Does Willis fancy that the speakers will be weeping at the tomb forever? Forever is, of course, hyperbole. (One wonders, by the by, what he would make of the logic of *perpetuo* at Juv. 10. 33–34 "perpetuo risu pulmonem agitare solebat / Democritus.") And finally, as there is a temporal contrast in 904 "ut es [*sc.* nunc] leto sopitus ∾ sic eris . . . ," so is there here: we have wept for you at the tomb; we will sorrow over you forever (*aeternumque*).

Later come examples from Propertius.

territa uicinas Teia clamat aquas

[Prop. 4. 8. 59 (p. 107)]

"This means," Willis writes, " 'Teia in panic cries out that there are aqueducts hard by.' " Means only, or necessarily, that? Willis does not explain that he is echoing here Goold's objections to the syntax of *clamare*. Hence no doubt his ". . . that there are. . . ." But hear Goold himself: "What ghastly Latin!" he exclaims, ". . . *clamat* is not the same as *poscit;* . . . *clamare* of shouts introduces direct speech."[11] The restriction is too severe. Shackleton Bailey had already cited Quintilian *Declamationes* 12. 6 "ut arma bello, ut aqua incendio inclamari publice solent."[12] Add Seneca *Epistle* 17. 3 "cum aqua (Gertz et Bücheler: *aliqua* codd.) conclamata est, quomodo exeat, non quid efferat, quaerit." I have borrowed this citation from E. Fraenkel, who continues: "Hier verhält sich *aqua conclamata est* zu *aquam clamare* genau wie *conclamatis latronibus* (Apuleius *Met.* 3, 27, 7) zu dem von W. Schulze, *Berl. Sitzgsber.* 1918, 501, n. 2 (*Kl. Schriften* 179 n. 4) damit zusammengestellten *latrones clamauit* (Petron. 14, 5). Weiter wird im Thesaurus Juvenal 3, 198 *iam poscit aquam* zitiert und schliesslich Plutarch 20, 7 οἱ δ' ὥσπερ ἐμπρησμῷ βοηθοῦντες ἐβόων ὕδωρ, was vermutlich das *aquam clamabant* einer lateinischen Vorlage wiedergibt."[13] So much then for the syntax; the real rub here is the plural, where we should have expected the singular, in a call for water. Taken, however, as a reference to the surrounding aqueducts, *aquas* is perfectly idiomatic and derives its meaning from the opening of the poem, "Disce, quid *Esquilias* hac

11. "*Noctes Propertianae*," *HSCP* 71 (1966): 61.
12. *Propertiana* (Cambridge, 1956), p. 257.
13. *Beobachtungen zu Aristophanes* (Rome, 1962), p. 31, n. 1; see also p. 32, n. 4.

nocte fugarit *aquosas* . . ." (1). Thus Phillimore renders, "Teia, terrified, screams for water—not far to seek in that quarter!" What, according to Willis, "editors like to imagine" the MS text means—"she called upon her neighbors for water"—is its meaning with Barber's conjecture *uicinis*. Let us put this conjecture, and Palmer's, and even Willis' refinement of Palmer's ("territa 'uicinae' Teia clamat 'aquam' ") in the apparatus; but let us not pretend for a moment that the problem admits of comfortable certitude. Diggle in his review of Willis assumed the proper attitude ("if the line is faulty") but went too far in labelling the Palmer–Willis conjecture "not Latin." Latin it is. And my colleague Professor J. P. Sullivan has a note, forthcoming in *Museum Criticum*, rebutting Diggle on the point.

> Certa loquor, sed nulla fides; neque enim Ilia quondam
> uerax Pergameis Maenas habenda malis.
> [Prop. 3. 13. 61–62 (p. 108)]

For the hexameter Willis accepts, by merely announcing that Goold "well sustains" it, Richmond's *neque uilia quondam*.[14] The *Pergameis* . . . *malis* of the pentameter he then calls "pure rubbish." "It could only mean," he assures us, " 'who ought to have been considered a true prophetess by the naughty Trojans.' " Strange that no other modern commentator, or one, bestows a thought on this "only" meaning and construction. But never mind: we are being prepared for a new emendation. Relying on Luck's *Pergamei* . . . *mali*, Willis proceeds to write—or rather to say that "Propertius wrote"—*Pergameis* . . . *mali*. A fact which might have dissuaded him, had he troubled to ascertain it, is that *Pergameus -a -um* is never used as a substantive in Latin verse.[15]

Maligners of the paradosis fail to tell us that *enim* is the *mot juste* for introducing a mythological exemplum.[16] And if Cassandra is to be identified adequately, *Ilia* seems wanted with *Maenas*. For this there are two reasons. First, *Maenas* in itself, *pace* the lexicons, does not mean "prophetess"; it means "a raving follower of Dionysus"—a follower, that is, of a Greek, not a Trojan, deity. For the epithet, compare Propertius 4. 1. 51 *Pergameae* . . . *uatis* (also of Cassandra). Second, those who remove the notion of raving, making *Maenas* "prophetess" rather than "raving woman," are removing a traditionally essential element of Cassandra's character, as witness *furor* in verse 65. The other element of her character, prophecy, is therefore left to reside in *uerax*. Phillimore's translation, by supplying "prophetess" with *uerax*, catches the distinction: "No, neither was the Trojan Bacchante in old days destined to be accepted as a true"—rather *truthful*—

14. The reading, in fact, of Richmond's late and nondescript MS—cod. Cantabrig. Bibl. Univers. Add. 3394. Which reading then begot which? The answer I reach is exactly the reverse of that reached by Goold, "*Noctes Propertianae*," p. 94. The original was *neque enim Ilia:* in the form *neque·n ilia*, with *enim* so abbreviated, this was all but certain to produce *neque uilia*. Professor W. Clausen has kindly furnished, *per litteras*, a stylistic objection to *neque uilia*. On the tendency of Augustan poets to avoid *neque*, see his remarks in "On Editing the *Ciris*," *CP* 59 (1964): 100. According to Schmeisser's concordance, Propertius has 204 instances of *nec*, yet only twenty-five of *neque*. In all but six of the latter *neque* is elided. In five of the six lack of elision conveniently produces a dactylic first foot; only the remaining 2. 28A. 5 ". . . neque crimina caeli" looks therefore to be unique. But here, as Clausen suspects, Propertius may have wished "to avoid the cacemphaton 'nec crimina.' "

15. See D. C. Swanson, *The Names in Roman Verse* (Madison, 1967), s.v.

16. See R. G. M. Nisbet and M. Hubbard, *A Commentary on Horace: "Odes," Book 1* (Oxford, 1970), ad 1. 22. 9.

"prophetess in the woes of Pergamum."[17] How then to take *Pergameis . . . malis?* Goold's statement that "the dative-ablative has no legitimate construction here" is far too categorical. Perhaps the words are, as Butler–Barber take them, ablative of attendant circumstance ("amid . . ."); otherwise, if they specify *uerax*, they may be ablative of respect or even, if they amplify *quondam*, ablative of time. For their meaning and their gender and number, neuter plural, compare Ovid *Ibis* 252 "sint tua Troianis non leuiora malis."

Under "Deliberate Falsification of a Sound Text" Willis instances Macrobius *Saturnalia* 1. 7. 37, a quotation from the *Annales* of Accius.

> Maxima pars Graium Saturno et maxime Athenae
> conficiunt sacra, quae Cronia esse iterantur ab illis,
> eumque diem celebrant. . . .
>
> [Accius *Ann.* frag. 3 Morel (p. 122)]

"Here the metre stumbled two scribes, who were not familiar with the synizesis which early Latin poets allowed themselves: the twelfth-century Florentinus has *huncque*, and the fifteenth-century Matritensis has *cumque*. One can only regret that the nineteenth-century Aemilius Baehrens proposed *conque*." But what about *this* synizesis of this form of *is* in this meter and genre? The reader may remember that forms of *is* are rare in dactylic poetry,[18] that some forms are rarer than others, and that the accusative masculine singular is among the rarest of all. Even Ennius, Accius' precursor, uses *sum* instead of *eum* in his *Annales*. And the consummate metrist Lucian Müller makes the following pronouncement: "porro haud quisquam dactylicorum praeter genetiuum et datiuum numeri singularis pronominis, quod est *is*, formas coegisse inuenitur. quod non credet casu factum esse qui sciet Ennium, ne illa quae sunt *eum*, *eam*, *eos*, *eas* una admitteret syllaba, dixisse *sum*, *sam*, *sos*, *sas*."[19] The *Thesaurus*, for its part, implies that the present text harbors the only example of monosyllabic *eum* in extant dactylic verse. Indeed, so chary of this *eumque* is Buchwald that, far from simply mentioning the conjecture *conque*, he is himself led to propose *em-* or *im-* or *sumque* (*TLL*, 7:458. 5–6). My intention here has not been to reject *eumque*, which I would in fact accept, but to accept it in a different spirit, a spirit of reservation based on an awareness of the evidence. A reasonable course for an editor would therefore be to protect himself by marking a *locus suspectus* and recording a conjecture *exempli gratia*. In his Teubner edition of Macrobius Willis did neither. More yet. Scornful in his conclusion ("one can only regret that the nineteenth-century Aemilius Baehrens proposed *conque*"), he unfortunately has the wrong target and the wrong century. *Conque* belongs to W. Morel and first saw the light in 1927 (in his revision of Baehrens' *Fragmenta Poetarum Latinorum*, hence perhaps the blunder).

17. For Willis, be it noted, "true prophetess" serves to translate *verax . . . Maenas*.

18. B. Axelson, *Unpoetische Wörter* (Lund, 1945), pp. 70–71.

19. *De re metrica poetarum Latinorum praeter Plautum et Terentium*² (Leipzig, 1894), p. 322, a sweeping pronouncement. For precise details, see now J. D. Mikalson, "Ennius' Usage of *Is Ea Id*," *HSCP* 80 (1976): 171–77. Important for us is not so much the Ennian **so-* as its implication—a strange intolerance in epic, subsequent and consequent, of oblique forms of *is*.

Under "Combinations of Words by Wrong Division" Willis provides just two examples, one of which is the following passage:

> Philosophia unde dicta sit apparet; ipso enim nomine fatetur. *Quidam et* sapientiam quidam ita finierunt ut dicerent diuinorum et humanorum scientiam; quidam ita: "Sapientia est nosse diuina et humana et horum causas."
>
> [Sen. *Epist.* 89. 4 (p. 88)]

Here is Willis' appraisal: "Thus the oldest manuscript, Bamberg. V.14 of the ninth century; the other manuscripts omit the second *quidam.* Without altering a single letter, Madvig wrote: . . . ipso enim nomine fatetur QUID AMET. Sapientiam quidam ita finierunt. . . . I am sorry to be less delighted with this emendation than the rest of the learned world seems to be. The observation *ipso enim nomine fatetur*, readily intelligible in itself, is not improved by the otiose addition of *quid amet*—otiose not only because Seneca's readers were perfectly familiar with the etymology to which he alludes, but also because philosophy has just been defined as *sapientiae amor et affectatio.* Also, *nomine fatetur* is a standard clausula, while *fatetur quid amet* is no sort of clausula at all. Finally, the second *quidam* is found only in B (according to Reynolds' critical apparatus), and without it the simplest emendation is to strike out the *et*, thus arriving at the text printed by Lipsius." One shares the rest of the learned world's delight: Madvig's emendation is brilliant. That *quid amet* should here become *quidam et*, given the following *quidam . . . quidam*, was almost inevitable. By contrast, that *quid amet*, which is so pertinent to the context, could be produced "without altering a single letter" defies all probability. One is surprised in any event that Willis, arguing as he does, omits to mention that *quidam et* might be a corruption of *quid amet*, which was (or which he might assume was) in origin an explanatory gloss. No matter: what misled *editores priores* was the loss in most MSS through haplography of the second *quidAM* after *sapientiAM*, not fastidiousness about Willis' mooted tautology and certainly not prose rhythm (to which they were indifferent). The clausula I will not press. I will simply observe that the second edition of the *OCD* (s.v. "Prose rhythm") states that Willis' "standard clausula" is "avoided by Seneca." And A. W. de Groot assigns it a frequency of but 1.5 percent.[20] More important, Willis' objection that *quid amet* would be "otiose" does not carry conviction. Strictly, after "Philosophia unde dicta sit apparet," even the bare "ipso enim nomine fatetur" would be "otiose." If it "apparet," what need of an *enim*-clause to explain? As for his point that "Seneca's readers were perfectly familiar with the etymology," so they were, but what was that to Seneca? In the same epistle, eleven lines below, we find him saying: "Sapientia est quam Graeci σοφίαν uocant. Hoc uerbo Romani quoque utebantur, sicut philosophia nunc quoque utuntur. . . ." Or take Cicero *Tusculan Disputations* 5. 9 ". . . hos se appellare sapientiae studiosos (id est enim philosophos)": would Willis delete the parenthesis as "otiose"? To delete explicit reference to the etymology of φιλοσοφ- is to obliterate a feature of style, one common even in Greek writers (Plat. *Symp.* 204A, *Rep.* 475B; Diog. Laert. 1. 12). The matter is illuminated—and one would think settled—by Isidore *Etymologiae* 2. 24. 1–3: "Philosophia

20. *Der antike Prosarhythmus* (Groningen, 1921), pp. 108–9.

est rerum humanarum diuinarumque cognitio cum studio bene uiuendi con iuncta . . . ipsud autem nomen Latine interpretatum *amorem sapientiae profitetur*. Nam Graeci φιλο- amorem, σοφίαν sapientiam dicunt." (Cf. also 8. 6. 2 ". . . iste interrogatus quid profitetur, uerecundo nomine philosophum, id est amatorem sapientiae se esse respondit. . . ."[21]) Notice especially that Seneca did not write, like the *grammaticus* Isidore, "ipso enim nomine fatetur amorem sapientiae." He wrote, like a man of letters, ". . . quid amet," an indirect question which would permit his readers to supply for themselves the object of *amet*. Compare, finally, Cicero *De officiis* 2. 5 ". . . sapientia . . . hanc igitur qui expetunt philosophi nominantur, nec quicquam aliud est philosophia, *si interpretari uelis*, praeter studium sapientiae. Sapientia autem est, ut a ueteribus philosophis definitum est, rerum diuinarum et humanarum causarumque, quibus eae res continentur, scientia. . . ." First a translation of φιλοσοφ· and then a definition, exactly as in Seneca. "Exemplis docendum erat," insisted Lachmann, "non optandum et fingendum." Why then in a textual problem like this one, where parallels of thought and diction are imperative, does Willis disdain them? The conspicuous scarcity of such parallels in the specimen passages of his book is in fact a capital defect. True, with parallels of types of corruption the book fairly overflows; but in criticism these parallels are secondary to those.

Sometimes in explaining corruptions Willis either errs or, where more than one explanation is possible, assigns only one. I make little of his statement (p. 84) that "*q* does not look much like *a*." "*a* is merely *q* without a tail," as Housman seems to have written for his benefit.[22] And why does he deploy two passages, Lucan 5. 190–92 and Virgil *Georgics* 2. 423–28, under the heading "Influence of the Context" in chapter 14, "Preoccupation with Other Matter"? These are errors of perseveration and belong in the preceding chapter.[23] In the same chapter one or two of his examples of "Literary Reminiscence" challenge demur. Consider the contention (p. 100) that PV's *aratro* in Lucan 7. 861 ". . . nec terram quisquam mouisset *arator*" was inspired by Virgil *Georgics* 2. 513 "agricola incuruo terram dimouit *aratro*." Maybe so. But did not Lucan's scribes more likely invert two letters, as Germanicus' did at *Phaenomena* 153 *arator/aratro?* Or, to be jocular, the scribes of PV might have kept *arator*—and denied Willis his observation—if they had remembered their Propertius (4. 1. 25 ". . . *movebat arator*"), or might have obliged him the less by remembering their Virgil through their Ovid (*Met.* 5. 341 ". . . unco glaeb*am dimouit aratro*") or their Ovid through their Isidore (*Etym.* 17. 3. 1). In a discussion of "Patterns of Internal Rhyme" Willis regards (p. 104) the variant reading *animos* at Ovid *Remedia* 147—"eripiunt omnes *animo* sine uulnere neruos"—as an accommodation to *neruos*. Again, maybe so.

21. It is clear that Seneca and Isidore go back ultimately to the same source: *Epist.* 89. 9 "Philosophiae tres partes esse dixerunt . . . moralem, naturalem, rationalem" ∾ *Etym.* 2. 24. 3 "Philosophiae species tripertita est: una naturalis . . . altera moralis . . . tertia rationalis."

22. *Classical Papers* (Cambridge, 1972), p. 418.

23. For a wider view of errors of perseveration, see my articles "*Apollonius Resartus:* A Study in Conjectural Criticism," forthcoming in *CP*, and "More on the Text of *Apollonius of Tyre*," forthcoming in *RhM*.

But can one rigidly exclude the influence of the preceding *omnes*, or a dittography of the *s* in the following *sine*? On page 143, in a chapter on "Attempts to Correct Metre," he questions, *more suo*, the reading of the OCT at Ovid *Amores* 2. 16. 40 *saxa cruore rubent*. He favors the variant *sanguine saxa rubent*. "A copyist's eye," he observes, "could easily have passed from *SAnguine* to *SAxa*, leaving a gap which was plugged in a very workmanlike way with *cruore*. On the other hand, I can see no very plausible process which would have led from *saxa cruore rubent* to *sanguine saxa rubent*." Why not? Could not a copyist's eye have passed, almost as easily, from *cRUore* to *RUbent?* The gap would then have been plugged by the more common word for "blood." Or perhaps there was no gap; perhaps the more common *sanguis* did but supplant, with meter necessitating a change in word order, the less common *cruor*. Compare *Corpus Glossariorum Latinorum* Goetz 4. 326 "cruentus: sanguinolentus," 4. 436 "cruor: sanguis." Nor, in a discussion of "Transposition of Words" (p. 147), are all Willis' examples, as he appears to conceive, clearly those in which a word has been accidentally omitted and then restored to the wrong place. Here he neglects Headlam's—or Porson's or Cobet's—*simplex ordo*.[24] By this mechanism words are rearranged, deliberately or inadvertently, according to the order they would have in prose. Probably to this we should attribute Ovid *Ars amatoria* 2. 277 "sunt uere nunc/nunc uere sunt" ("aurea *sunt uere nunc* saecula . . .") and 2. 471 "uolucres aer/aer uolucres" ("silua feras, *uolucres aer* accepit habendas"). Willis, incidentally, quotes only the transposed words and not their context; and in the case of *Ars amatoria* 2. 205, by quoting only "uictum nec/nec uictum" where the text reads *uictam ne*, he has rather oversimplified.

I subjoin some minor criticisms. On page 107, Willis states that "internal rhyme between unrelated words"—he means unrelated epithet and substantive—"is scarcely probable in Latin poetry of the Golden Age." And yet it does occur. In Propertius, whose text Willis is endeavoring here to emend, witness 1. 17. 5 "quin etiam absent*i* possunt tibi, Cynthia, uent*i*," 4. 11. 65 "uidimus et fratr*em* sellam geminasse curul*em*" and, in a pentameter, 1. 5. 20 "discere et exclus*um* quid sit abire dom*um*."[25] On page 136, Willis discusses Manilius 1. 422–23. Diggle drew attention to one error of fact ("Ellis examined the Matritensis not in 1906 but in 1893") in his review. Here is another: "The manuscripts read . . . *Timidi*." Willis has unwittingly repeated an error in Housman's first volume, an error now almost hopelessly ingrained through Housman's further remark (*praef*. xiii) that for Scaliger "to write *tumidi* for *timidi* in 1. 422 was a feat of easy brilliancy." What the manuscripts read is *tumidi* (see addenda, p. 98 of the 1937 reprint of vol. 1). In the discussion (p. 144) of Ovid *Heroides* 14. 91 "conatoque queri (et conata queri)," Willis might have quoted the other metrical makeshift, which is far more insidious, *conatoque loqui*. Same page, *Heroides* 15. 69 "et tanquam desint quae me sine fine fatigent (et tanquam desit quae me hac sine cura fatiget)":

24. See G. Thomson, "*Simplex Ordo*," *CQ*, n.s. 15 (1965): 161–75 (with references).

25. The interested are directed to B. O. Foster, "On Certain Euphonic Embellishments in the Verse of Propertius," *TAPA* 40 (1909): 34; K. Zelzer, "Zum Reim in der römischen Elegie," *WS* 79 (1966): 465–77; O. Skutsch, "Readings in Propertius," *CQ*, n.s. 23 (1973): 318.

had Willis but quoted the next verse, "accumulat *curas* filia parua meas," he would have furnished his readers an additional ground for condemning *hac sine cura*—poverty of diction.[26] Finally, it is absurd to say, at least without qualification, that the text of Catullus is "little better" than that of Propertius (p. 158).[27]

J. M. HUNT
University of California, Santa Barbara

26. On these two passages as handled in the most recent edition of the *Heroides*, see my review in *CP* 70 (1975): 217.

27. I make grateful acknowledgment finally to R. Renehan. Several points made in this review have come from him, and the discussion of Sen. *Epist.* 89. 4 (pp. 347–48) has come from him *in toto*.

BOOK REVIEWS

La faute tragique. By SUZANNE SAÏD. Textes à l'appui: histoire classique. Paris: François Maspero, 1978. Pp. 536.

Work on the early Greeks which comes to us from Paris—especially in a series edited by Pierre Vidal-Naquet—brings with it certain expectations, which in the present case will be disappointed or relieved, depending on the bias of the reader. This is not a work of structural analysis, but of old-fashioned philology in the best sense. The spine of the book is provided by a series of word studies: ἁμαρτία, ἄτη, ὕβρις, ἀδικία, and others, with their verbal and adjectival derivatives, are traced instance by instance through Homer and the tragic poets, with appropriate contextual material drawn from Attic prose and (to a small extent) from Aristophanes. Words, of course, have meanings only in contexts; here each instance is carefully placed within the work taken as a whole, so that we find in this book a number of interpretations of plays—some fuller than others—and of a number of prose works as well. The central topic of the book is *character* in Aristotle's sense, character as displayed in better and worse choices. Shifting evaluations of character in Homer and the fifth century are traced through analyses of diction and plot.

From one point of view this book is squarely in the Paris tradition. The whole is an elaboration of suggestions made by J.-P. Vernant: that tragedy can best be understood as placed between, and incorporating, older and newer modes of evaluating character, with resulting incoherences and contradictions. In the older mode, wrongdoing is defined in terms of objective damage, especially to the actor himself or to those with whom he is in solidarity; guilt is collective, so that punishment justly falls on others than the actor, and justice is associated with the retributive reciprocity of the *lex talionis*. Wrongdoing is a kind of culpable madness or folly, and actions are simultaneously attributable to the actor and to the god who constrains his action—without, however, relieving the actor of responsibility. In the newer mode, wrongdoing has more to do with subjective intention and the violation of a rule or standard; individuals are responsible for their own acts only, while justice has more to do with restitution than with retribution. Wrongdoing is often advantageous and may be undertaken with cool rationality; the acts of god are distinct from—and even in opposition to—the acts of man. The earlier mode of thinking is characteristic of the *Iliad;* it still appears in Euripides, but only to be criticized from the other point of view.

Saïd sees this transition as an extended process which can be traced, particularly through the sequence of the tragedians (with Sophocles, even in his last works, remaining firmly conservative). The process is not presented as a triumphant progress toward reason (or, as in Nietzsche, as a regress in the same direction), but rather as a shift through intermediate stages from one relatively stable and coherent view to another, equally coherent (if less stable) view created by Plato. The treatment is historicist, in that the poets are taken to represent their age, rather than as shaping it or standing in opposition to it; the organization, however, is not historical but by topics. After an initial section on ἁμαρτία in the *Poetics* and on attempts to use the term in relation to the *Oedipus Rex* (a section which forms, so far as I can see, no integral part of the argument), there follows a detailed study of the etymology and semantic field of ἁμαρτία. The next section is on the gradual attenuation of the notion that wrongdoing is something that damages the actor; S. then examines the gradual linking of responsibility to the intentional and the voluntary. The same process is then looked at from another point of view: wrongdoing, which had first been a violation of the privileges of god or man, becomes a violation of some law of man or nature. Finally, we hear of the gradual divorce of the advantageous from the just.

This topical order requires S. to treat the same texts several times, and there is some repetition. In addition, interpretations of the texts to which S. has devoted the most care—particularly the *Prometheus*, *Oresteia*, *Antigone*, *Philoctetes*, and *Hippolytus*—are broken up; the *Hippolytus*, for instance, is presented in seven distinct sections. The book is not, of course, about the tragedies, but about the background of tragedy; nevertheless, the interpretations of particular works (not only tragedies—S. is especially good on Antiphon's *Tetralogies* and Gorgias' *Palamedes*) are important in their own right, and it will repay the reader interested in a particular work to use the well-arranged index in order to trace that work through the argument.

A treatment of these themes in relation to these texts must often choose between being original and being right. S. has chosen the sounder course, and we are once again informed that Aeschylus was concerned with the relations between god and man, while Sophocles was more concerned with human things, particularly that special human creature called the hero; Euripides dramatized conflicts between reason and irrational forces. Even these familiar insights, however, are given new life by the mass and freshness of the detailed analysis brought to support them. The book has no startling thesis and is in a way intellectually modest; it nevertheless contains many original conclusions and small surprises and continually provokes further thought. The argument could easily have been crushed by the weight of documentation; in fact, the book is so lucidly written and carefully ordered (and so beautifully produced) that it carries us through.

This book, in short, is a major contribution to our understanding of tragedy and of the problem of evaluating action; it will surely be widely used by scholars and students for a generation at the least.

James M. Redfield
University of Chicago

Xenophon the Athenian: The Problem of the Individual and the Society of the "Polis." By W. E. HIGGINS. Albany: State University of New York Press, 1977. Pp. xv + 183. $15.00.

Xenophon (to paraphrase Wordsworth) has long been an author there was none to love, and very few to praise. Leo Strauss wrote extensively on him and with characteristic brilliance discovered subtleties and complexities which, even after his exposition, remain invisible to the common reader. J. K. Anderson's book (rather too casually written off here) is primarily biographical. Otherwise Xenophon has largely been a problem in *Quellenforschung* and chronology, or in rhetorical analysis, or has been discussed in terms of his intellectual limitations. Higgins, by contrast, evidently moved by a real affection for his author, shows us a Xenophon not only worthy of our respect as a personality but also of our attention as a thinker. A debt to Strauss is explicit and obvious, but this is a considerably more straightforward reading. The whole of Xenophon's work (except the *Cynegeticus*) is treated sympathetically, if rapidly; the resulting sketch (which claims to be no more) should send us back to Xenophon's text with a renewed eye for his merits.

For H., Xenophon wrote different kinds of books because he had different things to say. One of the merits of the book is its attention to generic constraints—which help to explain, for instance, differences between the *Agesilaus* and the *Hellenica*. At the same time, H. sees the corpus as a unity. For him, Xenophon, in youth a companion of Socrates, became a true Socratic only at the end of his life, after his experience of action and his observation (in exile) of events had brought home to him the meaning and importance of Socrates' teaching. At this point, now back in Athens, he began to write, perhaps prompted by his renewed contact with other Socratics, perhaps by his "reincorporation into the city." All of his works were, therefore, retrospective; taken together they constitute a kind of report on his own education, including his picture of the Master in the Socratic books, his ideal account of education and its consequences in the *Cyropaedia*, his (more or less fictionalized) pictures of men of action in the *Hiero* and *Agesilaus*, his account of himself in the *Anabasis* and of his times in the *Hellenica*. All the essays, including those on horsemanship, are worked into this pattern. The *Poroi*, for instance, turns out to be Socratic in inspiration: "self-knowledge is once again revealed as the basic constituent of proper growth." H. sees Xenophon as one who learned in a hard school to look beyond war to politics, and beyond politics to philosophy—a philosophy, it should be said, not of brilliant dialectics, but of sober forethought and moderation.

The account here given is obviously controversial to the last degree: it is not even clear (as H. admits) that Xenophon ever returned to Athens. H. complains of those scholars who "in methodological circles . . . arguing from the supposed facts of Xenophon's life obtained from his works . . . try . . . to use material so derived to explain Xenophon's ideas." He himself, however, is subject to the same objection. Yet it must be said that this view of Xenophon's development is not impossible and does lead to interesting interpretations—particularly of the *Anabasis*, here seen as a type of autobiographical *Bildungsroman*.

Careful argument and exact inference are not H.'s strength; he is not likely to convince any who begin by disagreeing with him. Many will, as he disagrees with many; in fact, his comments on previous scholarship (except for Strauss) are largely dismissive. His book will probably annoy some scholars, and on many points it leaves itself open to attack. It will be a pity if these flaws obscure the suggestive possibilities of H.'s imaginative approach.

The merits of the book, and its limitations, are well represented by the section on the *Constitution of the Lacedaemonians*. This section is also crucial to H.'s general thesis: that Xenophon was no laconizer, but rather a faithful adherent of Athenian values. Here, as elsewhere, H. offers a comparatively straightforward version of Strauss's view; whereas for Strauss the *Constitution* is "comic," for H. it is "ironic," a criticism of Spartan *nomoi* disguised as a compliment.

It is hard to know what to make of this; the arguments which H. advances are scrappy and of varying merit. H. points to various anomalies in Xenophon's presentation: Lycurgus' law on the age of marriage is no sooner stated than we are told of provisions for handling deviations from it; Xenophon's praise of eugenic arrangements and of Spartan theft seem contrary to his views elsewhere. The importance of private wealth at Sparta is explicitly denied but implicitly admitted. *Constitution* 9. 6 "seems rather flat" to H. (but not to me); 10. 4 and 10. 7 are, he thinks, inflated in their rhetoric.

H. takes *Constitution* 14 as an integral part of the text and asserts that the rest of the essay explains the decline there confessed. Sparta, says H., confused repression with virtue and thus exacerbated the appetites; competition was exalted, and citizen was thus made enemy to citizen. The Spartan was "taught submission and aggression all at once," and the checks imposed by the community produced a "paradoxical exaggeration of the individual."

All this is well observed; no doubt the Spartan *nomoi* had such weaknesses, which can be deduced from Xenophon's account of them. The question is: did Xenophon see these implications, and, if so, why did he make his case in such an extraordinary form? The irony, if it exists, seems inept in contrast, for instance, to Socrates' enthusiasm (in the *First Alcibiades*) for the riches of the Spartan kings and his praise (to Alcibiades!) of the impregnable chastity of their queens. This example is also debatable; but, if we take the text as ironic, we begin to enjoy Socrates' manipulation of Alcibiades, and to see more point in it. If H. were right, Xenophon's text, reread this way, should seem more coherent than before, more meaningful. I do not find it so. Surely the anomalies exist, and such explanations of them as Luccioni's I find unpersuasive; similarly, the relation of *Constitution* 14 to the rest is an unsolved problem. But I do not think that H. has solved it.

James M. Redfield
University of Chicago

Chance and Intelligence in Thucydides. By LOWELL EDMUNDS. Cambridge, Mass.: Harvard University Press, 1975. Pp. 243. $11.00.

Lowell Edmunds' book is a reappraisal of the concepts of foresight (γνώμη), expertise (τέχνη), and simple accident (τύχη) in Thucydides' *History*. In a subtle and provocative monograph E. studies and finally attempts to reconcile an antithesis that lies near the heart of Thucydidean metaphysics, namely, the limits of planning and the province of chance, for the politician and for the historian who interprets politics.

The first chapter argues, from a close exegetical study of the speeches, that "The Periclean policy is thus, as Thucydides presents it, consciously humanistic and historical" (p. 28); it trivializes chance by reducing it to mere human error and insists on the invincibility of knowledge and skill applied to human affairs.

Exemplifying this invincibility are the supremacy of the Athenian fleet, of Athenian democracy, and, finally, of the fifth-century Greek view of man as the master of his fate (as opposed to the archaic notion of an all-powerful Tyche whose vicissitudes men must bear as best they can). Such a maximum view of human freedom and skill carries with it the imperatives of constant progress and, in particular, of dedication to the polis as the ultimate achievement of social history to date. Hence the Athenians' famous ἀπραγμοσύνη: "born neither to take rest themselves nor to allow it to others" (Thuc. 1. 70).

In chapter 2 ("The Lacedaemonians and Chance") E. contrasts Pericles' policy with the alternative viewpoint embraced by the Spartans and by Nicias, who is portrayed as a Spartan in all but name because of his attitude toward chance and planning. In the Spartans, the operative facet of γνώμη is not planning but resolve; victory is predicted for the city whose resolve can surmount the inevitable reverses of war. The strategic concomitant of this outlook is to minimize the risk factor, and the irony of Book 7 consists in the calamity that overtakes Nicias precisely because of his efforts to avoid danger and safeguard success (εὐτυχία).

E. next considers the implications of the ideas of foresight, skill, and chance for Thucydides and the methodology of his history. A reexamination of the passages where the historian comments on his method (τέχνη) concludes that for Thucydides there are always two levels of discourse: the course of events, "history," where different cities and statesmen act on their varying estimates of chance and intelligence, and, on the other hand, the historian's interpretation of these events (τὸ σαφές). Complete rationality is possible only in historical interpretation, where chance can be at last eliminated in an intelligible interplay of situation and psychology.

This short treatise is the most sophisticated critique of Thucydides to appear in English for many years, perhaps since the Second World War. It is attuned to the considerable volume of continental writing on the subject; not only the conclusions but the techniques of French and German *Thukydidesforschung* underlie the discussion. It is therefore interesting to compare the conclusions of a recent study of the same material by Pierre Huart, ΓΝΩΜΗ *chez Thucydide et ses contemporains* (Paris, 1973), which came out too late for consideration by E. Huart's approach is lexicographical, yet on many points his views are close to those of the broader study. For example, Huart writes, "γνώμη devient le symbole de tout ce que peut réaliser l'homme par la force de sa réflexion" (p. 173). Indeed, the bald statistics for Thucydides' use of γνώμη (120 examples in Books 1–4, 54 in Books 5–8) effectively highlight E.'s conclusion that for a brief moment there seemed no limit to what planning could achieve. Long before the end of the war, however, this promise had faded, replaced by the more traditional stance of a Hermocrates or a Gylippus: "the victory (from the actors' point of view) of the traditionally moderate understanding of tyche" (p. 185).

One might take issue with the author on some points of detail. For example, the account of the idiom ὡς ἕκαστος on page 160 seems to rest on a confusion of the unspecified with the exceptional. As for E.'s general approach, one might cavil at the apparent relegation of the course of events in favor of the philosophy behind them. Was not Thucydides' interest more in history than in historiography, more in Themistocles' or Pericles' delineation of the frontiers between accident and deliberation than in his own perception of the pattern? "In der Begrenzung," said Goethe, "zeigt sich der Meister"—an aphorism just as true of this original and stimulating essay.

K. Adshead
University of Canterbury

Crassus: A Political Biography. By B. A. MARSHALL. Amsterdam: Adolf M. Hakkert, 1976. Pp. iii + 205.

Marcus Crassus and the Late Roman Republic. By ALLEN MASON WARD. Columbia and London: University of Missouri Press, 1977. Pp. xi + 323. $15.50.

The long prevailing view that M. Licinius Crassus was essentially a failure as a politician—less able, less astute, less decisive, or less courageous than his sometime allies and rivals for supremacy, Pompey the Great and Caesar—is, as T. J. Cadoux saw over two decades ago,[1] quite paradoxical. Crassus failed at Carrhae, not at Rome. We are told in a recent succinct summary of the old orthodoxy that Crassus recognized only belatedly that "unarmed power" was "insecure."[2] But the conference at Luca in 56 gave Crassus a great command against Parthia (his first military command since 71) and the opportunity, it would seem, to achieve predominance at Rome, if "armed" political power was what was needed (as the summary suggests). Was Crassus' power then "insecure" on the eve of his greatest success? Similarly, if we accept the traditional view, adopted by the same author, that Crassus' attempts to build up his power in the 60s against that of Pompey and the "*optimates*" all ended in failure, how are we to explain the importance of his support to the success of the coalition of 59 misleadingly called the "First Triumvirate" by moderns?

An apparent alternative to the old orthodoxy, offered by F. E. Adcock in a capsule biography of Crassus,[3] contributed only in a limited way to a more plausible interpretation of Crassus' career. Adcock, following R. Syme's suggestion,[4] presented Crassus as simply a conservative politician primarily interested in making money (p. v), and thus not really engaged in any rivalry with Pompey for predominance. Adcock's approach to the supposed evidence of sharp conflict between Crassus and Pompey in the 60s provided—or rather could have provided, since it was largely ignored—a useful alternative to the rampant speculation that continues to construct schemes on the part of Crassus and countermoves by Pompey or his allies with little regard for the lack of credible evidence. It is impossible, however, to follow Adcock when he argues that Crassus entered the coalition of 59 merely because of his interest in a share of the expected bribe from Ptolemy Auletes and his supposed financial involvement in the Asian tax farm (pp. 43–44), or that Crassus undertook the command against Parthia primarily for the sake of the anticipated booty (pp. 48–49). Adcock's treatment is more paradoxical than the old orthodoxy. Crassus, who appears to have reached the pinnacle of power, is portrayed as virtually indifferent to it. In any case, Adcock did not explain how

1. "Marcus Crassus: A Revaluation," *G&R* 3 (1956): 153–61.
2. E. Badian, *OCD*², s.v. "Crassus" (4).
3. *Marcus Crassus, Millionaire* (Cambridge, 1966).
4. Review of *Caesar* by M. Gelzer, *JRS* 34 (1944): 96–97.

Crassus came by the power that enabled him to pursue his supposed single-minded interest in riches.

It should cause no surprise, then, that we suddenly have three revisionist treatments of Crassus' career, all agreed that he was to some extent a successful politician, if on little else of thematic importance. Along with the two biographies under review, the first full-scale studies since A. Garzetti's long articles of World War II vintage,[5] we must consider E. S. Gruen's extensive, if selective, discussion of Crassus' political activities in his recent massive analysis of the political life of the failing Republic.[6] Rather, it is strange at first glance that such attempts at revision have been so long in coming—a historiographical puzzle to which Gruen provides the probable solution. Of the three treatments Gruen's is by far the most persuasive.[7]

Crassus' career has been misinterpreted, Gruen clearly implies, because of the prevailing misconception that politics in the 70s and 60s were polarized: on one side most of the prominent members of the senatorial oligarchy (the *optimates*, as the misguided, including Marshall and Ward, persist in calling this ill-defined collection of politicians), on the other Pompey and his following, including some renegade oligarchs, but only for anomalous reasons. All other centers of power were of only very secondary importance. On this reconstruction Pompey's strength against the entrenched power of the oligarchy derived only from the loyalty of his veterans (or the threat that he would actually use military force) and from his popularity with the masses, the consequence of his military prestige and his support of popular reform and reformers. His aim was domination of the state, or at least a personal preeminence inconsistent with oligarchic rule.[8] In this political context Crassus' pursuit of personal power to rival Pompey's would necessarily seem much less effective and successful than that of his principal foe. Crassus held no military command between 71 and 54.[9] His support of popular reform or would-be reformers, except for his collaboration with Pompey in 70, bore little fruit.

Political power was, in fact, far from polarized. Gruen goes too far in denying the existence of any clear lines of factional division in the 70s and at least the early 60s,[10] but even a superficial prosopographical analysis shows that the senatorial oligarchy was extensively divided against itself and that Pompey often had the

5. "M. Licinio Crasso," *Athenaeum* 19 (1941): 1–37, 20 (1942): 12–40, 22–23 (1944–45): 1–62.

6. *The Last Generation of the Roman Republic* (Berkeley–Los Angeles–London, 1974), pp. 2–3, 66–74, 83–120, etc. A brief but important earlier contribution to reinterpretation may also be noted here: R. J. Rowland, "Crassus, Clodius, and Curio in the Year 59 B.C.," *Historia* 15 (1966): 217–23.

7. This is not to endorse all of Gruen's more general theses, on which see (with some reservations) the review by A. Bernstein, forthcoming in *The Historian* (1979). This reviewer would like to thank Professor Bernstein for an advance copy.

8. This sort of interpretation goes back to E. Meyer, *Caesars Monarchie und das Principat des Pompeius* (Stuttgart, 1922).

9. Cadoux, "Marcus Crassus," p. 156, suggested that Crassus was "experimenting" with "the device of relying on imperium held by others," but it is not clear how this would have served to build up his personal power.

10. See B. Twyman, "The Metelli, Pompeius, and Prosopography," in *Aufstieg und Niedergang der römischen Welt*, vol. 1, pt. 1, ed. H. Temporini (Berlin, 1972), pp. 816–74. Gruen (*CW* 69 [1976]: 492) rejects the reviewer's results as paradoxical because of the argument that L. Lucullus and Pompeius were on good terms politically before 66. But there is nothing paradoxical in suggesting that political relations between the two changed with changing circumstances.

support of a powerful faction within the oligarchy.[11] And, in the light of such analysis, Crassus' power can at last be explained. Crassus' great influence in the Senate is well attested. Gruen argues convincingly (pp. 66–74) that it was based on his following in the lower ranks of the Senate among the *pedarii*, not on any special influence among the *principes*. With the latter divided, Crassus could hold the balance, as Cethegus had by apparently similar means in the 70s.[12]

Gruen's selective discussion of Crassus' political activities certainly left room for additional study. His argument is formally circular: Crassus' success in politics is important evidence for the fragmentation of political power that explains his success.[13] It is most unfortunate, then, that neither Marshall nor Ward made more than casual use of *The Last Generation* —both because the chance to test Gruen's argument on Crassus was missed and because neither biographer arrives at any plausible alternative explanation of Crassus' power and success in terms of the general structure of political life. Indeed, neither recognizes that past misinterpretation of Crassus' career probably derived in the main from misconceptions of what that structure was. Marshall suggests that Crassus has been neglected and thus misunderstood because scholarly attention has focused on Pompey and Caesar (pp. 1–2), but this mistakes a symptom for a cause. Ward in a sweeping argument *ad homines* contends that scholars have been all but universally misled by ancient prejudice against Crassus' means of acquiring wealth and his supposed undue interest in it, and by a common prejudice against losers (pp. 2–3).

Marshall simply does not see the importance of discussing the attested series of episodes that constitute most of what we know directly of Crassus' activities in the context of political structure. A footnote to a vague discussion of Crassus' persistent efforts to build up his personal connections and hence his power casually refers to Gruen's argument about Crassus' strength among the *pedarii* as an "interesting view" (pp. 16 and 23–24, n. 116). Elsewhere Marshall cites discussions by Gruen and this reviewer on relations between Pompey and the Metelli in the 70s as though our conclusions were fully compatible (pp. 60–61, n. 31), whereas, while Gruen argues that there was little or no conflict between the Metelli and Pompey before 67, the present writer contends that some of the Metelli were actually Pompey's allies. The two studies together raise the fundamental question of whether there were sharp lines of factional division within the Sullan oligarchy.[14] Marshall offers explicit comment on the structure of political life only in a brief discussion of the impact of the reforms carried out by Pompey and Crassus as consuls in 70 (p. 58). He rightly rejects the notion that the colleagues aimed to undo the Sullan settlement and hence finds it doubtful that they represented a "popular" movement opposed to the *Sullani*. Similarly, he discounts the old

11. Gruen, *Last Generation*, pp. 47–82; Twyman, "The Metelli," pp. 832–74. Neither discussion is meant to be superficial, but a casual reading will substantiate the argument in the text.

12. Gruen, *Last Generation*, pp. 39–40, 43–45, 66–74. On Cethegus, see Twyman, "The Metelli," p. 853, n. 189.

13. Circular argument is, of course, the bane of prosopography. See T. F. A. Carney, "Prosopography: Payoffs and Pitfalls," *Phoenix* 27 (1973): 156–79.

14. E. S. Gruen, "Pompey, Metellus Pius, and the Trials of 70–69 B.C.: The Perils of Schematism," *AJP* 92 (1971): 1–16; Twyman, "The Metelli," pp. 816–74.

anachronism of parties of *populares* and *optimates*. But we are not told what to put in the place of these old constructions. At times we seem to be in the late Republic imagined by C. Meier without any durable organization among the political elite,[15] yet Marshall does not eschew prosopographical construction of political factions (e.g., pp. 9–10, 95).

Marshall might defend himself against this criticism on the grounds that he merely meant to reconsider the direct evidence for Crassus' activities and to show that this evidence can be interpreted quite differently than it usually has been, without tackling the much more difficult problem of the political context. This sort of history as the explication of texts—a misconception all too familiar from the work of numerous classicists—is so common that Marshall cannot be much blamed for following the pattern. Our other biographer cannot be let off so lightly.

Ward's entire treatment of Crassus' career down to the formation of the coalition of 59 depends on his argument that politics were virtually polarized by the 70s and throughout the 60s—"the loyal optimate heirs of Sulla" standing against Pompey and his following. Ward's prosopography serves only to give this traditional construction a mechanistic rigor. Rivalries among *optimates* are treated as of strictly secondary importance, the support that some who ought to have been *optimates* gave Pompey as anomalous (pp. 5–45, esp. 8–13). Ward admits that there were other centers of power, although the faction of Cethegus is the only one he mentions (p. 13 and n. 24); he clearly thinks, however, that they were of little importance. It was by maneuvering between the two principal poles of power that Crassus, so Ward believes, built up his personal influence: now strengthening his position in the Senate, now using Pompey's methods in attempts to rival the latter's popularity or to control countervailing resources (military or otherwise) of power.

Ward may have meant to head off criticism that his reconstruction largely ignores Gruen's analysis of political structure in *The Last Generation* by the disarming admission that his work was "virtually complete" when that book appeared in early 1974 (p. vii). But this means that Ward was content to produce a dated work, rather than to revise it in order to take account of a quite different interpretation of the structure of political life in Crassus' time, an interpretation which calls his whole treatment of Crassus' career into question.[16] The point is not that Ward's view that politics were essentially polarized in the 70s and 60s is beyond defence (Gruen probably goes too far in the opposite direction), but rather that Gruen's analysis again leads to a persuasive explanation of Crassus' great influence, which Ward does not and cannot provide. He is well aware that Crassus' following in the lower ranks of the Senate was a principal source of his power (pp. 77–82), but why

15. *Res publica amissa* (Wiesbaden, 1966).

16. If one judges from some later additions, the work did not go to press until 1976. Page references to an article published by W. C. McDermott in 1977 (p. 41, n. 27, and elsewhere) were perhaps added in proof (see p. vii). There are references to works by B. A. Marshall (p. 18, n. 20, p. 214, n. 61) and T. N. Mitchell (p. 200, n. 26) that appeared in 1975. Missing, however, from the bibliography and notes are: T. N. Mitchell, "Cicero, Pompey, and the Rise of the First Triumvirate," *Traditio* 29 (1973): 1–26, and D. L. Stockton, "The First Consulship of Pompey," *Historia* 22 (1973): 205–18.

this should have been so if Ward's *optimates* generally dominated that council is not explained.

Ward seems in fact to have been loath to reconsider, or even fully defend, his dated view of the structure of politics in the 70s and 60s against any substantial criticism. At the risk of seeming petulant, we may consider his treatment of the reviewer's long discussion of the multifarious evidence of factional division among the *Sullani* from 80 through 66.[17] Comparison of that discussion of political alignments with Ward's will show that they are opposed on so many points that it would be tedious to set them out here. Suffice it to note that some forty-odd pages of complex analysis are dismissed by Ward in a single brief footnote with the comment that the reviewer's argument that Pompey was backed until the last of those years by the Claudii, *some* Metelli (including Metellus Pius), and other associated *nobiles* "fails to take into account the evidence linking Catulus [a political opponent of Pompey on several occasions] with the leading Metelli" (p. 36, n. 5).

The analysis that leads Ward to this conclusion is superficial. The evidence in question indicates some political connection between Metellus Pius and Catulus in 65 and perhaps in 87 (pp. 15–16). The later instance followed the quarrel between Pompey and Metellus' cousin L. Lucullus in 66 over the latter's arrangements in the East, a quarrel which arguably (at least) was the occasion of the final breakdown of past political friendship among the three.[18] The earlier instance—a mission by Catulus and his father to persuade Metellus to intervene against Cinna and Marius—might, directly contrary to Ward's interpretation, be taken to indicate that there was no close political connection at the time between Metellus and the political circle of the Catuli. Ward takes it for granted (pp. 14–16, 26) that Q. Metellus Creticus, who joined with Catulus' brother-in-law Hortensius in the defence of Verres in 70, represented the "senior Metelli"; the awkward fact that M. Lucullus, Lucius' brother, was prepared to testify against Verres is buried in a note (p. 42, n. 34).

As a defence against the charge of petulance, we may add that Ward not only casually dismisses the reviewer's work, but also ignores R. F. Rossi's demonstration that the speech attributed to Licinius Macer in 73 by Sallust (*Hist.* 2. 98. 1–3M) must be in part a fabrication and P. A. Brunt's discussion of the role played by L. Lucullus' enemies in the Senate in whittling down his great Eastern command (pp. 15, 45) The reviewer called particular attention to both studies.[19]

The central theme in discussions of Crassus' career proper (as opposed to the political context) has long been his rivalry, real or supposed, with Pompey. Only Adcock and now more thoroughly Marshall have argued that this rivalry has been at least greatly exaggerated and is probably to a large extent a fabrication of

17. See n. 11.
18. Twyman, "The Metelli," pp. 862–73, and above, n. 10.
19. R. F. Rossi, "Sulla lotta politica in Roma dopo la morte di Silla," *Parola del Passato* 20 (1965): 113–52, esp. 136–38; P. A. Brunt, "The Equites in the Late Republic," *Second International Conference of Economic History, 1962*, vol. 1 (Paris, 1965), pp. 117–49, esp. 148–49; Twyman, "The Metelli," pp. 852, 865–66.

political propaganda intended to impede or destroy the cooperation of the two principals in 59 and after. Ward follows the traditional approach.

Indeed, Ward's views on the structure of politics in the 70s and 60s naturally lead him to the premise, stated as such rather than as a hypothesis, that Crassus from the 70s onward was engaged in constant rivalry with Pompey for political preeminence or supremacy at Rome (pp. 99, 105). How could it have been otherwise (we may ask) if Crassus' ambition could have been realized only by supplanting Pompey as the principal opponent of the supposedly united *optimates?* In any case, the premise enables Ward to fill many pages with speculative and often circular argument on supposed maneuvers by Crassus in opposition to Pompey. For example, since Pompey evidently favored the *Lex Aurelia iudiciaria*, Ward suggests that Crassus supported the more radical measure alluded to by Cicero in the *First Verrine* (pp. 105–7). Similarly, Crassus may have been behind the plan of Roscius in 67 to appoint two commanders against the pirates (p. 114). The passage of the *Lex Manilia* in 66, we are told, was a "severe setback" for Crassus (pp. 116–19). Since Caesar was connected to Crassus, the former only appeared to be an ally of Pompey in 67 and 66 (pp. 124–27). And so on.

Marshall's discussion provides a useful corrective to the excesses of Ward's approach. Restricting himself throughout to the actual evidence of Crassus' political activity, Marshall argues quite plausibly that there is in fact no reason to suppose that in the 60s Crassus and Pompey were engaged in an embittered or even direct rivalry for power. The evidence that they were, he contends, is largely the product of the propaganda of opponents of their coalition (esp. pp. 36–41, 92–103). Marshall no doubt goes too far in denying that Crassus at some time joined Lucullus in blocking the ratification of Pompey's *acta* (App. *BC* 2. 9; probably in 60, but the chronological implications of this difficult passage need more careful consideration than they seem to have received). It is difficult to believe that Cicero would still have thought that Crassus and Pompey needed to be reconciled at the end of that year, as Caesar proposed to do, if there had been no serious conflict between the two (Cic. *Att.* 2. 3. 3). Nevertheless, Marshall's argument that Crassus went to Asia in 62 to strike an agreement with Pompey, an elaboration of Adcock's suggestion, is attractive, if beyond confirmation (pp. 92–94; cf. Ward, pp. 193–96).

Additional comment here on the treatment by our two biographers of the various episodes of Crassus' career seems unnecessary. The evidence is notoriously difficult, and scholarly agreement on many long-debated matters is probably unattainable. In any case, both writers generally handle these episodes along the thematic lines already discussed.

In summation: neither of these works can be judged a success, but both will be useful to specialists. Ward's discussion of the evidence and modern interpretation (but only through 1971!) is very thorough and occasionally offers some valuable insights. Marshall's attack on the common supposition of sharp rivalry between Crassus and Pompey in the 60s deserves careful consideration in a fuller context than the author chose to provide.

Briggs L. Twyman
Texas Tech University

Die Religionszugehörigkeit der hohen Amtsträger des Römischen Reiches seit Constantins I. Alleinherrschaft bis zum Ende der Theodosianischen Dynastie (324–450 bzw. 455 n. Chr.). By RABAN VON HAEHLING. Antiquitas, ser. 3: Abhandlungen zur Vor- und Frühgeschichte, zur klassischen und provinzial-römischen Archäologie und zur Geschichte des Altertums, vol. 23. Bonn: Rudolf Habelt Verlag GmbH, 1978. Pp. xii + 680; 8 tables in text.

This ambitious dissertation has three major objectives: (1) determination of the religious preferences of a large group of Late Roman functionaries, (2) assessment of the impact of religion on imperial appointments, and (3) application of prosopographical data to illuminate the policies of the emperors. The study begins with the final defeat of Licinius and the removal of a potentially severe constraint on Constantine, and proceeds through the Theodosian dynasty, the epoch of the first systematic legal exclusion of pagans from public office. The prosopographical sample comprises the *magistri militum*, praetorian prefects, urban prefects of Rome and Constantinople, prefects of Egypt, proconsuls of Asia, Africa, and Achaea, and the *comites Orientis*—roughly, the *illustres* and *spectabiles* of the *Notitia Dignitatum*, all of whom were appointed directly by the emperor. Notably absent are the consuls, and surprisingly so, in view of the author's explicit assumption that the Christian emperors intended their officials, by abandoning the old gods, to serve as models for the governed: if a proconsul of Africa could have such an effect on his provincials, then why not the empire's eponymous magistrates on the population as a whole? Von Haehling also omits the imperial court, pleading limitations of space and the existence of ongoing relevant research in Germany. Still, the court is a fruitful source for the author's themes and the omission is regrettable.

The sole concern of the prosopographical survey is religious profession, not sincerity or intensity of belief. Unlike the editors of *The Prosopography of the Later Roman Empire*, who occasionally note this item in their biographies, H. establishes a detailed set of methodological principles to guide his investigations. The most trustworthy indicators are literary statement, epigraphic attestation (either direct or symbolic), and evidence of the private construction or adornment of religious edifices and works of art. Many previously employed criteria must be discarded. For example, pagans often contemplated refuge in *conventicula Christiani ritus*, and Augustine affirms that this was their right. Similarly, the religion of the recipient of a law should not be inferred from the measure's content; notoriously, Theodosius I addressed some of his sternest anti-pagan legislation to Virius Nicomachus Flavianus. Nor should one base a determination on knowledge of an individual's family; Fl. Ablabius' son was a pagan, and instances of brothers divided in their loyalties are on record. Several types of evidence must be treated differently according to whether one seeks to demonstrate paganism or Christianity. Thus, while many Christians (e.g., Asclepius, a fifth-century African bishop) had pagan theophoric names, no pagan is known to have borne a name with Christian connotations. The author also contends that Christians never dedicated their literary productions to pagans, although the reverse was common (the exposition of this point is not satisfying). The most delicate methodological issues arise from the involvement of secular officials in ecclesiastical affairs. H. rightly distinguishes duties performed by the regular bureaucracy (financial grants, church construction, legal settlements, maintenance of public order) and those entrusted to special imperial representatives (intervention in dogmatic disputes, attendance at or participation in extraordinary religious assemblies). Assignments of the first type went to the appropriate bureaucrat, regardless of his religion. H. plausibly suggests, however, that religious knowledge must have been a prerequisite of the special emissaries. He adds that Christian factions would surely have disputed the presence of a pagan official and that no pagan is attested in such a role. Finally, anti-pagan activity sanctioned by the central authority: imperial directives of this nature were frequently carried out unevenly in the provinces, and H. argues that rigid enforcement implies a Christian functionary. Clearly, H.'s criteria are stringent, and the very conservatism of his approach inspires confidence in his conclusions.[1]

These conclusions are presented in a series of tables and a lengthy chapter devoted to analyses of individual reigns. H. estimates that his sample is 86 percent complete and that the religious preferences of slightly more than half of the attested functionaries are known with some degree of certainty; unfortunately, the statistical reliability of such a distribution is nowhere disclosed. For Eastern civil offices, H. counts 51 pagan tenures,[2] 87 orthodox Christian, and 8 Arian; for Eastern military offices, 9 pagan, 25 orthodox Christian, 7 Arian; for Western civil offices, 83 pagan, 104 orthodox Christian, 1 Arian; for Western military offices,

1. Occasionally, H. departs from his methodological strictures: for example, the assertion that Petronius Probinus (*cos.* 341) was a Christian on the basis of the indubitable adherence of his sister, Faltonia Betitia Proba, and son, Sex. Claudius Petronius Probus, to the Faith. Sometimes, doubtless because of the vast quantity of source material, discussions are incomplete. H. cites *benignus* and *sanctus* on *CIL*, 6. 1681 to classify Sex. Anicius Paulinus (*cos.* 325) among the Christian office-holders, apparently unaware of the *v(irgini) v(estali) sanctissimae benignissimae* of *CIL*, 6. 2131. Other considerations support the author's conclusion, but this obstacle should have been noted. The principle that Christians dedicated their literary works to Christians is invoked to prove that Acilius Severus (*cos.* 323), the individual to whom Lactantius dedicated several books of his correspondence, was a Christian. Since Lactantius had a deep interest in pagan literature, I do not see the necessity of the principle (although I agree with H.'s determination in this case). More important, H. uses Jerome (*De vir. ill.* 111 "Acilius Severus in Hispania, de genere illius Severi ad quem Lactantii duo epistularum scribuntur libri, composuit volumen . . .") to show that Severus was a provincial. He does not consider (1) that Jerome connects a relative of the consul, not the consul himself, with Spain, (2) that the Spanish property could have belonged to a distinguished *Roman* aristocratic house, and (3) that these two Acilii may well have been descendants of M.' Acilius Glabrio Cn. Cornelius Severus (*cos.* 152) and Acilius Severus, one of the Arval Brethren at the end of the second century (*CIL*, 6. 2099–2100). The point is important inasmuch as H. elsewhere claims (p. 515) that Sex. Anicius Paulinus was the only aristocrat of distinguished lineage to be converted during Constantine's reign. Another interesting piece of information omitted by H. is the probable marriage of L. Aradius Valerius Proculus *signo* Populonius (*cos.* 340) to a Christian; add to the bibliography O. Garana, "Il conte Valerio del sarcofago di Adelfia," in *Atti del I° Congresso Nazionale di Archeologia Cristiana* (Rome, 1952), pp. 157–69. For a few individuals, the discussion, though full, is unconvincing: for example, the attempt to prove that Fl. Thalassius, the *intime* of Constantius II, was not an Arian Christian simply because the emperor used him to communicate with Athanasius. Finally, a few complaints about the manner of presentation. Since the book has undoubted value as a reference tool, it is annoying to be referred to the bibliographies of other works for modern scholarship. Also, the arrangement of the prosopography chronologically by office, obviously designed to generate conclusions of broad historical importance, will force even the initiated to consult the index in order to find specific individuals.

2. These figures do not distinguish individuals; for example, a functionary who held three of the surveyed posts is counted three times.

8 pagan, 18 orthodox Christian, 3 Arian. Focusing on individuals rather than on tenures in office increases the Christian proportion somewhat, a fact which carries the interesting implication that pagans were more likely to hold several of the surveyed posts (the average pagan term was also longer). The Christian emperors, then, could not do without pagan officials, and H. offers three reasons for this phenomenon. Above all, the pool of qualified Christians was too small, especially in the West. In addition, it was characteristic of imperial policy not to offend heavily pagan areas such as Rome and Achaea. And, as the lists of prefects of Egypt under Constantius and Valens make clear, pagans were regarded as useful in areas of endemic inter-Christian strife. Because of these factors, the cumulative number of Christian officeholders remained a minority until the reign of Gratian.

Eastern pagan officials, according to H., were often associated with intellectual schools. Their prominence was due to the literary culture of the court, which created needs that Christians were unable to fulfill. The emperors could employ such men without jeopardizing the spread of Christianity because their paganism was unorganized and too esoteric to have mass appeal. Western paganism was different—more cult-centered and, owing to its permeation of various state institutions and ceremonies, more political. The author vacillates on the effectiveness of the Western pagans as a pressure group. On the one hand, he sees evidence of strength in the frequent appointment of pagans to the urban prefecture of Rome and the proconsulship of Achaea. In the final chapter of the book, however, the statement is milder. H. asks why pagans did not refuse to serve their Christian rulers and, after canvassing the possibility that pagans thought that participation in public life might benefit their cause, concludes instead that Western paganism, divided into numerous cults, many of which reflected a bygone political order, simply did not have the strength to resist.

H.'s discussions of individual reigns generally amplify, rather than transform, received opinion. The militant Constantius of the ecclesiastical sources is no less recognizable in his appointments. Julian did indeed oust Christians from civil offices, although a shortage of military talent and fear of usurpation prevented the extension of this policy to the army (ironically, a Christian stronghold at this time). If Julian went beyond his original intention and actually persecuted Christians, his officials—especially those who had themselves apostasized and were ever alert to exhibit their loyalty—must bear most of the blame. Valentinian I, aware that internal calm would facilitate completion of his chief task, pacification of the frontiers, was not doctrinaire in his appointments; the prosopographical record corroborates Ammianus' statement of the emperor's tolerance. Gratian, who ordered the removal of the altar of Victory from the senate house, was equally merciless in excluding pagans from key posts (except early in his reign, when Ausonius was influential). H. concludes that the two best-known Christian emperors of the period, Constantine and Theodosius I, shared a strategy of attacking pagan institutions rather than pagan individuals. Constantine relied on pagans because there were not enough qualified Christians, but he did exploit his prerogative to appoint the *praefecti urbis Romae* to establish incentives for the conversion of pagan aristocrats. No great paucity of Christians existed by the time of Theodosius, who used pagans to give his regime a "Nimbus von Geist und Bildung"

(p. 586). H. shows, however, that the concentration of pagan officials was greatest during the period of the estrangement of Ambrose and Theodosius and that their number declined rapidly after the reconciliation. Perhaps the author's most interesting contribution is his appreciation of Jovian. Not only did Jovian extricate the Roman army from Persia, but, by retaining some of his predecessor's officials while appointing fellow Christians to high office, he counteracted the religious polarization which Constantius and Julian had fostered. This cautious policy, dictated more by circumstance than by principle, set the tone for succeeding reigns.

"Wem Plotin einmal etwas zu Herzen gegangen ist, der weiss, welche Sünde und welche Torheit es ist, wenn man die Menschen dieser Zeit in Böcke und Schafe, Christen und Heiden sortiert." Although H. successfully challenges Wilamowitz' dictum, his division of the Late Roman world into pagans and Christians can blur as well as reveal. Consider the career of Domitius Zenophilus (*cos.* 333), an attested pagan. The present book allows two explanations for his prominence: scarcity of trained Christians and/or Constantine's desire to minimize pagan disenchantment with his government. Neither is cogent. Zenophilus was, in all probability, the subject of *ILAfr.* 456.[3] After terms in two *correcturae*, Zenophilus traveled as *consularis* to Numidia, where he presided over the trial which condemned Silvanus, the Donatist bishop of Cirta, as a *traditor* (320). Constantine seems to have dispatched him to Achaea, strategically located on the edge of Licinius' realm, sometime during the period of rising hostilities between East and West. Soon after Constantine's victory at Chrysopolis, Zenophilus assumed the proconsulship of Asia, which he occupied for two years. He then returned to Africa and remained there as proconsul for four years before becoming consul. An indefatigable official who served in strategic areas and at critical times, Zenophilus is best understood as a pagan supporter of Constantine. H.'s categories preclude apprehension of this loyalty. Knowledge of the process by which some pagans came to support the Christian emperors is vital to a complete understanding of the Christianization of the Roman Empire.

David M. Novak
Chicago, Illinois

3. For Zenophilus and the Constantinian period in general, see my "Constantine and the Senate: An Early Phase of the Christianization of the Roman Aristocracy," *Ancient Society* (forthcoming).

BOOKS RECEIVED

[Not all works submitted can be reviewed, but those that pertain to the subject matter of this journal are regularly listed under "Books Received." Offprints from periodicals and parts of books will not be listed unless they are published (sold) separately. Books submitted are not returnable.]

ASTIN, ALAN E. *Cato the Censor.* Oxford: Clarendon Press; New York: Oxford University Press, 1978. Pp. xi + 371; 2 maps in text. $39.00.

BABINIOTIS, GEORGE (ed.). *Bibliographical Bulletin of the Greek Language for the Years 1975 and 1976; Deltio Bibliographias tēs Hellēnikēs Glōssas gia ta Etē 1975 kai 1976.* Bibliographical Bulletin of the Greek Language, vol. 3. Edited by GEORGE BABINIOTIS. In collaboration with DIM. THEOPHANOPOULOU-KONTOU, P. ATHANASIADI, K. BAKAKOU, CHR. CHARALAMBIDOU, N. KALAMARA, EFT. KATSANTONI, P. KONTOS, G. MAGOULAS, P. MARKOPOULOU, University of Athens. Athens: Department of Linguistics of the University of Athens, 1978. Pp. 86. $15, drachm. 250 (paper). Orders: A. Kardamitsa, "Institut du Livre," Hippokratous 8, Athens 143, Greece.

BAGNALL, ROGER S., and WORP, K. A. *Regnal Formulas in Byzantine Egypt.* Bulletin of the American Society of Papyrologists, suppl. 2. Missoula, Mont.: Scholars Press, 1979. Pp. xi + 90. $6.00 (member's price), $9.00 (nonmember's price) (paper).

BAILEY, D. R. SHACKLETON (trans.). *Cicero: Cicero's "Letters to His Friends."* Penguin Classics. 2 vols. Translated with introductions by D. R. SHACKLETON BAILEY. Harmondsworth: Penguin Books, Ltd.; New York: Penguin Books, 1978. Pp. 495; 5 maps in text; 477 + 2; 4 maps in text. £2.25 each (U.K.), $5.95 each (U.S.A.) (paper).

BALTES, MATTHIAS. *Die Weltentstehung des platonischen "Timaios" nach den antiken Interpreten*, part 2: *Proklos.* Philosophia Antiqua, vol. 35, part 2. Leyden: E. J. Brill, 1978. Pp. x + 175. Fl. 48 (paper).

BANDIERA, MARIO. *I frammenti del I libro degli "Annales" di Q. Ennio: Riordinamento ed esegesi.* Con prefazione di PIERO SANTINI. Florence: Felice Le Monnier, 1978. Pp. xv + 109. L. 3,800 (paper).

BARNES, JONATHAN. *The Presocratic Philosophers.* The Arguments of the Philosophers. 2 vols. Vol. 1: *Thales to Zeno.* Vol. 2: *Empedocles to Democritus.* London–Henley–Boston: Routledge & Kegan Paul, 1979. Pp. xiv + 378; x + 353. $25 per volume, $45 the set.

BARRETT, DAVID, and SOMMERSTEIN, ALAN H. (trans.). *Aristophanes: "The Knights," "Peace," "The Birds," "The Assemblywomen," "Wealth."* Penguin Classics. Translated by DAVID BARRETT and ALAN H. SOMMERSTEIN. Harmondsworth: Penguin Books, Ltd.; New York: Penguin Books, 1978. Pp. 335. £1.25, $3.50 (paper).

BILLERBECK, MARGARETHE (trans.). *Epiktet: "Vom Kynismus."* Philosophia Antiqua, vol. 34. Herausgegeben und übersetzt mit einem Kommentar von MARGARETHE BILLERBECK. Leyden: E. J. Brill, 1978. Pp. xvi + 188. Fl. 64 (paper).

BLOMQVIST, JERKER. *Das sogenannte KAI adversativum: Zur Semantik einer griechischen Partikel.* Acta Universitatis Upsaliensis, Studia Graeca Upsaliensia, 13. Uppsala, 1979. Pp. 66. Kr. 33.50. Distributed by Almqvist & Wiksell International, Stockholm, Sweden.

BOUMA, HANS. *An Eye on Israel.* Photography by W. P. WEIJLAND. Translation by SIETZE BUNING from the Dutch edition (1976) of *Met het oog op Israël* (published by Uitgeversmaatschappij J. H. Kok N. V., Kampen, The Netherlands). Grand Rapids, Mich.: Wm. B. Eerdmans Publishing Company, 1978. Pp. 144; 69 ills. (photographs) in text. $7.95 (paper).

BROWNING, ROBERT. *The Emperor Julian.* Berkeley and Los Angeles: University of California Press, 1976 (first paperback printing 1978). Pp. xii + 256 + 12 ills. on 8 pls.; 3 maps in text. $4.95 (paper).

BULLITT, ORVILLE H. *Phoenicia and Carthage: A Thousand Years to Oblivion.* Philadelphia and Ardmore, Pa.: Dorrance & Company, 1978. Pp. xvi + 256 + 1 map (repeated) on endpapers; 5 maps + 4 ills. in text. $10.00.

BUNNENS, GUY. *L'expansion phénicienne en Méditerranée: Essai d'interprétation fondé sur une analyse des traditions littéraires.* Études de Philologie, d'Archéologie et d'Histoire Anciennes publiées par l'Institut Historique Belge de Rome, Tome 17. Préface de E. LIPIŃSKI. Brussels and Rome: Institut Historique Belge de Rome, 1979. Pp. x + 419 + 8 + 1 folding map + 2 pls.

The Cairo Codex of Menander (*P. Cair. J. 43227*). A photographic edition prepared under the supervision of H. RIAD and ABD EL-KADR SELIM with a preface by L. KOENEN. London: University of London, Institute of Classical Studies, 1978. Pp. 22 (unnumbered) + 54 pls. Folio; boxed.

CARLINI, ANTONIO et al. (eds.). *Papiri letterari greci.* Università degli Studi di Pisa, Istituti per le Scienze dell'Antichità, Biblioteca degli Studi Classici e Orientali, 13. Editi da ANTONIO CARLINI, GIOVANNA CALVANI, ROSANGELA CINGOTTINI, ADELE CONCOLINO MANCINI, PIERANGIOLO FABRINI, GRAZIELLA FANAN, DANIELA FAUSTI, TANJA LUZZATTO, DANIELA MANETTI, FRANCO MALTOMINI, FRANCO MONTANARI, AMNERIS ROSELLI. Introduzione di ANTONIO CARLINI. Pisa: Giardini Editori e Stampatori, 1978. Pp. 304. L. 12,000 (estero $20) (paper).

CASERTANO, GIOVANNI. *Parmenide: Il metodo, la scienza, l'esperienza.* Esperienze, 48. Naples: Guida Editori, 1978. Pp. 341. L. 12,000 (paper).

CHEYNS, ANDRÉ. *Éditions et traductions de l' "Iliade" et de l' "Odyssée": Bibliographie sélective.* Louvain, 1976. Pp. iv + 48 folia. Peut être obtenu en versant la somme de 150 Francs Belges au compte de chèques postaux 000-0968556-11 d'André Cheyns, Blijde Inkomststraat, 108, 3000 Louvain, Belgique.

CRAWFORD, MICHAEL. *The Roman Republic.* Fontana History of the Ancient World. Hassocks, Nr. Brighton, Sussex: The Harvester Press, Ltd.; Atlantic Highlands, N.J.: Humanities Press, Inc. (in association with Fontana), 1978. Pp. 224 + 8 pls.; 4 maps + 12 figs. in text. $18.50.

DELACY, PHILLIP (ed. and trans.). *Galen: "On the Doctrines of Hippocrates and Plato,"* First Part: Books I–V. Edition, translation, and commentary by PHILLIP DELACY. Corpus Medicorum Graecorum, V 4, 1, 2: *Galeni "De placitis Hippocratis et Platonis,"* Libri I–V. Edidit, in linguam Anglicam vertit, commentatus est PHILLIP DELACY. Berlin: Akademie-Verlag, 1978. Pp. 359. Mk. 98.

DELACY, PHILLIP HOWARD, and DELACY, ESTELLE ALLEN (eds. and trans.). *Philodemus: "On Methods of Inference."* Istituto Italiano per gli Studi Filosofici, La Scuola di Epicuro: Collezione di testi ercolanesi diretta da MARCELLO GIGANTE, vol. 1. Edited with translation and commentary by PHILLIP HOWARD DELACY and ESTELLE ALLEN DELACY. Revised edition with the collaboration of MARCELLO GIGANTE, FRANCESCA LONGO AURICCHIO, ADELE TEPEDINO GUERRA. Naples: Bibliopolis, 1978. Pp. 230. L. 18,000.

DESIDERI, PAOLO. *Dione di Prusa: Un intellettuale greco nell'impero romano.* Biblioteca di Cultura Contemporanea, 135. Messina and Florence: Casa Editrice G. D'Anna, 1978. Pp. 641. L. 12,000 (paper).

DREIZEHNTER, ALOIS. *Die rhetorische Zahl: Quellenkritische Untersuchungen anhand der Zahlen 70 und 700.* Zetemata, vol. 73. Munich: Verlag C. H. Beck, 1978. Pp. vii + 114 + 2. DM 40 (paper).

Epistēmonikē Epetēris, Tomos dekatos tritos (1974) kai Tomos dekatos tetartos (1975). Aristoteleion Panepistēmion Thessalonikēs, Philosophikē Scholē. Thessalonikē, 1974, 1975. Pp. 369; 421.

ERLER, MICHAEL (trans.). *Proklos Diadochos: "Über die Existenz des Bösen."* Beiträge zur klassischen Philologie, vol. 102. Übersetzt und erläutert von MICHAEL ERLER. Meisenheim am Glan: Verlag Anton Hain, 1978. Pp. xxi + 208 + 2. DM 40 (paper).

FRIEDRICH, PAUL. *The Meaning of Aphrodite.* Chicago and London: The University of Chicago Press, 1978. Pp. xii + 243; 1 map, 2 ills. + 4 charts in text. $13.95.

FYLER, JOHN M. *Chaucer and Ovid.* New Haven and London: Yale University Press, 1979. Pp. x + 206. $14.50.

GAUGER, JÖRG-DIETER. *Beiträge zur jüdischen Apologetik: Untersuchungen zur Authentizität von Urkunden bei Flavius Josephus und im I. Makkabäerbuch.* Bonner Biblische Beiträge, 49. Cologne and Bonn: Peter Hanstein Verlag GmbH, 1977. Pp. xvi + 361 + 3. DM 86.

GEORGACAS, DEMETRIUS J. *Ichthyological Terms for the Sturgeon and Etymology of the International Terms Botargo, Caviar and Congeners (A Linguistic, Philological, and Culture-Historical Study); Onomata Dēlōtika tou Oxyrynchou kai hoi diethneis horoi Botargo, Caviar kai Syngenē (Monographia Glōssoïstorikē, philologikē, me etymologikēn anaphoran eis tēn historian glōssēs kai politismou).* Pragmateiai tēs Akadēmias Athēnōn, tomos 43 (1978). Athens: Grapheion Dēmosieumatōn tēs Akadēmias Athēnōn, 1978. Pp. 330.

GIBSON, ELSA. *The "Christians for Christians" Inscriptions of Phrygia.* Harvard Theological Review, Harvard Theological Studies, no. 32. Greek texts, translation, and commentary by ELSA GIBSON. Missoula, Mont.: Scholars Press, 1978. Pp. xiii + 162 + 33 pls.; 2 maps in text. $5.00 (member's price), $7.50 (nonmember's price) (paper).

GIOVANNINI, ADALBERTO. *Rome et la circulation monétaire en Grèce au IIe siècle avant Jésus-Christ.* Schweizerische Beiträge zur Altertumswissenschaft, vol. 15. Basel: Friedrich Reinhardt Verlag, 1978. Pp. x + 129 + 2 maps. Fr. 38 (paper).

GLUCKER, JOHN. *Antiochus and the Late Academy.* Hypomnemata, vol. 56. Göttingen: Vandenhoeck & Ruprecht, 1978. Pp. 510 + 2. DM 90 (paper).

GOUKOWSKY, PAUL. *Essai sur les origines du mythe d'Alexandre (336–270 av. J.-C.),*

Tome I: *Les origines politiques*. Annales de l'Est publiées par l'Université de Nancy II, Mémoire n° 60. Nancy, 1978. Pp. 360.

Grant, Michael. *A View of the Etruscans*. Presidential address delivered to the Classical Association in the University of Edinburgh 30 March 1978. Reprinted from Proceedings of the Classical Association, vol. 75 (1978). Pp. 9–22.

Greenhalgh, Michael. *The Classical Tradition in Art*. London: Duckworth, 1978. Pp. 271; numerous ills. in text. $24.95 (hardcover), $9.95 (paperback). Distributed in U.S.A. by Southwest Book Services, 4951 Top Line Drive, Dallas, Texas 75247.

Griechische Handschriften und Aldinen: Eine Ausstellung anlässlich der XV. Tagung der Mommsen-Gesellschaft in der Herzog August Bibliothek Wolfenbüttel. Wolfenbüttel: Herzog August Bibliothek, 16. Mai bis 29. Juni 1978. Pp. 161; 56 ills. in text.

Gschnitzer, Fritz. *Ein neuer spartanischer Staatsvertrag und die Verfassung des Peloponnesischen Bundes*. Beiträge zur klassischen Philologie, vol. 93. Meisenheim am Glan: Verlag Anton Hain, 1978. Pp. vii + 41 + 2. DM 20 (paper).

Hamilton, Charles D. *Sparta's Bitter Victories: Politics and Diplomacy in the Corinthian War*. Ithaca and London: Cornell University Press, 1979. Pp. 346 + frontispiece (map); 1 map in text. $17.50.

Harris, William V. *War and Imperialism in Republican Rome 327–70 B.C.* Oxford: Clarendon Press; New York: Oxford University Press, 1979. Pp. xi + 293. $39.00.

Hartigan, Karelisa. *The Poets and the Cities: Selections from the Anthology about Greek Cities*. Beiträge zur klassischen Philologie, vol. 87. Meisenheim am Glan: Verlag Anton Hain, 1979. Pp. x + 121 + 1; 1 map in text.

Havelock, Eric A., and Hershbell, Jackson P. (eds.). *Communication Arts in the Ancient World*. Humanistic Studies in the Communication Arts. New York: Communication Arts Books, Hastings House, Publishers, 1978. Pp. xiv + 162. $12.50.

Hoevels, Fritz Erik. *Märchen und Magie in den "Metamorphosen" des Apuleius von Madaura*. Studies in Classical Antiquity, vol. 1. Amsterdam: Editions Rodopi, 1979. Pp. vii + 329. Fl. 65 (paper).

Hogan, James C. *A Guide to the "Iliad."* Based on the translation by Robert Fitzgerald. Garden City, N.Y.: Anchor Books, Anchor Press/Doubleday, 1979. Pp. vii + 309; 3 maps in text. $4.95 (paper).

Hood, Sinclair. *The Arts in Prehistoric Greece*. The Pelican History of Art. New York: Viking Penguin, Inc., 1979 (©1978). Pp. 311; 2 maps, 2 plans, 1 chronological table + 237 ills. in text. $12.95 (Penguin), $25.00 (Viking).

Iggers, Georg G. *Neue Geschichtswissenschaft: Vom Historismus zur Historischen Sozialwissenschaft: Ein internationaler Vergleich*. Vom Autor überarbeitete und erweiterte Ausgabe des Buches *New Directions in European Historiography*, erschienen 1975 in der Wesleyan University Press, Middletown, Conn. Ins Deutsche übertragen vom Autor, von Peter Th. Walther und Walter Theimer. Mit Beiträgen von Norman Baker und Michael Frisch. Munich: dtv (Deutscher Taschenbuch Verlag), Wissenschaftliche Reihe, 1978. Pp. 276 + 4. DM 11.80 (paper).

INDELLI, GIOVANNI (ed. and trans.). *Polistrato: "Sul disprezzo irrazionale delle opinioni popolari."* Istituto Italiano per gli Studi Filosofici, La Scuola di Epicuro: Collezione di testi ercolanesi diretta da MARCELLO GIGANTE, vol. 2. Edizione, traduzione e commento a cura di GIOVANNI INDELLI. Naples: Bibliopolis, 1978. Pp. 205. L. 10,000.

JACKSON, HOWARD M. (ed. and trans.). *Zosimos of Panopolis "On the Letter Omega."* Society of Biblical Literature, Texts and Translations, no. 14; Graeco-Roman Religion, no. 5. Missoula, Mont.: Scholars Press, 1978. Pp. vii + 64. $3.00 (member's price), $4.50 (nonmember's price) (paper).

JAKOBSON, ROMAN. *Six Lectures on Sound and Meaning.* With a Preface by CLAUDE LÉVI-STRAUSS. Translated from the French by JOHN MEPHAM. Cambridge, Mass., and London: The MIT Press, 1978. Pp. xxvi + 116. $13.95. Original edition published in France by Les Éditions de Minuit, 1976. English translation published in Great Britain by The Harvester Press, Limited, 1978. First MIT Press edition, 1978.

JANNI, PIETRO. *Etnografia e mito: La storia dei Pigmei.* Istituto di Filologia Classica, Università di Urbino; Filologia e Critica, 30. Rome: Edizioni dell' Ateneo & Bizzarri, 1978. Pp. 141. L. 5,000 (paper).

JANSON, TORE. *A Concordance to the Latin Panegyrics: A Concordance to the "XII Panegyrici Latini" and to the Panegyrical Texts and Fragments of Symmachus, Ausonius, Merobaudes, Ennodius, Cassiodorus.* Alpha–Omega, Reihe A: Lexika–Indizes–Konkordanzen zur klassischen Philologie, 37. Hildesheim and New York: Georg Olms Verlag, 1979. Pp. xi + 898 + 2. DM 158.

———. *Mechanisms of Language Change in Latin.* Acta Universitatis Stockholmiensis, Studia Latina Stockholmiensia, 23. Stockholm: Almqvist & Wiksell International, 1979. Pp. 133.

KAHN, LAURENCE. *Hermès passe, ou les ambiguïtés de la communication.* Les Textes à l'Appui, Histoire Classique. Paris: François Maspero, 1978. Pp. 205.

KERÉNYI, C. *The Heroes of the Greeks.* New York: Thames and Hudson, 1978 (reprint). Pp. xxiv + 439 + 76 pls. $7.95 (paper). Copyright Thames and Hudson 1959, first paperback edition 1974, reprinted 1978.

KESSELS, A. H. M. *Studies on the Dream in Greek Literature.* Utrecht, The Netherlands: H & S (HES Publishers), 1978. Pp. xi + 269.

KEYAN, ROSTAM. *The Evolution of Language.* New York: Philosophical Library, Inc., 1978. Pp. xv + 160. $7.50.

KRAMER, BÄRBEL, and HAGEDORN, DIETER. *Kölner Papyri (P. Köln)*, vol. 2. Abhandlungen der Rheinisch-Westfälischen Akademie der Wissenschaften, Sonderreihe: Papyrologica Coloniensia, vol. VII/2. Bearbeitet von BÄRBEL KRAMER und DIETER HAGEDORN. Opladen: Westdeutscher Verlag, 1978. Pp. 244 + 20 pls. DM 64.

KRAMER, JOHANNES (ed. and trans.). *Desiderii Erasmi Roterodami "De recta Latini Graecique sermonis pronuntiatione dialogus"; Desiderius Erasmus von Rotterdam: "Dialog über die richtige Aussprache der lateinischen und griechischen Sprache."* Beiträge zur klassischen Philologie, vol. 98. Als Lesetext herausgegeben, übersetzt und kommentiert von JOHANNES KRAMER. Meisenheim am Glan: Verlag Anton Hain, 1978. Pp. xiii + 236 + 2. DM 38 (paper).

LANG, MABEL L. *Socrates in the Agora.* Excavations of the Athenian Agora, Picture Book No. 17. Prepared by MABEL L. LANG. Dedicated to EUGENE VANDERPOOL. Princeton, New Jersey: American School of Classical Studies at Athens, 1978. Pp. 32 (unnumbered); 29 ills. in text. $1.00 (paper).

LECOUTEUX, CLAUDE (ed.). "*De rebus in Oriente mirabilibus* (*Lettre de Farasmanes*)." Beiträge zur klassischen Philologie, vol. 103. Édition synoptique accompagnée d'une introduction et de notes par CLAUDE LECOUTEUX. Meisenhem am Glan: Verlag Anton Hain, 1979. Pp. xxix + 108 + 2.

LEFÈVRE, ECKARD. *Der "Phormio" des Terenz und der "Epidikazomenos" des Apollodor von Karystos.* Zetemata, vol. 74. Munich: Verlag C. H. Beck, 1978. Pp. viii + 130 + 2.

LIVREA, HENRICUS (ed. and trans.). *Anonymi fortasse Olympiodori Thebani "Blemyomachia"* (*P. Berol. 5003*). Beiträge zur klassischen Philologie, vol. 101. Edidit, prolegomenis versione et commentario instruxit HENRICUS LIVREA. Meisenheim am Glan: Verlag Anton Hain, 1978. Pp. iv + 99 + 1. DM 19.50 (paper).

LOCASCIO, FERDINANDO. *Sulla autenticità delle epistole di Apollonio Tianeo.* Istituto Siciliano di Studi Bizantini e Neoellenici, Quaderni, 10. Palermo, 1978. Pp. 80.

LUNAIS, SOPHIE. *Recherches sur la lune,* 1: *Les auteurs latins de la fin des Guerres Puniques à la fin du règne des Antonins.* Études Préliminaires aux Religions Orientales dans l'Empire Romain, vol. 72. Leyden: E. J. Brill, 1979. Pp. xviii + 414. Fl. 188.

MARCOVICH, MIROSLAV. *Eraclito: Frammenti.* Biblioteca di Studi Superiori, 64. Introduzione, traduzione e commento a cura di MIROSLAV MARCOVICH. Traduzione dall'inglese di PIERO INNOCENTI. Florence: "La Nuova Italia" Editrice, 1978. Pp. xxii + 442 + 4. L. 25,000.

Materiali e contributi per la storia della narrativa greco-latina, 2. Perugia: Istituto di Filologia Latina dell'Università di Perugia, 1978. Pp. xx + 155. Deposito librario: Cadmo editore S. R. L., Largo dell'Olgiata, 15—00123 Roma.

Materiali e discussioni per l'analisi dei testi classici, 1. Rivista semestrale. Pisa: Giardini Editori e Stampatori, 1978. Pp. 227. L. 800 (paper). Un fascicolo, lire 4,800; estero, lire 7,000. Abbonamento annuo per l'Italia, lire 9,000; estero, lire 13,000. Fascicoli arretrati, lire 5,500; estero, lire 8,000. L'abbonamento comprensivo del n. 1 (1978) e dei nn. 2 e 3 (1979) è di L. 13,000; estero, lire 18,000.

MATHIESEN, THOMAS J. *A Bibliography of Sources for the Study of Ancient Greek Music.* Music Indexes and Bibliographies, no. 10. Hackensack, N.J.: Joseph Boonin, Inc., 1974. Pp. iv + 59.

MAZZEO, JOSEPH ANTHONY. *Varieties of Interpretation.* Notre Dame and London: University of Notre Dame Press, 1978. Pp. xiv + 178. $13.95.

MAZZINI, INNOCENZO (ed. and trans.). *Q. Gargilii Martialis "De hortis."* Opuscula Philologica, 1. Introduzione, testo critico, traduzione di INNOCENZO MAZZINI. Bologna: Pàtron Editore, 1978. Pp. 141. L. 7,500 (paper).

MCCLAIN, ERNEST G. *The Pythagorean Plato: Prelude to the Song Itself.* Stony Brook, N.Y.: Nicolas Hays, Ltd., 1978. Pp. x + 192; 57 charts and tables in text. $16.75. Distributed by: Great Eastern Book Co., 1123 Spruce St., Boulder, Colorado 80302.

McDONALD, MARIANNE. *Terms for Happiness in Euripides*. Hypomnemata, vol. 54. Göttingen: Vandenhoeck & Ruprecht, 1978. Pp. 335 + 1. DM 56 (paper).

MORANI, MORENO and GIULIA. *Per una lettura del mondo antico: Storia, valore, metodo degli studi classici*. Collana "Problemi didattici ed educativi," N. 24. Milan: Editrice Massimo, 1978. Pp. 174. L. 3,000 (paper).

NAGLE, D. BRENDAN. *The Ancient World: A Social and Cultural History*. Englewood Cliffs, N.J.: Prentice-Hall, Inc., 1979. Pp. xiv + 443; 12 maps + 66 ills. in text.

NEDERLOF, A. B. *Pyrrhus van Epirus: zijn achtergronden–zijn tijd–zijn leven (historie en legende)*. Amsterdam: Editions Rodopi N. V., 1978. Pp. xi + 329 + 1 folding chart; 14 maps + 14 ills. in text. Fl. 39.

OATES, JOHN F.; BAGNALL, ROGER S.; WILLIS, WILLIAM H. *Checklist of Editions of Greek Papyri and Ostraca*, Second Edition. Bulletin of the American Society of Papyrologists, Supplements, no. 1. Missoula, Mont.: Scholars Press, 1978. Pp. x + 63. $4.00 (member's price), $6.00 (nonmember's price) (paper).

OKSALA, TEIVAS. *Studien zum Verständnis der Einheit und der Bedeutung von Vergils "Georgica."* Commentationes Humanarum Litterarum, 60 (1978). Helsinki: Societas Scientiarum Fennica, 1978. Pp. 135. Mk. 40 (paper). Sale: The Academic Bookstore, P. Box 10 128, Helsinki 10.

OTT, WILHELM. *Metrische Analysen zu Vergil "Bucolica."* Materialien zu Metrik und Stilistik, 9. Tübingen: Max Niemeyer Verlag, 1978. Pp. xix + 170 + packet of 32 punched cards. DM 38 (paper).

———. *Metrische Analysen zu Vergil "Georgica."* Materialien zu Metrik und Stilistik, 10. 2 vols. Vol. 1: *Analysen und Übersichten*. Vol. 2: *Indizes*. Tübingen: Max Niemeyer Verlag, 1978. Pp. xvii + 320 + 4 packets of 16 punched cards each; vii + 163. DM 58; DM 32 (paper).

PARRY, HUGH. *The Lyric Poems of Greek Tragedy*. Toronto and Sarasota: Samuel Stevens, 1978. Pp. xiii + 241. $15.95.

PEROSA, ALESSANDRO, and SPARROW, JOHN. *Renaissance Latin Verse: An Anthology*. Compiled and edited by ALESSANDRO PEROSA and JOHN SPARROW. Chapel Hill: The University of North Carolina Press, 1979. Pp. xxix + 560. $24.

PINGREE, DAVID (ed. and trans.). *The "Yavanajātaka" of Sphujidhvaja*. Harvard Oriental Series, vol. 48. 2 vols. Edited, translated, and commented on by DAVID PINGREE. Cambridge, Mass., and London: Harvard University Press, 1978. Pp. ix + 506; vii + 527; 1 ill. in text.

PINTACUDA, MARIO. *La musica nella tragedia greca*. Cefalù: Lorenzo Misuraca Editore, 1978. Pp. 235. L. 4,000 (paper).

———. *Tragedia antica e musica d'oggi: La musica nelle rappresentazioni moderne dei tragici greci in Italia: Elenco cronologico delle principali rappresentazioni tragiche dal 1904 al 1977 in Italia*. Cefalù: Lorenzo Misuraca, 1978. Pp. 61. L. 1,500 (paper).

PITKÄRANTA, REIJO. *Studien zum Latein des Victor Vitensis*. Commentationes Humanarum Litterarum, 61 (1978). Helsinki: Societas Scientiarum Fennica, 1978. Pp. 164. Sale: The Academic Bookstore, P. Box 10 128, Helsinki 10.

QUIÑONES MELGOZA, JOSÉ (trans.). *Publii Ovidii Nasonis "Epistularum ex Ponto" libri quattuor; Publio Ovidio Nasón: "Epístolas desde el Ponto," cuatro libros.*

Bibliotheca Scriptorum Graecorum et Romanorum Mexicana. Introducción, versión rítmica y notas de JOSÉ QUIÑONES MELGOZA. Mexico City: Universidad Nacional Autónoma de México, 1978. Pp. i–cxxi + 1–100 + double pp. + cxxii–cclvi.

RAGLAN, LORD. *The Hero: A Study in Tradition, Myth, and Drama.* Meridian Books. With an introduction by WALTER KAUFMANN. New York: The New American Library, Inc., 1979. Pp. xix + 307 + 6. $4.95 (paper). First published in 1936 by Methuen & Co., Ltd.; revised American edition published in 1956 by Alfred A. Knopf, Inc.

Reading Greek. 2 vols. Vol. 1: *Text.* Vol. 2: *Grammar, Vocabulary and Exercises.* The Joint Association of Classical Teachers' Greek Course. Cambridge–London–New York–Melbourne: Cambridge University Press, 1978. Pp. xvi + 182; 72 photographs, 4 drawings, 5 maps in text: x + 368. $5.95; $9.95 (paper).

REEVES, JAMES. *Arcadian Ballads* [poems based on Ovid's *Metamorphoses*]. London: Heinemann, 1978. Pp. vi + 48. £4.95, $15.95. First published 1977 in a limited edition by The Whittington Press; this edition first published 1978. Heinemann Educational Books, Inc., 4 Front St., Exeter, N. H. 03833.

REHM, RUSH (trans.). *Aeschylus: The Oresteian Trilogy: A Theatre Version.* Melbourne: The Hawthorn Press, 1978. Pp. xii + 144 + 4 pls. $4.95 (paper).

RIIKONEN, HANNU. *Die Antike im historischen Roman des 19. Jahrhunderts: Eine literatur- und kulturgeschichtliche Untersuchung.* Commentationes Humanarum Litterarum, 59 (1978). Helsinki: Societas Scientiarum Fennica, 1978. Pp. 231. Mk. 60 (paper). Sale: The Academic Bookstore, P. Box 10 128, Helsinki 10.

RÖHRICH, WILFRIED. *Politik als Wissenschaft: Eine Einführung.* Munich: dtv (Deutscher Taschenbuch Verlag), Wissenschaftliche Reihe, 1978. Pp. 236 + 3. DM 11.80 (paper).

SAKALIS, DEMETRIOS TH. *Iōniko lektiko ston Platōna*, Meros A′: *Syntaxē.* Panepistēmio Iōanninōn, Epistēmonikē Epetērida Philosophikēs Scholēs Dōdōnē: Parartēma arith. 9. Iōannina, 1978. Pp. 220.